THE PILGRIMAGE ROAD TO

Santiago

THE COMPLETE CULTURAL HANDBOOK

DAVID M. GITLITZ

AND

LINDA KAY DAVIDSON

ST. MARTIN'S GRIFFIN ☙ NEW YORK

Quotations from original sources and pilgrims' narratives were
translated by David M. Gitlitz, unless otherwise indicated.

We thank the following for their permission to quote from their
publications:
   Italica Press for passages from William Melczer's translation of the
Codex Calixtinus Book V, the *Guide,* and from Thomas Coffey, Linda
Kay Davidson, and Maryjane Dunn's translation of the *Codex
Calixtinus* Book I's "Veneranda dies" sermon and Book II, *The Miracles
of St. James.*
   Pennsylvania State University Press for a translation of a 10th-c.
document by Jerrilyn Dodd in her *Architecture and Ideology.*
   Primavera Pers for James Hall's translation of Domenico Laffi's
narration of his three pilgrimages to Compostela in the late 17th c.,
published as *A Journey to the West.*

www.stmartins.com

Library of Congress Cataloging-in-Publication Data

Gitlitz, David M. (David Martin)
   The pilgrimage road to Santiago / David M. Gitlitz and Linda Kay
Davidson.—1st ed.
      p.   cm.
   ISBN 0-312-25416-4
      1. Spain, Northern—Description and travel.   2. Christian
pilgrims and pilgrimages—Spain—Santiago de Compostela.
3. Art—Spain, Northern.   I. Title.

DP285.G58 2000
946'.1—dc21

                                                              99-089860

10 9 8 7 6 5

THE PILGRIMAGE ROAD TO

Santiago

In 1974, 1979, 1987, 1993, and 1996 we walked to Compostela, accompanying groups of college student–pilgrims on academic medieval studies programs, sponsored successively by Indiana University, the University of Nebraska, Binghamton University, and the University of Rhode Island. This book began with our notes for those treks.

We dedicate this Handbook to Deborah and Abby Gitlitz and to all the other student pilgrims for their friendship, their infectious curiosity, their illuminating insights, and for fully indulging our enthusiasm for the Road.

CONTENTS

ACKNOWLEDGMENTS

The evaluations of artistic monuments and interrelationships between history, art, and pilgrimage are ours, based on decades of reading and hours of wonderful conversations with knowledgeable colleagues, priests and nuns, farmers and townsfolk, bartenders and jailers, local historians and mystics, hospitallers and vagabonds, *sabios* and *sapos*, whom we have encountered on the Road. Our several walking pilgrimages have given us insights unattainable by any other means. We have indicated source material and direct quotations where appropriate, of course. We take full responsibility for errors and omissions. We realize that there will be differences of opinion regarding some of our conclusions, and we welcome comments from readers that will help us prepare for subsequent editions of this book.

We especially thank Kristen Macnamara at St. Martin's Press and Jeanne Fredericks for having faith in the project; Christopher Hewitt, who did footwork for us in the library while we were on the Road in 1998; Ann Suter for her help with the Latin translations; and the University of Rhode Island librarians who helped us make deadlines. To Abigail Gitlitz, who did the artwork and maps for this volume, and to David Publow, who lettered them, we can only say, "Gracias, mil gracias."

PREFACE

When we first trekked to Compostela in 1974 we did not meet even one other pilgrim on the Road. In 1979 the only pilgrim we encountered was an elderly Frenchman who was fulfilling a vow made in the Second World War. To most people in the 1970s the pilgrimage Road was hardly more than a vague memory of a historical relic: "You know, in medieval times. . . ."

David's imagination had been fired by Walter Starkie's vivid account of his pilgrim experiences in the 1950s, and he had pulled together an American college group. Together we searched out the old paths, consulting army maps and asking directions from farmers plowing their fields with braces of oxen. Linda saw her first stork's nest (when *do* they return to Spain for summer?). We discovered Romanesque sculpture (what *is* that snake doing to that woman?). In the smallest villages we saw crumbling palaces and big barns of churches, and we wondered how these hamlets ever could have afforded to cut so much stone. Every kilometer generated questions.

For twenty-five years we have sought answers to those questions. In 1987 and 1993 we met hundreds of other pilgrims along the Road. In 1996, a Holy Year, more than 100,000 pilgrims walked the Road to Compostela. In their company we limped out of the Pyrenees, toasted our necks in the hot sun of the Meseta, and bowed under our backpacks as we struggled up the mountains to O Cebreiro. When our group stopped for a lesson, most walked on by. But every so often some fellow pilgrims would pause as we stared at a line of rocks in a seemingly empty field. "What are you looking at?" "That's where a Roman villa used to be," we answered. "See? That's the outline of an ancient building." Sometimes pilgrims clustered around our group as we retold the stories narrated on some church portal. Sometimes we drew a small crowd as we recited a medieval poem that recounted events that took place in the very building we were looking at. The urging behind all those pilgrim voices saying, "I wish we knew more," is why we have written this book.

Whatever your motive for making this pilgrimage, you will learn that the Road is more than dust and pain and friendships and the endlessly receding western horizon. It is history and poetry, snow-capped mountains and bloodred poppies, Romanesque capitals and Gothic spires, oak forests and sheep bells, and wedge-tailed black kites soaring overhead. Look up. Look around. If it takes you an extra few days to get involved with what you are walking through, in the long run you will judge it time well spent. You will learn what all of our pilgrim companions have learned on the Santiago Road: the going is more memorable than the getting there.

Our book is not a route guide. The Road to Santiago is so well marked now that it's hard *not* to find your way west without getting lost. You may have already chosen a route guide. For hikers, the translations of the Millán Bravo Lozano or the Valiña Sampedro guides and the shorter guide by the British Confraternity are all popular. There are special guides for bikers and motorists, and new guides seem to come out every other day. Neither do we suggest lodgings or restaurants. That sort of information goes out-of-date almost as fast as it is printed. And besides, with the modern boom in the pilgrimage, the numbers of *refugios* sprouting up all along the Road make it easy to find lodging almost anywhere.

What you are holding is your *Handbook* to the cultural contexts of the pilgrimage. It is meant to accompany your route guide, to be the second item you put into your knapsack. From the Pyrenean border between France and Spain we will walk with you, providing useful and interesting information about the history, people, natural environments, and artistic monuments that you are passing. At the back of the book you will find a timeline of monarchs and handy glossaries of the saints, artists, and artistic styles you will encounter every day. With luck, by the end of your pilgrimage you won't need the glossaries anymore. We have concentrated on things you would have seen if you had been a pilgrim in the Middle Ages, but we don't completely ignore modern times either. As you walk, it is what you see that engages your attention, so it will come as no surprise that our book focuses on the visual, particularly the splendid art arrayed along the Road. Since understanding what you see is a function of what you know, you will also find information about the historic, literary, and religious contexts of the pilgrimage and the pilgrimage Road.

So, as you pack up your gear, a couple of reminders. In the outside compartments of your knapsack, along with your water bottle, your route guide, and this book, stash a lightweight pair of binoculars and a small flashlight with a strong, focused beam for looking at monuments. Don't neglect to get your pilgrim's credential, or passport, which will admit you to the pilgrim *refugios*. The American Friends of the Road to Santiago [dgitlitz@aol.com] is pleased to supply you with one. Or you can pick one up at St.-Jean-Pied-de-Port or Roncesvalles, if you wish. If you are traveling other routes, you should be able to acquire one in one of the early larger towns or *refugios*. Don't forget to carry some money. But, most of all, fill your pockets with curiosity.

INTRODUCTION
THE PILGRIMAGE TO SANTIAGO DE COMPOSTELA

The story of St. James has been written so often as to be trite in its retelling. Honed over centuries of discoveries, interpretations, claims, and counterclaims, it lies somewhere between legend and fact, between superstition and belief. Yet whether it is true or only wished to be true, it has motivated pilgrimages for 1,000 years. It is why you are on the Road. What follows is the most prevalent version of the story of the Apostle James, with the addition of some historical material that is perhaps not quite so widely known.

James the Greater (Lat., Jacobus; Span., Sant-Yago, Santiago, Diego, Jaime, Jacobo) and his brother John, sons of Zebedee, were fisherman on the Sea of Galilee. The Gospels relate that James was the fourth person Jesus recruited (Matt. 4:21). The brothers had such bad tempers that they garnered the nickname *Boanerges* (sons of thunder; Mark 3:17). James is mentioned only a few times in the New Testament. James and John asked to be placed at Jesus's right-hand side in paradise (Mark 10:37), but the request was not met with enthusiasm.

The second part of the story has no biblical basis. Legend holds that just before His Crucifixion, Jesus divvied up the world among His Apostles, encouraging them to get the Word out as widely as possible. James was assigned the Iberian Peninsula. He traveled as far as Galicia, preaching as he went, but he seems not to have been very convincing, for he attracted only seven disciples. He decided to return to the Holy Land. On the way back, in Caesar Augustus (today called Zaragoza), he was visited by the Virgin Mary, reputedly her only miraculous apparition during her lifetime. She requested that a church be built there in memory of her Son, and she gave Santiago the pillar to which Jesus had been tied at His flagellation. James complied, erecting La Iglesia de la Virgen del Pilar, which is why so many Hispanic women are named Pilar.

Once back in the Holy Land, Santiago was beheaded by Herod Agrippa in 44 C.E., and thus became the first of the Apostles to be martyred (Acts 12:2); it is the only Apostle's martyrdom mentioned in the Gospels. Friends sneaked his body out of Jerusalem and put it on a boat that, with no sails, oars, or even sailors, according to some versions, traveled across the Mediterranean Sea, through the Strait of Gibraltar, and north along the Iberian coast. When the boat reached Galicia it stopped, and Santiago's disciples, somehow alerted that he was coming, took his body off the boat. There had not been time to ready a tomb, so they placed his body on a large stone that immediately curved to hold the holy relic.

The disciples searched widely for a place to bury Santiago. Finally they asked at the palace of Lupa, the area's queen. She set several trials for them, and each time the disciples miraculously met her demands. Finally, Lupa promised that they could bury the body in her lands if they could yoke two ferocious wild oxen on a nearby mountain. The oxen, aware that the corpse was holy, placidly allowed themselves to be harnessed. The disciples buried St. James on a hill.

There is no further word of St. James for nearly 750 years. Meanwhile the Iberian Peninsula was slowly Christianized. Visigoths replaced Romans. In 711, Muslims from northern Africa usurped power from the Visigoths, rapidly conquering as far north as central France before they were stopped. However, they left in peace some trivial groups of Christians hiding out in Iberia's northern mountains. This proved to be a mistake, as those small groups began armed resistance and slowly started pushing south. This so-called Christian Reconquest of the Peninsula took nearly 800 years.

About 813 the Christian hermit Pelayo heard music and saw lights shining over a small cave in the woods on Mount Libredón, some 17 km. from the port city of Iria Flavia, seat of Bishop Teodomiro. He dug on the site and found bones and parchment. Pelayo took the Bishop to the site and he authenticated the bones as those of the Apostle James and two of his disciples, Atanasio and Teodoro. Before very long the tomb began drawing pilgrims. Around the hillside a city grew up. The small chapel that guarded the relics eventually became the seat of a bishop.

In the 9th c. Muslims still ruled most of the Iberian Peninsula. They carried powerful relics of the prophet Muhammad with them into battle. Christians were delighted to be able to enlist divine aid on their own behalf with the relics of the only Apostle buried in Western Europe. Ca. 852, in the decisive battle of Clavijo near Logroño (a battle, by the way, that many historians now doubt ever occurred), the warrior Santiago, mounted on his white horse, appeared to lead the Christian armies in slaughtering their Muslim enemies. James was now not only Spain's Apostle, Santiago Peregrino, drawing pilgrims by the increasing thousands, he was Santiago Matamoros (Moor-slayer). All the more reason to visit his tomb and to donate large sums in his honor to insure his continued protection of Christian Spain. Kings, nobles, and commoners took the hint, and money poured in.

The pilgrimage started as a trickle but soon swelled to a flood, and Compostela grew to accommodate the crowds arriving daily (see ch. 88). You are part of a corpus of literally millions of pilgrims who have been drawn to this shrine. Some were moved by the spirit. Some by politics. Some came to enrich themselves on the pilgrim trade. Some came to be healed in the body. Some were sentenced to walk to Compostela in lieu of serving time in prison. Some had their expenses underwritten by their villages to go to pray for rain or relief from plague. Since the Middle Ages did not recognize the legitimacy of tourism or vacations, but did endorse pilgrimage, some came for the pleasure of travel, or to get away from the wife or the farm, or for the mere adventure of it. Often pilgrims left home for one set of reasons and discovered quite another set along the Road.

How many pilgrims were there? And how soon? Authenticity of some of the earliest documents is controversial. Some posit that Italian pilgrims visited sometime in the 7th c., even before the discovery of the relics, although that seems unlikely. In the late 9th c., 2 papal legates may have trekked from Italy, and a Muslim poet named Algazel may have visited. What is certain, however, is that by the mid-10th century a European pilgrimage tradition to Compostela was beginning to form. An Abbot Gotescalc of France wrote that he came in 950 "to beg mercy and help from God and Santiago." The abbot of a Catalan monastery made the journey in 959. Two years later the marquis of Gothia, Raymond II, was assassinated on the Road. According to a Viking chronicle, at least one Nordic pilgrim journeyed to Compostela ca. 968–71. A hermit from Armenia came in 983. By the middle of the next century, the pilgrimage had become big business as large groups of nobles, churchmen, and laypeople from all over Europe flocked to the Apostle's tomb. An infrastructure was developed. Hospices dotted the landscape. Laws were passed regulating the trade and chastising its abuses. The period of greatest pilgrimage activity, the 11th and 12th c., was not uncoincidentally the apex of popularity of the medieval veneration of holy relics. It was also the period of maximum effort to wrest control of relics from the Muslims, be these the Saracens fought by Crusaders on the roads to Jerusalem, or the Moors battled by Iberia's Christian knights along the precarious frontiers just south of the Santiago pilgrimage Road. In the late 12th c. the Spanish Military Order of Santiago was created—like the Orders of Saint John of Jerusalem and the Knights Templar—with a dual purpose: to wage war against the infidels and to protect pilgrims journeying to the holy places.

How best to get to Compostela? The compiler of the 12th-c. *Liber Sancti Jacobi*

(LSJ; see ch. 16) included some geographical indications in the work's fifth book. By the 14th c. we know of written guides for pilgrims coming from London, Venice, and Avignon; in the 15th c. for pilgrims coming from Italy and Belgium; and in the 16th c. from Flanders, Greece, and Armenia.

From earliest times, some pilgrims seem to have been compelled to chronicle their own personal experiences: not a guidebook for you, but a memoir about me. As you will discover in this book, we have not been immune to the temptation. Gotescalc's meager comments may be the first we have of an avowed pilgrim to Compostela. In the 12th c. the anonymous writer of the fifth book of the LSJ (sometimes identified as Aymery Picaud) made several personal observations on trails, water, people, and monuments from France to Compostela. An anonymous 14th-c. pilgrim described his experiences traveling by sea to Compostela. In the 15th c., writers from Austria, Germany, Italy, the British Isles, Poland, France, and even Armenia had a lot to say about their pilgrimages, and with time the numbers of memoirs increased. Some of these pilgrims, such as William Wey in the 15th c., approached the experience with deep belief in Santiago's divine role in Spain. He recounts 2 miracles that he witnessed along the Road and attributes them to Santiago's intercession. Others were equally as cynical: in the 16th c. the pilgrim Andrew Borde wrote: "I assure you that there is not one heare [hair] nor one bone of saint Iames in Spayne in Compostell. . . ." (204). The urge to keep a pilgrimage journal seems irresistible, as a visit to your local bookstore will easily confirm.

The Santiago pilgrimage boomed in the Middle Ages, decreased in volume during the religious reformations of the Renaissance, and dropped even further from the skepticism of the 18th-c. Enlightenment up through what some call the present postreligious age. But it has never stopped altogether. The numbers of guides and memoirs written during the last half millennium indicate that there has been constant pilgrimage activity focused on Compostela. Spain seems all along to have maintained the tradition of giving special attention to the pilgrimage during Holy Years (when the Saint's day, July 25, falls on a Sunday). Some official attention results from government commitment to honoring the Vow of Santiago (*voto de Santiago*), a promise to pay annual homage and economic tribute (*ofrenda*) to the Saint because of his intervention in the battle of Clavijo. Every July 25 some high-ranking officials of the Spanish government visit Compostela to deliver the national *ofrenda*. Dictator Francisco Franco took pride in the event during his near half century in power. King Juan Carlos and Queen Sofía have continued to make the visit in Holy Years. The practice is not new: Alfonso VII of Castilla went (1138); Alfonso II of Aragón visited (ca. 1195–6); as did Fernando III el Santo (1232); Carlos III de Navarra (1381–2, before he became king); Fernando and Isabel (1486); their daughter Juana and son-in-law Felipe el Hermoso (1506); their grandson Holy Roman emperor Carlos V (1520); and so on.

Wherever you are from, whatever reason motivates you to heft your knapsack and start walking west, when you reach Compostela you are entitled to wear the scallop shell, the universal insignia of a Santiago pilgrim. These days, when most pilgrims only walk west and then take modern transportation home from Compostela, people put on the shell when they start out. Medieval pilgrims liked insignia: pilgrims returning from Jerusalem brought palm branches, and were known as Palmers, while those returning from Rome wore the crossed keys of St. Peter, and were called Romers. How the relationship between the shell and the Santiago pilgrimage evolved is not entirely clear, but it started early. Scallop shells are found on medieval coats of arms and have been excavated in medieval pilgrim graves all over Europe. One theory is that because Compostela lies so close to the ocean and scallops are common on the Galician coast, early pilgrims could easily gather the shells and take them back home. Another version, recorded in the LSJ, says that one of the earliest of St. James's miracles was his rescue of a knight who had fallen into the sea. When the knight arose from his watery grave, he was covered with cockleshells, and thus they became linked with Santiago. You will see the shell everywhere, from a medieval gravestone in Roncesvalles to the myriad statues of Santiago Peregrino. The European Council has tailored an adaptation of the scallop shell as its markings along the Road. Wearing it identifies you as a member of the special confraternity of pilgrims to Compostela.

HOW TO READ THIS HANDBOOK

Because this Handbook is meant to provide you with the cultural contexts for your pilgrimage experience, the descriptive material in part I is organized geographically, to accompany you on your journey from east to west. Because you will encounter some things over and over again (e.g., St. Barbara, King Alfonso VI, Romanesque tympana, the sculptor Gil de Siloé), part II contains glossaries, tables, and sketches that will help you learn to identify key figures.

Part I: The Road

The Road to Santiago is not a single path. Pilgrimages have fixed end points, but they begin wherever people start walking. In the Middle Ages, pilgrims from all over Europe left their homes to head south toward Spain. Most of them eventually joined one of 4 major French roads funneling toward the Pyrenees Mountains that are the Iberian Peninsula's northern gate. There are several routes across the Pyrenees, but two were especially attractive: the western pass to Roncesvalles, and the central Pyrenean pass to Jaca. Some pilgrims crossed at Portalet, one valley east of the Jaca route, and since we like that road particularly well we have included it also. Once in Spain, the principal roads plunge south out of the mountains and then head west. They all unite in a small Navarran town called Puente la Reina, and from there a single major route strikes west to Compostela.

We start our descriptions of the routes at the French-Spanish border.

- Chapters 1–3 and 5–15 detail the Aragonese route that climbs from Urdos and Obanos, crosses the border at Somport, and descends through Candanchú to Jaca. From there pilgrims can follow the north or the south banks of the Río Aragón west into Navarra, so we detail both of these routes to Puente la Reina.
- Chapter 4 describes a second Aragonese route from Portalet to Sabiñánigo and then west to Jaca (ch. 5), where it joins the main Aragonese route.
- Chapters 16–22 explain the Navarran route leaving St.-Jean-Pied-de-Port, France, crossing the border at Ibañeta, descending to Roncesvalles and then to Pamplona and Puente la Reina.
- Chapters 23–87 proceed from Puente la Reina, where all of the major Roads come together, west through Navarra, La Rioja, Castilla, León, and Galicia.
- Chapter 88 treats Santiago de Compostela.

Some pilgrims drive, or bicycle, rather than walk, and their routes do not precisely coincide with the walking Road. Towns **bracketed [ ] in the route lists** are likely to be visited by wheeled pilgrims, but may well be bypassed by pilgrims on foot.

Many interesting or unique and important art works lie close to the pilgrimage Road, often tucked away in little villages, not marked on the usual pilgrims' route maps. On several occasions we suggest that you take time to veer off the Road for an excursion. These side trips are indicated by their separation, in boxes, from the main text.

Twice we have suggested that pilgrims deviate from the marked main Road for a day in order to visit a monument of extraordinary artistic and historical importance. These are chapters 7 (Santa Cruz de la Serós and San Juan de la Peña) and 33 (San Millán de la Cogolla).

We have designed this Handbook both for the relatively knowledgeable traveler and for the pilgrim who is not quite sure what to look at first. The pilgrimage Road offers significant monuments in every artistic style from 11th-c. Romanesque through 18th-c. Neoclassic, and in every artistic genre. At least once for every major style and genre, our descriptions will walk you through that style's major characteristics and suggest an appreciation of that particular monument's aesthetic qualities. Even if you have never looked seriously at art before, by the middle of your journey you should be able to recognize the styles without our cues. By the end, we hope you will have become a knowledgeable enthusiast. Sites in **boldface** are of special significance. If a monument is both **boldfaced and underlined**, it is not to be missed.

Along the way we insert scraps of legend, proverbs, traditions, historical information, and eyewitness accounts. Our goal is to make the apparently ordinary landscape in which you find yourself come alive. The stones you will walk over shine because they have been polished by a thousand years of pilgrims' feet, soon to include your own. You follow, and are part of, an ancient and venerable tradition, and we want you to enjoy the company of your fellow travelers, from the 12th-c. French cleric Aymery Picaud to the 17th-c. Italian cleric Domenico Laffi, from the 15th-c. German Arnold von Harff to the late-20th-c. Americans David Gitlitz and Linda Davidson.

Organization of Chapters in Part I

There are 2 types of chapters. Picture beads evenly spaced on a string. The beads are the good-sized towns where we usually spend the night. "Bead" chapters deal only with the overnight town. The string is the Road connecting the overnight towns, so the "string" chapters describe points of interest all along that day's route. Of course, pilgrims walk at different paces, and are interrupted somewhat randomly by the insurmountable opportunities that the Road can offer, so that the places you elect to spend the night may well differ from our choices.

Chapters dealing with the "overnight" towns follow this simple format:

• First we give pertinent historical information about the town.
• Next we detail the town's special relationship to the pilgrimage.
• Last, we list and then describe the monuments worth seeing. We generally begin in the center of town and list the monuments in a convenient order to visit.

Chapters describing the Road between major towns follow a slightly different format.

• The chapter heading gives the beginning and ending point of that day's journey.
• The route list presents in geographical order all of the towns you will pass through that day. Most of these towns are described in the text. Some, particularly in Galicia, are so small and insignificant—except to their 4 or 5 inhabitants—that we have not commented on them. The beginning and ending towns (treated separately in the "overnight" town chapters) are in capital letters to distinguish them from the others. Again, **boldface** or **underlining** indicates towns of extraordinary interest.
• The individual towns are discussed separately, generally following the history-pilgrimage-monument format. These visits are described in walking order, generally from east to west.

Maps: Interspersed in part I are maps at 3 levels of detail. The map of the overall Road is on pages xx–xxi. More detailed maps of the pilgrimage Road through each Spanish province are found at the beginning of the appropriate section. For the larger towns, monuments are indicated on schematic city maps at the beginning of that city's description.

Part II: The Reference Points

The part I Road descriptions include many references to historical figures, as well as a variety of specialized terms. Part II includes a list of abbreviations, a list of common Spanish words, basic information about the most common artistic styles, and alphabetical glossaries of the principal artists and saints (together with their artistic emblems, called attributes, and their feast days) you will encounter along the Road. Context will make it clear which glossary to consult. Part II also includes a chronological table of Iberian monarchs from 900 to 1500 to help you distinguish between the 8 King Garcías, the 11 King Sanchos, the 13 King Alfonsos, and the seemingly ubiquitous Urracas.

So . . . heft your pack and get going. As we sang in 1974, and several times since,

> The Road has no beginning,
> and the Road has no end.
> The towns they run together
> and they run apart again.
> Right now is the only moment,
> and Time is the time to go
> and make yourself a pilgrim
> on the Road to Santiago.

> ¡Buen camino!

The Pilgrimage

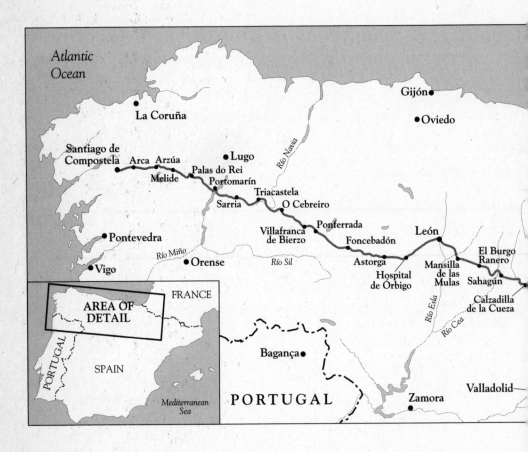

Atlantic Ocean

Gijón
Oviedo
La Coruña
Santiago de Compostela
Arca Arzúa
Palas do Rei
Melide Portomarín
Lugo
Triacastela
Sarria O Cebreiro
Ponferrada
Villafranca de Bierzo
León
Foncebadón
Pontevedra
Astorga
Mansilla de las Mulas
El Burgo Ranero
Sahagún
Hospital de Órbigo
Río Miño
Orense
Río Sil
Vigo
Calzadilla de la Cueza
Río Navia
Río Esla
Río Cea

FRANCE
AREA OF DETAIL
PORTUGAL
SPAIN
Mediterranean Sea
Bagança
PORTUGAL
Zamora
Valladolid

Road to Santiago

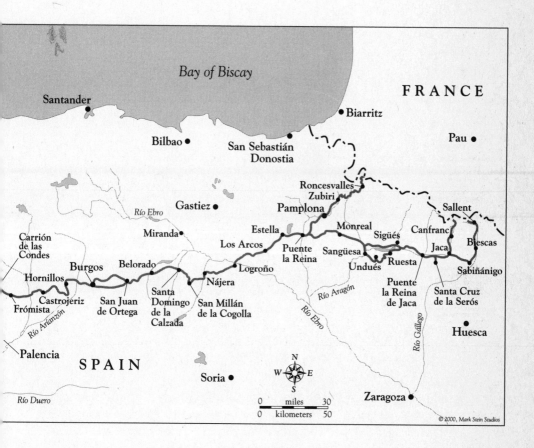

© 2000, Mark Stein Studios

PART I

The Road

1. Border → Canfranc

Route: Somport → Candanchú → **Santa Cristina** → Canfranc Estación → La Torreta → Canfranc

The central Pyrenees is a region of jutting peaks whose summits and upper slopes lie high above the tree lines. On the French side, north of the watershed axis, the valleys are wet, cold, and heavily forested. On the Spanish side, during the Pleistocene epoch massive glaciers scooped out U-shaped valleys perpendicular to the watershed divide, with lateral streams plummeting into the central valleys. The Spanish valleys drop rapidly into a much drier Mediterranean climate with markedly different vegetation: with each 200 m. of descent, 1 degree of mean annual temperature is gained, and several centimeters of annual precipitation are lost. The high valley walls all catch the winds and moisture and block the sunlight differentially, creating numerous microclimates. Overall, as you drop toward Jaca you will note a half dozen different ecosystems.

Several types of oaks are found in the upper valleys. The slopes and edges of the valleys are dense with heath-type plants: gorse (spiny, low, evergreen shrubs with yellow flowers), bracken ferns, Spanish broom, and heather. Along the streambeds are willows and poplars, and in the lower valley are thick tangles of briar. From midvalley almost to Jaca are thickets of boxwood (*boj; bojerales*). You will also see increasing quantities of wild herbs, particularly lavender (*lavanda*) and thyme (*tomillo*).

Along most of the descent, agricultural villages, spaced at 3- or 4-km. intervals, cling to small promontories or terraces that both offer protection and free up valuable bottomland for agriculture. The violent history of this region at the time the villages were established meant that there were almost no dispersed farmsteads.

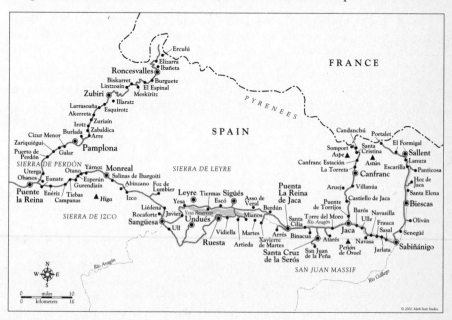

© 2000, Mark Stein Studios

Instead, peasants clustered their homes and barns for protection and walked daily out to their fields. Most of the isolated buildings you will see are modern.

✹ Somport The Somport pass (*Summus portus*; 1,640 m.) has been the preferred Roman route across the central Pyrenees ever since Cato conquered the Jacetania tribes around Jaca in 195 B.C.E. This relatively easy corridor from Oloron, France, to Jaca has been favored by merchants, pilgrims, and invading armies over the centuries. In the 4th c. the Vandals invaded through this pass. A century later the Visigoths swept through. In the 8th c. ragtag bands of Christians defended these heights against the Muslim invaders from the south, struggling to keep them from spilling into France. The 16th-c. Hapsburg kings fortified the pass against anticipated French invasions, but these did not come until 1809, when Napoleon's Mariscal Suchet swept through here on his way to occupy Jaca. When General Espoz y Mina finally ousted the French in 1814, they retreated along this same road. And modern bunkers from the time of the Civil War (see ch. 24) can still be seen along every pinch point leading up to the pass.

The pass also channeled most pilgrim traffic until the 12th c., when Navarran and Basque bandits were brought under control, making the much easier pass to the west through Roncesvalles safe. For most pilgrims, both medieval and modern, the entry into Spain was an emotional experience, for it meant that they had left their old lives behind and had reached the land of the Apostle. The breathtaking view of snowcapped peaks from the pass didn't hurt either.

The pass is marked by the Ermita del Pilar, built in 1992, and a modern pedestal decorated with the cross of Santiago.

At the border you are roughly 850 km. from Compostela.

✹ Candanchú (Camp d'Anjou). This was the camp established by the French Anjou dynasty that claimed sovereignty of the valley. At 1,560 m., today it thrives as a ski resort. Just below the town, on a spur of rock to the left of the highway, are scattered ruins of a castle erected early in the 13th c. for the protection of pilgrims. It was purchased by the king of Aragón in 1293 and abandoned in 1458. From the ruins you can see the glaciers of Candanchú and Rioseta. Look here, too, for Civil War bunkers.

The reddish conglomerate and sandstone La Raca cliffs on the east wall of the valley are fragments of the mountains that preceded the Pyrenees some 300 million years ago. To the south are the so-called interior mountains, recrystalized calcium deposits of the Devonian period, twisted by tectonic forces and dissolved and eroded by water in a karstic action that has created many caves.

✹ **Santa Cristina** The 12th-c. *Codex Calixtinus* (see ch. 16) in 1140 lauded the hospice of Santa Cristina—often referred to generically as simply El Hospital—as one of the world's 3 great pilgrim hospices:

> God has, in a most particular fashion, instituted in this world three columns greatly necessary for the support of his poor, that is to say, the hospice of Jerusalem, the hospice of Mount-Joux [a reference to San Bernardo, in the Swiss Alps], and the hospice of Santa Cristina on the Somport pass. [CC: Book V; trans. Melczer, 87]

Tradition holds that the original hospice was built by 2 pilgrims lost in the snow who were led to shelter here by a white dove carrying a golden cross. Documents, on the other hand, show that its founding was due to the collaboration of 2 princes, King Sancho Ramírez of Aragón (who visited here in 1078) and Count Gastón IV of Bearne, who died in 1130 while fighting the Muslims. Donations poured in, so that by mid-13th c. Santa Cristina owned some 14 churches in France and another 30 in Aragón, including property in places as far afield as Tarazona,

Calatayud, and Castejón. Numerous kings and popes contributed to its maintenance. In return, Santa Cristina maintained a network of smaller hospices in all of
the neighboring mountain passes. They all offered lodging, food, pasturage for the
pilgrims' animals, an infirmary, and money-changing facilities.

The hospice and priory of Santa Cristina prospered during the boom years of
the pilgrimage. But in 1569 its community of monks was moved to Jaca at the
request of the bishop, and in 1592 it was demolished and its stones used in building Jaca's new fortifications. The community maintained a small shelter for pilgrims during the summers until the 1835 general *desamortización*. Excavations in
1987–9 to the southeast of the Fuente de los Frailes revealed Santa Cristina's general
ground plan, including a monastery, church, and a hospice measuring 25 × 13 m.

Some 300 m. below the ruins are remnants of the Escarne Bridge, cited in documents dated 1586.

On the left, 2 km. before Canfranc Estación at the Coll de Ladrones, are extensive
late-19th-c. **fortifications** that incorporate a 1592 castle built as part of the defensive line anchored in Castiello de Jaca. The picturesque drawbridge and moat date
from ca. 1900. By the bridge below the castle used to stand the Ermita de San
Antón, completely demolished when the highway was built in 1888.

✱ Canfranc Estación A railroad connecting Spain and France through a great
Pyrenean tunnel was projected in 1853. But engineering difficulties and politics,
particularly the fear of invasion from the north, slowed the project, and actual
work did not begin until 1904. The railroad was not inaugurated until 1928.
Except for wartime, service continued from then until 1970, when an accident on
the bridge of L'Estanguet put an end to scheduled international service. As we
write, the tunnels are being reconditioned for modern use.

Canfranc Estación is a town built both by and for the railroad. Its great
esplanade was created with earth removed from the railroad tunnel, and the river
was rechanneled to permit the esplanade's construction. The town's population
swelled in 1944 when a disastrous fire devastated the ancient village of Canfranc,
further down the valley. The boom ended when the trains stopped running, and
the imposing railroad station was left to crumble to ruin. In the last few years Canfranc Estación has found new life as a ski center.

The reservoir and hydroelectric station below Canfranc Estación were built—
largely by manual labor—from 1957 to 1971.

Below Canfranc Estación the valley sides are composed of sedimentary rocks from
a 100-million-year-old sea. Pressures from the lifting of the Pyrenees folded the
rocks spectacularly. The imposing mountains to the left are Anayet (2,545 m.), La
Moleta (2,576 m.), and Collarada (2,886 m.) To the right rises the Pico de Aspe
(2,645 m.).

✱ La Torreta This picturesque castle, also called the Torre de Fusileros and the
Torreta de Espelunca, is an 1876 fortification built on the site of 16th- and 18th-c.
forts. On our last visit for the first time we found it open, splendidly restored to
become the Centro de Información del Túnel de Somport.

2. CANFRANC

HISTORY

Canfranc's name derives from *Campus Franci*, the field of foreigners. As the first truly habitable place on the Spanish side of the pass, Canfranc developed into a market and travelers' supply town. It was also a frontier control post, defending the entrance to Iberia and collecting road tolls, which in the early 11th c. Ramiro I donated to the Cathedral of Jaca. In the early 12th c. Alfonso el Batallador gave most of the town to Santa Cristina de Somport.

Unfortunately, little remains of medieval Canfranc, for almost the entire village was destroyed in a disastrous fire in 1617. Another fire in 1944 destroyed most of what had been rebuilt, and many of the citizens relocated to Jaca or to Canfranc Estación.

PILGRIMAGE

For centuries Canfranc's citizens rendered service to the Crown by keeping the Road open and assisting pilgrims rather than paying taxes, a privilege reconfirmed in 1440 by Queen María.

Canfranc had a hospice from at least the 12th c., probably near the ruins of a Romanesque church, documented in 1095, near the south end of the village.

MONUMENTS: 1. Mill. 2. Tower house. 3. Iglesia de Nuestra Señora de la Asunción. 4. Iglesia de la Santísima Trinidad.

1. Mill. On the left of the main street as you enter Canfranc, along the riverbank, are the ruins of an old mill. Across the street are the ruins of Canfanc's small 16th-c. castle, erected over a much earlier tower house.

2. Some remnants remain of another tower house in the center of town, probably the one built in 1341 by Pedro IV.

3. Iglesia de Nuestra de la Asunción. Built late in the 12th c., the church was given in 1202 by Pedro II to the Priory of Santa Cristina of Somport. Its original vaulting was destroyed in the 1944 fire.

4. Iglesia de la Santísima Trinidad. At the south end of town are the roofless ruins of a Gothic church built by a private citizen, Blasco de Les, ca. 1500. The interior has remnants of a Plateresque arch. Blasco also built a hospice here, of which nothing remains.

3. CANFRANC → JACA

Route: CANFRANC → **Villanúa** → Aruej → Castiello de Jaca → Puente de Torrijos →
JACA

From Canfranc, the Road descends on the left bank of the Río Aragón. Past the
cemetery you will cross a Romanesque bridge.

Between Canfranc and Villanúa the geology of the valley changes. Now the
rocks are marine sediments, sand and clay, slate and schist. These softer rocks permitted the glaciers to scoop out the deeper and wider valley that allows farming.

Just before Villanúa, to the east of the road is a small 5,000-year-old dolmen. At
the point where you can first see the concrete electric facility on top of the dam, it
lies 50 m. to the left of the path, in the middle of a broad field, in a circle of briars.
The site is 300 m. before the Cueva de Guixas.

The Cueva de Guixas (Witches' Cave) is one of many in the karst limestone formations near Villanúa. It was excavated in 1975, and human remains from 10,000
B.C.E to 300 C.E were discovered. If the entrance is locked, ask at the Ayuntamiento
in Villanúa.

✱ Villanúa The town's name derives from the fact that it was "newly" repopulated at the end of the 10ᵗʰ c. In 1097 Pedro I gave the town to the monastery of
Santa Cruz de la Serós. The Romanesque bridge at the entrance to town, documented in 1175, was rebuilt in 1963. Near it are the ruins of a former hospice. The
old part of Villanúa lies to the left of the river. The 13ᵗʰ-c. church of San Esteban
reputedly has a **Romanesque Virgin** and an image of **Santiago Peregrino**, probably
from the 15ᵗʰ c.

Beyond Villanúa the valley opens up into a geologic formation called flysch, characterized by soft sandstone and *lutita* rocks from the middle Eocene epoch, easily
folded by tectonic pressures. The valley contains lots of evidence of glaciation,
from the scarring on the cliff sides to the piles of gravel in the riverbeds, deposited
in ancient moraines.

✱ Aruej This tiny hamlet is private property. The 12ᵗʰ-c. church of San Vicente,
round-apsed and barrel-vaulted, was recently restored by its owner, who added a
family mausoleum near the bell wall. The hill to the west of the town, called Co-
lina de Santiago, was the site of an earlier settlement here. The largest house in
town, from the 15ᵗʰ c., has Renaissance windows and an 18ᵗʰ-c. balcony.

The valley from here down is intensely farmed, with wheat in the flatter fields
along the river and rye higher up. Most fields are left fallow every second year to
replenish the soil. Some fields serve for grazing, and some for growing hay for the
winter, a system known locally as *de diente y de siega* ("for teeth and harvest").
Since the 18ᵗʰ c., the valley has also raised potatoes. Stands of trees, especially oak,
are left for firewood and making charcoal.

✱ Castiello de Jaca When you reach this village you have descended to 921 m.
A town is mentioned here as early as 1042. The medieval town clings to a promontory both for defense and to leave the flat valley land for agriculture. The windows

in these typical Pyrenean stone houses tend to be oriented toward the south, for warmth, with balconies that permit the oblique winter sun to enter, but that cast shade in the summer and that protect from winter rain and snow. Balconies which block summer sun but allow winter sun in have been rediscovered in this century as a technique to create "passive solar" houses. The 2 styles of chimneys, the truncated cones of Aragón and the square box chimneys of France, hint at the town's hybrid origins. The bridge at the exit to town retains some medieval sections.

The Romanesque church of San Miguel Arcángel, like most in the valley, has been extensively reformed. Most of what remains is 16th c. Inside reputedly is a silver chest with a number of saints' relics that, according to local legend, were left by a pilgrim grateful for help received from townspeople. There is also a nice 1550 monstrance.

🚗 To the right of Castiello de Jaca, up the Lubiere Valley, is the town of Borau, and beyond it the *ermita* of San Adrián de Sasabe, with remains of a 1100–04 church, once half buried by floods and then restored in 1962. Originally it probably had a cloister. Notable are its carved capitals and the Lombard-style blind arches of its apse. Though the church seems isolated, it served as the region's cathedral in the 10th c. and produced 3 bishops. The remoteness of these lateral valleys reminds us of how beleaguered the Christian communities found themselves after the Muslim conquest, and what a stunning geographical and political advance the capture of Jaca was.

👟 Below Castiello, on the left bank of the Río Aragón where it is joined by the Río Ijuez and the Garcipollera Valley, are ruins of several *ermitas*. One is just past the railroad bridge on the road leading east into the Garcipollera Valley.

🚗 Nine km. up the Garcipollera Valley is the important 1072 Romanesque monastery of Nuestra Señora de Iguacel, with richly decorated capitals, stunningly high unbuttressed walls, and remnants of 13th-c. mural painting.

✽ Puente de Torrijos On the left bank of the river, across the railroad tracks, are the ruins of the Convent of Claraso and its church of Santiago. Just past km. 648 is a medieval bridge over the Aragón, and past it the 18th-c. Ermita de San Cristóbal (1796), built over an earlier church funded by Francisco Villanúa, an ink maker from Jaca.

Just outside Jaca, at the site of today's Hospital de la Salud, was a medieval leprosarium (see ch. 27).

As you approach Jaca you become aware that all of a sudden you are no longer hemmed in by the steep valley walls between which you have walked since descending from Somport. Jaca lies at the intersection of the narrow road to France and the broad, east-west road across Spain. It is the cork in the bottle. The first evidence of Jaca's military importance, both ancient and current, is an army base that guards the northern approach to the city.

4. BORDER → JACA

Route: GABAS → Portalet → El Formigal → SALLENT → Lanuza → Escarilla → Panticosa → Hoz de Jaca → BIESCAS → Oliván → Senegüé → SABIÑÁNIGO → Sasal → Jarlata → Frauca → Navasilla → Navasa → Ulle → Barós → JACA

❊ GABAS The last French town before the Portalet pass contains a 12th-c. Ermita de Santiago with modern additions based on medieval pilgrimage iconography. A man named Guillermo founded a hospice—long vanished—that once belonged to the monastery of Santa Cristina de Somport.

❊ Portalet The old pass of Portalet, 1,794 m. high, lies 2 km. east of the current highway and runs through a narrow, marshy mountain valley. At the center it is possible to find nearly adjoining rivulets running in opposite directions: north to France and the Gave River, and south to Spain, where they form the Río Gállego.

At the border you are roughly 880 km. from Compostela.

As you descend toward Sabiñánigo you will pass through several distinct geological and ecological zones. (1) From Portalet to Sallent: the axial ridge. The rocks are granite, composed of quartz, feldspar, and mica. Some are a compact *caliza negra*, a dense gray rock with veins of white. The jagged peaks and spongelike meadows harbor a variety of hardy low alpine plants, but almost no trees or shrubs. (2) From Sallent to Santa Elena: the *sierras interiores*. The gray rocks, frequently fine-grained in texture, contain tiny fossils of Cretacean marine microorganisms. The upper slopes are bare: the lower are thickly shrubbed. The valley is V-shaped, and its floor now sustains some minimal agriculture, but before the ski industry, local folk mainly herded sheep. (3) From Santa Elena to Senegüé: flysch formation. Here the rocks are softer, often composed of many fragments and pebbles cemented together with lime, and the glaciers have scooped out a U-shaped, broad valley, suitable for grain farming. (4) From Senegüé to Sabiñánigo: *margas*. These fine gray compacted sands line the east-west valley that stretches from Sabiñánigo nearly to Yesa. The valley floor is alluvial fans, washed from the surrounding hills. Fertile gently sloping fields alternate with deeply eroded gulleys.

❊ El Formigal This modern ski resort has a small late-10th-c. church transported from the nearby village of Basarán. A modern replica of the church tower of Larrede has been added to it.

❊ SALLENT A Roman bridge crosses the Río Gállego in the center of Sallent. During the Middle Ages, Santa Cristina de Somport also owned much of this town.

The ca. 1525 late Gothic **church of La Asunción** bears the coat of arms of Juan de Lanuza, the Aragonese royal official who paid for its construction. It has a beautiful starred vault. The 1537 Plateresque retablo was painted by Martín García and Antonio de Plasencia, followers of Pedro de Aponte, who was active in Aragón in the early 16th c. Typical of his Mannerist school are bright contrasting colors, a tendency toward chiaroscuro, and interesting background anecdotes. The contract for this retablo specified the iconography that the artists were to paint: the Crucifixion, Annunciation, Nativity, Epiphany, Resurrection, Ascension; Pentecost, Dormition, and Saints Benito and Bernardo.

An intricate gold late Gothic processional cross is to the left of the altar. To the right is the small chapel of La Virgen de las Nieves, patroness of mountain climbers. Although this church's interior has been thoroughly reformed, it preserves some Renaissance carving in this chapel: note the siren—half woman, half fish—and the floor-level rabbit.

A disastrous mudslide near Sallent on Aug. 7, 1996, killed more than 70 campers.

✳ Lanuza The 1897 church of El Salvador replaced an earlier structure. It was sacked during the 1936–9 Civil War (see ch. 24), and the few surviving pieces are in the Jaca museum. In 1975, when the reservoir was built, this entire town was expropriated and its 145 inhabitants relocated. The town is now being reconditioned for tourist purposes.

✳ Escarilla The Romanesque church of Escarilla has disappeared, though tradition recalls that it was decorated with scallop shells. The modern parish of San Joaquín has a nice Baroque retablo dedicated to San Sebastián.

From Escarilla you can follow the highway along the right side of the reservoir. We recommend the left side, through the yuppie ski town of El Pueyo de Jaca and through deep forests along the side of the reservoir. This road climbs 200 m. to **Hoz de Jaca**, from which there are spectacular views west toward the Peña Telera (2,764 m.) and east toward the Peña Blanca (2,556 m.), both snow-covered during much of the year. The town's small stone church dates from the 17th or 18th c.

Three km. past the reservoir, on the left bank of the Gállego, are the *ermita* and fort of Santa Elena.

> 📖 Local legend holds anachronistically that a Roman Christian, Santa Elena, fleeing the Moors, hid in a small cave near here. Her refuge was concealed by a spider web, miraculously woven for her protection: *Donde la araña tejió, Elena se escondió* ["Where the spider wove, Elena hid"].

Although an *ermita* stood here since at least the 13th c., the current structure dates from the 16th–18th c. Three hundred m. down the hill to the right, after crossing the bridge over the gorge, is a small megalithic **dolmen**.

> 📖 These megalithic (meaning "big stone") single-chamber tombs, called dolmens, were commonly formed of series of upright monoliths capped with large horizontal slabs, frequently with an entrance tunnel leading to a circular chamber. They were built between the 4th and 2nd millennia B.C.E, and are found all over western Europe, including the British Isles, and all over Spain, with their highest concentrations in Brittany and Galicia.

✳ **BIESCAS** Biescas is divided by the Río Gállego into the right-bank *barrio* of El Salvador and the left-bank San Pedro, named for their churches. A bridge has joined them since Roman times, although the current bridge is modern. The town was almost totally destroyed by fire in 1936 during the Civil War, although a few old buildings remain. Notable are the 16th-c. mansion of the Acín family, called *La Torraza*, in the San Pedro district, and the slightly more modern Casa de Pepe Estaún, in El Salvador, with an interesting carving of a two-tailed siren.
  • San Pedro. The church supersedes one destroyed in the 1936–9 Civil War.

• San Salvador. Only the 12th-c. apse survived the recent Civil War. Inside is a 16th-c. silver processional cross.

> The village of Gavín, some 2 km. east on Highway 220, was totally destroyed in the 1936–39 Civil War. There are ruins of a 12th-c. church; nearby, to the north of the paved road, is the tower of the 10th-and-11th-c. Ermita de San Bartolomé, formerly part of the monastery of San Pelayo de Gavín, with well-preserved horseshoe arches and interesting capitals.

✱ **Oliván** The region around Oliván was the center of *mozárabe* immigration in the 10th–12th c.

> The Muslim conquest introduced a new ruling class, but for the most part did not uproot the resident Christian population, who continued to function as organized—if second-class—citizens of the Muslim states. Although with time many Christians converted, those who did not were called *mustaribun*, which the Christian dialect deformed to *mozárabes*. Sporadic pressures on the remaining Christian communities provoked violent response. In the 830s in Córdoba some Christians defied Islam, denounced Muhammad, and actively courted martyrdom, in part to bolster the faith of a Christian community increasingly given to the imitation of Islamic customs and to conversion and mixed marriage. The 850s produced some 50 martyrs, most of whom were instantly revered by the Christians as saints. This provoked even harsher reactions from the Muslim leadership, which in turn led many Mozarab families to seek refuge in the Christian north, particularly in remote mountainous regions like the Serrablo where they felt they would be safe.
>
> The Christian culture they brought with them was a blend of preconquest Visigothic customs, infused with a nostalgia for the "happy times" before 711, and a fondness for Islamic culture, including Islamic aesthetics. They also brought a tradition of monasticism and sparked the hermit movement that was so popular in the 9th- and 10th-c. Christian mountain states. They introduced the heresy of adoptionism: to refute Muslim claims that Christians worshiped 3 gods, Mozarabs insisted that Jesus was not divine but only the adopted son of God. They also brought their own liturgy, which some Christians in the northern states distrusted as alien, and perhaps heretical.
>
> Later Muslim rulers, particularly 'Abd-ar-Rahman III in Córdoba in the mid-10th c., treated their Christian taxpayers with great tolerance. But the invasions of fundamentalist Almoravids (1086) and Almohads (1147) sent new waves of Mozarab refugees streaming to the north.

The 14 surviving churches nearby mix Visigothic, Spanish pre-Romanesque, French Romanesque, and Islamic techniques and motifs. Since Almanzor did not raid the valley, many of the earliest works remain. Several stylistic phases are discernible:

ca. 950: small, rectangular, unadorned churches, none of which are on the Road;

960–1000: horseshoe arches set into geometric frames (*alfiz*), with wood roofs, apses decorated with vertical rows of billets, and entrances through the south wall favoring doors with horseshoe arches (Busa, Larrede, and several others);

1000–1025: no horseshoe arches, no *alfices* (Orós Bajo, and others);

1025–1040: French influence in the strong bell towers and rounded apses deco-

rated with Lombard-Catalán blind arches (Oliván, Susín, and others). All of
these churches are notable for their absence of sculpted decoration, probably
reflecting the Islamic culture's ban on representing the human figure.

• **Orós Bajo.** 12th c., with one cruciform window in the Lombard style and
another which seems to be 13th-c. Romanesque. The apse is decorated with a
series of 7 arches on small columns.

Across the valley to the west is the village of Escuer, and above, at 1,124 m.,
sit the ruins of its medieval castle.

• **Oliván.** The church windows have horseshoe arches. Blind arches and a frieze
of cylindrical billets decorate the apse. The flat slate roof, typical of the region,
is weighted against the winds by a central capping of large stones. The village,
which like so many in the valley was crumbling into ruin as late at the 1970s,
has been lovingly restored by its inhabitants.

> From Oliván a 2-hour side trail climbs to **Susín**, a hamlet (*caserío*)
> whose church has double horseshoe windows framed by an *alfiz*. The
> apse is decorated with blind arches and a frieze of billets. The rest of the
> church is largely 18th-c. The interior retains vestiges of 18th-c. mural
> painting. The Romanesque murals from its apse are now in the Jaca
> museum (ch. 5).

• **San Juan de Busa.** The Mozarabic church, which stands alone in the countryside halfway between Susín and Larrede, has suffered few changes over the centuries. Its rectangular nave is covered with a wood roof. The original
door—now blocked in—has a horseshoe arch set into a low-relief squared *alfiz*.

• **San Pedro de Larrede.** Early 11th c., restored in 1935. Its horizontal lines balance perfectly with the verticality of its bell tower. Its entrance has a horseshoe
arch framed by an *alfiz*. An *alfiz* also frames its windows. There are blind arches
on its apse. The church is also notable inside for its barrel vault and 14th-c. baptismal font. Note the late medieval defensive tower on the hill east of the
church.

Larrede also contains the mansion of the López family with its coat of arms.

Beyond Larrede you can cross the suspension bridge and exit on the highway at
Senegüé. The small town of rich stone houses has a 17th-c. church of Nuestra
Señora de la Asunción whose tall tower can be seen for kilometers in every direc-
tion. Or you can continue down the left bank of the Gállego to **Satué**, with its
Romanesque-Mozárabe church. Its nave is covered with wood, its apse with a
quarter-sphere stone vault.

✳ **SABIÑÁNIGO** This strategic transportation crossroads in the central Pyrenees is
called *Sabiniacum* in several Roman itineraries. Little is known about it during
Visigothic times. The Muslim Abinyunash built a small castle to defend the crossroads. Sancho III of Navarra reconquered the area in the early 11th c. During most
of the Middle Ages it pertained directly to the Aragonese monarchy and thrived as
a market town and travelers' way station, although never to the extent of neighboring Jaca. Modern Sabiñánigo boomed with the arrival of the railroad in 1918.
The town was almost entirely destroyed in the 1936–9 Civil War. With the construction of the reservoirs in the 1950s, Sabiñánigo's access to cheap hydroelectric
and natural gas power contributed to rapid industrialization, as well as to the
depopulation of the surrounding agricultural region.

Sabiñánigo is the capital of the Serrablo region, which comprises the valleys of the Gállego and Guarga Rivers and their watersheds.

• **Museo Ángel Orensanz.** For any pilgrim interested in the culture of the small agricultural villages through which you will be passing over the next few days, this museum is a must. The ca. 1830 Casa Batanero, home of the sculptor Ángel Orensanz, has been lovingly restored. Each room displays artifacts, photographs, and exhibits that demonstrate some aspect of rural life in the Serrablo. Here you will see what lies inside the massive stone walls and the characteristic Aragonese round stone chimneys of the village houses. The chimney projects down into a massive square smoke catcher, over a stone or brick hearth surrounded by benches that are the center of family activity. Dozens of handmade kitchen artifacts hang from the walls and beams. The house contains bedrooms, workrooms, and storerooms. Fascinating photographs depict Pyrenean life as it was before the Civil War. Especially impressive is the display of wool, hemp, and linen cloth, and the hundreds of ingenious tools used to produce it. There is also a fine collection of photographs of *romerías*, local pilgrimages to the mountain *ermitas*.

🚗 East of Sabiñánigo along the Basa Valley, through Sardas, Osán, and Isún (with a Mozárabe church) is the **Ermita de Santa Orosia**, unofficial patron of the region, which is thronged with pilgrims each year on June 25. The festival is known for its unique dances.

From Sabiñánigo to Jaca we prefer a back road. It is not much longer and avoids all the highway traffic. You'll pass through several hamlets—Sasal, Jarlata, Frauca, Navasilla, Navasa, Ulle, and Barós—each with a small church (these are rarely open). The spectacular Romanesque murals from Navasa's tiny church are in the Jaca museum. The road, paved about halfway, runs due west between 2 lines of hills. To the right: jagged, bare, conglomerate rock with a layer of gray *marga* right next to the road. To the left: the much taller, forested slopes of the *terciario continental*, culminating in the immense massif of the Peñón de Oroel, to the southwest. These formations—results of ancient tectonic folding—will be visible almost all the way to Puente la Reina de Jaca.

5. JACA

Geography dictates Jaca's importance. The barrier of the Pyrenees separates Iberia from the rest of Europe. The easiest pass in the central Pyrenees, Somport, leads to Jaca. Almost all of the steep-sided, narrow valleys of the Pyrenees run north-south, impeding lateral communication. The first natural east-west route one encounters in Iberia is the valleys of the Aragón and Gállego rivers, separated only by a low ridge between Sabiñánigo and Jaca. Thus the promontory on which the city of Jaca is built dominates the junction of the most important natural roads in northern Iberia.

Because of its strategic importance, Jaca has been much coveted. Both Strabo (1st c.) and Ptolemy (2nd c.) mentioned the site. Pliny called the natives of this region *iacetani*, from which the name Jaca derives. Iberians minted coins here bearing the word IAK. In 195 a Roman garrison fortified the hill that controlled the Roman highway. Little is known about the region in Visigothic times. The Muslim occupiers also considered the site a stronghold.

After the early-8th-c. Muslim conquest, the meager Christian resistance holed up in the inaccessible mountain valleys of the north. The flat agricultural lands, and the major communication routes, lay entirely in Muslim hands. Jaca was a natural Christian priority of the reconquest wars, for its capture would mean that for the first time the Christians had broken out of their mountain prison. It was finally retaken at the end of the 8th c. by García Iñiguez I, ruler (758–ca. 802) of the neighboring Christian county of Sobrarbe. Ramiro I, who inherited the county of Aragón from his father, Sancho III el Mayor, established himself in Jaca, elevated the county to a kingdom, and in 1042 created a bishopric there. The charter (*fuero*) that was granted the city in 1063 served as a model for most of the kingdom, directly influencing the charters of Estella, Sangüesa, and Puente la Reina. Jaca served as the capital of tiny, mountain-locked Aragón until Huesca, the first Christian lowland reconquest, was recaptured from the Moors in 1096.

Medieval Jaca grew by stages clearly perceivable on the city map. The 10th-c. city grew around a fortified tower at the cliff edge. It lay between the modern Calle Oroel, the Puerta Nueva, and the 2 streets Siete de Febrero and Gil Berges. A second neighborhood grew up around the cathedral, and a third in the center of town, bisected by the Calle Mayor and Ramón y Cajal. By the 13th c. Jaca's wall followed what is now the streets of Regimiento Galicia, Jacetania, and Oroel: it had 23 towers and 7 gates.

Jaca was always a strategic prize. Navarra besieged it, unsuccessfully, in 1141. An English siege in 1366 also failed. Felipe II, worried about a French Huguenot invasion, fortified it in 1592. The French, who invaded through the Somport pass, captured it in 1809. The Spaniards who retook it in 1814 demolished the ancient city walls.

Medieval Jaca, like other prominent towns along the Road, had numerous neighborhoods (*barrios*) for the different ethnic groups who vied for commercial advantage. The Burnau (*burgo nuevo*) housed foreign merchants. The Jewish quarter was first located where the Ciudadela de San Marcos now stands, and later moved to the Barrio del Castelar, on both sides of the Calle Estudios. Jaca had 2 synagogues. After the 1492 expulsion one became an art school, and in the late 19th c. was converted to a garrison house, still called the Cuartel del Estudio.

JACA

PILGRIMAGE

The main altar of the cathedral holds the remains of Santiago's disciple San Indalecio. It bears the inscription: *Indaletii ossa theca tegit sidera mentem* ("The urn covers the bones of Indalecio; stars cover his mind").

As the first city of note south of Somport, Jaca was an important staging area for pilgrims and boasted several hospices. As early as 1084 King Sancho Ramírez is recorded as having financially supported the hospice of Sancti Spiritus. At least 4 other now-vanished hospices have left documentary evidence of their existence during the Middle Ages. By the early 1990s Jaca had again opened an Albergue de Peregrinos. Jaca's traditions of hospitality remain strong. The combined traffic of young pilgrims, skiers and hikers, and soldiers on leave insures a raucous nightlife. Pilgrims who have forgotten something essential at home can easily buy it in Jaca. Our daughters' favorite chocolate shop on the whole Santiago route is opposite the cathedral.

MONUMENTS: 1. **Cathedral.** 2. **Diocesan Museum.** 3. Iglesia de Santiago. 4. **Convento de las Benedictinas.** 5. Iglesia del Carmen. 6. Ayuntamiento. 7. Hospital del Espíritu Santo y de San Juan Bautista. 8. Clock tower. 9. **Ciudadela.**

1. **Catedral de San Pedro.** It may not look like much today, but this unprepossessing, dark little cathedral set the mode for churches all along the pilgrimage route. Take an hour or two to study its details, for you will see them replicated a hundred times along the Road. Little remains today of the original structure, but that little is a mecca for pilgrims and anyone with an informed interest in Romanesque art.

The church amalgamates French Romanesque and Iberian Mozarabic traditions. Construction may have been begun by King Ramiro ca. 1035, but clearly began in earnest ca. 1076 under Sancho Ramírez, and was finished in 1139. It suffered substantial damage in a 1395 fire. A 1430–5 campaign repaired the damage and added the chapels of Santa Orosia and Santa Cruz, but in 1440 the roof burned again. The current vaults were added in 1520–30, the sacristy in 1562. Rebuilding in 1790–2 destroyed the original Romanesque chevet. On the exterior, only the south and west portals and the southern apse retain Romanesque elements, but they are of monumental importance. In another month we will see this cathedral as it used to be, for San Martín de Frómista, on the plains of Castile, largely echoes Jaca in miniature.

Exterior:

- The western monumental **portico**, capped with a tower joined to the nave, was a relatively common French style introduced to Iberia with this church. It demonstrates a new preoccupation with proportion and technique characteristic of an experienced master and crew backed by ample resources. The concentration of decoration in the portico, the tympanum, and the capitals was also new to Spain. The larger-than-life Renaissance-style statues of 6 Apostles were taken from an earlier retablo on the main altar. The first on the right is **Santiago**.
- The west portal **tympanum**, executed ca. 1100, features a *crismón*, a paleo-Christian motif invented to distinguish Catholic monuments from those of the Aryans. Its symbolic design contains the cross, the chi-rho that begins the name *Christus* in Greek, and the alpha and omega indicating that Christ is the beginning and end of all things. The Jaca *crismón* is the earliest in Spain. It was imitated all along the Road and appears more than 50 times just in Huesca and Navarra. In Jaca it is flanked by 2 stylized lions and is labeled with a Latin inscription.

> 📖 The *crismón* inscription reads: *Hac in scultura lector, sic noscere cura: P, Pater; A Genitus, Duplex est spiritus almus: Hii tres iure quidem dominus sunt unus et idem.* ("Reader: in this carving take care that you learn the following: P = Father, A = Son, and the double [letter] = the Nourishing Spirit. The three are indeed the one and the same Lord.") The sculpted lions, symbol of Christ in the Apocalypse, are also inscribed. Left: *Parcere sternenti leo scit, xristusque petenti* ("The lion knows how to show mercy to the one prostrating, as Christ to the one calling on Him"). Right: *Imperium mortis conculcans est leo fortis* ("The lion is strong, trampling underfoot the empire of Death").

- The **south porch and portal** was assembled ca. 1600 with architectural elements of diverse ages taken from the cloister and other parts of the building. Many of the capitals are copies of originals in the cathedral museum, but two are worth particular note. On the left of the door is a well-executed **Balaam** on his ass (God caused the mistreated ass to speak [Num. 22:21–34]). On the right, Abraham's **sacrifice of Isaac** seems inspired by a similar capital in Frómista (proving that influences can run in both directions), that in turn was inspired by a Roman-Christian sarcophagus found near Frómista that is now in Madrid's

Museo Nacional de Arqueología. The high relief and graceful positioning suggest a sculptor from Toulouse. Isaac's face communicates anguish, reproof, and challenge at the same time. His right leg steps on his father's foot, as if to impede him from the murderous sacrifice. Abraham looks over his shoulder to the angel who brings him the message of salvation. What is most striking and rare about this dynamic capital is that the artist depicted Isaac nude and used the scene to study the musculature of the human torso.

• The outside of the **Apse of the Epistle** is all that remains from the sumptuously decorated building that set the **architectural vocabulary for Romanesque** decoration from the Pyrenees to Galicia. Its key elements are:

—a central narrow window flanked by columns topped by capitals and crowned by a semicircular, tubular arch (*baquetón*) and an external band of checkerboard decoration;

—checkerboard (*ajedrezado* or *taco*) decorations in horizontal bands (*impostas*) from the base of the window, from the top (*trasdós*) of the capitals, and under the eaves;

—narrow columns, serving both as buttresses and as vertical decorative motifs, counterpoint to the horizontal checkerboarding;

—decoration with flat metopes in between projecting corbels (*canecillos*), including human figures, grotesques, plant motifs, and groups of Islamic-inspired cylinders (*rollos*).

Interior:
This church did not set, but is clearly representative of, the basic design of early southwestern European Romanesque churches. Its principal elements are:

—basilica form with 3 naves, the central nave higher than the 2 lateral naves, and the naves separated by ranks of columns;

—barrel vaults, whose enormous weight is sustained in part by heavy supporting arches;

—naves ending in rounded chapels, vaulted with quarter-spheres;

—columns topped with decorated capitals mixing floral and figural motifs;

—in larger churches, a transept crossing in front of the main altar;

—a dome over the crossing, supported by squinches that reduce the square of the crossing to an octagon.

In addition, the interior of most Romanesque churches, including this one, would have been covered with bright mural paintings recounting biblical stories (see below). Jaca's transept, which does not extend beyond the naves, and the western narthex extending beyond the central nave are both classical in origin, and were not quite so widely imitated. The tower over the narthex-porch has precedent in the Mozarabic churches of the region.

• In the naves, note the unusual **alternation of grouped piers and columns**. With a strong flashlight and binoculars you will be able to determine that the capitals were carved by 3 separate sculptors: the master of Jaca, the master of doña Sancha's tomb (see below), and Maestro Esteban, genius of both the Pórtico de la Gloria in Compostela and the Pamplona Cathedral (see ch. 21).

• The current starred vaulting is 16th-c. The **dome** (*cúpula*) over the crossing, resting on conical or trumpet squinches (*trompas*) with its 4 intersecting ribs, is polemical: for some art historians it reflects Cordoban Islamic tastes; for others it anticipates the nerved arches of Gothic architecture. The original Romanesque semicircular apse has been replaced by a rectangular chancel of little interest.

• The main altar contains 3 silver urns: left—the remains of San Indalecio (see above); center—the 1731 sarcophagus of the virgin martyr Santa Orosia, of special veneration in the region; right—the remains of 2 early San Juan de la Peña Mozarabic monks, Saints Voto and Félix.

• Several of the chapels (considered counterclockwise from the west entrance), are worth a few moments.

Right nave:
　　—**Santa Ana**. In a solid, well-executed Renaissance grouping, Mary presents Jesus to his grandmother Santa Ana. The painted Pieta of the predella is flanked by Saints María Magdalena, Miguel, Juan Bautista, and Catarina.
　　—La Anunciación. Plateresque decoration.
　　—Cristo de la Salud. Realistic, life-size statue of Christ, object of significant local veneration.
　　—San Sebastián. With a Flamboyant Gothic doorway.
　　—**San Miguel**. The right side of the **Plateresque doorway** (1523) depicts San Roque with the crossed keys of St. Peter of Rome on his cloak, and the shell of the Santiago pilgrim on his hat. Note how he leans on his left leg and on his staff (now missing). On the left is San Cristóbal. San Miguel is in the center of this Italianate Renaissance retablo by Giovanni Moretto.

Chevet:
　　—**El Pilar**. This is one of the few internal vestiges of the original cathedral. The iron grille of tightly wound spirals reproduces a 12th-c. Romanesque chancel grille now in the cathedral museum. Intricate **capitals** from the early cloister support the altar table.
　　—Capilla Mayor and Choir. This 1790 painted addition to the cathedral now holds the organ and choir stalls.
　　—San Jerónimo. The Renaissance retablo echoes that of San Miguel.

Left nave:
　　—Santa Orosia. Six large 1780 paintings narrate the life of this local hermit-martyr-saint, patroness of Jaca.
　　—**La Trinidad** (or San Jerónimo). The entrance arch is transitional Plateresque-Baroque. The 1575 alabaster **retablo of the Trinity** by Juan de Anchieta has a nice Flamboyant Gothic frame, imitating Rome's Arch of Constantine. The composition is almost Baroque in its interplay on horizontals and verticals and its centripedal force, while the narrow and top-heavy upper story, and the rich Plateresque decoration, are grounded in Mannerism. The God figure of the Trinity is modeled on Michaelangelo's Moses.

2. **Diocesan Museum of Romanesque Painting**. Located in the Neoclassic cloister next to the cathedral, this is the best museum of Romanesque painting in Spain outside of Barcelona. It is easily worth a couple of hours of your time, and a couple of pages of ours. These paintings have been assembled from a number of small rural parish churches in the central Pyrenees. They were protected from ruin over the centuries because when artistic tastes changed they were covered with a cap of white plaster.

　　📖 In fresco painting the colors applied to fresh plaster penetrate to a depth of more than a centimeter. To prevent their deterioration in often remote villages, they have been removed by (1) fixing a cloth with an adhesive to the surface of the painting, (2) peeling the cloth with its thin coat of plaster from the wall, (3) gluing the removed painting to another surface for museum mounting, and (4) dissolving the initial adhesive and removing the cloth.

The splendidly mounted reconstructions in this museum give a sense of the paintings' original ambiance.

Romanesque mural painting of the central Pyrenees is prized for its vivid colors, its diversity of Old and New Testament themes, and the imaginative posing of the religious figures that are its subjects. Many of the fresco and tempera paintings offer glimpses of details of medieval life.

• The **Bagüés creation scene** (late 11th c.; prov. of Zaragoza). The Bagüés murals are one of the most complete sets surviving in Iberia. The various episodes of the Creation story—God with Adam, Adam naming the animals, the creation and blessing of Eve, her presentation to Adam, the serpent tempting Eve with fruit, etc.—are presented with a certain rigidity broken occasionally by dynamic details such as in the Slaughter of the Innocents and the Judas kiss (left wall). Here the placement of the figures creates tension, and the grimace of the man losing his ear to San Pedro's knife conveys strong emotion. Often the superimposition of figures, as in the Raising of Lazarus on the left wall, suggests an attempt to depict perspective. Unique in Spain is the substitution in the mandorla of the Ascension of Christ for Christ in Majesty.

• The **Ruesta Christ in Majesty** (late 12th c.; prov. of Zaragoza). You will encounter the ruins of Ruesta and of this church of San Juan Bautista later on the Road on the south bank of the Río Aragón. The iconography of this scene, immensely popular in the 12th c., is drawn from Apocalypse 4:2–8 and 5:8:

Lo, a throne stood in heaven, with one seated on the throne! And he who sat there appeared like jasper and carnelian, and round the throne was a rainbow that looked like an emerald. . . . Before the throne burn seven torches of fire, which are the seven spirits of God; . . . On each side of the throne are four living creatures, full of eyes in front and behind: the first living creature is like a lion, the second living creature like an ox, the third living creature with the face of a man, and the fourth living creature like a flying eagle. And the four living creatures, each of them with six wings, are full of eyes all round and within. . . .

The 4 beasts, often called the Tetramorphos, were taken to symbolize the 4 Evangelists and the themes of their Gospels: Matthew (man—the human qualities of Christ), Mark (lion—Christ's royal majesty), Luke (ox—Christ's sacrifice), and John (eagle—Christ's far-seeing omniscience).

• The **Navasa Christ in Majesty** (early 13th c.; prov. of Huesca, south of the highway connecting Sabiñánigo and Jaca). The depiction of the familiar scene is unusual in that the rather chubby Christ is seated on a cushion and lacks the surrounding mandorla. Below is a scene that conflates the Adoration of the Magi and the Flight into Egypt. Note the corporeal sense suggested by the strong geometry of the drapery. On the right, Luke's ox holds the Gospels in his hoof.

• The **Osia Coronation of the Virgin** (late 14th c.; prov. of Huesca, from the Ermita de Nuestra Señora del Rosario). Indicative of the new popularity of Marian imagery in the Gothic period, here Mary's coronation replaces the traditional Christ in Majesty. The lower register depicts Santa Lucía: presented to Pascasius, condemned to the bordello, resistant to a yoke of oxen brought to move her, her martyrdom and burial. The emphasis on architectural details in these scenes is unusual.

• The **Iguacel frontispiece** (c. 1300; prov. of Huesca).

> 📖 The Iguacel monastery, built in 1072 and given to San Juan de la Peña (see ch. 7) in 1094, became a major Cistercian center. Its church was one of the first in Aragón built in the European Romanesque style.

This altar frontal was found *in situ*, upside-down, where it was serving as an altar table. Its themes and style mark the transition from Romanesque to Gothic in Aragón. For example, the lightning bolt of the Annunciation uniting Mary with heaven is a Gothic motif. In the Byzantine-influenced Nativity scene the angels in heaven, the shepherds on the folds of the mountain, and the flocks below, form a sort of parenthesis between the earthly and divine in which the miraculous birth takes place. The disposition of the figures is particularly expressive. Note the doubt and reconciliation in the scene of Mary with Joseph.

The museum houses dozens of additional masterworks, especially Romanesque Virgins, stone capitals, and Gothic oil paintings on wood.

- The **capitals**. These are displayed up close at eye level and are well lighted, unlike the capitals in most of the dim, cavernous churches you will visit along the Road. Take a moment to appreciate some masterworks of very different styles. Contrast, for example, these three:
    —The capital on the right wall, next to the door to the chapter house, with its fat faces and curved drapery, relatively little detail but an overall sense of fluidity. It may be by the sculptor of San Juan de la Peña. Another by this artist is in Jaca's church of Santiago.
    —King David playing a rebec, surrounded by his backup musicians playing diverse instruments. Here the lines are much more angular, and the sculptor has chosen to emphasize fine detail.
    —The 3 headless women, probably adulteresses, given the snakes that are biting their breasts. These figures are more two-dimensional and very elongated, with drapery that emphasizes their verticality.

See if you can find other capitals by these same sculptors. Also take a look at the vast variety of treatments of the foliage on the Corinthian-style capitals.

- The **Virgins**. Romanesque Virgin Marys generally serve as a throne for the child-man Christ the King seated on their laps. Both have serious expressions and look straight forward; there is no interaction between them. The child's hand is often raised in blessing, or holds the Bible or an orb that signifies the world. Made of stone or wood, the figures were painted in bright colors. By contrast (there is a good example in gilt on the cloister wall), Gothic Virgins tend to be elongated, gracefully curved, and emphasize tender interaction between mother and child.

- The **paintings**. Late Gothic painting stressed elegant poses and engaging details. Our favorite here is the San Miguel from Otal. The fanciful demon is unable to influence Michael's weighing of 2 souls, even though, like a dishonest butcher, he puts his claw on the scale. The brocaded gilt background, the almost effeminate pose, and the rich costuming are all typical of this style.

3. **Iglesia de Santiago.** The 10th-c. church, destroyed by Almanzor, was rebuilt by Sancho Ramírez ca. 1088. It served as a parish church until 1614, when it was given to the Dominicans, renamed **Santo Domingo**, and substantially rebuilt. Much of the site, half hidden in the middle of the block between Calle del Ferrenal and Calle José M. Campo y Irigoyen, is now occupied by a school. Of the early

medieval church, only the Romanesque tower remains. Note the Mozarabic horse-shoe arch on the tower windows. The current church houses an 18th-c. retablo with a statue of **Santiago**. Just inside, to the right of the door, is an extraordinary **capital** from the early cathedral.

4. **Convento de las Benedictinas**. The convent was built in 1555 when the Benedictine nuns relocated to Jaca from Santa Cruz de la Serós, which you will visit in a day or two. Its crypt is the 12th-c. church of San Salvador, whose **Romanesque frescos** were transferred to canvas in 1965 and are displayed in the main church. Their themes are the Ascension (in which a standing Christ blesses his astonished Apostles), the Annunciation, the Visitation, the Nativity and Adoration, Epiphany, and the Presentation of Jesus in the Temple. Though the paintings are badly preserved, you can perceive their monumental intent and a variety of naturalistic details. The church's principal retablo contains José de Ribera's painting of San Mateo.

Toward the rear of the church is the extraordinarily expressive Romanesque **sarcophagus of doña Sancha**. Daughter of Aragonese King Ramiro I, widow of Count Ermengol III of Urgell, she was the founding abbess of the convent of Santa Cruz de la Serós (see ch. 7). One side depicts the canonical Jaca *crismón*. The other, by a different sculptor, shows the abbess being escorted to heaven inside an almond-shaped nimbus, an early representation of what was to become a common motif. She is escorted by her 2 widowed sisters, Urraca and Teresa, also nuns. Note the dynamic horsemen, griffins, and Samson wrestling with the lion.

5. Iglesia del Carmen. The Mannerist Baroque façade (1657) has Tuscan-style columns and escutcheons of the Carmelite order. There is a nice polychromed retablo on the main altar.

6. Ayuntamiento. Begun in 1544 in the Plateresque style, this Renaissance civic building has notable iron *rejas* in the windows.

7. Hospital del Espíritu Santo y San Juan Bautista. The current institution was founded in 1540. Note the eclectic Plateresque and Gothic decorations on the windows facing the Plaza del Hospital. The building, which served as a hospital for many years, is now again a pilgrim hospice.

8. Clock tower (*torre del reloj*). The clock tower formed part of an early Gothic royal palace that had been converted to a prison by the mid-13th c. Note the 15th-c. Gothic windows.

9. **Ciudadela**. Although the fort was begun in 1592 by Felipe II, who was concerned about a possible French invasion, it was not finished until 1641. Its designer was the noted Italian military architect Spannicchi. It was erected over the ruins of the extramural Burgo Nuevo. The immense pentagonal fort (260 m. per side!) features strong bulwarks, a drawbridge, and massive interior constructions. It is the only complete star-shaped fort in Spain. It is now a lovely park, in which we have frequently seen deer.

6. Jaca → Santa Cruz de la Serós

Route: Jaca → Torre del Moro → Atarés → Santa cruz de la Serós

✻ Torre del Moro This 14th-c. castle, also called the Torre de Boalar, has paired Gothic-style windows. Although no one knows its history, presumably it was constructed to protect the entrance to the valley.

Farmers in the narrow valleys south of the Río Aragón cultivate wheat and barley, raise sheep, and grow alfalfa and hay to feed their flocks in winter. Fork-tailed kites (*milanos reales*) patrol the skies over these valleys. Every time we have hiked through the oak forests that cover these hills we have heard the call of the cuckoo, although the small drab birds are secretive, and we have never knowingly seen one. The most notable geologic feature of these ridges is the narrow spines of hard sedimentary rock, raised vertical by tectonic folding and left jutting in the air by the forces of erosion that have washed away the surrounding softer rocks. These spines run from Sabiñánigo all the way to the beginning of the Yesa Reservoir at the border of Navarra.

✻ Atarés 840 m. This village, in the most fertile part of its valley, dates from at least the 9th c., when the area was repopulated by Count Galindo II. In 1188 Alfonso II of Aragón transferred title of the town to the nuns of Santa Cruz de la Serós. The church of San Julián incorporates the wall of a 10th-c. castle. It has a 15th-c. Flamboyant Gothic door.

7. SANTA CRUZ DE LA SERÓS AND SAN JUAN DE LA PEÑA

✴ Santa Cruz de la Serós

HISTORY

Santa Cruz de la Serós was founded ca. 1061 by Countess Sancha, daughter of Ramiro I of Aragón and widow of Count Ermengol III of Urgell. At first it was a dependency of the nearby monastery of San Juan de la Peña, but doña Sancha eventually made it independent and later Benedictine, the first convent for nuns in Aragón to come under the rule of Cluny. From its inception it served as a retirement home for upper-class widows—far enough from Jaca and Huesca so that they couldn't easily meddle in their sons' affairs, and close enough to the protective cliffs to offer a safe haven in times of trouble. Throughout the Middle Ages it was the most important women's convent in Aragón. In 1555 the whole community relocated to Jaca.

MONUMENTS: 1. **Convento de Santa María**. 2. **Ermita de San Caprasio**.

1. **Convento de Santa María**. The church is a splendid example of early Romanesque. The *crismón* with the 2 lions over the west portal is inspired by the Jaca Cathedral. The large, regularly cut stones of the nave (11th c.) and the apses and transept (12th c.) speak to the wealth that went into its construction. The whole building, and especially the tower, is exceptionally tall for a Romanesque church. You will need binoculars to view the corbels that sustain the roof, impressive in their variety and fine carving. A few of the flat metopes between the corbels are vestiges of what must have been an even richer display of decoration. The traces of polychrome remind us that the bare stone sculptures we appreciate today were in the Middle Ages a riot of color.

The massive nave is classic Romanesque. Look up—the barrel vault is held up by thick forming arches resting on decorated capitals, sustained in turn by tall columns. The horizontal lines of checkerboard decoration remind us that Jaca must have looked like this before its centuries of remodeling. But recalling what we saw in the Jaca Cathedral museum, we know that what strikes us today as imposingly sober was in the 12th c. covered with brightly painted narrations of biblical scenes.

Unique to this church is the large room hidden over the lantern vault that covers the crossing. The room—now reached by a modern spiral staircase in the nave that climbs to an upper staircase sandwiched between the walls—may have served as the abbess's quarters or as a hideaway for the nuns in times of danger. The **capital** on the west wall of this room, depicting the Annunciation, is a masterwork by the sculptor who carved doña Sancha's sarcophagus, now in Jaca. Note the corporeality of the angel under the drapes of his tunic and the subtle rhythm of the folds. The hair, mustache, and beard of Joseph, on the other side of the capital, make him look a little like a capuchin monkey.

Although the convent's cloister has disappeared, several of its capitals remain near the holy water font. One of the lateral retablos, from 1490, features a polychrome alabaster Virgin and scenes of Calvary and of the life and Dormition of Mary.

2. **Ermita de San Caprasio**. The hermitage is dedicated to 5th-c. San Caprasio, either the bishop of Arles (June 1) or the martyred bishop of Agen (Oct. 20). His

(their?) popularity is one more sign of French influence along the road. In the 11th c. the *ermita* had a single nave. In the 12th c. two more were added, as well as the external Lombard-Catalán-style blind arches that in addition to their decorative function serve as buttresses, allowing a thinner wall. The tower was added in the 13th c.

Over the centuries the village houses incorporated stones from the abandoned convent; you will find several finely carved, incongruous details here and there around town. One house sports a lintel with a cross and two lions; another has a *crismón*; several incorporate capitals.

The San Juan Massif forms a wall on the south side of the Río Aragón and literally towers over Santa Cruz de la Serós. For the pilgrim the 300-m. climb to San Juan de la Peña is an arduous detour, but well worth the time and effort. Not only is San Juan a spectacular monument of Romanesque art, it is a key to understanding the early development of the Spanish Church and the kingdom of Aragón.

✳ San Juan de la Peña

HISTORY

While the mountain barrier did not keep Muslim troops from overrunning the Aragón Valley, its many caves offered refuge both to religious hermits and to the meager Christian resistance. One legend—recounted in the 14th-c. *Chronicle of San Juan de la Peña*—holds that in the early 8th c. Juan Atarés established a small hermitage in a cave in the cliffs of the massif. Two centuries after his death, his work was continued by the brothers Voto and Félix, 2 *mozárabes* fleeing Muslim persecution in Zaragoza. They moved Juan's relics to a small church that they dedicated to San Juan Bautista. Around the year 920, the brothers Julián and Basilissa founded a monastery on the spot. From their mountain sanctuary the monks organized military resistance to the Muslim occupation of the region. They even appointed a king, García Jiménez, who built a small church here and designated it a cathedral, at that time the only one in Aragón. A competing legend says that a hunter from Zaragoza who was thrown by his horse over the rock face was saved by intercession of San Juan Bautista and in thanks dedicated a monastery to him on the site. Both legends assert that for 3 centuries San Juan de la Peña was a stronghold of religion and of arms, so important that it was targeted and largely destroyed ca. 990 in the raiding expedition of the Cordoban Almanzor.

The monastery was equally important to Christians, so reconstruction was immediate. Ca. 1025 King Sancho III el Mayor underwrote a substantial building campaign that included a new church, dedicated to Saints Julián and Basilissa. The church was entrusted with the realm's most sacred relic: the legendary Holy Grail.

> 📖 Tradition holds that St. Lawrence sent the Grail from the Holy Land to his hometown of Huesca, and that it was hidden in San Juan de la Peña when the Muslims overran the Peninsula. In 1399 the monks sent it to the Aljafería in Zaragoza, who sent it in 1437 to Valencia. Another tradition sites the Grail in O Cebreiro (see ch. 72).

Recent studies suggest a somewhat different early history, suggesting that the remote mountain hermitage of Julián and Basilissa had been long abandoned when in 1071 King Sancho Ramírez of Aragón established a new monastery on the site under the auspices of the Benedictines of Cluny. San Juan de la Peña was chosen for important church councils. One decreed that all Aragonese bishops had to come from this monastery. The second eschewed the Mozarabic-style worship for the Roman rite, which soon spread through all of Spain: on March 22, 1071, the monks here celebrated the first Roman liturgy mass on the Peninsula. From San Juan de la Peña the Cluniacs rapidly extended their sway over the Aragonese church.

📖 The Benedictine abbey of Cluny, founded in 910 in the forests of northern France, was from its inception a stronghold that, independent of any feudal influence, reported directly to the Pope. The superb organizational skills of its abbots (Peter the Venerable, and Saints Mayeul, Odilon, and Hugh), its political prominence, and its early reputation for strict adherence to the Benedictine rule, gained adherents all over Christendom. By 1010 its dependencies numbered well over 1,000. By 1160 they topped 3,000. Its abbots were allied with kings, and chose—or even became—the Pope. Throughout Europe, monarchs, like those of the Iberian kingdoms, were eager to have the principal monasteries in their realms affiliate with Cluny as part of their strategy of modernization, economic development, and control. By the end of the 11th c. the Cluniacs' temporal power had diluted their commitment to poverty and simplicty to such an extent that several splinter groups broke off. The most successful were the Cistercians (see ch. 10).

Unlike many Cluny dependencies, San Juan de la Peña's abbot reported directly to the Pope. He also had both voice and vote in the Aragonese *Cortes* (parliament). Donations of property poured in: at its height San Juan de la Peña owned outright more than 300 towns.

San Juan de la Peña also prospered politically. Kings were crowned at San Juan de la Peña, they went there to be blessed before battle, and they sent the women of the court there to be safe in time of trouble. Finally, they were buried there.

The rock stronghold was much too small for the community, so it added a second facility on the mountain top. After these buildings were destroyed in a fire, a major new monastery was built between 1675 and 1714. The French invasion of 1809 destroyed the mountain top monastery completely, and yet another new church, this time with a Churrigueresque front, was built between 1814 and 1828.

MONUMENTS: 1. **Old monastery**. 2. New monastery.

1. **Old monastery**. The site itself is stunning. The earliest parts were carved into natural caves in the bulging orange cliff, and later buildings were added in front, above, and below them, so that the whole complex today forms a jumble whose understanding gives pause to even the most three-dimensionally adept pilgrims. It is impressive when you approach by car on the road, and absolutely astonishing when you emerge upon it from the forest.

• The 9th-c. **Low church** (*Iglesia baja*), dedicated to Saints Julián and Basilissa, was consecrated in 922 and is typical of a small Visigothic monastery. Its simple church and small sleeping room are the earliest extant remains. The inscription over the door—*Porta per hanc coeli fit cuique fideli, si studeat fidei jungere jussa Dei* ("This will be heaven's door, through here, for believers who strive to conform their will to God's faith")—welcomes worshipers and reminds all, even the Aragonese monarchs, who is truly in charge.

In the apse are some remains of a ca. 1170 Romanesque **mural painting** with strong lines and colors (the same artist may have worked at San Isidoro, a monastery you will see in León). On the left dome, Saints Cosmas and Damian stand on a platform, their hands raised in supplication; above them rises heaven. In the corners there are 2 angels. Below, on both sides, executioners stoke a fire.

• The **Council chamber** (*Sala del concilio*), shaped from an early monastic dormitory, hosted the famous councils of the mid-12th c.

• The **Nobles' pantheon** (*Panteón de los ricos hombres aragoneses*) houses the remains of Aragonese kings and nobility from 1009 to 1325. The majority of the preserved tombs are 12th c., although their current arrangement dates from Carlos III's refurbishing in 1770. The Jaca *crismón* motif and the angels bearing a soul to heaven in a mandorla are typical of medieval funeral art. Other references on the tombs are to specific families. The cross with the roses on its end is the emblem of Pamplona's Iñigo Arista family; the shoes (*abarcas*) indicate the Abarca family of Garcipollera, northeast of Sabiñánigo.

• The **High church** (*Iglesia alta*), constructed in the late 11th c. and consecrated by King Sancho Ramírez in 1094, is early Romanesque in style. The front of the nave is vaulted by the mountain itself, and the apses, though prefaced with columns and blind arches, were carved out of solid rock. Curiously, here a single nave terminates in 3 apses, while they usually match 1 to 1. A Mozarabic horseshoe arch leads to the cloister.

• The chapels of Saints Voto and Victoriano, from ca. 1420, are in the Flamboyant Gothic style.

• The **Royal Pantheon.** The Neoclassic burial room was commissioned by Carlos III of Spain in 1770. The stucco frieze on the left represents various episodes of Aragonese history: the king granting a charter (*fuero*), the reconquest of Huesca, and the Battle of Ainsa, where a cross appeared miraculously on a live oak tree. Folk etymology holds that the name of the Sobrarbe region derives from this miracle; linguists counter that the region butts up against the Sierra de Arbe, which separates the Sobrarbe from Barbastro.

• The extraordinary **cloister**, sheltered by the rock overhang of the cliff, is worth the climb all by itself. Its dating is controversial, with estimates running from 1075 to 1200; most of the construction is probably late 12th c. The freestanding arcades of the cloister have been reconstructed several times, most recently in 1950. The column arrangement, whereby each of the corner capitals crowns 4 columns and the others crown pairs of columns, is common in French-inspired cloisters and is probably a Cluniac influence. The running decorative cornice and the semicircular arches between the columns, while not unique to San Juan de la Peña, are somewhat less common. On the walls are inscriptions from the 12th through the 16th c.

Before reading further, take a few moments to study the **capitals**, relishing their details and seeing how many different artists' styles you can discern.

Art historians call the most important of these sculptors the **Master of San Juan de la Peña.** Characteristic of his style are the short, almond-eyed, beatific smiling figures, arranged in semirealistic poses that—atypically for the normally static Romanesque—create a sense of wavy rhythm.

📖 The Master of San Juan de la Peña's work will also be seen later on the Road in the high sculpture on Santa María in Sangüesa (see ch. 12) and off the Road at San Pedro el Viejo in Huesca and in decoration at Santiago de Agüero and Egea de los Caballeros.

The north gallery begins with the Creation—and a newly knowledgeable Adam embarrassed at his nakedness—and ends with Christ calling the Apostles. Atypical for the period, this master artist seems to have given rein to his sense of humor: note the angel waking up one of the lazy Magi to get him on the road to Bethlehem. Though they are biblical scenes, several of the capitals offer typical glimpses of medieval life: a woman spinning with a drop spindle and distaff, a man plowing with a yoke of oxen, and a banquet table.

The symmetrically paired, oriental-style animals and monsters—here by another hand—are motifs common on capitals everywhere in the Romanesque period. No one knows precisely what their origin is, but many of the Spanish pairs seem derived from the Islamic ivory work produced in Andalucía and much prized by early medieval Christians.

2. New monastery. From 1674 to 1714 a large new brick monastery was constructed on the mountain top. The monastery was sacked and burned during the War of Independence. Parts have been recently reconstructed. It houses unremarkable images of Saints Juan Bautista, Benito, and Indalecio.

8. Santa Cruz de la Serós → Puente la Reina de Jaca

Route: Santa Cruz de la Serós → Binacua → **Santa Cilia de Jaca** → Puente la Reina de Jaca

✳ Binacua The area was occupied from at least Roman times, as evidenced by several carved stones from that epoch still incorporated into the village walls. The 11th–12th-c. church mixes the blind arches of the Catalán-Lombard style with elements derived from Jaca. The tympanum holds a *crismón* in the Jaca style.

✳ **Santa Cilia de Jaca** The village lies 100 m. north of the road, but is well worth a detour as an example of an early medieval planned town preserving interesting noble mansions, a bridge across the Río Aragón, and a memorable bakery.

Santa Cilia is documented as early as 989, when Sancho Garcés II donated it to San Juan de la Peña. The town was originally a walled oval some 200 m. south of the Río Aragón. In the 13th c. it was relocated to a tight 160 × 100 m. rectangle parallel to the river, with 3 east-west and 4 north-south streets. In the 14th c. a combination of floods, taxes, and disease nearly depopulated the town. The monks constructed a dike—remains of which are still visible—to protect the village from the river, but that did not help for long. At least one old bridge—probably more—also fell prey to floods, and the current bridge is of fairly recent construction.

In 1098 Pedro I extended a charter to the town to attract settlers. Though the village was never large, for most of the Middle Ages it was both religiously and commercially significant. The monastery of San Juan de la Peña established a priory by the river. This priory, extensively reconstructed in the 17th c., at one point administered 7 dependent churches in the region. The principal building was expanded into a **palace** with a paired Gothic window and enormous overhanging eaves, but San Juan's **coat of arms** can still be seen over the door.

Santa Cilia's 17th–18th-c. church has an elegant tower. Its principal retablo is ca. 1565.

A Gothic entrance adorns the *ayuntamiento*.

Near the road was the now-vanished Capilla de San Décimo, close to an inn nicknamed Venta Esculabolas, whose innkeepers were widely known as thieves. Your eyes won't find the inn, but your nose should lead you to Santa Cilia's excellent bakery.

9. PUENTE LA REINA DE JACA

The region around Puente la Reina de Jaca was reconquered in 833 by Galindo Aznárez I, who was related to the French Carolingian court. It was an independent county until 922, when it came under the sway of Navarra's Sancho Garcés. The region remained Navarra's until 1035, when it passed to Aragón. The area was an early center of monasticism, although little is left today. Santa Cilia's monastery has vanished, leaving only the priory, which is now a palace. North of Puente la Reina de Jaca, San Pedro de Siresa (in the Hecho Valley) and San Martín de Ciella (in Ansó) each housed 100 monks when they were targeted by Almanzor's raiders in the 990s.

Puente la Reina de Jaca also sits squarely astride the major east-west route from Pamplona to Huesca. However, before the 11th c. the village's importance was due to its location as a staging point on the main road from Zaragoza, through the Valle de Hecho and the Puerto del Palo, to France's Bearne region. Then in the 11th c. King Sancho Ramírez collaborated with the French counts of Bearne to open the easier Somport Road, and the valley thronged with pilgrims. Puente la Reina de Jaca may well be the "Osturit" mentioned in the 12th-c. *Guide*.

Yet, as far as medieval physical remains, Puente la Reina de Jaca is one of the least interesting towns along the Road. It has been flooded and fought over so often that nothing remains today except a gas station and a hotel.

This part of the Río Aragón Valley is known generally as the Canal de Berdún, and by geologists as the Interpyrenaic Depression. The San Juan de la Peña and Oroel massifs channel the river to the west. Periodic floods over the eons have deposited rich blue-gray alluvial soil in the valley floor. Rivers entering from the north have overlaid these soils with even richer alluvial fans. The intermittent protruding terraces, or small *mesas* of harder rock that have resisted the river's erosion, are utilized as village sites for their strategic value. Berdún is the most prominent example. The border between Aragón and Navarra runs through this valley: at one time there were defensive castles on almost every promontory on both sides of the river. For 2,000 years the valley land has been sown with wheat, and the breadth of the *mesas* permits modern mechanized agriculture. A secondary industry is sheep raising.

The bridge over the Río Aragón at Puente la Reina de Jaca was the easiest crossing point. From here the route divided, and pilgrims could follow either the north bank or the south bank to Sangüesa. There used to be later crossing points, but the river is now a reservoir. We have walked both routes and think that both are spectacularly beautiful and offer interesting monuments to visit, although we have a mild preference for the southern route, which is wilder, more distant from the truck traffic, and visits the abandoned castle town of Ruesta. The 2 routes are about the same distance and take about the same time. We will describe them both.

Route: Puente la Reina de Jaca → Berdún → Asso de Veral → Sigüés → Escó →
Tiermas → Leyre → Yesa → Javier → Sangüesa

The northern route to Sangüesa normally takes 3 days. Although much of it coincides with the modern highway, it passes some spectacular abandoned towns, the impressive monastery of Leyre, and the castle that was home to San Francisco Javier.

Three km. past Puente la Reina de Jaca, on the right, is the small *ermita* of San Babil, with meager Romanesque decoration around its door. Some 200 m. before Berdún, the Road passes the tiny Ermita de Santa María de las Eras.

✱ Berdún Berdún's superb strategic position on a jutting podium dominates the fertile agricultural plain on the north bank of the Río Aragón and commands the east-west road. From the 10th c. on, the village was a locus of contention. It was completely destroyed by Navarra in 1134. Rebuilt, it developed into an important market town. It was fortified again in the 16th c., then partly destroyed by Felipe V in 1720. During the 19th-c. Carlist Wars, villagers rebuilt the defensive walls.

Berdún still boasts several late medieval and Renaissance mansions with coats of arms. Berdún's 16th-c. church of Santa Eulalia reputedly has a nice Baroque organ (1738) and a Gothic retablo.

✱ Asso de Veral This fortified village, on a bluff just northwest of where the Río Veral enters the Aragón Valley, is documented from 1095. The church of Nuestra Señora de la Asunción occupies a small peak that once held a castle. A couple of the town's houses conserve 14th-c. windows.

✱ Sigüés In the Middle Ages the center of Sigüés was walled. A castle belonging to the Pomar family protected the north. It overlooked the riverbank some 100 m. north of the church of San Esteban. From the mid-19th to the 20th c. the town has shrunk to some 300 inhabitants. On our visits, Sigüés has always seemed to be home to large families of Siamese cats.

At Sigüés, the alternate French pilgrimage route from Mauleón, Tardets, and the Roncal Valley intersects with the main Aragonese Road through the Canal de Berdún. From the 14th to the 17th c. the town supported the pilgrim Hospital de Santa Ana located just south of the church. A 1628 document speaks of 2 small rooms, one for men and one for women, each with 2 beds. The document cautions the hospice-keeper to confiscate all weapons, to check to see if visiting couples are truly married, and to house people for a single night—unless they are sick—because "the hospice was not built as an inn." Furthermore, hospice-keepers should be married; if they are widows they should be accompanied by a son or brother over the age of 18.

The 12th-c. church of San Esteban has a *crismón* on its tympanum. Inside it, elegant starred vaults are in the Flamboyant Gothic style. The paintings on its Baroque retablo are overshadowed by intricate Solomonic columns.

✱ Escó Like Ruesta, on the other side of the Canal de Berdún, Escó was strategically located on the border between Navarra and Aragón and changed hands several times. For a while it belonged to San Juan de la Peña, and later to Leyre. Pedro II of Aragón gave it to Navarra in payment of a debt, but then recovered it when Sancho de Navarra died in 1234. Its castle was destroyed in 1363, and no traces remain. Its church of San Miguel is in ruins. The town's 300 inhabitants abandoned Escó when the Yesa Reservoir was built in 1962.

＊ **Tiermas** The town site is a natural: a perfect strategic location high on a rock pedestal overlooking the valley, with hot sulfur springs at its foot to attract tourists. In fact the thermal springs, now under the waters of the Yesa Reservoir, gave Tiermas its name. The Romans constructed baths here, and the town became a spa as well as a strategic way station on the Roman highway. Over the centuries, the unassailable cliffs surrounding the town were more important even than its odoriferous waters. Tiermas is mentioned in the 12th-c. *Guide* (see ch. 24). The town was fortified in 1201 by Pedro II of Aragón, and then given to the king of Navarra in pawn. It was returned to Aragón in 1234, and additional fortifications were built in 1283. At one time it was completely walled, and fragments of the walls remain. Unfortunately, like Escó, Tiermas was abandoned when the Yesa Reservoir was built. It is now a crumbling ghost town, with its Church of San Miguel in ruins. It's worth the climb for the atmosphere and the view.

West of Tiermas the enormous rock wall of the Leyre Massif closes the northern side of the valley. The tangled forests on the slopes are noted for their wild game, particularly boar.

＊ LEYRE

History

The Sierra de Leyre, also called the Sierra de Erraondo, that forms the unbroken north wall of this part of the Río Aragón Valley has been the home of hermits since Visigothic times. Legends have it that the 5th-c. hermit Adaldo preached Christianity to the pagan Basques in these mountains; that in the 7th c. San Marcial rose from abbot of Leyre to become bishop of Pamplona; and that ca. 715 San Babil, who ran a school here for Mozarabic children, and Leyre's Abbot San Lampadio were slain here by the Moors. But these may only be tales fomented by Leyre's later medieval monks, for whom it was politically important that Leyre be the oldest church in the region.

Other historical documents support the monastery's great age. The earliest, dated 842, refers to a monastery already 100 years old. When San Eulogio of Córdoba visited in 848, he found a large community and a library that even included a copy of the Qur'an. In 905 King Fortuño renounced his crown here, and in an impressive ceremony he said good-bye to his horse, stripped off his symbols of monarchy, removed his royal clothes, and donned a monk's habit. Aragonese royalty donated regularly to Leyre. King Sancho Garcés, in a gesture of gratitude for his defeats of the Moors, donated a tent, some mattresses, a tapestry, a silver chalice, and a horse, complete with a bridle and saddle decorated with silver. Other monarchs donated relics (see ch. 17). Leyre was the early pantheon of Navarra's royalty, as San Juan de la Peña was for the Aragonese. During Almanzor's 992 raids, Prince Sancho (later Sancho III el Mayor 1000–35) hid his family in Leyre. Sancho had friends who praised the Cluniac reforms at the monastery of Ripoll, and he sent Leyre's Abbot Sancho to study at Cluny in 1025. From the moment of his return, Leyre became a center of French influence, with brothers traveling back and forth to the French motherhouse; from Leyre the Benedictine movement spread through this part of Spain. Sancho III also supported building campaigns: the apse at Leyre begun during his reign was dedicated during the reign of his grandson, Sancho de Peñalén.

In the early 13th c., at the behest of King Teobaldo I, monks of the Cistercian Order replaced the Benedictines (see ch. 26). The 13th c., when Leyre owned some 38 towns, was the height of the monastery's wealth and influence. Later, as Castilla and Aragón became giants and Navarra became less of a major player, Leyre's fortunes ebbed. When the 1836 *desamortización* took effect, there was relatively little to dismantle. In 1954 the Diputación Foral de Navarra rehabilitated the abbey, and a community of Benedictines was invited to return.

> 📖 Leyre was the home of Spain's Rip Van Winkle, San Virila. The story goes that Virila, one of Leyre's early abbots, was unable to comprehend the concept of eternity. He went to the woods behind the abbey to meditate. He followed the sweet call of a nightingale to a fountain, where he lay down to nap. Later that afternoon he woke and returned to the abbey, which to his astonishment was much larger than when he had left. He knocked at the door, but the monk who answered did not recognize him, and had never heard of an abbot Virila. The monks searched the abbey's records and found that 300 years previous an abbot named Virila had been lost, and presumed dead, on the mountainside. The monks, quite naturally, believed that this was an elaborate practical joke, until the nightingale appeared from the woods with the abbot's ring. The saint's day is Oct. 1. This miracle was much sung in the 13th c., including in one of King Alfonso X's *Cantigas*. Not all is legend, for there actually was an historical abbot Virila in Leyre in 928. He went to Galicia for many years to do Church work there before returning to end his life at Leyre.

PILGRIMAGE

In the 11th c. the first Cluniac abbot, Sancho, opened a hospice in Leyre, and a chain of additional hospices in Ibañeta, Zubiri, Larrasoaña, and Roncal. Currently the abbey runs 2 hospices: one for clerics, and one for lay visitors.

MONUMENT: **Monastery and church**.

The crypt of the current church was built in the 9th c., and buildings were added or enlarged through the beginning of the Gothic period. The Benedictines were responsible for most of Leyre's splendid decoration. When the Cistercians added on to Leyre, they left the old Romanesque *cabecera* and sculpted portals in place. But they rebuilt the body of the church with an enormous Gothic nave, making their wealth and power visible in its massive size and perfection of form.

Exterior:
• The **west portal**. Dating from around 1150, the portal is unusual in that the pieces were not carved in a shop and then assembled, but rather carved *in situ*. Several figures are incomplete, as are the archivolts of the door leading from the cloister to the church, which suggests that lack of funds, or political events, halted the work.
    —The **tympanum,** depicting Christ surrounded by saints, may be by Maestro Esteban, based on the style of the monstrous birds with heavy feathers and bills, the curved palm leaves, and the treatment of the animals' feet and claws.
    —The **spandrels,** like those at Sangüesa, contain an anthology of themes. On the left spandrel: San Miguel slaying the dragon; Saints **Santiago**, Pedro, and Juan Evangelista; and the Transfiguration of Christ. In the scene of their martyrdom, the martyrs Saints Nunila and Alodia are running happily to be received by the hand of God. In the center another 2 martyrs are dispatched. On the right are Jonah, a demon trapping a soul, and diverse monsters,

together with the Visitation, Annunciation, and an angel sounding the horn of the Last Judgment.

—The **4 archivolts** offer one of the finest collections in Spain of figures representing common professions and even more common sins. Avarice clutches a fat moneybag. A drunkard—the face of gluttony—lifts 2 bottles at once. The sculptor (who may also have worked in Oloron-Sainte-Marie on the French side of the Somport pass) was especially talented in his depiction of animals and fish and his incorporation of classic models for the human figures.

—The **capitals** on the flanking columns continue the series of sins and demons. To the left of the columns is an image of **Santiago** surrounded by lions.

• The south portal and window capitals are early-12th-c., with a marked Compostela influence, particularly in the fauna. The flanking statues are probably Apostles. Neither they nor the 24 old men on the archivolts are of the quality of the central door.

• Viewed from the outside, the **3 semicircular apses** are unique. Pre-Jaca, pre-San Isidoro de León, pre-Santiago de Compostela, these early Romanesque apses show extraordinary command of technique in their massive, finely cut stones and their towering height. The model of 3 apses of equal height, innovative here, did not become the norm in later Romanesque, where the central apse is almost always higher. Simple corbels depicting animals and masks sustain the roof. The tower is part of the early construction, but the simple *espadaña* dates from the 14th c.

Interior:

• Parts of the **pre-Romanesque** *cabecera* may date from the 10th c. It was built over the much earlier crypt and consecrated in 1057. Compared to the well-cut stones and sophisticated contemporary engineering in Jaca or Santa Cruz de la Serós, this church is rude in appearance, and may have been built by the monks themselves without employing an architect. Note that the 2 lateral naves are of slightly different widths. A symbolic interpretation is that the difference deliberately reflects that of the 2 thieves crucified with Christ. Or maybe the architects or builders just calculated badly.

• The **nave** is Romanesque as high as the capitals. But in the late 13th c. a simple but massive Cistercian Gothic single nave replaced the 3 Romanesque naves of the early church.

> 📖 Medieval architects struggled to conduct to ground the weight of the stone vaults and high walls of their churches. If they failed, the weight of the vault pushed out the walls, and the whole structure came tumbling down. The solutions available to Romanesque architects, including thick walls and massive buttresses perpendicular to the walls, kept the churches for the most part relatively small. In the 13th c. the innovations of Gothic techniques permitted a jump in scale, both of height and width.

Nowhere in Spain (except perhaps the Cathedral of Gerona) is the contrast between the 2 styles quite so evident as in Leyre.

• The 2 altars are Neoclassic. On the right, a small funeral chapel holds an urn with the combined remains of Navarra's early kings. The image of Christ is late-14th- or early-15th-c.

• The 9th-c. **crypt** is one of Spain's finest and most unusual churches. Its simple doorway, with 3 narrow arches, leads to 3 narrow naves; the central (now divided in two) is higher and wider than the lateral naves. The columns are short, the **capitals** immense inverted pyramids with simple vegetable or geometric designs which seem to hearken back to prehistoric pagan decorative motifs, the arches elongated (*peraltados*) in the manner of Asturian art, slightly closing into horseshoes. The right apse holds the 14th-c. image of Bishop San Babil; the left, a 17th-c. statue of the Abbot San Virila.

✳ Yesa The village belonged to the Monastery of Leyre from the 11th c. The current parish church is modern. Near the highway is Yesa's late medieval church.

Two km. west of Yesa, you can see from the highway the ruins of the 11th-c. Roncaleses bridge across the Río Aragón, at the site of an earlier Roman bridge. It was destroyed in the 19th-c. Carlist Wars (see ch. 25). You can walk to the bridge, with difficulty, from the factory on the river's left bank, but the view is better from the main road to Sangüesa. The secondary highway that cuts south from Leyre toward Javier is much to be preferred by hikers, as it visits the family castle of Saint Francis Xavier.

✳ **Javier** San Francisco Javier was born here on April 6, 1506. His family's castle, dating primarily from the 16th c., is wrapped around a 10th-c. tower. Cardinal Cisneros laid it all to waste in the campaign to render Navarra powerless following that kingdom's forcible union to Spain in 1512. The castle complex was heavily restored as a Jesuit shrine and retirement home in the 20th c. Although San Francisco Javier's body is in Goa, India, the annual Javierada, on the first Sunday in March, brings tens of thousands of pilgrims to visit.

• **The castle.**

 —The Capilla del Santo Cristo contains a 14th-c. walnut **sculpted Christ** noted for its beatific expression. It is said to have shed blood at the moment of San Francisco Javier's death. On the walls of the chapel, which was formerly the family dining room, are late-15th-c. murals depicting the **Dance of Death**, a theme popular in painting in central Europe but rare in Spain. Just imagine young Javier facing this every morning at breakfast!

 —The central tower contains various medieval arms and a plaster model of the castle and its various defensive structures.

 —Several of the uppermost rooms have been outfitted as a museum of sacred art, with various statues of San Francisco Javier. For 3 centuries Jesuit missionaries to the orient have brought their souvenirs back to Javier, and their collections are often both peculiar and astounding.

• Iglesia de la Anunciación. In the parish church across from the castle is the 13th-c. Virgen de Echeverri, the 13th-c. font in which Javier was baptized, and portraits of St. Francisco Javier and the founder of the Jesuit order, St. Ignacio de Loyola.

11. Puente la Reina de Jaca →
Sangüesa II

Route: Puente la Reina de Jaca → Arrés → Xavierre de Martes → Martes → Mianos → Artieda → Vidiella → **Ruesta** → Undués de Lerda → Ull → Sangüesa

----

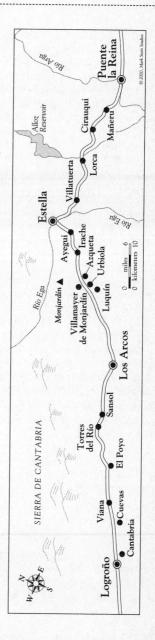

From Puente la Reina de Jaca, the medieval pilgrimage Road followed the south bank of the river, below the towns which occupy strategic outcroppings above the river plain, generally at places where small rivers have cut promontories as they descend to the Río Aragón. Their silhouettes from the valley floor are impressive. Today's path—much harder walking, but more scenic—stitches the mountain flank from village to village. These have changed little over the centuries. Their fortlike churches occupy the high ground; their street plans often indicate that they were once walled. Each village affords a spectacular view of the valley of the Canal de Berdún, as well as of the villages on either side.

The further west the Road goes the drier it gets. There are even occasional stands of live oaks (*encinas*). The edge of the valley is marked by wildly eroded gullies called *cárcavas*.

✳ Arrés The village, first cited in 850, has always been small: 34 hearths in the 15ᵗʰ c., 13 houses in 1845, and even fewer today. In 1090 King Sancho Ramírez of Aragón bought it from the Monastery of San Juan de la Peña. The small Monastery of Santa Columba de Arrés lay below the town in the 12ᵗʰ c., but today no sign remains. In the village, a 13ᵗʰ-c. tower house has 3 stories and a fine Aragonese-style chimney. The late-15ᵗʰ-c. fortress church of the Purísima Concepción still has arrow slits in the walls. In the cemetery is the 17ᵗʰ-c. Ermita de Santa Agueda. On the right as you leave Arrés are remains of an old mill.

The houses in Arrés are typical of village houses in most of the Alto Aragón. To stand against the snows and winds of winter, they are made of the sturdiest local material—stone—for both walls and roofs. Most are 2 stories and combine many of the functions of house and barn. Downstairs are storerooms for firewood, tools, foodstuffs, and utensils. Sometimes the downstairs doubles as a barn for a few animals. The family lives upstairs. The most important room is the kitchen, with a great hooded hearth leading to a massive conical stone chimney. Around the hearth formerly would be benches, where the family would gather to work, eat, and talk. Another more formal room tended to be reserved for parties: weddings, betrothals, and the like. Other rooms were used for sleeping (and some houses have a third story as well). The narrow attic both insulated against the cold and served for storage. Most now have bathrooms, but until recently, family members used the back courtyard (*cuadra*) or a chamber pot.

✱ Xavierre de Martes The village was given to the monastery of San Pedro de Siresa in 971, and later to the Cathedral of Jaca. After changing hands several times, in 1443 it was sold to San Juan de la Peña. There are ruins of a 13th-c. *ermita* of San Xavierre, which was abandoned in 1785 and restored as an active church in 1917 by the landowner. One can perceive the ruins of an ancient village in the fields surrounding the church. A medieval bridge that once spanned the stream disappeared in the floods of 1988.

✱ Martes The town occupies a strategic promontory over the gully (*barranco*) of the Río Tobo. From 1096 it belonged to San Juan de la Peña. Its large castle (32 × 35 m.) stood on a nearby spur until the 16th c. The town's street plan suggests that a wall once enclosed it, and that its church, Nuestra Señora de las Candelas, stood just outside the wall to the north. Several Gothic houses remain, including the old Casa Consistorial with a paired window with canopial arches. Unlike villages in the rest of the valley, Martes's houses have tile roofs made of the region's good clay, or slate roofs cut from local quarries. Many have substantial eaves or carved lintels. In the center of town is an old fountain.

Beyond Martes, just to the north of the highway, the corral of Calcones marked the 11th-c. frontier between the kingdoms of Aragón and Navarra (and now between the provinces of Huesca and Zaragoza). Just south of the mountain ridge is Bagüés, which from 1030 also belonged to San Juan de la Peña. By 1488 it had shrunk to 8 houses. Its Romanesque church of San Julián had fine frescos that are now in the Jaca museum.

✱ Mianos Founded in the 10th c., from 1113 to 1831 this town was another of San Juan de la Peña's properties in the valley. In 1849 it had 212 inhabitants, quadruple the current number. On the top of the hill is an ancient, fortified seigniorial property, with a palatial house, plaza, cemetery, and defensive structures.
Mianos's 12th-c. Church of Santa Ana was reformed in the 16th c. by extending the nave and adding a sacristy and chapel. It has an interesting coffered ceiling with 7 carved beams resting on figural corbels. The 3 retablos are 16th-c. Best is the Hispano-Flemish **retablo de San Sebastián** that narrates the Saint's life, arraignment, flagellation, and martyrdom. A magnificent Plateresque canopy covers the retablo.

✱ Artieda Artieda is documented from the 10th c., when it was donated to Leyre. In the 12th c. it had a castle. The circular medieval town plan is clearly discernible. The 12th-c. church of San Martín was much reformed in the 16th c., when a starred nerve vaulting was added to its early barrel vault. Two chapels were added at the same time, as were the entrance and the high choir, which rests on carved *ménsulas*. The 2–story old pilgrim hospice stands 50 m. west of the church at 20 Calle San Martín.

Just north of the highway was the former priory of Santa María de Artieda. It belonged to Leyre in the 11th c. and was later given to Santa Cristina in Somport. All that remains is the fountain of Santa María.

> Two km. north of Artieda, on a terrace over the river, is the Ermita de San Pedro, on the site of a former Roman town or large villa. Roman remains found near the Ermita de San Pedro include a fort, houses, mosaics, and a pottery kiln. In the north wall of the hermitage are several Roman stones, including a Corinthian capital.

South of the highway in the 11th c. was the village of Vidiella, now vanished. Just beyond, on the right, was the Ermita de San Juan Bautista, belonging to San Juan de la Peña.

✳ RUESTA

HISTORY

Muslims established Ruesta after the 711 invasion. It was abandoned during their general retreat in the 10th c., then taken by Sancho Garcés I of Navarra, who in 911 fortified the cliff overlooking the rich Canal de Berdún. The site was of such strategic importance that Almanzor targeted it during his northern campaigns at the end of that century.

Ruesta belonged to Navarra until 1054, when Ramiro I captured the Esca Valley for Aragón. During most of the Middle Ages it prospered as an agricultural center, a fortified border town, and as a minor commercial center. It even attracted a small Jewish community, which was responsible for provisioning the castle in times of attack.

In the 19th c. Ruesta had 100 houses of families who farmed the fertile land along the river below the city. When, in the 1950s, the Yesa Reservoir flooded that land, the town was doomed, and it was finally abandoned in 1959. In the late 1990s it was being reconditioned as a prospective tourist center.

PILGRIMAGE

We know of 1 medieval hospice, associated with the Iglesia de San Jacobo. Beyond the bridge at the exit from Ruesta was a fountain called the Fuente de Santiago.

MONUMENTS: 1. **Iglesia de San Juan de Ruesta.** 2. **Castle.** 3. Iglesia de Nuestra Señora de la Asunción. 4. Ermita de San Jacobo.

1. **Iglesia de San Juan de Ruesta.** This small church, some 300 m. prior to entering Ruesta, was built in the 10th c., perhaps as a small hermitage. Soon it was incorporated into the monastery of San Juan de Maltray. In 928 the king attended an important assembly here, and you can picture his entourage's tents pitched in the fields around this humble church. In the late 10th c. the monks took advantage of Almanzor's raids to relocate to Cluny (see ch. 7). When the region was quiet again, ca. 1025, Navarra's King Sancho Garcés el Mayor brought them back and charged them with the restoration of Maltray. Ramiro I took the area for Aragón in 1054, and Sancho Ramírez, the great internationalist of early Aragonese history, had the Roman rite introduced here (see ch. 7). Toward the end of the century the community relocated permanently to San Juan de la Peña.

This church's Romanesque mural paintings from ca. 1016 are in the Jaca museum.

2. **The castle**. The castle was military rather than palatial. Of its 45 × 35 m. rectangle, only some slabs of wall and a few of the crenellations remain. The tower, with its arrow slits, is in reasonable condition.

3. Iglesia de Nuestra Señora de la Asunción. The 11th-c. tower indicates its nature as a fortress church. The church formerly had 4 retablos, one of them dedicated to Santiago. The 16th-c. entrance resembles another in nearby Sos del Rey.

4. Ermita de San Jacobo. This small Romanesque church is documented from 1087, when King Sancho Ramírez donated it to the French community of Suave Majeure in Guyenne. It maintained a pilgrim hospice. The *cabecera* of the church was constructed ca. 1055 and the nave about 30 years later. The entrance retains some figured capitals, and there are traces of its 18th-c. mural paintings on the east wall of the eastmost room.

Ruesta still contains some 15th–19th c. nobles' mansions with coats of arms. Near the town entrance, for example, is the palace of the Marqueses de Lacadena.

Past the Ermita de San Jacobo you will climb Mount Fenerol to the site of the abandoned town of Serramiana. Some foundations of long-vanished houses remain. During most of the Middle Ages this entire zone belonged to Leyre.

Once on the heights the landscape changes dramatically. These dry, rolling farmlands, with soils too poor and terrain too rough for large-scale mechanized agriculture, grow mostly cereals: wheat, barley, oats, and a little corn. There is also a diminishing herding industry.

✳ UNDUÉS DE LERDA

HISTORY

The Roman highway from Jaca to Sangüesa crossed these heights, and a stretch of pavement can be seen to the northeast of the village. Until 1646, when they were joined, Undués and Lerda (which belonged to Leyre) were separate towns. Undués de Lerda sits high on a massif overlooking the valley of the Río Aragón, north toward Leyre and west toward Sangüesa. Its importance as a strategic outpost on the border between Aragón and Navarra led to its having been intermittently fortified and frequently destroyed. Its 12th-c. church of San Román has gone, as has its 13th-c. castle. Today Undués's medieval wall has vanished, but its outline remains in the near-solid circle of houses surrounding the town's 2 plazas and central church.

In 1900 the village had 480 inhabitants. In 1993 and 1996 some of the older residents told us that they recalled when Undués farmed 3,000 sheep and 800 cows, which they walked to market at the one of the 4 regional fairs held in Lumbier, Sos, Sangüesa, and Tafalla. Well into this century the town maintained 2 schools, 1 for boys and 1 for girls. But the Civil War and later the growth of the industrial cities has emptied the village. Current population is about 30—and that only on weekends, when the city folk come back to their parents' old houses to relax.

PILGRIMAGE

The principal pilgrim Road followed the river along what is now covered by the Yesa Reservoir and crossed several now-vanished bridges. The few pilgrims who ventured to these heights were most likely lodged in the church or with private families.

MONUMENTS: 1. Iglesia de San Martín. 2. Ayuntamiento. 3. Mansions.

1. A local stone mason, Miguel de Redondo, built the church of San Martín in 1592. It has some interesting touches of Mudéjar-Gothic tracery, a 13th-c. baptismal font, and a 16th-c. retablo. Note the carved wooden corbels that support the high choir.

2. The 15th-c. Ayuntamiento, or city hall, rebuilt in the 17th c., has been refitted recently as a pilgrim hospice. We had the privilege of inaugurating the crisp new beds in 1993, while the smell of fresh varnish still hung in the air.

3. Several substantial late Gothic or Renaissance mansions attest to the town's brief period of prosperity. At the northwest edge of town, near the exit toward Sangüesa, is a house where San Francisco de Asís reputedly stayed on his pilgrimage to Compostela in 1214. The modest structure preserves its Aragonese-style chimney and a medieval paired window.

At the border between Aragón and Navarra a modern sign welcomes pilgrims and gives information about the route. On the hill to the north was the medieval town of Lerda, documented as belonging to Leyre as early as 880. The frontier town prospered until well into the 12th c., but seems to have been destroyed and abandoned in the 14th-c. strife between Navarra and Aragón. Nothing remains.

👟 Beyond Lerda, also to the north, is the whitewashed Ermita de Nuestra Señora del Socorro, the sole surviving remnant of the more than 30 hermitages that sprang up in the Middle Ages around Sangüesa.

According to legend, the Virgin appeared on the *ermita* hill in an olive tree to cheer up the Christian troops about to enter battle against the Moors. The Christians captured the Muslim leader near Yesa and, while they were debating what to do with him, a woman from nearby Roncal cut off his head.

The ancient hermitage was rebuilt in the 16th c., the 18th c., and again in 1967. Its Renaissance retablo has a late Gothic seated Virgin, which is the unofficial patron of the region. Villagers from all over the region make pilgrimage here each Sept. 8.

✳ Ull Further still, the base of the flat-topped 490-m. hill immediately to the north was the site of a Roman town, and the hilltop above it the site of the medieval town of Ull. In the early 12th c. Alfonso el Batallador gave the town to Sangüesa. It was destroyed during a French attack in 1283, and by 1301 is cited as abandoned.

The rolling fluvial soils of this area are interspersed with deposits of clay and gravel. The popular architecture of the Navarra valley towns along here mixes stone, brick, adobe, and wood construction. The principal agriculture crop is cereal, mainly wheat, with an occasional interspersed vineyard for local consumption. You will find the pilgrimage Road's first olive trees a little beyond Ull.

At the entrance to Sangüesa, on a hill to the north of the Road, are what remains of the medieval hospice and basilica of San Babil, founded early in the 14th c. The regularity of the stonework around the semicircular arched door attests to its former wealth. Sangüesa's Retired Citizens' Association restored the hermitage in 1991. The small Baroque retablo contains an image of San Babil and is topped by the coat of arms of Navarra.

12. SANGÜESA

HISTORY

Bronze Age silex arrowheads and scrapers, some of them 5,000 years old, have been found on terraces along both sides of the Río Aragón around Sangüesa. About 500 B.C.E a Basque-Celtic town was established on an easily defended crag just to the north of the paper mill, where the village of Rocaforte is now. Romans later conquered and considerably enlarged the town. If you look on the last bay of the Pamplona side of the bridge you will see a reutilized Roman funeral stele: *Cornelia iucunda / sibiet cornelio feliciet / cornelio firmiano / libertis* ("Cornelia Iucunda had this tomb built for herself and for her 2 sons Felix and Firmo"). In the 9th c. a castle on top of the crag formed the border between Christian Pamplona and the Muslim territories to the south. The crag changed hands numerous times over the next 150 years. The castle has long since vanished.

Sancho Ramírez relocated Sangüesa to its current site by the river in the late 11th c. As a river town along a key transportation route, Sangüesa's boom years began with his construction ca. 1089 of a bridge spanning the Río Aragón. In 1121 Alfonso el Batallador extended the Fuero de Jaca to Sangüesa, offering attractive incentives for the settlement of Frankish merchants.

When Navarra and Aragón split on the death of Alfonso el Batallador in 1134, Sangüesa found itself on the border. In 1171 Sancho el Sabio of Navarra capped the Arangoiz hill just to the left of the west side of the bridge with a castle, and surrounded it with a new suburb called El Castellón. (This castle was abandoned in the 15th c.; extant remains are from 19th-c. Carlist forts.) The older city, on the east bank, acquired a surrounding wall, pierced by 4 gates. The massive fortifications reflect Sangüesa's strategic position as a border town during several centuries of near-continual warfare against Aragón. The fortifications were almost entirely destroyed in Cisneros's campaign to disarm Navarra after its forced annexation to Spain.

> 📖 When Fernando el Católico died in 1516, the last Navarran monarch, Jean d'Albret, conspired to recover the crown. The Spanish regent, Cardinal Cisneros, sent an army that destroyed Albret's troops near St.-Jean-Pied-de-Port, just north of Roncesvalles. Cisneros followed this with an order that all Navarran forts capable of serious resistance were to be razed to the ground.

Like other strategically located towns along the great northern road, Sangüesa grew with the pilgrimage and became an important market center. The street leading to the bridge naturally became the Rúa Mayor, and even today is the major commercial artery. Among the immigrants attracted by the commercial opportunities was a small Jewish community. We know that Jewish travelers were accommodated in a Jewish hospice near the synagogue. In the 13th and 14th c. each section of town was dominated by the monastery of one of the major religious orders: Carmelites (around La Nora), Franciscans (at the end of the Rúa Mayor), Dominicans (at the north end, by the castle), and Mercedarians (in the south). Each district had its own parish church and its own hospice for pilgrims and other travelers. The city plan of early medieval Sangüesa can be seen easily on a map. The streets that formed the perimeter road (*ronda*), just inside the wall, are San Miguel, Genaro Vallejo, J. de Berrueta, and B. Armendáriz.

In 1665 Sangüesa was officially made a city, which allowed it to establish its own civil and criminal courts. During the War of Succession (1710) the party favoring the Austrians over the eventually victorious Bourbons occupied the city. From 1808 to 1812 French troops occupied and pillaged the city, before being driven out by General Espoz y Mina. The city suffered additional damage during the Constitutional disturbances of the 1820s, and the Carlist Wars of midcentury (see ch. 25), during which it changed hands, was fortified, and sacked various times.

Unfortunately, in addition to the wartime destruction, much of medieval Sangüesa has been swept away by periodic major floods of the Río Aragón (1330, 1430, 1739, and 1947). Construction of the Yesa Reservoir in 1959 seems to have solved the problem. The current metal bridge was erected in 1892.

PILGRIMAGE

The bridge of San Martín crossed the Río Irati north of Sangüesa near Rocaforte from ca. 1089 until 1971, when it was swept away by a flood. It carried pilgrim traffic from Tiermas and the Canal de Berdún toward Monreal. However, the attractions of Sangüesa itself drew many pilgrims to the route along the south bank of the Río Aragón, through Ruesta, Undués, and Ull.

Sangüesa's 13 documented medieval hospices are all gone. Perhaps the most notable was San Nicolás del Arenal, whose site is now occupied by the convent of the Comendadoras del Santo Espíritu. The hospice and chapel were donated in the mid-12th c. to Roncesvalles. Its splendid Romanesque capitals are now dispersed in the convent of the Comendadoras, the Casa de Cultura, the portal of Pamplona's Cámara de Comptos, and the Museo de Navarra in Pamplona. Outside the walls was the Hospice of San Lázaro for lepers (see ch. 27), supported—as were most hospices—by a *cofradía*, or brotherhood of citizens, who contributed time and money to the care of travelers and the sick.

MONUMENTS: 1. **Iglesia de Santa María la Real**. 2. Palacio-Castillo del Príncipe de Viana. 3. Palacio de Añués. 4. Palacio de los Iñiguez Abarca. 5. Palacio de los Sebastianes. 6. Palacio de los París Iñiguez Abarca. 7. Iglesia de San Francisco. 8. **Iglesia de Santiago**. 9. Hospital de Santiago. 10. **Palacio de Vallesantoro**. 11. **Iglesia de San Salvador**. 12. Palacio de los Iñiguez de Medrano. 13. Convento del Carmen.

1. **Iglesia de Santa María la Real**. The early Romanesque church was built on the site of King Sancho Ramírez's 11th-c. palace. Alfonso el Batallador, who repopulated the town in the early 12th c., gave the church and what remained of the palace to the Hospitallers of San Juan de Jerusalén. The 3 *cabecera* apses are from ca. 1131. The naves, transitional between Romanesque and Gothic, are ca. 1200, and the graceful tower was finished a century later. The battlements remind us that the church was attached to Sangüesa's defensive wall. The church suffered considerable damage in the 19th-c. Carlist Wars (see ch. 25), when it served as a barracks for the liberals' army. It was extensively restored in 1922.

Exterior:

• **West Portal**. The massive, monumental portal is often interpreted as symbolic of the international character of the Santiago pilgrimage, as it draws on elements of Romanesque sculpture from the far corners of Europe. It is most likely neither a unified 13th-c. construct nor a semirandom 13th-c. anthology, but rather a series of building stages, each with its own characteristics.

—Earliest is the **top row of Apostles**. It was most likely raised to its current position ca. 1155 when the tympanum, archivolts, and figured columns were carved. These Apostles show some stylistic affinities with the Jaca Cathedral as well. The style of the almond-eyed Christ in Majesty sur-

SANGÜESA

rounded by the Tetramorphos suggests that it is by the Master of San Juan de la Peña. The 12 Apostles are similar in their rigid poses, hieratic expressions, and protuberant eyes. Since most of the Apostles had not yet been fixed with their artistic attributes, it is hard to distinguish among them, with the exception of Peter with his keys, and barefoot **Santiago**, who holds a pilgrim staff. The 2 smaller figures, second and third from the right in the lower register, are from another sculptural series.

—The **figured columns** are transitional between 2 styles: their rigid poses

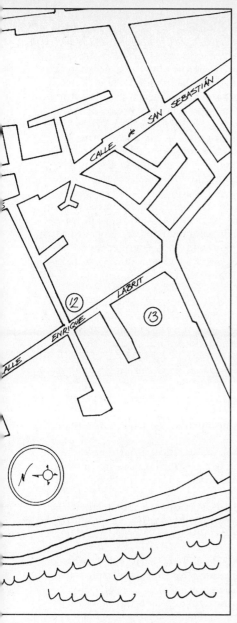

and hieratic expressions derive from Romanesque norms, while their elongated shapes and positioning on the columns anticipate Gothic developments. The tunics of the 3 Marys on the left, with zigzag edges and long draped sleeves, closely resemble the queens at Chartres. On the right are Saints Pedro and Pablo, and the hanged Judas, whose depiction here on a monumental portal is unique in Spain and may be inspired by the hanged Judas in Autun. The Burgundian sculptor signed the work on Mary's book: *Leodegarius me fecit* ("L. made me").

—The **capitals** mix Old and New Testament themes: the Annunciation and Visitation (a single Virgin takes part in both scenes), the Presentation in the Temple, and on the right, the Judgment of Solomon.

—The **tympanum** repeats the Christ in Majesty of the upper arcade but places Him in the context of the Last Judgment, with angels sounding the trumpet and dispatching the saved to Christ's right and the damned to His left. This is the only Navarra ensemble with this iconography, which is common in France (there are good examples in the pilgrimage churches of Moissac, Conques, Cahors, and Beaulieu-sur-Dordogne, among others). The representation of good and evil on San Miguel's scale is unusual. Rather than the standard Spanish doubling of the human soul, with good represented as a serene praying figure and evil as a demon or grimacing figure, here the right balance holds a dove (the Holy Spirit?) and the left, a serpent. The nude couple about to be engulfed by the jaws of Hell, with the woman's breast typically bitten by a snake, represents the sin of carnality. Although there is no attempt at perspective or verisimilitude in the composition, the highly rhythmic arrangement of these figures is an impressive example of the best Romanesque.

—On the **lintel**, Apostles flank the Virgin. **Santiago**, identified by name on his arch, is second from the left. Note the varied decoration on the columns separating the Apostles.

—The **archivolts** are extraordinarily diverse in their subjects. On the inmost are sins: avarice, lust, and the like. Many of the most graphically punished sinners are women, reflecting the Church's 12th-c. tirades against women as partners of the Devil. The second portrays professions or possibly the months of the year: a blacksmith; slaughtering animals; cutting wood; the March ram of Aries; the April bull of Taurus. The other 3 continue the mix: a prophet, a bishop, a **pilgrim** (third figure from the right on the middle archivolt), jugglers and acrobats, the January water jug of Aquarius, adulterous women (attacked by snakes and toads), and so forth.

—The **spandrels** contain an anthology of sculpture, most likely assembled from works donated to the church by passing pilgrims from various parts of Europe. Several of the figures may once have been part of the archivolts.

The right spandrel: The animals on the top 2 rows resemble similar figures in San Juan de la Peña and San Pedro el Viejo in Huesca. The laced rope is a common Merovingian pattern. Another figure, leaning on a tau-shaped staff, probably represents a **pilgrim**. Two of the right spandrel's figures may come from the **Sigurd cycle of Norse mythology**: Sigurd sticks his sword Nothung into Fafner, in his guise as dragon, who guards a hoard of gold; Regin makes the sword on an anvil; Sigurd gives Regin Fafner's heart in payment; Sigurd works Regin's bellows. Without going so far afield, other art historians see here merely an assemblage of fairly common 12th-c. motifs: the knight fighting a dragon (as at Estella, Ujué, Artaiz, Puente la Reina, and Irache), the armorer, etc. This theory is supported by the fact that the figures are by different hands, and their arrangement is chaotic.

The left spandrel: Several of the figures on the top 2 rows seem to represent vices. In the second row a knight thumps somebody (A crusader beating an infidel? Santiago killing a Moor? Sigurd dispatching Fafner?). In the third row are Adam and Eve and, next to them, Cain and Abel. Another set of figures represents the Evangelists: John's eagle (third row), Luke's ox (top row), and Mark's lion (third row on right spandrel).

• The windows on the 3 apses and the west wall facing the river are Jaquesque (see ch. 5). Note the capital (restored) of the artist self-consciously carving the base on which he stands. The corbels, with the exception of those on the apse nearest the entrance, are 20th-c. reproductions modeled after those of the Ermita de San Adrián de Vadoluengo 1 km. to the south.
• The spired and crenellated octagonal 13th-c. **Gothic tower** rises over the transept crossing.

Interior:
• The lantern vault rising over the crossing is notable for its height and simple elegance.
• The naves are Romanesque to the height of the capitals, from where they were continued in the early Gothic style. The capitals in the nave are mostly simple and foliated, although some depict symmetrical animals in the San Juan de la Peña style.
• The semicircular apses of the *cabecera* are derived from the Jaca Cathedral. These **capitals**, too, seem to echo Jaca. Several biblical stories are expounded, while others represent vices, such as avarice. The nude women with clawed feet swoop out of 12th-c. antifeminine rhetoric.
• The early 16th-c. main retablo contains the late-13th- or early-14th-c. silver-covered **Virgen de Rocamador**, especially venerated by French pilgrims. The large Baroque Assumption in the center was added in 1774.
• The right nave contains a fine Baroque wood crucifix. The Capilla de San Miguel contains 16th-c. carved plaques and a retablo dedicated to the Virgen del Pilar. On the left is a 15th-c. Gothic San Blas.

2. Palacio-Castillo del Príncipe de Viana. Built along the city's northern wall ca. 1280, this was the intermittent home of Navarra's monarchs, especially those of the house of Champagne, and the site of several political assemblies (*cortes*). In the 1430s Queen Blanca of Navarra took refuge here during Juan II's wars against Navarra. In the 1440s don Carlos, prince of Viana, lived here for 2 years, remodeling the palace to suit his passion for parties. His 55 personal servants included many musicians.

The merchants' palaces along Sangüesa's main streets have not yet all been restored, but they are all worth your attention. The defining characteristic of

Sangüesa's bourgeois style are the broad, decorated eaves (*aleros*), so be sure to look up.

3. **Palacio de Añués.** This 15th-c., crumbling Flamboyant Gothic mansion is the first of 4 monumental palaces along the Calle Mayor. The windows display some fine Gothic tracery. The coat of arms includes the ermines of the Añués family, the cauldrons of the Olletas, and the crescent moons of the counts of Javier.

4. **Palacio de los Íñiguez Abarca.** This 1601 mansion is a late example of the Renaissance style. The enormous coat of arms contains the wolf and tree of the Íñiguez, and the band, hounds, and fleur-de-lis of the Paris family. Most of the artist's creative energy seems to have gone into the oversized eaves. In this house, in 1639, was born José Íñiguez Abarca, a Cordoban Inquisitor.

5. **Palacio de los Sebastianes.** This 15th-c. late Gothic mansion belonged to the Sebastián family, who were merchants and moneylenders. One of the Sebastián descendents emigrated first to France. From there the family spread to Holland, and later to the United States, where, according to a local historian, a daughter, Elizabeth Bastiaen, became the wife of President James Monroe in 1786, cited in U.S. biographies as Elizabeth Kortright.

In 1503 Enrique Labrit (or d'Albret, see above), the last Crown Prince of Navarra, was born here. His parents, Jean and Catherine, were so committed to the pilgrimage that they asked 2 passing German pilgrims to stand as godparents, and named the child Enrrich after one of them. Jean and Catherine, the last Navarran monarchs, were deposed by Fernando el Católico in 1512. In 1516 they failed in their bid to retake the crown and died shortly thereafter in exile in France.

6. **Palacio de los París Íñiguez Abarca.** Check out the astoundingly ornate eaves on this 16th-c. Renaissance-style palace. On the coat of arms: a Moor's head (Puente), tree and wolf (Íñiguez), 2 keys (Paris), 2 shoes (Abarca), and the cross of Santiago.

7. **Iglesia de San Francisco.** King Teobaldo II founded the Franciscan community in Sangüesa in 1266 with monks from the monastery in Rocafuerte (Sangüesa la Vieja, some 6 km. to the north). In 1530 and 1551 the Cortes Generales of Navarra met here. In 1898, a half century after the *desamortización*, the monastery was given to the Capuchin order.

The current church dates mainly from the 16th c.; it was restored in 1960. The simple portal is Gothic. Inside, there is fine Gothic vaulting and window tracery. The single nave and square apse are typical of churches of the mendicant orders. One of the chapels holds a 17th-c. statue of San Antonio de Padua, probably carved in Granada. The monastery's best feature is its 14th-c. beamed cloister, which now houses a small museum with a collection of medieval funeral stelae.

8. **Iglesia de Santiago.** Begun in the 12th c., this fortress-church with its crenellated tower formed part of the southeastern defenses of the city. Government troops used the church as a barracks during the third Carlist War in 1875 and largely destroyed its interior. Its current state is the result of a 1966 restoration campaign.

Inside, the nerving on the transept vault is characteristic of the transition from Romanesque to Gothic. But the most interesting aspect of this church is the 4 images of Santiago Peregrino that greet pilgrims here. The **polychrome Santiago** on the doorway, replacing the vanished Romanesque tympanum, is 16th c.; the large head, curly beard and hair, the self-contained expression, and the rounded pleats of the drapery mark its Romanist influence. Excavators in 1964 discovered a large early 14th-c. **Gothic Santiago** as well, whose pose, large head, and draped tunic speak of French influence. It may well have been carved by the sculptor of the Christ on the portal of nearby San Salvador. It is now in the main apse.

On the main Baroque-Rococo retablo, constructed by a local artist in the 18th c., there is a Renaissance statue of **Santiago**, undoubtedly from an earlier main altar, with 2 kneeling pilgrims at his sides. Note also the central 16th-c. image of Nuestra Señora de Belén, flanked by the patron saints of Navarra, Fermín and Francisco Javier.

The Capilla de San Román has a Rococo retablo with nice statues of Saints Román and Lorenzo. On one of the squinches of the chapel is a graceful half bust of **Santiago**, painted al fresco early in the 18th c. (the others are Saints José, Babil, and Sebastián).

The baptismal chapel, off the left nave, has a marvelous 16th-c. retablo of San Eloy, funded by the silversmiths' guild.

9. Hospital de Santiago. The house directly across the plaza, displaying symbols of the pilgrimage (shells, staves, bottle gourds, etc.), was the Hospital de Santiago, documented from the 16th c., but undoubtedly of earlier origin.

10. **Palacio de Vallesantoro** (also called Ongay, or de las Marquesas). This 17th-c. Baroque palace, Sangüesa's most opulent, has **magnificent eaves** supported by wooden corbels representing bizarre animals resting their paws on human heads. There are also Indians, flowers, and exotic fruits. The doorway displays decorative motifs that seem derived from colonial American Baroque. Its mixture of wood, brick, and stone is characteristic of the style adopted by Sangüesa's merchant elite in the 17th c. The building is now the Casa de la Cultura.

11. **Iglesia de San Salvador.** This 13th-c. church near the town wall has a 16th-c. narthexlike porch and a nice doorway derived from the Cathedral of León's Portada de la Virgen Blanca (even to the man with the bellows firing the infernal cauldron). The tympanum depicts Christ in Majesty displaying his wounds flanked by the Virgin and San Juan. The lintel portrays the Last Judgment. Naked souls push open their tombs; the staidly dressed elect line up to be admitted to heaven; naked sinners are thrust into the jaws of hell. Christ's almond eyes, ringlets, and perpendicular ears all suggest it was carved by the same sculptor who did the large statue recently discovered in the church of Santiago.

📖 The Last Judgment was the favorite tympanum topic for late Romanesque and early Gothic sculptors. As such it replaced the early Romanesque's Christ in Glory surrounded by the 4 Evangelists and their symbols. The Last Judgment was commonly comprised of 5 scenes, each with traditional emblems or episodes:

—The resurrection of dead: Gabriel, often accompanied by other angels, blows the trumpet signaling the end of days (Matt. 24: 29–31) and prompting tombs to open (John 5: 28–9; 1 Cor. 15:52; Thess. 4:16) and the dead to come back to life.

—Christ as judge: He sits on a throne of glory (Matt. 25: 31), a crown on His head, His right hand raised in blessing.

—The separation of the damned from the elect: on Christ's right are the souls to be saved and on His left, the damned (Matt. 25:33).

—The weighing of souls: frequently the Archangel Michael holds the scales (Dan. 12: 1–2). Sometimes a demon, like a dishonest butcher, pulls on the sin side of the balance to increase its weight.

—A vision of paradise and hell: heaven is most often shown as ranks of humans and angels with beatific smiles. Hell is more picturesque: struggling souls are herded by grotesque demons toward a monstrously gaping mouth. Sometimes they are plunked into a boiling cauldron. Often graphically apt punishments fit the sins of gluttony and sexual excess.

Inside the church, behind the 1608 Romanist-style main retablo, are remnants of Gothic painting. There is a nice Renaissance high choir with Plateresque decoration, and a fine 16th-c. organ. On one wall of the Capilla de San Sebastián (left aisle) is a Hispano-Flemish painting of San Antonio Abad.

12. Palacio de los Iñiguez de Medrano. 16th c., with interesting eaves.

13. Convento del Carmen. Destroyed in 1378 and rebuilt in the late Gothic style in the 16th and 17th c., the building was a military barracks and hospital in the 19th c. and now houses the Conservatory of Music and a clock museum. Its best features are the Gothic portal, whose columns narrate the cycle of Christ's birth, and the Gothic cloister.
Behind the convent is a remaining stretch of the 13th-c. town wall.

1 km. south along the road to Sos del Rey is the small Romanesque church of **San Adrián de Vadoluengo,** which used to maintain a hospice. The complex belonged to Cluny from 1141 and was a refuge for the Benedictines of Leyre when Cistercians replaced them in the 13th c. By the mid-15th c. it was in private hands. The surviving barrel-vaulted church conserves nice capitals and a simple *crismón* on the Jaca-style portal, a Romanesque tower with graceful windows, and an interesting collection of **corbels,** including a bleary-eyed drunk drinking from a barrel and a woman displaying her pudenda.

13. SANGÜESA → MONREAL

Route: SANGÜESA → Rocaforte → [Liédena] → [Foz de Lumbier] → Izco →
Abínzano → [Idocín] → Salinas de Ibargoïti → MONREAL

✳ **Rocaforte** This intersection, where 3 Roman roads come together—the road to Zaragoza and the Ebro Valley, to Jaca and the Somport pass, and to Pamplona and Roncesvalles—is the site of the original town of Sangüesa. Below it today is a sprawling paper factory. During the 9th and 10th c. the castle that formerly capped Rocaforte's limestone hill marked the frontier between Muslims and Christians. In the 11th c., once the Christians deemed the region safe, building began in earnest, and 3 successive neighborhoods were established from the top of the hill on down. By the middle of the next century, however, with the Muslim threat pushed far to the south, Sangüesa la Nueva, in the city's current location, offered economic advantages and soon eclipsed the old site. Cardinal Cisneros destroyed Rocaforte's castle in 1516. General Espoz y Mina defeated the French here in 1812 in one of the first actions that brought to an end Napoleon's occupation of the country. The former city of Rocaforte is now only a hamlet.

The parish church of Santa María de la Asunción contains a new statue of **Santiago Peregrino.**

Just north of Rocaforte, on the hillside above the road, is the Oratorio de San Bartolomé (also called San Francisco), a remnant of a monastery that has existed here since 1098, when Pedro I of Navarra and Aragón had it built to commemorate a victory against the Muslims.

According to tradition, San Francisco de Asís, on pilgrimage to Compostela in 1214, left one of his brother monks here with a sick companion. These two founded the first Franciscan monastery in Spain. The principal Franciscan community moved from here to Sangüesa la Nueva ca. 1300, but a small community persisted here until the 1835 *desamortización*, when the building became a family residence. Since 1962 the Franciscan Community of Olite has taken care of the property. The small church, wholly enclosed by the rectangular stone building and walls of the monastery garden, reputedly conserves some fragments of Gothic mural painting.

> 📖 According to legend, St. Francis set his staff in the ground near the oratory, and it blossomed into a mulberry tree that over the centuries bloomed whenever there were Franciscans in residence and dried up during their absence. Its leaves and berries had curative powers, and children who wore a bag of dried leaves around their necks were protected against fear of the dark.

St. Francis is said to have constructed a small fountain at the foot of the hill alongside the Road. The remnants of structures visible today are mostly from the 18th c.

📖 Residents of the region believed that the waters from St. Francis's fountain were curative, especially for women who had recently given birth. Some say that when he was returning from Compostela, Francis left his scallop shell here for pilgrims to use as a drinking cup.

🚗 Liédena Liédena sits on a hill that controls access to the valleys of the Irati and Salazar rivers, which join here. Sancho el Mayor donated the town to Leyre. The town has several seigniorial buildings with a characteristic local style: sturdily quoined corners, walls constructed of rubble or small flat stones, and massive slabs of rock framing the windows.

The church of Santa María de la Asunción, refurbished in 1889, contains several high-quality 16th- and 17th-c. sculptures. Like many churches between here and Logroño, a porch, practical protection against the summer sun and the chill rains of winter, covers its entrance. Pilgrims who were unable to find beds in a hospice often spent the night under these porches.

In Roman times this part of the valley was intensively farmed, and fragments of Roman buildings and of pottery have been found on nearly every rise of ground. Three km. beyond Liédena, to the east of the modern highway, are the excavated remains of a 1st–4th-c. **Roman villa**, whose mosaics are in the Museo de Navarra in Pamplona. Directly across the valley are the ruins of a Roman bridge spanning the Irati River at the entrance to the Foz de Lumbier canyon, reached by an alternate road departing from Liédena.

👟 Foz de Lumbier A stunning alternate route follows the north bank of the Río Irati to the ruined bridge, referred to locally as the Devil's Bridge (*Puente del diablo*), and then through the Lumbier Canyon (*foz*). The canyon's microenvironment is home to several endangered species, such as colonies of vultures.

✳ Izco Like many of the hamlets between here and Puente la Reina, Izco contains a half dozen large stone farmhouses with their outbuildings, a few more modest homes, and a church. One of the large homes here displays a coat of arms with the chains of Navarra (see ch. 17). The entrance of the San Martín church, in a transitional style between Romanesque and Gothic, has several rough-figured capitals.

✳ Abínzano The hamlet is cited in early-12th-c. documents. The church of San Pedro dates from the 13th c.

🚗 Idocín The village lies on the highway north of the walking Road. In the 11th c. the area around Idocín contained a number of small monasteries. It is dominated by Mount Izaga, on top of which the Romanesque Ermita de San Miguel still perches. The early Gothic doorway of Idocín's church of San Clemente has a few rough capitals. The leftmost appears to be a **pilgrim** leaning on a staff.

📖 Idocín's most famous son was General Francisco Espoz y Mina (1781–1836), a farmer who became a guerrilla leader hero of the 19th-c. War of Independence against the French. He defeated the French in more than 40 pitched battles and rose to the rank of general. The French responded by burning his family's house, the ruins of which still remain. After the war, when Fernando VII drove the liberals from Spain, Espoz y Mina had to emigrate. Later, during the first Carlist War in 1834, he again distinguished himself fighting against Zumalacárregui.

✳ Salinas de Ibargoïti This tiny village, like many in the region, is now a bedroom community for Pamplona. We were told in 1998 that of the ca. 150 villagers, only 4 still farm. The late Gothic church has a nice starred vault.

14. MONREAL

The name Mons Reallus or Mons Regalis relates to the royal castle, built by Teobaldo I of Navarra in the mid-13th c. It used to stand on the hill behind this village; its ruins—including what seem to be some Roman foundations—are still up there among the pines.

Although King García Ramírez IV extended a charter (*fuero*) to the town in 1149 in an attempt to attract foreign businessmen and foment economic growth, Monreal soon lost out to Sangüesa in the struggle for regional economic dominance. Nonetheless, during most of the Middle Ages it had 3 distinct neighborhoods: Jews to the east, *Francos* to the west, and local *Navarros* in the center, around the church of San Martín. A second church, at the west edge of town, no longer exists. Neither does the medieval wall, erected in the 14th c., long since swept away by floods and war.

MONUMENTS: 1. **Bridge.** 2. Iglesia de San Martín.

1. At the entrance to Monreal are a picturesque 2-span **Gothic bridge** and minor remains from the former city wall.

2. The modern church of San Martín contains a baptismal font resting on Romanesque capitals.

Route: MONREAL → Yárnoz → Otano → Ezperún → Gurendiaín → Tiebas →
Campanas → Enériz → **Eunate** → Obanos → PUENTE LA REINA

As you leave Monreal, you will see a pointed mountain to the southwest called the
Higa de Monreal. On top is the small Ermita de Santa Bárbara. This area saw a lot
of fighting during the 19th-c. Carlist Wars (see ch. 25).

✳ Yárnoz The town once belonged to the Knights of San Juan de Jerusalén. The
village's 15th-c. fortified tower dominates the 3 valleys that intersect here.

✳ Otano The Knights of San Juan de Jerusalén also owned Otano. Two arches
remain from the Romanesque bridge over the Río Elorz, and the main street is the
ancient pilgrimage Road. The 16th-c. church of San Salvador (or Ascensión) reputedly contains a retablo with a Gothic Virgin. The quarries on the slopes of the
Alaiz Mountains are the modern town's economic base. Yet, to judge from their
crumbling buildings, the towns between here and Puente la Reina do not yet seem
to display the pride of place and recent investment in reconstruction that typify the
villages of the Pyrenees.

✳ Ezperún The tiny church of María de la Purísima Concepción, a palace, the
houses, and outbuildings are all now a private farm. From here you can see to the
north the sprawling suburbs of modern Pamplona.

✳ Guerendiaín The old church of San Juan Bautista was rebuilt in the 16th c.

✳ Tiebas Two km. east of Tiebas are the ruins of the 13th-c. Gothic castle of
Navarran Kings Teobaldo I and II. In 1263 the monarchy traded certain properties
to the Monastery of Roncesvalles in order to obtain title to this land for the castle.
The following year Teobaldo II extended the charter (*fuero*) of Estella to Tiebas to
encourage commercial growth, but the town never really took off. In 1378 Pedro
Manrique burned the town during the Castilian dynastic wars. There was some
reconstruction, but prosperity did not come, and when the railroad reached nearby
Olite in the 19th c. this town all but died.
  The Romanesque-Gothic church of Santa Eufemia contains a nice choir with
14th-c. sculptures.

✳ Campanas (aka Venta de Campanas). The former church, now a hermitage,
is dedicated to San Nicolás de Bari. It once had a pilgrim hospice.

The reddish soils of these valleys south of Pamplona support agriculture based on
wheat, grapes, and asparagus. But in each village today at most a half dozen people still farm. Most of the rest work in Pamplona. The distant hill on the right is
the Puerta de Perdón, recently capped with windmills that generate a substantial
portion of Pamplona's electricity.

✳ Enériz The village contains several stately homes. The church of the Magdalena, built in 1763, has a 17th-c. Romanist retablo. Nearby are the *ermitas* of
Santo Domingo, San Juan, and Santa Catalina.

✳ **Eunate** This small **octagonal church** is one of the most important Romanesque monuments in Navarra. Its Basque name means "house of 100 doors." The church's origins and function are somewhat obscure, although it is commonly associated with the Knights Templar, whose churches frequently reflected the octagonal structure of the Church of the Holy Sepulcher in Jerusalem (see ch. 68). Excavations around this church have turned up a number of graves with scallop shells, presumably identifying them as pilgrim remains. A 1607 lawsuit suggests that the church may have been built by a locally prominent family as a burial chapel. Until modern times it was maintained by a brotherhood (*cofradía*) of Santa María, whose members were buried between the church and the circling wall.

Several curious, unique, and largely unexplained features make this 13th-c. church a fascinating puzzle. One is the surrounding **arched wall**. Its paired **capitals** have early Gothic characteristics, but largely Romanesque imagery: vegetables, monsters, and musicians with enormous heads and fiddles. Several of the plain prismatic capitals look as if they were never finished. A column from ground to roofline defines each angle of the octagonal church. The **corbels of the apse** portray enormous faces whose turbans and Negroid features suggest that they are meant to be Moors. The inside is asymmetric (probably a function of the tower), with crossed arches in the **cupola** related to Islamic Cordoban or Templar art. Here some of the capitals have faces with beards twisted like snail shells. Judging from the **masons' marks**, some 9 different stonecutters worked on this church.

📖 Getting the right stones in the right shapes to the right places was a complex and expensive process, requiring both artistic and administrative skills. For large churches, a master quarryman might supervise dozens of cutters who freed the blocks from the ground using chisels, hammers, and saws. Scores of laborers hoisted the loose blocks and laid them out to be shaped. Skilled stonecutters, using wooden templates manufactured by a master mason and his crew, shaped the stones carefully so that they would fit precisely into the wall or column for which they were destined. It was all piecework, so each cutter marked his stones with his personal logo so that he would be paid for every piece he had produced and the master quarryman would be paid for every stone cut in his quarry. Carters urged their lumbering oxen to truck the finished stones to the work site. Carpenters built scaffolds, derricks, and windlasses to hoist the stones into place. Mortar makers combined sand, lime, and water to produce cement of just the right consistency for each part of the job. Masons laid the shaped stones in courses, testing with their levels and plumb lines to make certain that all angles were square. Blacksmiths were at hand to manufacture, repair, and sharpen everybody's tools. In the later stages of construction, sculptors fashioned the capitals, tympana, gutters, gargoyles, corbels, and delicate stone tracery. The sculptors were often itinerant artisans who spent two or three months at a work site and then moved along the pilgrimage Road to find another church under construction. Since in the 12th c. nearly every town of note in Spain was building a new church, there were few places on the Road between the Pyrenees and Compostela where you would have been out of earshot of the clink-clink-clink of chisel against stone.

✳ **Obanos** In the Middle Ages this substantial town at the junction of the 2 main routes to Santiago controlled several churches and hospices. From 1234 the assembly of Navarran nobility, called the Infanzones de Obanos, met here to protest treatment by Navarran kings. Their coat of arms, which hangs on the church, bears the motto: *Pro libertate patria gens libera state* ("Let the people be free so that the patria may be free").

Obanos is famous for its mystery play dedicated to Saints Guillermo and Felicia, written by Canónigo Don Santos Beguiristáin and performed since 1965 on the Sunday following Corpus Christi.

> 📖 Guillermo, a duke in Aquitaine, made a pilgrimage to Compostela with his sister Felicia. As they were returning, Felicia declared her desire to become a hermit in Amocain (near Elía, in northern Navarra). Guillermo, angered that she would not return to the French court, tried to take her from the hermitage by force. Raging at her rejection, he killed her. Instantly contrite, he returned to Compostela to pray, and on his second journey homeward he decided to remain in Obanos, where he wept for his sister until his death. He was buried in the Ermita de Nuestra Señora de Arnótegui, located south of Obanos.

The church of San Juan Bautista contains Guillermo's skull, encased in silver. When his tomb was opened, among his bones was found a Santiago medal, now kept in a silver reliquary. On the Thursday of Holy Week, watered wine is passed through the reliquary and distributed to villagers.

The 1911 neo-Gothic church incorporates a 14th-c. portal with a typically Gothic narrow frieze of capitals depicting hunting scenes. Inside are 18th- and 19th-c. retablos. One contains the 13th-c. seated Virgen Blanca. In a delicate touch, repeated in several early Gothic Navarran Virgins, her left hand grips the corner of her robe. There is a splendid late-16th-c. crucifix, larger than life-size, with a dramatically muscled Christ. In the sacristy are a seated Romanist-style San Juan Bautista and a masterfully composed standing Virgin, Child, and San Juanito by the 16th-c. sculptor Juan de Anchieta.

At the edge of Obanos is the Ermita de San Salvador, by tradition the juncture point of the 2 medieval Roads to Compostela.

Just beyond Obanos, dominating the countryside from a hill south of the valley road, is the Ermita de Nuestra Señora de Arnótegui y San Guillermo, restored in 1964.

The Road that crosses the Pyrenees in Somport joins the Road from Roncesvalles just outside of Puente la Reina. To celebrate the 1965 Holy Year, Gerardo Brun was commissioned to cast the statue of **Santiago Peregrino** now found at the crossroads. When we hiked in 1974, this was a quiet country junction; the statue is now flanked by hotels and restaurants.

Route: Puerto de Ciza → Erculú → Elizarra → [Valcarlos] → Ibañeta →
Roncesvalles

The Puerto de Ciza road enters Spain through the easiest pass in the western Pyrenees. For the Romans, this was the Via Traiana, which linked Burdegala (Bordeaux) with the gold mines of Asturica Augusta (Astorga, in western León). We will refer to the Via Traiana often during the next 761 km. Two traditional routes cross the border here. The lower route through Valcarlos and Ibañeta, traced by the modern highway, invited trouble, since it offered many opportunities for easy ambush of travelers. The higher route, to the east and over the high ridge, was preferred by the Romans—who hated being surprised—and by safety-minded pilgrims, and it is the route marked out as the hiking trail today.

Erculú (Erreculuch), on the ridge to the east, just before the summit as you climb up from St.-Jean-Pied-de-Port, is the remains of a Roman triumphal monument marking the defeat of the Aquitanians by Agrippa and Mesala (38–27 B.C.E). All that is left is the base, a rubble-filled circle of large stones 21 m. in diameter and 3 m. high. Erculú also had a small pilgrim hospice for travelers caught in the mountains at night.

The scarcity of alternate routes for pilgrims invited abuse. The author of the *Veneranda dies* sermon in the 12th-c. *Codex Calixtinus,* for example, insists that "the toll collectors at the gates of Ostabat or Saint-Jean or Saint-Michel at the foot of the Pass of Cize, who take unjust tolls from them, are thoroughly damned. No tongue, in fact, can narrate how many evils they have brought upon pilgrims. Hardly anyone passes through there who is not robbed by them." [CC: Book I; trans. Coffey et al., 48–9]

📖 The *Liber Sancti Jacobi* (*Book of Saint James*) is a mid-12th-c. compendium in Latin of material centered on the cult of Santiago and the pilgrimage to Compostela. The *Codex Calixtinus* (CC) is the oldest surviving manuscript of the LSJ. It is housed in the Santiago de Compostela Cathedral. The Calixtus claiming to be author of the manuscript's opening letter is Pope Calixtus II, a boyhood friend of Compostela Archbishop Diego Gelmírez. Since this Pope died 2 decades before the work was compiled, the attribution is clearly false.

The work contains 225 folios, divided into 5 books, each having a different focus.

—Book I contains the liturgy and hymns for the Saint's feast days. Several of the hymns contain some of the earliest examples of polyphony. The *Veneranda dies* ("A day to be honored") sermon speaks extensively about the pilgrimage to Compostela, its merits, pitfalls, and glories. It offers glimpes into the life of the 12th-c. pilgrims.

—Book II contains 22 miracles wrought by Santiago all over medieval Christendom. Most took place between 1064 and 1135 and include miraculous cures, resuscitation from death, release from imprisonment, aid in battle, rescue from drowning, and forgiveness of sins. Recipients of these miracles include men, women, and children (although men predominate); they are of varied social classes and professions, as well as nationalities (although the French outnumber all others combined).

—Book III is one version (of 2 offered in the CC) of the miraculous *translatio* (translation, or movement) of the martyred Santiago's body from the Holy Land to the Galician shore.

—Book IV, allegedly narrated by Turpin, Charlemagne's archbishop at Rheims, recounts the exploits of Charlemagne and Roland as they battle the Muslims on the Iberian Peninsula. It is a version of the epic *Chanson de Roland*, and it was quite popular in the Middle Ages. We cite it as the *Turpin* chronicle.

—Book V, popularly called the *Guide,* is the only extant 12th-c. guidebook to the pilgrimage route to Compostela. It includes what to do once the pilgrim has reached the Saint's tomb. Interspersed are bits of personal narrative, including invective against some of the Peninsula's inhabitants and praise for others. It cautions about commercial scams, unclean foods, and bad water. It describes monuments and holy places meriting visits. Most of these sites are French, leading scholars to think the author of Book V was a Frenchman, perhaps a man named Aymery Picaud, although the ambiguous manuscript reference to him may only mean that he carried the book to Compostela.

—Appended to the CC, hastily written, is the sole surviving text of "Dum Pater familias," which has become the most famous of pilgrim hymns.

At the border between France and Spain, at a place where the cross and chapel of the French epic hero Roland (see ch. 17) traditionally stood, and where one can for the first time see into Spain, pilgrims would fall to their knees, plant small wooden crosses in the ground next to the cross of Roland, face west toward Santiago, and pray for their safe journey. Domenico Laffi in 1673 described his emotions at this point on his journey:

We stood up, and when we had come out of the little chapel we turned around and glanced back at France saying "Good-bye: God only knows if we will ever see you again!" And saying this, when we took our first steps down the mountain, tears came to our eyes and a certain nostalgia came into our hearts. And that is how we were for an hour, without being able to speak to one another, as we walked downward toward Roncesvalles. [Laffi; ed. Crespo Caamaño 83. Trans. Gitlitz]

✳ Elizarra At the left of the path are the minimal ruins of the former chapel of Elizarra.

✳ Valcarlos The Carlos of this Valley of Carlos is Charlemagne, whose troops fared poorly in this narrow gorge. This ancient village on the modern highway had an important pilgrim hospice, now vanished. Its medieval church of San Juan has also disappeared. The stone bridge is where the last Carlist pretender of Spain abandoned the Peninsula in 1875, thus ending the Carlist Wars (see ch. 25).

The current church is dedicated to Santiago. In front of it is a modern nonrepresentational monument to pilgrims, which looks more like a monument to war dead. We've been told that the recumbent pilgrim is not dead, merely exhausted.

✳ Ibañeta The 1,300-m.-high Ibañeta pass was where an 11th-c. *ermita* belonging to the Monastery of Leyre (see ch. 10) once stood. Here, too, was the famous monastery and hospice of San Salvador, founded in 1127 by the bishop of Pamplona, Sancho Larrosa. Pilgrims in the mid-12th c. referred to this chapel as the *Capella Caroli Magni*, but by the end of the century, people had come to believe this to be where Roland sounded his horn, and renamed it the *Capella Rollandi* (see ch. 17). In addition to the chapel there was a hospice—still documented in the 17th c., where many pilgrims spent the night before descending to the monastery of Roncesvalles.

Today's modest chapel still has a bell to guide pilgrims on foggy days. Nearby is a modern granite monument to Roland. Just below it you can see a bunker from the 1936–39 Spanish Civil War.

17. RONCESVALLES

HISTORY

From its inception until 1984, the monastery of Nuestra Señora de Roncesvalles belonged to the Order of San Agustín. It now pertains to the archbishopric of Pamplona. As the front porch of Spain, as the legendary site of major events in the epic of Charlemagne and Roland, and as one of the most important hospices along the Road to Santiago, it continuously attracted substantial support over the ages. At its height it owned land, churches, hospices, and villages throughout Spain, and in Portugal, France, Germany, England, and Scotland.

CHARLEMAGNE AND ROLAND

Roland (known in Spanish as Roldán, in Italian as Orlando), the hero of the French medieval epic *Chanson de Roland*, is inseparably linked with Roncesvalles. The facts, as recorded in 9th-c. chronicles, are that on August 15, 778, the rear guard of Charlemagne's army suffered a disastrous defeat in the narrow defiles of the pass over the Pyrenees, probably at the site known now as Valcarlos, which derived its name from the events. It is unclear whether the attackers were Muslims or Basque *Navarros* and whether the attack was strategic or mere banditry. Poets of the 11th c. transformed the story to fit their conceptions of society and of war: armies were led by noble heroes who perished only at the hands of other heroes or archvillains, preferably in single combat. Thus were born the 12 Peers of France, among them Roland—as personification of knightly virtue—and the traitor Ganelon. The new vision required an open field of battle, and the encounter was literarily relocated to the heights of Erro, a little further south into Spain, and the soldiers on both sides were considered to number in the tens of thousands. With the 12th-c. boom in pilgrimage, throughout most of Europe Roncesvalles became synonymous with Hospice and Monastery, and in the popular imagination the events of Roland's death were relocated to its immediate vicinity. The rock that the dying Roland split while trying to break his sword Durandarte, to keep it from falling into Moorish hands (the *peña partida*), was imagined to be the site where Charlemagne built the Sancti Spiritus chapel, in truth the monastery ossuary. The chapel was then reinterpreted to be the burial chamber of the 12 Peers. In these revisionist histories Charlemagne's expedition was not motivated by French political expansion, but by the desire to wrest control of the pilgrimage Road from the Saracens (despite the historical fact that Santiago's bones had not yet been discovered). This vision is enshrined in the 12th-c. *Codex Calixtinus*'s fourth book, known as the *Turpin* chronicle.

> 📖 These French stories and relics are indicative of the strong Frankish interest in northern Spain from Charlemagne's time in the late 8th c. right up until the forcible incorporation of Navarra into modern Spain in 1512. The historical Charlemagne personally directed intermittent military campaigns in Iberia from 785 to 815. Since the invading Muslim armies had reached all the way to Poitiers before being stopped by Charles Martel, Muslim control of the northern Peninsula was perceived as a direct military threat. France's strategy was to create a buffer zone, a French March, between the infidels and the Pyrenees. This zone was linked to Aquitaine and stretched from Navarra to Cataluña. In the times when Frankish control was strong, adven-

turers and businessmen, Gascons from the north and learned Jews from the Muslim south, flowed into the borderlands, particularly Barcelona, which by the end of the 9th c. was recognized as an independent county (*condado*). French clergy set up a translation school near there in Ripoll. The ties between the Spanish kingdoms and France continued through the epoch of the pilgrimage. The Benedictines of Cluny, and later the Cistercians of Clairvaux, Gallicized Spanish Catholicism and brought with them architects, sculptors, and poets adept in the new French styles. Spanish monarchs extended special privileges for immigrating French businessmen.

The Road to Compostela, known also as the French Road, brought hundreds of thousands of French pilgrims trooping through Spain, staying in hospices run by the French and worshiping in churches dedicated to the Virgins of Le Puy and Rocamador and to French saints such as San Martín de Tours.

PILGRIMAGE

The hospice at Ibañeta, rendered unusable by the violent weather of the pass, was moved to Roncesvalles in 1132 by the bishop of Pamplona, Sancho Larrosa, and King Alfonso I el Batallador of Navarra. As a pilgrim hospice, but also as the major hostelry between France and the kingdom of Navarra, it was naturally open to everyone. A Latin 12th-c. hymn, called "La Pretiosa," includes these verses:

> Its doors open to the sick and well,
> to Catholics as well as to pagans,
> Jews, heretics, beggars, and the indigent,
> and it embraces all like brothers.

Other stanzas describe how monks would wash the feet, cut the hair, and trim the beards of pilgrims; how volunteer women would tend the sick; and how any pilgrim who was so (un)fortunate as to die in Roncesvalles would be buried in Sancti Spiritus.

Pilgrims were fed well in monastery hospice refectories like Roncesvalles, but only after the appropriate religious niceties were taken care of. A 16th-c. description tells how at sunset the friars of Roncesvalles processed into the refectory, where the hungry pilgrims stood waiting in a long line in front of the tables. The principal canons and prior ascended to the high table at one end of the room. The prior prayed for the poor, for pilgrims, for the Church, the Pope, the monarchs and Spanish nobility, and for all those, both Spanish and foreign, who had contributed to the monastery's support. As a cleric in the high pulpit read out each name in turn, the assembled throng recited a Hail Mary or an Our Father. Finally, one of the friars, or some particularly honored guest, went down from the high table and distributed to each of the pilgrims his or her ration of bread (after first kissing the loaf). Other friars distributed wine, and then eventually the main dish.

As late as the 17th c., well into the decline of the pilgrimage, the Roncesvalles hospice was hosting 25,000 pilgrims per year. One of them was the Italian priest Domenico Laffi (see ch. 25), whose diary notes that when they arrived at the monastery they were singing the solemn Mass, in the Spanish style. The only instruments they had were bagpipes of various kinds. "They made a deafening noise that could easily be heard a mile away. The organ pipes are made of tin and wood and when it is played they, too, sound like bagpipes with drones." [Laffi; trans. Hall (1997), 107]

MONUMENTS: 1. **Real Colegiata**. 2. Cloister. 3. Museum. 4. Capilla de Santiago. 5. Capilla de Sancti Spiritus. 6. Granary.

1. **Real Colegiata.** A *colegiata* is a hybrid institution: a church headed by an abbot and with a community of both monks and secular canons (i.e., priests not affiliated with a monastic order). This Real Colegiata was built by Sancho VII el Fuerte and consecrated in 1219; it was restored from 1940 to 1945. It is one of the earliest pure Gothic monuments in Spain. Though the church is early, it shows a complete mastery of the Gothic forms. The structure was revolutionary in Spain for its expanses of windows, its triforium gallery, and the 10 rose windows over the triforium. The aisles are divided by alternating thick and thin columns, from which rise alternatively 1 or 3 nerves to sustain the vault. The church's 3 naves and polygonal apse are covered with delicately nerved vaulting. The windows in the right nave depict Navarran saints Veremundo and Fermín. They were designed in Münich during the 1940s reforms.

• The **Virgin of Roncesvalles**. The wood statue, covered with silver, was brought to Roncesvalles in the 13th c. from Toulouse. Well into the 18th c. the image was kept behind a curtain and revealed to pilgrims only with elaborate ceremony. Now it is located in the center of the altar area. It was officially crowned as Navarra's patroness in 1960.

• The **baldachin**. Above the Virgin, setting her dramatically apart from the rest of the church, is a unique and ornate silver canopy called a **baldachin**. Roncesvalles's original baldachin vanished eons ago: this one, placed here in 1945, is an exact copy of the baldachin in the Cathedral of Gerona.

> 📖 The word *baldachin* derives from "Baldac"—the medieval term for Baghdad—the source of silk cloth imported for ecclesiastical canopies.

2. **Cloister.** When a massive blizzard obliterated the Colegiata's Gothic cloister in the 17th c., this unadorned replacement was built. Its most notable feature is the annexed 14th-c. **chapter house**, a tall, airy structure covered with delicate nerves resting on corbels (*ménsulas*) in the shape of angels.

• The chapter house contains the **tomb of Sancho VII** el Fuerte. This Navarran king masterminded the decisive victory over the Muslims at Las Navas de Tolosa in 1212 that opened up Andalucía for the first time to Christian reconquest. The battle is depicted in the modern window in the chapter house. Both this king's nickname—*el Fuerte* ("the Strong")—and the effigy on his tomb reflect his extraordinary height of 2.25 m. (7'4").

Roncesvalles holds 3 sorts of relics: religious, historic, and *Chanson de Roland*-ic. The most interesting of the historic are the **chains of Christian prisoners freed at Las Navas**. These lie on cushions in the chapel at the foot of Sancho's tomb.

> 📖 At the battleground of Las Navas de Tolosa, in 1212, the Muslim general Miramamolín was protected by a wall of slaves chained in a circle around his tent. The story goes that Sancho VII himself spurred his horse to vault the wall, leading his knights to capture the tent and the general and to free the Christian prisoners. Henceforth the chains were incorporated into the coat of arms of Navarra [and later into Fernando and Isabel's escutcheon of united Spain (see ch. 24)]. An enormous emerald that the King took in booty was likewise set into the shield's center.

3. **Museum.** The museum is small, only 1 large room, but it contains some extraordinary works, including the other 2 categories of reliquaries. Reliquaries are ornate

constructions of precious metals or carved and painted wood that contain relics, fragments of saints' bones, or physical objects associated with Jesus or Mary.

📖 Relics were very important to medieval Catholics, who believed that some of the aura of divinity associated with Christ or the saints remained in their bones, or in the objects associated with them. Venerating the relic, visiting it, or honoring it by adorning it with precious metals was seen as a form of worship, and put the worshiper in direct contact with the divine. Crusaders brought back tens of thousands of relics from the Holy Land. Kings preferred them to gold. Pious thieves stole them for their home churches. The power of important relics drew pilgrims, and belief in Europe's most significant relic, the nearly complete body of 1 of Jesus's 12 Apostles, launched the great pilgrimage to Compostela. Monasteries and churches all along the Road proudly exhibited their most sacred relics to the visiting pilgrims.

• Holy relics. Among Roncesvalles's prizes are a 14th-c. Gothic reliquary (discussed below) that contains bits of bones of more than 30 saints, a 15th-c. reliquary carved to look like a saint's arm, and a 16th-c. gold reliquary with 2 thorns from Jesus's crown of thorns.

• French relics. Given Roncesvalles's pride in its centrality to the French epic of Roland, it stands to reason that the monastery would house not only saints' relics, but also some tangible relics of Charlemagne's expedition and of Roland's death. Monks showed pilgrims these 3 trophies:

—The legendary **Roland's horn**. Known as the Oliphant, this carved ivory trumpet is one of 2 battle horns held by the monastery.

📖 Once Roland had split the rock with his sword Durandarte, the *Chanson* states that he blew blasts on his ivory horn to summon Charlemagne to his aid. He blew so hard that he cracked the horn on one side. But the traitor Ganelon persuaded the French king that Roland blew his hunting horn every day at that hour, so that Charlemagne rode on, leaving Roland to his fate. [CC: Book IV, ch. 21]

—Roland's maces. We saw them, hefted them, and swung them around our heads in 1974. Pilgrims like Arnold von Harff and Domenico Laffi also reported seeing the maces and oliphant; Harff noted, without comment, that he had also seen the Oliphant in Toulouse. On our most recent visit in 1998 they were no longer on display, and no one could tell us where they had been stashed.

—**Charlemagne's chessboard** (*ajedrez de Carlomagno*). Not really a chessboard and having nothing to do with Charlemagne, this 14th-c. complex reliquary, probably from Montpellier, is made of gold-plated silver over wood, with applications of translucent enamels. The enamel is produced by firing vitreous material of various colors that have been laid over gold or silver bases of different thickness on which the desired motifs have been etched. The piece is extraordinary in the variety of colors and tones achieved. The 32 square compartments faced with rock crystal contain bits of saints' bones, wrapped in cloth, each with an identifying label. The relics are arranged so as to suggest the Last Judgment and Redemption of humanity. Note the enameled symbols of the 4 Evangelists.

• Retablos. The museum also contains many panels and paintings taken from retablos.

—One 17th-c. panel depicts a pilgrim saved from attacking wolves by intercession of the Virgin.

—The most unusual painting is the **triptych of the Crucifixion**, identified as 16th-c. northern European. However, the faces of the triptych's several images of Christ, the good thief, and a number of the lesser figures appear to be oriental. Below the cross is a melee of exotic figures, ostentatiously caparisoned horses, and grotesque courtiers who appear to have nothing to do with the sacred scene. On the right panel is the betrayal, with a redheaded Judas (red is the color of the Devil) and a dozen dehumanized, monstrous figures. St. Peter wields his knife, but is shown faceless. On the left panel, Jesus is shown preaching, but the background is filled with exotic birds and animals, including a monkey—the symbol of parody—and flying above it a dove, clearly the Holy Spirit. In the foreground kneel the sober donors and their families, who seem to have been painted first, and then overpainted with the grotesques. We have never seen anything like it.

—**Romanesque missal.** Take a moment to look at the prayer book whose carved silver covers are reflected in a mirror lying under the book. One cover shows a scene—derived from the Apocalypse—that you will see dozens of times between here and Compostela. Christ sits in Majesty, His right arm raised in blessing, His left holding a book that proclaims that He is the beginning (alpha) and end (omega) of all things. He is surrounded by a nimbus (here diamond-shaped) and 4 creatures who represent the 4 Evangelists. (see ch. 5).

4. Capilla de Santiago. The bell in this 13th-c. Gothic chapel was rung at night to guide late-arriving pilgrims down from the Ibañeta Pass.

In 1974 we crossed the Pyrenees in heavy fog, got lost at the summit, and came down in the valley of Orbaiceta, 10 soggy km. to the east. About midnight, wandering in the forests in a clothes-drenching rain, we were about to give up and take shelter by some fallen logs when we heard Roncesvalles's bells tolling—we had alerted them when we would be coming—and gratefully followed the sound to the monastery.

5. Capilla de Sancti Spiritus (Silo de Carlomagno). The 12th-c. central ossuary held the bones of pilgrims who died crossing these mountains, although a widespread medieval legend held it to be the crypt of Charlemagne's soldiers killed here in battle. The center has been restored and a modern altar placed on top of the ossuary.

6. Granary. This late medieval granary is now an exhibition hall. The monastery's wealth was—among other things—agricultural, and it owned several large rectangular silos (*claverías*). You will see 2 more between here and Pamplona, in Larrasoaña and Trinidad de Arre. These buildings also occasionally functioned as pilgrim hospices.

18. RONCESVALLES → ZUBIRI

Route: RONCESVALLES → **Cruz de Peregrinos** → Burguete → El Espinal → Mezkíritz → Biskarret → Lintzoaín → [Erro] → [Agorreta] → ZUBIRI

✳ **Cruz de Peregrinos** Some 300 m. outside of Roncesvalles toward Burguete is a 14th-c. Gothic pilgrims' cross. Its base is a Renaissance capital representing Navarran king Sancho el Fuerte and his wife Clemencia. The cross was brought from further up the mountain to this site in 1880.

Unlike the central Pyrenees, which have jagged and bare summits with deeply glaciated valleys (see ch. 2), the western mountains are gentle, consisting of rolling hills and ridges that drop to broad tectonic depressions. In these basins are the major market towns like St-Jean-Pied-de-Port. Streams descending into these basins from the high meadows have frequently cut deep, V-shaped valleys, so steep-sided that many are true gorges.

The summits, which receive the highest precipitation and ultraviolet radiation, the strongest winds, and the widest daily and annual temperature variations, harbor a variety of alpine plants. They are the preferred summer pastures for herders of the region. The intermediate slopes tend to shrubby thickets, some cut for silage or for winter bedding for animals. The most common plants are gorse, heath, bracken, ling, and broom. An occasional hardy palm or even banana tree can be found tucked away along a protected wall. The flat land along the rivers is intensely farmed, with rye, hay, and (in modern times) potatoes the predominant crops, although increasingly these fields are being turned into small pastures for horses and cows. Some of the intermountain basins are broad enough to lend themselves to modern mechanized agriculture.

The trees that flourish highest up, such as on the slopes just above the monastery of Roncesvalles, tend to be beeches. Below them grow several varieties of oaks: *marojos* with deeply indented leaves and rounded tips, gall oaks (*quejigos*) with shallowly indented leaves and pointed tips, and *robles* with barely indented rounded leaves. Near the villages each spring, people harvest from these trees, trimming the branches for firewood, fences, or tools, and leaving the stubby trunks to regenerate next year's crop. Lines of the trimmed trunks are sometimes left as fences. Poplars and willows, and sometimes ash or maple, border the rivers themselves, and any spot left untended goes quickly to briar. If you hike in late July you can eat your fill of blackberries.

✳ **Burguete** The town is located at the junction of the Arce and Urederra Rivers on an upland plateau some 800 m. high. Its original name—Burgo de Roncesvalles—reflected its dependency on the monastery. In the Middle Ages the town's importance entitled it to be represented in Navarra's parliament (*cortes*). Burguete's economy was based on the pilgrim trade, and it was known for its shoemakers and barbers. Little is left of the medieval town because it suffered a disastrous fire in the 14th c., but it conserves its single long street, typical of the medieval pilgrimage Road towns. The flat-tiled sloping roofs of the houses are designed to shed the Pyrenees' heavy winter snows; their white-painted exteriors reflect a southern French architectural style. Burguete's modern church of San Nicolás de Bari conserves a Baroque doorway.

Below Burguete, the Road crosses a small Romanesque bridge over the Río Urrobi. A little further on is one of the sites traditionally identified as the location of the massacre of Charlemagne's troops by the Saracens. According to chapter 21 of the CC's *Turpin* chronicle (see ch. 16) (whose inflated numbers challenge the imagination):

> While Charlemagne crossed the pass with Ganelon, Turpin, and 20,000 Christians, Roland, Oliveros, and 20,000 additional Christians formed the rear guard. Marsilio and Beligando [Muslim captains] rode out at dawn with 50,000 Saracens from the woods and hills where, by [the traitor] Ganelon's advice, they had been hidden for two days and nights. They divided their army in two groups: one of 20,000 men, and the other of 30,000. The 20,000 began a surprise attack against our rear guard. But shortly our men turned back against them, and after fighting them from dawn until tierce [9:00 A.M.], vanquished them all: not one of the 20,000 managed to escape alive. But immediately thereafter, the other 30,000 attacked our men, who were without energy and exhausted on account of such great fighting, and [the Saracens] wiped them out, from the smallest to the largest.

✳ El Espinal The village was founded in 1269 by Teobaldo II of Navarra to help defend pilgrims from robbers who made this stretch of the Road difficult. There is a new bust of him in the plaza, dedicated in 1969. The town belonged to Roncesvalles until the 1835 *desamortización*. The modern church is dedicated to San Bartolomé. Although some of the houses have dated lintels, most look like modern chalets, a sign of the increased prosperity of the region.

Alto de Mezkíritz. At 922 m., this pass divides the watersheds of the Arce and Erro Rivers. The river valleys that descend from the Pyrenees' central ridge all flow south, and generally slightly east, eventually to join the Río Ebro. Since the pilgrimage Road runs southwest from here to Pamplona, you must cross 3 of these small rivers and the mountains that separate them. If instead you followed the Río Arce south you would join the Aragonese pilgrimage route near Sangüesa. If you followed the Erro, you would end up in the same place.

As you start down from the Mezkíritz pass you leave the last beech groves you will see along the Road.

✳ Mezkíritz Although architecture in this valley tends to be sober, one family in this village in 1787 treated themselves to an elaborate Baroque façade for their house. In front of the village's new indoor *frontón* (jai alai court) is an ultramodern monument to the town's ballplayers (*bostkirolari*).

✳ Biscarret For the 12th-c. *Codex Calixtinus Guide*, Biscarretum was the end of the segment of the Road that began in St. Jean. It was never a large town. A 15th-c. tax census recorded only 19 families: 5 noble and 14 laborer. The heavy pointed arches of the 13th-c. church of San Bartolomé are transitional between Romanesque and Gothic.

✳ Lintzoaín This village's 13th-c. church of San Saturnino has a Romanesque portal of very little interest. The interesting buildings are the houses and their lintels over the front doors bearing 18th- or 19th-c. dates.

Tradition holds that 2 km. southwest of the church, to the left of the Road, a rock 3 m. long, now buried in brambles, recorded the exact measure of Roland's pace.

🚗 Erro This small village on the paved highway, some 222 m. below the Alto de Mezkíritz, once belonged to the Monastery of Leyre, 60 km. to the southeast. In the 11th and 12th c. it was the center of the county of Erro. Its ancient church and cemetery sat high on the rock west of the village. One of the old noble houses in town conserves its coats of arms. Erro's current church is dedicated to San Esteban. Just beyond Erro, near km. 29, is another bunker from the 1936–39 Civil War (see ch. 24).

Alto de Erro. The 801-m. pass over this hill had an inn, the Venta del Puerto. Its meager ruins are now a cattle pen. From here you drop precipitously through pine forests to the Arga Valley.

19. ZUBIRI

In Basque, Zubiri means the "Town of the Bridge." The village is cited in a 1040 document, when King García el de Nájera donated it and its small monastery to the Benedictine monastery of Leyre.

The current Gothic bridge over the Río Arga probably replaces earlier ones. Local tradition holds that cows that walk 3 times around the bridge's central pillar—which reputedly contains the relics of Santa Quiteria—are protected against rabies. The Italian pilgrim Domenico Laffi (see ch. 25) had rough going in Zubiri:

> ... there was no footpath nor any access to a proper road. At last, after surviving many difficulties and often in danger of falling over, we arrived at the Bridge of Paradise. Though I think of it as the Bridge of Hell.
>
> It spans a big, deep river that runs between two high hills. It is shaded by dense trees so that the water, though it is clear, in fact looks black. It is so fast-flowing that it fills the traveller with fear and trembling. The bridge is guarded by soldiers, better described as thieves and murderers. As it is a deserted spot they will strip passers-by of their belongings. Persons of high rank are made to pay, that is, made to give them a 'tip.' Anyone who refuses gets brutally treated. They will break open our head with their sticks and will sometimes get rid of people by making the river their grave. [Laffi; trans. Hall (1997), 113–4]

Near the Zubiri bridge was a leper hospital called the Hospital de la Magdalena. Nothing remains.

Just past Zubiri is the Magna Company's large factory, which processes magnesite for use in making synthetic rubber and fertilizer.

20. ZUBIRI → PAMPLONA

Route: ZUBIRI → Illaratz → Esquirotz → [Urdaniz] → **Larrasoaña** → Akerreta → Zuriáin → Irotz → Zabaldica → [Arleta] → Arre → [Huarte] → [Villava] → Burlada → PAMPLONA

The villages from Zubiri to Pamplona each have very few houses, while the houses themselves are of enormous size. The villages are located 2 or 3 km. from each other, on crags 30 to 50 m. above the valley floor. This was for defense, and because in medieval times the scarce bottomland along the river was reserved for farming.

The houses are 3 or 4 stories tall, often with the animals downstairs and the attic given over to a dovecote or hayloft. They are broad structures, with long sloping roofs, often resembling Swiss chalets. Notice the varied styles of chimneys. The truncated conical chimneys, capped with stone and with windowlike holes to let out the smoke, resemble the ones you would see in the Aragonese Pyrenees. Houses that belonged to noble families often bear an ancestral coat of arms over the door. Sometimes a wooden balcony overhangs the door, to shade from the summer sun and to protect from the cold rains and infrequent snows of winter. Look for fanciful touches of decoration on the balconies. Windows tend to be small to preserve internal heat, and are often shuttered against the elements. A few houses still have their stone or concrete clothes-washing basins next to the front door. What in other cultures would be outbuildings—sheds and barns and storage rooms—here tend to be incorporated into the main building or in tacked-on structures.

✳ **Illaratz** Just past this minuscule village is an old church, now incorporated into a private dwelling. To the right is the medieval bridge leading to Urdaniz.

✳ **Esquirotz** This village has a number of noble homes, some of which preserve their traditional stone façades, and others that appear recently plastered and whitewashed in the southern French style.

🚗 **Urdaniz** On the highway. In the 14th c. this small village was inhabited exclusively by members of the minor nobility. Just past town is a small bridge where a foreign pilgrim woman was found dead in 1391. In such cases all personal effects belonged to the Crown, but in this instance King Carlos III donated the 9 francs found in her pocket, and the money from the sale of her horse, to the Monastery of San Agustín in Pamplona.

✳ **Larrasoaña** In the 11th c. Larrasoaña had an Augustinian monastery that belonged to Leyre. The town grew to sufficient importance to be mentioned in the 12th-c. *Guide* (see ch. 16) and in 1174 to be given a charter (*fuero*) that encouraged immigration and economic development by foreigners, who were called *Francos* without regard to where they actually may have come from. Its 14th-c. bridge, called the Puente de los Bandidos, seems to have been a good place for robbing travelers. Two pilgrim hospices—San Blas and Santiago—, each with its supporting brotherhood (*cofradía*), were in operation at either end of the town well into the 18th c. They have since disappeared.

What has survived is the former Clavería de Roncesvalles, a long monastery warehouse opposite Larrasoaña's church. It conserves its small cross of Roncesvalles behind some bushes below the north window. Some believe that it, too, functioned as a hospice. Its 5 interior Gothic arches are supported by external buttresses (see ch. 10). The downstairs was originally 1 room, but a 16th-c. document mentions stables on the first floor and 11 small rooms on the second. The building now serves as a private home.

Larrasoaña's undistinguished 13th-c. church is dedicated to San Nicolás de Bari. Its long main street contains a number of 15th- and 16th-c. wealthy homes, some of which bear coats of arms. A 2-span medieval bridge crosses the Río Arga here.

✳ **Akerreta** Small village, large houses, good view. Precisely the same as can be said of most of the villages in this part of the Arga Valley.

✳ **Zuriáin** This town, in a strategic position at a pinch point in the valley, has a church dedicated to San Esteban, rebuilt in the 16th–17th c. Over the door there is a small, painted Crucifixion in naïve style. A census in 1428 counted 3 houses in the hamlet, noting that one was occupied by a woman separated from her husband. By the 19th c. it had grown to 15 houses.

✳ **Irotz** The church is dedicated to San Pedro. A 3–span Romanesque bridge leads back across the Arga.

✳ **Zabaldica** The plain 12th-c. church is dedicated to San Esteban and conserves some simple geometric painting over the door. In the Middle Ages the town developed 2 centers, one around the church, and the other below, along the Santiago Road.

🚗 **Arleta** On the highway. The early medieval hamlet was abandoned in the 14th c. and registered 1 large house in the mid-16th. It has since doubled in size. The larger of the 2 houses in this hamlet—now private property—is the Palacio del Señorío, with a paired window in its Gothic tower. The tiny church is dedicated to Santa Marina.

✳ **Arre** The site, just past Arleta where the Río Ulzama slices between 2 hills, is strategic. The Roman road from Pamplona to Bordeaux crossed the river here on its way to Roncesvalles, and another angled off toward the Valle de Baztán. In medieval times the Miravalles hill was topped by a castle controlling both the Ulzama and Arga Valleys. You pass over the Río Ulzama on a Romanesque bridge that connects directly to a right-angled arch under a monastery: an ideal control point for all traffic between Pamplona and the mountains.

The monastery, hospice, and *clavería* (granary) of Trinidad de Arre formerly belonged to the Monastery of Roncesvalles. This is the most complete medieval monastery/hospice complex remaining in Navarra. Inside the courtyard are remains of the old hospice, similar to those of Roncesvalles and Larrasoaña: a long rectangular building, with internal Gothic arches supported by strong stone buttresses. Today this church still maintains a pilgrim hospice.

Trinidad's 1507 bylaws still survive. Villagers were to provide the hospice "with bread for the entire year, a half-pound per person, for all the pilgrims who arrive at the hospice at night, above and beyond the [usual tax of] 12 bushels of wheat" (Huidobro y Serna 1:657).

Just below the bridge is a dam, millrace, and several old mills, the site of Roncesvalles's 12th-c. *clavería*, and a 13th-c. fulling mill for making felt. The once small town of Trinidad is now part of Pamplona's continuously increasing belt of suburbs, and its old section—nearly intact when we hiked through in 1974—has largely been replaced with apartment houses. As we prepared this book we noted that 4 more old houses were being demolished.

🚗 Huarte To the east, on the highway. Huarte is dominated by a crag called El Monte San Miguel, on which a castle once perched.

📖 Since St. Michael is the warrior archangel, many churches and castles perched in strategic locations are named for him. For the same reason he was frequently named patron saint of a city or kingdom, as in the case of Navarra.

Huarte's church of San Juan Bautista contains a 16th-c. Plateresque retablo and a 14th-c. image of the Virgin.

🚗 Villava To the east, on the highway. There are some minor Roman remains near town. The town appears in medieval documents from the 12th c. By the mid-13th c. several fulling mills are documented, and the town prospered from the manufacture of felt. The current San Andrés church is 17th-c. Several of Villava's houses display coats of arms. The Ayuntamiento's 1545 escutcheon depicts the chains of Navarra (see ch. 17). At Calle Mayor, 51 is the Casa Motza, dated 1558, one of Navarra's few remaining Renaissance civil portals. The medallions depict the owners, don Pedro de Andosilla el Mayor and his wife doña Francisca Solchaga.

✳ Burlada This once tiny village is now an industrial suburb of Pamplona and Navarra's third-largest town. At the rotary beyond Burlada you leave the highway that climbs to Pamplona and cross the floodplain of the Arga River that Pamplona has preserved as parkland. Near the end of the plain on your left is a modern house fancifully decorated in scallop shells. Just beyond is the 14th-c. Magdalena bridge. It was restored in 1965 and given a stone cross by the city of Compostela. This was the site of the long-since-vanished leprosarium of La Magdalena, located, as always, outside the city walls (see ch. 27). As you view the city walls from the bridge it is easy to appreciate Pamplona's commanding strategic position on a bluff over the intersection of the Arga and Sadar rivers.

21. PAMPLONA

HISTORY

Geography explains Pamplona's prominence. On a high, defensible bluff, it controls both the entry to Iberia from France through the Pyrenean Puerto de Ciza and the French road's intersection with the east-west Via Traiana, the first lateral route encountered after crossing the Pyrenees. As such, it met the Roman ideal. In 75 C.E. the Roman general Pompaelo ordered that his camp be built over the ruins of a Basque settlement on the bluff. Excavations of the cathedral cloister have uncovered remains of Roman houses, a forum, markets, and baths. Legends state that the town was Christianized by disciples of Santiago and later by Saints Saturnino (Cernín) and Fermín.

The city prospered under the Romans and later with the Visigoths. Muslims took it in 718. Two centers of resistance to the Muslim occupation remained in the mountains: one, near Pamplona itself, was mainly poor, fiercely independent Basque mountain men; the other, near Leyre, was Gascon farmers who had migrated there from France. Pamplona itself was Muslim until 799, when Christian citizens rose up, killed their governor, Mutarrif, and elected a Basque to govern them. Pamplonans felt themselves caught between pincers: Omayad Muslims to the south and Charlemagne's Franks to the north. Basques and Franks fought each other as much as they each fought the Muslims, and their feuding is probably one of the causes of Charlemagne's late-8th-c. historical expeditions to Spain on behalf of the Gascons and for his legendary defeat at Roncesvalles.

> 📖 Charlemagne's expeditions were later recast as heroic French intents to help the Iberian Christians wrest control of the Santiago pilgrimage Road from the Muslims. Thus, according to chapter 2 of the 12th-c. CC *Turpin*, Charlemagne spent 3 months besieging Pamplona in 734, without being able to breach its walls. In despair, he sought help from above: "Oh, Santiago! If it is true that you appeared to me, let me conquer this city!" At which point Pamplona's walls, like those of Jericho, came tumbling down.

It is important to remember that the early Reconquest was not in most senses a religious war. Rather, regional strongmen—warlords, in other societies—pacted, raided, and married, and built defensive towers for one central purpose: to expand their personal holdings. When it came to land, religion didn't count all that much. Pamplona in the 9th c. is a case in point. A Basque strongman named Íñigo and his son Íñigo Íñiguez (or Íñigo Arista) had taken Pamplona from its Carolingian governor.

> 📖 The *ez* in Castilian names is a patronymic: Enrique son of Pedro = Enrique Pérez. In the early Middle Ages last names changed with each generation. Thus Enrique's own son Fernando would be Fernando Enríquez.

Íñigo Íñiguez sought alliances by marrying one of his daughters to García Galíndez of Aragón and the other to Musa ibn Musa, of the Banu Qasim clan, who happened to be his half brother. In 824 the French Carolingians sent Count Aznar from their fiefdom of Jaca in an abortive attempt to take Pamplona back. From then until the early 850s, Christian Íñiguez and Muslim Musa together helped Pamplona maintain its tenuous independence.

The nobility elected the earliest Navarran kings, who were concerned with staving off the Muslims and preserving their own autonomy. The fifth king, Sancho Garcés I, who took the throne in 905 when his brother Fortuño abdicated to become a monk in Leyre, defeated the Muslims at Monjardín, married his daughter to Fernán González, the hero of Castilian independence, and made Pamplona his capital. Fearing growing Christian power, Cordoban caliph 'Abd ar-Rahman III destroyed the town in 924. Christians rebuilt. Toward the end of the century King Sancho el Mayor, who invited the Cluniac Benedictines to Leyre (see ch. 10), granted Pamplona its *fuero*. In 1084 Sancho Ramírez V drove the Muslims definitively from the region and—for a short time—merged his kingdom with Aragón.

Alfonso el Batallador (1104–1134) invested heavily in Pamplona's repopulation, granting another *fuero* that created financial advantages for foreign—principally French—immigrants. Before long, Pamplona had both French and Jewish quarters alongside its Basque, Gascon, and Mudéjar neighborhoods. The different *barrios* got along like cats in a sack. They ringed themselves with walls and towers to keep neighbors at bay. King Sancho VII el Fuerte (1194–1234) attempted to pacify the city, but was only moderately successful. In 1276, riots destroyed large portions of the city.

During most of the Middle Ages there were 4 principal ethnic neighborhoods. The Navarrería, around the cathedral, had the best natural defenses. It was the first area resettled and was the district reserved for the native Navarrans (Basques). Its southeast corner, just west of today's bullring, was the Jewish quarter. In 1154 Sancho el Sabio charged the bishop with protecting the Jewish community and granted him the right to settle Jews in any of his lands with 1 condition: that the Jews of Pamplona and Estella, the 2 major commercial towns, were to remain free and enjoy the same privileges as the *Francos*. It worked well for a while, but the Pamplona riots of 1276 wrecked the Navarrería and almost completely destroyed the Jewish *aljama*. Jews did not resettle in the city until 60 years later.

San Cernín was mainly French, immigrants attracted during the 11th and especially the 12th c., drawn by Alfonso I el Batallador's 1129 *fuero* that granted the *Francos* attractive rights:

> They shall pay no tolls anywhere in the kingdom; they shall enjoy free pasturage and the right to cut wood on all the mountains and meadows belonging to the King or to [the Cathedral of] Santa María, for as far as they can walk in one day; they may hold a market in the flats of Brañáin. No Navarro, cleric, soldier or prince may live in their district. They have the exclusive right to sell bread and wine to pilgrims; . . . the bishop shall select their mayor from three candidates whom the residents shall propose. [Arraiza, "Pamplona"]

The San Cernín district is located in and around the diamond bisected by the Calle Mayor. The *Francos*' tendency to group by street according to profession has left its mark on the names of modern Pamplona's Calles de Bolserías (purse makers), Carnicerías (butchers), Calceteros (sock makers), Caldererría (tinkers), Pellejería (leather workers), Zapatería (shoemakers), etc.

San Miguel, an enclave within the Navarerría that belonged to the Knights Hospitaller, was its own separate jurisdiction up until the 1276 riots. A donation in 1125 established a large pilgrim hospice here in front of the cathedral, then under construction.

The newest district, called both the Burgo Nuevo (new, that is, in 1110) and the Población de San Nicolás (the name of the church in its center), mixed *Francos* and *Navarros*, most of them engaged in pilgrim trades.

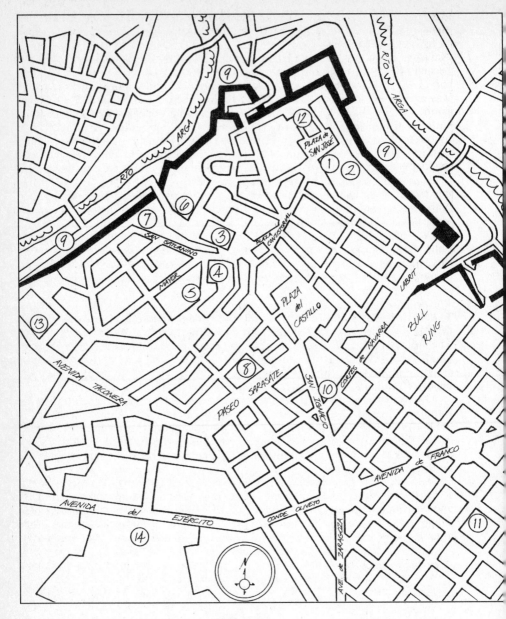

PAMPLONA

Each *barrio* had its own laws, customs, and even language. For the most part they feared and hated each other, fortified their neighborhoods with walls against each other, and fought—more or less continuously—from the 11th until the 15th c. One reason that Pamplona has so little early medieval architecture is the periodic fires that destroyed the warring *barrios*. In each reconstruction modern innovations were introduced. Most of the streets in each enclave, for example, were straightened in 1324. Then in 1422 Navarra's King Carlos III created a single city administration and had the internal walls torn down. One curious result of this growth process is that Pamplona, unlike many cities and towns along the pilgrimage Road, does not have one sole main commercial street.

In a way, Pamplona's political history is the history of the tiny kingdom of Navarra. When Sancho VII el Fuerte died without issue, Teobaldo I of Champagne became king, and from 1234 to 1329 Pamplona and Navarra were French territory. Castilla, Aragón, and France vied for control of the tiny state. For a stretch it was independent, but allied with the French and governed by the French Evreux family (1329–1425). In the 15th c., with rulers from the French house of Foix, it suffered bitter wars of succession. Navarra resisted being dragged into the new union of Aragón and Castilla that created modern Spain, until Fernando el Católico battered down Pamplona's walls by cannon fire in 1512 and incorporated the kingdom against its will.

Pamplona's strategic importance has made it a frequent military target, destroying most of the medieval buildings that escaped the fires. It was occupied by Napoleon's troops from 1809 until October of 1813. It was besieged by Carlist troops during 1873–4 (see ch. 25).

Each year on July 7, Pamplona celebrates its patron, San Fermín, by running bulls through the streets and then holding bullfights. Hemingway's celebration of this festival gave it international prominence and turned it into the overtouristed, overcrowded, drunken rite of passage that it is today.

PILGRIMAGE

Pamplona was the first large city encountered by pilgrims entering Spain over the Puerto de Ciza and as such was a place to rest, see the sights, and reprovision. The numbers of pilgrims who stopped here, and the variety of local groups (churches, nobles and royalty, guilds, brotherhoods) competing for prestige by assisting pilgrims, insured that there were plenty of hospices. Some have left behind documentary or physical evidence.

The Hospital de San Miguel de la Catedral was founded in 1086. King Sancho Ramírez ordered that of each cord of wood entering the city, 1 piece should go to the hospice. For a time it only admitted women. In the 13th c. it provided 50 beds. In 1310 García de Calzaín donated to it "100 *sueldos* for shoes for poor *romeros del camino*." In the 16th c., with the decline of the pilgrimage, it shrank to 8 beds on the first floor "to receive pilgrim women who are going to Santiago."

Santa Catalina de la Catedral was founded in 1327 for pilgrim men. Traffic was so heavy that it maintained 2 facilities, one for Spaniards (Calle Dormitaleria, 13), and one for foreigners (Calle de la Compañía, 3). The brotherhood (*cofradía*) that supported it counted King Carlos III and the wife of the crown prince of Viana among its members. A 1534 logbook records much random data about its clientele:

> 3 sick poor people from Flanders. . . . A beggar from Montalban with 3 wounds, coming back from Santiago; he stayed 3 days. . . . May 1: 4 very sick poor people on their way back from Santiago, 3 from Bordeaux and 1 a Flemming, and 3 of them were nearly dead, so much so that the Flemming stayed 12 days. . . . The day of Our Lady of September a poor man from Toulouse coming back from Santiago fell ill here and 9 days later he died. . . . The cleric Mosén Peire was salved and purged. [Arraiza, "Pamplona"]

By the early 19th c. traffic had all but stopped. Between 1818 and 1828 this hospice lodged only some 40 pilgrims per year. It went out of business with the 1835 *desamortización*.

The Hospital de la Magdalena was situated outside the walls to accommodate pilgrims who arrived at night after the city gates closed.

Santa Catalina de San Cernín functioned for a largely French clientele from the 13th c. until 1564. Run by nuns, it was sometimes called the Hospital de Duennas.

We know the names of at least 3 others: San Miguel, of the parish of San Nicolás; San Lorenzo; and in the Navarrería district, Corpus Christi. In the 17th c., as in many cities along the Road, all the hospices were incorporated into one municipal Hospital General, with food served in the Cathedral kitchen (see below). Domenico Laffi (see ch. 25) was one of the pilgrims who ate there in the 1670s:

> While they are singing High Mass they feed 12 pilgrims just inside the door of the church at a table made ready for them. They make all the pilgrims go to the kitchen door and the cook gives each one a bowl of broth. . . . When they all have their bowlful, they are made to stand in single file and go in procession through the church, carrying their bowl of soup. On reaching the table each one sits at his appointed place. Then they come with a large basket of bread and give one to each pilgrim. Next, another comes with a big cauldron of meat, and gives one piece to each; behind him is another who brings a slice of pork to each one; then finally they bring wine, and give a jug to each. [Laffi; trans. Hall (1997), 119–20]

Of course, not every hospice experience was a good one. CC Miracle 6 relates what must have been an all-too-common abuse:

> With his wife and two small children seated on a horse, [a] pilgrim arrived at the city of Pamplona. However, when his wife died there, an evil innkeeper nefariously took the goods that the man and wife had brought with them. The pilgrim, deprived of his wife and completely fleeced of his money and the horse on which he was transporting his children, began his journey again, bearing his children in his arms with great suffering. [CC: Book II; trans. Coffey et al., 70–1]

The story, however, has a semi-happy ending. The pilgrim is befriended by Santiago himself, who lends him a donkey and who appears to him at journey's end to report that "your wicked innkeeper in Pamplona is about to fall headfirst from his seat and die . . . [and] be condemned for all eternity." We have always been treated well in Pamplona, and we always stay there an extra day to savor the city's fine collection of art and architecture, not to mention its delightful array of restaurants.

MONUMENTS: 1. **Catedral.** 2. **Museo Diocesano.** 3. **Ayuntamiento.** 4. **Iglesia de San Cernín.** 5. Cámara de Comptos Reales. 6. Iglesia de Santo Domingo. 7. **Museo de Navarra.** 8. Iglesia de San Nicolás. 9. Walls. 10. Iglesia de San Ignacio. 11. Iglesia de San Miguel. 12. Convento de Carmelitas Descalzos. 13. Convento de Agustinas Recoletas. 14. **Ciudadela.**

1. **Catedral.** The first cathedral (begun in 1004) was replaced by a Romanesque structure (1104–42), one of whose architects was Maestro Esteban, who carved the Puerta de las Platerías in Santiago. This building collapsed in 1390. Some remnants of his work here are in the Museo de Navarra. The current Gothic building was begun in 1394. As always, a good flashlight and binoculars will enhance your tour.

Exterior:
  • West façade. Neoclassic, by Ventura Rodríguez ca. 1783. Sober and massive, so devoid of ornamentation that it seems more suited to a civic structure than to a Catholic church. Fans of this style praise the harmonious proportions, the interplay of forms of the colonnaded portico, the recessed balconies, and the bell towers. The left tower contains—at 12 tons—the second-largest bell in Spain.
  • Portada de San José, through which one enters the north transept, is 15th-c. Gothic and conserves 2 superb wood doors.

Interior:
- The basic plan adheres to the French Gothic model: a Latin cross, with 3 naves, a transept, and an ambulatory with radiating chapels.
- The main altar contains the Romanesque **Virgen del Sagrario**, in front of which the kings of Navarra were crowned. The 12th-c. wood image has been totally encased in silver except for the faces and hands of the Mother and Child. She is covered by an elegant Gothic baldachin (see ch. 17), similar to the one on the 1285 French reliquary in the museum.
- The **mausoleum** of Carlos III el Noble and his wife Leonor de Trastámara, by Jean de Lomme of Tournai (1417), in the center of the cathedral, is considered one of the best-executed early 15th-c. tombs in Spain. Note the Burgundian realism, the delicacy of the small figures on the base, and the idealized expressions on the faces of the dead couple. She has dogs at her feet, symbolizing fidelity; his feet rest on the lion of royalty.
- The Renaissance **choir** was carved by Esteban de Obray and colleagues in the late 16th c. Obray is known for his command of the human form. Observe the musculature of the **torso of San Jerónimo** (eighth from the right), who holds a stone in his hand and has a lion at his feet. **Santiago** is fifteenth from the right.

📖 In the 17th c. Domenico Laffi was impressed by this church's music: "They make music with two choirs, both on the same side of the church. One is composed of singers, the other of various instruments, that is to say, harps, zithers, spinets and an organ with many pipes. . . . They make a great melodious noise that can be heard from far off." [Laffi; trans. Hall (1997) 119]

- Several of the chapels contain significant works of art. Start from the south transept entrance, and go counterclockwise.
  —First chapel. San Gregorio. Fine Renaissance images, especially of San Antonio Abad, on the lower right, with his iconic pig. The grille or chapel screen (*reja*) that encloses the chapel is a particularly fine example of this Spanish cast-iron art form.

📖 Spanish artisans in the late 15th and the 16th c. built on an ironworking tradition that had developed great sophistication in both Christian and Muslim Spain. Their crowning achievements were chapel screens (*rejas*), produced by the hundreds for churches and monasteries all across the Peninsula. They combined forging, casting, and hammering techniques to produce complex artifacts combining Flamboyant Gothic, Mudéjar, and Renaissance Plateresque aesthetics. The size of these screens (the larger ones exceed 9 m. square) and their wealth of design exceed anything else in Europe. Frequently the *rejas* are composed of several horizontal bands of balusters, decorated by friezes of hammered, intricate scrolls, *putti*, and floral or geometrical figures. They are often topped with elaborate crests, featuring human figures and coats of arms. Colors are achieved through silvering or gilding the ironwork, and sometimes by painting. You will see hundreds of *rejas*, including some of Spain's best, between here and Compostela.

  —Second chapel. Renaissance Pieta, in red and blue. The symmetry and triangular composition echo Italian models.
  —Tenth chapel, in the rear on the left. The retablo (ca. 1610) narrates the life of **San Juan Bautista**. This is a masterpiece of high-relief Renais-

sance panels. The half-clothed San Juan permitted the sculptor to study the human form. Note the tendency to symmetrical arrangements of figures and the use of background props to enhance the theatricality of his presentations. The Renaissance crucifix, dated 1577, is by Juan de Anchieta.

—Eleventh chapel, in the rear on the right. Santa Catalina. Several panels on this retablo are first-rate, especially the Massacre of the Innocents, which manages to convey a sense of a moment frozen in time even while it attempts to depict movement. The upper register contains a **Santiago Matamoros.**

—Twelfth chapel. The Gothic wall tomb ably depicts mourners expressing their grief in a variety of poses.

Cloister:
Constructed from 1280 to 1375, the cloister shows a strong French influence in its delicate complex pillars and finely nerved vaults. It has been called the best exhibition of French Gothic style in Spain and one of the finest cloisters in Europe. Several of its features are extraordinary.
- Just to the left of the entrance is a 13th-c. *reja* forged from fragments of chains brought back by Christian prisoners liberated after the 1212 battle of Las Navas de Tolosa (see ch. 17).
- **Tympanum of the Death of the Virgin**. Typical of 14th-c. Gothic tympana is their obsession with detail. The people in these crowded scenes are individually expressive and are arranged in ensembles that stress each individual's role in the narration. The complex groupings, of different heights and widths, are masterfully balanced in a harmonious whole. Along the way, the sculptor allows us to look closely at styles of clothing, furniture, etc. This doorway is called the *Puerta Preciosa*.
- **The Three Kings**. Note the liveliness of these 14th-c. figures.
- **Tympanum of the Virgen del Amparo** (or Dormición). The door (ca. 1335) leads to the north transept. This strange, asymmetrical construction, broken by a strong vertical line, is nonetheless bound together by the bent backs and heads of the 3 mourning men. Above the Virgin, God receives her soul in His hands. The tympanum shows traces of its painting, reminding us that most medieval sculpture was originally brightly colored.
- **Capilla de Barbazana**. Built by Bishop Arnaldo de Barbazán; served as the chapter house. Note the star-shaped vault. Underneath the chapel is a crypt—at the time of writing closed to visitors—that served as the pantheon of notable bishops, including the founder. If it is open, make sure you see its delicate central octagonal pillar and nerves that radiate like palm leaves.

2. **Museo Diocesano.** Not only does it contain some real treasures, it permits you to see parts of a cathedral complex not normally accessible to visitors. The museum is installed mainly in 14th-c. rooms that were the kitchen and refectory. In the 17th c. these kitchens served pilgrims residing in the Hospital General. It is not likely you will ever see a larger **kitchen chimney**. The refectory, or dining hall of the cathedral community, has a pulpit on one wall, from which a cleric would read some religious text while the community ate in silence. The **pulpit's** intricately carved base contains scenes from the legend of the hunt for the unicorn. The room's finest feature is its colored *ménsulas*, containing an anthology of scenes of medieval daily life, animals and hunting scenes, as well as a few surprising grotesques.

Among the museum's many masterpieces is the ca. 1285 **French reliquary**. It is unique in its design, its perfect technique, and its extraordinary attention to detail. An angel sits on the edge of the empty tomb, pointing out to the 3 Marys that Christ has risen, while 2 tiny sleeping soldiers sit by the detritus of their gambling.

Note the women's medieval costume and the 4 figures' delicate facial features and elegant poses.

A second 14th-c. **reliquary**, with a fragment of the True Cross, is notable for its elaborate system of buttresses, windows, and arches, as well as its combination of silver and enamel. It was sent to Carlos III el Noble from Paris in 1401.

In addition, there are several 14th- and 15th-c. processional crosses, and a good collection of seated Romanesque and Gothic Virgins from rural churches in the diocese. For an explanation of the differences in style between Virgins of these 2 periods, see ch. 5's description of the Jaca museum collection.

3. **Ayuntamiento**. The façade is one of Spain's finest examples of Baroque civil architecture.

4. **Iglesia de San Cernín**. The cult of San Saturnino, centered in the great pilgrim-age church of Saint Sernin in Toulouse, reminds us again of the strong French influence in Navarra. The first church built here was Romanesque. But civil strife—note the 2 defensive towers—led to various rebuildings. Most of what remains is 13th-c. Gothic. Its **polychrome tympanum** depicts the Last Judgment and is flanked by interesting historiated capitals narrating the Christian cycle from the far left's Annunciation to the far right's Christ leading souls from the mouth of hell.

Inside, its single nave leads to 7 chapels in the *cabecera*. On the right wall are 2 14th-c. stone figures, brought in from the covered atrium: one is **Santiago Pere-grino**—complete with a scallop shell on his wallet—assisting a child pilgrim. Over the street entrance is a mounted unusual Crusader knight, directed on his way by the hand of God. Nobles from the other Iberian kingdoms were directed by the Pope to conquer their own Muslims in the south rather than participate in the Cru-sades to retake the Holy Land. Navarra was closely allied with France, and many Navarran knights went to Jerusalem with the French Crusaders.

The Baroque Capilla de la Virgen del Camino, really an entire separate church, contains a silver-encrusted image of this patroness of the city of Pamplona.

📖 Legend holds that the image of la Virgen del Camino—which had been in a small *ermita* in the village of Alfaro—appeared mysteriously one day in 1487 on a roof beam of San Cernín. For 2 years villagers tried to return it to the *ermita*, but each night it miraculously returned to Pamplona, where at last a chapel was built to house it.

---

5. Cámara de Comptos Reales. 14th-c. Gothic house. Starting in 1364, when Car-los II el Malo established the mint, Navarran coins were pressed here. Some of the machinery is now in the Museo de Navarra. Note the paired Gothic window and the Romanesque doorway in the patio.

6. Iglesia de Santo Domingo. 16th c. It once belonged to the University of Santiago de Compostela. Its doors are decorated with scallop shells and **Santiago Peregrino** stands on its main retablo.

7. **Museo de Navarra**. The building, with a 1556 Plateresque façade, was formerly the Antiguo Hospital de Nuestra Señora de la Misericordia. Among its archaeo-logical exhibits, Roman mosaics, medieval sculptures, paintings, and metalwork, are several masterpieces, including:
• **Sculptures by Maestro Esteban from the Romanesque cathedral**. Carved between 1140 and 1150. Two *ménsulas* with lion heads. Six extraordinarily intricate, sinuous **floral doubled capitals** with vegetable motifs. Three <u>histori-</u>

ated capitals from the vanished cloister depict the trials of Job, the Descent from the Cross, the Shrouding of Christ, and Judas. They are unique for Spanish Romanesque in the way they use every square inch of space, interweave multiple scenes, and communicate movement, while giving lavish attention to every detail. The capital with the 2 birds biting their legs was imitated all over Navarra and appears along the Santiago Road to the west as well.

• A superb collection of **Gothic mural painting** brought from various Navarran churches (for a discussion of fresco painting, see ch. 27). Like 12th- and 13th-c. Romanesque painting, it still uses strong colors and strong lines, but it is radically different in its conception of space. Figures are placed into complex scenes, interacting with one another in believable ways. Architectural forms are often used to frame the scenes, and background detail is generally minimal. The best artists in this style, and the best are represented in this museum, are adept at communicating strong emotions: pathos (note the mourning women to the left of Christ from the **Pamplona Cathedral mural**), or tenderness (the birth of Jesus from **Olite**). The emotions seem to be derived as much from the geometrically rhythmic poses, the curved bodies, and the strong contrasting colors, as they do from the facial expressions. The delicate curves of the 4 women in the **Olite Annunciation** eloquently convey the Gothic idealization of noble women. The same artist depicted a realistic scene of **shepherds**: a sheepdog, a goat eating leaves from a tree, a bagpiper whiling away the December evening. In the Pamplona mural, the soldiers beneath the mourning women are ingeniously posed, and their feet break through the painting's frame. The **Gallipienzo** soldiers include an obvious Moor.

• A 1055 Cordoban Islamic **ivory chest** made for the relics of Saints Nunila and Alodia. Note the intricate arabesques of foliage, the combination of Christian iconography and Mudéjar frames, the hunting scenes, paired animals, and the square Arabic Kufic script.

• Fragments of carved stone and plaster from the former mosque of Tudela.

• A black-and-white mural depicting Carlos V's 1547 military victory over German Protestant troops. You can't miss the contrasting sense of Renaissance pageantry and the horrors of cannon warfare.

• Goya's **portrait** of the Marqués de San Adrián and a portrait of the playwright Leandro Fernández de Moratín.

8. Iglesia de San Nicolás. Two 13th-c. transitional Romanesque-to-Gothic doors. The church conserves an air of having been a fortress.

9. Walls. The northern face of the bluff—site of the earliest Roman and Navarran settlements—retains its 16th-c. fortifications, with several strong bulwarks now turned into parklike promenades. The Portal de Francia remains pretty much the way Laffi described it ca. 1670: a very strong gate, preceded by "a great moat which you cross by way of a large wooden bridge." [Laffi; trans. Hall (1997), 119]

10. Iglesia de San Ignacio. This unremarkable 17th-c. church has historic interest. It marks the site where a young knight named Ignacio de Loyola was wounded in the defense of Pamplona on May 20, 1521. While recovering, the wounded knight asked for novels of chivalry to read. Instead, his friends brought him the Bible and some saints' lives. Ignacio decided to become a soldier of Christ and went on to found the Jesuit Order. This church's ornately plastered Baroque dome and vaults are worth a look.

11. Iglesia de San Miguel. This modern church preserves a superb Plateresque **retablo** by Juan de Anchieta, formerly in the cathedral.

12. Convento de Carmelitas Descalzos. The community of Carmelite monks relocated to this site inside the walls in the 1640s.

> 📖 The Carmelite Order began in Crusader times with hermit monks on Mount Carmel, near Haifa. Pope Honorius III licensed them as a mendicant order in 1226. Muslims expelled the Crusaders from Mount Carmel in 1291, and several groups of monks made their way back to Europe. Like many medieval monastic Orders, the Carmelites evolved in directions their founders had not intended, acquiring property, accepting posts outside the monastery, and involving themselves in secular affairs. Attempted reforms in the 15th c. failed. But in the 16th c. an extraordinary Spanish Carmelite nun and mystic, Teresa of Ávila, rededicated her convent to a life of prayer and poverty, symbolized by exchanging their shoes for sandals. The Discalced Carmelite movement spread to the male order, in part with the help of Teresa's colleague and friend John of the Cross.

The exterior is largely hidden by modern buildings. The church is typical of 17th-c. monastery architecture. It is laid out as a Latin cross, with a rectangular chevet, and lateral chapels interconnected by semicircular arches that serve as lateral aisles. The clean white walls are set off by Tuscan-style columns, decorated with carved plaster capitals, and cornices. The cupolas and vaults of plaster decorated with geometric designs in the Mannerist fashion are found in many Carmelite monasteries. The Capilla de San Joaquín is encrusted with profuse Rococo decoration. There is a sober Neoclassic cloister.

13. Convento de Agustinas Recoletas. This early-17th-c. convent facing the Plaza de Recoletas has a severe, almost Neoclassic façade. The main retablo has several noteworthy statues that seem overpowered by massive, profusely decorated Solomonic columns.

14. **Ciudadela.** The star fort of La Ciudadela, at the south end of the city, was begun under Felipe II and completed a century later following the most advanced theories of the French military engineer Vauban (1633–1707). It was captured by the French during the Napoleonic invasion of 1808.

Route: PAMPLONA → **Cizur Menor** → Galar → Zariquiégui → Puerto de Perdón → [Basongaiz] → **Uterga** → Obanos → [**Eunate**] → PUENTE LA REINA

The flats between Pamplona and the Sierra del Perdón are where chapter 12 of the CC *Turpin* chronicle sets the decisive battle between Charlemagne and the Muslim chief Aigoland. "Aigoland marched his army out of [Pamplona] and, leaving them below its walls, went with 60 of his lieutenants a mile from the city. The armies of Aigoland and Charlemagne were in a splendid plain next to the city, 6 miles wide by 6 miles long. The Santiago Road separated the 2 armies." After an exchange of insults, the champions of the two armies clashed. Twenty Christians killed 20 Muslims. Then 40 more slew their rivals. Then 100, and 200, and 1000. Finally Aigoland acknowledged that his defeat signified the superiority of Christianity and forthwith converted with all his survivors.

This valley, the Llanura de la Taconera, was the site of several monuments, now vanished. The basilica of San Juan de la Cadena had a cemetery for deceased pilgrims. The village of Acella, which has left no trace, had a convent of Augustinian nuns. The valley is also where Pamplona used to hang felons convicted of theft.

✳ **Cizur Menor** The ca. 1200 **Church of San Miguel** with its fortified tower was part of the Monasterio de los Hospitalarios de San Juan de Jerusalén, established here in 1135 with 7 brothers in residence.

📖 The Order of the Hospitallers may be the most important military-religious Order to come out of the Crusades. Service-minded knights organized themselves in the 11th c. to aid sick pilgrims to the Holy Land and to assist in the war for Jerusalem, which fell to the Crusaders in 1099. In 1113 Pope Pascal II recognized the Order and its twin mission of service to pilgrims and war against the infidels. Before long the knights were known as the Hospitallers of St. John of Jerusalem.

The Crusader kingdoms soon began to lose ground to the Muslims, and with each defeat the Hospitallers relocated their headquarters and took on a new name. By 1197 they were called the Hospitallers of St. John of Acre. When Acre fell in 1291 they moved to Cyprus; from there they conquered Rhodes in 1309, making the island their headquarters. When the Turks took Rhodes in 1522, they relocated to a tiny strategic island controlling the straights between Sicily and Tunis, and became the Knights of St. John of Malta. They played a key role in routing the Turkish navy toward the end of the 16th c., especially in the 1571 battle of Lepanto (the fight in which Cervantes, the author of *Don Quijote*, lost the use of one hand). Since then the Order has dedicated itself to helping pilgrims and to shepherding its business interests. When Napoleon dislodged them from Malta in the early 19th c., the Order's administrative center relocated to Rome.

Throughout the Middle Ages the Hospitallers of St. John, in their various guises and under various names, provided important support services to Santiago pilgrims in Spain.

The church's cloister, and most of the monastery's dependencies, disappeared after the 1836 *desamortización*. When we made our first pilgrimage through here in 1974, the church, after more than a century of use as a grain silo, lay largely in ruins. It has since been restored. The transitional Romanesque-Gothic door has a tympanum with a *crismón* (see ch. 5). The nave, with its cylindrical vault and massive sustaining arches, is wholly Romanesque. The keystone of the vault of the chapel on the right has the coat of arms of the Beaumont family in combination with the chains of Navarra (see ch. 17).

In front of this church the rectangular building with towers on each end once served as a pilgrim hospice; it is now a private home. A document dated 1508 records that it offered 6 beds for poor pilgrims.

The simple 12th-c. Romanesque church of Saints Emeterio y Celedonio, whose portal also has a *crismón*, was recently restored. Columns with simple capitals bearing vegetable motifs sustain the cylindrical vault.

🚗 Two km. west on the highway, Cizur Mayor's 14th-c. church of San Andrés has a nice 16th-c. retablo and an elegant *reja*. Two km. further west, in **Gazolaz**, is Nuestra Señora de la Purificación, whose 13th-c. porch has an array of splendidly carved capitals. The tympanum of the portal, decorated with the classic Jaca-style *crismón*, is supported by the heads of a lion and a bull, both devouring sinners.

✳ Galar The Road passes about 1 km. west of this town, well worth the short detour. A tympanum with 3 coats of arms has been added to the Romanesque portal of the church of San Martín, and additional coats of arms adorn the walls of the nave. Inside is a 16th-c. crucifix on which Christ has sharply defined anatomy and a face expressive of suffering. The right transept houses a retablo narrating the martyrdom of Santa Agueda.

🚗 To the west on the highway is the cluster of houses and ruins of a 16th-c. church known as Guendulain. Although we found it seemingly abandoned in 1974, it has now been partly restored as private property. The massive house next to the church was the 16th-c. palace of the Cabo de Armería. A medieval pilgrim hospice located here was supported by a Cofradía de Santiago.]

✳ Zariquiégui The hamlet prospered in the 12th and 13th c., before being largely wiped out in 1348 by the bubonic plague. In the 15th and 16th c. several 2-story mansions with horizontal lines and massive semicircular arched portals were built. A few of them retain the Baroque coats of arms added in the 17th and 18th c.

The 13th-c. Romanesque church of San Andrés, remodeled in the 16th c., has a portal with 6 palm-shaped capitals and a tympanum with a *crismón*. Inside is a roughly carved Gothic Virgin and Child, in the 14th-c. style characterized by the Virgin's warm, human expression and the V-shaped folds of her dress. The 17th-c. Romanist main retablo features the judgment and martyrdom of San Andrés.

In 1974 David was leading our band of 7 pilgrim women in single file out of Zariquiégui when, turning a corner, we came upon an old man half-dozing on a stone wall as he tended his 2 dozen sheep. As we tramped past, the shepherd, clothed entirely in brown corduroy with a black beret on his head, blinked his eyes in a double take and saluted us with a version of a 15th-c. Carolingian ballad about Lancelot that he adapted *ex tempore* to the circumstances:

Nunca fuera caballero	Never was there a knight
de damas tan bien servido	so well served by dames
como este peregrino	as this pilgrim was
cuando de Francia vino.	when from France he came.

This ballad must have been one of Cervantes' favorites too, for in 1615 he has Don Quijote quote it in Book I, chapter 13. How nice to see that some literary traditions, like some pilgrimages, never die.

Just before the pass you will find a fountain that recalls the Fuente Reniega legend. An exhausted, hot, and thirsty pilgrim was tempted by the Devil with water if he would renounce his faith. The pilgrim resisted, and Santiago miraculously appeared to lead him to this fountain, where the Saint offered him water from his own scallop shell.

🚗 In Astraín, on the highway just north of the pass, the 13th-c. Gothic church of Santos Cosme y Damián, remodeled in the 16th–18th c., contains an image of the Virgen del Perdón. Until the late 19th c. there was a pilgrim hospice in the town as well. Two massive, horizontal Renaissance palaces remain in the town, one with a showy Baroque coat of arms.

✳ **Puerto de Perdón** An Ermita de San Cristóbal and the Basílica de Nuestra Señora del Perdón were located here in medieval times. The Basilica ran a pilgrim hospice, documented as functioning as late as 1816. They are all vanished, replaced in 1994 by a gargantuan line of 40 windmills with capacity to generate 20 megawatts of electricity annually for Pamplona while effectively destroying the medieval aura of the Navarran landscape. Energía Hidroeléctrica de Navarra (EHN) has also placed a statue of Santiago pilgrims along the ridge and a bird observatory on the summit.

🚗 Basongaiz On the highway. In 1288 the town belonged to the Hospitalarios de San Juan, whose cross remains on the lintels of several houses and the chapel.

✳ **Uterga** The current popular architecture of this medieval town, like many along this stretch of the Road, features 3-story whitewashed houses with red tile roofs and massive stones framing the windows. The *retablo mayor* of the 16th–18th–c. church of La Asunción contains some nice Romanist-style Renaissance reliefs depicting scenes from the life of the Virgin and a **Santiago Peregrino**. Most of the rest of the art in the church dates from the late 19th and the 20th c.

Of Uterga's 5 medieval *ermitas*, only San Nicolás, next to the cemetery, remains. The main street conserves several massive, square 18th- and 19th-c. mansions.

🚗 Just below Uterga lies the village of Muruzábal. The church of San Esteban (14th–17th c.) contains the Retablo de los Santos Juanes (ca. 1500), a
masterpiece of Hispano-Flemish art, with lively, richly colored paintings of
Saints Andrés, Mateo, **Santiago**, Catalina, Agueda, Bárbara, and Quiteria set
against interesting background scenes. The Baroque main altar holds a fine
late-16th-c. Romanist-style Virgin and Child. In the village are a 16th-c.
palace and *ermitas* of San Blas, Santa Lucía, and San Pedro de Auriz.

✶ Obanos See chapter 15, Monreal → Puente la Reina.

👟 **Eunate** [See chapter 15, Monreal → Puente la Reina. Though a visit
to **Eunate** will add an hour for the walking pilgrim, it is well worth the
detour to visit this 12th-c. octagonal, Romanesque-Mudéjar funeral chapel.]

✶ The *ermita* on the peak of a hill to the left as you near Puente la Reina is Nuestra Señora de Arnótegui.

The Road that crosses the Pyrenees in Somport joins the Road from Roncesvalles
just outside of Puente la Reina. To celebrate the 1965 Holy Year, Gerardo Brun
was commissioned to cast the statue of **Santiago Peregrino** now found at the crossroads. When we hiked in 1974, this was a quiet country junction; now it is subur-
ban.

23. Puente la Reina

History

In the early Middle Ages several independent towns existed in the flats along the Arga River, which had to be crossed by anyone following the Roman road west to Castilla. Too deep to ford, the river spawned numerous small ferries that served and exploited travelers. No wonder that when a queen of Navarra financed a bridge in the 11th c., urban development centered at the entrance to that bridge. The growing town, whose Basque name was Gares, took the name Puente la Reina. No one knows precisely which queen was responsible, doña Mayor, wife of Sancho III, or doña Estefanía, the wife of his successor García el de Nájera.

In 1122 Alfonso el Batallador laid out a town with parallel streets perpendicular to the river and granted a charter encouraging repopulation. A wall enclosed the entire town. By the late 11th c. Puente la Reina had a large *Franco* quarter, with its parish church of San Salvador. Puente also had a small Jewish district. A synagogue is documented in 1315, and in 1345 2 Jews, Juce Abalfaza and Simuel Nahamán, were burned alive in the plaza as sodomites. As in most new cities in Navarra, each ethnic group kept to its own quarter, but in the markets you could hear Navarran (the local variety of Spanish), French, Occitaine-Provenzal, Hebrew, and of course Basque. In 1142 King García Ramírez gave the town to the Knights Templar, to whom it belonged until their expulsion from Spain and dissolution in the early 14th c. (see ch. 68).

Between the 1366 census and the early 19th c., Puente quintupled in population by growing vertically. Note the number of solid stone 14th- and 15th-c. one-story houses topped with 2 or 3 later stories in very different styles. In the 16th and 17th c. these are generally farmhouses with the third story used for silage. A few manor houses, with brick galleries in the upper stories, are from the same period, and tend to be double the width of the farmhouses. In the late 17th and 18th c. several apartment houses were built to house multiple families.

Pilgrimage

In the Middle Ages, as now, businesses catering to pilgrims lined Puente's main street, the Rúa Mayor. A 1235 document characterizes the street as "populated with pilgrims" (*poblada de los romeus*).

A Templars' hospice, documented in 1146, had permission to sell bread and wine to pilgrims, but had to lodge them for free. The Trinitarian Order supported a hospice from the early 13th c. A hospice of San Lázaro (see ch. 27) is also documented. The Iglesia del Crucifijo also ran a hospice called Santa María de los Huertos. Documents from 1350 indicate that a man named Jacques de Troya, a French pilgrim from the Champagne, was hung for stealing money, books, and clothes from other pilgrims there. In 1447 Juan de Beaumont, chancellor of Navarra and prior of the knights of St. John of Jerusalem, founded a hospice for pilgrims. One of the brothers in the *cofradía* gave the hospice the town of Mañeru, together with its lands, rents, workers, bread, wine, and firewood. The hospice's custom was to ring the church bells 40 times in the evening at 9 and 10 o'clock to guide pilgrims who might still be on the road. Pilgrims were entitled to one night's lodging on their way to Compostela, and 2 nights on the way back. Pilgrims would wash off their road dust before entering the town at a spring—now a fountain— outside the church of the Crucifijo. The 18th-c. monastery built on the site of the former hospice has been occupied since 1917 by a school run by the Padres Reparadores.

The Italian pilgrim Domenico Laffi described in some detail his entrance into Puente la Reina in a way that makes clear how universal are the experiences of hiking pilgrims: difficulty in finding comfortable lodging, closed monuments, and the dual demands of religion and tourism:

> We passed through a great forest, finally reaching Puente la Reina. . . . After taking a short walk through the town and seeing its fine buildings and churches we looked for an inn to lodge. But we could find nothing because the place was already full of people and there was nowhere for us. . . . We looked for lodging in many places but in vain. But then God, who never abandons anyone, reminded us that at the entrance to the town, at the distance of no more than a gunshot, there was a little chapel in the middle of the open road. We decided to go there in order to sleep inside. When we arrived we saw a peasant standing at a window looking at us. We begged him to give us lodging, promising to pay him however much he asked. The man, moved either by interest or compassion, came down, opened the door to us and made us very welcome, seeing we were dressed as priests. . . .
>
> He led us into the house and wanted to give us bread. But we would not take it, because of the expense, since he was very poor and we had already bought some. But he gave us good wine to drink and then we went to bed. This bed consisted of four heaps of vines spread on the ground and covered with a blanket. Thus we settled down as best we could. In the morning, half crippled, we went to the principal church to see if we could say mass, but could find no one. [Laffi; trans. Hall (1997), 122–3]

Like Laffi, in 1979 we had trouble locating lodgings in Puente la Reina. That day was pilgrim Maryjane Dunn's turn to find us beds, or someone's floor, or a comfortable hayloft. Every place she tried turned her town. Maryjane looked so lost that finally a young woman in blue jeans stopped her bicycle to ask if she could help. "Come stay with me and my sisters." she offered, "It's not too far and we've got plenty of room." Maryjane, supposing she was a farm girl from large family, followed her to her house at the edge of town and was astonished to find that it was a convent, and that the blue-jeaned samaritan and her "sisters" were all nuns. The pilgrim girls spent a comfortable night with their newfound friends, while David, who was of the wrong gender to be included in the invitation, flopped in a bunk over a bar in town. (On the cover of this book, Maryjane is the pilgrim in the red jacket.)

MONUMENTS: 1. **Iglesia del Crucifijo**. 2. Convento de los Padres Reparadores. 3. Calle Mayor. 4. **Iglesia de Santiago**. 5. Iglesia de San Pedro. 6. **Bridge**. 7. Convento de las Comendadoras del Espíritu Santo.

From Puente la Reina we all walk together to Compostela, but we came to Puente by a variety of routes. Those of you who crossed the Pyrenees at Portalet have seen some wonderful Mozárabe churches. You, and the pilgrims who crossed at Somport, have seen lots of Romanesque art on your route through Aragón. Those of you who crossed at Roncesvalles have visited some Gothic churches of the first magnitude. In other words, you may find it useful to skim the art material in the sections of this book that deal with the routes you did *not* walk.

1. **Iglesia del Crucifijo**. This church was formerly called Santa María de las Huertas (or de la Vega). It belonged to the Knights Templar until the early 14th c. and later maintained the 15th-c. hospice described above. During the Carlist Wars (see ch. 25), the church and monastery became a barracks and were also used as a prison and munitions arsenal. The church is now attached to the 18th-c. monastery of the Padres Reparadores, an Order of German origin.

The 12th-c. tympanum is largely floral, with designs probably derived from Byzantine ivories. Surprisingly, each of the columns and each of the archivolts is of a different design.

The original 12th-c. Romanesque church had a single nave. A second, Gothic, nave was added in the 14th c. The church was originally named for the 12th-c. **Romanesque seated Virgin** with the adult-child Christ on her lap, stylistically one of Navarra's oldest. The original image was kidnapped some years ago. Although it was later recovered, the church now displays a replica that is inaccurate in some details. Surviving fragments of the 14th-c. paintings from the apse are now in the Pamplona Museo de Navarra.

The early 14th-c. **crucifix** for which the church is now named is an odd Y-shaped cross. This emotive image, its face half-masked by its long hair, its wounded arms raised in triumph or supplication, is unique in Spain. It combines stylistic currents from Cologne, Germany (the 2 intertwined strands of the crown of thorns, the multiple wounds, the high-relief veins and arteries, drapery exposing the right knee) and 13th-c. Italy (the serene pathos and pain expressed in the face, the long hair parted in the middle, the sunken stomach).

2. Convento de los Padres Reparadores. The 18th-c. monastery occupies the site of the medieval Templars' hospice. The arched porch connecting to the Iglesia del Crucifijo across the street was reconstructed in 1951. Note how efficiently it channels all traffic toward the center of town.

3. Calle Mayor. The narrow, shop-lined street retains its medieval character. As you walk down its length you will see nearly 3 dozen 15th- and 16th-c. portals, many with their coats of arms. The open space (atrium) in front of the Iglesia de Santiago was the site of the medieval food market, until a larger market square was opened further along the street in the late 16th c. Toward the west end of the street, near the bridge, are a series of Baroque decorated eaves, as in Sangüesa.

4. **Iglesia de Santiago**. The church was in existence prior to 1142.

Exterior:
The Romanesque doors remain, but the rest of the church dates from ca. 1543, with an elegant Baroque tower from the 18th c.
• The **south portal**, with its Mudéjar-influenced multilobed arch, is related to some churches you will see in the next few days: Estella's San Pedro de la Rúa and Cirauqui's San Román. Its wealth of sculpture is indicative of major investment in a major monument. The lobes of the arch, rather than the usual tympanum, bear the principal figures. Second from the top in the center is God the Father. Christ, set against a chi-rho and an alpha-omega in the fashion of the Aragonese *crismón*, stands in the center over the door (see ch. 5). The 5 archivolts depict sins, professions, calendar symbols, and a host of heavenly and human figures. Surprising are the number and variety of monsters: demons fought by saints (with halos), grotesque heads atop the columns (including 2 that seem to be swallowing their columns), and monsters cramming souls into the jaws of hell (right side of the door). On the left spandrel, the figure of a man fighting with a lion may illustrate the classic struggle between body and soul; a similar scene is visible on the second archivolt. Unfortunately, the door has deteriorated to the point where many of the images can no longer be identified.

Interior:
• The large chestnut slabs on the floor of the church that cover the sepulchers are common in Navarra.

📖 You will see hundreds of funeral monuments in churches between Puente la Reina and Compostela. Prestige, and cost, increased the nearer you were to the main altar. The cream of society built their family chapels off the lateral aisles. In addition to funding construction, this generally required establishing an endowment to support in perpetuity the offering of masses for the deceased's soul.

• The monumental Baroque late-17th-c. central retablo (with several 18th-c. Rococo additions) is dedicated to **Santiago**. The lower plaques narrate the **apparition of the Virgin to Santiago** (see intro.) and his later **martyrdom**, flanking an assemblage of saints' relics. The 18th-c. central image of the pilgrim saint is of academic taste.

📖 *Retablo* is derived from *retro-tabulum* ("behind the altar"). The vogue for these large, theatrical backdrops to the mass began in late Gothic times and lasted well into the 19th c. By whatever route you came, you have already seen dozens, and you will see more in almost every Spanish church between here and Compostela. You will soon be able to recognize the basic types:
—Gothic (14th–15th c.). Often combine painting and sculpture; frequently a set of painted scenes around a central sculpted figure; usually surrounded with an architectural frame constructed of intricate tracery, sometimes with small canopies (*doseles*) over individual figures.
—Renaissance (16th c.). Combine narrative plaques with sculpted freestanding figures set into architectural niches; arranged in vertical and horizontal rows separated by classical architectural motifs; clean structural lines; generally an ordered narrative sequence, left to right, top to bottom.
—Baroque (16th–18th c.). Theatrical; heightened sense of movement; decorative and narrative elements mixed together; massive, elaborate architectural frames tend to dominate the sculpted figures; complex or broken structural lines; Solomonic (twisted) columns; emphasis on the Eucharist gives prominence to the arks in which the host is kept (*sagrarios*); little decorative figures stuck onto everything (*putti*, vegetable motifs, angels); lots of gold leaf.
—Neoclassic (18th–19th c.). Massive classical architectural forms, with sober, clean lines, frame individual statues; painting tends to predominate; more marble (or faux marble) than gold-encrusted wood.

• The 18th-c. lateral retablos are dedicated to San Antonio, la Virgen del Carmen, and la Virgen del Rosario (which contains an excellent 14th-c. seated Virgin and Child: unity of composition is suggested by the similar faces and the raised right arms). The retablos of the transept are dedicated to the Virgen de la Nieve, la Inmaculada, and San Antonio Abad.
• On the left aisle a late-14th-c. image of **Santiago Peregrino** with tousled hair is known in Basque as Santiago Beltza, the black saint. The dramatic drapery clutched in the Saint's left hand offsets the static quality of the image. The curly beard, the arched eyebrows, and the half-open mouth are typical of 14th-c. Gothic sculpture. Facing it is a nice 14th-c. statue of San Bartolomé.
• The sacristy contains segments of chains of Christian prisoners released after the 1212 battle of Las Navas de Tolosa (see ch. 17), brought to Puente la Reina

by Rodrigo Jiménez de Rada. You will also find bits and pieces of diverse retablos and some striking metalwork, including a vessel inscribed as having been made in Mexico.

5. Iglesia de San Pedro. This 16th-c. church at the corner of what was the medieval wall contains the image of Nuestra Señora del Puy (see ch. 25). She is called locally la Virgen "del Chori" (or Txori), stemming from a miracle having to do with when the image was located in a tower that used to stand in the middle of the bridge.

> 📖 In 1825, 1834, 1840, and 1842–3 a strange lark (locally, a *txori*) used to fly around and around the statue of the Virgin. Bells began to ring by themselves. When local worshipers approached in procession, their joyous noise did not scare off the bird. In 1834 General Viamanuel laughed at the "miracle" and forbade the celebration of the *txori*, which he had put in a cage. Shortly afterward, he was taken prisoner in one of the battles of the Carlist Wars.

The interior of this church has 3 superb Baroque-Rococo retablos. The profusely ornamented central retablo, ca. 1696, features images of Saints Pedro, Pablo, and Andrés. The Rococo retablo on the left features San Babil (a 16th-c. Renaissance image). The retablo of the Virgen del Chori and San Blas stands on the right. The stone image of the seated Virgin and Child is 16th c., late Gothic in style. Other retablos are dedicated to Nuestra Señora de las Nieves and the Betrothal of the Virgin.

6. **Bridge**. Its 6 graceful arches, with their abutments pierced by windows both for aesthetic reasons and to lighten the weight of the structure, is one of Europe's most graceful Romanesque bridges.

7. Convento de las Comendadoras del Espíritu Santo. Across the bridge, the large convent on the left of the highway has occupied this site in the suburb of Zubiurrutia since the 13th c. In the Middle Ages it maintained a pilgrim hospice. The current church, built in 1754, contains some late-18th-c. **Rococo retablos** and a **painted dome** crowded with figures, foliage, architectural forms, cherubs, cornucopias, and allegorical figures of the 3 cardinal virtues: faith, hope, and charity. The main retablo, ca. 1759, contains a number of superbly executed Baroque images, contrasting the seminude figures of penitential saints with the dramatically flowing drapery of the bishop saints. The church is occasionally open around noon.

> 🚗 Five km. north of Puente la Reina is the Señorío de Sarriá, an estate known for its wines.

24. PUENTE LA REINA → ESTELLA

Route: PUENTE LA REINA → Mañeru → **Cirauqui** → [Alloz] → Lorca → **Villatuerta** → ESTELLA

Across the bridge, beyond the Convento de las Comendadoras del Espíritu Santo, pilgrims follow the Arga River and zigzag up the heights on the remnants of a Roman road, much more of which could be seen through the 1980s, before the "improvement" of this part of the route.

On the hilltop called Eunea, near a modern picnic area, are minor ruins of the Order of San Juan's Priory of Bargota and its hospital, one of Navarra's most handsomely endowed. It welcomed pilgrims from 1239. Although the priory housed mainly brothers, the Order of San Juan also admitted women, and 2 nuns looked after the hospice. The Order also ran a school for local children at the site. When the Order moved its house to Puente, ca. 1440, the site began to decline. A single hermit looked after pilgrims in the hospice, which continued to function until 1724.

✳ **Mañeru** At the entrance to Mañeru is a late-16th-c. roadside cross. In the 12th and 13th c. Mañeru belonged to the Knights of San Juan de Jerusalén. Most of the seignorial houses lining its mazelike streets are from the 16th to the 19th c. They display as fine a series of coats of arms as one finds on the pilgrimage Road. One stately house incorporates the façade from the 13th-c. Ermita de Nuestra Señora del Rosario.

The Neoclassic late-18th-c. church of San Pedro replaced one that in the 13th c. belonged to the Order of San Juan. Its most interesting internal architectural feature is its rounded dome. In addition to an engaging seated Santa Bárbara, and some interesting reliquaries, there is a finely sculpted 16th-c. Romanist style crucifix. The figure of Jesus was carved with realistic anatomy and a serene face.

As you exit from Mañeru, note the house whose window is decorated with scallop shells.

Halfway to Cirauqui, in a field just north of the modern highway, are the ruins of the Romanesque Ermita de Aniz, all that is left of a medieval town and its church of La Asunción, first documented in 1192.

✳ **Cirauqui** This Basque name means "nest of vipers," probably referring to the town's location on top of a rocky ledge apt to house serpents—or bandits. Both the architecture and the street plan reveal that the town grew in 3 stages: in the 9th c. around the church of San Román; in the 10th and 11th c. on the hillsides south of the church of San Román; and in the 14th c. around the church of Santa Catalina. You climb to the high churches through a Gothic arch in the old city wall, along steep streets that maintain their medieval ambiance. As you climb, note the many 16th–19th-c. mansions with their coats of arms over the door.

MONUMENTS: 1. **Iglesia de San Román**. 2. Civil War monument. 3. Iglesia de Santa Catalina. 4. **Roman road and bridge.**

1. **Iglesia de San Román.** The 12th-c. Romanesque church was rebuilt and enlarged in the 17th c.

Exterior:
• **Mudéjar portal.** You will recognize how closely this early Gothic portal resembles the Romanesque portal of Santiago in Puente la Reina. The 10 lobes of its **Mudéjar-style arch** are decorated with Cistercian-style rope nets, repeated geometric forms, and flora. Each of the 9 archivolts bears a different geometric design. On their keys are 5 Christian symbols: the hand of God, an angel bearing the cross, the Lamb of God symbolizing the Eucharist, a star, and the mystic crismón representing Christ's name and role. The **capitals**, which flow together in the Gothic fashion to make a continuous frieze, are filled with animals, people in various poses, and vegetable motifs. On one jamb is a gorgeous siren, half woman, half fish, erotically caressing her hair to lead mankind to the sin of lust.

Interior:
Inside the church are several fine **retablos**, with Renaissance-style carvings in heavy Baroque architectural structures, featuring twisting, grape-covered Solomonic columns.
• Retablo de San Francisco Javier. Left aisle, ca. 1700, Baroque.
• Retablo de la Virgen del Rosario. Left aisle, 1700–30, Baroque, with a statue of **Santiago** in the upper story.
• Retablo de San Román. Main retablo, 1702–6, Baroque. The central image of San Román is 13th-c.
• Retablo de San Juan Bautista. Right aisle, late 17th c., with an airy, elegant San Cristóbal carrying the infant Christ, several scenes of the life and death of San Juan Bautista, and smaller statues of Saints Antón, Agueda, and Fermín.
• At the end of the left nave is a Roman funerary stone reutilized as a column.
• On the left wall of the nave is a large painting of the missionary San Francisco Javier ministering to diverse peoples.
• The sacristy contains some elegant, intricately carved 16th-c. **silver processional crosses.**

2. Next to San Román's portal is a Civil War monument from the Francisco Franco dictatorship period (1936–75). It invokes the apotheosis of the martyred José Antonio, founder of the fascist Falange movement, and lists Cirauqui's soldiers "fallen for God and for the Fatherland" (*caídos por Dios y por la Patria*).

📖 As the Spanish Republic (1931–9) increasingly secularized Spanish government and increased the role of the middle and lower classes in governance, and as strident philosophical and political divisions rendered it less and less effectual, the conservative elements in Spanish society looked for a way to reverse what they saw as literally diabolical trends. On July 17, 1936, about half of the Spanish army revolted. Within days they controlled all of Castilla la Vieja, Navarra (with support of the Carlists; see ch. 25), Galicia, most of Andalucía, major cities like Zaragoza, Sevilla, Córdoba, Valladolid, and Cádiz, and most of the traditional Santiago pilgrimage Road. The insurgents called themselves Nationalists, and their ideology was drawn from the fascist Falange party. By October, Francisco Franco had emerged as their commander in chief. Supporters of the government, called Loyalists or Republicans, formed a Popular Front to oppose them. In the opening days of the war each side massacred thousands of presumed civilian leaders of the other persuasion. As the attempted coup turned into a long civil war, each side sought and achieved foreign support: the Nationalists from fascist Germany and Italy, the Republicans from the Soviet Union, the Communist Party, and the International Brigades of volunteers. For 3 years the 2 sides slugged it out, until nearly a million people had lost their lives. In March 1939, Franco's troops entered Madrid after a 3-year siege, and by April 1 the war had ended.

These monuments, which listed only the soliders and civilians killed on the Nationalist side, were ubiquitous until Franco's death, when many towns removed or trashed them. Navarra, a stronghold of the Falange during those years, is often an exception, and you will see several of these symbols along the Road. Note how in its escutcheon the Falange calls up the symbols of Hapsburg Spain, which in Falangist ideology embodied centralized national power on behalf of Counter-Reformation militant Catholicism, together with the suppression of regional cultures. The columns bear Carlos V's motto: *Plus Ultra*.

📖 The Pillars of Hercules marked the exit from the Mediterranean Sea to the Atlantic. For ancients they signaled the end of the known world and traditionally bore the inscription *Ne plus ultra* ("No one goes further than this"). Carlos V, who ruled in the Americas and southeastern Asia, was proud of the fact that he had indeed gone further.

The escutcheon groups the castle of Castilla, the lion of León, the bars of Aragón, and the chains of Navarra, with the pomegranate of Granada below them. The yoke and arrows were King Fernando and Queen Isabel's personal symbol.

📖 The yoke ("Y" for *yugo* and *Ysabel*) suggested that with their marriage Aragón and Castilla pulled together. The sheaf of arrows ("F" for *flechas* and *Fernando*) symbolized strength in unity. The Spanish Falange during the 1920s adopted this device to indicate their legitimacy as the continuers of traditional Spain. Until Franco's death it was placed at the entrance to every Spanish village.

3. Iglesia de Santa Catalina. As we write, this early-13th-c. church, extensively modified in the 16th c., again appears to be undergoing restoration. The capitals of the early Gothic door, typically merging into a continuous frieze, appear to depict scenes from the infancy of Christ, although they are much deteriorated. We could not enter, but in the past, the church contained several interesting retablos depicting the Virgen del Pilar (late-18th-c. Rococo, with a ca. 1600 Virgin), San Blas (17th-c. Romanist), Santa Catalina (early-18th-c. Baroque, with an elegant statue of the Saint, sword in hand), and San Juan Bautista (early-17th-c. Romanist).

A new covered *frontón*, or jai alai court, stands in front of the church.

4. **Roman ruins.** At the exit from Cirauqui, a recently restored stretch of **Roman paving** leads down the hill to a **Roman bridge**. Although almost the entire pilgrim-

age Road follows the Roman Via Traiana, these are by far the most spectacular remains. You will follow Roman paving, with some stretches repaired or rebuilt in the Middle Ages, most of the way from here to Lorca.

> 📖 Roman roadbeds differed little from today's. Surveyors determined the best routes. Excavators scooped out a shallow trench, which construction crews—often local slaves—filled with a layer of gravel, then tamped-down sand. The borders were marked with large blocks, set vertically into place. The roadbed itself was laid with closely fitted paving stones, with wedge-shaped stones driven in to clamp them together. The roads were cambered (e.g. slightly higher in the middle) to facilitate drainage. Sometimes the larger roads, near cities, were paved with two colors of stone to delineate the lanes of traffic. If the road was to cross a marsh, wooden pilings would be driven into the mud and then a causeway built up on top of them. One you will see later, just west of Castrogeriz, is still capped with the low stone arches that kept the legions and merchants up out of the mire. Small streams were routinely bridged with simple stone arches: you will pass a dozen between here and Compostela. Larger rivers were spanned with monumental structures that emphasized, as did the entire highway system, the unassailable might of Rome.

Some 2 km. beyond Cirauqui, the Road crosses a small, early Gothic bridge. Beyond it at the top of the hill to the south lie the ruins of the abandoned town of Urbe, documented from the 11th to the 18th c. The flat-topped hill just south of the ruins is a pre-Roman *castro*.

> 🚗 **Alloz** Alloz lies a few km. north of Lorca, past Lácar, on a hill over the Salado Valley. The nearby church of Santa María de Eguiarte conserves capitals depicting the birth and infancy of Christ that appear to be by the same sculptor who worked on the north portal of San Miguel in Estella.

At km. 34.3 the Road veers right to cross the remnants of a **Gothic bridge over the Río Salado**, the site of one of the 12th-c. CC *Guide*'s most picturesque incidents, and one of the few in which the author lets his first-person narrative voice be heard:

> Beware from drinking its waters or from watering your horse in its stream, for this river is deadly. While we were proceeding towards Santiago, we found two Navarrese seated on its banks and sharpening their knives: they make a habit of skinning the mounts of the pilgrims that drink from that water and die. To our questions they answered with a lie saying that the water was indeed healthy and drinkable. Accordingly, we watered our horses in the stream, and had no sooner done so, than two of them died: these the men skinned on the spot. [CC: Book V; trans. Melczer, 88–89]

✱ Lorca The name derives from the Arabic term for battle (*alaurque*). In 920 Sancho I of Navarra was defeated here by a Muslim named Muhammad Abenlope (whose name, *ben-Lope* [son-of-wolf], hints that he, too, might have been Basque). The hamlet, which controls the pass between Cirauqui and Estella, is typical of Road towns in having a single east-west main street. Several mansions sport Baroque and Rococo coats of arms.

The late-12th-c. church of **San Salvador**—its interior much remodeled—has a Romanesque apse in a style that suggests that it may have doubled as a fortification. It formerly belonged to Roncesvalles. It contains a fluted Romanesque baptismal font. The 1560–70 *retablo mayor* is transitional between the Plateresque and Mannerist styles. Stuck incongruously among its religious images are figures of Leda and the swan and a sleeping Eros. The retablo on the right aisle has a theatrical 18th-c. Baroque **Santiago Peregrino.**

A hospice, founded in 1209 and dedicated to Nuestra Señora de Roncesvalles, used to stand in front of the church.

✱ **Villatuerta** Many small Roman sites have been found near this town. In 1061 the Navarran king Sancho el de Peñalén gave the town to Leyre. In the 1330s the monarchy awarded the town to 2 noble families for services rendered, and in 1342 turned around and bought it back from them, only to give it to 2 other nobles 26 years later. Medieval Villatuerta developed in 2 centers: one on the hill between the parish church and San Román, and the other along the banks of the Río Iranzu. Two arches of a small Romanesque bridge remain from these early days.

Villatuerta's late-14th-c. Church of La Asunción retains a Romanesque fortified tower. Inside are graceful Gothic vaults with carved keystones. Several columns are topped with figural Romanesque capitals: warriors with shields, swords, and lances; a centaur; a dragon; and a bishop. The superb Renaissance **retablo**, late 17th c., narrates scenes from the life of San Veremundo: a miraculous mass and a battle against the Moors.

> 📖 Veremundo, an abbot of the Irache Monastery west of Estella, was born either here or in nearby Arellano. The 2 towns take turns guarding the Saint's relics: 5 years in each church.

Lateral retablos from the 1590s are dedicated to Saints Catalina and Miguel. Two sizable **fragments of Gothic mural painting** remain on the side walls. A Romanesque doorway from the crumbling Ermita de San Román was mounted on the right wall some years back. Recent restorations have also turned up some ancient colored tiles.

Many hermits lived in these hills in the 10th and 11th c. There are traces of the *ermitas* of Saints Ginés, Román, Salvador, Cristóbal, and Lucía. The few material remains of their culture are in the Museo de Navarra in Pamplona. One km. west of Villatuerta stood a small 11th-c. monastery belonging to Leyre. The remaining structure, the Ermita de San Miguel, is a landmark that can be seen for many km. in every direction, but little of interest remains in the building except a simple stone cross. Two other primitive, low-relief carvings of an angel and the crucified Christ were taken to the Museo de Navarra.

25. ESTELLA

HISTORY

Estella sits astride a craggy bend of the Ega River. In Basque it has 2 names: *Lizarra* (Old Church) or *Erizarra* (Old Town). Its importance began in 1090, when King Sancho Ramírez decided to build a commercial center here for foreign merchants and to encourage the settlement of *Francos*, who flocked to the town from French Auvergne and Limousin. He was also determined to entice the increasing pilgrim traffic to pass through Estella. The city was granted a charter (*fuero*) ca. 1076 and another in 1164. A Thursday market is documented the same year. By the end of the 12th c., the nucleus, called *Stella*, had incorporated the parishes of San Juan and San Salvador and had grown large enough to merit an entry in the *Codex Calixtinus*: "Estella, where bread is good, wine excellent, meat and fish are abundant, and which overflows with all delights" (CC: Book V; trans. Melczer, 86). And about the same time Peter the Venerable wrote: "In Spain there is a noble and famous fortified city [Estella] which by its location and the fertile land that surrounds it, and for the large population which inhabits it, is far superior to the other fortified towns in the region" (*De miraculis* Book 1, ch. 28).

Farmers near town specialized in olives, grapes, and orchards. Further out were wheat and grazing lands. In 1365 Carlos II invited experts from Zaragoza to set up a wool-weaving facility in Estella. But the biggest industry was the production of leather. We could still see the ruins of the tanneries in the late 1970s before a park was cleared in front of the Santo Sepulcro Church.

Medieval Estella was well defended, with castles on each of her 4 hills. The Lizarra castle was on Puy hill: remnants of its foundation walls were used as a fort during the 19th-c. Carlist Wars. Zalatambor, begun ca. 1090, disappeared in an enormous explosion in 1572 when Navarra's remaining castles were destroyed to concentrate the kingdom's defenses in Pamplona. Estella's largest castle sat on Belmecher de Ordoiz, a knoll above the Monastery of Santo Domingo, today marked by a cross. It was the last holdout against the Castilians in the 1512 war that incorporated Navarra to the united kingdom of Spain. There was also a watch-tower, called the Atalaya, on the hill above the Rocamador Church. As in Pamplona, Estella's churches were built with an eye toward defense, as evidenced by the thick walls and towers of Santo Sepulcro, Santo Domingo, and San Pedro de la Rúa. You will find scraps of other 12th- and 13th-c. walls in various parts of the city.

Again similar to Pamplona, within a hundred years of its founding, Estella had developed into 3 distinct, separately walled, and often warring neighborhoods: San Pedro, San Juan, and San Miguel, each with its own council. *Navarros* (both Basque- and Romance-speaking), *Francos*, and Jews lived separately. As Estella's political importance grew, the kings of Navarra built a palace by the riverbank and convened *Cortes* here in 1237. Weekly markets were held on the left bank in the Barrio de San Miguel, and an annual fair in the fall drew traders and moneylenders, wholesalers, and artisans from all over southern Europe. Before long Estella rivaled Burgos and Medina del Campo as a commercial center. A 1366 tax census showed 7,100 hearths, categorized as follows: 10% clergy, 16% tax-exempt *hidalgos* (lower nobility), 23% merchants (*Francos y ruanos*), 47% laborers, 3% Jews, and 1% Moors.

Estella's Jewish quarter was one of the 5 largest in Navarra. Even so, in the 12th c. Judah Halevi unsuccessfully warned the poet Moses ibn Ezra from going to so remote a place, which he compared to living among wolves, bears, and lions. The *aljama*, or Jewish quarter, was originally on the hill over what is now the highway tunnel, but in 1135 these prime properties were taken by the city, and the *aljama* was moved nearer the castle of Zalatambor. In a later period Estella's Jewish community had a separate synagogue for women—the only known case in Spain. By 1264 the Jewish population had swollen to 110 families, some 10% of the city's population. Documents indicate that most Jews worked in the clothing business, or as silversmiths or ink makers, but that some were farmers. A Jew named Jonás made a chess set for King Carlos III el Noble in 1402. A few achieved prominence: in the late 14th c. Estella's Leví family administered Navarra's taxes, and Rabbi Jucé Orabuena was court physician to the Navarran monarchy. As in much of the rest of Spain, Christian-Jewish relations in Estella tended to oscillate. In the 1328 Navarra civil war, much of Estella's Jewish community was massacred. The poet Menahem ben A'aron ibn Zérah vividly described how during the riots his father, mother, and 4 brothers had their throats cut, and how he survived thanks to the intervention of a compassionate Christian soldier. The 5 men found guilty of instigating the riots had their hands cut off and were then publicly hanged in Estella. Attempts were made to rebuild the community, but in the countrywide anti-Semitic riots of 1391 it was largely destroyed again. In the 15th c. Estella's remnant Jewish population seems to have been better accepted. When Navarra finally expelled its Jews in 1498, most of Estella's Jews converted to Christianity rather than leave their homes.

The 14th and early 15th c. dealt harshly with Estella. Wars with Castilla and squabbles between local noble clans took their toll, as did the periodic decimation of the Jewish community. The black plague that struck in 1348, 1362, 1380, 1400, and 1420 reduced the city from its 829 hearths in 1366 to 431 in 1427. From the 16th to the 18th c. Estella prospered again as a center of commerce, printing, painting, and sculpture. In the 19th c. it was the center of the Carlist movement, and house #13, Plaza de los Fueros, served as the principal residence of the last Carlist pretender, Carlos VII.

📖 The unpopular Spanish king Fernando VII, childless in 3 marriages, had a daughter with his 4th wife, María Cristina de Borbón, in 1830. That left Fernando's popular, conservative Catholic brother Carlos out of the line of succession. When Fernando died in 1833, Carlos's followers—adherents of the traditional Salic Law that gives preference in royal succession to male heirs—founded the Partido Apostólico. With the slogan *Rey, Religión y Fueros* ["King, Religion, and Local Law"], they rebelled against the Crown. There were 3 bloody eruptions called the Carlist Wars over the next half century. They centered in the conservative north and east: Navarra, the Rioja, Cataluña, and Levante—areas with strong regional cultures. Several key events occurred in or around Estella. The city was taken by Zumalacárregui's troops in 1835 and served as the chief Carlist stronghold during the whole of the first Carlist War. The Carlist armies, led by don Carlos himself, began their unsuccessful march on Madrid from Estella on May 15, 1837. The Treaty of Vergara ended the war in 1839. When don Carlos died, the mantle of Carlism passed to his son Carlos, and eventually to his great-grandson Carlos.

The short second Carlist War, fought in 1869, had little effect on this region. The third lasted from 1871 until 1876. In 1873 Estella was again taken by force by the troops of the new pretender don Carlos, who subsequently established his headquarters in the Plaza de los Fueros. In November the Carlists beat back an assault in the Battle of Montejurra. The Republicans threatened again in June of the following year, and Estella's citizens—

carrying all of their moveable goods—took refuge in the hills. After 3 days of fierce fighting, the Republicans were trounced in nearby Abárzuza and Estellans filed back into the valley. At the foot of the Montejurra Massif, don Carlos reviewed 18,000 of the triumphant Carlists, all decked out in the red beret of Navarra. It was the last great success of the Carlist cause. In February 1876, after beating the remnants of the Carlist forces in the Estellan hills, General Primo de Rivera entered the city. Don Carlos fled to France, and Alfonso XII and the Bourbon dynasty were firmly in control. But although the wars were over, the movement lived on, at least symbolically. Even today in certain regions of the north the red berets of the Carlist faction are worn as a symbol of adherence to aggressive Catholic conservatism and regional autonomy.

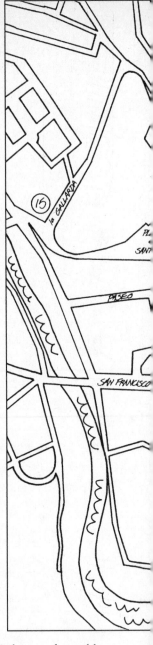

PILGRIMAGE

Up through the end of the 11th c., when Estella began to prosper, pilgrims generally avoided the dangerous narrow defile of the Río Ega where the city now stands. Instead, they hiked southwest from Villatuerta to the bridge across the Ega at Zarapuz (a hamlet documented from the late 10th to the 17th c.) and then over the hills to the Monastery of Irache. But with the growth of the town in the 12th c., the preferred route shifted north to Estella.

As befit a major center, Estella had numerous hospices for pilgrims. In each of the major parishes a brotherhood (*cofradía*) maintained a hospice, providing beds and rudimentary meals. In 1374 Carlos II financed the hospice of Ordoiz, 1 km. from Estella on the Pamplona road. From the 12th c. the leprosarium of San Lázaro (see ch. 27) stood near the Pamplona gate (the *crismón* from its door is in the Pamplona museum). There were so many *Francos* doing business in Estella, and so many French pilgrims passing through, that Estella had churches dedicated to the French cults of the Virgin of Puy, San Martín de Tours, San Nicolás (the patron of Lorraine; the church was closed in the 16th c. and has now disappeared), and the Virgin of Rocamador. The Cofradía de Santiago, called Los Sesenta, served pilgrims going both to the French shrine of Puy and to Compostela. With the 16th-c. decline of the pilgrimage, these hospices fell on hard times, and in 1524 Carlos V ordered the 11 remaining hospices to combine into one, the Hospital de Santa María de Gracia. In 1624 its successor moved to a site in the Calle de la Imprenta, near the church of San Miguel. Still, when Laffi visited in 1673, he was favorably impressed with Estella's hospitality:

> This is a beautiful town that lies on both sides of a great river. . . . There are some fine large houses and monasteries, in particular the Monastery of the Redemption where they provide charity to all pilgrims, consisting of bread and wine. In the castello they give alms of money to those pilgrims who are going to St. James of Galicia. [Laffi; trans. Hall (1997), 123]

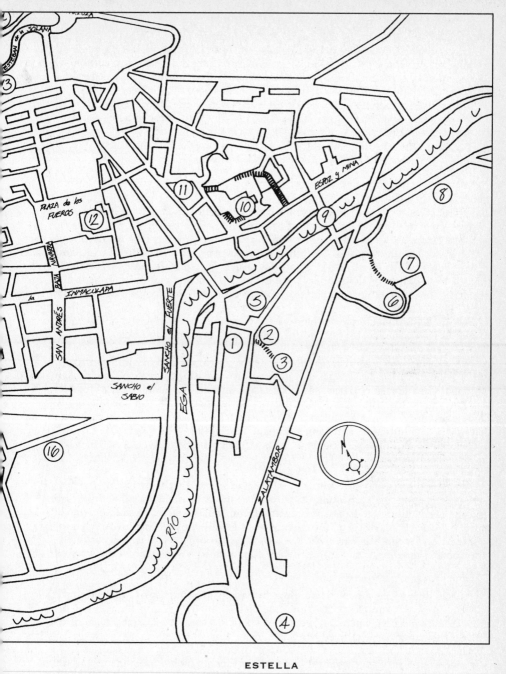

ESTELLA

Domenico Laffi (1636-ca. 1700) was a priest from Bologna, Italy, who made 3 pilgrimages to Santiago de Compostela in the late 1600s. The first experience must have been positive, for he repeated the journey in 1670, in the company of a painter named Domenico Codici, and then wrote a book summarizing his impressions from the 2 pilgrimages. He commemorated the 1673 publication of *Viaggio in Ponente* by repeating the journey a third time, accompanied by an Italian friar, Giuseppe Liparini. A revised edition of his book, incorporating his experiences and observations from his third pilgrimage, appeared in 1681. It was reprinted several times over the next fifty years. Laffi's memoir is often vivid with descriptions of local color, narrations of his personal experiences, and insights into the character—and characters—of pilgrimage. The *Viaggio* is a valuable chronicle of pilgrimage customs in the period between the Reformation and the Enlightenment. We quote from him several times in the course of this book.

Estella's 1164 charter had a special section prohibiting abuses of pilgrims, which included provisions like this one: "If any pilgrim or merchant is lodged in a house and should lose his baggage, and should say to the host or his wife or children: 'You took my baggage and you are a thief, or a thief's accomplice,' and the host should respond 'No,' then he must prove this by judicial trial; and if he is defeated, he shall return what was stolen in triplicate, and shall pay 60 *sueldos* to the king for the robbery, and 60 *sueldos* for judicial costs. If he is not defeated, the pilgrims or merchants shall pay the 60 *sueldos* to the city officials."

In 1759 a German couple on their way to Compostela was delayed in Estella by the wife's giving birth. They named the baby Francisco Santiago Liscler.

MONUMENTS: 1. **Palacio de los Reyes de Navarra**. 2. Old Ayuntamiento. 3. **Iglesia de San Pedro de la Rúa**. 4. Iglesia de Rocamador. 5. Palacio de los San Cristóbal/Casa de Fray Diego de Estella. 6. Iglesia de Santa María Jus del Castillo. 7. Iglesia de Santo Domingo. 8. **Iglesia de Santo Sepulcro**. 9. "Romanesque" bridge. 10. **Iglesia de San Miguel**. 11. Hospital de Santa María de Gracia. 12. **Iglesia de San Juan Bautista**. 13. Iglesia de San Pedro de Lizarra. 14. **Iglesia de El Puy**. 15. Convento de las Concepcionistas Recoletas. 16. Convento de las Clarisas.

Estella's wealth during the centuries of pilgrimage attracted artists of the first rank, so that this small city contains per square meter as many monuments worth visiting as any along the Road. We always spend 2 nights here, so as to devote an entire day to art and history. Unfortunately, in Estella most churches are open for viewing only during the half hour prior to mass, so time your visits accordingly. Schedules of masses for the entire city are supposed to be posted on every church door.

1. **Palacio de los Reyes de Navarra**. Built by Sancho el Sabio toward the end of the 12th c., this rare example of Romanesque civil architecture is in the style of the palaces in the French Benedictine center of Cluny. Despite its name, no documents suggest the monarchs ever lived here.

The original building had a single floor. Nonetheless, the upper stories were added in such a way as to create a harmonious façade, with 4 monumental arches capped by the second story's series of 4 sets of 4 delicate arches, framed by doubled columns and a horizontal protruding eave with its corbels. The palace's pride is its **capitals**. Three mortal sins are depicted on a single capital: lust on the right side; avarice on the front, in which hell is an iron kettle boiling on a demon-tended fire; and sloth on the left. In the Romanesque period, laziness—understood as distraction from piety or duty—is often represented as the seductive power of secular music, demonized by showing the musicians as animals (a goat plays a harp on a corbel in Irache, just up the Road).

📖 The nasty 7 mortal sins are anger, avarice, envy, gluttony, lust, pride, and sloth. The 7 virtues, much less frequently depicted, are faith, hope, charity, temperance, prudence, fortitude, and justice.

The most important capital depicts a scene from the French epic *Chanson de Roland*, in which **Roland fights with Ferragut** (see ch. 17). Their names, as well as the sculptor's, are visible: *Pheragut, Rollan, Martinus me fecit*. The detailed chain mail and the contrast of the Muslim Ferragut's round shield with the elongated shield of the Christian knight are realistic details reflecting the Spanish Reconquest environment. The story of this battle, which traditionally took place near Nájera (see ch. 31) is featured in the CC *Turpin*. The close ties between Navarra and France meant that this story was popular here. On the Road it appears in the cloister of Irache and on the pilgrim hospice in Navarrete.

The building now serves both as the tourist office and as a museum housing the works of the local painter Gustavo de Maeztu (born 1887), who is known for his vibrant colors. Outside, in the center of the Plaza de San Martín next to the palace, is a 16th-c. fountain.

2. Old Ayuntamiento. The Council of the *Francos* met at this site from the 11th c. through the next 800 years. The current Renaissance town hall has interesting eaves. Inside are remains of the 12th-c. chapel of San Martín.

📖 Estella used to celebrate 12 annual municipal festivals, which bankrupted the Council. They decided to suspend 9 of the festivals. To compensate, the Ayuntamiento put up a retablo in the chapel of San Martín depicting the 9 de-festivaled saints, and funded a mass on the eve of each of the 9 saints' days.

3. **Iglesia de San Pedro de la Rúa**. This 12th–13th-c. fortified Romanesque church dominates the Barrio de los Francos. Among San Pedro's treasures is a fragment of the True Cross and a shoulder bone of San Andrés.

📖 Legend has it that in 1270 a Greek Santiago pilgrim fell ill in Estella's Hospice of San Nicolás. He died, and, when he was buried in the pilgrim cemetery in San Pedro's cloister, the grave glowed. When it was opened, the astonished clerics discovered the fragment of the *lignum crucis* and the bone of St. Andrew, as well as the pilgrim's crosier and gloves, revealing that he was not a common pilgrim, but the bishop of Patras.

In 1523 Carlos V swore in this church to uphold the ancient city charters, then heard mass with 100 men dressed in white livery, and donated 200 ducats to charity.

Exterior:
 • The daring tower clearly shows its 3 phases of construction. The heavy square blocks of the base formed part of the Romanesque church's defenses. The central portion frames the large 14th-c. Gothic west window. The crowning bell tower is early-17th-c.
 • The monumental late-12th-c. **doorway**, at the top of a lengthy staircase, is a strange mixture. The framing cylindrical arches, the finely elaborated floral,

mythological, and abstract capitals, and the zigzag motif are all found in French Norman churches. The interlaced and lobed arches suggest Mudéjar art. (You have seen this already in the church of Santiago in Puente la Reina and in Cirauqui's San Román.) The figural art in the center of the 5 archivolts is symbolic: the hand of God blessing with 3 fingers suggests the Trinity, the lamb is the Lamb of God, and the *crismón* is Christ's special emblem. The centaur on the right door jamb, by contrast, together with the erotic woman-siren spreading her two tails, remind sinners of the human predilection for bestial lust.

Interior:
- The 2 side naves are from the original church; the central one was replaced after the 1572 explosion.
- The Romanesque central apse's 3 great **niches** are unique in Spain for their size and 3 tiers of windows. The windows are 19th-c., as is the peculiar twisted column with the snakes.
- One of its ca. 1150 narrative **capitals** picturesquely narrates the torments of sinners in hell. Others depict fighting knights, soldiers confronting demons, and tangles of vines enclosing human figures, as in San Miguel, across the river.
- The retablo is 15th-c.
- The choir stalls are 17th-c.
- The apse chapel, with the 13th-c. Virgin from Santa María Jus del Castillo, was once the monarchs' special chapel. Note also the 12th-c. statue of Nuestra Señora de Belén, brought from the Santo Sepulcro Church.
- The Rococo Capilla de San Andrés, added in 1596, was paid for by Felipe II and the bishop of Pamplona. It has a lovely Baroque 1706 grille (*reja*). The wall paintings narrate the story of the Byzantine bishop's pilgrimage, death, and burial in Estella. Until the 1979 theft, the chapel housed the relics of St. Andrew left by the bishop of Patras: a 13th-c. bishop's crosier from Limoges and a 12th-c. Byzantine crucifix. We remember them well enough to recognize them if we spot them in a pawn shop one day.
- In a niche on the left aisle is the **13th-c. crucifix** reputedly found floating in the river in front of the Santo Sepulcro Church (see below). The simple, stylized face projects both suffering and resignation.
- The Capilla de San Nicolás de Bari, one of the most popular saints on the Santiago Road, contains a 14th-c. image of the saint and a Mannerist retablo depicting several of this saint's miracles: saving drowning men, granting a dowry, and rescuing besieged soldiers.
- The Capilla del Rosario has a 17th-c. Mannerist retablo depicting various scenes from the life of the Virgin. In its center is the 14th-c. pregnant **Virgen de la O**. On the wall nearby is an early-14th-c. Gothic crucifix (formerly in Santa María Jus del Castillo), a classic of its genre. Characteristic of this style are the curved body; long loin cloth with elegant, angular drapes; stylized prominent ribs; pathetic narrow face with small mouth, straight nose, and hieratic expression.
- Note also the 12th-c. Romanesque baptismal font. Its decoration probably represents the 4 rivers of Paradise feeding the Tree of Life.

> 📖 The 4 rivers, the Pison, Gihon, Tigris, and Euphrates, were believed to emanate from a single rock, and thus constituted a ready symbol for the 4 Gospels flowing from Christ.

- In the sacristy are several distinguished gold and silver pieces, including a splendidly worked Renaissance chalice.

Cloister:

Unfortunately, when Zalatambor castle was blown up in 1572, large chunks landed on the cloister. The 2 remaining sides of the **cloister** contain a superb collection of <u>**Romanesque capitals**</u> on top of paired columns. At least 3 sculptors' hands are visible: the birds and knots of the west gallery, as well as the twisted group of 4 columns, resemble those of one of the masters of Santo Domingo de Silos (Province of Burgos). It is worth spending a good deal of time with these capitals as they are masterworks, they establish stylistic patterns that you will see repeatedly on the Road, and they present a nearly complete overview of the biblical, animal, and vegetable iconography that you will see dozens of times between here and Compostela.

The historiated capitals of the north gallery are by 2 masters schooled in the traditions of the pilgrimage Road. The capitals were probably executed ca. 1175 and are of the quality—and some perhaps the same hand—as those in the old Cathedral of Pamplona. Their iconography is principally New Testament, with a sprinkling of monsters and miscellaneous scenes of contemporary life. Although many capitals were lost when the castle blew up, the remaining capitals indicate that in addition to the life of Christ, another series depicted the martyrdom of various saints, 3 of which remain (Lawrence, capital #6; Andrew #7–8; Peter #9). Curiously, the 8 scenes dedicated to Andrew were carved approximately 100 years before (!) the bishop of Patras arrived with that saint's shoulder bone.

As is common in the Romanesque style, each capital depicts 4 scenes, often episodes of a single story or aspects of a particular topic. Some of the more complex capital faces contain multiple scenes, linked by encompassing background devices. This sculptor was particularly adept at depicting interactions among figures and their emotional reactions to events. His architectural renderings are more tangible than the usual Romanesque sketched skyline silhouettes of buildings.

The stories:

2. N: Christ with his cross visits Limbo, frees Adam and Eve, who step on Satan; demons carry a basket with the souls of the condemned. E: Christ is entombed by Joseph of Arimatea and Nicodemus. S: Christ tells María Magdalena not to touch him. W: The 3 Marys visit the tomb.

3. N: The soldiers give Herod severed heads. E: The Massacre of the Innocents. S: Herod sends 3 soldiers. W: The 3 Wise Men visit Herod.

4. N: Angels inform the shepherds. E: The Visitation (Mary visits Elizabeth); the Birth of Christ; the Virgin hands the child to a midwife; St. Joseph. S: The Annunciation (note that the open book says *Ave María*). W: Adoration of the 3 Wise Men.

5. N: Seated boy grasps lions (Daniel? Salvation?). E: Soldier with a shield; animal with a tail that becomes heads (allegory of the struggle against evil?). S: 2 riders on strange beast (men given to sin?). W: 2 combatants with shields and swords; 2 nude boys wrestle, watched by a seated, 2–headed quadruped (probably an allegory of anger).

6. N: Emperor Decius condemning St. Lawrence. E: Martyrdom of Lawrence by fire (note the inscription: *Passio Sci Laurentii es hic*); angels receive his soul. S: Saints Lawrence and Hipolitus. W: Lawrence gives church's treasures to the poor (note the inscription: *hic tradit S. Laurentius thesauros*).

7 and 8. The story of Saint Andrew, listed in the chronological order of the episodes: 8. S: A man is interrogated by a bearded judge. N: Andrew, bound, is between a judge and a young man (Andrew defends him from incest?). E: Egeas puts Andrew in prison, where he preaches to a crowd; the inscription reads: *Hic jubet eum Egeas incarcerari*. W: Andrew on the cross. 7. E: Andrew on the

cross, nude, preaches to a larger crowd; the hand of God blesses from above; the woman next to Andrés could be Egeas's wife Maximilla, whom he converted. N: Men before a judge (plea to free Andrew? or request his body?). W (much deteriorated): Andrew near death; Maximilla kneeling; angels take his soul. S. Andrew dead; Egeas killed in the street by a demon.

9. E: Saint Peter before Herod Agrippa, with his prison on the right. N: Peter taken to prison. W: 2 soldiers guard him; an angel approaches, takes him by the hand. S: Jerusalem.

4. Iglesia de Rocamador. This church, near the San Nicolás Gate, maintained a hospice and was especially popular with French pilgrims. It was founded in 1201 by Sancho el Fuerte in thanks for a Christian victory in Morocco, and financed by a tax paid by Estella's slaughterhouse. The only remnant from the early Romanesque church is the central apse with its decorated corbels. The rest, including the image on the main entrance, dates from 1691. The church contains a sculpted 17th-c. **Santiago Peregrino** in the Romanist style (solid volume, hair in large curls, clenched lips), and a fine late-12th-c. richly dressed image of the Virgin. It now houses a community of Capuchin monks.

> 📖 The shrine of Rocamadour, in a gorge in Quercy in central France, is one of Europe's popular pilgrimage destinations. Legend has it that Zaqueo the Publican was visited by the Virgin on her death. She told him to go to Galia and build a hermitage. He called his cave Amator Rupium (Roc-Amadour) and took along an image of the Virgin that he had carved and Saint Luke himself had painted. Centuries later in 1166, the abbot of Mont-Saint-Michel found Zaqueo's incorrupt body, and the pilgrimages began. Perhaps to appeal to the numbers of French pilgrims on the Santiago Road, Rocamador churches multiplied along the route in towns like Sangüesa, Hornillos, and Astorga.

5. Palacio de los San Cristóbal. The 1561 Plateresque house has nice plasterwork, eaves, and patio. Two fine Renaissance heads are in semicircular frames on the façade. The Franciscan mystic Fray Diego de Estella, a member of this noble family, lived here. The palace, recently restored, now houses the Casa de Cultura. The 2 busts represent Hercules and Venus.

> 📖 Diego de Estella (1524–78), nephew of San Francisco Javier, gained prominence as an intellectual. Felipe II appointed him Court Preacher. Two of his books had profound influence on Catholic philosophy and mysticism of the period: *Treatise on the Vanity of the World* (*Tratado de la vanidad del mundo*) and *Most Devout Meditations on the Love of God* (*Meditaciones devotísimas del amor de Dios*).

6. Iglesia de Santa María Jus del Castillo. In 1145 King García Ramírez, in a gesture to atone for his sins, confiscated the synagogue that occupied this site and ceded it to the bishop of Pamplona to build a new church, to be called Santa María y Todos los Santos. Its location near the castle facilitated its serving for a time as a royal chapel. Until 1881 it was a parish church, and at that time declining population led to the parish's merging with San Pedro de la Rúa, and its subsequent ruin. Its façade is 17th-c. Inside, it preserves the only 12th-c. pre-Gothic vault in Estella, whose keystones depict Christ in Majesty and the Virgin and Child. The apse has been recently restored.

7. Iglesia de Santo Domingo. The early Gothic monastery was built ca. 1258 next to the Jewish neighborhood. Teobaldo II of Navarra once held *Cortes* here. In the 13th c. the monastery ran an important school that even taught Arabic. A large wall, remnants of which remain, linked it to the castle of Belmecher. Another wall, built with money extorted from Estella's Jewish community, separated it from their *aljama*. Because of its proximity to the castle, the convent served as a secondary residence for Navarra's royalty and was expanded and decorated at their expense. Harmed in the 1809 French occupation, it was abandoned in 1839 after the *desamortización*, and it fell to ruin. Recently partly reconstructed, since 1981 Santo Domingo serves as a senior citizens' home.

For a 13th-c. church, the width of its naves is impressive: 10 massive Romanesque-style buttresses sustain the weight of its roof. Because of the steep slope on which the church is built, its various parts are on different levels.

8. **Iglesia de Santo Sepulcro.** The church was built by wealthy merchants prior to 1123 and served as a burial ground for the *Franco* community. Its founding involves a common medieval anti-Semitic legend in which a crucifix, thrown into the river by a spiteful Jew, floated to this particular spot and refused to be moved to any other. The crucifix has since acquiesced to reside in San Pedro de la Rúa. By the late 19th c. this neighborhood had been largely abandoned, and the church was closed definitively in 1881.

The 1328 **façade** depicts the Last Supper, the Crucifixion, the 3 Marys, and Jesus's descent into hell. The theme—Christ's sacrifice and the saving power of the Eucharist—is reinforced by the 2 **bearded Jews** who sustain the tympanum, as if to show how the New Law both supersedes and is sustained by what went before. The theme continues in the figures alongside the cross, where 1 man's face shows devotion and another rejects Christ by an act of will, covering his eyes. They may well be the centurion who recognized Jesus as the son of God (Matt. 27:54, Mark 15:39; traditionally called St. Longinos) and another whom folklore holds to have refused to recognize Christ's divinity. These early Gothic scenes are notable for their variety of details, vivid expressions, and the movement of their figures. Yes, **Santiago Peregrino** is there on the upper course of Apostles. Another is on the left side of the door. Both have scallop shells on their purses.

If you look carefully, you will see that this portal—like many 14th-c. Gothic assemblages—has many curious details. Among the figures on the capitals over the left row of Apostles is a farmer leading a pig. On the capitals to the right of the Last Supper are a dozen or more fanciful beasts. Our favorite is the monster with a second face on his belly (near the third Apostle on the right side).

9. "Romanesque" bridge. Built in 1973, it attempts to replicate the original that was destroyed in 1873 during the Carlist Wars.

10. <u>Iglesia de San Miguel</u>. Because San Miguel Archangel leads the heavenly armies against the Devil's minions, medieval churches dedicated to him often occupy strategic high ground and—like France's famous Mont-Saint-Michel—are half church and half castle. This church controls the eastern approaches to Estella along the river. The restrictions imposed by its site make its north portal the principal entrance. Begun prior to 1145, it has been reformed and expanded many times.

Exterior:
- The <u>**north portal**</u>, among Spain's richest displays of Romanesque sculpture, is largely the work of a single sculptor around 1170 (exceptions: the 8 Apostles on the spandrels are earlier, and the high reliefs below them are later). Most probably an upper story was destroyed in the 1512 war that incorporated Navarra into the rest of Spain. The relatively small door is made grandiose by the 5 cir-

cling archivolts sustained by columns, carved capitals, and a decorative band on top of the capitals (*imposta*), which is prolonged on the flanking walls and creates a strong horizontal line. As almost always in the Romanesque, the sculpture is subordinate to the architectural forms. The overriding theme of the portal is the Last Judgment.

• The tympanum shows Christ in Majesty in an undulating mandorla, surrounded by the Tetramorphos, with the cautionary inscription: *Nec Deus et nec homo presens quam cernis imago, sed Deus est et homo quem sacra figurat imago* ("This present image you see is neither God nor human, but God it is and man whom this holy figure represents").

• The corbels sustaining the tympanum are ferocious lions devouring the souls of sinners. They echo Maestro Esteban's in the Pamplona Cathedral in style.

• The archivolts. The nearest to God bears 6 angels with incensaria. The next one, 20 paired old men of the Apocalypse with their musical instruments. The third, prophets with scrolls. The fourth, scenes from the life of Christ, including the blind man cured at Jericho, the Wedding at Cana, María Magdalena, the Baptism. The fifth, Christian symbols and episodes from the New Testament and saints' lives, including: the beheading of San Juan; San Martín dividing his cape; Herod and Salome; the martyrdom of San Lorenzo; the *crismón*; San Pedro receiving charity, detained, and martyred; and the stoning of San Esteban. The outermost, furthest from God, invites sinners to ponder the torments of hell: 2 greedy men are dragged by ropes while another greedy couple, money bag in hand, are hauled to hell by a goat-demon; an adulterous woman rides a devil-goat while another is bitten by snakes and toads (as on the Palace of the Kings and Santa María in Sangüesa); monkey-musicians play seductive melodies that horrify churchmen and parents, then as now.

• The capitals on the pillars reputedly are the earliest in Spain to arrange the episodes of Jesus's life in strict chronological sequence: Annunciation, Visitation and birth, Angels with the shepherds, Adoration, Presentation, Flight to Egypt, Slaughter of the Innocents, and Herod. The last 2 capitals on the right are masterpieces, depicting hunters and their prey enmeshed in tangled thickets of vines. The fluid, intricate composition is reminiscent of capitals from Pamplona's vanished Romanesque cloister.

• The **high reliefs** of the jambs, added later, are also masterpieces of Romanesque sculpture. On the left (Christ's right) **San Miguel slays the dragon** of the Apocalypse before a second, admiring angel, and in a separate scene **weighs souls** (shown as kneeling children) between God (the bosom of Abraham) and a demon. The tenderness with which Michael takes the hand of the elect soul mirrors a similar scene at Autun, in France. This frieze is extraordinary for the almost Hellenic grace of the head of God, the serene, static quality of the figures, and the sophisticated treatment of the drapery. The hatching on the wings to represent feathers may be derived from Byzantine ivories. Note also St. Michael's shield with the chains of the coat of arms of Navarra.

• The frieze on the right depicts the Resurrection, the empty sepulcher, and the arrival of the 3 Marys with unguent jars. Note the women's closely fitting cowls and the sophisticated drapery of their robes, one of which is held shut by the third Mary's hand.

• The 8 Apostles on the jambs, probably from an earlier door (ca. 1185) that was later mounted as an upper register, recall those of Sangüesa.

• Note also the medieval ironwork on the doors.

• The 14th-c. Capilla de San Jorge, on the terrace, contains a ca. 1500 effigy of St. George on horseback.

Interior:

• The naves are Romanesque to the level of the capitals. The vaults and airy triforium are 13th-c. Gothic, while the lacy vaults of the central nave are 16th-c.

• At the west end of the left transept the 1406 Aragonese-French Gothic retablo portrays Santa Elena identifying the cross. The donors (the royal architect Martín Pérez and his wife) are depicted at Helena's feet. Note the bright reds and blues and the elaborate draperies typical of the Aragonese-Catalán style. The panels depict the legend of the Holy Cross.

The stories on the retablo from the top left:
1. The Byzantine emperor Constantine dreams that he will conquer under the sign of the Cross.
2. The dream comes true; Constantine vanquishes Magencio in 312.
3. His mother, Elena, consults with Jerusalem elders about the location of the Cross.
4. (2nd row). Elena finds the Cross and those of the two thieves.
5. Elena, with donors and Cross.
6. She learns which is the True Cross when it resurrects a dead woman.
7. The Cross is returned from Persia to Jerusalem in the 7th c. by Emperor Heraclio.
8. Heraclio returns the Cross to Calvary.

• A painting in the right transept depicting the Mass of San Gregorio shows Diego de Eguía and his family, who captured this fortified church for Fernando el Católico in the 1512 Navarra war. Eguía had 30 children, 26 of whom lived. The 13 boys and 13 girls all came to hear mass in this church.
• The principal retablo is early-18th-c. Baroque, with a central 16th-c. image of San Miguel defeating the dragon.
• Right nave: the shoemakers' guild retablo of San Crispín and San Crispiniano was donated by the guild in 1601. The 2 saints were martyred by boiling.
• The sacristy contains a particularly fine collection of 16th–18th-c. ecclesiastical metalwork, including chalices and processional crosses.

11. Hospital de Santa María de Gracia. In the Calle de la Imprenta, near San Miguel. The pilgrim hospice built here in 1624 consolidated several others in the city. Its abandoned single-nave church, invisible from the street, has little artistic merit. Next to the door, sustained by angels is a coat of arms of the city of Estella, a star framed by chains, topped by a jeweled crown.

12. **Iglesia de San Juan Bautista.** Built by Sancho el Fuerte (1194–1234) in the Plaza de los Fueros, and transformed radically over the years by wealthy parishioners. Externally, little of the old church remains except the Romanesque north portal and the transitional Romanesque-Gothic south portal. The rest dates from 1902. Inside is an early-13th-c. Romanesque baptismal font, and a nice Gothic Crucifixion. In a chapel off the left aisle is a small retablo with an early-17th-c. **Santiago Peregrino.**
The most important work is the **retablo** with sculpture by Juan de Beauvais and Pierre Picart (begun 1563). At the base, Ezequiel, David, Moses, and Daniel dramatize how the Old Law sustains the New. The upper stories are all saints and scenes from the life of the Holy Family. The lower right panel contains another **Santiago Peregrino.** The architectural design combines both Plateresque decorative elements and the sober overall structure of the new Romanist aesthetic. Picart's contract specified that for the decoration he "must carve only angels and seraphim and winged children and little heads and leaves and natural fruit, and no horses, beasts, or grotesques" (Marías, 248).

📖 Michelangelo and his school were the principal stylistic inspiration for Spain's so-called Romanist sculptors, who produced thousands of Counter-Reformation altarpieces in the last 40 years of the 16th c. The movement was particularly fertile in Navarra and La Rioja. Working mainly in wood, although sometimes in alabaster, they carved bulky, stolid, majestic, decorous saints and Old Testament figures. Their rounded faces, clenched lips, thickly curled locks, and muscular torsos all projected strength. They were set into monumental Renaissance retablos. Often the retablo's columns of niches were narrow, cramping the figures while maintaining an overall sense of verticality. The Counter-Reformation urged conformity in doctrine, and distrusted individual, impassioned religious expresion. Thus the saints of the Romanist school tend to look pretty much alike, with bright colors, favoring reds and blues, grandiloquent gestures, and heroic poses, but little of the emotion that infused 16th-c. Spanish mysticism or the Baroque style that was evolving at the same time.

13. Iglesia de San Pedro de Lizarra. Documents cite the existence of this church in 1024, prior even to Sancho Ramírez's repopulation of the area. The current structure dates mostly from the 14th c. and contains Romanesque elements in the apse, a 16th-c. sacristy, and a 17th-c. Baroque tower among the ruins. Its most notable feature is a large **Roman funeral stele** embedded in its south façade.

14. **Iglesia de El Puy**. Legend holds that ca. 1085 some shepherds found an image of the Virgin in a cave on this hill in front of which stars were falling. Another legend states that although they tried to move the image to San Pedro de la Rúa, it would not budge, and so they built a church here named Le Puy—after a famous French shrine.

📖 From the 5th c. Le Puy-en-Velay, in south-central France, had a popular Marian sanctuary, in itself an important pilgrimage destination. By the early Middle Ages the church had become a cathedral. The village is dominated by an 82-m. lava pinnacle (called "the peak," or *le puy*), on top of which perches the ancient chapel of St.-Michel d'Aiguilhe. Le Puy was so important that it gives its name—*Via podense*—to one of the 4 major Santiago pilgrimage Roads through France. From the 11th c. on, we find many secondary churches dedicated to the cult of the Virgin of Le Puy in both France and Spain.

In 1174 this popular hilltop shrine was given by the bishop of Pamplona to the 60 *Cofrades* of Santiago to administer. Historians posit a series of later churches (Romanesque, Gothic) on the site, and then a 17th-c. Baroque church that had fallen into terminal ruin by the 1920s. The current building, begun in 1930, was inaugurated in 1949.

Stylistically, the **silver-covered wooden Virgin's image** is problematical: some say it is Visigothic—which makes it much earlier than the legend of its finding— and some say it dates from the 13th or 14th c. Either way, La Virgen del Puy was named patroness of the city in the 17th c. Among El Puy's relics is a finger bone reputedly of the Evangelist St. Mark.

15. Convento de las Concepcionistas Recoletas. This austere Baroque brick convent was built between 1688 and 1731. It was funded by Paula María de Aguirre, a rich heiress who became a nun against her widowed mother's wishes and gave

her father's fortune to the Order to construct a complex replicating the convent in Agreda where she had done her novitiate. Its façade features 4 enormous coats of arms: the lower two of the donors (the wolf suckling two cubs is the Aguirre emblem), the upper two of the Franciscan Order. The convent's use as a military barracks during the 19th-c. wars destroyed much of its original art, but it now houses several interesting small retablos.

16. Convento de las Clarisas. Franciscan nuns have had a convent on the flats by the river since the 13th c. The current complex, fruit of 15th- and 17th-c. building campaigns and still a cloistered convent, has 3 splendid **Baroque retablos**, with the most deeply carved twisted Solomonic columns that we have ever seen.
  • Retablo de la Santísima Trinidad, ca. 1700, right transept. The retablo's glory is its profuse, high-relief decoration, and the curious depiction of the Holy Trinity at its center: God the Father and Christ seated side by side, floating on a curlicued, angel-filled cloud, with the dove of the Holy Spirit above their heads.
  • Main retablo, ca. 1679. The architect, Juan Barón, played with receding planes of focus to create a varied texture that highlights the 6 principal sculptural groups: Saints Catalina and Bárbara, above them Francisco de Asís, Clara (with a forceful sense of movement), and Antonio, and the crowning Calvary.
  • Retablo de la Inmaculada Concepción, ca. 1700, left transept. The figure of the Virgin has intricately detailed drapery.

If you have time, Estella has some other religious buildings of note. Two favorites:
  • Convento Antiguo de San Benito el Real. Next to Santa Clara on the river plain. Largely abandoned, with interesting bits of Renaissance and Baroque architecture.
  • Convento Nuevo de San Benito. Next to El Puy, on the hill. A nice collection of silver and gold work in the sacristy.

26. Estella → Los Arcos

Route: ESTELLA → Ayegui → **Monastery of Irache** → Azqueta → **Villamayor de Monjardín** → Urbiola → **Luquín** → LOS ARCOS

The large massif to the southwest of the Road is Montejurra. The conical mountain to the northwest is Monjardín. The cliffs on the north horizon are the Montes de Cantabria; they separate this part of Navarra, and later the Rioja, from the Basque Provinces.

✳ Ayegui King Sancho el de Peñalén gave the town to the monastery of Irache in 1060. Townsfolk paid taxes to Irache in wine, wheat, and labor. The early-17th-c. church of San Martín de Tours, replacing an earlier church on the hill above the village, was extensively revised in the Baroque style in the 18th c. It contains a 14th-c. Virgen del Rosario and a French-Gothic crucifix with characteristically schematic anatomy and deeply lined ribs.

On the Montejurra heights outside of town you can see the Ermita de San Cipriano, which contains a late Gothic image of the Saint.

✳ **Monastery of Irache** This ancient abbey seems to have followed the Benedictine rule since Visigothic times, even though its earliest documentation is from 958. Here King García el de Nájera built the first pilgrim hospice in Navarra in 1052–54. Irache's greatest leader was its abbot San Veremundo.

> 📖 San Veremundo was born ca. 1020 in Villatuerta or Arellano, neighboring towns that still dispute the honor. He succeeded his uncle as abbot, leading Irache from 1052 to 1092. Veremundo, with the aid of his friend King Sancho Ramírez, built Irache into one of the richest and strongest abbeys in Navarra. In 1969 he was declared Navarran Patrón del Camino de Santiago.

When Sancho el Fuerte returned from the Battle of Las Navas de Tolosa in 1212, he hung his share of the chains of the released Christian prisoners (see ch. 17) from the towers of Irache.

> 📖 In the late 11th c. Benedictine monks in several parts of Europe thought that their Order had gone soft and that reform—in the direction of greater piety, poverty, and service—was called for. In 1098 Robert of Champagne founded the first Cistercian abbey at Cîteaux, 24 km. south of Dijon. St. Bernard (1090–1153) began his own breakaway group at Clairvaux, a little way to the north. From the very first, these new communities attracted a large corps of dedicated young monks, and when the parent group at Cîteaux incorporated the Order of San Bernardo in 1112, the Cistercian Order rapidly became the most potent monastic force in Europe, counting more than 2,000 abbeys by the mid-13th c. Alfonso X's compilation of Spanish law in the late 13th c. was explicit about the reasons for this revolution:

"The order of white monks of Cisteles . . . [superseded] the monks of San Benito, who began in great poverty. For this reason the Church in Rome had given them many privileges and powers. But because some of them later went on to have vassals, and villages, and castles and churches, and tithes, and offerings, and accepted the oaths of fealty of their vassals as well as their properties, and assumed the role of judges to hear their lawsuits . . . the Church thought they should leave all this, for if not they would revoke all of the privileges and powers they had been given by reason of their poverty and the hard life in which the order had begun." [Partida 1, Título 7, Law 27]

The monastery entered a period of decline from the 13th to the 15th c., but in 1522 another Benedictine community, brought from Valladolid, infused new vigor. A school was established, and the Benedictine university in Sahagún was transferred to Irache in 1605, where it continued to grant degrees in philosophy, canon law, letters, medicine, and theology until the early 19th c. When Laffi visited in the late 17th c. he found what we find today: "a large and magnificent Benedictine monastery. It is very wealthy and seems like a town itself because it has a big surrounding wall and is very large." [Laffi; trans. Hall (1997), 123] Napoleon's troops occupied the buildings in 1809. During the 19th-c. Carlist Wars (see ch. 25) Irache was a hospital. It now houses a community of Padres Esculapios.

Exterior:
• The exterior presents an **imposing silhouette**, in which the unmodified, grandiose, pre-12th-c. Romanesque construction is clearly seen. Under the eaves of the *cabecera* the trilobed arches recall those of San Pedro de la Rúa in Estella. The exterior of the church contains various expressive capitals and corbels cautioning against the excesses of sin. Particularly engaging is a grotesquely fat monk turning his head to steal a drink from a wineskin. Another—reminiscent of the Palace of the Monarchs in Estella—shows a goat harpist, indicating the seductive power of secular music.
• The **Byzantine-style lantern tower**, with its central cylinder and its 4 corner cylinders, is related to lantern towers in Salamanca, Toro, and Zamora. Historians speculate that an eastern Mediterranean pilgrim architect may have left his mark on these churches. The **Herrera-style tower** from 1609, to the left of the west entrance, echoes those of the Escorial.
• Puerta de San Pedro. This 12th-c. portal, on the monastery's north side, contains several expressive capitals: fantastic animals, harpies, a centaur, San Martín dividing his cloak, etc.
• West entrance. The 13th-c. late Romanesque west entrance is simple, as per the Cistercian norm, with **finely carved stylized floral capitals**. The maze to the left of the door contains a cross; the maze on the right the Lamb of God. Over the door is a *crismón* sustained by the hand of God. The escutcheon of the Spanish monarchs (see ch. 24) over the door dates from ca. 1600.

Interior:
The church is impressive in its **Cistercian simplicity**.

Everything that we find charming in the Romanesque, the Cistercian St. Bernard of Clairvaux found sinfully distracting. "What utility can there be in so many ridiculous monsters, that misshapen beauty and pleasing misshapenness, especially on the walls of the cloisters, under the eyes of the of the cloisters, under the eyes of the monks who are engaged in reading? What use have these primitive monkeys, these fierce lions, these monstrous centaurs, these half-men, these spotted tigers, these fighting warriors, these horn-blowing hunters? Here one sees many bodies beneath a single head. On one side there is a four-footed beast with a serpent's head; on another, a quadruped's head with the tail of a fish; here, a horse with the hindquarters of a goat; there, a horned beast with a horse's body. In short, on all sides there is such a large and prodigious diversity of animals, that the marble stones make better reading than the books. One could pass the whole day here admiring the details of each one instead of meditating on God's Law. Oh, my God! Even if one were not embarrassed by these miserable creations, why is there no shame at such foolish expense?" [*Apologia ad Willelmum*, ch. 12]

• The apse and lower portions of the naves are Romanesque. The naves were vaulted in the early 13th c. in the new Gothic style but give no hint of the height and airiness that the Gothic style was intended to achieve, since the architect supported the vaults with massive arches still conceptually Romanesque.
• Irache's **apse** is unique: a great semicylinder, divided into 3 stories, with large Romanesque-style semicircular windows, and—very unusual for the period—circular windows. The placement of the windows, of the blind arches, and of the horizontal bands of decorations creates a harmonious ensemble that gives an increasing sense of lightness in its upper stories. In the morning the sun pours in and the stone glows the color of gold. The right transept shines with light filtering through a cruciform central window screened in the Mudéjar style. The stylized, rounded figures on the **capitals** flanking the apse depict fighting knights (left) and the 3 Wise Men. The transept was revaulted in the 16th c. with a hemispheric cupola imitating its original Romanesque dome, while preserving the Romanesque keystones: the hand of God, a trumpeting angel, the martyrdom of San Estéban, and what appears to be the baptism of Christ. The squinches sustaining the dome represent the Tetramorphos—the 4 Evangelists—as human figures clothed in detailed, flowing robes, capped with symbolic heads. The high choir, in the back of the church, is a tour de force for the flatness of its Plateresque arch.
• The central apse houses the 12th-c. silver- and gold-encrusted Romanesque image of **Santa María la Real**. The right apse has a statue of Abbot San Veremundo.
• The **Plateresque cloister** (1540–74) resembles that of San Zoilo in Carrión, with its thousands of intricate depictions of Old and New Testament figures, saints (especially San Benito), kings, and mythological themes (Prometheus, Hercules, etc). The oldest sections, which are the north side and the adjoining segments of the east and west wings, are peopled with energetic, dramatic figures contrasting with others in the saccharin, Italianate style. The remainder of the cloister is more Romanist (see ch. 25).
• The New Cloister. This was the center of the university. In the strong sunlight, sheltered from the wind, grows one of the stately palm trees you will see in similar environments along the Road. Nobles of the Middle Ages cultivated them to demonstrate the oriental taste they had acquired on the Crusades or in the battles in Andalucía.

✳ Azqueta In 1128 the abbot of Irache gave this town to the knight who had caught in Logroño the thieves who had stolen the monastery's treasure. The village's circular structure derives from its medieval walls. The 16th-c. church of San Pedro, with its modern tower, has Flamboyant Gothic vaults, a nice Romanesque baptismal font, and an early-17th-c. Romanist retablo. The sculptor seems to have used the angel of the Annunciation as an opportunity to study the naked human form.

Fuente de Moros Just before Villamayor is a Gothic fountain/cistern, restored in 1991. As the name implies, local legend holds that it is a much earlier Islamic construction.

❋ **Villamayor de Monjardín** The castle of San Esteban de Deyo crowns the hill above this town. The castle's base is Roman, but it has been repeatedly reconstructed over the centuries. It was the last major stronghold of the Banu Qasi Muslims in this region until King Sancho Garcés captured it in 914. However, the CC *Turpin*, as a propaganda vehicle for French interests in Iberia, avers instead that Charlemagne captured it from a Navarran king.

> 📖 In chapter 16 Charlemagne supposedly defeated in Villamayor de Monjardín the Navarran prince Furré, who lived in the Monjardín castle. The Emperor marched with his troops from Puente la Reina, and thousands of soldiers on both sides met their deaths before Charlemagne carried the day and went off to fight Ferragut in Nájera. Before the battle Charlemagne asked God to indicate which of his soldiers would die the next day. When the troops put on their armor, 150 men were marked on their backs with a glowing cross. Charlemagne had them stay behind to protect his camp, but on returning from battle, found that they all had mysteriously died.

On the site of the castle today is the small Baroque Ermita de San Esteban, constructed from the castle's square-cut stones, many with masons' marks (see ch. 15).

The church of **San Andrés** is largely Romanesque, with its sides supported by 4 slender buttresses, and its unusually high apse sustained by 4 delicate pillar-buttresses. The Baroque tower dates from the 17th c. The monumental **Romanesque entrance** has a series of capitals with pairs of symmetrical animals, the Virgin and Child, and a fight between 2 knights, as in Estella and Irache. The *crismón* on the keystone recalls Jaca. Inside is an extraordinary Romanesque silver **processional cross** from ca. 1200. One side depicts the Crucifixion, the other the Lamb of God (*Agnus Dei*) with its head in a cross-shaped nimbus and bearing the Bible and the standard of Christ. Four pairs of saints under arches are at the cross's 4 extremities.

> 📖 Legend has it that when Sancho Garcés I was preparing to attack the Moors on Monjardín, a goatherd saw a goat that seemed frozen in place. He used his sling to scare off the circling vultures and went to investigate. He found a cross with one of his stones imbedded in its arm. Remorseful, he swore that he would rather have lost the use of his own arm than have done damage to the cross, and with that his arm became immobile.

The warehouselike building on the outskirts of town is the Castillo de Monjardín winery, known for its white wines. In recent years grapes have largely replaced the white asparagus for which this region is famous.

❋ **Urbiola** The town is north of the paved road. The 16th-c. church of San Salvador houses a Gothic Virgin. A hospice for poor pilgrims was established here in 1226 by the Knights of San Juan.

✹ **Luquín** The town, some of whose houses display impressive, oversized coats of arms, is just south of the paved road.

The medieval Church of San Martín Obispo, with its 13th-c. tower, was reconditioned in the 16th c. in the Greco-Roman style. Its 1730s **doorway**, in bad disrepair, is an ostentatious Baroque retablo housing an image of San Martín and an enormous coat of arms bearing the emblem of St. Peter and the papacy. It is typical of Baroque doors of this period in Navarra with its freestanding fluted columns, a double cornice, interplay of straight and curved lines, plain and highly decorated surfaces, and diverse textures. Inside the church are 3 18th-c. **Baroque/Rococo retablos** with well-executed details.

At the other end of town is the 18th-c. Basílica de Nuestra Señora de los Remedios, which replaces a 12th-c. predecessor. Its **doorway**'s best feature is the ornate foliate plaque over the entrance, set off by the broken lines of the architectural frame. Inside, the early-18th-c. **Baroque *retablo mayor*** is remarkable for its accomplished details and sense of harmonious whole. The unusual double arch in the center shelters 2 manifestations of Mary—Nuestra Señora de los Remedios (13th-c. Gothic) and Nuestra Señora del Milagro (16th-c. Flemish Renaissance), with a chubby, naked Jesus embracing her neck. The lateral **Retablo del Resucitado** contains an elegant 1795 Christ, whose beautiful face and gently modeled flesh are typical of that period's academic style.

Agriculture in the reddish, sandy soil of this undulating plateau until recently was mainly wheat. It is now being replaced by 3 cash crops: sunflowers, grapes, and asparagus. Note how the asparagus fields are mounded to produce white asparagus: the stalks grow entirely underground, and are cut before they have a chance to develop their green color in the light.

The path skirts to the right of some low, pine-covered hills called the Cogoticos de la Raicilla and then slices through them along the Río Cardiel to emerge in Los Arcos.

27. LOS ARCOS

HISTORY

The ideal geographical site—the Odrón River, a defensible hill, good farmland, on a natural transportation route—means that Los Arcos has been inhabited since Roman times, when it may have been known as Curnonium. Five Roman tombs were discovered near the small *ermita* at the entrance to the town.

Sancho Garcés I, ca. 914, retook Los Arcos from the Muslims. During the 1067 battle of Valdegón between the Kings of Navarra, Aragón, and Castilla—all named Sancho—the archers of Urancia (this is the town's name in CC *Turpin*) fought so well that the winner, Navarra's Sancho el de Peñalén, conceded the town an escutcheon with bows (*arcos*) and arrows and gave the town its current name.

By the mid 12th c. Los Arcos was protected by a castle on the hill northeast of town. Its location near the frontier with Castilla made Los Arcos a frequent military target. Alfonso X took it by force in 1274. It was later returned to Navarra. The town was arbitrarily annexed to Castilla yet again in 1463 in the settlement of a dispute between Juan II of Aragón and Enrique IV of Castilla. Like many important towns in the region, it suffered substantial destruction in the 19th c. with the Napoleonic invasion and the Carlist Wars.

Two battles took place at Los Arcos during the first Carlist War (see ch. 25). In the opening actions, the popular Carlist general Santos Ladrón took a stand against the Queen's troops in Los Arcos. On Oct. 11, 1833, his forces were routed. He was taken prisoner, summarily judged guilty of sedition, and shot. By early 1835 the Carlist general Zumalacárregui, who had not yet been able to capture any fortified positions held by the government, finally acquired a cannon. The first castle they attacked was at Los Arcos, but the bombardment was insufficient to dislodge the Queen's troops. So Zumalacárregui prudently relaxed the siege, allowed his enemies to escape, and then occupied the town with pride as if he had taken it by force.

Because it was on the pilgrimage Road and it was so near the Castilian frontier, Los Arcos became a toll-collecting station and a place to change money. In 1175 Sancho el Sabio authorized a weekly market and moved to draw settlers by equalizing rights between locals and *Francos*. For the next 3 centuries it flourished as a market center, as the town's many rich merchant houses attest. Los Arcos also attracted a small Jewish population and was termed by the late-15th-c. pilgrim Künig von Vach a "city of Jews." As late as the 17th c. Laffi commented on the town's wealth: "This is truly a well-fortified place, and well kept and there are plenty of things like fruit and vegetables in the main square, and good bread" [Laffi; trans. Hall (1997), 125].

Los Arcos projects a medieval aura, even though most of the mansionlike houses date from the 16th and 17th c. The city plan—long streets parallel to the river, cut perpendicularly by short connecting streets—resembles that of Sangüesa and Viana. Several of the small plazas have ancient arcades, with the overhanging houses supported by stone pillars or massive wooden beams.

The hill east of the town, where the castle once stood, is made of twisted layers of sedimentary rock shot through with veins of white calcium, into which family wine cellars (*bodegas*) have been excavated.

PILGRIMAGE

The Camino de Santiago enters through the Plaza del Pozo and continues west along the Calle San Antón through the Plaza de las Frutas and the Plaza Santa María to exit through the Arco de Felipe V. King Teobaldo II's will in 1270 donated 10 escudos to a pilgrim hospice in Los Arcos. This may have been the Hospital de Santa Brígida, still located at the back of the parish church.

MONUMENTS: 1. **Iglesia de Santa María de la Asunción**. 2. Arco de Felipe V. 3. Ermita de San Blas.

1. **Iglesia de Santa María de la Asunción**. The church was constructed over a period of 600 years, from the 12th through the 18th c., though little remains of the early church, begun ca. 1175. The Greco-Roman architectural style predominates. The internal decoration of this church offers a good opportunity to compare classic Spanish Baroque with its Churrigueresque and Rococo variants.

📖 Much Italian 15th-c. Renaissance architecture sought to imitate the clean lines and simple geometric shapes of buildings from classical antiquity. Fifteenth-century architecture in Spain gravitated toward a different aesthetic, complicating shapes and decorating plane surfaces with both geometric patterns echoing Islamic art and the intricate mazelike filigrees of Flamboyant and Flemish Gothic. The ongoing Spanish taste for complexity of structure and intricacy of decoration made the leap from Renaissance to Baroque a much shorter jump in Spain than in many parts of Europe. As styles evolved in Spain from 1500 to 1750 we can perceive several phases which often overlapped in time, and sometimes even coincided in a single artistic creation, as here in Los Arcos.

Mannerism (last two-thirds of 16th c.). A reaction against the equilibrium and coldness of Renaissance classicism. Characterized by twisted, elongated figures, dramatic lighting effects, aggressive use of color, and dramatic contrasts of scale.

Baroque (late 16th–early 18th c.). Hightened sense of theatricality in all genres; mixed media; sculptures and paintings spilling out of their assigned frames; colossal scale; emphasis on movement and tension; broken lines; overpowering architectural frames.

Churrigueresque (late 17th–early 18th c.). An extravagant Baroque style popularized by José Benito de Churriguera and his brothers. Features façades and retablos with twisted columns and elaborate leaf work.

Rococo (18th c.). Originated in France as a reaction to the excesses and grandiloquence of Baroque. Presumed delicacy and refinement based in curving, asymmetric design motifs of scrolls, shells, flowers, and branches. Often introduced oriental motifs.

Exterior:
• The superb Renaissance **tower** by Jan and Martín de Landerrain was finished in 1590. Note the graceful proportions of the 4 stories, each slightly smaller than the former, the ornamental buttress supporting the belfry and lantern vault, and the Plateresque detailing in the gargoyles and urns.
• The late Plateresque entrance (ca. 1560) has archivolts with angels, saints, and Apostles (look for **Santiago** on the right of God). In the niches are San Pablo and an expressive San Pedro, whose energetic posture, flowing beard, and angularly draped robe recall Michelangelo.

Interior:

• The profusion of **Baroque decoration**, on the vaults and walls and especially the superb series of retablos, makes this one of the most stunning Baroque churches on the Santiago Road. The ornate, painted **plasterwork** of the cornice and the quarter sphere of the dome is typical of 18th-c. Navarran Baroque in its combination of foliated motifs and cherubs.

• José Bravo's **painted murals** high on the walls were justified in the church's 1742 budget request because paintings "are very useful, very beautiful, and permanent," and because "they are found in all the best churches." The paintings in the choir, some 20 years later, tend toward the Rococo.

• The late-17th-c. walnut **main retablo** is one of the pilgrimage Road's best. While most retablos are funded by the Church or by wealthy donors, this one was paid for by Los Arcos's town council. It is of regular geometric Romanist design capped with an innovative, Baroque 3-paneled quarter sphere. The retablo depicts various scenes from Christ's Passion, the life of the Virgin, and the Apostles, who are the sustaining columns of the Church. Look for **Santiago** on the bottom left. Note the Apostles' crystal eyes. The highest figure is San Ignacio de Loyola. The pelican on the central tabernacle is an icon of Christ's sacrifice.

• In the center of this retablo is the seated image of **Santa María de los Arcos**, whose geometric simplicity, serene oval face, and angular drapery with folds below the knees are all typical of 14th-c. French Gothic Virgins.

• On its left is the 1718 profusely ornamented **retablo de San Juan Bautista**, constructed by Juan Angel Nagusia. The broken lines and surging shapes link the retablo's diverse spaces and create a sense of tense equilibrium. The Romanist-style central statue, ca. 1627, echoes Juan de Juní's in the Salamanca Cathedral. San Juan is flanked by his parents, Saints Zacarías and Isabel.

• The 1718 retablo de la Virgen del Rosario (at the end of the right transept) has some finely decorated convoluted columns.

• **Retablo de la Visitación.** The retablo mixes sculpture, architectural figures, and painting in the classic 15th-c. Aragonese style. The predella contains Old Testament notables, with the David (second from the right) suggesting a portrait of Fernando el Católico! San Blas crowns the retablo.

• The **retablo of San Francisco Javier** is on the left in the chapel next to the transept. The titular saint is flanked by Saints Apolonia and Lucía, and smaller statues of Saints Isidro and an especially graceful **Roque**, dressed as a Santiago pilgrim. This retablo is in the 18th-c. Churrigueresque style.

• Opposite, to the right, is the 1710 retablo of San Gregorio Ostiense, who died in Logroño in 1041. It is capped with a representation of souls in purgatory. The altar table is Rococo.

• The mid-18th-c. Rococo **organ**, built like a small retablo, is considered to have the best sound in Navarra. In 1979 we were lucky enough to have the parish priest play it for us and then give us a tour of the organ's innards.

• The late-16th-c. Plateresque polychrome oak **choir stalls** depict with Mannerist touches a variety of biblical scenes and saints. You should easily find the pilgrims **Santiago** and **Roque**.

• The ends of the transept are covered with 18th-c. silver plaques, creating the sense of a curtained salon.

• The 1560s Flamboyant Gothic cloister is a poor imitation of those of Nájera and Pamplona. Its best feature is the decorative keystones on the vaults. On the north side a semicircular arch remains from the Romanesque church.

2. Arco de Felipe V. At the west end of town, facing the small bridge over the Odrón River, this ca. 1700 arch is all that remains from Los Arcos's defensive system.

3. Ermita de San Blas. This 12th-c. hermitage is located on the road to Viana across a small bridge over what the 12th-c. *Guide* calls the "fatal water" of the River Odrón. It is now part of a private home, although the Romanesque apse is still visible. The *ermita*, formerly dedicated to San Lázaro, once supported a hospice for lepers.

📖 What we know today as leprosy is caused by the bacillus *Mycobacterium leprae*, but in the Middle Ages a variety of disfiguring diseases were lumped under the term *leprosy*. Leviticus 13:45, in the context of ritual purity, proscribes harsh treatment for lepers: "The leper . . . shall wear torn clothes and let the hair of his head hang loose, and he shall cover his upper lip and cry 'Unclean, unclean.' He shall remain unclean as long as he has the disease; . . . he shall dwell alone in a habitation outside the camp." Because the disease was considered highly contagious, and ostracism had biblical sanction, in the Middle Ages lepers were generally prohibited from entering towns. Their hospitals, or leprosaria, often named for San Lázaro in honor of the leper cured by Christ, were located outside the gates. Lepers were made to carry sticks and begging bowls, and a bell or rattle or clapboards to bang together to warn of their approach. A leper wanting to buy something had to touch it with his stick.

Inside this *ermita* is a small 18th-c. retablo with a central figure of San Blas.

Among Los Arcos's other monuments are:
- The Convento de Concepcionistas (formerly of the Capuchinos). The small, sober 17th-c. church contains retablos and paintings of minor importance.
- Ermita del Calvario. On a hill overlooking the city, at the end of a Via Crucis. This 18th-c. chapel has a small Baroque retablo.

28. Los Arcos → Logroño

Route: Los Arcos → Sansol → **Torres del Río** → El Poyo → **Viana** → Cuevas → Cantabria → Logroño

----

As you leave Los Arcos, the town in the distance on the left is El Busto.

✱ Sansol This hamlet, named for the Cordoban martyr San Zoilo, used to belong to the monastery of the same name in Carrión, 210 km. west along the pilgrimage Road. Sansol was probably the site of the "Hospitium" mentioned in the 12th-c. CC *Guide*. Here, too, was the now vanished chapel of Santa María de Melgar, belonging to the Hospitallers of Saint John. The village contains several splendid Baroque palaces with monumental façades festooned with coats of arms: Calle Real, 4 (16th c); Calle Mayor, 11 (17th c; the staircase has a painted cupola); Calle Real, 2, Plaza de la Iglesia; and Barrio Nuevo (all 18th-c).

The Baroque 18th-c. church of San Zoilo has a dome painted with the Ascension of Christ to heaven. The church contains a 16th-c. baptismal font, a 14th-c. Gothic sculpture of San Pedro from a nearby hermitage, and a number of small Baroque retablos.

✱ **Torres del Río** Given the number of eminently defensible high places nearby, Torres del Río's location deep in the narrow gully of the Linares River is unusual. Existing before the Muslim occupation, and then retaken by the Christians with Monjardín ca. 914, Torres del Río belonged to the Monastery of Irache in 1109. The citizens of the village in the 14th c. bought the monastery out, and from then on the town pertained directly to the monarchy. Several of the village's houses sport massive 18th-c. coats of arms. According to chapter 6 of the CC *Guide*, drinking water from the River Linares can be fatal. In our experience it is not—but the wine tastes better.

MONUMENTS: 1. **Iglesia del Santo Sepulcro**. 2. Iglesia de San Andrés.

1. **Santo Sepulcro**. The origins and affiliations of this church remain somewhat obscure. Because of its odd design, many believe that during the 12th c. the church of Santo Sepulcro, which had a small monastery next to it, belonged to the Military Order of the Knights of the Holy Sepulcher in Jerusalem, aka Knights Templar, who had established a priory in Logroño by 1144. A fundamental question relates to the building's original function. It may have been a funeral chapel, since excavations around the church have turned up several tombs. Others consider it to be a beacon, given the lantern vault over the dome and the circular staircase that leads up to it. Presumably a fire could be lit in the evening to guide night-traveling pilgrims, though this seems improbable given Torres's location deep in the valley. Or it may simply have been a monastery church.

Exterior:
- The building is extraordinarily well proportioned. The octagonal cylinder, flanked in rigorous symmetry by 2 smaller cylinders, is divided harmoniously into 3 stories.
- A variety of vegetable and zoomorphic corbels support the eaves.

Interior:
- The inside, too, is well proportioned. The altar niche (which resembles the prayer niche, or *mihrab*, of a mosque) is matched by the annex containing the cylindrical staircase, and the distance from each to the center of the octagon is exactly the same. The width of the dome is precisely the height of the walls. The height of the dome is precisely the height of the first story of the church proper, to the height of its capitals. The octagonal plan and the striking crossed arches of the Islamic-style cupola bear a resemblance to those of the church of the Crucifijo en Segovia, which was the Spanish motherhouse of the Knights Templar, and the small churches of Eunate and Santo Espíritu in Roncesvalles. The **arches of the cupola** may echo those of the Mosque of Córdoba or the Aljafería of Zaragoza.
- The themes of the capitals are Christ's death and resurrection. The triple structure over Jesus's empty tomb may allude to Jerusalem's Church of the Holy Sepulcher.
- The 13th-c. crucifix's geometricized anatomy and the flexibility of its body are characteristic of the transition from Romanesque to Gothic, while the stylized expression is almost Byzantine in character.

2. Iglesia de San Andrés. The crosses on this late-16th-c. Renaissance parish church indicate that it, too, may have belonged to the Order of the Knights of the Holy Sepulcher. Its mid-17th-c. *retablo mayor* mixes Renaissance naturalism with Romanist Mannerism. The alternating relief panels and freestanding sculptures are reminiscent of those of Gregorio Hernández.

✼ El Poyo The name is derived from the Latin *podium*, a projecting point or high place. The exhausting climb to El Poyo, one of the highest points on the Road, has made it a perfect resting-place for travelers. Its small Trinitarian monastery has existed since at least the 12th c. In 1303 it was given to the Monastery of Roncesvalles, which administered it until penury in 1814 forced the monastery to sell it. El Poyo also maintained a hospice from at least the 14th c. until its destruction in the 19th-c. Carlist Wars. The church, restored after its partial destruction in the wars, reputedly contains a 14th-c. image of Nuestra Señora del Poyo, with Jesus on her knee holding the Book of Life. Legend holds that it was stolen 3 times by citizens of Viana, but always returned miraculously to El Poyo.

These heights afford pilgrims their first view of La Rioja. The mountain range to the left is the Sierra de la Demanda, and its highest peak, San Lorenzo, often shines with snow well into the summer. The sandy valleys, eroded remnants of an alluvial plain, are perfect for the cultivation of the grapes that have made this region famous. Several Roman villas were nestled into these hills. One, north of the paved road near km. 77, is likely the town Ptolemy called Cornava. Both Roman and Celtiberian remains were found at another site, north of the road at km. 83. Nothing is left to see at either site.

✼ **Viana**

HISTORY
Sancho VII el Fuerte founded Viana in 1219, consolidating several villages onto the hilltop. He walled the town as a bastion facing Castilla. In 1274 Castilian king Alfonso X el Sabio besieged it for 2 months without success. In 1275 it withstood another long siege. Over the centuries it bounced back and forth between the kingdoms. In the 1360s dynastic wars it was occupied first by the Trastámaras and then by the forces of Pedro el Cruel. In 1378 a treaty ceded it to Castilla; in 1423 another gave it back to Navarra. That year Carlos III el Noble founded the Principality of Viana, a semiautonomous area within his kingdom that would be ruled

by the crown prince as a kind of training ground (much as Wales has served the British monarchy). His immediate purpose was to secure the succession for his grandson Carlos (supported by the Beaumontés party) against the supporters of Juan II of Aragón, husband of his deceased daughter Blanca (supported by the Agramontés faction). In 1461 Castilla's Enrique IV, aided by the French, besieged Juan II here for 9 months. When Juan saw the situation was hopeless, he had to force the citizens to surrender. In thanks for their support he added to their escutcheon the motto "Very noble, illustrious, and loyal" (*Muy noble, muy ilustre, y leal*).

During the later Middle Ages Viana's economy, like that of so many merchant towns along the pilgrimage Road, boomed. French and Jewish artisans and merchants flocked to the town. The Torriviento neighborhood (on a low hill to the southeast of the current town) was the Jewish quarter. Along with so many of Navarra's *aljamas*, it was torched in 1329, reestablished in midcentury (in the 1366 census 45 of Viana's 265 hearths belonged to Jews), decimated again in the riots of 1391, reestablished once again, and then eliminated with the expulsions at the end of the 15th c.

Viana went to war again in 1507 in the struggle to see who would rule Castilla. Viana's role is marked by the heroism of Cesar Borgia, whose bust is in the Plaza and whose bones lie in the Church of Santa María.

📖 Cesar Borgia was the son of Aragonese cardinal Rodrigo Borgia (later Pope Alexander VI). By his early twenties, Cesar Borgia was feared as one of the most powerful warlords in Italy. A black legend, derived both from Italian loathing of the Spanish and from Cesar's true character, had made his name synonymous with murder, rape, incest, robbery, and treachery. In 1506, after decades of fighting in Italy, generally against Spanish interests, Borgia was captured and imprisoned in the Castle of La Mota, near Valladolid.

Castilla and Aragón had been united by Fernando and Isabel's marriage, but then Isabel's death forced the question of who would succeed her. Fernando could rule through their mad daughter, Juana. The other contender was the 7-year-old Hapsburg prince Carlos V, the son of Juana and her husband, Philip the Fair. The French, fearing the Hapsburgs, allied with Fernando. The Italians, fearing both but detesting the Spanish (who controlled the Italian Peninsula from Naples south) even more, backed the Austrians. When Philip the Fair suddenly died, Cesar Borgia plotted with Maximilian of France to bring Carlos V to Spain. Borgia escaped from La Mota by sliding down a rope, injuring himself in the process. He recovered in Pamplona and was soon back on the battlefield. In February of 1507 he was called to direct the defense of Viana against the besieging troops of Count Louis de Beaumont. Borgia held the town; Beaumont the castle.

On the stormy night of March 3 Borgia learned of the imminent reinforcement of the castle by Beaumont supporters. Unable to rally the defenders of Viana to sortie with him, he rode out to confront the troops alone. Beaumont, seeing him approach, remarked, "Who is that mad man?" and sent out a patrol to engage him. When Borgia's body was found in the morning, it had 25 wounds.

Viana's economy continued to boom from the 16th through the 18th c., as can be surmised from the number of impressive civic buildings erected during that period. In 1630 Felipe IV raised the town to the rank of city. During the Carlist Wars (see ch. 25), Viana was the site of devastating battles in 1834, when it was taken by Zumalacárregui, and 1873, when don Carlos's forces captured it.

PILGRIMAGE

Two famous pilgrims commented on their passage through Viana. In the late 15th c. Künig von Vach noted 4 pilgrim hospices. In the 17th Laffi recorded his happiness on seeing "such a fine town with a beautiful church, so well ordered that it wanted for nothing. It has a splendid door with the most beautiful reliefs" [Laffi; trans. Hall (1997), 125].

MONUMENTS: 1. Walls. 2. **Iglesia de Santa María de la Asunción**. 3. Ayuntamiento. 4. Iglesia de San Pedro. 5. Casa Consistorial. 6. Iglesia de San Francisco. 7. Basílica de la Soledad.

1. The city's walls—in some places with a Roman base, although much reconstructed over the centuries—remain nearly intact, giving Viana the appearance of one of the most imposing fortified towns on the pilgrimage Road. The castle, located at the edge of the southeast corner of the hill, had its defenses destroyed by Cardinal Cisneros in 1515 in his campaign to disarm Navarra. By the late 16th c. houses were built incorporating segments of the wall, which is today in many areas encased within other structures.

2. **Iglesia de Santa María de la Asunción**. The main structure was built from 1250 to 1329, with a 16th-c. tower and façade.

Exterior:
• **South Portal**. This monumental Plateresque construction by Juan de Goyaz and successors, begun in 1549, is in the form of a retablo that combines scenes of the Passion and Redemption with secular themes like the Labors of Hercules and Renaissance grotesques. The 39 plaques that support the frieze suggest the triumph of virtue against evil. The 4 large plaques that flank the door are noted for their varied composition: Christ praying in the garden of Gethsemane has 2 superimposed scenes; the Annunciation has strong diagonals, emphasized by the huge jar of lilies, a symbol of virginity; the birth of Christ has a circular composition; while the road to Calvary is oppressively jumbled around the figure of Jesus. These, and the Virgin and Child of the tympanum, are delicately detailed and impart the Renaissance sense of calm, self-possessed grandeur.

The strongly contrasting second story presents the Crucifixion against an unadorned background, with each of the figural groups standing alone in scenes which alternate simple and complex compositions. God the Father reaches out in blessing on the dome, the rich texture contrasting with the lower scene.

This is the portal that so impressed Laffi.
• East Portal. The 14th-c. Gothic tympanum depicts the Virgin between 2 angels.

Interior:
• The 3 Gothic naves, of unusual height, are vaulted with elaborate tracery, and the **gallery with triforium** is the best in Navarra.
• Several of the 13th- and 14th-c. capitals of columns in the north nave have well-executed foliage. Among the figures on the capitals of the south nave are a monk filling a pitcher and a squatting man. The keystones are decorated with images of the Virgin, Santa Catalina, the Agnus Dei, and a variety of other Old Testament figures and Christian symbols. The striking baptismal font in the baptistry is also the work of Juan de Goyaz.
• The 1664 **main altar retablo** combines Plateresque elements with 17th-c. Baroque. The twisted columns, intricate frames, and detailed narrations convey a sense of crowded magnificence. The Virgin is flanked by the 12 Apostles, who function as both pillars of the church and as columns of this retablo. Stylisti-

cally the retablo shows evolution from Renaissance Romanist forms toward the Baroque. Anatomies are covered with flowing drapery, hair is dramatically curled, gestures are theatrical, symmetries are exaggerated, and the whole is encompassed in rich 3-dimensional decorative forms.

• Renaissance and Baroque lateral altars depict Saints Catalina, Bartolomé, Félix, José, Francisco Javier, and Lorenzo.

• The walls of the 16th-c. Capilla de la Magdalena, in the ambulatory, were painted in the Baroque style in 1730–1. The Trinity, the Virgin, and the 3 Theological Virtues are all portrayed in complex architectural settings. Its Neoclassic *templete* displays a 1704 statue of the penitent María Magdalena, clothed in a formfitting reed mat.

• The **Capilla de San Juan del Ramo** has fine **Neoclassic frescoes** in oil and tempera painted in the 1780s by Luis Paret depicting the life of San Juan Bautista. The paintings flanking the entrance show Zacariah foretelling Elizabeth's pregnancy and the Virgin's visit to Elizabeth. The seated female figures on the squinches of the dome represent John's virtues: Holiness kneels before a cross; Wisdom carries the Book of Knowledge and turns her face to receive inspiration from the Holy Spirit; Constancy holds a column and sword; and Chastity drives off a naked Cupid while her left hand holds a basin of water, perhaps for the proverbial cold shower. Although the allegories in the dome have been damaged by humidity, thanks to the 1965 restoration you can still make out the contrast between the Old and New Testaments, and the allegory of Fertility—which the artist suggests results from prayer and confidence in God. Other scenes narrate John's life: his penitence in the desert, his preaching, his support of the Lamb of God, and his arrest. The pictures are a masterpiece: the horizontal lines of the principal actors are given depth by strong diagonals and architectural or landscape backgrounds. The poses, gestures, and treatment of the figures echo Michelangelo, but have a grace and delicacy typical of Neoclassic painting, while the wide-ranging palate staves off the general Neoclassic ambience of coldness. Sculpted Neoclassic plaques depict other scenes from John the Baptist's life and martyrdom.

• The 1631 retablo of **Santiago** in the ambulatory focuses on episodes from Santiago's life and miracles, including the **apparition to Santiago of the Virgen del Pilar,** Santiago preaching to his disciples, his martyrdom, and a magnificent **Santiago Matamoros,** with a strong head framed by curly hair and beard. It also depicts some scenes from the life of Christ.

• The sacristy, with a fine 1711 Byzantine-style cupola, contains a notable collection of Renaissance church vestments.

3. Ayuntamiento. Imposing Baroque façade with massive lateral towers, 2–story colonnade, and an imposing central escutcheon (1673–88).

4. Ruins of the Iglesia de San Pedro. This oldest church in Viana, of pure Gothic construction, dates from the early 13th c., when its tower was incorporated into Viana's fortifications. In the 1740s the church added a Baroque portal shaped like a great niche. The portal is framed by a triumphal arch and decorated with plaques of diverse themes and textures, which interplay with columns and arches of contrasting surfaces and lines. Look for an angel carrying the papal cross, a seated San Pedro, the dove of the Holy Spirit, and 2 cherubs holding a flowery bouquet. This church was used as a barracks in 1833 in the Carlist Wars, and 10 years later collapsed. When we visited it in 1998, we found that its ruins had been consolidated and turned into a municipal park. The fact that it is only half-standing affords you a good look at Gothic construction techniques.

5. Casa Consistorial. Seventeenth-century monumental Baroque façade.

6. Iglesia de San Francisco. This 17th-c. monastery has an elegant Baroque façade featuring the interplay of various cubic spaces. It was sacked in the 19th-c. Independence Wars and abandoned in the great *desamortización* of church property. It was later reconditioned as a hospital and school, and now functions as a retirement community. The administration permits visits to its unremarkable cloister with its 18th-c. well, though when we visited in October of 1998 the church itself was closed to visitors. It is reputed to contain a number of Baroque and Neoclassic retablos from the ruined church of San Pedro. Its most notable features are a 17th-c. painted *trompe l'oeil* retablo of the Virgen de Guadalupe, which seems three-dimensional, and a *trompe l'oeil* window through which a tiny figure spies on worshipers.

7. Basílica de la Soledad (Hospital de Santa María de Gracia). Calle Mayor, 18. Built in the 15th c. and modified in the 16th c., this ex-hospital includes a small church and a great meeting room. It is more parallelogram than rectangle, given the limitations of the urban property, and is sustained by columns and huge wooden beams.

✳ Cuevas Only the 17th-c. Ermita de la Virgen de las Cuevas remains of the medieval town that, according to a 1302 document, used to belong to Roncesvalles. In front is a picnic area, and a small stream that marks the boundary with La Rioja.

✳ Cantabria This is the name of the flat-topped *mesa* overlooking the old bridge into Logroño. On top are remains of pre-Roman, Roman, and medieval settlements, including a massive defensive wall with vestiges of towers and a gate. A steep path leads up the *mesa* from the eastern side, behind the factories, and another descends from the northwest edge of the *mesa* to the municipal cemetery, just before the bridge. We prefer this route to the marked Road for the ruins, the view, and because it avoids a lot of highway. The cemetery walls are inscribed with an admonishing *memento mori*.

29. LOGROÑO

HISTORY

The Celtiberian town of Varea, 3 km. below the Logroño bridge on the right bank of the river, marks the furthest point inland that the Ebro is navigable. In Roman times the town boomed (see sidetrip). Sancho Garcés of Navarra and Orduño II de León retook Logroño from the Muslims in 755. It grew slowly as a small agricultural town belonging to San Millán de la Cogolla.

Sitting on the triple frontier between Aragón, Navarra, and Castilla/León, Logroño and the surrounding region of La Rioja was a prize to be courted, or a plum to be picked. In the 11th c. Logroño was held by Alfonso VI of Castilla and defended by Count García Ordóñez, who was one of Alfonso's lieutenants, as well as being his brother-in-law. He was also the curly-haired man the *Poema de mío Cid* calls el "crespo de Grañón" (v. 3112). The Ordóñezes were longstanding enemies of the Vivar family, and Rodrigo Díaz de Vivar (El Cid), during his exile from Castilla, conspired with the Muslim king of Zaragoza to unsettle the Castilian border. The *Crónica de Cardeña* says he attacked the town in 1073 and then, loaded with booty, retired 60 km. downriver to the castle of Alfaro.

Alfonso VI wanted Logroño strong, prosperous, and loyal. He built a bridge over the Ebro at the city, and in 1095 he gave a charter (*fuero*) to Count García Ordóñez that was designed to attract settlers to the region and to foment economic activity.

> Logroño's *fuero* had some revolutionary clauses, in the main intended as incentives, and it became a model for early medieval Castilian charters. It freed peasants from forced labor on their lords' estates and limited other abuses of the nobility. It ordered that uncultivated lands be expropriated and sold to new farmers. In compensation, the nobles were given monopoly rights over certain activities such as the manufacture of iron arms and tools, and over certain institutions like mills and communal ovens. The *fuero* also established free rights of pasturage and of water, both for irrigation and for fishing. Most important in terms of development was that it freed commerce from certain taxes, such as highway tolls and import duties.

As the town grew, its value increased to its enemies. In fact, few Spanish cities have been fought over as much as Logroño, which helps explain why so few early medieval monuments are left. Aragón's King Alfonso I el Batallador took it by force. Castilla's Alfonso VII captured it in 1134. Sancho el Sabio of Navarra took it in 1160, and promptly strengthened the walls and issued an even more favorable *fuero*. Nevertheless, Logroño was retaken in 1176 by Alfonso VIII for Castilla. A 1336 attack from Navarra was heroically beaten back by 4 brave men who stationed themselves at the end of the bridge. But in 1369 Logroño fell to Navarra, initiating a period of intense warfare. By 1375 it was held by Pedro Manrique, whose sympathies lay with Pedro I the Cruel of Castilla.

> 📖 The Navarran king, Carlos II el Malo, offered a 20,000-doubloon bribe to Pedro Manrique to open the gates to Navarra. When he was informed, the Castilian king instructed Manrique to let the Navarrans in, but to take them prisoner once they had entered. The plan worked perfectly, except that Carlos el Malo waited in safety on the other side of the bridge to see how his troops fared, thus escaping capture.

Logroño stayed in Castilian power until 1460, when Navarra, with the help of Aragón, briefly retook it, only to lose it almost immediately to Enrique IV, who incorporated it, and the Rioja, definitively to Castilla. But there were still battles to come. A 1521 French attack—part of a campaign to conquer Navarra—was beaten back by Carlos V, who added 3 fleur-de-lis to the city's escutcheon. In the 19th c. Logroño was taken by Napoleon's troops. It suffered greatly in the 1808–12 War of Independence, and then was occupied again in 1833–4 in the Carlist Wars. No wonder that the Rioja, courted for so long by so many violent suitors, has welcomed its post–Francisco Franco status as one of Spain's Autonomous Regions.

Its position on the Ebro River is in many ways the key to both Logroño's strategic importance and its prosperity. Its only entry in the 12th-c. *Guide* states that in Logroño "there is a large river called Ebro which is healthy and abounds in fish" (CC: Book V; trans. Melczer, 89). As the gateway to Castilla, and to Aragón's Ebro Valley, it was a market center of the first order, attracting merchants from all over Iberia, as well as Franks and Jews. As Künig von Vach remarked in the late 15th c.: "This is the first city in Spain. . . . There you will know other money. That's the end of *coronados*, for you will have to learn to recognize *malmedis* [*maravedís*]."

Medieval Logroño was a fortified rectangle parallel to the river, traversed by 2 long streets, the Rúa Vieja and the Rúa Mayor, which are still the major commercial streets of the old city. The Jewish quarter, located outside the walls between the Cadena Gate, the San Gil parish, and the river, was wiped out in the 1391 anti-Semitic riots that swept through Spain. In the early 15th c. a small new Jewish community was established on 7 streets bounded by Muros del Pósito (now Avenida de Viana), Carmelitas (Avenida de Navarra), and Calle del Siete (Muro de Cervantes).

PILGRIMAGE

Almost nothing remains of the many hospices for pilgrims in Logroño. We know the names of several: San Juan de Dios, Santiago, San Roque Amador, and outside the walls the leper hospice San Lázaro (see ch. 27). The Rúa Mayor was the Camino de Santiago. Among its many churches, the pilgrims' favorite was Santiago el Real, in front of which there is still a pilgrims' fountain. The scallop shell adorning the house across the street indicates its affiliation with the pilgrimage, perhaps as the site of a former hospice. The Hospital de Roque Amador, further down the Rúa, was taken in 1569 to become the palace of Logroño's Inquisition. An assessor's document speaks of a large downstairs room, 7 × 40 m., and upstairs a reception room, and a hall of 8 × 13 m.

LOGROÑO

opening onto 6 small rooms, one with a fireplace and a bathroom, and all of which were constructed of plaster-covered stone.

Arnold von Harff, a German pilgrim from Cologne, reminds us in 1497 that travelers—even pilgrims—were put out by the paperwork and expense of crossing international borders. "In this town of La Grunea [Harff never mastered Spanish] they search to see what goods you have, for you have to pay duty on them, and for your horse you pay two reals as duty . . . and you must take a letter with you that you have brought such a horse, of such appearance and size, with you into the country. Otherwise when you want to leave the country again, by whatever exit, they will take your horse as stolen or purchased" (Harff; trans. Letts, 268).

MONUMENTS: 1. Bridge. 2. Walls and Puerta del Camino. 3. Iglesia de Nuestra Señora del Palacio. 4. **Iglesia de Santa María la Redonda**. 5. **Iglesia de San Bartolomé**. 6. **Iglesia de Santiago el Real**. 7. Convento de La Merced. 8. Palacio de Espartero. 9. Casa de la Inquisición (Biblioteca Pública).

1. Bridge. The medieval predecessor of the bridge that you cross from the east was commissioned by Alfonso VI, repaired in the 11th c. by the engineer Santo Domingo de la Calzada, and rebuilt by his disciple San Juan de Ortega. The current bridge dates from the 19th c. Legend holds that the monastery just before the bridge was endowed by the grateful father of a girl cured by San Francisco de Asís.

2. Walls and Puerta del Camino. The plan of medieval Logroño can easily be seen on a modern city map. Fragments of the 12th-c. walls are visible in Calles San Gregorio, Carmen, Bretón de los Herreros, and Once de Junio. The only remaining city gate, on the city's west side, is called the Puerta del Camino. Guess which Camino. Carlos V rebuilt it ca. 1520 and had his enormous coat of arms placed there so everyone would know that the Hapsburgs had taken over.

3. Iglesia de Nuestra Señora del Palacio. The church (aka Santa María la Real) was commissioned in the mid-12th c. by King Alfonso VII, who donated one of his palaces to the Hospitallers for a church. Almost nothing remains from the 12th c. The early Gothic arches, the transept, some capitals with human heads high up in the entryway, and the hexagonal spire are all 13th c., with probable French influence from Auxerre or Chartres. The tower is 14th c., and the cloister 15th.

The inside of the church is all chopped up, with the west end capped by numerous tiny cupolas and the east end with elegant Flamboyant Gothic vaults. The *altar mayor* has a 16th-c. retablo by Arnao de Bruselas that shows a curious imbalance, with exterior columns and a top row of figures disproportionate to the other structures. Note the curious Last Supper, in which Christ and the Apostles crowd around a tiny folding table. In the left aisle is the 13th-c. Romanesque image of the **Virgen del Río Ebro** by the Burgundian sculptor Leodegarius. Legend states that a washerwoman found it in the Ebro late in the 19th c.

4. **Iglesia de Santa María la Redonda**. This is a "concathedral," that is, it shares a bishop with the cathedrals in Calahorra and Santo Domingo de la Calzada, the only such case in Spain.

Exterior:
• The **Baroque façade and towers** were built by Martín de Beratúa between 1752 and 1756. The façade creates an interplay of plain and decorated surfaces with high and low relief, the fluted and complex columns, heavily decorated squinches (the triangular pieces sustaining the half-shell of the dome), and the dome's decorated coffers. The towers' lower stories are plain, so as not to compete with the façade, and as they rise they progress to increasingly intricate decorated surfaces.

Interior:
• The interior is curiously organized, with the areas behind the altar and behind the choir constituting seemingly separate churches. The nave is from the 15th c. The church is vaulted with the intricate Flamboyant Gothic stars popular in the Rioja in the 16th c.

• The main retablo is Baroque, with massive Solomonic columns and architectural excesses that somewhat overpower the few statues for which they supposedly are frames. You'll see a retablo in the same style, but much better executed, in Navarrete, a few hours' walk west of Logroño.
• On the right aisle are 10 **Hispano-Flemish paintings** by Andrés Melgar and Francisco Alonso Gallego, whose work combines a late Gothic love of detail with Renaissance colors and structures, particularly the use of the triangle as an organizing principal. You'll see more of these 2 artists' work in Santo Domingo de la Calzada.
• On the left side, at the front of the church, is a small Hispano-Flemish retablo depicting the **Adoration of the Magi**. Its organization verges on Baroque, with 2 centers of interest: the 5 figures grouped around the infant Jesus on the left side of the painting, and the broader grouping of the Holy Family on the left counterbalanced by the 3 Magi—standing, kneeling, leaning forward—on the right. This grouping focuses attention on the Black King, whose prominence on center stage is another innovation.
• Further down the left aisle is a set of Renaissance paintings with glowing colors—primarily rose and red—and Italianate figures. The Virgin placing the chasuble on San Ildefonso is particularly well done, and the Pieta is very moving.
• The church behind the altar contains a painted **crucifixion by Michelangelo**, and the white marble tomb of local hero General Baldomero Espartero.

📖 In the first Carlist War, which ended in 1839, General Baldomero Espartero distinguished himself as the leader of the liberal monarchist forces of Regent María Cristina (Queen Isabel II was still a child). After he was named Duque de la Victoria and made a government minister, he forced the Regent into exile, and for 2 years served as regent-dictator of Spain. In 1843 a revolt forced him into exile.

The area at the west end of the church behind the choir is Rococo, with a painted dome and a half dozen gaudy Rococo retablos against the walls.

5. **Iglesia de San Bartolomé**. The 13th-c. church is transitional Romanesque-Gothic. Its strategic bell tower overlooking the Ebro was destroyed in a French attack in 1521, and later restored in the Mudéjar style with some delicate brick latticework.

Exterior:
• The entrance's 15th-c. door (set into 13th-c. framing arches), though much deteriorated, retains vestiges of its former glory. Its tympanum and lintel were lowered to provide additional light to the high choir. The **tympanum** focuses on the Crucifixion and its consequences. Angels bear symbols of Christ's Passion, while Christ sits as judge, listening to the advocacy of the Virgin and San Juan Bautista.
• The jambs narrate the **life and martyrdom of San Bartolomé**. On the right side, right to left: Bartholomew curing King Polemón's daughter; converting his court; breaking idols; taken prisoner before Astiages; and preaching. On the left, from left to right: his flagellation; martyrdom by flaying (this scene is particularly graphic); the Saint with his skin over his shoulder; and Astiages tearing his garments.
• On the capitals and above the arches, tiny figures seem to play among the Gothic vegetation. Our favorites are the angel driving Adam and Eve out of Eden and the shepherds learning of Christ's birth, with an *hórreo* (Spanish-style corncrib) in the background.

Interior:
- The interior has been recently and spectacularly restored, so that you will see the stone elements of construction in all their functional purity (even as you realize that in their original state they would have been covered with brightly painted biblical scenes). The apse is Romanesque in the Jaca style. The arches over the crossing are the earliest Gothic, with heavy, slightly pointed forming arches holding up the weight of the vaults. The capitals are still Romanesque in their size and motifs.

6. **Iglesia de Santiago el Real**. The church sits astride the Santiago Road as it passes through Logroño. By legend, the church was built over another commissioned by Ramiro I in the 9th c. after the battle of Clavijo. Archaeological investigations revealed the remains of a crypt from that epoch. The current building dates from the 15th and 16th c.
- Its entrance boasts a monumental 17th-c. **Santiago Matamoros** and **Santiago Peregrino** over the door.
- Inside, its enormous single nave is vaulted with a complex Flamboyant Gothic web of nerves—like many in Logroño—and a fine star over the altar. The early-17th-c. retablo of the *altar mayor* features a 16th-c. **Santiago**, and a late-13th-c. Virgen de la Esperanza, which was added to the retablo in 1966. At the rear of the church, in front of the choir, is an iron grille (*reja*) with the large red cross of the Order of Santiago (see ch. 60) in the center.

7. Convento de La Merced. The 16th-c. convent is now the Diputación General de la Rioja. The façade is elegant and the simple cloister, where the Riojan legislature now sits, even more so.

8. Palacio de Espartero and Provincial Museum. This is the 18th-c. Baroque palace to which General Espartero retired. Its treasures include Roman artifacts from the Rioja, several Gothic paintings from San Millán de la Cogolla, a Hispano-Flemish 15th-c. **retablo of Santa Ana** that includes a painting of the infant Jesus playing with young St. John the Baptist and **Santiago** (with his pilgrim staff), and the "Misa de San Gregorio," attributed to Roger Van der Weyden.

9. Casa de la Inquisición (Biblioteca pública). When the Logroño Inquisition Tribunal was established in 1569, it took over the old Hospital de Rocamador, accommodating the building to its uses. Contracts from that period exist for renovation of a main hall, a secret interview room, doors for 26 cells (but windows for only 12), a dispensary, and a small tower, as well as for plastering, fixing roof beams, repainting, and the like. Prisoner complaints about blockage of light in the narrow windows led in 1571 to chopping down an apple tree in a next-door garden. The building included temporary cells for holding prisoners still to be tried, and a *Cárcel Perpétua* for those who had been convicted. The Logroño Inquisition building was destroyed during the French occupation in 1814. The building occupying its former site is Logroño's public library.

📖 The Spanish Inquisition, founded in 1478, did not cease operations until 1834. It had a dozen or so regional tribunals, of which Logroño was one. At first the Inquisition pursued mainly converts from Judaism who were thought to still practice their former religion, but over its 350 years it directed most of its attention to Protestants, *Moriscos*, heretical mystic groups like the *Alumbrados*, bigamists, homosexuals, and abuses of the clergy such as extorting sexual favors in the confessional. In the early 17th c. there was a flurry of activity concerning witches, and 6 unfortunate women from the Navarran town of Zagarramurdi were burned alive in the square in front of the library in 1610.

🚗 Verea Three km. east of Logroño, on a flood plain above the union of the Iregua and Ebro Rivers, was the major prehistoric village of Verea. It prospered under Roman occupation. The ancient writers Strabo and Ptolemy mentioned it, and Titus Livius called it the strongest city in the region. As early as the 2nd c. B.C.E coins were minted here. The Roman city was destroyed by the Visigoth Leovigildo in the late 6th c. The village is home of the cellars of the Marqués de Murrieta winery.

🚗 Clavijo Eighteen km. southwest, on the slopes of the Laturce Mountains, Clavijo occupies a spectacular and strategic promontory over the Ebro and Iregua Valleys. It was here in 844 that **Santiago** allegedly appeared to help the Christians in a battle between Ramiro I and 'Abd ar-Rahman II. In 960 Count Fernán González may have been held prisoner for a time in this castle. The central tower and several stretches of wall remain in the castle ruins, and the view alone is worth the drive up. If you have 2 extra days it is equally worth the walk.

30. LOGROÑO → NÁJERA

Route: LOGROÑO → Pantano de la Grajera → Hospital de San Juan de Acre → **Navarrete** → [Sotés] → Ventosa → Alto de San Antón → Poyo de Roldán → [Tricio] → NÁJERA

✳ Pantano de la Grajera The Río Iregua was dammed in 1883 to create this reservoir, a welcome oasis after the seemingly endless industrial suburbs of Logroño. Look closely and you will distinguish 8 separate ecological zones around the reservoir.

1. The reservoir itself. The water is rich in aquatic plants, including lilies, which serve as pasture for several varieties of fish (tench, eels, black bass, and perch). Birds found here include herons, gulls, terns, ducks (mallards and red-crested pochards), and grebes.

2. Reeds (*carrizal*), cattails (*aneas*), and cane. Reeds are thickest at the tail of the reservoir, serving as a nesting area for many species of birds. Look for coots (black water birds with a white stripe over the nose), moorhens (same with an orange stripe), and rails feeding among the reeds. The incredibly melodious drab bird perched on a reed is probably a great reed warbler (*carricero tordal*). Look for several species of frogs and toads, as well as muskrats.

3. Salt slopes. The scaly white patches are formed by seasonal evaporation and are devoid of all but a few low, scrubby plants. White and yellow wagtails scrabble for insects here. Three types of long-billed, long-legged birds peck here in the sand: they are distinguished by their leg color: redshanks, greenshanks, and yellowlegs.

4. Bank trees. There are several clumps on the low banks that are seasonally flooded: willows and white poplars, occasionally matted with blackberry briars. Around the administration building are a number of imported species. Several types of woodpeckers and flycatchers nest in the tree hollows here. Look for lizards in the matted vegetation.

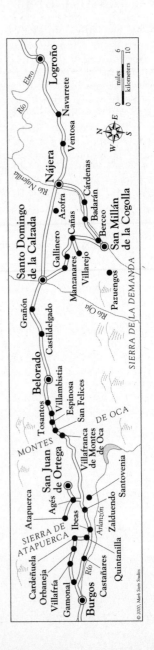

© 2000, Mark Stein Studios

5. Thickets of kermes oaks (*carrascas*). Thick, matted oaks in impenetrable tangles are the natural vegetation of this region. Thrushes and tits frequent these tangles, which are prominent on the low hill southeast of the reservoir.
6. Bush (*matorral*). This thrives on the steep, eroded, dry hillsides. The most common plants are thyme (*tomillo*), gorse (*aulaga*), aster (*jarilla*), and esparto (*Lygeum spartum*, aka *albardín*). This is a good area to look for larks and assorted snakes and lizards.
7. Cultivated areas. Grapevines, rye, and barley are the most prominent crops. You may see partridges or quail foraging among the stubble.
8. Pine groves. Reforestations have included maritime pines (*pinos carrascos*) and a few cyprus trees. Beginning in 1987 Logroño's Ayuntamiento has planted black poplars *(chopos)*, willows, lindens (*tilos*), and maples (*arces*). Look for bright yellow goldfinches and striped dull yellow serins.

✳ Hospital de San Juan de Acre The ruins of this hospice can be seen just before Navarrete on the west side of the *autopista*. María Ramírez, mother of the bishop of Osma, founded the hospice in 1185. It flourished through the Middle Ages and well into the 16th c. A 1568 report mentions a church, choir, atrium, and hospice, but adds that the hospice roof was in such bad repair that only the lower floor of the hospice was habitable, and that only 3 beds were available for pilgrims. Its destruction was finished off during the first Carlist War. In 1886 the portal of the hospice was rescued by moving it to the west end of Navarrete to serve as the entrance to the cemetery, where you will see it later on. When the hospice ruins were excavated in 1989–90, the floor plan revealed a typical small Romanesque church with a Gothic semi-octagonal apse, a combination unique in the Rioja.

✳ Navarrete

HISTORY
Navarrete is laid out in a semicircle of concentric streets around the foot of the hill called Cerro Tedeón, a pattern you will see later in Burgos, Castrogeriz, and other fortified, hill-clustering towns. An early fortified tower on the hilltop was enlarged and strengthened by Alfonso VIII ca. 1195. This king invested heavily in Navarrete and gave it a *fuero*. Although as a frequently disputed border town between Castilla and Navarra it was walled and castled, nothing remains, as the fortifications were destroyed in the early 16th c. in the war to incorporate Navarra into Spain (see ch. 25).
Navarrete is known for its wine and mushroom industries. Both utilize the numerous caves (*bodegas*) carved into the hill behind and under the town. Its ceramic industry has been important since Roman times.

PILGRIMAGE
As with many pilgrimage towns, the main street is the Santiago Road. In its exact center is the church of La Asunción. And, as in the wealthier pilgrimage towns, 17th- and 18th-c. mansions line the street. Pilgrims enter Navarrete through the Puerta de Santiago, with its 14th-c. image of **Santiago Matamoros**. Several of the city's streets preserve ancient buildings and covered arcades. In the Calle de la Cruz there is a reutilized capital from the Ermita de San Pedro which depicts 2 medieval knights and a squire, and which may represent the battle between Roland and the giant Ferragut (see ch. 31).

MONUMENTS: 1. **Iglesia de La Asunción**. 2. **Cemetery**.

1. **Iglesia de La Asunción**. If you have the misfortune to pass through Navarrete at an hour when the church is closed, you may be tempted to walk on. Resist the

temptation if you can! Wait for the church to open, or hunt up a key, because La Asunción contains one of the most stunning **Baroque retablos** in all of Spain.

The church was constructed over 2 earlier temples in 1583–1625 by Juan de Vallejo, a modernist schooled in the Burgos Cathedral. He brought Renaissance-style coffered barrel vaults and Plateresque decorative motifs to the Rioja for the first time. Its tower was begun in the 15th c. and not finished until well into the 18th. In the sacristy is an early-16th-c. triptych of the Assumption, attributed to Ysenbrant, which includes portraits of the donors. The church's 1702 image of Nuestra Señora del Sagrario reputedly contains a fragment of the True Cross. But all of this pales next to Navarrete's main retablo, executed 1694–98 by Fernando de la Peña.

📖 If you currently think that Baroque is not your favorite style, or if you find it so massive and confusing you don't know where to look first, we invite you to enjoy the visual feast in 6 steps:

Take in the whole. Stand in the middle of the church and see how the retablo is organized into streets (vertical) and rows (horizontal). Let its **structures lead your eyes** where they will. From mid-church the Navarrete retablo carries your eyes upward to the central panel of the Assumption of the Virgin, which gives the church its name. Here several triangular shapes urge your eyes toward the center. The pinnacle of the central niche that holds the image of the Virgin is one. The Virgin's white mantel is another. The twisted columns themselves, though they rise vertically from floor to vault, seem darker on the outsides, and lighter as your eyes travel toward the center. The painted panels, almost all of them featuring reds and blues, seem brighter toward the top. Now walk up close, right in front of the retablo, and see how it envelops you, from side to side and from top to bottom, and how now the lines lead your eyes to the figure of God the Father at the retablo's top.

Look at **the individual lines.** Baroque designers were fond of straight lines that were not exactly straight, creating tension or an interplay of forces. Here the vertical columns have a spiral, twisted form, and are wound with vines and covered with thick bunches of grapes (this type of column is called Solomonic, since people believed that they originated with Solomon's temple). The horizontal lines which separate the retablo's rows would be straight if you looked straight at them from midway up the back wall, but from floor level they are broken, zigzagging across the composition.

Look for **harmony and balance.** Here none of the individual architectural elements, or images, draws undue attention by being disproportionate to the others or dominant in size or texture. Instead there is a harmonious interplay of textures and tones: low- and high-relief images; painted and gilt surfaces; panels dominated by reds and blues, with the accenting whites and golds of the *putti* (the little angels); flat bare areas that reflect the light and thick encrustations of gold with sparkling highlights.

Look for **linking structural elements** that tie the retablo together. The Solomonic columns and zigzag horizontals are one. So are the freestanding, high-relief figures, placed in various parts of the retablo—high and low, right, left and center—to invite your eyes to consider them as a set. The low-relief panels have the same effect. Moreover, each of the panels has a similar structure, with figures on the left facing figures on the right, almost always converging in a triangular composition in the center.

Look at **the framing devices.** In the best Baroque, each individual area of focus is framed by the elements that surround it. And as the eye wanders outward it finds successive frames framing the internal sets of frames. Choose any panel, any statue. See how the gilt architectural elements, arranged symmetrically around a vertical axis, draw your eyes to the focal point. Pick a few more focal points of different sorts and see how the same framing principles apply. Curiously, at the same time that the architectural elements frame the images, in many cases the images also frame the architectural elements. In the best Baroque neither the frames nor the focal points dominate each other; rather, they combine in interlocking sets of harmonious constructions.

Look at **the details**. Let your eye wander from focal point to focal point: the clothing of the 3 Magi, the musical instruments of the angels in the Assumption panel. In the best Baroque retablos, both the architectural elements and the images will be finely detailed and interesting in and of themselves, so that almost any square-meter section could be hung by itself on a museum wall with pride.

The Navarrete ensemble offers a few special touches. The lateral retablos, at the end of the 2 aisles, seem to prolong the central retablo and contribute to the wraparound effect. Several things identify them as separate constructions: their columns have zigzag fluting instead of Solomonic spirals. Their colors are subtly different, as are their general organizing principles. Particularly fine is the crucified San Andrés, on the right, whose zigzag body plays off of the fluting of the columns. But, as with the best Baroque, they create tension through ambiguity: they both are part of the whole, and are not; both *sic et non*.

2. **Cemetery**. The cemetery was built in 1886 in the former suburb of Villarroya. The early-13th-c. Romanesque entrance came here from the Hospital de San Juan de Acre in 1886. The **historiated capitals** are extraordinary. One depicts the epic battle between Roland and the giant Ferragut (see ch. 31). On another, St. George slays the dragon of sin. Two depict **scenes of pilgrimage**: 2 pilgrims eating and drinking, and 1 pilgrim washing another's hair. Another shows a yoke of oxen plowing. Trashed in a corner of the cemetery behind the gate is the former monument to members of the Falange party from Navarrete who were killed before and during the 1936–9 Civil War (see ch. 24).

Near the cemetery is a monument by sculptor Miguel A. Sáinz to the pilgrim Alice de Craemer, who died in 1986 while cycling to Compostela.

👟 **Sotés** The Road passes to the right of this village, which is worth a short detour. Its 17th-c. Church of San Martín contains 4 superb Romanist **retablos**, a 13th- or 14th-c. **Romanesque Virgin**, and a graceful 18th-c. image of **Santiago Peregrino** with shells and crosses on his hat and cloak.

✱ Ventosa The parish church is dedicated to San Cernín.

✱ Alto de San Antón Six km. from Navarrete, the Road climbs over the Alto de San Antón (699 m.) where, to the right of the walking path, one still finds ruins of the medieval monastery and hospice of San Antón.

Along this trail you should be able to distinguish 2 sorts of oak trees: kermes oaks (*carrascas*) with spiny, leathery oval leaves almost like holly; and gall oaks (*quejigos*) with oval leaves bearing sawtooth indentations. The compact conical shrubs with wicked spines are juniper; you may see jays (*arrendajos*) and blackbirds (*mirlos*) feeding on their berries.

Looking southwest from these heights you can see the Sierra de San Lorenzo (2,262 m.) rising behind the valley of the Najerilla and the monastery of San

Millán de la Cogolla. The forested slopes of the Pico del Cuento (819 m.) to the north are the Dehesa de Navarrete, a regional nature preserve.

✴ Poyo de Roldán Two km. before the Yalde River, just prior to the road to Alesón, is the Poyo de Roldán (Poroldán), another of the sites identified as the place where Charlemagne's paladin Roland fought and slew the giant Ferragut. In one version of the legend, Roland killed the giant not with the dagger through the navel as per the CC *Turpin* (see ch. 31), but rather by heaving an enormous rock at him. In that version, the Poyo is that rock.

🥾 **Tricio** The marked entrance to Nájera is ugly, and we prefer a short detour to the south of the paved highway to the village of **Tricio**, built over the ruins of an ancient Iberian city. The Romans destroyed the city during the 2nd-c. conquest and built their own city of Tritium on the flats east of the hill. The city became important enough to mint coins there in the 2nd c. B.C.E. Some mosaics and funeral stones have been excavated near the Ermita of **Nuestra Señora de los Arcos**, a national monument incorporating numerous Roman architectural elements into its construction. A slit in the door allows you to look inside even when the monument is closed. A good flashlight makes viewing the details easier.

Tritium also produced fine red ceramics, local copies of the Italian Roman *sigillata* ware, so called for the embossed seals that identified the potter. Tritium's ceramics, stamped TSH, are found all over the Iberian Peninsula and even in other parts of Europe.

In Tricio in October of 1833 General Santos Ladrón de Cegama captained an uprising that began the first Carlist War in Navarra (see ch. 25). He was subsequently captured near Viana and executed in Pamplona.

31. NÁJERA

HISTORY

Nájera (from the Arabic meaning "between cliffs") is strategically located to control both the east-west Compostela Road and the fertile plains to the north. Orduño II of León and Sancho Garcés I of Navarra reconquered the region from the Muslims in 923. A Christian castle, built over Islamic and—judging by shards of pottery we have seen on the hilltop—Roman predecessors, crowned the summit of the jagged red hills west of the city. Navarra's King Sancho Garcés III el Mayor (1004–35), a great patron of the pilgrimage Road, favored Nájera for his court, and here he minted the first Christian coinage in reconquered Spain. Much of Spanish law derives from the charter (fuero) he issued to the town. The Rioja region was annexed to Castilla in 1076, when Fernando I divided his kingdom among his children. A bridge built across the Najerilla River ca. 1090 by San Juan de Ortega (over the remnants of an early Roman bridge) channeled commercial traffic through the city.

Nájera's history is intimately bound up with that of the Monasterio de Santa María that King García III el de Nájera (1035–54) founded in the mid-11th c. With his patronage it soon became one of the most prosperous in the region and the site of the Navarran royal tombs. The church also ranked as a cathedral. When Castilla captured the Rioja in 1076, an epic feud began. Castilian king Alfonso VI, at the urging of his wife Constance of Burgundy, donated the monastery with all its dependencies to the Benedictines of Cluny in 1079. The bishop of Nájera was so angry he transferred the bishopric physically to Calahorra, down the Ebro River toward Zaragoza, but he did not relinquish his claim on the Monastery of Santa María. The dispute percolated for centuries. When a later bishop of Calahorra requested the Pope's intervention and the Pontiff declined to act, the bishop accused Santa María's prior of the crime of simony. In 1163 the bishop personally invaded the monastery, assaulted several monks, and stripped the altars and the library of their valuables. The Pope responded by excommunicating the bishop, and the king of Navarra banned the bishop from entering his kingdom. Shortly after that, Castilla and Navarra went to war over La Rioja, and the new prior of Santa María profited by courting both sides. In 1214 Diego López de Haro, recognizing the near total ruin of the monastery, endowed a new building:

> Since we are so grieved to see how the majority of the monks of Nájera's church are ill, and have been living in want and misery for a long time, and have no prior or anyone else to look after them, for their benefit and sustenance we rebuild for them and donate to them our palace called the Enfermería. . . . [López de Haro; cited in Alvarez-Coca González, 25]

The monastery and the town alternated between prosperity and ruin. It was an important market town, which meant that throughout most of the Middle Ages the monastery profited because 25% of the profits of the weekly Thursday market went into the church's treasury. For a time Nájera had a sizable Jewish community, of whose neighborhood—located south of the monastery between the cliff and the river—nothing is left. In an extraordinary gesture of equanimity, Nájera's late-11th-c. fuero equalized the fines for killing a noble, a cleric, or a Jew at 250 sueldos (it only cost 100 sueldos to indemnify killing a commoner). But then in the 1368 dynastic wars Pedro I defeated Enrique II here (and by-the-by slaughtered most of Nájera's Jewish population); an official sent by Pedro confiscated the monastery's gold and silver to help pay the costs of the war. Although Santa María never regained its former wealth and prestige, in 1633 it still controlled 84 smaller monasteries in various parts of northern Spain. Some 40 years later, the Italian pilgrim Domenico Laffi had nothing but praise for Nájera:

> This is one of the finest towns to be seen in this region. It lies in a plain and has a broad river flowing through it. It is spanned by a fine bridge connecting two parts of the town on the west side. There is a very steep hill, all of bare rock, which overshadows the town in such a way that half of it is sheltered from rain and sun, except until about mid-day. It is a really beautiful place and well supplied with everything. They are busy all day constructing many buildings, together with churches. There are three squares. [Laffi; trans. Hall (1997), 128]

During the 19th-c. War of Independence, the city was sacked by the French. In the 1970s and 1980s it boomed again as the center of a thriving furniture-making industry. But in the 1990s, as the factories close, Nájera again seems to be falling into hard times.

📖 The Neoclassic poet Esteban Manuel de Villegas (d. 1669) was from Nájera. His collection of poems entitled *Eróticas o Amatorias* (Nájera: 1628) introduced the sapphic verse form into Spain.

PILGRIMAGE

Although at one time Nájera had 2 churches dedicated to Santiago, neither survives. Nájera supported several pilgrim hospices. San Lázaro, located near the bridge and administered by the monks of San Millán de la Cogolla, originally cared for lepers and continued in operation until the 19th c. The Hospital de la Abadía was founded in 1055. The German traveler Künig von Vach, who visited Nájera late in the 15th c., had mixed reactions to local hospitality:

> There they give willingly for the love of God. In the hospices you can have everything you want, except in the Hospital de Santiago: there the people are very mocking. The women in the hospice yell at the pilgrims a lot. But the food is good.

French pilgrims tended to associate Roland's legendary defeat of Ferragut with Nájera. The events are narrated in detail in chapter 17 of the 12th-c. CC *Turpin*.

📖 In brief, Roland's defeat of Ferragut: The emir of Babylonia had sent 20,000 Turks and the giant Ferragut, who was of the race of Goliath, stood 7 m. high, and had the strength of 40 men, to combat Charlemagne in Spain. Ferragut rode out of Nájera and challenged the French to put up their best knight in single combat against him. Ferragut seized Ogier, the first to try, and dragged him back to the city. Another 20 similarly failed. Then Roland himself begged to try his luck. They furiously fought for 3 days, marked by periods of truce and amicable conversation about their professed religions. Ferragut let slip that his only vulnerable point was his navel. At last the two agreed to fight a final time, with the winner to be whichever of them professed the true religion. Ferragut fell on Roland, thinking to crush him with his weight, but the French hero stuck him with his dagger—guess where. When Ferragut died, Roland successfully captured Nájera and released the Christian prisoners.

MONUMENTS: 1. **Monasterio de Santa María la Real.** 2. Iglesia de Santa Cruz. 3. Iglesia de San Miguel. 4. Iglesia de Santa Elena.

1. Monasterio de Santa María la Real. In 1044 Navarran king García III was hunting along the banks of the Río Najerilla. His falcon pursued a dove into one of the caves in the mountainside. When the King followed, he saw a strange light emanating from the deep recesses of the cave. Exploring, he found nestled against the cliffs an ancient wood sculpture of the Virgin Mary with a bell and a vase with fresh lilies at her feet. García ordered a chapel to be built, and later a church and monastery, to whose consecration in 1052 came the kings of Castilla, León, Aragón, and Sobrarbe, the count of Barcelona, the bishops of Narbonne, Pamplona, Alava, Nájera, and sundry lesser folk. Of this early church, only 1 capital and 2 windows remain. Also in the 11ᵗʰ c. the relics of the Cordoban saint Colomba were brought to the monastery. Like most Spanish monasteries, Santa María was abandoned in 1835. Since 1895 it has been entrusted to the Franciscans, who have been responsible for the reconstruction of the current building complex, which for the most part dates from the 15ᵗʰ c.

Exterior:
• King García said, "Build me a church," and geography dictated the rest. The monastery's exterior is undistinguished. The remaining bits of the early Romanesque apse are on the monastery's southwest corner against the cliff. You can see 2 windows, 1 with a semicircular Romanesque arch and 1 with a keyhole Mozárabe arch.
• A spacious patio on the east side of the church today serves as the principal entrance.

Interior:
A doorway from the patio takes you into a modern corridor that served as our dormitory during our 1979 pilgrimage. Now there is a ticket booth. Eventually the corridor will lead you to the Claustro de los Caballeros, and from there to the church and caves.
• A *trompe l'oeil* painted **Renaissance dome** caps the stairwell at the entrance to the cloister. Look closely at its three-dimensionality, and you will see that it hasn't any. The pelican in its center is a symbol of Christ's sacrifice. A polychrome Hapsburg 2-headed eagle adorns the door to the cloister.
• The **Claustro de los Caballeros** (Knights' Cloister; early 16ᵗʰ c.) contains some of the most delicate, innovative late Gothic stone **filigree work** in Spain. Each arch is decorated with a different lacy pattern. The patterns cast by sunlight against the cloister walls are striking. As you walk you will see the tombs of many nobles.
• On one wall of the cloister the **tomb of Mencía López de Haro** (ca. 1280) faithfully depicts her lavish clothing and a procession of professional mourners, or *plañideras*. Diego López de Haro's tomb (ca. 1240) depicts monks and elegant courtiers in a burial procession.
• An intricately carved Plateresque wooden door leads from the cloister to the church.

The church itself has 3 principal areas worth visiting: the cave and pantheon, the main altar, and the high choir.
• **The cave.** Go past the tombs all the way into the cave and admire its red conglomerate rock shot through with veins of white quartz. At its deepest point you will see a vase of lilies and a copy of the statue of the Virgen de la Rosa. This is where King García III found the original vase and statue.
• **Pantheon of the Navarran Kings.** In the 16ᵗʰ c. a Plateresque pantheon was

constructed to hold the 30 tombs. The tombs themselves date from the 10th to
the 13th c. They include the tombs of:

—King Sancho Abarca (970–994; second on right as you face the door).
He fought against both Almanzor and Conde Fernán González, the founder
of Castilla. His queen was doña Urraca, daughter of Fernán González.

—King Sancho VI el Sabio (d. 1194; fifth from right). Known as a builder,
after the reconquest of the north from the Muslims he repopulated Estella
and Pamplona, as well as several other important northern cities like San
Sebastián, Laguardia, and Vitoria.

—King García III el de Nájera (1035–54; first on left). He founded this
monastery and at one point controlled all of the Rioja, Navarra, the Basque
Provinces, and parts of Burgos, Soria, Zaragoza, and Huesca. He founded
Spain's first military order, the Orden Militar de los Caballeros de la Terraza,
named to honor the vase of lilies that he had found in the cave. He died in
the battle of Atapuerca against his brother Fernando, king of Castilla.

> 📖 Although the Order of La Terraza never amounted to much—prob-
> ably because Navarra was soon cut out of the Reconquest efforts by
> Aragón and Castilla, who formed a joint border to Navarra's south—3
> other military-religious orders, all organized in the 12th c., played crucial
> roles in the Christians' drive south.
>
> The Orden de Calatrava, organized in 1158 by King Sancho III and
> Raymond, abbot of the Cistercian abbey of Fítero, was instrumental in
> the conquest of Andalucía. In recompense, the Castilian monarchs dele-
> gated vast stretches of the newly conquered lands for the Order to admin-
> ister in the Crown's name, which insured that Calatrava would become
> one of the wealthiest and most politically powerful associations of nobles
> on the Peninsula.
>
> Another group, formed in the mid-12th c., was confirmed in 1177 as
> the Order of San Julián del Pereiro. In 1218 its name changed to the
> Order of Alcántara, when that strategic bridgetown fell to the Christians.
> It became one of the most potent forces in Extremadura.
>
> A third group, which coalesced in the 1160s, eventually became
> known as the Order of Santiago (see ch. 60). Its administrative center in
> León made it a force in Castilla la Vieja, and its castle in Uclés, delegated
> to it in 1175 by Alfonso VIII, led to the Order's dominance in the lower
> *Meseta* of Castilla la Nueva.
>
> Members of all these Orders called themselves *frailes* and took monk-
> like vows of chastity, poverty, and obedience, none of which they took
> very seriously. Each of the military Orders elected a master (*maestre*) and
> several commanders (*comendadores*), positions which soon became
> hereditary. The Orders were the most powerful political and military
> force in Spain until Fernando de Aragón personally assumed the master-
> ships in the late 15th c. in his drive to concentrate power in the Crown.

—King Sancho IV el de Peñalén (1054–76; second on left). He substituted
the Roman liturgy for the Mozarabic rite (see ch. 7), reconquered much of
Zaragoza, and died at the hand of his brother Ramón, who threw him off a
cliff in Peñalén (now Funes, Navarra).

—King Ramiro García, son of García el de Nájera (fourth on left). This
man's son married one of the Cid's daughters.

• **Doña Blanca's tomb.** The best tomb, now relocated to a prominent spot in
front of the pantheon, is the **tomb of doña Blanca de Navarra.**

📖 García Ramírez el Restaurador's daughter Blanca was born in 1135 and was destined to live as a pawn in the dynastic politics of the age. Engaged at age 5 to Prince Sancho of Castilla and then at age 14 to King Ramón Berenguer of Aragón, she was nonetheless married to Sancho at age 16. She died 5 years later giving birth to Castilla's future king Alfonso VIII.

One side depicts the parable of the wise and foolish virgins, the Magi, the judgment of Solomon, and the Slaughter of the Innocents. The other side features a Pantocrator (Christ as judge; rarely found on tombs), around which are grouped the Tetramorphos and Apostles, together with the dying queen and the royal family. Contrast the static scene of the slaughter (hieratic expressions: no trace of grief or pain; no attempt at perspective) with the incipient perspective of the scene of the Queen's death (angel behind the bed, in front of the tree). The best parts of the tomb may well be the work of the Burgundian sculptor Leodegarius, who worked in Sangüesa and carved nearby Logroño's image of Nuestra Señora del Palacio.

• The main altar. The 18th-c. Baroque *retablo mayor* depicts the miracle of the Virgin in the cave and **Saints Benito** and **Escolástica** (founders, respectively, of the male and female orders of Benedictines), with monarchs kneeling. The central **sculpture of the Virgin** is reputed to be the one found by don García in 1044. The golden, jewel-studded crown it bore for centuries has long since disappeared (1 ruby is now in the crown of the Queen of England), and the current, stylized wood crown dates from 1948.

• The **high choir**. The high choir is located on the level above the caves. In 1998 it was open to the public during only 2 brief periods each day. But those periods are worth waiting for. The wood **choir stalls**, dating from the last years of the 15th c., were probably executed by Andrés and Juan de Nájera, or possibly by the Amutio brothers, new-Christians (i.e., of Jewish descent) who worked in the region. Over the door to the choir stalls the 3 young men in Jewish dress are considered to include self-portraits of the artists. Another Jewish reminiscence are the shields with the crossed circumcision knives (seat 23). The extraordinary choir is a transitional work, with Renaissance low-relief carving of saints and Old Testament figures in classic poses set into complex late Gothic **tracery**, different on each seat back. Over the abbot's chair stands the imposing figure of King García el de Nájera. Note also the rich misericords, the half-seats against which the monks rested while singing the holy offices. While individualized portraiture is rare in Gothic choir stalls, there are several good examples in Nájera: the 2 black men in one of the upper friezes and the portrait of a nobleman on one of the misericords.

2. Iglesia de Santa Cruz. Founded in 1052, the current church was consecrated in 1611 and was later reconstructed. Its sacristy houses a 13th-c. Gothic crucifix.

3. Iglesia de San Miguel. Built in 1489, it now houses the Casa de Cultura.

4. Iglesia de Santa Elena. 16th c., has a splendid Baroque **retablo**, with a central image of 4th-c. ruler Constantine's mother, Saint Helena (Santa Elena).

32. NÁJERA → SAN MILLÁN DE LA COGOLLA

During most of the Middle Ages there were 2 principal routes from Nájera west. One proceeded more or less directly to Santo Domingo de la Calzada. The second detoured to the south to visit the important relics at the monastery of San Millán de la Cogolla before veering back to Santo Domingo de la Calzada. We much prefer this second choice. San Millán's architectural monuments are superb. The literature produced there by the 13th-c. monk Gonzalo de Berceo is the most important written in Spain in that century. The site is idyllic and well worth lengthening your pilgrimage by a day—or maybe more, if you take advantage of all that San Millán has to offer.

To complicate matters further, there are 2 routes leading to San Millán from Nájera (described in this chapter). There are also 2 routes from San Millán to Santo Domingo (described in ch. 35). And—wouldn't you guess?—there are 2 ways of reaching Santo Domingo directly from Nájera (described in ch. 34).

Route 1: Nájera → Cordovín → Berceo → SAN MILLÁN DE LA COGOLLA

The shortest and most scenic walking route follows the Najerilla River south past the caves along the cliff, then turns west at the first creek, the Río Cordovín, that enters the Najerilla. A dirt road follows the north bank of the creek to the village of Cordovín. Exit toward the southwest by the cemetery and, once you have gained the heights, strike out southwest through the wheat fields toward the notch in the Sierra de San Lorenzo that shelters the 2 monasteries of San Millán.

Route 2: NÁJERA → Cárdenas → Badarán → Berceo → SAN MILLÁN DE LA COGOLLA

This route follows the Najerilla upstream for 6 km. until it is bridged by the paved road that leads west to San Millán through the towns of Badarán and Berceo.

✸ **Badarán** The main street contains several 16th- and 17th-c. mansions with coats of arms. The parish church of La Expectación, built early in the 17th c. and restored in this century, contains a Baroque retablo. Some scattered Roman remains lie on a hill over the town called—not inappropriately—Sobrevilla.

This is good wine country. The family vineyards that line both sides of this road are planted with both *garnacha* and Spain's native *tempranillo* vines. If you pass through here very early in the spring you may see farmers pruning the vines and gathering up the cut twigs (called *sarmientos*) to use as firewood. If you hike a little later, you will notice the waxy green new leaves sparkling in the sunlight. If you come in the fall you will see how the *garnacha* leaves turn bright red and the *tempranillo* leaves bright yellow. And you may see the farmers handpicking the tiny blue grapes and putting them into flat crates or baskets. In all of the villages in this region you will see cavelike family wine cellars cut into the hillsides near, and sometimes under, the towns.

The fertile soil and the year-round river that parallels the paved road on the south have made this valley prime farmland for at least 2,000 years. Approximately halfway to Berceo, at the point where a dirt farm road intersects the paved road from the right, is the site of a former Roman villa of which nothing is left but a few scattered potsherds.

✳ Berceo The late-18th- or early-19th-c. church of Santa Eulalia has an 18th-c. painting of **Santiago Matamoros** in one of the lateral chapels. The village's other monument is the 17th-c. Ermita de Santa Potamia, one of San Millán's disciples. Her relics now repose in the monastery of San Millán de Yuso.

33. SAN MILLÁN DE LA COGOLLA

HISTORY
The Saint
According to his biographer San Braulio, San Millán was born in 473 in the village of Berceo. As a young shepherd he heard God's call and had a vision in which his zither became a pen and the mountainous landscape of the Sierra de la Demanda to the south became God's beautiful kingdom. He was tutored by San Felices and, after a brief stint as a priest during which he gave away most of his church's assets, he retired to a cave to be a hermit. His fame as a holy man spread, and the cave soon became a pilgrimage site where Millán worked many miracles, multiplying bread to feed the crowds of worshipers, exorcising demons, and the like. Bishop Dídimo of Tarazona, who had ordained him priest, asked him at age 70 to take on parish duties, but Millán preferred the solitary life of his cave, where he died at age 101 and was buried.

The Monasteries
The first small monastery at the site of San Millán's hillside cave may have been built during the Saint's life. In any case, by the year 640 a small religious community was housed there, and over the next 2 centuries the community grew and prospered. Though from ca. 750–923 the region was under Muslim control, Christian institutions continued in relative peace, and manuscripts from the monastery's scriptorium from that period still exist.

In 923 Kings Sancho Garcés I of Pamplona and Ordoño II of León wrested the region from the Muslims, fortified the frontier, and donated properties to the monastery of San Millán de la Cogolla. Fernán González, in his struggles to carve Castilla from León, did likewise. Competition between Castilla and Navarra resulted in San Millán's accruing many lands, vineyards, villages, as well as fishing, lumbering, and pasturage rights. The new kingdom of Castilla adopted San Millán as a kind of patron, and by the end of the 10th c. the monastery, enlarged with new stone buildings, was the most prestigious religious institution in the region. Its cattle grazed all over La Rioja. Its scriptorium produced splendid manuscripts like the *Codice emilianense de los Concilios*, written in 992, whose 476 illuminated folios are now in the Escorial. It attracted pilgrims, and donors fought to be buried close to the Saint's cave. When the Muslim chief Almanzor raided northern Christian strongholds, San Millán was a prime target. It went up in smoke in the summer of 1002.

The *wazir* Muhammad ibn Abu 'Amir rose to power in a chaotic dynastic struggle in the Caliphate of Córdoba ca. 976. With an army of Berber troops and Mozarabic Christian mercenaries, over the next 26 years he led a total of 52 expeditions against the Christian kingdoms of the north. For his successes he was given the nickname "Victorious through Allah" (*al-Mansur bi-Allah*, which the Christians shortened to Almanzor). For the most part these raids were not political or religious wars: they were sallies in search of booty; and demonstrations of power to extort protection money (*parias*). In the 10th and 11th c. almost all the wars and alliances between Christians and Muslims had to do with issues of power or money. In fact, in return for an annual fee, Almanzor lent Bermudo II of León Cordoban troops for his struggles against Ramiro III. Sancho II of Navarra hoped to protect his kingdom by sending one of his daughters to be Almanzor's wife, even though she had to convert to Islam. And Almanzor's own rebel son took refuge, and sought support, in Christian Castilla.

Almanzor raided the richest targets of Iberian Christendom. In 985 he swept up the Mediterranean coast and burned Barcelona. In 987 he laid waste to Coimbra, León, Zamora, and Sahagún. In 997 he pillaged Santiago de Compostela, dismantling the wood cathedral doors to use for shipbuilding, and carrying off the bells to hang in the great mosque in Córdoba. In 1000 he plundered Burgos. His 1002 raid on La Rioja was his last great expedition, for he died of illness later that year in Medinaceli. Almanzor's triumphs were the swan song of the Cordoban Caliphate, for soon after the warlord's death al-Andalus broke up into competitive small states known as *taifas* (whose boundaries for the most part are reflected today in the individual provinces of the southern half of the Iberian Peninsula: Sevilla, Cádiz, Badajoz, Almería, etc.). He also changed the face of northern Spain. After his death, power—and the income from *parias*—began to shift to the Christian kingdoms. In the 11th c. everything that Almanzor had destroyed had to be rebuilt, which explains why you will see so much Romanesque architecture along the pilgrimage Road.

Rebuilding San Millán was a high priority. In 1030 Sancho III commissioned a new silver ark for the relics of the Saint and ordered the monks to adopt the rule of San Benito. In 1052 a 9-year-old girl named Oria [Aurea] from the village of Villavelayo took up residence in a tiny cave next to Millán's shrine. She reported numerous visions of the Virgin. By the time of her death ca. 1069, when local witnesses swore she had been taken to heaven by Saints Agueda, Cecilia, and Eulalia, Oria had become revered locally as a saint for her humility and her self-inflicted suffering. Her relics lay on the monastery's altar until the invading French army stole them in 1809.

The 11th c. in Europe was the apex of both pilgrimage and organized monasticism. Legend has it that King García III el de Nájera tried to remove San Millán's relics to Nájera, where they would be more accessible to pilgrims, but miraculously they would not budge (version 1: they became as heavy as stone; version 2: the oxen drawing the cart with the reliquary would not go beyond the valley; persuasive version 3: he met armed resistance). The abbot Domingo, who had opposed both the King's program of monastic reform and his desire to remove the relics to Nájera, was forced to leave San Millán for the more remote monastery of Silos in Castilla. In his *Vida de Santo Domingo de Silos*, the poet-monk Gonzalo de Berceo (see below) gives voice to the community's displeasure with the royal attempt to strip San Millán of its most precious possession:

Rei, bien te consejo como atal sennor	King, I advise you to act like a king;
non quieras toller nada al sancto confessor,	don't try to steal from the holy confessor;
de lo que ofrecist non seas robador:	don't rob what you yourself donated:
si non, veer non puedes la faz del Creador.	if not, you'll never see the Creator's face. (stanza 154)

Even though he forced the Abbot out, the miracle impressed the King, who ordered a splendid new monastery—Yuso—to be built in the valley. The monks consecrated Yuso in 1067 and placed Millán's relics on the altar in a new gold-and-ivory ark.

The old Visigothic world of mountain hermits was gone. The new world of Roman liturgy, international Romanesque art, Roman script, and monastic prosperity was at hand. The region boomed. Gold, paid by the Muslims as *parias* to keep the Christian armies from destroying their lands, financed new churches all over La Rioja. In 1090 San Millán acquired the relics of San Felices from Bilbao and commissioned another gold-and-ivory ark. Donations of all sorts poured in: 46 separate donations from 925 to 1025, and 765 donations over the next hundred years.

But by the beginning of the 13th c. the boom was over. The strategic frontier had moved south, and the royal families invested elsewhere. From 1125 to 1225 San Millán received only 55 donations. Lawsuits between the sees of Calahorra, Nájera, and Burgos stripped San Millán of many assets. Other local shrines—Silos, Abelda, and Valvanera—vied with San Millán de la Cogolla for patronage. Although there was another brief period of boom in the 16th and 17th c., the glory days had passed. The early-19th-c. *desamortización* broke up the remaining holdings and the library.

 The *desamortización* (expropriation, or disentailment) of Church property was a product of the violent clashes between liberal-monarchists and conservative Catholic regionalists that also plunged Spain into the chaos of the Carlist Wars (see ch. 25). From the time of the Cortes de Cadiz (1810–14) attempts had been made to return unproductive landed estates, both religious and civil, to productive use and ownership by the farmers themselves. Early in 1835 the liberal minister Martínez de la Rosa banished the Jesuits. His successor, Juan Alvarez Mendizábal, an archliberal economist and Mason, decided to salvage the nearly bankrupt nation by banishing all the major religious orders (except those running hospitals or schools) and seizing their property. Within a short time the monastic cloisters were empty, and much of the national artistic patrimony had been put on the auction block, to the enrichment of museums and private collectors all over the world. Many of the working monasteries you will visit have been revived in the last 130 years or so, frequently by communities of monks or nuns of different Orders from the ones who were evicted in the 1830s. The last in the series of 19th-c. expropriation laws was promulgated in 1860. Some of the monasteries' artistic wealth was fortunately preserved *in situ*, some has been partially reassembled at great cost, some has been approximated by analogous collections, and some is just lost forever.

When the Augustinian Order was assigned responsibility for San Millán de la Cogolla in 1878, little remained. When we visited in 1974 only 12 monks were left of a community that at its medieval peak had counted 20 times that number. During our 1987 visit one of the 12 died, and an old woman in the village sang us this irreverent ditty: *Muere el monjito, dicen los demás: una queja menos, una ración más* ("One little monk dies, and the rest declare: that's one less mouth to gripe, and one more meal to share"). In the 1990s the monks gave a 99-year lease on part of the monastery to a major hotel chain. In return they got a general overhaul of the whole crumbling complex, including hot running water in their cells for the first time in more than 1,300 years.

Gonzalo de Berceo

This monk held several administrative posts in San Millán de la Cogolla. We know him as the most famous poet of Spain's 13th c. His works in rhymed Castilian quartets are religious monuments of significant literary merit. They provide a splendid introduction to medieval Spanish spirituality. They also reflect the fiscal and political concerns of his monastery. Berceo's *Vida de San Millán* (written ca. 1228–46) followed Braulio's version of the Saint's life, but also stressed the debt of gratitude—and annual contributions—owed for Millán's helping Fernán González best the Moors. His biographies of Santo Domingo de Silos and Santa Oria built the reputation of his monastery as a pilgrimage site in its own right, well worth a detour from the main Compostela pilgrimage Road. His Spanish rendition of miracles attributed to Mary, the *Milagros de Nuestra Señora*, begins with a lyrical, allegorical description of earthly paradise.

Yo maestro Gonçalvo de Verceo nomnado,	I, Master Gonzalo, of Berceo
yendo en romería caecí en un prado,	while on pilgrimage happened upon a meadow,
verde y bien sencido, de flores bien poblado,	green and sweet smelling, filled with flowers,
logar cobdiciaduero pora omne cansado.	a desirable place for an exhausted man. (stanza 2)

The Riojan Eden that he describes detail by detail over the next 13 stanzas strikes us as very much like the meadows a couple of km. upstream from the monastery where we always spend at least a day reading from Berceo's works and washing our clothes.

Berceo's poems are written in an artfully naïve style, salted with local vocabulary and local color. His self-consciousness and his pride in himself as a poet in the Castilian language are both new factors in medieval Iberian poetry. Also, like a good native son of La Rioja, he was fond of the local wine.

Quiero fer una prosa en román paladino,	I want to tell a story in common Romance,
en cual suele el pueblo fablar con so vezino;	the language folks use to talk to their neighbors
ca non so tan letrado por fer otro latino.	for I am not so learned to be able to write in Latin.
Bien valdrá, como creo, un vaso de bon vino.	I believe it is worth a glass of good wine.
	(*Vida de Santo Domingo*, stanza 2)

MONUMENTS: 1. **Suso**. 2. **Yuso**.

1. **Monasterio de Suso**. Built to incorporate the caves of the hermits San Millán and Santa Oria, **San Millán de Suso's** construction spans 7 centuries. A small Visigothic temple enclosed the caves perhaps as early as the 6th c.; it was expanded into a pre-Romanesque 2-nave basilica, consecrated in 959. Sacked and burned by Almanzor in 1002, the basilica was enlarged by Sancho III el Mayor early in the 11th c. You should make sure to see:
• The front porch with tombs overlooking the valley. The front row of tombs contains the bodies, but not the heads, of the 7 Infantes [Princes] de Lara.

📖 The Infantes were victims of a famous family feud at the time of Castilla's 10th-c. secession from León. Their uncle treacherously betrayed the 7 sons and their tutor to the Muslims, who cut off their heads and presented them for identification to their already imprisoned father. Later a half brother of the princes avenged their death by slaying the uncle. This tale is a favorite subject of Spanish medieval balladry. Historians long debated if the story was true, and if the Infantes were buried here or in nearby Salas. In the late 16th c. both sets of tombs were opened: in San Millán they reputedly found 7 headless bodies, and in Salas 7 bodiless heads wrapped in cloth.

The **reutilized Roman tomb** in the center holds the body of the Infantes' tutor, Nuño Salido. The remaining 3 tombs reputedly held 3 Navarran queens: Toda, wife of Sancho Garcés I (905–25); Jimena, wife of García Sánchez el Temblón (994–1000); and Elvira (Mayora) wife of Sancho III (1000–35).
• The doorway from the porch to the naves is flanked by 2 **marble capitals** in Islamic style, most likely reutilized from some other site.
• The southernmost caves, used from the 6th c. by monks as living quarters, were later reutilized as a **cemetery**.
• The central cave contains an *oratorio* (prayer chapel) of San Millán, a tri-lobed Visigothic altar niche, and the Saint's early-12th-c. <u>**Romanesque tomb**</u>, one of Spain's finest. Note the idealized reclining figure of the 101-year-old Saint, the Visigothic-style sacramental robes with the unusual cross (repeated in the valley on Yuso's Baroque main portal), and the monastery escutcheon. Four angels guard the tomb corners. The seated, bearded figure with a book open on a bookstand may well be San Braulio, Millán's biographer. The other human figures represent people who, according to Braulio, were miraculously aided by the Saint: a blind man whose vision was restored and a child brought back from death. The tomb appears to be by 2 hands: Millán and Braulio are clearly indi-vidualized, while the other figures are treated more generically (long, straight noses; small foreheads; round, pupil-less, protuberant eyes).
• The north cave houses the Chapel of Santa Oria. There is a small window grille through which visitors passed food to her.
• The 2-nave basilica has **domed apses** constructed in the style of the Mosque of Córdoba. King Sancho III had the naves extended in the 11th c., curving them to fit the contour of the mountain. The **horseshoe arches** were probably built by Mozarabic workmen. On the doorway to the apse is some of the calcium fused by Almanzor's 1002 fire. Blue Talavera tiles highlight an ancient fragment of a wooden **beam**.

📖 According to legend, when monastery workmen were building a silo they cut one piece of precious timber too short. San Millán sent them to lunch, and when they returned it had grown to the required length (echoing the miracle attributed to Jesus in the apocryphal Gospel of the Infancy of Jesus, attributed to St. Thomas). Touching it is reputed to effect cures.

2. **Monasterio de Yuso.** Nothing is left of the original Romanesque monastery, built when King García el de Nájera moved the monks down the mountain from Suso in the mid-11th c. The current Renaissance monastery of **San Millán de Yuso** is often called the Escorial of the Rioja. The nucleus was built from 1504 to 1540, with a cloister added in 1554. Mountain runoff caused the church's north chapels to fall in 1595. A century later saw extensive remodeling in the Baroque style: the

tower (1633–7); Pablo de Basave de Marquina's Baroque façade (1642); the monumental staircase and the Salón de los Reyes (Monarchs' Hall; ca. 1690).

Exterior:
- The huge plaza was added from 1698 to 1752 as a protective measure.
- The exterior façade is adorned with a 1689 statue of a mounted San Millán slaying Moors. The serrated sword and Benedictine habit distinguish him from Santiago.

Interior:
- The **Salón de los Reyes,** the first room visited on the standard tour, displays paintings by Fray Juan Ricci (ca. 1653) of 4 major benefactors of San Millán de la Cogolla: Fernán González, who authorized the *voto de San Millán* that taxed the kingdom annually for the monastery; Sancho el Mayor, who made major donations; García el de Nájera, considered the founder of the monastery of San Millán; and Alfonso VII of Castilla, another major donor.

  Three plaques on the wall contain quotations from the *Glosas emilianenses.* These earliest written examples of both the post-Latin Spanish and Basque languages were found as translations and notes in the pages of some of the monastery's 10th-c. manuscripts.
- The church is more interesting for what it contains than for its architecture.

  —The **painting on the main altar's retablo** depicts San Millán in the battle of Hacinas helping Fernán González to slay Moors. They are surrounded by Saints Ildefonso, Domingo de Silos, Oria, and Gertrudis. Ricci's depiction of the **Assumption** shows how well he had assimilated the palate, composition, dramatic gestures, and drapery of El Greco. The predella depicts the legend of King García el de Nájera's abortive attempt to transfer San Millán's relics.

  —The richly carved 16th-c. walnut **pulpit.**

  —The 1640 choir stalls.

  —The choir's 1676 large, ornate *reja* (iron grille) by Sebastián de Medina.

  —Francisco Bisou's 1767 Rococo *trascoro* that divided the lay public from the worshipping monks. It contains 8 superb statues of saints related to Millán: Braulio (his biographer); Felices (his teacher); Aselo, Geroncio, Citonato, Sofronio, and Potamia (his disciples); and Oria (with a tower and a dove she saw in one of her visions).

  —The Baroque **sacristy,** whose retablo is dedicated to Nuestra Señora de los Angeles, surrounded by angels and the saints whose writings established various points of doctrine relating to the Virgin (Ildefonso, Anselmo, Bernardo, and Ruperto). Four youngsters with cornucopias offer the Virgin the products of the 4 seasons of the year.

  —Capilla del Rosario. Ricci's paintings include the Virgin of the Rosary and Christ presenting the rosary to Saints Benito and Miguel Florentino; Santo Domingo de Silos freeing captives; and San Benito with his disciples Saints Plácido and Mauro.

In the rest of the monastery complex, you will want to see:
- The cloister, built in transitional Gothic-Plateresque style by Andrés de Rodi, was never finished, although the doorway is dated 1554. Largely mediocre paintings narrate in great detail the life of San Millán.
- The library, formerly one of northern Spain's best, was scattered in the 19th-c. *desamortización* and now houses a small, painfully reassembled collection.
- The museum, containing extraordinary Mozarabic **reliquaries** commissioned by Abbot Blas in the late 11th c. French soldiers despoiled the reliquaries in 1809. Many precious stones and ivory panels were lost, while other ivory pan-

els eventually landed in museums in St. Petersburg, Berlin, Florence, Washington, and New York.

    —The **Arca de San Felices** probably dates from the late 11th c. Four ivory tablets depict scenes from the life of Christ.

    —The <u>Arca de San Millán</u>, funded by King Sancho Garcés IV of Navarra in 1067. Though the style is Germanic (and the St. Petersburg plaque gives the artisan's name as Engleman, working with his son Rodolfo), the horseshoe arches are clearly Spanish. The Pantocrator on the front includes 2 kneeling men at prayer: Abbot Blas and the chronicler Friar Munio. The 22 ivory plaques are remarkable for their narrative detail about San Millán's life and miracles as reported by San Braulio.

  📖 The stories on the ivory plaques:

1. An angel indicates to the sleeping Millán the road he must take to visit San Felices; smiling Felices invites Millán to rise, in an act of humility blessed by the hand of God.

2. Millán warns the citizens of Cantabria (near Logroño; see ch. 28) of the upcoming destruction of their city by King Leovigildo. In the second panel he prepares to decapitate Abundancio, who had scoffed at Millán's prophesies.

3. An angel tells Millán of his impending death. Disciples lay him in his tomb.

4. A disgruntled man complains that there is no food for the minions whom Millán has told to stop and pray, and Millán asks God's help. The lower panel is divided: one scene depicts the food miraculously provided; the second shows a young child, resurrected from death by Millán's intercession, playing with the altar mantel to the astonishment of her parents.

5. A demon, expelled from a penitent's home by Millán's intervention, reacts by throwing stones. The exorcised couple act with gestures of surprise uncommonly expressive for early Romanesque art.

6. The bed of the sleeping Millán is set afire by demons, who in the second panel beat each other with clubs as a smiling, wakened Millán looks on.

7. Blind penitents reverently approach Millán's tomb. In the lower panel a priest cures Eufrasia's blindness by applying oil from the Saint's lamp.

8. The Saint's gesture cures the kneeling paralytic Barbara. Below, we see her standing with a gesture expressing gratitude.

9. With his staff the Saint drives a devil from the mouth of a deacon; below, the grateful penitent kisses Millán's hand.

10. The Saint feeds a prayerful crowd by multiplying the meager food at hand. The second panel depicts the same miracle.

11. The Saint, surrounded by his disciples Saints Aselo, Eroncio, and Sofronio, offers mass.

12. The Devil rebukes aged Millán for living with women; Millán defeats the Devil in a wrestling match near Suso.

13. Two thieves steal Millán's horse; they are struck blind, and return the horse.

34. NÁJERA → SANTO DOMINGO
DE LA CALZADA

Route 1: NÁJERA → Azofra → SANTO DOMINGO DE LA CALZADA

Route 2: NÁJERA → Azofra → Alesanco → **Cañas** → SANTO DOMINGO DE LA CALZADA

Route 1. This is the one-day route marked out for modern pilgrims.

✳ Azofra Near Azofra took place the (perhaps legendary) battle in the early 960s between Count Fernán González, the founder of Castilla, and King Sancho de Navarra.

Azofra is a somewhat atypical Road town, for it has 2 long main streets. One, arching by the church, is the pre-12th-c. pilgrimage Road. It was superseded by the second, which is now the highway. No traces are left of the church of San Pedro, its cemetery, nor of the town's 12th-c. pilgrim hospice, founded by a doña Isabel in 1168.

Azofra's current church of Nuestra Señora de los Angeles, which was formerly used for pilgrim burials, has a nice floral Flamboyant Gothic vault and contains images of the pilgrims San Roque and **Santiago**. As we write, it is undergoing restoration.

Two houses near at the west edge of the village have enormous Baroque coats of arms. On the other side of the road is a 1975 monument to the Virgen de Valvanera, who is venerated in a monastery some 30 km. to the south. Just beyond on the right is a pilgrims' fountain.

Route 2. We suggest that you detour through Cañas, which has a superb Cistercian monastery and museum. This adds about 5 km. to the direct route to Santo Domingo de la Calzada.

✳ Alesanco The village has a 16th-c. Iglesia de la Asunción.

✳ **Cañas** Santo Domingo de Silos (1000–1073) was born here. The Cistercian convent of **Santa María de Cañas** was founded in 1170 by the count of Haro and his wife—soon widow—Aldonza Ruiz de Castro, who retired to the convent with all of her goods and with expectations of luxury. Her daughter the Beata Urraca López de Haro (1170–1262) became abbess. Legend has it that San Francisco de Asís stayed here on his way to Compostela. The monastery prospered all through the Middle Ages and then fell to ruin. It was restored 1943–75. The nuns of Cañas make and sell interesting pottery.

The convent follows the typical Cistercian monastery plan, organizing the community around a large central cloister. The 13th-c. church is the typical Latin cross with 3 semicircular apses, lit by **enormous windows**. The church's 16th-c. **Plateresque retablo** was carved by Guillén de Holanda and painted by Francisco Alonso Gallego and Andrés Melgar. **Santiago Peregrino** is on the upper left. Note also both the 14th-c. Gothic Virgin and the crucifix.

The chapter room (*sala capitular*) contains Urraca López de Haro's extraordinary 13th-c. tomb. Note the abbess's crook of office, the 2 angels with censers by her head, the novices at her feet, and the extraordinary funeral procession winding around the sarcophagus. Near the dying queen the mourners' faces are twisted in grief. Several of the women on the reverse side wear tall, elaborate head coverings.

The church museum houses a collection of images of saints and a superb display of monastic life, with models of monasteries and a history of the Cistercian Order.

An additional detour 1 km. south of Cañas will bring you to the village's 16th-c. hermitage. Along the tiny paved road is what has to be the most enigmatic monument in Spain. In a hayfield a solitary stele reads: *Aqui se detuvo la mula del obispo Sancho MXL* ("Here is where Bishop Sancho's mule paused in 1040"). Someday we hope to meet a descendant of Bishop Sancho, or the mule (we know that neither should have descendants, but we can dream), and discover the story behind this 11th-c. pause.

From Cañas you return to Azofra and the main road. There, about 1 km. west of Azofra, you will pass a medieval roadside cross and *rollo*—where malefactors were hung. A little further along, about halfway to Santo Domingo, just past a sharp curve on the highway, is the site of the now-vanished Hospital de Bellota, run by the Orden of Calatrava in the 12th c. At the entrance to Santo Domingo is another plain cylinder *rollo*.

35. San Millán de la Cogolla → Santo Domingo de la Calzada

Route 1: San Millán de la Cogolla → **Cañas** → Azofra → Santo Domingo de la Calzada
(This route follows the highway. Because Cañas and Azofra are discussed in chapter 34, they are not treated here.)

Route 2: San Millán de la Cogolla → Pazuengos → Villarejo → Manzanares de Rioja → Gallinero de Rioja → Santo Domingo de la Calzada

---

One km. south of Yuso on the road toward Mount San Lorenzo, at the intersection of a creek on the right, take the trail that leads due west and climbs steeply to a small pass before descending into the village of Pazuengos.

✳ Pazuengos The village of Pazuengos is today remote. From the 8th to the 11th c. it served as an important border stronghold initially between Christians and Muslims, and then between Castilians and Navarrans. In the mid-11th c. it was held by Navarra, but in 1063 Fernando I of Castilla encroached, occupied the village, and restored the castle's fortifications. Rather than go to battle over the issue, the 2 kings decided to submit the dispute to judicial duel: whichever side's champion defeated the other in individual combat would prove that God—and right—was on his side. Before assembled representatives of the 2 kingdoms, the experienced Navarran knight Jimeno Garcés lost to a 23-year-old Castilian nobody, Rodrigo Díaz de Vivar, whom the jubilant Castilians granted the title Champion (*Campeador*). Years later he would be called by the Arabic term for Great Lord: El Cid.

The trail leads north, along the ridge, past a new dirt-strip airport, before descending through horse pastures and thick oak forests to Villarejo. Several times along here we have heard wild boar snuffling in the brush, but we have never been (un)lucky enough to see one. A firm dirt road leads to Manzanares de Rioja and Gallinero. Directly to the south are the twin peaks of La Retuerta and Merrinasque (each about 1,150 m.).

✳ Gallinero The village is thought to be the source of the chickens that took part in Santo Domingo de la Calzada's miracle of the "hanged innocent" (see ch. 36).

When it rains, the fields around Santo Domingo can turn into a sticky quagmire, as the Italian pilgrim Domenico Laffi found out ca. 1670:

> We found a woman weeping bitterly who begged us to go with her. We were a bit suspicious because we had been told about women in these parts who, under some pretext or other . . . lead travellers to where men are lying in wait to assassinate them. . . . But we were persuaded by her flood of tears, and followed her into a nearby field, where she had two donkeys stuck in the

mud in a deep bog. We gave her a hand and after much time and effort dragged them out. Whereupon she began laughing and crying all at once. . . . Then we continued on our way to Santo Domingo de la Calzada, four long leagues away. [Laffi; trans. Hall (1997), 129]

36. SANTO DOMINGO DE LA CALZADA

HISTORY

Prior to the 11th c. the Road west from Nájera led through tangled, bandit-infested forests and swamps. It was transformed from one of the most dangerous segments of the Road to one of the safest because of the efforts of an extraordinary man.

Domingo García was born in the nearby town of Viloria ca. 1019. He gave up sheepherding to become a monk, but he did so poorly in his studies in the monasteries of Valvanera and San Millán that he was not allowed to continue. Nonetheless, resolved to a life of religious service, in 1034 he became a hermit in the forests bordering the Oja River. A dream directed him to join San Gregorio Ostiense in his labors to improve travel conditions in the Rioja region. They worked together for several years; when Gregorio died, Domingo returned to Oja and dedicated the rest of his life to serving pilgrims.

His first task was to make a stone bridge over the Oja. Next, the Saint used a heavy sickle (*hoz*) to cut 37 kilometers of road through the forests that choked the region from Nájera to Redecilla del Camino. When he stopped to pray, angels continued to chop timber with the sickle.

> 📖 Here is another version of the legend: the citizens of nearby Ayuela gave Domingo permission to log as many trees as his sickle could cut in a day. The miracle: he made only one cut, felling a single tree, but by sundown the Saint had all the wood he needed.

King García III Sánchez el de Nájera (1035–54) gave Domingo permission to accommodate an old ruined fort as a pilgrim hospice. From this meager beginning a small village grew up. By the end of the 11th c. the village's older section, flanking the Road from the east leading to the church, was already referred to as the "barrio viejo." In 1076 King Alfonso VI captured the Río Oja region for Castilla, referring to it officially for the first time as La Rioja. Alfonso favored civic improvements like roads and bridges and actively supported the work of Domingo who, with his disciple Juan de Ortega, built numerous bridges and improved the Road west. From the first, his town was laid out deliberately with the east-west pilgrimage Road as its focus. Domingo devoted the last years of his life to erecting a church in the village, in which he was buried when he died ca. 1109. In those days the town belonged to Domingo's abbey and was called an *abadengo*.

Ever since the early 10th c., when the founder of Castilla, Fernán González, beat back a Navarran incursion at Valpierre, a few km. to the northeast, this part of La Rioja has had strategic importance in the defense of the eastern frontier of Castilla. Despite Alfonso VI's heavy investment in the village, Santo Domingo de la Calzada was retaken in 1120 by Navarra's King Alfonso el Batallador. Alfonso VII of Castilla and León re-recaptured it in 1134 and put it under the jurisdiction of the Calahorra Cathedral. The town changed hands 3 more times before becoming a permanent part of Castilla in 1143. The town prospered in the 12th c. with the flow of pilgrims. When Domingo's church burned in the mid-12th c., a larger building was quickly erected and named a *colegiata*. In 1227 Pope Honorius III transferred the bishopric here from Calahorra (see ch. 31 and below). In 1250 Fernando III el

Santo asserted royal jurisdiction over the town, which became a *realengo*, and in 1333, recognizing its growing economic importance, Alfonso XI elevated it to a city.

In 1364 Santo Domingo de la Calzada was a focal point in Pedro I el Cruel's losing war against Enrique de Trastámara. To secure the city, Pedro built an enormous wall, 1.6 km. in perimeter, with 38 towers and 7 gates. This wall stood largely intact until 1886. What remain are fragments of 8 towers, 300 m. of the wall, and 2 gates, all in the northwest corner of the old city.

PILGRIMAGE

The city's principal hospice was founded by the Saint himself and is discussed below. The town's major claim to fame, of course, was the relics of Santo Domingo himself. But in the 15th c. at least 1 pilgrim, the German Arnold von Harff, expressed doubts as to their authenticity.

> In the chief church, on the right hand as one enters, lies St. Dominicus in person in a fine large and lofty grave, whose body and grave were also shown us in Benonia [Bologna] in Lombardy, in the monastery of preaching friars. I leave God to decide these disputes among priests, who never allow that they are wrong. [Harff; trans. Letts, 268]

The Miracle Legend

The miracle of the "hanged innocent" was a staple of St. James's miracle lore by the early 12th c. A version is collected in the *Liber Sancti Jacobi*. Though most versions site the miracle in Toulouse, a Riojan tradition locates the story in Santo Domingo de la Calzada and attributes the miraculous events not to Santiago, but to the Riojan Saint. Though there are many variations, in general the story goes like this: A family of German pilgrims (father, mother, and son) making their way toward Compostela spent the night in Santo Domingo de la Calzada. When the innkeeper's daughter propositioned the son, he spurned her (he was, after all, on pilgrimage). She took revenge by convincing a friend to hide some of the church silver in the young man's pack. The next day she notified the authorities. They arrested the pilgrims and found the silver. As a result, they hung the young man for theft. In medieval times executed criminals were left on the gibbet to rot as a vivid warning of the wages of sin. The parents continued to Compostela and on their way home came again to Santo Domingo de la Calzada. Sick at heart, they approached the gibbet, where to their astonishment their son cheerfully greeted them, explaining that St. James—or in some versions Santo Domingo—kept him alive by supporting his weight the whole time. Miracle! The parents ran to inform the city official that their son was still alive. The official, who was roasting chickens for dinner, scoffed at their news, retorting that their son was as alive as his roasting chickens. Whereupon the chickens reincorporated themselves, feathers and all, and flew cackling away: *Santo Domingo de la Calzada: do cantó la gallina después de asada* ("Santo Domingo of the Road: where after it was cooked the chicken crowed"). Literalists like ourselves wonder who fed him during the month, and how come nobody else in town noticed he was alive.

A piece of the gibbet is displayed high in the cathedral transept over Santo Domingo's tomb. The chickens that cackle from their coop in the west transept of the cathedral are—legend has it—descendants of the resuscitated roasters. Late-15th-c. German traveler Künig von Vach, although skeptical of many aspects of the pilgrimage legends, was apparently enchanted with this miracle, and he wrote in his diary:

> Don't forget about the chicken next to the altar. Consider it well; think that God can do miracles. I know well that it is no lie that the chickens escaped from the spit, because I myself have seen the room where they began to walk and hearth where they were roasted.

Domenico Laffi, who trekked through ca. 1670, also believed the chickens to be miraculous.

> These creatures eat only what is given to them by pilgrims going to Galicia. It must be bread—and only bread that they have found for the love of God, for if it be bread that has been purchased, they will have nothing to do with it and would rather die of hunger. [Still, he adds, the chickens will accept one subterfuge:] When there are no pilgrims passing by, there is a woman who looks after them. She goes through the city dressed as a pilgrim, begging for alms, and thus they are provided for. [Laffi; trans. Hall (1997), 129]

A version of this story is included in CC: Book II, the collection of the Saint's miracles. In fact, the "hanged innocent" legend was one of the most popular miracles associated with the Road, and examples in various genres are found all over Europe. For example, the whole story is narrated in a multipanel 15th-c. Flemish retablo now in the Indianapolis (USA) Art Museum. In Tafers, Switzerland, a private chapel built ca. 1769 displays the story in multiple scenes painted on its external walls. The 19th-c. English poet Robert Southey's long poem "The Pilgrim to Compostella" (sic) also relates the tale.

MONUMENTS: 1. Catedral. 2. Monasterio de las Bernardas. 3. Monasterio de San Francisco. 4. Hospital/Parador. 5. Ayuntamiento.

1. Catedral

The first church, begun in 1098 and consecrated by the bishop of Nájera in 1106, had been commissioned by Alfonso VI of Castilla, who gave land for the edifice, personally set the first stone, and was buried there when he died in 1109. Santo Domingo was the architect and mason for this first church, of which only traces remain in the apse. A second building campaign, with a marked French Romanesque influence, lasted from the mid-12th to the mid-13th c. Several cities in the region disputed the right to house the cathedral, and in 1227 Santo Domingo won out, for a time, when the bishopric was transferred from Calahorra. (Currently Santo Domingo shares co-cathedral status and a peripatetic bishop with Calahorra and Logroño.) By the 14th c., when the pilgrimage boom had largely passed, the church had begun to crumble, and the bishop offered indulgences to donors to its restoration . . . and to its fortification, for, with the exception of the rose window, the 14th-c. additions tend to be defensive structures, perhaps reflecting the political crises in Castilla and the fluctuating border of Navarra. The nave was reroofed in the 16th c. Some of the side chapels were added at later dates.

This church is worth several hours, and we devote several pages to it. It contains a good anthology of styles. Its best art is very good indeed, and many pieces are directly related to the pilgrimage Road.

Exterior:
- The 69-m. **Baroque tower** was built in 1762 by Martín de Beratúa. Typical of his style is the simple square base topped with an ornately decorated octagon. Curiously, the tower stands alone, across the street, entirely detached from the cathedral buildings, the only such we will see along the Road.
- The apses. A master carver and his disciples sculpted the **corbels and capitals** of the apse. Among the usual array of monsters and vices are a hunchback, a man playing a stringed instrument, a jolly glutton cramming bread into his mouth, a man wrestling a lion (flesh versus spirit?), San Martín exemplifying Christian charity by dividing his cape with a pilgrim, and 2 elegant, surprisingly realistic female heads.
- West portal. 13th-c. transitional Romanesque-Gothic, devoid of decoration.

The portal is covered by an atrium, built in the 14th c., which also serves as a defensive tower.

• South portal. Beratúa erected it in the Neoclassic style ca. 1769. The 3 saints over the door are Domingo de la Calzada, Emeterio, and Celedonio. On the left flanking wall is an escutcheon with the Hapsburg eagle.

Interior:

• The ambulatory, with its radiating chapels and clerestory, is typical of the great pilgrimage churches. The **pillars** are simple, with those **in the transept** radiating nerves as if each were a stately palm. The oldest vaulting (Gothic-*ojival*, 13th c.) is in the apse. The transepts were revaulted in the 16th c. in the Flamboyant Gothic style, with each vault exhibiting a slightly different pattern.

• The main altar. When Forment's Renaissance retablo (see below) was removed in the early 1990s, extensive, high-quality, unique Romanesque constructions were revealed. The altar is separated from the ambulatory by <u>decorated pillars</u> (ca. 1148–80), a unique arrangement in Spain, recalling the pilgrimage churches of Vézélay and Conques. The principal motifs on the pillars are Jesse's Tree, David playing a rebec (his feet crossed like the Compostela David), a roll with 7 seals, and the Holy Trinity, with God the Father holding the Son in his arms, between Mary and the sacred host. Each of the pillars is topped with a **frieze**. Among the most interesting is the allegory of the **wise and foolish virgins**, the former carrying lamps right side up, the latter carrying them upside down, with puzzled expressions on their faces wondering why the lamps did not remain lit. (The apse and its capitals are described below.)

• The **choir** was begun in 1521 by Andrés de Nájera, who supervised the work and carved the bishop's throne, and Guillén de Holanda. The overall design is Plateresque; the figures show the idealized realism, grace, and solidity of mature Renaissance sculptors. Each of the saints is explicitly named, so this is a good opportunity to test your knowledge of the saints' attributes. You will easily recognize the barefoot pilgrim **Santiago**. The variety of decorative motifs and designs is stunning, and different on each seat. You can easily spend a couple of hours delighting in the animals and monsters on the hand rests, the etched designs on the misericords, the varied patterns of the seat backs and crests, and the tiny figures to the right and left of each folding seat.

• The *trascoro* that separates the choir from the main church was carved ca. 1530 by Andrés Melgar and Francisco Alonso Gallego. It narrates episodes from the **life of Santo Domingo**. The central panel is the traditional medieval representation of this Saint, showing him surrounded by the poor and by captives (for whose freedom he is believed to intercede). The 8 remaining panels, beginning at the top and reading left to right, show:

1. A battle in the dynastic war of 1360 between Pedro I el Cruel and Enrique de Trastámara that threatened to destroy the city. When the concerned citizenry came to the church, hands emerged from the Saint's tomb and announced that Pedro would become the city's protector.

2 and 3. The miracle of the "hanged innocent," here attributed to Santo Domingo.

4. The Saint maintained a garden to feed pilgrims, but a shepherd came in every day and ruined the crops. The shepherd became twisted, hunchbacked, and deaf, but when Domingo responded to his pleas for forgiveness, he became whole again.

5. A pilgrim sleeping by the road is run over by a cart taking stone for Domingo's bridge over the Oja. San Juan de Ortega sees this and tells Domingo, who restores the pilgrim to life.

6 and 7. Two pilgrims believe Domingo has treated them badly. They beat him and throw him into a fire. The next day they leave the city, argue, and kill each

other with swords. A dog finds a severed hand and takes it to Domingo, who prays for them.

8. Domingo cares for pilgrims.

• **Santo Domingo's tomb.** On the church's main level, the 12th-c. Romanesque reclining **statue of Domingo** is covered by a Flamboyant Gothic *templete* designed by Felipe Vigarny and built by Juan de Rasines in 1513–14. Scenes from the Saint's life are carved along the side. They recount several miracles attributed to him, including the "hanged innocent" miracle. In other scenes Domingo revives an official killed working on the Oja bridge, is mistreated by neighbors who feel his building encroaches on their rights, welcomes grateful prisoners released through his intercession, distributes charity, revives the dead son of a pilgrim couple, and has heaven punish the shepherd who destroyed his garden.

On the ornamental grille hangs a small **sickle**, now chased with silver, reputedly the one Domingo and his angels used to chop out the pilgrim Road. The statue of Santo Domingo with his chickens in the silver arch was executed in 1789 by Julián de Sanmartín. The chains and handcuffs hung from the top of the *templete* are from freed prisoners.

The crypt is underneath. In it are a plain 13th-c. tomb of Santo Domingo and 3 13th-c. Romanesque statues: Domingo with a captive at his feet, the face and beard resembling those on his reclining statue on the tomb; San Juan Evangelista; and San Pedro, who is especially well portrayed, with a sense of movement and fluidity, with differentiated cloth that suggests observation from life. These last 2 statues were discovered when the Forment retablo was dismantled for restoration.

• The chapels. Beginning from the south entrance and going counterclockwise:

—Capilla de **Santiago** (1565 retablo) and San Pedro (1630 retablo).

—Capilla de San Andrés. The retablo's central image of San Andrés shows the vigor and elegance typical of the Renaissance Romanist style. The **Plateresque tomb** by Guillén de Holanda typically lavishes detail on the clothing worn by the deceased bishop and on the pillow under his head. The monk reading from the book is a masterpiece of Renaissance idealized realism.

—**Romanesque chapel** in the apse. If Romanesque architects erred and made their windows too large, the wall collapsed. The solution here was to divide the window with a triangular support: outside they look like 2 windows, inside like one. Each support is capped with a small statue of one of the biblical patriarchs: Abraham, Isaac, and Jacob.

The image in the center of this chapel is the 13th-c. Nuestra Señora de la Calzada.

The **decorative capitals** in this chapel include the Epiphany, the Flight to Egypt, and several finely worked monsters. An episode unique to this church is a story from the pseudo-Matthew of the Apocrypha: **lions threaten Mary**, and Jesus reassures her that they only come to pay respect at her feet. On the **Annunciation** capital (third pillar enclosed in wall, left of the center apse), the Virgin is shown in multiple roles: as potential Mother of God (the Angel points to her womb while old Joseph reflects on his dream) and also as queen of heaven (2 angels crown her at the moment of the Incarnation). You will see a similar rendition on Compostela's Puerta de Platerías. In the **Assumption** capital (right transept) the Virgin, usually raised vertically to heaven, is reclining, as in this capital's model in the cloister of Pamplona's cathedral.

—Capilla de San Bartolomé. Here you can see remains of the Romanesque apse terminating the north aisle.

—Entrance to the sacristy. Remains of a Romanesque chapel, now with Neoclassic decoration.

—**Damián Forment's retablo**. This ca. 1538 retablo covered the main altar until the 1990s. Forment carved the base in alabaster and the upper stories in walnut (later painted by Andrés Melgar). Trained in Italy and in the Flemish Gothic style, Forment opted for the new Renaissance aesthetic in this retablo. In Burgos and Astorga you may see its equal, but on the Santiago Road you will never see better.

📖 You will see these 6 characteristics over and over again on the Renaissance retablos between here and Compostela.

Like the best works of its genre, the **narrative program is coherent** (the history of Salvation, from God the Father and Adam and Eve on top to the 4 Evangelists at the bottom).

In the narrative scenes, Old and New Testament **biblical stories combine with classical figures** like sirens, tritons, and centaurs, alluding to the struggle between good and the evils of vice. The dozens of Italianate *putti* remind viewers of the saving power of love. Some of them hold up pelicans (which symbolize Christ's sacrifice), or ride on sirens and dolphins (triumph over sinful desires), or merely play (suggesting the delights of heaven).

The **gilt architectural elements frame but do not overpower** the scenes.

The figures are in **high relief**, emphasizing movement and dynamic postures.

Scenes are conceived as **expressive tableaux**, the details superbly carved and painted, the architectural sets and props cleverly integrated into the narrative structure. The supporting figures and the decorative motifs are executed with the same lavish expressiveness and care for detail as the principal figures.

Each block can be enjoyed as **an independent work of art**, while **simultaneously** each plays a key role in a larger, **integrated** work of art, balancing color, line, and movement.

📖 The dozen or so artists whom Forment trained while constructing this retablo went on to create many significant works in La Rioja. On the Road you will see works of two of them: Natuera Borgoñón (who carved this choir), and Guillén de Holanda (who worked on this choir and executed the Cañas retablo).

—Capilla de la Verónica. This tiny chapel contains a superb late-15th-c. German **statue of the Veronica.**

—Capilla de la Magdalena. Plateresque iron grille (*reja*) attributed to Cristóbal de Andino. The late-15th-c. **tomb** of Pedro de Carranza, schoolmaster of the Cathedral of Burgos, is attributed to Felipe Vigarny. It is remarkable for its realistic details. The early-16th-c. **retablo by León Picardo** is characteristic of late Hispano-Flemish style. Picardo typically fills his compositions with large, stubby forms adorned with elaborate fashions.

📖 When León Picardo's patron Count Pedro de Ayala was imprisoned for his part in the 1520 Comunero revolt against young Charles V, Picardo took him a bowl of porridge every day for 3 years.

—Entrance to cloister. Note the double window in the Gothic-Mudéjar style.

—Baptismal chapel. Severe Herrera Renaissance style, ca. 1650.

—Capilla de Santa Teresa. Late-15th-c. ornate iron *reja*. Sculpted 15th-c. tombs. The 2 **Hispano-Flemish paintings** were only recently discovered. They include 24 scenes by the Master of Belorado (ca. 1500) showing characteristic sober harmonies of color, lavish gold brocaded backgrounds, late-Gothic or Renaissance architectural settings, and folkloristic natural details. This chapel was rededicated to Santa Teresa after her death in 1582.

—Capilla de Hermosilla. Contains the tomb of San Jerónimo Hermosilla, martyred in 1861 in Vietnam (canonized in 1988), and 16th-c. painted wood panels with scenes from the life of Santo Domingo. On the retablo are fine Renaissance statues of Saints Lucía and Catalina.

—**Chicken coop** (*Hornacina del milagro*). The stone coop dates from ca. 1460. In former times pilgrims pushed crumbs into the cage. If the cock and hen both ate, the pilgrims believed they would have safe a journey to Compostela; if not, they might die on the Road. Nowadays some pilgrims believe that if a feather falls from the cage into a pilgrim's hand they will have good luck. On the wall to the left are more chains from released prisoners.

Cloister:

Built in 1326–46; reformed in the Plateresque style in 1517–50. The burial niches date from the 15th and 16th c.

The cloister is now a museum. Among the many displays are detailed explanations of **how a retablo is developed,** from the lobbying for the contract to the festival following its unveiling. You will also find archaeological artifacts, sculptures collected from small towns in the vicinity, Gothic painting (our favorite depicts vigorous monks watching the **Mass of San Gregorio**), and 2 stunning **Apostles** from a mostly vanished Romanesque Apostolate. Three Renaissance masterpieces are also displayed. Adriaen **Ysenbrant's triptych** depicts the Mass of San Gregorio and on the side panels San Antón and a young, energetic Santo Domingo de la Calzada. An anonymous **Epiphany**'s left panel depicts Saints Juan, **Santiago,** and Pedro watching Moses and Elijah appear with Christ under a figure of God the Father. In the background of the **Annunciation triptych** you can see the tower of the Antwerp Cathedral under construction.

2. Monasterio de las Bernardas. Founded in 1610 by the bishop of Calahorra and his 2 nephews, the bishops of Cesarea and Oviedo, and it contains the alabaster tombs of all three. These days the sisters maintain a hospice dedicated to Santa Teresita.

3. Monasterio de San Francisco. This former monastery, outside the walls in the southwest corner of town, was built in the 1570s in the Herrera style, dominated by classical geometric shapes rather than decoration. The principal stone retablo is also carved in that style. It serves as the mausoleum of the monastery's founder, Fray Bernardo de Fresnada. The polychrome Last Supper is noteworthy. As we write, the monastery is undergoing restoration and is inaccessible. Ca. 1670 the pilgrim Domenico Laffi also found it closed, but only because it was the Franciscans' dinner hour. The sacristan had him come back later and then fed him and his companions a meal of bread and fish.

Much of the monastery is now a hospital administered by the Hijos del Inmaculado Corazón de María.

4. **Hospital/Parador**. In the early days Domingo himself used to feed pilgrims at a large table set up alongside the river, which came to be known as the "mesa

del santo." As the town grew, he constructed a formal hospice, and when he died in 1109 he left it all his goods. Although the building was rude, with only holes for windows, tradition holds that when pilgrims ate at his long wooden table, not a single fly came in. This hospice was replaced in the mid-15th c. by a modern building that served pilgrims for the next 300 years. Eighteenth-century pilgrims write of a large, columned building organized around a cloister, with a crocodile skin hanging from one of its ceilings. There was a central patio with a well. The main building probably had 3 naves (of which 2 remain today). The French pilgrim Manier says they gave him broth, beans, and decent bread, but that the bed was awful. By the 1730s, as pilgrim traffic dropped off, the hospice began to take in the poor and the sick, of whom there was never a shortage. A century later, when monastic property was expropriated in the great *desamortización*, the hospital moved to the Convento de San Francisco, and the old building was abandoned. By the 1950s it was in terrible shape, and might have been lost had it not been refurbished in the late 1960s as a Parador Nacional.

5. Ayuntamiento. The Renaissance, balconied town hall bears the coat of arms of Carlos V.

🚗 The region around Santo Domingo de la Calzada was important in prehistoric times. Leiva, northwest of the city, was a prehistoric center. Herramelluri, 2 km. south, was a Celtiberian town at least through the 3rd c. Neither site offers much to see now.

37. SANTO DOMINGO DE LA CALZADA → BELORADO

Route: SANTO DOMINGO DE LA CALZADA → **Grañón** → **Redecilla del Camino** → Castildelgado → [Viloria de la Rioja] → Villamayor del Río → BELORADO

Leaving Santo Domingo, you cross a bridge over the gravel banks of the Río Oja, which gives the region its name.

Halfway between Santo Domingo and Grañón, near km. 43, was a little stone cross, la Cruz de los Valientes, raised in memory of Martín García. Local legend has it that at the beginning of the 19th c. this champion from Grañón defeated the best defender of Santo Domingo in a battle to decide which of the 2 towns was to own a property called Ballana. He asked the town to say an Our Father for him yearly on the anniversary of the contest, and even though the cross is gone, as late as the 1950s they still did!

✳ Grañón

HISTORY

Grañón's hill controls the east-west road in this part of the valley, so it has been inhabited nearly forever. Celtiberian burials have been found on the hill. The Roman settlement here was called Libia. In the early Middle Ages Grañón was a frontier town; a reference to it is found in a document dated ca. 884. The hill was probably fortified by Fernán González in the early 10th c. as part of the Castilian defenses against Navarra. The old fortifications can easily be traced in the compact, oval shape of Grañón's street plan. As the town's commercial importance grew, it attracted a sizable Jewish population. Grañón's population reached a peak in the 16th c., with nearly 1,300 people; only a few less lived there in the 19th c. Today the population is nearer 500. Remnants of the town's former wealth can be seen in the 18th-c. houses with coats of arms in the *barrio* of Santiago, through which pilgrims enter the town.

PILGRIMAGE

Grañón evolved as a typical Road town whose east-west axis is the main street and whose 2 other main streets parallel the pilgrimage Road. Though it doesn't look like much today, at one point Grañón had 2 monasteries (Santo Tomé and San Miguel) belonging to Santo Domingo de la Calzada. The medieval pilgrims' hospice (founded 1085) was located on the northeast corner on the Plaza del Hórreo, north of the San Juan church. Nothing remains of the old hospice, but a new hospice has been constructed next to the church in approximately the same location.

MONUMENT

The **Church of San Juan Bautista**, dating from the 14th c., was part of a now-vanished monastery. The exterior is undistinguished. The simple baptismal font (inscription dated 1099), with an interesting decoration of leaves and cylinders, is all that remains from the original Romanesque church. The current church was constructed over a period of 400 years and has nice Baroque retablos. The *retablo* *mayor* (constructed 1545–6) by Natuera Borgoñón and Bernal Forment is inspired by Damián Forment's masterwork in Santo Domingo. The figures are well articulated, with good details (e.g., their curly hair) and with good color.

At the south edge of the village is the 16th-c. Ermita de los Judíos whose relief of the placing of the Crown of Thorns, with its several exaggerated Jewish figures, may have given the tiny church its name.

👟 Two km. south of town, in a small woods, is the late-17th- or early-18th-c. **Ermita de Carrasquedo**, built on the site of a 12th-c. hospital. The Baroque retablo, by Diego de Ichazo, concentrates our attention on the central image. The chapel is filled with 17th- and 18th-c. large painted ex-votos thanking the Virgin for various favors received.

The oak forest here is a regional park called the Dehesa de Grañón.

Just beyond Grañón, after crossing the tiny Río Villarío Medio, the Road leaves La Rioja and enters Castilla. The landscape changes dramatically to looming sandy gray hills, almost entirely devoid of trees and of grapes. Welcome to wheat country.

✳ **Redecilla del Camino** Redecilla, like Grañón, developed in the 11th c. as a pilgrimage Road town, with its single east-west street, the Calle Mayor. The rivulet just west of town is the Río Reláchigo. The second house on the left incorporates the ruins of an ancient *ermita*.

The Church of **Nuestra Señora de la Calle** has an 18th-c Rococo interior. The must-see here is a monumental baptismal font in the Romanesque Byzantine style, perhaps influenced by the Mozarabic style. It is perhaps the most important font on the pilgrimage route. It depicts heavenly Jerusalem resting on 8 columns with towers. A serpent coils around the base, probably signifying the triumph of the Church over the Devil.

South of the church, at Calle Mayor, 27, is the Hospital de San Lázaro, in recent years converted to a pilgrim hospice. In the 16th c. a French pilgrim named Jean died there. The parish had an auction to raise the money to bury him, but his clothes were in such bad shape that there were no bidders, so the parish itself had to pay for the burial. They buried him in the choir for 400 maravedís.

✳ **Castildelgado** The town plan and land-use patterns suggest that this was a Roman town. A document dated 926 calls the town Villa de Pun. In 1136 Alfonso VII of Castilla commissioned a hospital here, next to the church of Nuestra Señora la Real del Camino. No traces remain. In the 16th c. the town was renamed for the bishop of Burgos, Jerónimo Gil Delgado, a local boy made good who served as a delegate at the Council of Trent.

The church of San Pedro is 16th-c. Gothic, containing Churrigueresque retablos. The tomb of Bishop Delgado is also here.

The 14th-c. Ermita de Santa María del Campo reputedly contains a wood monstrance and a 13th-c. folding polyptych.

👟 Viloria de la Rioja Domingo de la Calzada was born in 1019 in a house in front of the church, which still has the font where he was baptized.

✳ **Villamayor del Río** This medieval hamlet, arrayed around the church of San Gil, has declined noticeably from the 125 inhabitants noted in the 1830 census.

38. BELORADO

HISTORY

The site has been occupied since Roman times. By the mid-10ᵗʰ c. Bilforado was already a substantial Christian city. In 1116 Alfonso I el Batallador fortified the town against his stepson and rival, Alfonso VII el Emperador. Its strategic importance comes from the fact that it sits in a narrow pass flanked by steep cliffs, and that it guarded the frontier between Castilla and La Rioja.

Belorado's boom years may have begun in 1116, when Alfonso I granted the town a *fuero* and authorized, for the first time in Castilla, an annual fair. Belorado's economic strength by the 13ᵗʰ c. may be seen in the fact that it had 8 churches. Like many market towns along the Road, it had separate neighborhoods for the 4 ethnic groups that flocked there for the commercial opportunities: *Francos*, Christian Castilians, Jews, and Muslims, each neighborhood with its own traditions and judges.

> 📖 Many Muslim families remained behind here and in many other northern towns after the Christian Reconquest. They tended to work as farmers or in the building trades. Almost every Christian city in the Middle Ages had its *morería*.

The Jewish quarter was in the Calle de San Martín (now called Raimundo Miguel), and its importance was marked when Alfonso I granted equal legal rights to Christians and Jews. During most of the Middle Ages, Belorado's Jews and Muslims were exempt from city taxes and required instead to keep one of the city's defensive towers in good repair. Another curious law required Belorado's Jews to name 2 men to sweep the city streets every Thursday, in return for which the Jewish community was permitted to pasture their cattle on city lands and cut firewood in the municipal forests.

Belorado's modern tanneries and leather factories are coming onto hard times. As we write, every fifth house in the old part of the city seems to be in ruins, which permits glimpses of medieval construction techniques. Note the heavy wood framing beams and the rubble-filled walls.

PILGRIMAGE

Like many pilgrimage towns, Belorado had hospices at both ends, outside the walls to accommodate pilgrims arriving late in the evening after the city gates had been shut. To the east, near the Ermita de Belén, was the Hospital de los Caballeros. Documents speak of its existence in the 11ᵗʰ c. A donation in 1171 gives it to the Cathedral of Burgos. To the west was the Hospital de San Lázaro (or Misericordia), documented from the 16ᵗʰ c. No traces remain of either one.

MONUMENTS: 1. Ermita de Nuestra Señora de Belén. 2. **Iglesia de Santa María**. 3. Caves. 4. Castle ruins. 5. Iglesia de San Pedro. 6. Iglesia de San Nicolás. 7. Iglesia de San Francisco. 8. Convento de Santa Clara.

1. The Ermita de Nuestra Señora de Belén, often rebuilt, has an 18ᵗʰ-c. retablo.

2. **Iglesia de Santa María**, outside the walls, across the Verdancho creek, was originally a chapel of the castle. Its central nave dates from the 15ᵗʰ c., while the lateral

naves are somewhat later. The stone retablo features both a **Santiago Matamoros** and a **Santiago Peregrino**. There is a nice ivory Christ, a three-generational grouping of St. Anne with the Virgin and Child (1591), and a **Romanesque Virgin**.

3. The caves in the cliff east of Belorado were once inhabited by saintly hermits. Local legend has it that one of them was San Caprasio (sometimes called San Pacasio), bishop of Agen, who, disgusted with the secular world, retired to this cave. Today the caves are all private property; a local artist inhabits one.

4. Castle ruins. Not much is left, but if you hike up at sunset there is a panoramic view of town below and of the storks' nests on the *espadaña* of Santa María.

After wintering in Africa, pairs of storks—they mate for life—return to their previous year's nests in Spain in mid-March. They lay from 2 to 5 eggs, which hatch after a 4-week gestation period. The parents work hard to keep the chicks supplied with fish and lizards and such: for the first month the babies cannot even stand, and they do not leave the nest for 2 months more. Most families return to Africa in August, but a few choose to winter over.

5. Iglesia de San Pedro. This church in the Plaza Mayor was rebuilt in the 17th c. The Rococo retablo was carved in 1767 by local sculptors. Half the year it is topped by a statue of San Vitores, a local martyr who holds his severed head in his hand. The other half of the year the statue resides in the Ermita de Belén. Local folk chant this verse: *San Vitores / perdió la cabeza / en Quintanilleja* ("San Vitores lost his head in Quintanilleja").

6. Of the church of San Nicolás only the ruined Plateresque door and clock tower survive.

7. Iglesia de San Francisco. This former convent was founded in 1250 and rebuilt in the 16th c., when it hosted San Bernardino de Siena on his pilgrimage to Compostela. It is now a private dwelling.

8. Convento de Santa Clara. The convent is outside the walls, where the Road crosses the Tirón River. Local legend says that it was built over an *ermita* to the Virgen de Bretonera, which had been destroyed by the Muslims. In 1358 Pope Inocencio VI gave the site to the Franciscan nuns.

39. Belorado → San Juan de Ortega

Route: BELORADO → Tosantos → Villambistia → **Espinosa del Camino** → **San Felices de Oca** → **Villafranca de Montes de Oca** → Montes de Oca → [Valdeafuentes] → SAN JUAN DE ORTEGA

On the west side of Belorado, just before the bridge, is an old millrace and mill.

✳ **Tosantos** This village, which has existed from at least the late 10th c., was purchased in 1414 by Belorado. A 16th-c. census counted some 200 inhabitants, far more than today.

The 17th-c. church of San Esteban contains an interesting 16th-c. Romanist wood retablo.

The Ermita de Nuestra Señora de la Peña is cut into the rock on the north side of the road beyond the city. Legend holds that in 712 an image of the child Jesus was hidden under a bell in this cave to protect it from the conquering Muslims. The image, however, is from the 12th c. It passes the winter in the *ermita* and the summer in San Esteban.

✳ **Villambistia** The 17th-c. church holds a 16th-c. retablo. The Ermita de San Roque has a small Rococo retablo. The Road near this town conserves some stretches of medieval pavement. Many of the houses in Villambistia and neighboring towns clearly show their half-timber and stucco construction.

✳ **Espinosa del Camino** The 16th-c. church of La Asunción reputedly contains a 1657 retablo and a **12th-c. image of San Indalecio,** one of Santiago's 7 Spanish disciples.

✳ **San Felices de Oca** These ruins, in the middle of a wheat field 1 km. before Villafranca, are all that is left of a major Mozarabic monastery, begun early in the 9th c. It was favored by the early counts of Castilla. Diego Porcelos, the man who reconquered and resettled Burgos, was buried here. All you will see now is a single undistinguished arch from the Mozárabe church, hardly enough to tell you that at one time this monastery was one of the principal religious institutions in north central Spain. *Sic transit gloria mundi.*

✳ **Villafranca de Montes de Oca** There is evidence of pre-Roman Iron Age settlement near Villafranca in the gorge of the Oca River from as early as 700 B.C.E. The large Roman city of Auca, in the flats along the river just north of the village, is said to have covered over 40 hectares.

Legend holds that Santiago himself named San Indalecio the first bishop of Auca. The first historically documented bishop was Asterio, who attended the 589 Council of Toledo. The rapid Muslim conquest of the area in the early 8th c. left the Christian population largely in place, and for a time Oca continued as seat of the bishop, probably until the destruction of the city in the late 8th c. For nearly the next 300 years the church was administered from several small town centers like Valpuesta, Amaya, Muñó, and Sasamón, until Sancho III relocated the see to Oca again in 1068. The town's glory was fleeting, for only 7 years later the see was moved to Gamonal, on the outskirts of Burgos. Today Villafranca has about 180 residents, with more on the weekends.

MONUMENTS: 1. Castle. 2. **Iglesia de Santiago**. 3. **Hospital de la Reina**.

1. Of the castle, located just south of the current cemetery, little is left. Here was also the site of the first Oca cathedral, dedicated to Santiago.

2. **Iglesia de Santiago**. The modern structure (1790–1800) replaces several earlier churches. The retablo was brought from the church of San Francisco in Belorado. It narrates the life of San Francisco, and includes a superb **Santiago Peregrino** and an Ecce Homo. The holy water font is a shell from the Philippines.

3. **Hospital de la Reina**. Its location at the eastern end of 2 difficult days of walking makes Villafranca a perfect place for a hospice. Alfonso III built one here in 884, of which no trace remains. In 1270 a doña Violante founded another, also vanished, except for some foundation stones discovered in recent excavations. Juana Manuel, Enrique II's queen, created another in 1380. Her large donation gives the current building one of its names, Queen's Hospice. San Antonio Abad, to whom it was dedicated, is the other name. King Felipe III donated 100 ducats toward its maintenance. The hospice was built in various phases. In the 15th c., or earlier, the hospice had a small rhomboidal entrance patio, flanked by some administrative rooms, a small porticoed patio, and some storage rooms in a basement. In the 16th c. an annex was built off a long hallway next to the church. It included a chapel and some dormitory rooms. In the 18th c. a kitchen was built at the end of the hall past the dormitories. On the north side of the hospice there was a small, detached burial chapel.

Like most *hospitales*, it also cared for the sick. An order from 1733 directs that rosemary be burned every day to alleviate the smell. As late as 1822 the hospice maintained 14 beds for men, 4 for women, 4 for priests, and 14 for the sick (5 for women and 9 for men). Four other beds were reserved for distinguished guests. The large staff was comprised of an administrator, a chaplain, a guard, a major-domo, and a full set of servants.

This *hospital* seems always to have thronged with pilgrims. A register for the year 1594 logs 16,767 pilgrims, on some days more than 200. In 1495 Künig von Vach noted that it had a big kitchen stove, with benches all around for pilgrims to warm themselves, and that it was known for the quality of its feather beds. Laffi, in the late 17th c., was impressed by the food. The building must have been very dark, for several extant documents speak to the purchase of lamps.

Today there is not much left to visit. The main entrance displays the coat of arms of the Catholic Monarchs (see ch. 42) and the eagle of San Juan Evangelista. It has a small chapel dedicated to San Antonio Abad.

✳ Montes de Oca In the local dialect, *monte* indicates not a mountain, but a hilly, desolate, scrubby wasteland. The Montes de Oca are certainly that: rolling, pine- and oak-covered hills and gullies, thick with heather and broom, host to "mushrooms of unbelievable size, as big as a large straw hat" [Laffi; trans. Hall (1997), 136]. It was also known for its wild animals and thieves. There are no distinguishing geographical features to guide the pilgrim. Laffi got lost here. So did the pilgrim Walter Starkie in the 1950s. We got lost near here in 1974, before the modern pilgrimage Road was marked.

The rolling hills, described in the Castilian epic *Poema de Fernán González* as "a fierce mountain" rise to a height of 1,150 m. and divide the watersheds of the Ebro, which flows to the Mediterranean, and the Duero, which empties into the Atlantic. The *Poema* makes clear that this *monte* was also the traditional eastern border of Castilla with Navarra.

Estonçe era Castiella un pequeño rincón,	At that time Castile was a poor corner;
era de castellanos Montes d' Oca mojón	Montes de Oca marked the frontier (171ab)

The steeply sided gully that cuts through the center of the region is known as the Puerto de la Pedraja, since it offers an inverse mountain: a steep descent, followed by a climb. At its eastern edge is a small monument to men from Burgos assassinated in 1936 during the Civil War whose bodies were dumped in this spot.

📖 Insurgent rebel forces rose against the Republican government on July 18, 1936. During the preceding months every political faction in the increasingly anarchic cities and villages attempted to summarily eliminate the leadership of opposing factions. The commonest technique was to burst in late at night, hustle the victim into a car, and take him for a ride, a short journey from which he never returned. In the morning heaps of bodies would be found in nearby dump sites. The massacres intensified during the weeks following the uprising, as lines and loyalties hardened and those with the upper hand strove to eliminate possible opposition. Some of the very worst atrocities were perpetrated by the fascist right wing in Burgos. During July and August of 1936, witnesses speak of discovering dozens of bodies every single day along the Arlanzón River, in the Montes de Oca, on the hill by Burgos's castle, and on the forested grounds of the Cartuja de Miraflores.

👟 **Valdeafuentes** Six km. before San Juan de Ortega, on the highway 1 km. south of the walking Road, is the small 13th-c. Ermita de Valdeafuentes that maintained a small pilgrim hospice from 1187. In the Middle Ages this was the site of a Cistercian priory and small village. The current Gothic ruin has been fitted out with modern statues of **Santiago**, San Millán, and Santo Domingo de la Calzada.

40. SAN JUAN DE ORTEGA

HISTORY

Juan Velázquez (ca. 1080–1163) was born to a humble family in Quintana Ortuño near Burgos. As a young man he became a disciple of Domingo de la Calzada, and helped him construct bridges in Logroño, Santo Domingo de la Calzada, and Nájera. When his mentor died in 1109, Juan went on pilgrimage to the Holy Land. On his way home he was shipwrecked. He prayed to San Nicolás de Barí, whose relic he had with him, that if the Saint would intercede to save him he would devote his life to helping pilgrims. On his return to Spain, Juan chose the notoriously dangerous and difficult wastes of the Montes de Oca as his mission and developed the Road from Villafranca to Burgos. He took the name Ortega from the Latin word for "thistle." His hospice in the wilderness was dedicated to San Nicolás.

By 1130 Juan's hospice in the woods had attracted the attention of powerful benefactors. Alfonso VII of Castilla donated the taxes from the town of Milanés. Alfonso visited the monastery several times, chose Juan as his personal confessor, and eventually granted him rents from most of the Montes de Oca region for his support. In 1138 Pope Innocent II offered his personal protection. Juan died in 1163, and in 1170 Alfonso III put the monastery under the protection of the Burgos Cathedral. Despite the early royal patronage and its importance to pilgrims, the hospice and small monastery struggled through the Middle Ages until 1431, when Bishop Pablo de Santamaría (see ch. 42) charged the Jeronymite Order with its maintenance. The church and monastery were enlarged. In 1462 Pedro Fernández de Velasco, the count of Haro, paid for a new baldachin over the Saint's tomb, and later the monks developed a pharmacy that was known throughout the region.

Over time, San Juan de Ortega came to be thought of as patron not only of hospice keepers, but also of children and of barren mothers. The reason is that when his tomb was opened, there was a pleasant odor, and out flew a swarm of white bees, which were interpreted to be the souls of unborn children that the Saint was keeping safe pending their incarnation in the wombs of the faithful. Among the women who trekked to the site was Isabel la Católica, childless queen of Castilla, who came to the monastery to pray for a son and heir. She took home an arm from the monastery's ivory crucifix as a souvenir. When at last she conceived, she named the boy Juan. After his death, she again came to pray, and when her next child was born, she named her Juana.

PILGRIMAGE

In the 16th c. the hospice was reported to have 16 beds. In the 1670's Laffi reported that "the fathers are wealthy and are very charitable to pilgrims" [Laffi; trans. Hall (1997), 136].

Monastery records from 1756 log 114 miracles granted up to that date to petitioners who had sought the intercession of San Juan de Ortega or San Nicolás de Bari here.

> Three of the granted miracles directly concern pilgrims:
> 1. Irish pilgrims were praying near the sepulcher for their dead 7-year-old child and laid some apples on the tomb. The child asked for one.

2. A French pilgrim named Vadovin, whose twisted feet could barely drag him along and whose arms were so deformed he could not even feed himself, was cured here.
3. A deformed pilgrim entered on crutches, vowing not to leave until he was well. All of his colleagues could hear the noise his nerves made stretching.

When we first visited San Juan with a group of pilgrims in 1974, Father José María Alonso Marroquín, parish priest of Agés, had to come and open up the semi-ruined monastery so that we could lay our sleeping bags on the floor. At that time, pilgrim groups were so rare that he arranged for us to be interviewed on the radio when we reached Burgos. Since the early 1980s, with the rebirth of the modern pilgrimage, the Church has assigned Father Alonso to San Juan full time to tend to pilgrims. His garlic soups, shared communally at the hospice's long table, have become legendary.

MONUMENT: **Church of San Juan de Ortega.**

Exterior:
• **Apses.** The oldest part of the church, the 3 12th-c. apses, may have been built by San Juan de Ortega himself, or at least under his direction. Their regularly cut stones and fine sculpture attest to early substantial investment in the enterprise. The **corbels** and **capitals** are particularly fine.
• The rest of the church was erected in the 15th c. by Juan de Colonia, the architect of much of the Burgos Cathedral.
• The façade bears the coat of arms of San Juan's patron, Bishop Pablo de Santamaría.

Interior:
• The church follows a plan laid out by the Saint: a Romanesque central apse, transept, and 3 semicircular apses, as in Jaca and Frómista.
• **Capitals.** One of the capitals of the right apse depicts the battle between Ferragut and Roland (see ch. 31). On the left of the apse, an extraordinary **triple capital** narrates the **Annunciation, Visitation, and Nativity.**

It is believed that the positioning of the Annunciation capital in the left transept has a calendrical function, since the Annunciation receives a ray of sunlight at twilight on the equinoxes of March 21 and September 22.

• **Tomb of San Juan de Ortega.** The Flamboyant Gothic baldachin, with its complex arches and delicate tracery, is attributed to Juan de Colonia. The alabaster tomb was carved in 1474 by Gil de Siloé. The panels narrate scenes from the life and miracles of San Juan.
    —Several robbers steal a cow; while trying to escape they are lost in a fog; in the morning they find themselves at the Saint's door.
    —San Nicolás de Bari appears to San Juan during the storm at sea.
    —At the opening of San Juan's tomb, white bees fly out.
    —Juan receives arriving pilgrims and sends his nephew Martín to bring them food. There is none. Juan sends Martín back to the pantry, and this time he finds it filled with bread.
• The **crypt.** Underneath the Gothic tomb is a **crypt** containing the **Romanesque tomb** of the Saint. The iconography is typical of the late 12th c. The Saint lies on

his deathbed attended by grieving monks in architectural frames, with angels emerging from clouds to receive his soul, shown as a small figure whose posture reveals his acceptance of his death. On another side 4 angels sustain the Lamb of God. On the tomb cover is Christ in Majesty in a mandorla, surrounded by the Tetramorphos.

• The Capilla de San Nicolás was financed by Queen Isabel in 1477. The *reja* is from 1580. The 18th-c. retablo, devised as a large reliquary, depicts in the center San Nicolás de Bari (as bishop) and San Juan de Ortega (as an Augustinian monk).

• Retablo de las Animas. Six panels depict tortured souls in hell and in purgatory, with Jesus and the Apostles above them.

• Plateresque Retablo de San Jerónimo. The retablo narrates how Jerome— during his time as a hermit in the desert—removed a thorn from a lion's paw. In gratitude, the lion served him by taking care of his donkey. When the beast was stolen by passing merchants, the lion served as beast of burden, until at last it was able to recover both the donkey and the merchants' camels. It is patent that this sculptor never saw real camels. In the left-center, Jerome—who loved to read the classics—is flagellated by angels who remind him that he is a Christian, not a Ciceronian.

Modern-day pilgrims have access to a portion of the old monastery that has been fitted out as a *refugio*. It also has a simple 15th-c. cloister and a tiny interior cloister. From the *refugio* window we have several times seen owls (*lechuzas*) sitting on the roof of the barn behind the monastery.

The village today is tiny and nearly deserted. What is left of the monastery is medium-sized and slowly undergoing restoration. But to get an idea of the enormity of San Juan de Ortega's former holdings, devote an hour to taking a walk all around the monastery wall. What this wall encloses was just the inner pasturelands and monastery gardens. Beyond the wall, the woodlot was most of the hill to the north, and the monastery pastures filled the valley.

41. SAN JUAN DE ORTEGA → BURGOS

Route 1: SAN JUAN DE ORTEGA → Agés → Atapuerca → Cardeñuela de Río Pico → Orbaneja → Villafría → Gamonal → BURGOS

Route 2: SAN JUAN DE ORTEGA → Agés → Atapuerca → Cardeñuela de Río Pico → Quintanilla-Ríopico → Castañares → BURGOS

Route 3: SAN JUAN DE ORTEGA → Santovenia de Oca → Zalduendo → Ibeas de Juarros → Castañares → BURGOS

You have to cross or skirt the Atapuerca Massif in order to reach Burgos. From San Juan de Ortega to the top of the massif the road is wild and beautiful, if steep. From the western slopes of the massif to the center of Burgos you are likely to find the city's industrial suburbs dusty, noisy, and interminable. With the exception of the Gamonal church, they are also relatively boring. Route 1, which bears the Road markings and is the most traditional, therefore strikes us as the most tiresome. We much prefer either of the other routes. Route 2 brings you into the city not through the blocks of factories and ranks of apartment houses, but through 5 km. of shady parkland south of the Arlanzón River. Route 3 skirts the massif and is therefore longer, but also enters Burgos through the park.

Route 1:
    As you come out of the forests from San Juan de Ortega, you will see on the heights east of Agés the 18th-c. Ermita de Nuestra Señora de Rebollar. As you walk through this valley's towns, you will note that many of the houses have stone first stories and timber-framed upper floors, with plaster-covered rubble-filled walls.

✳ Agés In 1052 King García el de Nájera (Navarra) gave the village to the monastery of Santa María la Real in Nájera. A marker at the entrance to the church says that he was buried here after his brother Fernando I of Castilla killed him in the Sept. 15, 1054, battle of Atapuerca, halfway between the 2 towns. The site is known locally as Fin de Rey (King's End). García's body was later moved to the royal pantheon in Nájera. Agés isn't much today, but in the early Middle Ages it was large enough to have a small Jewish community.
    The 16th-c. Gothic church of Santa Eulalia de Mérida, undergoing reconstruction as we write, reputedly contains a Rococo retablo.

Halfway to Atapuerca, before the Road crosses a creek, on the left is a 1–arch bridge built by San Juan de Ortega.

✳ Atapuerca This was one of the earliest recovered towns during the reconquest wars, with a small Christian population already by ca. 750. In the early 12th c. Alfonso VI gave the town to the Hospitallers of San Juan de Jerusalén in support of their mission to wage war against the infidels and to protect pilgrims. The wealthier homes in this town are built entirely of stone. The 15th-c. church is dedicated to San Martín.

From here the Road ascends to the top of the limestone Atapuerca Massif. From the heights medieval pilgrims saw for the first time the immense flatness of the Castilian Meseta. We can see the flatness of the landscape, but are more likely to notice the enormity of the suburbs of Burgos stretching endlessly before us.

In one of the caves that honeycomb the massif, archaeologists found the oldest human remains in Europe.

> 📖 José María Bermúdez de Castro and his team have been excavating in these caves since 1994. They have discovered fossils of early humans dating from 127,000 to 1,000,000 years ago. The vast quantity of human bones in these caves to date represents more than 90% of all pre-Neanderthal remains found in Europe. Indications are that some of the bones come from a previously unknown subspecies of homonid, *Homo antecessor*, who may be the common ancestor of Neanderthals and modern humans.

Since the discoveries the caves have not been open to the public.

✳ **Cardeñuela de Río Pico** The first cluster of houses after descending from the Atapuerca heights is the village of Cardeñuela. Its church of Santa Eulalia, whose *espadaña* (bell wall) holds 2 large bells, has a Renaissance entrance with an image of the Saint.

✳ **Gamonal** In the early 11th c. Castilla's principal bishopric was in Auca (Villafranca de Montes de Oca; see ch. 39). In a move to centralize power in what was to be the new center of the kingdom, Alfonso VI transferred the see in 1075 to Gamonal, offering a former palace of Fernando I and the adjoining church of Santa María. Gamonal is now a bedroom community contiguous with Burgos itself. A few bits of the old city can be seen among the blocks of apartment houses.

Gamonal's church, the 14th-c. Nuestra Señora la Real y Antigua, is preceded by a covered atrium next to which stands a 13th-c. defensive tower. The church's tympanum depicts the Coronation of the Virgin. The doorway is framed with the castles and lions of Castilla and León, and the 15th-c. Mudéjar-style door is inlaid with geometric designs. Inside the church you will find a classic 1-nave Latin cross with transept and a square apse. Its vaults are influenced by those of the Burgos Cathedral: crossing nerves with a longitudinal central nerve and an 8–pointed star in the vault of the apse.

In front of the church is a 16th-c. Gothic roadside cross with figures of **Santiago**, Saints Pedro and Andrés, and Christ tied to the column. In the center of the street is a striking 1992 rusted iron monument dedicated to people who donate blood.

Route 2:

A trail leads across the Castilian Meseta from the Quintanilla Church to Castañares, in the Arlanzón Valley. From there it connects with the path that runs through the stately trees of the parkland south of the Arlanzón River.

✳ **Castañares** The village is documented from the late 10th c.

Route 3:

This route, slightly longer but easier walking, skirts the Atapuerca Massif and joins Route 2 in Castañares.

✳ **Santovenia de Oca** This ancient village is documented from the 10th c. Its church of Santa Eugenia sits on a hill in its center. At the west end of the village is a small medieval bridge over the Río Vena.

✱ Zalduendo This late medieval town has suffered much change as it has been cut by modern highways. The church is dedicated to Nuestra Señora de la Asunción.

✱ Ibeas de Juarros This is an early settlement that belonged to the Cathedral of Burgos until the mid-13th c., when it was given to the Military Order of Santiago (see ch. 60). Its church is dedicated to San Martín.

42. BURGOS

Romans fortified the hill overlooking the Arlanzón River. The site seems to have been of minimal importance in Visigothic and Muslim times. In the 9th c. Alfonso III of León built a small castle over the Roman ruins. After Moorish raiders devastated the area in 922, a tiny county called Castilla, having recently seceded from León, appointed 2 judges, Laín Calvo and Nuño Rasura, to rule over the area and to defend it from the Muslims and from Ordoño II of León. These two, together with Nuño Rasura's nephew Fernán González, are considered the founding fathers of Castilla, widening its borders and strengthening its government. From the start, Burgos was Castilla's most important city.

As a small buffer state between León, Navarra, and Aragón, young Castilla was much fought over. Sancho el Mayor of Navarra captured it in 1029 and left it to Fernando I el Magno, the first medieval Christian ruler to preside over the whole of the north in 1 semiunified kingdom. Unfortunately, Fernando's will divided the north among his 3 male children: Alfonso VI (León), García (Galicia), and Sancho II (Castilla). Daughter Urraca was given the city of Zamora. Sancho went to war against Alfonso and his powerful sister, Urraca. When Sancho was assassinated in Zamora, Alfonso was widely held to be responsible. One of the leaders of the Castilian nobility, young Rodrigo Díaz de Vivar, later known as El Cid, forced Alfonso to swear in Burgos's church of Santa Gadea in 1072 that he had had nothing to do with the crime. The King's rage led to Rodrigo's banishment, described in the opening of Spain's great medieval epic, the *Poema de mío Cid*. The poem is specific about Burgos's urban geography. For example, when the Cid found himself exiled by Alfonso VI, he rode with his men first to the cathedral. Then, forbidden to remain within the city, he and his men pitched their tents on the gravelly south bank of the Río Arlanzón.

Partiós' de la puerta, por Burgos aguijava	He left the doorway, and spurred through Burgos
llegó a Sancta María, luego descavalga,	he came to Santa María, and there he dismounted,
fincó los inojos, de coraçon rrogava.	he fell on his knees, and prayed with all his heart.
La oración fecha, luego cavalgava,	When he'd finished praying, he rode off,
salió por la puerte e Arlançón passava,	he exited the city gate and crossed the Arlanzón,
cabo essa villa en la glera posava,	near the city, he set up on the gravel bank,
fincava la tienda e luego descavalgava.	when his tent was pitched he dismounted. [51–7]

The political fortunes of Burgos have varied with the wars and whims of Castilla's monarchs. Alfonso VI permanently located the bishopric in Burgos in 1075, donating for a Romanesque cathedral—now vanished—the land on which Fernando I had built a palace. Eventually he made peace with the Cid. Alfonso VII made Burgos his principal residence. He also began the Monastery of Las Huelgas. Burgos prospered, and in 1150 the Muslim traveler Idrisi lauded the city:

Burgos, a large city, is divided by a river into 2 parts, each with its wall, and in one of them the Jews predominate. It is strong and rich, it has commercial establishments, markets, warehouses, and is frequented by many travelers, both as a way station and as a final destination. It has many vineyards, and in its region are numerous well-appointed towns. [Idrisi, 145]

Fernando III began the Gothic cathedral in 1221, and the city boomed, even though for a brief period Sancho IV shifted the center of royal favor southwest to Valladolid. During the late 14th-c. dynastic wars, Burgos sided with Enrique de Trastámara in his victorious war against Pedro I el Cruel, and in fact Enrique (who reigned 1369–1379) was crowned at Las Huelgas. A century later, in the wars between Enrique IV and his half sister Isabel la Católica, Burgos eventually went with young Isabel. She often resided in the city, which had become central Spain's principal commercial center. Isabel and Fernando received Columbus here after his second voyage in 1497. In the Comunidades revolt of 1520, which pitted the urban bourgeoisie against the new Hapsburg King Carlos V, Burgos was a center of opposition to the monarch. The city's decline began when Madrid was declared the permanent capital of Spain in 1560. Yet 2 more wars left their imprint on Burgos. Napoleon occupied the city from 1808 to 1813 and destroyed what was left of the medieval castle. And General Francisco Franco made it his operations center during the 1936–9 Civil War (see ch. 41): his headquarters was the Palacio de Munguiro, Paseo de la Isla, #37, an 1883 brick, neo-Gothic town house.

The extreme temperatures of the Burgos region do not favor agriculture: "Nine months of winter, and three of hell" (*Nueve meses de invierno y tres de infierno*) goes a local proverb. Instead, Burgos's prosperity, as Idrisi noted, depended on commerce, and that depended on transportation. Burgos sits at the eastern edge of the great plateau of the Meseta Alta. It has a pivotal location on the Road to Santiago. Good roads connect it to the port cities of Laredo, Santander, and Castro Urdiales, 150 km. to the north, thus linking the wool-producing Meseta to the textile centers of England and Flanders. By the early 14th c., Burgos merchants were regular visitors in London and Bruges. Castilian monarchs abetted Burgos's commercial growth, abolishing duties for goods imported by foreign merchants. As the unofficial capital of the kingdom, a bureaucracy of scribes, administrators, and tax farmers congregated in Burgos, soon becoming its leading citizens and investors. Although there was no manufacturing in the region, local produce and artisanry were traded. Documents attest to the presence of surgeons, doctors, money changers, and lawyers, as well as artisans like millers, charcoal makers, dyers, tile makers, and wood and salt merchants. By the mid-13th c. a large market flourished on the banks of the Arlanzón outside the walls. The fish market, originally alongside the cathedral, was relocated to the riverbank next to the bridge.

Almost from its inception Burgos was a cosmopolitan city. Castilians, Basques, Aragonese, and Franks occupied the parishes to the east. There were 2 Moorish quarters. The earliest, or upper, *morería*, was near what is now the Seminario Diocesano. But so many Muslims moved to Burgos during Enrique IV's reign that the *morería* had to be expanded in the flats along the river near what is now the Centro Cultural Francisco Salinas. The Moorish cemetery was on the south bank between Las Huelgas and the river. The earliest Jewish quarter occupied the ground between the *morería* and the castle, with the modern Calle de Embajadores the border between the neighborhoods. Later a second *aljama* of Jewish merchants grew up near the Puerta de San Martín along the pilgrimage route through the city. While most of the Jews were artisans or small businessmen, a few worked for the monarchs as tax collectors and became very wealthy: the Burgos Jewish community paid 3 times the taxes of any other Castilian *aljama*.

📖 In an episode in the *Poema de mío Cid* that plays on standard medieval Christian anti-Semitic stereotypes, the poverty-stricken Cid raises money to provision his exiled soldiers by borrowing from Burgos's Jewish money-lenders, and then tricks them by offering a chest filled with worthless stones as security and requiring their oath not to look in the chest for a year.

Con vuestro consejo bastir quiero dos archas	With your help I want to provide two chests
incámos las d'arena ca bien serán pesadas.	we'll fill them with sand so they'll be heavy
cubiertas de guadalmeçí e bien enclaveadas.	covered with tooled leather and well nailed.
Los guademeçís vermejos e los clavos bien dorados.	The leather will be red, and the nails of gold.
Por Rachel e Vidas vayádes me privado:	Go for me to Raquel and Vidas in secret.
	(85–9)

The Jews provided the gold, which the Cid never repays, at least not in the *Poema*.

Burgos was also home of the prominent Santamaría family, who, as Jews in the 14th c. and as Christian converts in the 15th, played important roles in Castilla's political and ecclesiastical history. The most influential was Shelomo Halevi/Pablo de Santamaría (1350–1435).

📖 Shelomo Halevi received a classic Jewish education, impressed the community with his wisdom and learning, and became their precocious chief rabbi. In 1390, moved by the preaching of San Vicente Ferrer, he and his children converted. Shelomo, now Pablo de Santamaría, took a doctorate in Paris, dissolved his marriage with his still-Jewish wife, took religious orders, and went to Avignon, where he became friends with the schismatic Pope Benedict XIII. In 1403 he was named Bishop of Cartagena. The bishop carried out a number of thorny political assignments for King Enrique III, and after the king's death he formed part of the Council of Regents. In 1415 he became Bishop of Burgos. Pablo's best-known book, *Scrutinium scriptuarum*, purports to prove the superiority of Christianity over Judaism. Legend makes him responsible for the 6-pointed star on the cathedral's west façade. (It is legend because the façade predates him, and because the 6-pointed star was a standard decorative motif in medieval Christian and Islamic art that did not become the iconic symbol of Judaism until the 19th c.) Pablo's son Alonso de Cartagena succeeded him as Burgos's bishop.

Burgos's Jewish community was decimated during the 1391 anti-Semitic riots that swept through Castilla.

Burgos's modern growth began with the Civil War, when the Franco government established textile factories here to replace the Catalán factories under Republican control. In the 1960s chemical, textile, metallurgy, and other heavy industries were attracted to the government-sponsored Burgos Development Zone.

PILGRIMAGE

No Spanish town had more pilgrim hospices than Burgos. In the late 15th c., Künig von Vach counted 32, some 25 of which still existed in the 18th c. They were founded by royalty and by private citizens, by merchant guilds, and by religious and military orders that competed in offering services to pilgrims.

The earliest known hospice was San Juan Evangelista (aka Alberguería del Emperador), founded prior to 1085 by Alfonso VI. Its charter mandated a chapel to serve as a burial place for pilgrims. By 1097 it had grown to a monastery administered by the Benedictines, and in 1128 Alfonso VII donated it to the bishopric. It had 12 beds and a chapel dedicated to San Lesmés. After its destruction in the Trastámara wars, the hospice was rebuilt in 1479 and extensively renovated in 1626. Its 50 beds and its pharmacy were supported by the Cofradía de Mercaderes de Burgos. It was closed in the 17th c. West of the city the monumental and still extant Hospital de Rey (see below) owes its founding to Alfonso VIII at the end of the 12th c. By 1212 it belonged to Las Huelgas and was administered by the Order of Calatrava. Burgos's patron saint, Adelelmo Lesmés, a Benedictine who helped Alfonso VI reconquer Toledo, also founded a hospice for pilgrims. A doña Elvira la Cordobanera founded one ca. 1337 with 18 beds, 8 of them reserved for women; its caretaker—according to her will—was to be a "person of good name and good soul." She also donated 50 pairs of shoes per year "for pilgrims going to or coming from Compostela." A wool merchant, Pedro Pérez, founded another hospice in 1346. Burgos's blind people successfully lobbied the city council in 1312 for an *hospital* dedicated to their needs. The dean of the Cathedral Council founded a pilgrim hospice that also treated lepers (see ch. 45), a rarity for a hospice inside the city walls. Two extramural hospices also treated lepers: the Hospital de San Lázaro de Malatos (1165) near the bridge; and Villayuda, founded by Alfonso VIII, that still had 8 beds in the 18th c.

No matter how eager you are to reach Compostela, Burgos is not a town to rush through. It contains a staggering wealth of art, more than any other city along the Road. We usually spend 6 hours with our pilgrims in the cathedral alone. Since many monuments are open only before mass, it will take a minimum of 2 days to see even the most important. And the art is of such high quality that even for the wildest enthusiast it may stretch the word "insatiable" to its limit. We have described 17 monuments below, and at the end of the chapter we've listed some others that in almost any other city would have made the must-see register.

Twice we have been fortunate enough to be in Burgos for Corpus Christi. The procession is one of the most impressive we have ever seen. The consecrated host rides through the streets on an enormous cart made of silver brought back to Europe by Columbus. After high mass, Burgos's famous giants—puppets almost 2 stories tall—dance in the streets. They also dance during the festival of Saints Peter and Paul (June 29), which we have also been fortunate enough to hit twice.

MONUMENTS: 1. **Catedral**. 2. **Iglesia de San Nicolás de Bari**. 3. Arco de Fernán González. 4. Castle. 5. Iglesia de San Esteban and **Museo del Retablo**. 6. Arco de San Esteban. 7. Iglesia de Santa Agueda. 8. **Casa de Miranda and Archaeological Museum**. 9. **Arco de Santa María**. 10. Statue of the Cid. 11. **Casa del Cordón** and Capitanía General. 12. **Iglesia de San Lesmés**. 13. **Cartuja de Miraflores**. 14. **Monasterio de las Huelgas**. 15. Iglesia de San Gil. 16. Paseo de la Isla. 17. **Hospital del Rey**.

1. **Catedral**. Take your time with this cathedral, for it is the richest anthology of medieval art styles and genres that you will find along the Road. Buy the ticket to enter the various chapels and dependencies. Bring your binoculars and flashlight. Perhaps reserve your visit to the main altar for a high mass, when the retablo will be spotlighted and the organ will make all of the dim recesses of the chapels vibrate with music. Make several visits and focus your attention each time on 1 or 2 artists

or areas. Burgos's cathedral is like a box of exquisite bonbons: no one, no matter how fond of chocolate, can do their flavors justice by eating them all in one sitting.

Architects of large medieval churches strove to affect worshipers with a sense of wonder and awe. In Burgos they exceeded their expectations. For openers, think of the unprecedented size of this church. In the 13th c. it stood not among today's multistory offices and businesses, but instead rose seemingly miraculously from amid the 1- and 2-story houses that constituted the horizontality of medieval towns. If you can, picture Burgos's urban landscape as a plain from which enormous pinnacles, the spires of her churches, soared skyward as visible links with heaven.

The Gothic cathedral was begun by Fernando III el Santo and his building bishop, Mauricio.

📖 Mauricio (ca. 1175–1238) was born in Medina de Pomar, probably of an English merchant immigrant family. During his education in Paris, various ambassadorships, and participation in the Fourth Lateran Council, he developed an enthusiasm for the new French style of Gothic architecture. After serving as archdeacon in Toledo, he was elected bishop of Burgos in 1213 and played an active role in Castilian politics. He lobbied successfully for a mammoth new cathedral to replace Alfonso VI's **Romanesque** construction.

With the monarchs and court in attendance, the first stone was laid on July 20, 1221. Mauricio oversaw the initial construction, hiring masons, carpenters, carters, smiths, and artisans of all types. More importantly, he raised funds, even contributing part of his own fortune for the labor. Pope Honorio III conceded indulgences (forgiveness from sins) for major contributors to the building fund. The first mass in the new building was celebrated in 1230. Work continued at Bishop Mauricio's accelerated pace even after his death in 1238. The ceiling vaults

BURGOS

were closed in 1243, an amazing 22 years after construction began. To a large extent, the cathedral's sense of harmonious unity is due to this man's vision and vigor.

Though it never lost its 13th-c. Gothic character, the structure was enlarged, reshaped, and adorned for the next 500 years, with significant examples of Gothic, Plateresque, Renaissance, Baroque, and Rococo art. The silhouette of its soaring towers and the pinnacles of the Capilla del Condestable (see below) are one of the distinguishing features of the Burgos skyline.

Exterior:

• **West façade.** Despite the late-17th-c. mutilation of its 3 monumental portals, the west façade is stunning for its size, harmony, and self-confident Gothic design based on a subtle interplay of lines: vertical (towers, columns), horizontal (balconies and friezes), and pyramidal (Gothic arches and the arch of the rose window continuing to the lateral doors). See how the stone becomes progressively lighter and airier from the lower masses of solid stone to the filigree of the towers and spires. The rose window's 6–pointed star is a common Gothic motif. The Virgin at the top is by Juan de Colonia, who also finished the German-style openwork towers (1442–58). The 8 kings in the arcade—from Fernando I to Alfonso XI—remind people in the new Gothic fashion of the links between royal and divine power. Many of the sculptures on the tower are Gothic masterworks, noted for the graceful simplicity of their poses, that convey a strong sense of spirituality. Who do you think that is on top, riding a horse, sword in hand?

The central door was known as the Portada Real, through which royalty entered in procession. It is also called the **Puerta del Perdón**. The current door is a 1663 addition in the Greco-Roman style that unfortunately jars with the rest of the composition. The 4 monumental statues depict Bishops Asterio and Mauricio and Kings Alfonso VI and Fernando III. The side portals depict the conception and the coronation of the Virgin.

• **South portal: Puerta del Sarmental.** This ca. 1230–40 portal at the south end of the transept shows strong French influence. The door is divided by a mullion (*parteluz*) bearing the restored statue of a bishop, possibly the founding bishop Mauricio. The **tympanum**'s simple Christ in Majesty, surrounded by the symbolic Tetramorphos, is a Romanesque motif, executed here in the earliest Gothic style, that combines the representation of real things with idealizations important exclusively for their symbolic value. Look, for example, at the Evangelists writing at their desks. The Christ is so similar to one at Amiens that they may be by the same sculptor. A different artist executed the frieze over the door. Its depiction of the **12 Apostles**, devoid of any anecdote, is the earliest of the Burgos Cathedral's external sculptures. The archivolts continue the reference to the Apocalypse (see ch. 5) with the array of angels and old men. The jambs, linking the Old Testament to the New, portray Moses and Aaron, and Peter and Paul.

• The exterior wall of the Capilla del Condestable bears enormous coats of arms of the Velasco-Mendoza family in an ornate, late Gothic frame.

• **North portal: Portada de la Coronería.** This mid-13th-c. façade at the north end of the transept, now somewhat deteriorated, presents good examples of early Gothic monumental sculpture. The Virgin and Saint John intercede for humanity before Jesus, human in His nakedness and suffering, but also divine judge on His throne, accompanied by angels bearing the instruments of His Passion. The theme continues in the Judgment and weighing of souls on the lintel. Sinners are punished horrifyingly on the inner archivolt. As at Chartres, Apostles are arrayed on the jambs.

📖 Early Gothic sculpture differs from the Romanesque you have been seeing in several ways. It has moved away from static, hermetic, idealized forms toward a representation of the particular. Many of the figures still project a sense of otherworldliness, but the details of their faces, hands, and clothes are real and immediate. The figures often inhabit real spaces: tops of towers, walls, balconies, and the like. Frequently the figures interact with each other. The emphasis is less on the symbolic value of the figures (as in the Romanesque Christ in Majesty surrounded by 4 animals representing the Evangelists), and more on narrative cycles: figures telling stories.

• North side: Puerta de Pellejería. This Plateresque composition, begun in 1516 by Francisco de Colonia, afforded access from the leatherworkers' street and the higher neighborhoods of the city. It is one of the first monumental ensembles in Spain to show transition to the new Renaissance style. The sculptures of the 4 saints flanking the door—Andrés, **Santiago**, Juan Bautista, and Juan Evangelista, whose martyrdom is shown in the panels above—are still Gothic in concept, but the decorative motifs, introduced into Spain via books of engravings, are infused with the new classicism.

Interior:
The inside of this cathedral is so immense that it is easy to get lost. Once you buy the ticket that will admit you to the principal areas, we suggest a visit in this order: (A) center of the cathedral, main retablo, transept, and choir; (B) chapels, counterclockwise, beginning at the south door, or the Puerta del Sarmental; (C) cloister and museum.

• General plan; vaults. The cruciform floor plan is typically Gothic, executed here in grandiose proportions. The 3 naves are separated by massive columns that sustain the nerved vaulting. The stained-glass windows rise above an arcaded triforium. The architectural techniques for handling weight and height are French: the pillars, triforium, and series of flying buttresses have direct models in Coutances, Bourges, Saint-Denis, and Paris. Also in the French fashion, the lateral aisles extend into an ambulatory, from which radiate a number of hexagonal chapels. The transept was rebuilt by Juan de Vallejo (1539–67) after a disastrous fire. Most striking is Vallejo's 1568 daring openwork **lantern vault**, 54 m. high, built in the Mudéjar style. King Felipe II said it was the "work of angels, not of men."

• **Main altar.** The Renaissance **retablo** (1562–80) was designed by Rodrigo de la Haya. The style is monumental Romanist: 7 vertical columns and 4 horizontal stories narrate the life of the Virgin. Many of the sculptures are by Rodrigo's brother Martín, with the central Coronation of the Virgin by Juan de Anchieta. Note the solidity of the figures and the realistic attention to the architectural settings of the groupings. The central silver-encrusted figure of Santa María la Mayor is Hispano-Flemish (1464) and projects the sweetness and serenity of the late international Gothic style.

• In the crossing of the transept are the **tombs of the Cid** and his wife **doña Jimena**, brought here in 1921 from San Pedro de Cardeña (8 km. to the south).

• **Choir.** In 16th-c. Spain it was fashionable to close the nave with a choir, breaking up (and for the modern taste, spoiling) the view. The lateral <u>stalls</u>, in walnut, by Felipe Vigarny, Andrés de Nájera, and friends (1507–12) are notable for their Renaissance realism. The end stalls and bishop's throne (1586) show a more mannered, idealized heroic view. Every surface of each chair is covered with unique designs. Spend some time examining the backs, seats, armrests, side panels, decorative motifs, and crowning frieze. Don't miss the Virgen del Pilar, on one of the north side seats, or the urinating angels.

In the center of the choir, the 13th-c. **tomb of Bishop Mauricio**, founder of the cathedral, is copper over wood, with encrustations of precious stones and Limoges-style enamels. The choir has 2 organs, one Baroque and the other Neoclassic.

• Chapels. Some 15 chapels circle the naves and ambulatory of the cathedral. As if that were not enough to glut the eye, other significant works flank the aisles in between the chapels and decorate the outside of the choir and *trascoro*. We describe them going counterclockwise from the Puerta del Sarmental.

—1. Capilla de San Enrique. 1670–4. Hyperdecorated, with 2 domes. The 13th-c. funerary frontals have rows of saints under arches. The central tomb is that of a canon who served the Condestables (see chapel 4). The superbly emotional **Ecce Homo** is of the school of Gil de Siloé.

—2. Sacristy. Baroque (1762–5). Fray José de San Juan de la Cruz's **dome**— one of the best carved plaster ensembles in Castilla, garishly painted in 1870— depicts the Coronation of the Virgin.

—3. Capilla de Santiago. Built 1521–34 by Juan de Vallejo. The *reja* (1696) is capped with a **Matamoros**, and with sculptures of Adam and Eve and the Annunciation, thus pairing the birth of sin with the birth of redemption. The retablo by González de Lara (1772) has another statue of **Santiago Matamoros**.

—4. <u>Capilla del Condestable</u>. This chapel is one of Europe's great treasures, a schoolbook of the transition from Gothic to Renaissance styles, and almost by itself justifies a visit to Burgos.

📖 Don Pedro Fernández de Velasco and his wife doña Mencía de Mendoza, the Condestables de Castilla, were among the dozen or so most powerful nobles of 15th-c. Spain. Juan I had created the post of *condestable* in 1382 for the chief administrator of the realm, a sort of prime minister, who, among other things, lead the troops in battle and held the keys to the city where the monarch was in residence. In the mid 15th-c. the post was given to the Velasco family, the counts of Haro, which held it for several generations, and enriched themselves mightily with Burgos's burgeoning wool trade. At their height the Velascos controlled 258 towns in Castilla la Vieja.

Pedro ordered the chapel in 1492, stipulating that the architects should follow the instructions of the countess doña Mencía. In 1495 she entrusted her son, Bernardino, the second Condestable, with finishing the work. In time, the third Condestable, Íñigo, took over. Finally came Pedro, the fourth. The bulk of the work was executed in the mid-1520s.

The capilla's octagonal shape, the plain surfaces of the walls bearing the coats of arms, the sense of depth created by the triforium, the windows and daring cupola, all contribute to a sense of unity and harmony, despite the variety of decorative elements it contains. Don't miss the tiny details, such as the hundreds of small animals ensconced in the carved leafy decorations of the chapel.

The chapel contains more major works of art than do most museums. At the entrance you will see:

—The Renaissance *reja* by Cristóbal de Andino (1523).

—The façade by Simón de Colonia. The savages who sustain the scenes of the Birth and Presentation are repeated in large size on the chapel walls.

—Two 14th-c. tombs just inside the door. They display typical funerary iconography: professional mourners on the earlier tomb, religious symbols on the later one.

—The Mudéjar-Gothic <u>openwork dome</u> by Simón de Colonia. The architect shows off by having the dome's weight transferred to the pillars by delicate nerves that cross in midair. The 8-pointed openwork star, of Mudéjar inspiration, is filled with Flamboyant Gothic tracery.

—The <u>sepulcher of the Condestables</u> (1525–32) was carved from Italian Carrara marble. Authorship is disputed (Vigarny, Alonso Berruguete, and Juan de Lugano are all possibilities). The sculptor lavished attention on the details of the clothing, armor, hair, and pillows. The veins on the dead constable's hands look as if they could still carry blood. If the dog at doña Mencía's feet smelled food, it would bark.

—The **retablo de Santa Ana** (right), begun by Gil de Siloé and finished by his son Diego, has 3 stories and is framed in the Hispano-Flemish filigree style. Angels bear the escutcheons of the Velasco and Mendoza families. In the center, the **Santa Ana** by Gil de Siloé shows many realistic details: the child-Virgin seems to want to leave Ana's lap, leaning forward toward the book. The images have elegant hands. Gil de Siloé also carved the predella with its small seated figures, the women, with round faces, tiny eyes, and smiling mouths, carrying their books and palms of martyrdom. Their hair is done up in an anthology of late-15th-c. coiffures. He also carved the 7 female saints:

—**Bárbara**: her tower is the same as in the Cartuja retablo.

—**Catarina**: in the center, with her broken wheel.

—**Dorotea**: on the left, with the roses; notice her rapturous expression and her intricately styled hair.

—**Inés**: left side, a lamb at her feet.

—**Isabel**: John the Baptist is at her feet.

—**María Egipciaca**: seated, with a book. She shows Gil de Siloé's attention to minute details such as the complicated folds of cloth in her lap and the delicate detail work on the book in her hand. The desert saints were generally shown nude, with long hair providing minimal modesty.

—**Elena**: with her cross. Her trancelike expression seems that of a woman lost in a world of ideal beauty that we can contemplate, but not enter.

Diego de Siloé is responsible for the central **Christ and angels** (1520–3). The head with half-closed eyes, the sharp nose, the half-open mouth, and the curly hair are signatures of Diego de Siloé's work. While Gil is late Gothic, Diego was profoundly influenced by the Italian Renaissance. Typically Italian are the studied anatomy of the idealized nude; the circular composition, and the balanced structure, with the angels supporting Christ's arms; the contrast between the brows wrinkled in pain and the quiet emotion of the angels turning away their heads. Diego de Siloé's **María Magdalena** (with her unguent jar) is strikingly different from his father's women: notice the round eyes, full fleshy lips, angular nose, and the vertical falls of drapery.

—The **retablo of the principal altar** (1522–6) was executed by Diego de Siloé and Felipe Vigarny, who were paid 1,500 ducats for their labor. It was painted in 1526 by León Picardo. Its theme is the Presentation of Jesus in the temple. The Renaissance flair for drama sets the scene between columns, as on a stage. The central altar acts as the focal point for the 2 converging groups. On the left, the woman's basket, doves, and diagonal drapery folds indicate the direction of her walking. The figures are grouped with an eye to realism. See how Vigarny's Simeón stretches out his arms to receive the child Jesus, while Anne, with her index figure emphasizing her words, draws near the group. As Diego de Siloé's Mary takes Jesus from Joseph, look at the triangle formed by head, arm, and child. Though the right figures are Diego de Siloé's and the left are Vigarny's, the ensemble works harmoniously. Also by Diego de Siloé: Jesus tied to the column (head lowered, a Michelangelo-like gesture), the Dolorosa (with delicate hands), and San Juan. By Vigarny: Christ praying in the garden, the angel on the column, and Christ on the road to Calvary.

Vigarny's are the figures of the **Church** (left) and the **Synagogue** (right). Church has a young face and arrogant posture, emphasized by her protruding chin and the fact that her body and face turn in different directions. The cross, chalice, and monstrance typically part of this scene are missing. By contrast, Synagogue's face is that of a blind old man, grimacing. His turban is oriental. His book has verses from Exodus 34:33 (Moses covers his head with a veil to announce the Law to his people) and 1 Corinthians 10:12 (Paul warns of the destruction of those who do not accept Christ).

Three marvelous groupings at the base of the retablo are by Diego de Siloé. In the Annunciation Mary, caught by surprise, seems unstable. The Birth includes classic ruins and a kneeling Italianate Virgin with long, expressive hands. The **Visitation** places the 4 women in an architectural setting. The Virgin, with classic face, raises her cousin, the tension of lifting communicated by the drapery folds. The strong diagonal line of the 3 heads is balanced by the fourth woman and by the architecture. This interplay of broken lines is characteristic of Italian 15th-c. painting.

To the right of this altar is a stone **Santiago Peregrino**.

—The **retablo de San Pedro** (left) depicts the edifice of faith presided over by Pedro and the Apostles, sustained by saints, and defended by the preaching orders. Armored San Jorge (top right) here is the ideal Christian knight. This retablo was built in the 1520s to counterbalance the Santa Ana retablo.

Like most in this chapel, it is a collaborative work. Diego de Siloé carved the San Sebastián (the tree with its knots and its roots in the air is characteristic), Juan Bautista (see how well he differentiates age and emotional states), Juan Evangelista (elegant, idealized, eyes fixed on his visions), and **Jerónimo** (aged nude, wrinkled skin, agonized face, and toothless mouth combine to produce extraordinary realism). Vigarny's are the **San Benito** (realistically plump), **Santiago** (expressive face, posture showing his exhaustion), Pablo, Andrés, Francisco, and Domingo.

—The **coats of arms** of the Mendozas and Velascos, the families of the Condestables. Above them, in the triforium, men and women in furs. This may reflect the period custom of dressing as savages the family servants who presented the family's coats of arms at festivals.

—The chapel contains several stellar paintings. The **triptych** is attributed to **Gerard David** (15th c.). The Van Dyck-like **Christ in Agony** is by Mateo Cerezo. The painting of **María Magdalena** is by Giovanni Pietro Ricci.

—*Trasaltar*. As you leave the Capilla del Condestable you will see the back of the cathedral's main altar. Parts of the 5 **high-relief panels** are much deteriorated by "stone cancer," although the central scenes remain pretty much untouched. The 2 exterior panels in the Baroque style are by Pedro Alonso de los Ríos (1681–3). The 3 in the center are by **Felipe Vigarny**, whose transitional art combines 2 styles. The crowded background scenes are late Gothic. The corporal reality of the figures and the classicist decoration on the gates of the city show Renaissance influence. The crowd surrounding **Jesus on the road to Calvary** seems a Renaissance urban rush hour. The ensemble works as a dynamic grouping, while each individual figure communicates a sense of isolation before the transcendental event.

Giovanni Pietro Ricci's mid-17th-c. paintings flanking the carved panels are noted for their splendid coloring, their inset details that often seem like miniature still lifes, and their dramatic compositions. The panels portray Saints Céntola (losing her breast), Casilda (basket of flowers), Victoria (leaning against an angel), Antonio de Padua (his serenity contrasting with the vigor of the witness to his mystic vision), and Francisco (receiving the stigmata).

—5. Capilla de San Gregorio. This chapel contains 2 nice 14th-c. tombs. Bishop Hinojosa's tomb (d. 1327) depicts contemporary funerary processions, whose excessive emotional displays were banned by Church authorities in 1344. Bishop Fontecha's tomb (d. 1351), sculpted after the ban, shows his body accompanied by angels, religious figures praying over him, and a stately procession.

—6. Capilla de la Anunciación (aka San Antonio Abad). The retablo (1540) is by disciples of Diego de Siloé.

—7. Capilla de la Natividad. Paid for by a family that made its fortune in Perú. The Renaissance retablo by Martín de la Haya and colleagues (ca. 1583) shows a strong influence of both Gaspar Becerra and Michelangelo.

—In between Capillas 7 and 8 is the tomb of Pedro Fernández de Villegas, the work of Simón de Colonia (1503). It is richly decorated with the Fernández escutcheons, and scenes from the life of the Virgin are set in filigree-like moldings.

—8. Capilla de San Nicolás. Retains only a deteriorated 13th-c. tomb and a wooden 13th-c. altar frontal with the typical Romanesque icons of Christ Pantocrator, the Tetramorphos, and Apostles.

—Escalera Dorada, at the end of the north transept. In 1519, access to the cathedral through this door was facilitated by this innovative staircase by Diego de Siloé. Its overall plan and profuse decoration recall Italian models, even though it predates Michelangelo's similar construction in the Laurentine palace. The combination of textures from the white marble and black-and-gold staircase is particularly striking. For Renaissance masters like Diego de Siloé, something functional—like a staircase—could be just as much a work of art as a painting or a sculpture.

—9. Capilla de Santa Ana, or La Concepción. Built by Juan and Simón de Colonia, 1447–48.

The retablo, by Diego de la Cruz and Gil de Siloé (before 1487) represents the Tree of Jesse, an unusual retablo subject. Jesse sleeps; from his chest springs a tree with the kings of Judah who, as the house of David, are the ancestors of Mary. She appears with Jesus high in the center. Below Mary, her parents San Joaquín and Santa Ana embrace chastely, suggesting Mary's Immaculate Conception. The Church (open-eyed, chalice, intact staff) and Synagogue (blind, tablets of the Law, broken staff) attend the Virgin. The figures in this retablo, with their Flemish face types, are not as skillfully executed as those on the retablo in the Cartuja de Miraflores (see below).

The sepulcher of Bishop Acuña was Diego de Siloé's first major commission in Burgos, executed on models he had seen in Italy. He imparts a sense of horizontality with the curved walls of the bed, the tripartite structures, and the corners adorned in the Italian fashion. The reliefs depict the 7 Virtues and a Sibyl.

📖 From the mid-13th c. the diocese maintained a school for the *Niños de Coro*, the children who served in various liturgical functions in the cathedral, and who also swept, dusted, replaced candles, and like tasks. In the 1470s this school was a pet project of Bishop Acuña, who underwrote it with personal funds.

In the wall in front of the retablo is the archdeacon's tomb, with its narration of the birth of Christ, by Gil de Siloé. Diego de Siloé executed the small stone retablo of Saint Anne with the curious central image of Anne teaching the young Mary, seated on her mother's lap, to read.

—10. Capilla de Santa Tecla. Baroque (1731–6), with a profusely decorated Rococo ceiling and an exuberant retablo showing the martyrdom of Santa Tecla and Saints Antonio Abad, Domingo de la Calzada, and a Santiago Matamoros. The chapel contains a 13th-c. Byzantine baptismal font decorated with Apostles under arches.

—Papamoscas. High on the wall in the northwest corner of the nave, this clock (of uncertain date) is a symbol of Burgos. Every quarter hour the Martinillo figure hammers on 2 bells. At the hour the figure over the clock flaps his mouth like a German nutcracker (the name *Papamoscas* means flycatcher).

—11. Capilla del Santo Cristo de Burgos. Day in and day out, this chapel of the Black Christ is the cathedral's greatest focus of religious fervor. Legend holds that the sculptor was Nicodemus (according to John 19:39, one of the people who helped lower Christ's body from the Cross); that the statue was found floating in the sea; that the nails, thorns, hair, and skin are real; and that the image must be shaved every 8 days. The 13th- or 14th-c. image, which was in an Augustinian monastery until the 1835 *desamortización*, is hyperbolized so frequently in pilgrims' diaries, from Baron Rozmital (1466) on, that it must have been an obligatory visit. Several mention hundreds of candles and refer to 3 curtains being drawn aside with much ceremony to reveal the statue.

> 📖 For the 17th-c. pilgrim Domenico Laffi, "this holy image would move the very stones to compassion. . . . One cannot deny that this is the true and real likeness of Christ, so lacerated by the scourge that his human aspect is lost. St. Nicodemus, inspired with divine love and contemplating at all hours the death of the Lord, had his likeness imprinted in his heart and before his eyes." [Laffi; trans. Hall (1997), 137]

—12. Capilla de San José (aka La Presentación). Felipe Vigarny (1521). The *reja* by Cristóbal de Andino is transitional Gothic-Renaissance. The dome imitates the openwork of the Capilla del Condestable. The alabaster **tomb of Gonzalo de Lerma** (1524–5) may be Felipe Vigarny's most expressive work. The exaggerated realism of the serene wrinkled face and hands contrasts beautifully with the low-relief decoration on the robe and brocaded pillow.
—13. Capilla de las Reliquias. Rococo, 18th c. Most of the Apostles and numerous other saints have bits of bone venerated here.
—14. Capilla de San Juan de Sahagún (formerly, Santa Catalina). Begun in 1316, the chapel's large size and square shape reflect that it was designed to be a chapter house. The vault's elegant 8-pointed star of nerves resting on decorated corbels is an early example of what became an immensely popular model.

> 📖 The missionary Juan de Sahagún, canonized in 1690, had been a priest in Burgos before entering the Augustinian Order.

—15. Capilla de La Visitación. Designed by Juan de Colonia. You can compare the simple star-shaped nerves of the vault (1442–5) with the Flamboyant vaults that grew progressively more complex over the next 100 years. The masterful **sepulcher** of Bishop Alonso de Cartagena is later than its base. Gil de Siloé sculpted extraordinary facial features and lavished attention on the details of the Bishop's robes and the staff and miter. The kneeling page with the open book alludes to Cartagena's great literary achievements.

> 📖 Bishop Cartagena (1384–1456), also known as Alonso de Santamaría, was the son of Bishop Pablo de Santamaría, the former rabbi who had converted in 1390. Known for his intellect, Alonso made his mark as poet (mediocre), writer (prolific), philosopher (accomplished), and politician (extraordinary). He was so impressive in seminary that upon graduation he was named Chronicler of Castilla, and in that position he became a confidant of King Juan II, who sent him on several embassies as

a peacemaker. After an extended stay in Italy, where he breathed the heady airs of the Renaissance, he returned to Spain as bishop of Cartagena and then in 1435 of Burgos, where his house became a kind of unofficial university of humanism. Alonso pumped energy into modernizing the clerics and the aesthetics of the Burgos Cathedral, and he is largely responsible for its being today an unparalleled treasure of early Renaissance art and architecture. At the age of 70 he went on pilgrimage to Compostela and, taking ill on the return journey, died at home in Burgos.

Cloister:
• The **entrance** can be dated to ca. 1270. On the **tympanum** is the Baptism of Christ. The jambs link Old and New Testament figures related to the coming of the Messiah: Isaiah and King David (right), and the Annunciation (left). The lintel's castles and lions link the Castilian monarchy to the divine. The archivolts continue the theme of Christ's genealogy. The walnut door leading from the cathedral (probably by Gil de Siloé) depicts Saints Peter and Paul and Christ's entry to Jerusalem and descent to Limbo.

The 13th-14th c. cloister is an enormous 40 m. per side. It now functions as a museum of medieval religious sculpture. Among other works, you will see 13th-c. full-size **portraits of King Alfonso X** and **Queen Violante** exchanging marriage vows.
• The Capilla de Santa Catalina. The doorway's castles and lions mirror those of the cloister's entrance. The Deposition on the tympanum retains some of its colors. To the right of the door is a stone **Santiago Peregrino**. Inside is a delicate 8-sided vault.
• The Capilla de Corpus Cristi. The tympanum parallels that of the Puerta de la Coronoría (see above), with the 4 angels surrounding Christ bearing the instruments of his Passion. The **kneeling donors**, among the earliest such in Spain, are the diplomat Juan Estébanez and his wife. The **chest** on the wall is reputedly the one in which the Cid passed off sand for jewels when he deceived Burgos's Jewish moneylenders. Diego de Siloé's **Christ tied to the column** masterfully depicts Christ's suffering and resignation.
• The **chapter house** (early 14th c.). The vaults rest on corbels with painted representations of saints. The entrance sculpture parallels that of the main cloister entrance. The 14th-c. **ceiling** is a **Mudéjar** construction of interlacing geometric patterns, still retaining their red and purple paint, and their cavities set with stalactite-like carvings (*mocárabes*). The walls are covered with 16th-c. Flemish tapestries.

2. <u>Iglesia de San Nicolás de Bari</u>. A predecessor church is documented in 1163. In the 15th c., when the present building was erected, it became the showpiece of the merchant guilds, many of whose members had business offices in Florence. They contributed lavishly to the adornment of its altars and built their family tombs along its sides.

Exterior:
• The tympanum contains an enthroned San Gil, San Sebastián showing the wounds from his arrows of martyrdom, and the Burgos martyr San Vitores, head in hand.
• The wood panels on the entrance door depict San Nicolás rescuing 3 young men from drowning in a tub, and presenting a dowry to some young women.

Interior:
- The **stone retablo by Simón de Colonia** (begun in 1505) was commissioned by the merchant Polanco family. It is a stunning example of retablo-cum-funeral niches. Its concept—huge geometrical shapes crammed with infinitely varied detail, like a tapestry hung in the front of the church—is so grandiose as to be overpowering. It is so dominated by its architectural elements that the fine sculpture on the human figures is easily lost. You will want your binoculars here. The lateral columns present Apostles (**Santiago** is paired with San Andrés), saints, and biblical scenes under intricate Flamboyant Gothic canopies (*doseles*). In the center, a circular Coronation of the Virgin is surrounded by choirs of angels, San Miguel, and the Evangelists, with San Lucas as a painter at his easel, painting the Virgin. The central effigy is San Nicolás, flanked by diverse scenes from his life: the storm at sea, the 3 youths, the dowry, and the perfume emitting from his sepulchre. Simón de Colonia also carved the high relief of **Santiago Matamoros** on the right side of the retablo.
- The lateral Baroque retablo contains 8 earlier panels (1480–1505) of the school of Fernando Gallego with scenes from the life of San Nicolás. We see the Saint anonymously giving charity and admonishing his father not to tell; rescuing condemned innocents; and the captive Adeodatus, homesick, dropping his cup at the feast of a heathen king, then being transported home. The panels of the Annunciation and Slaughter of Innocents, above San Nicolás, are more Flemish in style, with crowded compositions and tangled drapery in the Flemish fashion. The Innocents look like 15th-c. schoolboys.

3. Arco de Fernán González. This Renaissance commemorative arch (1592) is dedicated to the founding father of Castilla.

4. The castle. Erected over the ruins of a Roman fortification, the castle has suffered innumerable changes through the ages. As befits the principal fortification of an important city, the castle saw its share of history. In the 10th c., King García of Navarra was held prisoner there. Alfonso VII of Portugal took it by force in 1127. Alfonso VII of Castilla married Berenguela de Cataluña here in 1178 and converted the musty old fort to a royal palace. In the 13th c. it was Alfonso X's favorite site for executing the condemned. In the 15th-c. dynastic wars it was taken by the forces of Juana la Beltraneja (1474), and then retaken by Fernando of Aragón. The Catholic Monarchs strengthened its defenses, adding a tunnel that connected with the city. Their grandson, Carlos V, used it as a jail for prisoners taken during the Comunero revolt. In 1808 it was captured by Napoleon, and it was blown up on June 13, 1813, by a defeated French garrison that chose suicide over surrender. 1990s sensitivity to the tourist industry has led to its extensive restoration.
The nearby Mudéjar Arco de San Martín remains from the city's 12th-c. walls.

5. Iglesia de San Esteban and **Museo del Retablo**. Built in the 13th–14th c., the church was damaged in the dynastic wars (1475–6). The rose window was rebuilt in 1479. The tower, a casualty of the castle explosion of 1813, has been since rebuilt. The doorway, flanked by pinnacles, resembles that of the cathedral cloister. The sharply pointed **tympanum**, similar to tympana of that period in the cathedral cloister, is divided into 2 stories. Above, Mary and St. John intercede with Christ the Judge, as on the Coronería doorway. Below are the life and martyrdom of St. Stephen. See the hand of God at the top. Inside, the high choir is by Simón de Colonia (1502–6). The tomb and the pulpit are works of Pedro de Gumiel (ca. 1514), with his typically Italianate grotesques.
Inside this former church is now the **Museo del Retablo**, displaying 18 retablos from the 15th through the 18th c., collected from churches in the province of Burgos. Although none is of stellar quality, the museum's best feature is that you can view the retablos up close to study their fascinating details. Several include figures

of the pilgrims **Santiago** and San Roque. Upstairs in the high choir is a collection of gold, silver, and enamel chalices and processional crosses, clearly demonstrating the evolution in metalwork from pre-Romanesque and Mozárabe styles through 18ᵗʰ-c. Neoclassic.

> 📖 The small Romanesque ivory cross from San Juan de Ortega is armless. One arm was given to Isabel la Católica as a souvenir of her visit to the monastery to pray for relief from her barrenness; another went to Pope Adrian VI.

6. Arco de San Esteban. This 12ᵗʰ-c. entrance through the city wall was enlarged in the 15ᵗʰ c. It shows Mudéjar characteristics.

7. Iglesia de Santa Agueda (Gadea). The present 15ᵗʰ-c. church supersedes the one in which Alfonso VI swore to the Cid that he had nothing to do with the murder of his brother Sancho II. A popular 15ᵗʰ-c. ballad (*romance*) describes the scene in detail:

En Santa Gadea de Burgos,	In Santa Gadea de Burgos,
do juran los hijos de algo,	where the nobles swear their oaths,
allí toma juramento	that's where the Cid
el Cid al rey castellano,	takes an oath from the Castilian king
sobre un cerrojo de hierro	[with his hand] on an iron lock
y una ballesta de palo.	and a wooden crossbow.
Las juras eran tan recios	The oaths were so severe
que al buen rey ponen espanto.	that they terrified the good king.

The church's 15ᵗʰ-c. stone retablo has a **Santiago Peregrino** on the left. Some fine fragments from 16ᵗʰ-c. retablos line the walls.

8. **Casa de Miranda and Archaeological Museum.** The mansion was built in 1545 for the canon Francisco Miranda. The Plateresque triumphal arch of the entrance and the elegant patio are classic examples of Spanish urban Renaissance architecture. So are the shift from the first story's stone to the upper story's brickwork, the cylindrical towers flanked by pinnacles, and the window on Calle de Miranda with the humanistic motto: *Veritas et pacientia omnia vincunt* ("Truth and patience conquer all"). Now an archaeological and medieval art museum, the building holds many masterworks, including Roman and Muslim pieces, Gothic and Renaissance paintings, and coins. There is also a section of an early church from Tardajos, a village that you will pass when you leave Burgos. Make sure to see:
- The Silos altar frontal. 12ᵗʰ-c. Romanesque copper altar frontal, adorned with a Christ in Majesty and several saints. The bodies are enameled in the French Limoges style and have high-relief copper heads. This is one of the best enameled altar frontals in Spain.
- The **tomb of Juan de Padilla**. The tomb is by Gil de Siloé.

> 📖 Juan de Padilla's grandfather, the Marqués de Villena, was one of Castila's most important nobles. He backed young Prince Alfonso in his war against his half brother King Enrique IV. Juan was Queen Isabel's favorite page, and she was crushed when he died in 1491 at age 20 in the war against Granada.

9. **Arco de Santa María.** Across from the cathedral's Puerta del Sacramental, this was the principal gate of the city in the 14th c. After the Comunidades revolt, victorious Carlos V enlarged and decorated the gate as an object lesson in victor's politics.

📖 The so-called Comunidades War was part of the death throes of medieval feudalism. It began in 1518 in the Cortes de Valladolid, when the representatives from several cities moved to limit royal power and expand the power of the legislative body. Some cities, like Toledo, sought autonomy on the Italian model. The movement turned armed and ugly at the accession of 20-year-old Hapsburg Carlos V in 1520, adding to the urban revolt a veneer of loyal Spaniards rebelling against a foreign king. By 1521 the Comuneros had lost several key battles (Tordesillas, Ampudia, Torrelobatón) and their leaders had been decapitated. Some of their bodies were displayed on this gate as cautionary reminders of the importance of loyalty to the Crown.

The gallery of Judges and Heroes, designed by Francisco de Colonia and Juan de Vallejo, was not finished until 1553. Its purpose was to situate the new Hapsburg King Carlos V in the midst of Burgos's and Castilla's traditional heroes: the founding count Diego Porcelos, the judges Laín Calvo and Nuño Rasura, and the heroic knights Fernán González and the Cid, all under the sheltering wings of the city's Guardian Angel.

Later monarchs climbed on the bandwagon. Allegories were painted under the arch for the entry of Felipe III into Burgos. He didn't come. So they were repainted in 1679 for the ceremonial entry of Carlos II.

The inside of the building has been accommodated as an exhibition hall. Two architectural remnants from the original gate reflect late medieval, Christian nobility's taste for Islamic art. The ceiling of the Sala de Poridad is a Mudéjar *artesonado* of complex geometric design. And the wall of the main hall displays a large fragment of intricately carved plaster (*ataurique*) complete with Qur'anic verses in Arabic script. A good replica of the Cid's sword Tizona is also on display.

10. Statue of the Cid. The statue of the warrior Cid and his steed Babieca is a 1950s work of Juan Cristóbal. The battle cape of this imposing statue of Spain's most famous medieval warrior seems to float in the wind, leading to the monument's local nickname: *el murciélago* (the bat).

The bridge over the Arlanzón is adorned with modern statues (ca. 1955) relating to the history of the Cid. On the west, 4 warriors familiar to readers of the *Poema*: Alvar Fáñez, Martín Muñoz, Martín Antolínez, and Diego Rodríguez. On the east, 4 of the Cid's close associates: Bishop Jerónimo, Abbot Ben Galbón of Cardeña, San Sisebuto, and Rodrigo's wife, doña Jimena.

11. **Casa del Cordón** and Capitanía General. The palace was built in the 15th c. for the Condestable de Castilla, Pedro Fernández de Velasco (count of Haro), the man whose tomb is the center of the cathedral's Capilla del Condestable. In the 15th c. the Velasco family owned most of the provinces of Burgos and Logroño, some from ancestral holdings and some as a reward for political service to Kings Juan II and Enrique IV in their incessant civil wars.

The decorative cord is typical of Franciscan architecture. The family escutcheons and emblems of unicorns and the anagram of Jesus—IHS—are accompanied by the mottoes: "A good death gives honor to an entire life" (Velasco) and "To love God surpasses all things" (Mendoza). There is a nice Renaissance patio reached through an elegantly decorated doorway.

📖 Ferdinand and Isabella usually resided here during their visits to Burgos, and here they received Christopher Columbus on his return from his second voyage in 1497. Philip the Fair, the husband of their daughter Juana and the father of Carlos V, died in this house, precipitating Juana's madness. The *Cortes* that added Navarra to the Spanish union was celebrated here in 1515. After the battle of Pavia, the French king François I was held prisoner here. Carlos V, before his retirement to the monastery of Yuste, stayed here. And subsequent kings Felipe II, III, IV, V, and Carlos II also resided in the house during their visits to Burgos.

The Casa is now a bank. The basement, preserving not one trace of late medieval character, is used as an exhibition hall.

12. **Iglesia de San Lesmés**. This church honors the patron of Burgos, San Lesmés. In 1387, military strategists deemed that an earlier version of this church was so near the city wall "that it could be used by the king of Navarra as a scaling ladder giving access to the city." So they knocked it down and rebuilt it in its current location. The core of the current building dates from 15th c., but it has been modified many times.
   • The Capilla de los Salamanca is the funerary monument of a merchant family named Salamanca. The polychromed wood **retablo** is well proportioned and well executed.
   • The 1533–6 pulpit displays fine Baroque medallions.
   • The **tomb of San Lesmés,** in the center of the crossing, is another of Burgos's superb Plateresque funerary alabaster sculptures, with unbelievably realistic details.

13. **Cartuja de Miraflores**. Burgos's first Carthusian monastery was built on the site of the Miraflores palace and hunting lodge of King Enrique III el Doliente, given to the Carthusians by King Juan II in 1441.

📖 San Bruno started the Carthusian Order in the Alps with 6 monks in 1084. Its rule (the set of regulations that govern a Catholic Order) is among the most severe. The monks live as quasi hermits, in cells separate from each other, and in silence. They gather only to pray, to eat, and to work, but their central activity is solitary meditation and study. Their 3 major houses in Spain (Granada and El Paular, north of Madrid, in addition to Burgos) are all highly decorated artistic monuments.

The monastery was intended to supersede Las Huelgas as a pantheon for the tombs of Castilian royalty. Enrique IV, who came to the throne in 1454, had other concerns, and the project sat on the back burner until Queen Isabel chose it as the perfect location for the monumental tombs of her parents and her brother, the unfortunate Prince Alfonso, who died in the midst of the war against Enrique IV. They were the last royal entombments in the north, for Isabel and Fernando were subsequently buried in Granada, and the Hapsburgs preferred Felipe II's Escorial.

Isabel put her corps of Flemish architects and sculptors to work on the project. Juan de Colonia began the design. At his death Garci Fernández de Matienzo took over. When he died of plague in 1478, Simón de Colonia brought the main church to completion. As the solution to his dual mission—a church for a simple, contemplative Order that also would serve as a royal pantheon—he opted for a single high spacious nave without lateral chapels.

By 1497, when Arnold von Harff traveled to Compostela from Cologne, it was already a tourist site, for he wrote in his journal: "About half a mile across the river Moneta, there is a fine Carthusian monastery on a little mountain called *ad millas flores*. In it lie buried all the kings and queens of Castille" (Harff; trans. Letts, 270).

Exterior:
• The typical late-15ᵗʰ-c. façade is adorned with the escutcheons of the founders, the lions and castles of Castilla, and the diagonal bar being swallowed by 2 dragons (*la banda engulada*) of the Trastámara family. The Pieta on the tympanum alludes to the spirit of the Carthusian Order.

Interior:
• The church's single elegant nave has splendid Flamboyant Gothic vaulting with decorated keystones.
• The stained-glass windows were brought from Flanders in 1484.
• The church has 2 separate choirs. The **monks' choir stalls** were carved in 1558 by Simón de Bueras, a disciple of Berruguete, following the 1505–12 drawings by Felipe Vigarny, who did the stalls of the cathedral.
• The triptych on the right is by Roger Van der Weyden.
• Each of the 40 backs of the **priests' choir stalls** (1489) has a different Gothic tracery design.
• The **Anunciación**, by Pedro Berruguete, ca. 1500, plays with space within space in the Flemish fashion. The medallions on the frame show Italian influence.
• <u>Tombs by Gil de Siloé</u>
    —The **tombs of King Juan II** and his wife **Isabel de Portugal**, the parents of Alfonso and of Isabel la Católica, were commissioned by Isabel. After 4 years of work, they were finished in 1498. Several of the individual figures were later broken off and dispersed; you will find the Santiago in New York's Cloisters Museum. The tomb was originally polychromed; look for traces of paint on the King's head. The symbolism is traditional: the lion for courage, the dog for fidelity. Gil de Siloé's style mixes late Gothic, Flemish Renaissance, and Spanish Mudéjar, all of which strove to fill every frame and cover every surface with intricate detail. His delight with detail is independent of any sense of proportion or symmetry. Favoring incision over modeling, he covers the surface with webs of finely carved lines. On the other hand, his treatment of drapery is mannered, with deep, convoluted folds, and twisting, jagged lines. His faces tend to be serene in expression, with heavily lidded eyes, prominent cheekbones, and deep wrinkles. The figures project late Gothic modesty, good taste, and extraordinary wealth.
    —The alabaster wall **tomb of** kneeling **Prince Alfonso** portrays the prince with the same facial features as his parents. The sculptor paid extraordinary attention to the texture of the textiles.
• The **retablo**, also by **Gil de Siloé**, is of wood, gilded with gold brought back on Columbus's second voyage, and later painted by Diego de la Cruz. It was finished in only 4 years (1496–9). Rather than the traditional columns and rows, its upper register is organized like a great rectangular tapestry, with a circular medallion dominating the center, similar to but earlier than the one in La Iglesia de San Nicolás. Its subject is the redemption of humanity by Christ, and its symbolism is complex. Christ is the center of redemption. The cross is sustained by God the Father and the Holy Spirit. Above is a pelican, which symbolizes Divine Love. Mary and the Beloved Disciple are at the cross's base. In the circles at the angles of the cross are scenes from the Passion. The cross is surrounded by a crown of angels. At the sides are Saints Peter and Paul, pillars of the church. The 4 Evangelists are shown with the Apostles Matthew and John above, the non-Apostles Luke and Mark below. The 4 triangles inside the Evan-

gelists hold four doctors of the Church: Augustine, Ambrose, Gregory, and Jerome. In the higher corner circles, the Annunciation and the Adoration; in the lower, the Last Supper and Christ's Imprisonment.

The lower register centers on the tabernacle of the Eucharist and is divided into sections by 4 saints: John the Baptist (patron saint of King Juan II and favorite of Isabel), Magdalena (a Carthusian favorite), Catalina (name of Juan II's mother and of Isabel's daughter), and **Santiago** (protector of Spain and her royalty). At the corners are the monarchs: Juan II, guided by **Santiago Peregrino**, and Isabel de Portugal, protected by St. Elizabeth. The escutcheons of Castilla and Portugal hang over them. The composition's effect is to overpower the worshiper, although the individual details are not always of the quality of Gil de Siloé's other work.

• The Cartuja's remaining treasure is the 17th-c. image of **San Bruno** by Manuel Pereyra, so realistic that it is said that the only reason it does not speak is that it is Carthusian.

14. <u>**Monasterio de las Huelgas**</u>. Access to the interior is by guided tour only.

In 1175 Alfonso VIII turned the grounds of one of his rural palaces into a convent. It was to be run by the Cistercian Order, but there was a catch: the convent reported directly to the King. He named it Las Huelgas (*holgar* means to take pleasure). His goal, the ironic opposite of the Cistercian ideal, was to create the world's most sumptuous convent, an opulent refuge for widowed nobility. His queen, Eleanor (Leonor) Plantagenet, who was the daughter of English King Henry II and sister of Richard the Lion-Hearted, was made its first prioress. She fixed the number of noble lady members at 100 and decreed that they be called *Señora*, and not *Sor*.

📖 For centuries the Monastery of Las Huelgas served as a kind of boarding school for the daughters of the nobility who, as Alfonso X's *Cantiga* #303 points out, were pretty much like everybody else's children:

Costum' é que as menynas	It is normal for little girls
Que ena orden criadas	brought up in religious orders
Son, que grandes travessuras	to do very naughty things
Fazen algunas vegadas;	from time to time;
Poren freiras que as guardan	for which the sisters who take care
Lles dan, per que castigadas	of them punish them
Sejan y non façan cousas	so they won't do things
Per que caian en errança.	that will make them fall into error.

The convent church, built from 1180 to 1230 next to Alfonso's palace, nods to Cistercian simplicity and decorative motifs featuring vegetation rather than human figures, but it shows off its wealth in its vast size. Today it houses a community of Bernardinas who guide visitors through the complex.

From the 12th to the 14th c. Las Huelgas also served as the royal Pantheon. So many of these men spent their lives fighting the Muslims along the southern frontier that it is particularly striking to find that their funeral chamber adopted Mudéjar decorative motifs in the woodwork of the cloister ceiling, the carving on the tombs, and the textiles in which the deceased monarchs were wrapped.

• The church's plan—3 long naves ending in a T whose rectangular chapels form a kind of transept—is derived from the Cistercian motherhouse in Cîteaux. Today the cloistered part of the convent begins with the naves, set off from the transept by a wall painted with scenes depicting the 1212 battle of Las Navas de Tolosa, in which Fernando III initiated the successful reconquest of Andalucía.

• The main retablo (Baroque, 1655). The Assumption of the Virgin is flanked with enormous Solomonic columns and the images of Saints Bernardo and Benito, typical in Cistercian Benedictine churches. The kneeling monarchs are the founders Alfonso VIII and Leonor.
• **The tombs.** Untouched for centuries, many of the royal tombs were opened in 1942–3, revealing a treasure of crowns, jewelry, and textiles (a selection of which you will see later in the museum section). The best tombs are:
　　—Tomb of Fernando de la Cerda (d. 1275). A wall niche with a 13th-c. Crucifixion and a tomb covered with castles and lions. Additionally, since his mother was Aragonese, it bears the bars of Aragon.
　　—**Double sarcophagus of Alfonso VIII and Leonor** (d. 1214). Combines the castles of Castilla with the 3 lions of the Plantagenets. The triangles on one end show the King giving the nuns their charter, and on the other end the cross. The Queen's tomb depicts Calvary and angels carrying her soul to heaven.
　　—Tomb of the nun Berenguela (d. 1279). Actually, this tomb was carved for her grandmother, who was queen. It displays various biblical scenes.
　　—Tomb of María de Almenara (d. 1196). Funeral scenes in a style transitional from Romanesque to Gothic.
• The 13th-c. **Descent from the Cross** is an unusual and emotive ensemble that conservatively still includes the 4-nail crucifixion common in the Romanesque period.
• The late-12th-c. Romanesque "Claustrillas" Cloister is the oldest extant part of the convent. It conserves its 15th-c. **Mudéjar roof beams.**
• The nearby Mudéjar-style Capilla de la Asunción was part of the former royal palace. Its mere existence in this European Cistercian monastery is eloquent testimony to the dual aesthetic allegiance of the late medieval Castilian monarchs. Its walls are covered with **Almohad Mudéjar tracery** (*ataurique*)—the best examples you will see along the Santiago Road—and polylobed arches.
• The 14th-c. statue of **Santiago Matamoros**, with an articulated right arm bearing a sword, was used to dub knights into the Order of Santiago. Beginning with Fernando III in 1219, medieval Castilian monarchs were dubbed knights by this statue here in Las Huelgas.
• The **Capilla de Santiago,** built in 1275, has **Mudéjar-style plasterwork** and a stunning, inlaid **Mudéjar ceiling.** Again, the commitment to this aesthetic in a chapel of this Saint seems striking.
• The Gothic cloister of San Fernando (1240–60) has twinned columns topped by a single capital. The capitals, transitional between Romanesque and Gothic, are light and airy.
• The chapter room has delicate columns and 9 cupolas.
• Nearby rooms have more gorgeous **Mudéjar plaster tracery work.**
• The Museum of Cloth contains samples of shrouds and garments found when the tombs were opened (others are in the Cleveland [Ohio] Museum of Art). The museum displays a minute inventory of the contents of the coffin of Alfonso X's son, Prince Fernando de la Cerda. The pine coffin had a silver cross on the lid; gold medallions, covered with 2 pieces of tunic, were draped with his cloak, which was decorated with castles and lions; on his head was a cap with the escutcheon of Castilla and León in coral, gold, and pearls; his face was covered with green brocade. His left arm was folded across his chest, while his right arm held a broadsword; his fingers bore rings and ribbons. His shoes had decayed, but the spurs remained.

📖 Prince Fernando was married at age 6 to a daughter of King St. Louis of France. He and his brother began a civil war against his father, and he was killed at age 19.

15. **Iglesia de San Gil.** The church is located in the commercial quarter, which in the 12ᵗʰ c. grew just inside the east wall of the medieval city. It is documented as early as 1163, although the current building dates from the 13ᵗʰ–14ᵗʰ c. The chapels were rebuilt in the 15ᵗʰ c., while the stairway leading to the main portal was the result of an 1834 bequest. The portal depicts the Virgin and San Gil, and has a simple rose window. The south doorway, now filled in, narrates the Epiphany and the Flight to Egypt.

The church has dozens of fine tombs and contains large retablos whose themes are the Betrothal of the Virgin and the Mass of San Gregorio. A 16ᵗʰ-c. **Santiago** and San Jerónimo are on one of the panels on the right side of the retablo.
  • Capilla de la Navidad (left nave). This Plateresque chapel is noted for its **Renaissance retablo,** its nearly flat openwork cupola like an overhead rose window, and its vaulting. It was built in 1523, after getting city permission to extend through the city wall. It houses the tombs of various members of the influential Castro family.
  • Capilla de Nuestra Señora de la Buena Mañana (left apse). So called because of the early hour its chaplain was required to say mass. Its retablo, probably from the workshop of Gil de Siloé, shows the dominant characteristics of late-15ᵗʰ-c. Burgos art: the minute attention to detail typical of Flemish Gothic and the sense of plasticity of German sculptors of that period. The chapel displays ecclesiastical vestments (*ternos*).
  • Capilla de los Reyes Magos (right apse). Contains a fine late Gothic retablo (probably by Gil de Siloé), fine tombs, Sebastián Ducete's superb 17ᵗʰ-c. **Christ tied to the column,** and an 18ᵗʰ-c. San Pedro.
  • A statue of the **Dolorosa** by **Gregorio Hernández** (right transept). This master sculptor's work is so modern in tone that the image looks as if it had been carved only a few years ago.
  • The **Cristo de las Santas Gotas.** According to legend, during the 14ᵗʰ-c. wars of Pedro the Cruel, this Christ sweated 14 drops of blood. The image is characteristic of 14ᵗʰ-c. Gothic Crucifixions, which accentuate the suffering caused by Christ's painful wounds.

16. **Paseo de la Isla.** This long park was created to reclaim the Arlanzón riverbank, which had long been a wasteland of stinking drain-off from Burgos's wool-washing plants. The shady promenade has been decorated with fountains and with bits of ancient architecture from crumbling churches in the diocese, including one nice Romanesque portal.

17. The **Hospital del Rey.** At the western exit to the city, it is now the Faculty of Law. It was founded in 1195 by Alfonso VIII and entrusted to the Knights of Calatrava (under the Order of Cister), as supervised by the abbess of Las Huelgas.

📖 Alfonso X el Sabio commemorated the foundings of both the *hospital* and the convent in his *Cantiga* 221.

Et pos tornous a Castela	Later he returned to Castilla
De si en Burgos moraba	and resided in Burgos

> *E un Hospital facia*   and he founded a Hospice
> *El, e su moller labraba*   and his wife founded
> *O Monasterio das Olgas.*   the Monastery of Las Huelgas.

The Hospital was headed by a prior. His official staff included 12 *freiles* of noble origin, who had to be at least 30 years old, 8 nuns at least 35 years old, a sacristan, an organist, presbyters, 2 doctors, a surgeon, a bonesetter, and some interpreters. Alfonso X legislated its hospitality:

All the pilgrims who pass by on the French Road and other roads, whatever their origin, no one shall be refused there, and all shall be received; and they shall have every necessary thing there to provide them with food, drink, and lodging, at all hours of the day and night, whenever they arrive. And all who wish to lodge there shall be given good beds with bedclothes . . . ; and any man or woman who arrives sick shall be provided men and women to take care of them, and to quickly give them food and anything they might need, until they recover or die.

Künig von Vach, in the late 15th c., said that the monks here "give you food and drink until you are satiated." Laffi, ca. 1670, observed that "for its size [it] seemed like a city in itself. . . . It holds 2000 people" (Laffi: trans. Hall (1997), 141).

The current buildings date from the 16th–18th c. The monumental entrance is testimony to the Hapsburgs, with Carlos V's twin columns of Hercules, the 2-headed Hapsburg eagle, and the coat of arms of united Spain. Seated in the central niche is **Santiago**.

Inside, to the left, is the entrance to what was the 13th-c. church, with an early Gothic stone door now filled with 2 monumental **wood panels** (perhaps by Juan de Valmaseda), depicting a knight praying between Santiago and San Miguel, and a **group of 3 generations of walking pilgrims**. The upper register's penitent Adam and Eve show a Renaissance fascination with the human form.

In the hospice's cemetery was the Ermita de San Amaro, named for a French pilgrim who dedicated his life to this hospice. Excavations have found many pilgrim graves.

In addition, if you still have time and energy, or if you decide to move permanently to Burgos, the following are worth a look-see:
• Iglesia de La Merced. 15th-c. church by Juan de Colonia.
• Convento de Santa Dorotea. 15th-c. church, with a Gothic doorway by Simón de Colonia and Baroque retablos.
• Iglesia de San Lorenzo. Massive Baroque façade.
• Iglesia de Santos Cosme y Damián. Baroque retablos.
• Convento de Santa Clara. Baroque retablos.
• Hospital de la Concepción. 16th-c. Renaissance façade; was once a pilgrim hospice.
• Iglesia de Santa Ana. Begun by Juan de Colonia in 1477, with a superb retablo by Gil de Siloé.
• Convento de Carmelitas Descalzas. With *mementi* of its founder Santa Teresa de Ávila.
• Ayuntamiento. 18th-c. Neoclassic town hall.
• Paseo del Espolón. A good place to relax from all of the above, on a shaded esplanade by the river, known for its outdoor cafés.

Route: BURGOS → Villalba → **Tardajos** → **Rabé de las Calzadas** → HORNILLOS

As you exit Burgos, the large building across the river is a prison where many political prisoners were held during the later Franco years. So many young dissidents got a sophisticated political education here that the prison earned the nickname "La Universidad."

✳ **Villalba** (aka Villava, Villalbilla) The bridge over the Arlanzón River, reconstructed in the 17th c., is called Puente del Arzobispo. Here Alfonso VI, running to escape some thieves, fell from his horse. He invoked the Cristo de Benaver (a 12th-c. image still found in the church of Palacios de Benaver, some 14 km. to the northwest), and managed to save himself. The *espadaña* of the Iglesia de la Asunción generally is capped with a stork's nest.

✳ **Tardajos** An 18th-c. stone cross greets you at the east entrance to this ancient town. This is the former Roman Augustóbriga, located at an important junction of Roman roads (the east-west Via Traiana and the north-south road that connected Clunia with Julióbriga, now Retortillo, on the Cantabrian coast). On the hill to the right, just past the river, are said to be minimal ruins of a Celtiberian *castro*. Excavations turned up ceramics and coins. North of the hill was a Roman villa in which a statue of Venus was found. We have not located traces of either.

Tardajos was important in the reconquest of the Castilian Meseta, and in the 9th c. its castle formed part of the defensive perimeter against the Muslim south. The street plan makes clear Tardajos's 2 medieval neighborhoods: an original walled nucleus, with the church at its center, and a newer neighborhood to the east.

According to a 929 document, the town was large enough to have 3 churches. Remains of the earliest,

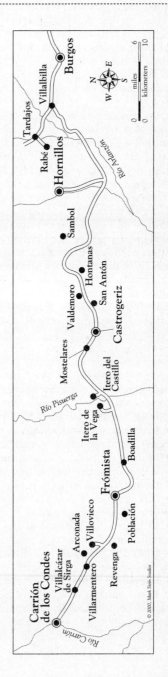

destroyed by lightning in 1783, are in the Burgos Archaeological Museum. The 12th-c. church of La Magdalena, whose hospice was donated by the Countess Mayor to the Burgos Cathedral in 1182, reputedly hosted San Francisco de Asís during his pilgrimage to Compostela. This church, too, has disappeared without a trace. The modern Monastery of the Paulian Fathers occupies the site of a former palace belonging to the archbishopric of Burgos.

The monastery church of Santa María was begun in the 13th c., but most construction occurred later, with the Flamboyant Gothic vaults dating from the 16th c. Inside are 5 Baroque retablos. The central retablo contains 4 reutilized Renaissance panels and a central image of the Virgen de las Aguas, venerated especially in the spring when local farmers pray for rain. The left rear retablo has a nice pilgrim San Roque. Santa Teresa took communion in this church in 1582.

✳ **Rabé de las Calzadas** The medieval pilgrimage Road traversed swampy ground between Tardajos and Rabé, an impediment that led to a popular jingle:

De Tardajos a Rabé,	From Tardajos to Rabé
libéranos Domine.	may God deliver us.
Y de Rabé a Tardajos,	And from Rabé to Tardajos,
no te faltarán trabajos.	you will not lack for troubles.

The village belonged to the Burgos Cathedral until 1675. It had a castle on the hill just south of the village. As you enter town, to the right is a 17th-c. palace, whose symmetrical façade features 2 small towers. Rabé's church of Santa Marina conserves its 13th-c. entrance with a zigzag archivolt. The church contains a tiny Romanesque relief of the Crucifixion. The heights above the town were the site of the now-vanished Ermita de Santiago. At the west end of town, just before the cemetery, is the undistinguished Ermita de Nuestra Señora del Monasterio. These days farmers here raise a lot of turnips.

To the right of the path, before Hornillos, just before the paved crossroad, used to stand the Leprosarium of San Lázaro (see ch. 27).

Motorists may take routes to either side of the old pilgrim Road from Burgos to Castrogeriz. Several of the small towns on these rolling mesas have monuments worth a few moments' pause.

🚗 Olmillos de Sasamón The 1440 Gothic castle belonged to Pedro de Cartagena, son of Burgos's *converso* Bishop Pablo de Santamaría, whose coat of arms remains on the castle. The late Gothic church of La Asunción (1540–1610) has a cohesive, impressive style and delicately nerved vaults. It is unusual for all 3 naves to be of the same height. The entrance is in the style of Herrera. The Baroque retablo holds a 14th-c. Virgen.

🚗 Sasamón The town is 2 km. north of the paved highway. Built over the Celtiberian and Roman towns of Segisamon, the village has remains of 3 small Roman bridges. Caesar used it as a base during his 1st-c.-B.C.E. war against the Cantabrians. It was a bishopric during the 10th–12th c. It conserves remnants of its medieval walls and a gate with the royal escutcheon. **La Iglesia de Santa María la Real** is a major Gothic monument, with 5 naves, a 13th-c. portal related to the Sarmental of Burgos's cathedral, a cloister attributed to Juan de Colonia, a statue of San Miguel by Diego de Siloé, a Plateresque retablo dedicated to **Santiago**, and a collection of tapestries. Its Ermita de San Isidro contains a fine 16th-c. processional cross.

🚗 Hormaza The church has a nice triptych whose central Pieta was painted either by Gerard David or a talented disciple. Hormaza's castle is crumbling.

In 1979 we spent the night in the village as guests of a family whose son, despite having to study for his seminary examinations, took the time to teach Linda how to milk the family cow. We will never forget the taste of that fresh milk in a cup of steaming coffee.

From Olmillos de Sasamón the paved road leads through and across desolate mesas (*páramos*) sown with wheat. You will pass Rosaleda de San Nicolás (a cluster of houses, one of which includes the apse of a Romanesque church); Villandiego (with a row of wine cellars, called *bodegas*, built into the hill); and Castellanos de Castro.

44. HORNILLOS

The town has existed since ancient times. In fact Hornillos's undistinguished church of San Román, just north of the town center, crowns a small hill that was the site of a pre-Roman *castro*. The town's name, derived from Fornellos, suggests that it was once the site of a kiln or smelting furnace. In 1156 Alfonso VII founded a monastery here, which he donated to the French monastery of Saint-Denis. In 1181 his successor, with words specifically identifying Hornillos as a pilgrimage town, transferred ownership of "the village called Fornellos, located on the St. James Road between Burgos and Castrogeriz" to the French monastery of Rocamador.

The remains of the medieval hospice and convent of Rocamador are still found in a field 150 m. northwest of the town. The monks also maintained a small hospice of San Lázaro for lepers (see ch. 27), whose ruins are just before town to the south of the Road.

Hornillos's main street was the pilgrimage Road. Carved on the first house on the right after the first crossroads in town are the cross of Santiago and a chalice. This was the former Hospital de Sancti Spiritus.

45. HORNILLOS → CASTROGERIZ

Route: HORNILLOS → Sambol → Hontanas → Valdemoro → **San Antón** → CASTROGERIZ

Halfway to Sambol, on a mesa 100 m. south of the Road, is the Despoblado de la Nuez. The corral is all that remains of the small 12th-c. abbey of the Hospitalarios de San Juan de Acre.

✳ Sambol There is a modern pilgrim hospice in this small oasis watered by the icy spring of San Boal (Baudillo). There are, however, no plumbing facilities. Across the gully are minimal remains of the monastery of San Baudillo, a dependency of San Antón de Castrogeriz, and later of Oña and San Pedro de Cardeña. San Baudillo was founded before 1068.

✳ Hontanas The town's name relates to the numerous springs in the area. The center of town is dominated by the mostly-14th-c. Church of the Inmaculada Concepción. A large house on the left, called the Mesón de los franceses, was another former hospice of San Juan and has recently been remodeled as a pilgrim *refugio*. In the 1670s Laffi found the wildness of the surrounding Meseta much more impressive than the town itself:

> It lies hidden in the valley of a little river, so that you scarcely see it until you have reached it. Moreover it is small, wretched and poor. There are ten or a dozen huts, roofed with straw, that look like winter refuges from the snow, though they are occupied by shepherds. They have a strong palisade round the huts to guard against wolves which come at night to attack them. . . . There are so many of them that you see them in packs, like flocks of sheep, both in the daytime and at night. So whenever you want to cross this desert you must do it in the middle of the day when the shepherds are out with their huge dogs. . . . Having reached this wretched place by the evening, we ate a little bread with garlic. . . . Then we went to bed on the ground because there was nowhere else. We were allowed to stay in one of the huts, after we had paid for our lodging in advance. [Laffi; trans. Hall (1997), 143]

✳ Valdemoro On a hillside to the north of the walking road, about 2 km. beyond Hontanas, are minimal remains of the village of Quintanilla de Valdemoro, documented in the 12th c. The only sizable ruins are of the church of San Vicente.

✳ **San Antón** The ruins are what remain of a monastery and *hospital* of the Order of San Antón. Alfonso VII helped underwrite the founding of this *hospital* and church in 1146, though the current buildings are mainly 14th and 15th c. At its height the complex included a church, convent, hospice, mill, orchard, and dovecotes. The institution had substantial royal support, as well as donations from grateful citizens.

📖 The Order of San Antón (St. Anthony, San Antonio Abad) was founded in 1093 in St.-Didier-de-la-Mothe when the hermit Anthony's relics were taken there and a man named Guérin, whose child suffered from a burning affliction seemingly akin to leprosy, prayed to St. Anthony and the child was cured. The symptoms of St. Anthony's fire—the burning sensation, bluish color, loss of circulation and eventually gangrene, as well as loss of mental functions—suggest ergot poisoning, caused by eating barley bread infected with a fungus generating the alkaloid ergotine. This plague, whose onset is documented in the 10th c., reached epidemic proportions from the 11th to the 14th c. The disease could often be alleviated by change of diet (eliminating barley bread and increasing intake of wine, which dilated the veins) and vigorous exercise: e.g., pilgrimage. The hospices of San Antón, credited with curative powers, sprang up along Europe's major pilgrimage routes. The Order also treated cases of leprosy, which was likewise thought to be cured by pilgrimage. Well, if it did not cure it, at least it got the presumably contagious lepers out of town.

Ergotism's symptoms additionally resembled those of a porcine disease that the Order also attended. This may explain why San Antón is often shown accompanied by a pig. Since lepers had to announce their approach by banging 2 boards together or ringing a bell, the bell is another emblem of this saint. The Order adopted as its symbol a tau, said to resemble the mark the angel placed on the doors of Egyptian Jews to exempt them from the plague that killed firstborn sons. The Order's members wore a blue Tau on their black habits, and they fed pilgrims with bread marked with the Tau. At its height the Order of San Antón administered as many as 369 *hospitales* in Europe. The Order was disbanded in 1787.

The archway spanning the pilgrimage Road is similar to numerous French pilgrimage hospices and to the Spanish complexes in Puente la Reina and Trinidad de Arre, outside of Pamplona. Pilgrims arriving too late at night to enter this hospice were welcome to sleep under the porch. Each evening the monks laid out food for them in the niches in the wall in front of the porch, all that remains of the monastery's hospice.

The portal preserves remnants of what must have been spectacularly carved archivolts, capped by an image of the Virgin. At the west end of the ruins are remains of the rose window and tile plaques with the insignia of the Order of San Antón. Note the French and German coats of arms still preserved on the ruins.

46. CASTROGERIZ

Location, location, location. The steep-sided mesa, eroded to form a small, impregnable island in the sea of grain of the Meseta Alta, has been fortified since at least Celtiberian times. From its heights Romans guarded the road to the Galician gold mines. The Visigoths called it Castrum Sigerici. In the 9th and 10th c. these rugged mesas were the front between the 2 warring cultures, and Castrogeriz changed hands several times before being definitively reconquered by the Christian Nuño Núñez ca. 912. It was even held for a while by Fernán González. In 974, Christians encouraged repopulation of the area by issuing a *fuero* establishing in Castrogeriz a Second Grade of Knighthood (*Caballería de segunda clase*) that could be joined by any soldier—noble or not—who owned a horse.

For 4 centuries Castrogeriz prospered as a fortified way station and commercial center on the pilgrimage Road. It attracted many French merchants and numerous Jews, who are documented in the town as early as 974. The city's *fuero* included the unusual proviso that anyone who killed a Jew would be treated as if he had killed a Christian. A building known locally as the "synagogue" is across the street from the present *albergue*. In the later Middle Ages the town was home of the powerful counts of Castro. The town's decline began when it picked the losing side in the 1521 Comunidades War.

PILGRIMAGE

As in Burgos and Navarrete, the pilgrimage Road, the city's principal street, flanks a fortified hill, here a 2-km. arc. In Castrogeriz's heyday this street linked 5 churches and 7 pilgrim hospices. In 1497 the German Arnold von Harff noted that pilgrims rightly called "Castresory . . . the long town" (Harff; trans. Letts, 270).

Occasionally in the old chronicles one finds hints of just how dangerous pilgrimage could be and of how unscrupulous people preyed on pilgrims. The 12th-c. *Historia compostelana* narrates how in 1118 some of Queen Urraca's messengers tried to slip past Castrogeriz, which was at the time held by her enemy and estranged husband Alfonso I el Batallador of Aragón:

> What happened? When the two legates—that is, the two Pedros, one the prior of Compostela, the other a cardinal—reached Castrogeriz, despite the fact that they traveled in pilgrims' clothes, they were instantly seized by Aragonese robbers. They stole their 120 ounces of gold, their horses, their clothing, their money, and everything else they had with them for the journey. [Book II, ch. 4.2]

Pedro the prior was eventually ransomed for 70 marks of gold. We don't know what happened to Pedro the cardinal.

Excavations under the plaza, in the old cemetery of San Esteban, found a 14th-c. pilgrim skeleton complete with habit, scallop shells, and English and French coins.

MONUMENTS: 1. **Ex-colegiata de Santa María del Manzano**. 2. Iglesia de Santo Domingo. 3. Iglesia de Santiago de los Caballeros. 4. Iglesia de San Juan de los Caballeros. 5. **Castle**.

1. **Ex-colegiata de Santa María del Manzano**. The church owes its founding to a miracle: as Santiago was passing by, he saw a vision of the Virgin in an apple

tree, and he was so excited that he leaped heavily onto his horse. The hoofprints can be seen in a rock outside the south door. The church belonged to the Benedictines of San Millán de la Cogolla from 1050 until 1173, when its jurisdiction was transferred to the bishop. King San Fernando III's mother, Berenguela, endowed the current building in 1214. It prospered later under the patronage of the counts of Castro. The vaults were rebuilt in the 16th c. and the *espadaña*, in the 18th.

Exterior:
The west door displays 2 large figures from a Gothic Annunciation. The rose window has 15th-c. stained glass donated by Cardenal Iñigo López de Mendoza.

Interior:
• The Rococo main altar houses the 14th-c. stone Virgen de Nuestra Señora del Pópulo and 6 Rococo **paintings by Antonio Rafael Mengs**, who worked in Castrogeriz from 1768 to 1779.
• The 13th-c. **Virgen del Manzano**, of polychromed stone, is the miraculous image celebrated by Alfonso X in 5 of his *Cántigas*, the religious songs that touted various sites along Alfonso's portions of the Santiago Road.

> 📖 Several of the miracles described in the *Cantigas* have to do with this church's construction. *Cantiga* 242 tells how a man slipped while working on one of the vaults, and how the Virgin gave him strength to hold on by his fingertips. *Cantiga* 249 tells how another mason, who worked not for salary but for love of the Virgin, was saved from a fall. *Cantiga* 252 narrates how when workmen were digging the foundation to the "church called Almazan, at the edge of the town," the sand caved in, killing many of them, but that when the survivors prayed to the Virgin their colleagues were resuscitated. Finally, *Cantiga* 266 recounts how when workmen were putting up scaffolding to build the tower and main portal a large falling beam would have crushed them if the Virgin had not held it up.

• The church contains several fine tombs, including the **sepulcher of doña Leonor** de Castilla, wife of Alfonso IV de Aragón, assassinated in the Castle of Castrogeriz in 1359.

2. Iglesia de Santo Domingo. The Gothic Dominican church is now a museum, housing Romanesque and Gothic Virgins, ivories, church vestments, jewelry, and 6 large 17th-c. Bruges **tapestries** woven following designs by a disciple of Rubens depicting the 5 Liberal Arts: Philosophy, Grammar, Astronomy, Music, Mathematics, and a compendium of the 5.

3. Iglesia de Santiago de los Caballeros. This ruined church retains its late **Romanesque doorway**. The **carved skulls** warn passers-by to heed the inevitability of death.

4. Iglesia de San Juan de los Caballeros (west exit of town). This 13th-c. Gothic fortified church has been stripped of its external decoration. The 3 naves, of near equal height and with starred vaults supported by palmlike columns, were rebuilt in the 16th c. by Rodrigo Gil de Hontañón. There are many well-carved tombs, including those of the Mujica family.
The church's masterpiece, in the funerary chapel of Juan González Gallo (1517), is the painted **Flemish retablo** from ca. 1530 by Adriaen Ysenbrant. Its

principal themes are the Mass of San Gregorio and the Annunciation. The chapel also has a baptismal font attributed to Diego de Siloé.

The 14th-c. cloister has **painted roof beams**, and coats of arms of the Gómez de Sandoval family, who were lords of Castrogeriz from 1426 to 1476.

5. **Castle.** As scattered fragments of pottery make clear, the castle's origins are pre-Roman, although by legend it was constructed by Julius Caesar or Pompey. Its successor Visigothic fort was destroyed in the Islamic conquest. Christians and Muslims disputed the hill for centuries until the Christians finally won out. The castle was rebuilt in the Middle Ages by the Condes de Castro, and later it served as the home of the Díaz de Mendoza family. The climb to the top is exhausting, but well worth the view. From below, the hill looks like a mountain; from the top, you can see that it and the surrounding mesas were once part of an absolutely level plain, eroded out over the centuries.

Other sights:
• In the fields to the south of Castrogeriz are the ruins of the convent of San Francisco, built over the former palace and gardens of Pedro el Cruel.
• To their southwest is the Convento de Santa Clara, founded by Alfonso X. The current church dates from the 14th c., but with much subsequent rebuilding.
• Several of the *bodegas*, the wine cellars cut into the castle hill, have multiple interconnected subterranean chambers. If you are fortunate, someone may give you a tour.

47. Castrogeriz → Frómista

Route: Castrogeriz → Mostelares → Itero del Camino → Itero de la Vega → **Boadilla del Camino** → Frómista

The San Miguel Bridge across the Río Odra retains some arches from the 12th c. The Road across the flats traverses a **Roman causeway**, raised above the marshy ground by a long series of arches. The Road then ascends a steep, flat-topped hill (*páramo*) called Mostelares. Two-thirds of the way up, it goes through a thick stratum of mica, mined here by the Romans. A monument now marks the summit.

✳ Itero del Camino (aka Itero del Castillo) The town is on the east bank of the Río Pisuerga, a few hundred m. north of the marked pilgrimage Road. In the early Middle Ages the town was fortified to protect the wheat-rich Tierra de Campos from Moorish raiding parties. The Río Pisuerga in former times was the border between Castilla and León, as noted in the 13th-c. *Poema of Fernán González:*

Estonçe era Castiella un pequeño rincón;	At that time Castilla was a poor corner
era de castellanos Montes d' Oca mojón;	Montes de Oca marked the frontier
e de la otra parte Fitero el fondón . . .	Fitero limited the other. (171abc)

The village's name also indicates its status as a border town: *petra ficta* meaning "fixed stone"; *ficta* evolved to *fita* to *fitero* to *itero*.

In 1174 Count Nuño Pérez de Lara founded a pilgrim hospice here to be administered by the Cistercians. It was later run by the Hospitallers of Saint John.

Of the castle only a 10-m.-wide square tower remains; beam holes in the interior walls show that it once had 4 stories. As of this writing, 2 large cracks run all the way through it, and it may not be standing when you read this. The walls of the castle proper were torn down in the 18th c. to build the village church, which has some intricate Baroque and Rococo retablos. The medieval churches of San Millán and San Nicolás are largely in ruins.

In the early 12th c. doña Urraca donated land just east of the bridge for the **Hospice of San Nicolás**, assigning it to the Benedictines of San Millán de la Cogolla. The Italian Confraternita di San Jacopo di Compostella di Perugia has recently restored it as a pilgrim *refugio*. Drinking water is obtained from the nearby Fuente del Piojo (Flea's Fountain).

The **bridge** (*Pons Fiterie* in the CC *Guide*) over the Río Pisuerga today is the border between the provinces of Burgos and Palencia. It was commissioned by Alfonso VI in the 11th c. to assist pilgrims. Its 11 arches have been reconstructed frequently. Beyond the bridge begins the Tierra de Campos, of which chapter 7 of the CC *Guide* says: "This country is full of treasures, of gold and silver; it abounds in fodder and in vigorous horses, and it has plenty of bread, meat, fish, milk, and honey. On the other hand, it is poor in wood and full of evil and vicious people."

📖 The Visigoths, who conquered Roman Spain in the early 5th c., called the rich wheat lands around Palencia the *Campi Gothorum* (the fields of the Goths). The name stuck. Today this agriculural plain, comprising much of Palencia and Valladolid with parts of León and Zamora, is known by 2 versions of the name: the Campos Góticos or the Tierra de Campos.

✳ Itero de la Vega The 1557 church of San Pedro retains bits of a 13th-c. Gothic portal. At the entrance to the village the 13th-c. Ermita de la Piedad contains a nice image of **Santiago**. Time has swept away the village's other 2 documented *ermitas*.

🚗 Seven km. north is the site of the 1068 battle of Llantada between Alfonso VI of León and Castilla's Sancho II, who was assisted by Rodrigo Díaz de Vivar, the Cid.

✳ **Boadilla del Camino** (aka Bobadilla) The town is cited in a 10th-c. document and appears to be older. The circular street plan indicates the location of the medieval fortifications. In the late 15th c. Enrique IV granted the village its independence from the lords of Melgar and Castrogeriz. To celebrate, the village erected a **Gothic gibbet** (*rollo*, or *picota*) in its plaza so that they could hang their own local malefactors without any noble intervention. The 16th-c. **Iglesia de Santa María de la Asunción**, often reconstructed, has a Plateresque 16th-c. retablo and a 15th-c. Gothic Crucifixion. The **pulpit** mixes Gothic, Mudéjar, and Baroque in a mélange common in the region. There is also a Romanesque **baptismal font**.

In former times Boadilla offered many services to pilgrims. In the 13th c. the town was large enough to support a monastery and 4 churches. The church dedicated to Santiago stood on the hill just east of town near the cemetery. The Hospital de la Puente, 50 m. from the small bridge leading to the barrio de Santiago, is documented in the 13th c. The Hospital de la Visitación appears in 16th- and 17th-c. documents.

The fields around Boadilla are filled with dovecotes (*palomares*), erected for 3 practical purposes: doves eat insects that eat crops; dove droppings fertilize the crops; and doves are good to eat. The dovecotes are circular or square adobe structures with rows of niches inside for the doves to build their nests. Early or late in the day you will see the doves swirling over the villages in dense flocks. Although dovecotes are common in the Tierra de Campos in the Province of Palencia, those of Bobadilla are particularly ornate. This may be a legacy of the *Morisco* farmers resettled in this region after the Alpujarras revolt of the 1560s (see ch. 53).

From just beyond Boadilla until you reach Frómista, the Road skirts the Canal de Castilla.

📖 Fernando el Católico was the first to suggest that canals be dug on the flat Meseta Alta of Castilla for irrigation, transport, and to provide waterpower for mills. The plan languished until the 1750s, when Carlos III's minister, the Marqués de la Ensenada, launched what was to be a nearly 50–year effort to dig 4 major canals through the heartland of the Tierra de Campos. By the time Spain finished building the canals, railroads had replaced canal barges as the principal movers of heavy goods. But the canals have continued to provide water for irrigation and for power for the century and a half up until our day. The area around Frómista is a prime example: the 5 locks noted in an 1855 report powered a mill, 2 flour factories, and 2 fulling mills (*batanes*) for making felt. In 1986 the canal water flowing through locks crossed by the Camino de Santiago was rerouted into pipes to produce electric power for local factories.

🚗 Eleven km. south of Frómista is the cheese-making town of Támara, where in a 1037 battle Vermudo III of León lost his troops, his horse Pelayuelo, his kingdom, and his life to Fernando I of Castilla. The resulting Pact of Támara united the 2 kingdoms for the first time. A branch of the pilgrimage Road went through the town, and by the late 12th c. Támara had a pilgrim's hospice run by the knights of Saint John of Jerusalem. In 1516 the bishop of Palencia warned them to take in only "credentialed foreign pilgrims, and not to house them longer than two days unless they be in dire need." Támara boasts several small monuments:
* The village center conserves its medieval core, a porticoed plaza, and also bits of 11th-c. walls and one of the city gates.
* The floor plan of the Ermita de la Virgen de Rombrada is early Romanesque, perhaps with vestiges of Visigothic.
* The 13th-c. church of San Miguel was a Benedictine monastery.
* The 14th–16th-c. Iglesia de San Hipólito el Real has nice retablos, a *reja*, a Gothic baptismal font, choir stalls, and a sonorous organ. Its tower is Herreran in style.

48. FRÓMISTA

HISTORY

Two words explain Frómista: wheat and pilgrimage. The center of the richest grain-growing area in Iberia, and one of the breadbaskets of the Roman Empire, even the town's name is most likely derived from the Latin word for cereal, *frumentum*. Frómista was established by the Celts, farmed by the Celtíberos, the site of a Roman *villa* or farming community, and then of a Visigothic town. Muslims burned the town but did not establish a settlement here, most likely because the region's flat terrain did not offer easily defensible sites. For years the area around Frómista was a kind of no-man's-land. Christians gained definitive sway in the 10th c., and in the next century doña Mayor, countess of Castilla and wife of Sancho III el Mayor, invested in Fromísta's repopulation. In 1118 doña Urraca donated the village to the Cluniac Benedictines of Carrión de los Condes. For 300 years Carrión controlled the monastery while the town was run by its own lords and citizens. The inevitable conflicts ceased in 1427 when the entire town became the property of the Gómez de Benavides family.

The 1391 coordinated attacks against Castilla's and Aragón's Jewish population for the most part skipped Frómista. Refugees swelled the town's Jewish community to some 200 families, most of whom lived near the Church of San Martín. In the 15th c. Frómista thrived as a regional market center. Its decline began in 1492 with the expulsion of the Jews. The synagogue in the San Martín neighborhood became the Iglesia de la Cruz. Overall, Frómista's 15th-c. population of 1,000 households had shrunk to 521 by 1591, and by the mid-18th c. to 217.

> 📖 When Laffi's pilgrim group marched through Frómista ca. 1670 he recorded in his diary vivid details about the difficulties of living on the Meseta Alta: "[Frómista] is so big it is like a city, but there is a terrible famine since, because of the locusts, they have not been able to harvest neither wheat, the vines, nor fruit, nor anything. It is wretched to see these places so desolate because of these creatures. At night all the inhabitants of the area go out through the town with wooden clubs and kill the locusts which collect under the walls during the day, covering them so that they appear to be painted black. At night they fall to the ground because of the cold, and they then come and kill them." [Laffi; trans. Hall (1997), 144]

The Canal de Castilla brought water to the region in 1773 and reversed the economic decline. For the last 2 centuries Frómista has again prospered as an agricultural center.

Few vestiges of medieval Frómista remain. Stone is scarce in this region, and adobe does not last.

PILGRIMAGE

Medieval Frómista had 2 now-vanished hospices for pilgrims: Santiago and Los Palmeros. The modern hotel is located on the site of Los Palmeros, in the plaza behind the statute of San Telmo. The orchard known as the Huerto de los Romeros, just to the north of the Church of San Pedro, is the site of a medieval pilgrim cemetery.

> 📖 The term *palmeros* referred originally to Holy Land pilgrims who brought back palm branches from Jerusalem, but by the late Middle Ages it had become a generic term for pilgrims. *Romeros* is another word for pilgrims, in this case indicating pilgrims to Rome.

MONUMENTS: 1. **Iglesia de San Martín**. 2. **Iglesia de San Pedro**. 3. Iglesia de Santa María del Castillo. 4. Statue of San Telmo. 5. Ermita de Santiago del Otero.

1. **Iglesia de San Martín**. Construction of the church, and of the monastery (now disappeared) of which it was a part, was underwritten in 1066 by the widow of Sancho el Mayor of Navarra, doña Mayor, whose church-building family is also responsible for the Cathedral of Jaca and San Isidoro of León. From its conception, this church was to be special, worthy of the pilgrimage Road. Architects from Jaca designed it as a reduced-scale replica of the Jaca Cathedral. The large, evenly cut stone blocks had to be brought from elsewhere at great expense. The masons, architects, sculptors and—presumably, since it has all been lost—painters who worked on it were all masters of their crafts. Although heavily, and some say clumsily, restored, San Martín remains the purest extant example of the 3–nave, rounded apse Jaca style of Romanesque.

Exterior:
• The debt to Jaca is seen in the clear separation between the 2 levels of roof; the narrow, slit windows; the octagonal cupola; the rounded apses; and the extraordinarily rich series of **corbels** and square **metopes** supporting the roof. With your binoculars you can see the details of the grotesques, the animal and vegetable motifs, the geometric knots, and the sirens. The twin towers are a San Martín innovation. Given the dominance of the Jaca model, the lack of tympana on the portals is strange.

Interior:
• The look of clean simplicity reflects the modern restorers' tastes: in the 11th c. the walls and vaults would most likely have been covered with vivid fresco paintings. Note the Jaca-style semicylindrical vault resting on a checkerboarded decorative band (*imposta*) and the alternating cruciform and complex pillars. The cupola rests on squinches, which permits the insertion of windows to give more light than in Jaca.
• San Martín contains the best series of **capitals** (100+) and **corbels** (315) in all Castilla. Note the preponderance of vegetable motifs, with Jaca-style palms, and Byzantine-influenced rolled cylinders. The **narrative capitals** are striking for their themes and quality of workmanship. (A map inside the church identifies each scene and its location.) The capitals in the *cabecera* and the apses were carved by the so-called first Master of Frómista, who also probably worked in the Jaca Cathedral. The capitals in the naves, while they are still extraordinarily varied, seem to have been done by a less-inspired disciple—the second master—who was not quite as adept in his rendering of the classic human figure.
• In the apse is a 16th-c. statute of **Santiago Peregrino**.

2. **Iglesia de San Pedro**. 16th-c. Gothic, with graceful vaults and some mediocre paintings attributed to Mengs or to Ribera. The church houses a small **museum**, with panels and 29 paintings attributed to Fernando Gallego's school. These come from the Church of Santa María's ca. 1480 Hispano-Flemish **retablo**. There are some superb details, such as the angels in the Nativity scene and the nudes of Adam and Eve in the Garden of Eden.

3. Iglesia de Santa María del Castillo. In 1378 Fernando Sánchez de Tobar, the Admiral of Castilla, commissioned a church next to his castle here. It was supplanted by a Plateresque structure begun ca. 1530. In the early 18th c. a Neoclassic Herrera-style tower was added.

> 📖 A Eucharistic miracle is associated with this church. A man had been excommunicated for not returning money borrowed from some Jews. Years later, in 1453, he lay on his deathbed. He was unable to lift the consecrated Host from the paten until he was reinstated to the Church, upon which the Host entered his mouth on its own accord. For centuries a reliquary with the stubborn Host was exhibited to pilgrims. A stele commemorates this miracle in the church, as does the name of the street on which it is located: Calle del Milagro.

4. Statue of San Telmo (1970). Pedro González Telmo (born here in 1190, buried in Tuy, France) is possibly the San Telmo, or St. Elmo, who is the patron saint of sailors.

> 📖 Other claimants to the St. Elmo name are 4th-c. bishops from Campagna and from Syria. Even more likely is that Elmo comes from Ermo, the abbreviated Italian form of St. Erasmus. St. Elmo—whoever he was—was associated with an atmospheric phenomenon, the discharges of electricity from the tops of masts of ships during storms, called St. Elmo's fire.

5. Ermita de Santiago (aka Ermita del Otero). This small rectangular church, rebuilt with Baroque touches in the 17th c., is located across the railroad tracks in the direction of Astudillo.

✳ Población de Campos The town has existed since at least the 11ᵗʰ c. In the 12ᵗʰ it belonged to the Order of San Juan, and in the 13ᵗʰ it was held by one of Alfonso X's brothers, don Felipe. A 16ᵗʰ-c. document records macabrely that "In this town Enrique Cook was drawn and quartered the night that the King Felipe II spent in Frómista." A hospice administered first by the Templars of Villasirga and then by the Hospitallers of Saint John used to stand on the town's main street, the Calle Francesa. Another, which stood at Calle de las Escuelas, 17, still displays the crossed keys of San Pedro over the door.

In a little park on the left as one enters town is the 13ᵗʰ-c. Romanesque Ermita de San Miguel, which once belonged to the Knights of Malta. The façade has a nice Gothic arch. The Church of Santa María Magdalena contains an 18ᵗʰ-c. Baroque retablo, a Romanesque baptismal font, and the 13ᵗʰ-c. image of the Virgen del Socorro. West of the church, and below the level of the street, is the hermitage of La Virgen del Socorro, restored in 1973. On the floor inside are several interesting tombs.

The medieval Road on both sides of town has been wiped out by recent redistribution of the agricultural land.

✳ Revenga de Campos Alfonso VIII gave this village on the Ucieza River to the monks of San Zoilo in Carrión in 1213. The church of San Lorenzo is Baroque.

✳ Villovieco To avoid the highway, here we cross the creek and proceed along its right bank through Villovieco, with its Renaissance church of Santa María, to the Ermita de Nuestra Señora del Río. According to legend, when a flood swept away the village of Tablares in 1101, this image of the Virgin swam upstream and stopped at this site. The *ermita* has an airy Neoclassic interior.

Halfway from the *ermita* to Villasirga is the Humilladero del Santo Cristo de la Salud, a roadside oratory. Through the window in the door you can see a nice Gothic Christ.

✳ Villarmentero de Campos The town is presumably named for the person responsible for its repopulation, Armentarius.

The early 16ᵗʰ-c. Church of San Martín de Tours preserves its **Mudéjar-style ceiling** (a weatherworn sample can be seen on the porch) and a good Plateresque retablo with an image of San Martín dividing his cape.

A hospice in the Calle Francesa was maintained by the Cofradía de la Vera Cruz as late as 1674. A later hospice is documented at Calle Ramón y Cajal, 14: it is the first house on the left entering the village from the highway from Revenga.

Three enormous pine trees (*pinos doncales*) next to the river are a marvelous source of both shade and pine nuts.

✳ Villalcázar de Sirga

HISTORY

The town's original name was Villasirga (*sirga* means road; i.e. the pilgrimage Road). Later, given the castlelike aspect of the church, it was changed to Villalcázar de Sirga (*alcázar* means castle). According to tradition, ca. 1157 Castilian king Sancho III invited the Knights Templar (see ch. 68) to protect the Santiago Road. They established their base (*bailía*) in Villalcázar and within 40 years had constructed a monumental, fortified church and residence complex. Curiously, however, surviving documentation does not mention the Templars in Villasirga until 1307, a mere 5 years before their expulsion from Iberia, which suggests that the town—like many others in the region—was protected not by the Templars but by the Orden de Santiago. In the 14th c. the town was large enough to have 3 parishes (some ruins of San Pedro survive as a granary and warehouse). In the later 14th and the 15th c. it belonged to various noble families. In the 18th c. war, famine, disease, and emigration severely reduced Villalcázar's population.

PILGRIMAGE

The CC *Guide* does not mention Villasirga, since at that time the Road from Frómista to Carrión passed to the north through Arconada, where Count Gómez Díaz had built a hospice in 1047. The medieval documents refer to a Templar's hospice in the Calle Grande and another run by the Orden de Santiago from 1527. Yet a third was maintained by a local *cofradía*. With the construction of the church of Santa María and Villalcázar's hospices, and with the fame of the miracles worked by the Virgen Blanca in the town, the Road shifted, and Villasirga became a minor pilgrimage goal in its own right.

In great part this was due to the 427 songs written in the second half of the 13th c. by (or under the direction of) Castilla's King Alfonso X the Wise, who was a strong booster of *Vila-Sirga, ú faz a Virgen muitos miragres assí com'a ela praz* ("Villasirga, where the Virgin works many miracles, as is her pleasure"; *Cantiga* 313). The King dedicated 12 *cantigas* (poems in the Gallego language) to the Virgen Blanca "who is in a church in Vila-Sirga, which is two leagues from Carrión" (*Cantiga* 31). At the time of the King's writing, the main route must have still passed east of Villasirga, for *Cantigas* 278 and 253 each speak of a pilgrim who detours ("desvou-sse do Camino") to visit the church. Several of the miracles narrated in the songs concern the pilgrimage:

> 217: an unrepentant French pilgrim could not physically enter the church until he had begged the Virgin to forgive him. This *Cantiga* is explicit about how the Road served as an international conduit of information: "people carried the news through all of Spain and even to Rocamador."
>
> 218: A crippled German pilgrim who saw the "great number of pilgrims going to Santiago from his country" (*víu que gran romaria / de gente de sa trra a Santiago ya*) decided to hobble along with them, and although he found no cure in Compostela, he was granted his miracle in Villasirga on the return trip.
>
> 253: A sinner from Toulouse was sentenced by his abbot to walk to Compostela carrying with one hand a 24–pound iron weight to lay on Santiago's altar. In Villasirga he rested it on the altar and prayed for pardon. The weight split in two, and since no one could lift either piece, he was free from his obligation.
>
> 268: After prayer to the Virgen Blanca and "lighting many candles as is the pilgrims' custom," a French pilgrim recovered the use of her paralyzed body.
>
> 278: A blind man recovered his sight after a vigil, and the Virgen Blanca's fame drew blind men from all over western Europe.
>
> 313: Italian pilgrims, sailing to Spain to bring a chalice to Compostela, were saved from a storm by the Virgen Blanca after Saints Peter, Nicholas,

Matthew, and James had ignored their prayers. The chalice can be seen in the treasury.

355 is a variant of Santo Domingo de la Calzada's "hanged innocent" miracle, in which a man bringing a finely carved chair to Villasirga was unjustly accused of theft by a spurned village woman, was hanged, but then was saved by the Virgin who holds him up with the chair.

Cantigas 227, 229, 232, 234, and 243, also refer to this church, telling how the Virgin rescued a man from prison, restored hearing and speech to a deaf mute, blinded some Moors who wanted to destroy the church, helped a nobleman from Treviño find his prized hunting falcon, and saved other nobles from hunting accidents.

MONUMENTS: 1. **Iglesia de Santa María la Blanca**. 2. Ayuntamiento. 3. Mesón de Pablo.

1. **Iglesia de Santa María la Blanca**. Most of the construction dates from the late 12th and early 13th c., with the major decorative programs from the late 13th. Legend holds that in 1157 Queen Blanca de Castilla, the wife of Sancho III, donated some of her jewels for the refurbishment of the church and its dedication to the image of the White Virgin. The fortified tower, cloister, chapter house, residences of the Knights Templar, pilgrim hospice, silos, stables, and the enormous surrounding wall, with its towers, gates, etc., were lost in the Lisbon earthquake of 1755 and in 1808 in the war against the French. The west end of the church, damaged in the quake, collapsed in 1888. Even with all this vanished, the portions that remain are monumental.

Exterior:
• The huge porch is modeled on the Burgos monastery of Las Huelgas. The 2–tiered late-13th-c. frieze is unusual. In the upper register the Apostles surround Christ in Majesty and the Tetramorphos. The lower frieze features the Virgen Blanca on her throne approached by the 3 Wise Men on the left, with San José and the Annunciation on her right. The scenes are not interactive. Rather, each of the large figures is isolated in its niche as on an altar frontal or the portal of a cathedral. Although these figures are clearly in the Gothic tradition, they recall the Romanesque portals you have seen in Estella and the one you will see next in Carrión.
• At the west end you can see where the 3 naves were walled up after the 1888 collapse, which destroyed what travelers before then described as the "Puerta del ángel." With your binoculars you can see several tiny statues that were salvaged and set on the roofline: the center image is of the Sacrifice of Isaac, with the angel staying Abraham's hand.

Interior:
• The church's curious design features a double transept, with 5 naves in the *cabecera* narrowing to 3 west of the transepts. At the crossing are 4 large stone sculptures, from the same period as those on the entrance, and undoubtedly relocated here from some other portal. Curiously, San Pedro, the Virgin, and San Miguel are all treading on dragons (the angel of the Annunciation stands on a lion). Scattered throughout the church are other statues from the same period and perhaps the same portal.
• **Main altar**. The retablo combines 3 separate styles. The Calvary, on top, was carved ca. 1300. The lowest line of figures, the bench, was carved in the Renaissance style ca. 1560. The faces tend to be superbly rendered; the bodies less so.
    The body of the **retablo** is a late example of the Hispano-Flemish style, ca. 1535–40, by the so-called Sirga Master, who was a disciple of Pedro Berruguete. Each panel or figure is covered with a canopy of delicate Gothic

tracery. Most of the figures are set against Renaissance-style landscapes. The highest tier relates important miracles involving Jesus and Mary: the Mass of San Gregorio, the delivery of chasuble to San Ildefonso, Christ's supper with the leper Lazarus, and Christ's appearance to his mother. The central tiers depict the **life and Passion of Jesus**. These are extremely well done: interesting compositions, finely executed details, full of color and movement. While they narrate the episodes of the Passion in complex landscapes crowded with figures, they invariably focus our attention on the central figure of Christ or Mary. In the Ascension (lower right), Christ disappears into a cloud, leaving his footprints behind, while the astonished Apostles (including **Santiago** dressed as a pilgrim) stand gaping. The side panels depict 6 full-length saints: Francisco, Juan Bautista, and Pedro (left), and Benito, Cipriano, and Andrés (right). The 13th-c. **statue of the Virgen Blanca** occupies the center.

• The **holy water font** near the entrance was refashioned from a 14th-c. stone relief showing a knight taking leave of his lady. The arms show him to be a member of the military Order of Alcántara.

• Left of the main altar is an early-16th-c. **retablo de San Antonio**, by the "Calzada Master." The half saints are Agueda, Augustín, Brígida, and Zoilo. Hispano-Flemish-style rigid fabrics hang behind the heads. The frames, backgrounds, and captioned scrolls are all Gothic, but the composition, colors, and treatment of the human figures have been influenced by the new Renaissance styles.

• The carved plaster pulpit is another transitional Gothic-Renaissance work. Among its statues is a **Santiago Peregrino**.

• The Capilla de Santiago. A knight of the Order of Santiago endowed this chapel in the transept with the rose window.

Its ca. 1530 retablo depicts 9 scenes from the **life of Santiago**. The central image, a ringleted Santiago with his head thrown back and an open book in one hand, is probably by Juan de Valmaseda. The 4 panels on the left have to do with James's encounter with the magician Hermogenes and his subsequent struggles with a host of demons.

> 📖 Hermogenes was a magician whose power came from the Devil. The medieval legend, recorded in the LSJ (Book I, ch. 9) and the *Golden Legend* tells how Hermogenes sent his agent Philetus to confound Santiago, but that when Philetus observed the Apostle working miracles, he became one of James's disciples. Hermogenes, furious, imprisoned Philetus, but Santiago set him free. Hermogenes sent demons to bring Santiago to him, but, instead, the demons took the magician to Santiago, who treated him well, set him free, and gave him his own walking staff as a holy protection against the demons. Hermogenes, like Philetus, signed on as a devout Christian, burning his library of magic as a sign of his conversion.

On the right are Santiago's arrest, decapitation, and the translation of his body to Galicia. This is the most detailed exposition of Santiago's life between the French border and Compostela.

The chapel also holds several images of the Virgin, including the Virgin of Alfonso X's *Cantigas*. The curious **statue of the Virgen de la O** depicts Mary both pregnant and with the child Jesus in her arms.

The chapel's **3 tombs**, resting on carved lions, are masterpieces.

—The tomb of **Felipe**, brother of King Alfonso X, was sculpted in 1274 by Antón Pérez de Carrión.

📖 As a fifth son, never hopeful of the throne, Felipe was destined for the Church. He studied in Paris with Albertus Magnus and Thomas Aquinas and, on his return to Spain, progressed from canon in Toledo and abbot in Valladolid to become in 1248 the first archbishop of newly reconquered Seville. But the young man's interests lay elsewhere, and in 1258 he was given permission to leave holy orders. He took up the cause of Princess Cristina of Norway, who had been engaged to wed Alfonso X when the King declared that he would divorce his current wife, Violante, because she was barren. Cristina made the long journey to Spain, but Alfonso decided not to go through with the divorce. To salvage Cristina's honor, Felipe married her. In 1269, 11 years after her death, he married Leonor Ruiz de Castro y Pimentel. But he never forgave his brother for his shabby treatment of Cristina, and rose up against him in rebellion on several occasions, seeking allies in Navarra, Portugal, and even the Muslim kingdom of Granada. Felipe died—to his brother the king's great relief—in 1274.

The polychromed stone tomb is an anthology of 13th-c. funeral customs. His wife is shown taking her leave, and then on horseback accompanying the funeral procession of monks, musicians, and professional mourning women (*plañideras*). Two women watch from a window. The prince's horse carries his arms, reversed in a sign of mourning. The reclining figure of the prince carries a falcon. Two lines of castles (from his father Fernando III) and eagles (from his mother Beatriz de Suabia) surround the tomb.

—The **tomb of doña Leonor Ruiz de Castro**, Felipe's second wife, depicts her carrying a pepper, a pun on her name Pimentel. Or it could be a heart. Her tomb, too, details 13th-c. funeral customs: her death, the funeral cortege, mourning, and burial.

—The **tomb of the Grand Master of the Templars** is older than the others. This is probably the man who built the *bailía*.

—There is also a more sober mid-14th-c. tomb of knight Juan Pérez. At its head Christ crowns the Virgin, accompanied by angels. At its feet there is a badly preserved small altar to Santiago.

2. Ayuntamiento. This originally was the palace of the counts of Villasirga. It was rebuilt as the town hall in the early 18th c., incorporating bits of the Church of Santa María.

3. Mesón de Pablo. This restaurant, across the plaza from the church, specializes in "medieval" banquets, and is decorated with pilgrim paraphernalia. One rainy June day in 1974, before the regeneration of the pilgrimage, the Mesón was hosting a wedding banquet. Our group, in pilgrim regalia, strode in wet and bedraggled, astonishing the guests with the anomaly that in these modern times there were still pilgrims on the Road. Invited to join the feast, we paid for our meal by singing the 12th-c. Latin hymn of Santiago, "Dum Pater familias" (see ch. 16) and other medieval pilgrim songs.

50. CARRIÓN DE LOS CONDES

HISTORY

In Roman times the city on the bluff a little north of today's Carrión was known as Lacobriga. The Visigoths, who held the city next, left tombs in the cliff banks both north and south of Carrión. Muslims, who conquered the area ca. 713, built a castle here, on the site now occupied by the Iglesia de Belén.

Carrión figured large in 11th-c. Castilian history, and during the Middle Ages it was one of the wealthiest and most important towns in north central Spain. In its heyday, the city's 13 parishes housed 10,000 people. Carrión's prosperity came first from agriculture. The Islamic geographer Idrisi in 1150 called it "a flourishing middle-sized city with abundant harvests" (145); and the CC *Guide* termed it "a well-managed and industrious town, abundant in bread, wine, meat, and all kinds of produce" [CC: Book V, trans. Melczer, 86]. It also benefited from the commerce that accompanied the development of the Road. Its international character attracted a sizable Jewish population.

Alfonso VI of León took refuge in Carrión's church of Santa María after his defeat by his brother Sancho II of Castilla. This was before he had Sancho murdered on the ramparts of Zamora, earning the enmity of much of Castilla and in particular the Cid (see ch. 42). According to the epic *Poema de mío Cid*, Carrión was home of the villainous counts who married and mistreated the Cid's daughters, and in whose (dis)honor the city is called "de los Condes."

After the Condes, one of Carrión's 2 most famous medieval citizens was a poet, Sem Tob ibn Ardutiel ben Isaac de Carrión.

   📖 The 14th-c. rabbi and poet Sem Tob is best known for his *Proverbios morales* (*Moral Proverbs*, ca. 1355). This long poem is the only medieval literary work by a Spanish Jew in the Spanish language. It gives advice for living a sane life in perilous times. His sources were Islamic, Jewish, and Christian. His plaintive plea to be taken seriously by his Christian neighbors is a sign of the intensification of Christian anti-Semitism during the 14th c.

Non val el açor menos	The falcon is not worth less
nor nasçer de mal nido	for being born in a lowly nest,
nin los enxemplos buenos	nor are good exempla
por los dezyr judio.	just because a Jew says them. (stanza 64)

He also wrote in Hebrew several philosophical works, among them the "Battle between the Pen and the Scissors."

The second of these famous citizens was also a poet: don Iñigo López de Mendoza, the Marqués de Santillana (1398–1458).

The Marqués de Santillana was an early Renaissance figure who distinguished himself as a warrior, a politician (enemy of Álvaro de Luna, the powerful prime minister of Castilla), a bibliophile (his collection is now in the Biblioteca Nacional in Madrid), and as a literary critic and poet. He was one of the earliest poets enamored of the Italian Renaissance and is credited with introducing the sonnet form into Spain. His balladlike *serranillas* detailed some of the more grotesque manifestations of rural sexuality.

PILGRIMAGE

Because legend holds that Charlemagne camped here during his campaign to wrest control of the pilgrimage Road from the Moors, Carrión was particularly popular with French pilgrims. It had as many as 14 pilgrim hospices: 1 at the eastern entrance (Sancti Spiritus), 2 along the pilgrim Road in the city (Santiago and Santa María del Camino, which was in the Plaza de Santa María, where the telephone company now stands), 5 in various other parts of the city (Palmeros, Corpus Christi, and others named for Saints Pedro, Julián, and Miguel), as well as 6 more across the river on the Road to Calzadilla (Todos los Santos, de la O, de la Herrada, and Saints Lázaro, Torcuato, and María). The largest, Santa María del Camino, had 12 beds. Its roof was capped by a weathervane shaped like a rooster, which continues to crown the municipal hospital. The remains of the 13th-c. hospice of Todos los Santos can be seen in the stonework opposite the Church of San Zoilo. Nearby, next to a smithy, was the Hospital de la Herrada, founded before 1209 by Gonzalo Ruiz, majordomo of Fernando III and one of the 2 strongest nobles of the Tierra de Campos. Ruiz's 2 wives and 13 children supported this hospice with numerous donations of lands and rents.

In 1584 the Diocesan Seminary sued to take over the Hospital de la Herrada, alleging that "since with changing times the pilgrimage has waned, the endowment is being spent not on pilgrims but on vagabonds, fallen, doctrine-less people of whom one can expect little, who spend their time traveling between the 6 or 7 hospices in the region that were intended for pilgrims, and incurring a cost in this hospital each month of 8 or 10 measures of bread." The king agreed to the transfer, stipulating only that "if times change again, and the endowment should be again needed for pilgrims, that it be so restored." This evidently happened, for in 1789 the endowment was supporting an administrator and his servant, 2 bread makers, 2 workmen, a sacristan, a doctor, a surgeon (bonesetter), a druggist, a carter, and 2 iron workers, as well as providing bread, eggs, wine, and cash payments to indigent pilgrims.

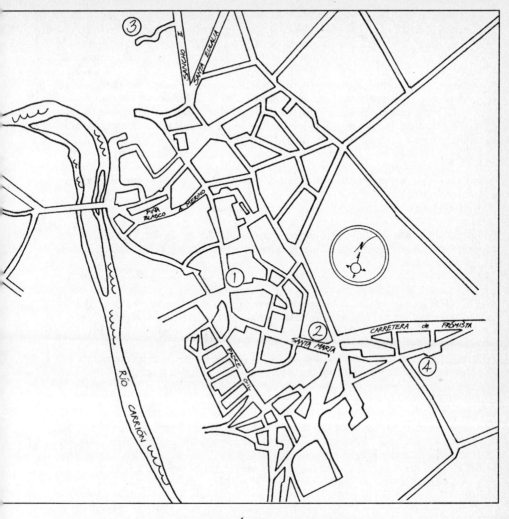

CARRIÓN DE LOS CONDES

MONUMENTS: 1. **Iglesia de Santiago**. 2. **Iglesia de Santa María del Camino**. 3. Iglesia de Nuestra Señora de Belén. 4. Real Convento de las Clarisas. 5. **Monasterio de San Zoilo**.

1. **Iglesia de Santiago**. The 12th-c. church was destroyed by fire during the War of Independence against the French. An 1845 reconstruction spared the **façade**, one of the masterpieces of Castilian Romanesque monumental sculpture.

• The **frieze**. Interest is focused on the stern-faced **Christ in Majesty** that may have been inspired by a frieze in Cahors executed in the style of Saint-Sernin of Toulouse. The head is better than the body, and the stylized clothing suggests that of Castilian nobility. The disposition of the figures recalls Romanesque altar frontispieces and may even be modeled on the Silos reliquary now in the Burgos Archaeological Museum. In turn, the Carrión Christ was imitated in a half dozen façades elsewhere in Castilla (unfortunately none of them directly on the Road).

• The **archivolts**. The **24 old men of the Apocalypse** was a motif popularized by both the Cluniac Benedictines and the Dominican Orders. There are 2 more sets on the Road, in León and in Compostela, and many more on other Spanish churches as well. The extraordinarily varied and realistic Carrión set represents medieval occupations. Among them you will see a tailor, a cobbler, a dancer-acrobat-contortionist, a violist (with crossed legs, as in Santo Domingo de la Calzada and in Compostela) transported by his music, a professional mourner, 2 men fighting (round shields are often associated with Muslims, elongated shields with Christians, as in the royal palace in Estella), a woman with a zither, a monk reading from a book, a scribe writing, and a blacksmith working a bellows.

• The **capitals**, whose themes exalt charitable acts, are well executed. Note the leper Lazarus being attended by dogs; a Jew with his legally mandated conical hat removing a person from a chest; a rich man in torment, and the beggar Lazarus raised to glory.

• The inside contains a small museum of sacred art.

2. **Iglesia de Santa María del Camino** (aka Santa María de la Victoria). This church dates largely from the 12ᵗʰ c. It celebrates the defeat of the Moors on this site by Vermudo I.

📖 The legend of the 100 virgins is associated with the victory over the Moors. Each year Christian king Mauregato was required to surrender 100 virgins (in some versions only 30) to their Moorish overlords in tribute. When the Christians prayed to be freed of this burden, a herd of bulls attacked the Moors and chased them off. A plaque in the church commemorates the event, as do a painting and a capital on the south porch.

Exterior:
• The **porch** is earlier than the façade of La Iglesia de Santiago. Centering on the Adoration, it also depicts the Epiphany, Herod, the 3 Wise Men, Samson and the lion, and a knight who may be **Santiago**. The 4 bulls on the jambs and the women on one of the **capitals** refer to the legend of the 100 virgins.

Interior:
• The lateral aisles and apses are Romanesque, with checkerboard bands and window treatments derived from Jaca. The central nave was revaulted in the Neoclassic style, and the principal apse is from 1685.

• Of special note in the church are a good Romanesque Virgin and a 14ᵗʰ-c. Gothic crucifix.

3. Iglesia de Nuestra Señora de Belén. This unremarkable church occupies the site of the former medieval castle. People here relate that it was taken from the Moors by smuggling soldiers into the fort inside coal carts, a variant of the Trojan-horse strategy. The carts appear on the city's escutcheon. The medieval Jewish quarter was located near this church.

4. Real Convento de las Clarisas. Little remains from the 13ᵗʰ-c. church that tradition holds was founded in 1231 by 2 colleagues of Santa Clara. The church, rebuilt in the 17ᵗʰ c. with a gift from Felipe III, contains a Baroque retablo fronted with some Talavera tiles, a nice Pieta by **Gregorio Hernández**, and a small museum of Franciscan memorabilia.

5. **Monasterio de San Zoilo.** Located on the west bank of the river Carrión, San Zoilo is a monument of major historic and artistic importance. At its peak it

administered a network of 7 hospices. It was founded in the 10th c. by Conde Gómez Díaz and his wife Teresa and dedicated to St. John the Baptist. It was renamed in 1047 when their son brought them the relics of the Cordoban martyr San Zoilo.

> 📖 The son of Gómez Díaz and his wife was said to have assisted the Emir of Córdoba, who asked him if he wanted gold and silver in reward; the son preferred the relics.

The monastery of San Zoilo was given to Cluny in 1076 by widowed Countess Teresa Peláez and became the second most important Cluniac monastery in Castilla after Sahagún. One of its dependencies was the monastery of San Martín de Frómista, donated in 1118 by Queen Urraca, who had a close relationship with the Monastery of San Zoilo. When Bishop Mauricio brought the skull of Santiago the Lesser to her from Jerusalem, she deposited it here for safekeeping while she waited for the Galician war to subside so she could carry it to Compostela. In the 13th c. the monastery owned much of the town, including Carrión's mosque, and King Fernando III freed citizens, be they Christians, Muslims, or Jews, from paying royal taxes—so they could pay the monastery directly.

San Zoilo declined in the 14th and 15th centuries, surviving for a time by pawning part of its artistic patrimony. In the 16th c. it was restored and enlarged by the Benedictines of Valladolid. Then, like most Spanish monastic possessions, it was abandoned during the 19th-c. *desamortización*. Later it housed a small community of Jesuits and then a school. Most recently the monks' quarters have been turned into a luxurious hotel.

> 📖 A miracle is associated with this church: a blind pilgrim was brought to the monastery to sleep, but instead he stood vigil before the church's relics, and with morning he found his sight restored.

Exterior:
• The monumental 17th-c. **façade** depicts St. Louis, king of France, and Saints Juan Bautista, Benito, Bernardo, and Zoilo, along with the coats of arms of various prelates and abbots.

Interior:
• The **Renaissance cloister** was begun by Juan de Badajoz the Younger in 1537 and finally finished in 1604. Its **ceiling** is magnificent, with over 200 intricately carved arch keystones (*claves*) of patriarchs, prophets, kings, saints (especially the life of San Benito), and a wide variety of other topics. Of course **Santiago** is there. It is a dizzying collection of high-quality Renaissance busts, the best you will see along the Road.
• An early **Romanesque doorway**, probably belonging to the ancient Capilla de San Juan Bautista, was discovered in 1993, hidden behind a plaster wall. Its marble columns and 4 narrative capitals: reptiles (sins), Balaam's ass (the sinner repentant), a soul saved by angels, and a grape harvest (the Eucharistic miracle) appear to be by a sculptor who worked in Frómista.
• The tombs. Here are the sepulchers of the descendants of the counts of Carrión who bedeviled the Cid. There are several plain sepulchers from the 11th and 12th c. and some decorated tombs of the 13th c. as well.

Other monuments in Carrión include the churches of:
- San Andrés, with 16th-c. choir stalls from the nearby Abby of Benevívere.
- San Francisco, with several good tombs.
- San Juan del Mercado.
- San Julián.

As you cross the Río Carrión, look north to the gravel island. Is the painted-stone mosaic of **Santiago Peregrino** that we saw in 1998 still there?

51. Carrión de los Condes → Calzadilla de la Cueza

Route: CARRIÓN DE LOS CONDES → [Benevívere] → [Calzada de los Molinos → Cervatos de la Cueza → Quintanilla de la Cueza] → CALZADILLA DE LA CUEZA

Flat is one word that comes into most pilgrims' minds along this stretch of the Road. *Treeless* is another. *Monotonous* is a third, but that one is flat-out wrong. The very desolation here is impressive. The grain fields lining both sides of the Road change color with the sky or the ripples of the wind. We have often counted 30 or more different species of wildflowers along the roadside here. Hawks and kites accompany us overhead, and once, in 1983, we saw a rare turkey-size bustard (*avutarda*), with its grey head and buff breast, pecking for insects in the wheat stubble. There is variety here, but it is subtle, and a lot depends on the light. As the old saying goes, "the landscape of Castilla is in her sky."

The mountains that on a clear day are visible in the north are part of the Cantabrian Range that forms the northern boundary of Spain's Meseta Alta. Several of the towns in this region are named *Calzada* (meaning "road"; i.e., the Roman or pilgrimage Road) or *Quinta* (from the Latin *quintus*, an hacienda or large farm with several families in residence, so called because they traditionally paid a fifth of their annual production in rent.).

Two km. from Carrión and 500 m. to the north of the hiking road are the ruins of the Abadía de Santa María de Benevívere, founded ca. 1065 by Diego Martínez Sarmiento de Villamayor, the majordomo of Alfonso VIII. Administered by the Augustinians, it ran the pilgrim hospice of San Turcuato. All that remains here now is a barn. Its

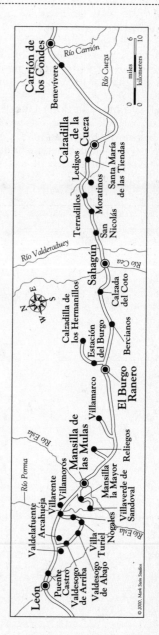

carved tombs are in the Palencia museum. One tradition locates near this abbey the "field of lances" episode in the *Song of Roland* (see ch. 55).

🥾 Calzada de los Molinos 500 m. to the south of the hiking road. As you cross the bridge into town you will see an old mill on your right. The 18th-c. Church of Santiago (incorporating earlier remnants) reputedly contains a Hispano-Flemish retablo with Old Testament prophets and Saints Agueda and Lucía, an unremarkable image of Santiago, and a Mudéjar-style coffered ceiling (*artesonado*).

🥾 Cervatos de la Cueza Juan de San Martín, the father of José de San Martín, the liberator of Latin America, was born here in 1728. Cervatos's pyramidal brick church tower stands on a bluff and can be seen for miles. The church, and a second brick tower, have crumbled to dust within the memory of Cervatos's inhabitants. A villager told us in 1998, with a tear in her eye, that "it used to be a glory to look at them" (*daba gloria verlas*).

🥾 Quintanilla de la Cueza In this village, as in many along the Cueza River, the bell tower stands next to the cemetery, not the church.

Just north of Quintanilla are remains of a **Roman villa and baths**. The extensive constructions, including several well-preserved mosaics, testify to its having been a major relaxation center on the Roman road to León and the Bierzo mines. These are the best Roman ruins along the pilgrimage Road and are not to be missed.

52. CALZADILLA DE LA CUEZA

HISTORY
   The tiny adobe villages of the Tierra de Campos have changed significantly in the last 25 years. When we first walked through Calzadilla in 1974 no roads to the town were paved; perhaps a third of the houses were inhabited, and the rest were falling apart. Adobe was the only material in use. The one-room school, too, was vacant and crumbling. Since there were no children in the village, we were allowed to sleep on the school's wood floor. The town had no bar, no restaurant, and no source of water except one nearly dry well. By lying on the ground, and extending a dipper as far as we could reach, we could draw up just enough to wet our lips. Compare that to what you see around you now.

PILGRIMAGE
   The hamlet is a typical Road town, with a single, long, east-west street. A 3-bed pilgrim hospice, third house on the left as you enter the village (Calle Mayor, 32) was located here.
   In 1996 we were fortunate enough to find Calzadilla in full fiesta. The town's former citizens had come back from their jobs in León or Madrid or Oviedo for the weekend's festivities, swelling the village population to, say, 50. The little kids and teenagers were decked out in folk costumes. A folklore group, hired from León, performed traditional dances on the widest of the town's 3 cross streets and then invited the kids, and us pilgrims, to join in. The parents and grandparents beamed. Wine flowed. That night, in one of the village's shed-like barns, another band played modern dance music until nearly dawn. Even so, by 8:00 the next day, our pilgrim group was walking gingerly westward, thankful that the strong morning light was at our backs, and not in our bloodshot eyes.

MONUMENTS
   The tower by the cemetery has been recently restored. The current parish church of San Martín houses a retablo formerly in the nearby Abbey of Santa María de las Tiendas.

   A small Roman settlement called Viminacio occupied the mesa called Castro Muza to the north of the highway just west of the bridge over the River Cueza.

   The wine cellars (*bodegas*) at the foot of the mesa have doors made from old threshing sleds (*trillos*), flint-embedded wood platforms that oxen or horses would drag across the harvested wheat to crack the hulls. The wheat would be threshed by tossing it into the air so that the wind would blow the lighter chaff to one side and the heavier grains of wheat would fall to the ground in a pile (whence the saying: "to separate the wheat from the chaff"). The flat area on which the wheat was threshed was called the *era*, a name you will often see on street signs and other geographical indicators.

Route: CALZADILLA DE LA CUEZA → Santa María de las Tiendas → Ledigos → Terradillos de los Templarios → Moratinos → San Nicolás del Real Camino → SAHAGÚN

✱ Santa María de las Tiendas In 1182 Alfonso VIII authorized Bernardo Martín to build a monastery here, at the site of a small hospice known as *Las Tiendas* ("the tents"), probably because of a military encampment on the site. In 1190 Martín gave it to the Order of Santiago and set up an endowment to support the Order's defense of the kingdom's borders. The Order built a small residence-monastery here. Pedro Fernández and his wife donated 5,000 *maravedís* to create an endowment for the hospice in their 1222 will. Other codicils in the will destined money for the Order's motherhouse in Uclés, for a hospice in Toledo, and for a priest to offer a daily mass in Compostela. Ca. 1670 the Italian pilgrim Laffi found here "a very large and wealthy hospice called *Ospitale del Gran Cavaliere*. Here they give pilgrims a *passada* of bread and wine and cheese, of which there is plenty in this region, because of the many herds. They also gave us cottage cheese and a loaf of bread each" [Laffi; trans. Hall (1997), 145]. The institution seems to have hosted travelers well into the 19th c. The abbey is now an abandoned farm, with a crumbling neo-Gothic plaster chapel. The former church's retablo is now in the parish church in Calzadilla. The coat of arms designates the Sandoval family.

Across the road to the northwest are the ruins of what in 1974 was the pilgrimage Road's most ornate adobe dovecote. Every time we hike by, less and less of it remains, though in 1998 you could still see fragments of its former intricate decorative motifs.

✱ Ledigos Archbishop Diego Gelmírez of Compostela extorted the gift of Ledigos in 1130 from King Alfonso VII.

The church of **Santiago** has a nice image of the Saint.

✱ Terradillos de los Templarios In the late 13th c. the village evidently belonged to the Knights Templar under Alfonso López de Haro. Its Church of San Pedro reputedly has an early Gothic crucifix. This town and the next seem to have been among the few in the region that did *not* support a pilgrim hospice.

✱ Moratinos The town's name suggests that at one time it had a Muslim, or converted Muslim, population.

📖 In the 1560s the *moriscos* (Muslims nominally converted to Catholicism) of Andalucía rebelled when the Christian authorities began demanding strict adherence to their new religion. After a decade of war in the Alpujarras Mountains, south of Granada, the *moriscos* were banished from Andalucía and resettled in the flatlands of Castilla, where they would supposedly find guerrilla warfare impossible. Here they farmed and hired out as builders, which is why there are so many Muslim-style churches and dove-

54. SAHAGÚN

HISTORY

The name Sahagún derives from San Facundo. The bodies of the 4th-c. martyrs Saints Facundo and Primitivo were buried near the Río Cea, and their tomb was marked by a Visigothic church. This area, the heart of a rich agricultural region, was a focal point of the wars between Muslims and Christians. Muslims destroyed the Visigothic church in 833. A Cordoban monk rebuilt it in 872 and added a monastery. Muslims retook the region in 883, only to lose it again to Alfonso III el Magno, who entrusted its rebuilding to Abbot Valabonso in 904–5. The monastery offered refuge to Mozarabic Christian monks fleeing Muslim persecutions in Córdoba and became a center of Mozarabic resettlement in León. Sahagún was important enough to be targeted by Almanzor in 987, and its rebuilding after his death was a Christian priority.

By the mid-11th c. Sahagún was the most important Christian religious and economic center in León outside of the capital city. King Alfonso VI (who reigned 1065–1109) was educated here, took refuge here during his wars with his brother Sancho, wed his third wife, Costanza de Borgoña, here, and ultimately was buried here with all 4 of his wives. In 1078 he invited the Benedictines of Cluny to take charge of the monastery. The Cluniacs sent an abbot named Robert, who became an enthusiast for the Mozarabic rite and who condoned the king's current extra-marital liaison. Pope Gregory VII yanked him in 1080 and sent another Cluniac, Bernardo de Sauvetot, who pushed the international Roman rite and put an end to the king's dalliance. Under Bernardo, Sahagún soon became the center for Cluniac reform in the entire kingdom. Alfonso VI gave the town its *fuero* in 1085. Its text highlights the cosmopolitan nature of the town, for it extends rights to Gascons, Bretons, Germans, Englishmen, Burgundians, Normans, Provençals, Lombards, and men from Toulouse, among others. The same year, the old Roman Puente de Canto bridge was rebuilt to facilitate commerce and pilgrimage. The town prospered. When the Muslim chronicler Idrisi visited in 1150 he found "a well-populated, strong city, of pleasing aspect and comfortable lodgings" (145).

Sahagún's geography facilitated its economic growth. The fertile rolling hills were rich in cattle and grain, its river valleys nourished orchards and vineyards, and its key location on the Road made it a natural market center. Both monarchs and abbots worked to build—and tax—its economic clout. In 1155 it was given the right to hold an annual market for 3 consecutive weeks, an unheard-of length of time. A hundred years later, when Alfonso X guaranteed the safety and rights of all merchants traveling to Sahagún be they Christians, Muslims, or Jews, this had been reduced to a 15-day fair.

The town was segmented according to the origin of its citizens—Franks, Muslims, Jews, and old-time Christian residents of the kingdom of León—but it grew so fast that additional districts sprang up outside the walls. Eventually the Christian population was so large that Sahagún had 9 parishes, each with its own Romanesque church. Four survive today. Sahagún's present triangular shape reflects medieval competing neighborhoods and the walls that surrounded them.

Most of the Christian and Muslim families were small farmers who supplied the city and the monastery. In addition, many Muslims worked in the construction trades. In the dry lands of León, farmers lived on the economic margins. Documents note loans as small as a single bushel of wheat, to be repaid after harvest. Since even these small loans were secured by real estate, debtors easily lost owner-

cotes in this region. The Church continued to carp about their nonassimila-
tion to Catholicism, and the monarchy continued to consider them a threat.
In 1609 they were all uprooted and expelled from the Peninsula.

Like many Road towns, Moratinos's single street, running east-west, is named for
the pilgrimage: *Calzada francesa*. The small Church of Santo Tomás is of little
artistic merit.

✳ San Nicolás del Real Camino This village also belonged to the Templars
until 1183, when they traded it to Alfonso VIII for some other lands. The church
of San Nicolás de Bari, rebuilt in the 18th c., reputedly has a 13th-c. Virgin and
Child and another, in the Baroque style, on the retablo. From the 12th c. this village
had a pilgrim hospice, located down the hill near the river next to the village cemetery at Calle de la Esperanza, 30. It could accommodate up to 13 lepers (if more
arrived, they had to wait until others left).

At the top of the hill beyond San Nicolás pilgrims get their first view of the kingdom of León and the welcoming grain silo of Sahagún. At the bottom of the hill a
small bridge crosses the Valderaduey River, whose Iberian name—*Val de Aratoi*—
means "flat fields." Just north of the bridge over the Valderaduey was a small
Roman town; there are a few remains in the area known locally as Despoblado de
Boadilla. This tiny river is the border between the kingdoms of Castilla and León.

Just across the highway bridge, to the north, is the **Ermita de la Virgen del Puente**,
whose exterior is a splendid example of the Sahagún Mudéjar style (see ch. 54). In
the Middle Ages an Augustinian-run pilgrim hospice and pilgrim burial ground
were located here. Inside reputedly is an image of the Virgen del Puente, but we
have never had the luck to find the building open. In front of the *ermita* are
remains of the old Roman bridge, half buried in silt.

ship of their property and were converted to tenant farmers serving the monastery, whose holdings grew larger and larger.

From the beginning of its boom, Sahagún attracted Jewish immigrants. Some came from the south, seeking refuge from the Almoravid persecution of non-Muslim minorities. Others were attracted by the commercial opportunities offered by the fairs and the Road. Their neighborhood was north of the town, near the Cornudillos gate, between the tanneries and the Moorish quarter. Ironically, the synagogue was on the Calle Santa Cruz. The Jews were jurisdictional pawns, claimed by both the Crown and the Abbey, each promising protection, each levying taxes, and each extorting special contributions. Relationships were also tense between the Jews and the Christian merchants with whom they competed. It did not help matters that Church law prohibited Christians from lending money for interest, and people of all stations depended on the Jews for loans. Riots in 1127 killed many Jews in the abbey and surrounding towns. The nationwide convulsions of 1391 killed many more. By the time of the 1492 expulsion, only 30 Jewish families remained in Sahagún.

All the while, private donations to the monastery and the incorporation of outlying religious institutions to the Cluniac network fed Sahagún's rapid growth. At its height, the Abbey controlled over 90 other monasteries throughout Spain. In power, its abbots rivaled kings. It stands to reason that relations between the powerful abbots and the town and the king were generally strained.

   📖 In 1111, burghers protested to the king that their abbot was a despot. The king failed to act, but the abbot retaliated by excommunicating the townsmen and going to Rome to get an order to force them to obey him. While he was gone, the burghers assaulted and pillaged the monastery. In 1117 the Pope issued an order demanding that they return the booty, but it is unclear whether they ever did.

In the late 11th c. Abbot Bernardo established a school, which became a university in 1348 and continued to function until the 17th c., when it was transferred to Irache (see ch. 26). Sahagún had a huge scriptorium, and many important books, such as the famous illuminated manuscript of the Beato de Osma, were penned here. But with the gradual shift of monastic power from the Benedictines to San Bernardo's Cistercian Order, the fortunes of the monastery of San Facundo and the town began to decline. Today nothing remains of the monastery's former splendor, while the town has become a small, dusty market center amid the wheat fields of the Meseta Alta.

PILGRIMAGE

As a major religious and commercial center, Sahagún maintained various hospices. In the late 11th c. the monastery's Abbot Julián was patron of a 70-bed facility run by 2 monks from the abbey. In the late 15th c. Künig von Vach counted 4 hospices and noted that Sahagún's water was bad. Laffi, 150 years later, praised Sahagún's religious establishments:

Among the religious houses there are two which are particularly rich and handsome, one Benedictine and the other the Observantine Franciscans. We went to the monastery of the Benedictines to see the refectory, which is such that I cannot believe any other could be finer. It has a vaulted ceiling of carved wood which is most magnificent and worth seeing by anyone. The monks gave us supper and treated us with great esteem. [Laffi; trans. Hall (1997), 145–7]

SAHAGÚN

MONUMENTS: 1. **Monasterio de San Facundo**. 2. Arch of San Benito. 3. **Iglesia de San Tirso**. 4. **Iglesia de San Lorenzo**. 5. **Convento de las Madres Benedictinas**. 6. Iglesia de San Juan de Sahagún. 7. Iglesia de La Trinidad. 8. **Santuario de la Peregrina**.

1. **Monasterio de San Facundo**. As noted above, almost nothing remains of what was at its height one of the richest and most powerful monasteries in Iberia. The original late Roman construction over the tombs of the martyrs Saints Facundo and Primitivo has vanished, as has the later Visigothic church. In 872 Alfonso III of Asturias underwrote a building campaign to which the founder of Castilla, Fernán González, also contributed. A few Mozarabic-style capitals from this early period remain, but they have been widely dispersed (you will see some here in the church of San Lorenzo, and in León in the San Marcos Museum). Alfonso VI gave the monastery of San Facundo

to Cluny in 1078; his son-in-law Raimundo de Borgoña oversaw the beginning of its period of greatest construction, which lasted from 1099 until the beginning of the 13th c. Eventually San Facundo was so immense that it had 4 separate cloisters.

Among Sahagún's most famous monks were San Juan de Sahagún (1430–79), now the city's patron; Fray Bernardino de Sahagún (1499–1590), missionary to Mexico, who might be considered the first modern anthropologist; and Fray Pedro Ponce de León (1514–84), pioneer teacher of deaf-mutes.

In the last half millennium San Facundo's fortunes have ebbed. French soldiers, quartered here in 1812, destroyed much of the monastery, and after the 1835 *desamortización* the remainder burned. Today the paltry ruins house the barracks of the Guardia Civil.

All this aside, San Facundo was Spain's most influential monument in the **Romanesque-Mudéjar style**, which flourished in the 12th and 13th c. Its general characteristics can be seen in these ruins and in Sahagún's other remaining churches. The key elements are:

—Adoption of the standard basilica floor plan of 3 naves, without a transept, culminating in 3 semicircular apses.

—Construction in brick, which was the favored building material of Spanish Muslims even in those areas where stone was plentiful. An exception: many of these churches began the *cabecera* of the churches in stone, and then finished off the upper courses in brick.

—Roofs resting on wooden beams, not stone vaults.

—Thin walls and minimal buttressing, possible because brick walls are lighter than stone, and because the churches lack heavy stone vaults.

—Large bell towers, often elaborated with geometric designs and arches.

—Minimal use of decorative sculpture, such as on tympana, capitals, and friezes. This may be related to the Islamic styles that respect prohibitions against representation of the human form.

—Decorative elements with an emphasis on horizontal rather than vertical lines.

—Incorporation of Islamic decorative elements, such as (1) bands of semicircular arches, and (2) polylobed Islamic-style arches, which are (3) often interlaced; sometimes bands of (4) alternating red and white brick; (5) geometric panels set in a square or rectangular frame (*alfiz*); (6) recessed planes creating decorative interplay of light and shadow; (7) decorations constructed of bricks laid vertically, diagonally, or at 45° angles.

Among the ruins you will see a tower, finished in 1835, that now serves the city as clock tower. There is a Neoclassic façade (see #2, below). The crumbling early-12th-c. chapel of San Mancio is being restored as we write. Most of what was once covered by monastery buildings is private housing, a park, and a wide street.

2. Arch of San Benito. The 1662 arch was the façade of the Monasterio de San Facundo's church. Two rampant lions sustain an enormous Hapsburg coat of arms. On the back of the arch are remnants of 1 Romanesque column and a couple of round windows.

3. **Iglesia de San Tirso**. This Romanesque-Mudéjar church was built prior to 1123.

Exterior:
- The north entrance and portico date from the 19th c.
- The enormous tower includes arches and windows of varied numbers and sizes. The stone pillars in the hollows of the tower are a link with European Romanesque traditions.
- The apse shows Sahagún's characteristic Romanesque mix of stone and brick construction.
- The **tower** and apse fell in 1945 and were reconstructed from photos.

Interior:
- The brick horseshoe arches spanning the nave are unusually large.
- A 13th-c. tomb—perhaps that of one of Alfonso X's granddaughters—has recently been placed in the center of the nave. The iconography is typical of the period. A Christ in Majesty is surrounded by the Tetramorphos. Angels surround the *Agnus Dei*, and others receive the soul of the deceased woman. A collection of mourners, monks, courtiers, and professional wailers (*plañideras*) parade around the tomb.

4. **Iglesia de San Lorenzo**. A church of this name is mentioned in a document in 1110, but the current building appears to be early 13th c. A 1253 reference says that during that year's riots someone "took refuge with all his men in the church of San Lorenzo, where one of them was killed by an arrow that came in through a window." The church's concept and execution are Romanesque, despite occasional appropriations from the Gothic style that was becoming popular as it was built.

Exterior:
- The church has many typical elements of **Sahagún Romanesque-Mudéjar**. A series of blind horseshoe arches circles the apses. The 4-story tower over the crossing has arches and windows of varying size and number.
- The north Gothic door is set into an *alfiz*, with 4 recessed arches taking the place of archivolts.

Interior:
- Cruciform pillars sustain the wood roof.
- Among the church's art are a 13th-c. San Sebastián and a 15th-c. image of the Virgin. Don't miss the Capilla de Jesús. Its 1730 **retablo** incorporates 8 16th-c. low reliefs by Juan de Juní, which were brought here from a now-vanished monastery.
  Next door to this church is the Cofradía de Jesús building that houses the images paraded during Holy Week.

5. **Convento de las Madres Benedictinas**. Consecrated in 1184, the church is in the early ogival style. The plain exterior, devoid of any decorative motifs, has been completely rebuilt.

Interior:
- The pillars on the altar, awkwardly attached, were probably designed prior to the stylistic transition.
- The small, eclectic **Museum of the Madres Benedictinas** displays a <u>monstrance</u> (*custodia*) by the early Renaissance master goldsmith Enrique de Arfe. As is typical of the metalwork transitional between the late Flemish Gothic and the Renaissance, the smiths strove to imitate every church architectural detail in miniature. Here you will see delicate flamboyant arches and exquisitely detailed and expressive individual figures, particularly the Virgin and child Jesus.

The museum also contains the statue of La Virgen Peregrina brought here from El Santuario de la Peregrina (see below).

• Attached to the museum is a **Baroque chapel** that houses an exquisite **Churrigueresque retablo** and the tombs of Alfonso VI and his 4 wives.

📖 The Convent's nuns have sweet voices. We like to go early in the morning to hear them sing matins—and take another long look at the Churrigueresque retablo—before walking west toward Burgo Ranero.

---

6. The Iglesia de San Juan de Sahagún is Neoclassic in style, with a brightly painted façade that recalls those of Andalucía. It houses the urns with the remains of Saints Facundo and Primitivo, and 2 lovely alabaster retablos.

7. The Iglesia de la Trinidad has recently been converted to a pilgrim hospice.

8. **Santuario de la Peregrina.** The church, begun in 1257 in the Gothic-Mudéjar style, is all that remains of the Franciscan monastery founded on a bluff outside the town walls. The church's name comes from a legend, recounted in Alfonso X's *Cantiga* 49, about how pilgrims here saw a bright light and a woman with a glowing staff in her hand who was sent to guide them.

Exterior:
• The exterior is in shabby shape, but you should walk all the way around it to enjoy the **decorative brickwork**. You will find several Mudéjar elements immediately identifiable. Note particularly the elegant frieze of blind **horseshoe arches**. Around back you will also find the excavated foundations of some of the monastery's former buildings.

Interior:
• The brick *cabecera* and the lobed arches continue the Mudéjar influence, even though most of the rest of the church was refurbished—and not very well—in the Neoclassic style.
• The 17th-c. painting of the **Virgin as Pilgrim** is by Luisa Roldán.
• The large painting in the apse commemorates the reconciliation in Rome between the warring Franciscan and Benedictine Orders.
• The funeral chapel of Diego Gómez de Sandoval (d. 1455), whose tomb is no longer there, contains inlaid **plaster panels** of exquisitely carved Islamic geometric designs (*atauriques*) that still retain traces of their original colors. With the possible exception of the *atauriques* in Las Huelgas Monastery in Burgos, these are the best you will see along the Road. They give an idea of what the Mudéjar ceiling in San Benito that Laffi so admired might have looked like.

Several of Sahagún's treasures are housed in the National Archaeological Museum in Madrid. Among them are a Romanesque stone Virgin in the Cluniac style and an abbot's throne, the earliest dated Spanish throne with animal claws as feet.

🚗 Five km. southeast, Grajal de Campos was the home of the 15th-c. Comendador Mayor de Castilla, Hernando de Vega. The family's 16th-c. **castle** dominates the village.

🚗 Five km. southwest is **San Pedro de las Dueñas,** whose splendid 12th-c. Romanesque-Mudéjar church preserves in its interior several Romanesque **capitals** and a **crucifix** by the Renaissance sculptor Gregorio Hernández.

55. SAHAGÚN → EL BURGO RANERO

Route 1, the pilgrim Road: SAHAGÚN → Calzada del Coto → Bercianos del Real Camino → EL BURGO RANERO

Route 2, the Roman Road: SAHAGÚN → Calzada del Coto → Calzadilla de los Hermanillos → Estación del Burgo → EL BURGO RANERO

In 1974 and 1979 we found this stretch to be utterly desolate. Walking for many hours on the ancient pilgrim Road with no terrestrial points of reference except the wind in the thistles and the distant tinkling of sheep bells had a strong impact on all of us. El Burgo Ranero, at the end of the day's hike, rose before us like an oasis. In 1987 we found this section had been "improved" by bulldozing and graveling a pilgrim path, building a car road next to it, planting trees every 10 m., and putting in concrete benches and picnic tables. The changes make it impossible to lose perspective, and the mystic effect of the Castilian plain seemed to have been lost. In 1993 and 1996, at Calzada del Coto we switched to the Roman Road, north of the railroad tracks, and we recovered our sense of wonder. Today, unfortunately, along much of this stretch the *Autovía de León* is within sight or hearing of the pilgrims. The Roman Road is slightly longer, but we still like it better.

Route 1, the southern, or pilgrim, Road:

Leaving Sahagún, you will cross the Río Cea. Until 1992, the bridge commissioned by Alfonso VI in 1085, the Puente de Canto, was the only bridge.

The forest immediately across the river is the legendary site of Charlemagne's Field of Lances. The episode is found in chapter 8 of CC's *Turpin* (see ch. 16). Charlemagne, in his efforts to make the Road safe for pilgrims, is pursuing the villain Aigoland:

> They caught Aigoland in a region called Campos, next to the River Cea, in some meadows that are a flat fertile plain. Later, by order of Charlemagne and with his help, the excellent large basilica of the martyred Saints Facundo and Primitivo was erected there.... Then the night before the battle some Christians, carefully preparing their arms for the battle the next day, stuck their lances into the ground, straight up, in front of the camp.... At dawn the next day, those men who in the coming battle were to receive the palms of martyrdom for their faith in God found that their lances had grown bark and were covered with leafy branches. Astonished beyond telling, and attributing the miracle to God's divine power, they cut them off at ground level. From the staves whose roots remained buried later was born the great forest that even today can be seen in that place.

Turpin reports that 40,000 Christians died in losing the next day's battle. Today the site is the municipal camping area, although presumably the trees are of later vintage.

The region west of Sahagún has no distinguishing geographic features and is not described by any of the medieval itineraries. In the early 1670's Laffi found only horror on this stretch: "We came across a dead pilgrim. Two wolves had begun to eat his body, so we chased them off and continued towards El Burgo Ranero. When we arrived there it was evening. We went to see the priest and asked him to go and recover the body" [Laffi, trans. Hall (1997), 147]. Nicola Albani, who trekked to Compostela from Naples in 1743, had to hire a local guide for this stretch to keep him from getting lost.

✳ Calzada del Coto In the early 10th c. the village was given to Sahagún's monastery of San Facundo, in whose possession it remained until 1849. The church is dedicated to San Esteban.

One km. before Bercianos you will find on the left the small Ermita de Nuestra Señora de Perales, site of a medieval hospice administered by the monks of Cebreiro.

✳ Bercianos del Real Camino The name suggests that when the area was reconquered it was repopulated with people from León's Bierzo region (which may help explain why Cebreiro's monks ran the hospice mentioned above). The village of Bercianos was given to the monks of Sahagún in 966. At the entrance to town is the tiny Capilla de San Roque. The brick and adobe tower of the Church of El Salvador has collapsed since we walked this route in 1987.

Route 2: the Roman, or northern, Road, also called the Via Traiana:

✳ Calzadilla de los Hermanillos The little brothers (hermanillos) in the town's name were Benedictine monks affiliated with Sahagún.

MONUMENTS: 1. Ermita de la Virgen de los Dolores. 2. Iglesia de San Bartolomé.

1. Ermita de la Virgen de los Dolores. Built by monks sent from Sahagún, the ermita shows traces of Mozarabic-style brick construction. It was restored in the 16th c. and contains an emotive image of the Virgin with the crucified Christ lying in her lap.

2. Iglesia de San Bartolomé. Entirely rebuilt in the 16th and 17th c., the main altar has a nice 16th-c. Crucifixion scene and a statue of San Bartolomé stamping on a demon.

56. El Burgo Ranero

HISTORY

Two folk etymologies interpret the town's name. One suggests that burghers here sold frogs (*ranas*) from the town lagoon. The second is that in the midst of this splendid wheat country the town was originally called El Burgo Granero ("Granary City"). The town appears in documents as early as 1126. Wheat and wool sustain the town, and several major *cañadas*, the sheep paths over which the herds migrate to the northern mountain pastures in summer and return to the steppes in winter, pass through the village.

📖 Wool was Castilla's biggest business during most of the Middle Ages. The reconquest of the Duero Valley in the early 10th c., and then of Toledo in 1065, opened up vast new grazing lands to the Christians. And Europe beyond the Pyrenees was a lucrative market. The growing European population needed to be clothed; cloth manufacturing in Flanders and Italy was increasingly sophisticated. Black-faced merino sheep, introduced from North Africa, were resistant to the extremes of climate in Iberia and were efficient producers of wool. A system quickly evolved in which the herds grazed in lush northern mountain pastures during the summer, while the plains of the Meseta were growing wheat, and were then brought south to winter in the wheat stubble. Villagers made their living tending the sheep, but the herds—sometimes as large as 40,000 head—were owned by nobles, prelates, the military Orders, and the monarchy. The whole business was heavily regulated and heavily taxed.

The biggest problem was grazing rights during the *transhumancia*, the migration of the vast herds from the northern mountains to the pastures of the south. In the 13th c. the Honorable Council of the Mesta was set up to build, maintain, and police the long sheep roads, called *cañadas*. There were three main *cañadas*: (1) from the mountains of Castilla and León south to Salamanca and Extremadura; (2) from the mountains of La Rioja south and west to Burgos, Palencia, and the southern Meseta Alta; (3) from the mountains of Cuenca south to the Meseta Baja, often called La Mancha. The major *cañadas* were 80–100 m. wide, bordered by strong walls. And of course there were hundreds of smaller *cañadas*. Flocks might travel 20–25 km. in a 24-hour period. Shepherds were contracted for a full year, 6 months of which would be spent away from home. As the ancient folksong relates:

Ya se van los pastores	The shepherds are going
ya se van marchando	the shepherds are marching off
más de cuatro zagalas	more than four village girls
quedan llorando.	are left behind weeping.

Transhumancia still goes on, though today largely by truck. Still, at several places between El Burgo Ranero and Astorga you will see where the pilgrimage Road is crossed by ancient *cañadas*. The wind can carry the sound of sheep bells for many km., and if you are lucky, the sound will accompany you along this stretch of the Road.

When we first visited El Burgo Ranero in 1974 the pond was full of frogs, but most of the houses were empty. There was no paved road to the village, and the trains stopped infrequently. One of the few brick houses in town was owned by an old couple, doña Plasencia and don Benjamín, who kindly let our pilgrims sleep on their floor. The younger villagers seemed to be in their 60s, and there were far more sheep, and maybe more mules, than people. Today the paved road, the frequent rail service, and the modest economic gains that permit mechanized agriculture have brought a small measure of prosperity to El Burgo. The population is still small, most of the houses are still empty, but you will see many new houses and several large agricultural warehouses and granaries.

The priest hereabouts serves several neighboring villages. El Burgo built him a fine new house in the 1980s, but when for various reasons he decided to live in one of the outlying towns, the house became the pilgrim hospice.

PILGRIMAGE

The main street was called the *Camino francés*. Ca. 1670 Laffi remarked on the town's poverty: "We went to an inn, but it was such a poor one that we had to sleep on the floor, for the inhabitants of the village are all herdsmen, who live in huts roofed with straw" [Laffi; trans. Hall (1997), 147].

MONUMENT

The dilapidated church of San Pedro once contained a Romanesque Virgin that is now in the museum of León's Cathedral.

57. EL BURGO RANERO → MANSILLA DE LAS MULAS

Route: EL BURGO RANERO → Villamarco → Reliegos → MANSILLA DE LAS MULAS

Route 1, the southern, or pilgrim, Road, and route 2, the northern, or Roman Road, diverge at the pond in El Burgo Ranero and rejoin just before Villamarco. Both routes parallel the railroad tracks. As with the trek from Sahagún to El Burgo Ranero, and for the same reasons, we recommend the Roman Road.

There is nothing special to observe in these windswept steppes except the spectacularly lonely plains and the kestrels (*cernícalos*), black hawks (*rateros*), and kites (*milanos*) that cruise the updrafts looking for lunch among the grain fields. Villages are few and far between. You may meet a shepherd or two along this stretch or, in the proximity of the villages, some old people out for a walk.

✴ Reliegos In Roman times the village was called Palantia, and 3 military roads converged here. As far as we know, no visible traces of the Roman settlement are left. A medieval village here is cited from 916, and in 1043 Fernando I donated the town to the Cathedral of León.

58. Mansilla de las Mulas

History

The Roman town plan is evident: a rectangular wall; gates in the middle of each side; principal streets bisecting the town east-west and north-south, crossing in a central plaza housing the principal municipal and religious buildings. In fact, the town's Roman name (*mansella*) indicates that it was a small estate or a midway stop in the Via Traiana leading to León. Thus Mansilla's escutcheon, featuring a hand (*mano*) on a saddle (*silla*), is etymologically ersatz. The second half of the town's name reflects the fact that from the 10th c. Mansilla was known for its mule market: animals raised in the mountains of León were sold as farm animals to the *campesinos* working the Tierra de Campos.

Retaken from the Moors and repopulated in the 10th c., it was granted a *fuero* in 1181 by Fernando II of León, who refortified the city. The walls were rebuilt again in the 13th and 14th c. In the 12th c. Mansilla had a castle that belonged to the dukes of Benavente until Enrique III captured it in battle in 1394 and had it destroyed. At its height, Mansilla had 2 monasteries and 7 parishes. As a major commercial center along the Road, it attracted a Jewish population, whose *aljama* was south of the current Ayuntamiento.

The heroine of the famous 17th-c. picaresque novel *La pícara Justina* was from Mansilla. The author, Francisco López de Úbeda, lived in the corner of the plaza at the northwest edge of town.

The village has several graceful plazas with walks shaded by columned arcades, and it is worth a concerted stroll. The riverbank offers shade, and the river itself is nice for swimming—well, wading and splashing around.

In 1974, our pilgrims went into a bar in Mansilla to slake the afternoon thirst, when the mayor of the town came over and "arrested" us for wearing shorts. The mayor, obviously a bit of a joker, admonished us with this verse:

Ha prohibido el alcalde	His honor the mayor
de Mansilla de las Mulas	of Mansilla de las Mulas
que ande la gente	forbids people walking
medio desnuda.	around town half nude.

Our 7 pilgrims couldn't tell whether we were seriously in trouble or not. After an awkward moment David, who is also addicted to stringing rhymes together, replied in kind:

Mejor que vayamos	It's better to walk around
vestidos de este modo	dressed that way
a que no caminemos	than if we went walking
desnudos del todo.	entirely naked.

End of crisis and beginning of an afternoon of many shared glasses of wine. A footnote: in 1979, 5 years after this incident and 4 years after General Franco's death, we observed that bathers of both sexes in the river went topless.

Pilgrimage

At various times in the Middle Ages Mansilla had 4 pilgrim hospices. No traces remain.

The 18th-c. French pilgrim Manier called Mansilla a "little nothing" kind of village, where the walls were made of yellow mud. He was impressed, though, seeing the villagers harvesting red beans, so spicy in flavor that they were called "peppers."

MONUMENTS: 1. **Iglesia de Santa María.** 2. Iglesia de San Martín. 3. Exconvento de San Agustín. 4. **Walls.**

1. **Iglesia de Santa María.** The church contains a 13th-c. Christ originally in the cathedral in León. The retablo shows both Renaissance and Baroque elements arranged in a novel circular fashion. The church's small museum of statues contains a nice Flemish San Roque as pilgrim. As we write, the church is undergoing reconstruction.

2. Iglesia de San Martín. The scraps left from this 14th-c. church have been incorporated into the recently constructed Casa de Cultura. The doorway's arch is transitional between Romanesque and Gothic. The Herrera-style stone tower seems to serve as a dovecote.

3. Ex-convento de San Agustín. For as long as we have known them, the open-air ruins of this destroyed convent have served as a handball court (*frontón*).

4. **Walls.** More than three-quarters of the **medieval walls** remain. In parts they are 3 m. thick. Most were built by Fernando II of León as part of his line of fortifications against Castilla. The construction is typical of 12th-c. fortifications in the Tierra de Campos, using the Mudéjar techniques with clay, brick, and rubblework. Two gates are left: the best is the Arco de la Concepción on the city's east side.

> Most of the walls you will see on the pilgrim Road are urban and easily lost among the traffic and blocks of apartment houses of cities like Burgos, León, and even Santo Domingo de la Calzada. For a sense of what a medieval walled town really looked like from the outside, walk through the fields to the west of Mansilla, preferably in the late afternoon when the declining sun makes the walls glow gold.

> Nearby is the 10th-c. monastery of **San Miguel de la Escalada**, perhaps the best-preserved and most interesting Mozarabic monastery in all of Spain. An earlier Visigothic church on the site had been destroyed by the Muslim invaders. After the reconquest of this area, Alfonso III built San Miguel for the Christian monks fleeing persecutions in Córdoba. Nonetheless, a dedicatory Latin plaque (dated 913) suggests it was the monks themselves who erected the building, without the help of royal donations or public taxes:
>
> > This place, of old dedicated in honor of the archangel Michel and built with a little building, after falling into pieces, lay long in ruin until Abbot Alfonso, coming with his brethren from Córdoba his fatherland, built up the ruined house in the time of the powerful and serene prince Alfonso. The number of monks increasing, this temple was built with admirable work, enlarged in every part from its foundations. The work was finished in twelve months, not by imperial imposition or impression of the people, but by the insistent vigilance of Abbot Alfonso and the brethren, when García already held the scepter of the realm with Queen Mumadona in [913] and consecrated by Bishop Genedius on November 13. [trans. Dodds, 50]

The building is an extraordinary example of "repopulation architecture," which continues Asturian building techniques with strong influences of Visigothic, Carolingian, and Islamic architecture. The walls seem Asturian: quoined at the corners, with frame-and-fill construction that utilizes brick in the upper registers to reduce the weight. The basilica church has a south **gallery with 12 horseshoe arches** whose style, and whose **capitals**, resemble the mosque of Córdoba. The capitals are tied to the columns by a stone *astrágalo* of twisted rope, which also seems to show Asturian influence, as it resembles those of the early churches of Naranco and Valdediós in Oviedo. The interior conserves an extraordinary **chancel screen**, graphically demonstrating how in the Mozarabic rite the altar was separated from the congregation.

> The Third Council of Toledo in 589 spoke clearly to the tripartite division of a Mozarabic church. "Observe this order: The bishop and the priest take communion in front of the altar, the other clerics in the choir, and the public outside the choir."

The dimly lit, small, horseshoe-shaped presbytery behind the screen further shielded the mysteries of the altar from the laity.

The Romanesque tower was added in the late 11th c. Curiously, archaeological excavations have turned up no sign of the monks' habitations or cloister.

One km. north of Mansilla was a Roman bridge. The first bluff on the right of the León highway, just before the gas station, is called Villasabariego. It was the site of the Astur city of Lancia, captured and garrisoned by the Romans in 26 B.C.E. in their wars to dominate the Peninsula. The fields below them are still called Sollanzo (*Sublancia*). Archaeologists are excavating the site.

59. Mansilla de las Mulas → León

Route 1: Mansilla de las Mulas → Villamoros de Mansilla → Puente de Villarente → Arcahueja → Valdelafuente → Puente Castro → León

----

Route 2: Mansilla de las Mulas → Mansilla la Mayor → **Villaverde de Sandoval** → Nogales → Villa Turiel → Valdesogo de Abajo → Valdesogo de Arriba → Puente Castro → León

----

Route 1 is marked, and it is the most common way to walk from Mansilla to León. We prefer Route 2 for the Romanesque ruins of Villaverde, the adventure of fording the Río Porma, the bucolic nature of the small villages away from the highway, and the spectacular view of León from the summit of the ridge before you descend to Puente Castro.

Route 1:

The first bluff to the east, above the gas station, was the Castro of Villasabariego, site of Lancia, capital of the Astures (see ch. 58).

The big bridge over the Río Porma, extant in medieval times and often repaired since, is noted by most pilgrim narratives, including the 12th-c. CC *Guide.*

✳ Villamoros de Mansilla A classic medieval Road town whose main street gives the town its alternate name, Villamoros del Camino Francés.

✳ Puente de Villarente Over the centuries, the tiny town has supported several pilgrim hospices. Across the bridge on the left, the 2-story building with the large arch was a hospice. In 1536 the archdeacon of Triacastela set up an endowment for the hospice in his will:

> Because of the great need there was in that place, which was largely uninhabited, and because it was on the French Road, and because when the river which flows there is high it impedes the passage of pilgrims and other travelers, and since because there is no place to lodge they suffer greatly in their persons and sometimes risk their lives, and because it is a great service to God and work of charity to provide remedy to all this, I determined to act, and to build the hospice to the state in which it now finds itself, so that God our Lord and his Blessed Mother may be served, and in it works of charity may be performed now and forever.

You cross the Canal del Porma to Arcahueja and Valdelafuente. One km. past Valdelafuente, the Portillo hill divides the watersheds of the Ríos Porma and Torio. The summit is where the 15th-c. cross that is now in front of San Marcos in León once stood.

> 📖 López dè Úbeda's narrator, the roguish Justina (see ch. 58), notes that on this hill stood the statue of a capon, with the inscription: "The capon combines the worst of mankind with the worst of womankind" (Book II, part II, ch. 1).

✱ Puente Castro A Roman fort once stood here. Puente's bridge is Roman in origin and has been repeatedly rebuilt.

> 📖 The bridge of Puente Castro did not impress Francisco López de Úbeda, who called it "a genteel antiquary of smooth cobblestones, badly constructed but much praised, because the citizens of León have baptized it as one of the five wonders of the world" (Book II, part II, ch. 1).

The town is also called Castro de los Judíos (*Castro judaeorum*). There is documentary evidence of a Jewish presence on the hill as early as 905, and excavations have turned up many Hebrew gravestones, some of which, dated ca. 1100, are in León's San Marcos and Diocesan museums. On this hill on July 23, 1196, the combined troops of Aragón and Castilla attacked León. After 2 days of fierce fighting, the invaders took the castle, burned the Jewish quarter and synagogue, and carried off nearly the entire Jewish populace as captives. Although León quickly retook the hill, the Jewish community relocated from this relatively isolated spot to the city proper.

The parish church contains a fine 16th-c. processional cross of the school of Enrique de Arfe with finely wrought thorns, small figures of dragons, and an expressive, anatomically detailed Christ.

Pilgrims enter León through the Barrio de Santa Ana, which in medieval times was extramural and had a leprosarium.

Route 2:

✱ Mansilla la Mayor This 10th-c. agricultural village belonged to the nearby Monastery of Gradefes in the 13th c.

✱ **Villaverde de Sandoval** In 1142 Alfonso VII and his wife Berenguela decided to found a monastery here at the junction of the Ríos Esla and Porma. They donated the land to their majordomo Count Ponce de Minerva and his wife Estefanía, who built the current monastery complex and gave it to the Cistercians in 1167.

> 📖 Legend has it that the warrior count, returning from a long imprisonment by the Muslims, adopted the guise of a pilgrim for the journey home. During his absence his wife had been spending her days at the nearby monastery of Carrizo performing the ritual washing of feet for pilgrims. She was astonished one day when she recognized the feet and then the face of her husband, who had stopped at Carrizo his last night before going home.

Fires in 1592 and 1615 severely damaged the structures, which were then abandoned after the 1835 *desamortización*. They are now part of a private farm complex.

Many parts of the 12th–13th-c. Romanesque structures remain, as does the 1462 Gothic vaulting. Several sculptures representing monks adorn the doorway's 15th-c. capitals, while its tympanum depicts the Crucifixion, the Virgin, and a praying abbot. The cloister, half crumbled, has a Romanesque door with a zigzag arch. The church, in much better shape, is large and airy. There has to be a reason why the retablo's lateral doors are decorated with elephants, but it escapes us. You can go through the doors, however, to catch a rare glimpse of the back of a retablo and view how it is put together.

> 📖 In the courtyard outside this monastery we have several times coincided with vast herds of sheep and goats waiting to be trucked to their summer pastures in the mountains to the north (see ch. 56).

One km. upstream from the monastery you can cross the icy Porma River via a shallow ford. The inconvenience of the crossing may give you a new appreciation for why medieval samaritans like Juan de Ortega and Domingo de la Calzada got to be saints for building bridges. Once through the marshes and stands of poplar on the west bank you will come out to a farm road that will lead you through a string of small agricultural villages: Villa Turiel, Valdesogo de Abajo, and Valdesogo de Arriba. In the center of this town you leave the paved road and take the dirt road to the west up a steep hill. At the top of the ridge is a breathtaking view of the distant city of León. This is the only perspective we know about that gives the sense of how the twin spires of the cathedral soar above the rest of the city. The pass was the site of a small Roman outpost, judging from the remnants of ceramics and roof tiles scattered among the thistles and lavender along the Road here. From the pass a dirt road eventually leads you down to join Route 1 before the Puente Castro bridge.

60. León

HISTORY

León was founded by the Romans in the year 70 to protect the Galician gold mines against the indigenous populations of Astures and Cantabros. It was also the base for the Roman conquest of the Suevi in northwest Spain, a struggle that took more than 350 years. The city was the seat of the Seventh Legion, whence the name *Le[gi]ón*. From its founding, León was the Roman capital of northwest Spain, with the emperor's legate in residence. The old part of León reflects the plan of the Roman fortified city: 20 hectares enclosed by a giant wall, principal streets north-south and east-west exiting the walls through 4 gates. Oddly, except for the wall and some baths under what is now the cathedral, no major Roman buildings have been found. León's importance also led to the founding there of the first bishopric in Spain, some 200 years before Christianity became the legal religion of the Roman Empire.

In 585, in the struggles among the invading Germanic tribes, the Visigoth king Leovigildo took León as he defeated the last Suevi resistance. Islamic invaders conquered it 712. It remained in Muslim hands until ca. 846, when it was reconquered by Ordoño I of Asturias, who constructed several churches. His successor welcomed Mozarabic refugees from the south to the city. The Mozarabic monastery of Santiago, located just east of the present cathedral, housed both men and women. In the 10th c. Alfonso III el Magno, who pushed the Leonese border south to the Duero River, set up his Tribunal of Justice in front of León's cathedral. His son Orduño II transferred the Asturian court to León, built a royal palace, and deeded the site of the old Roman baths to Bishop Fruminio for a new cathedral. By this time the city was definitively the capital of the new kingdom of León, which subsumed the old kingdom of Asturias. Unfortunately, the subsequent 10th-c. monarchs were weak: Ordoño III, Sancho I the Fat, and the hunchbacked Orduño IV the Evil all paid protection money to the Cordoban caliphs to sustain a precarious peace.

Meanwhile, the city grew. The coinage used in the burgeoning markets reflects the city's diverse character: French coins, Leonese *sueldos*, and Cordoban *dirhems* paid for Byzantine textiles and jewels, Cordoban ivories, and the agricultural products of the Leonese *meseta*. The 10th-c. prosperity ended in 988 when Vermudo II the Gouty sought Islamic help against his rebellious brother Ramiro III. Vermudo's troops were crushed, and the raiding hordes of Almanzor leveled the city, even tearing down most of the Roman wall. Muslims again occupied the city. As a result, nothing remains today of the 10th-c. building boom.

After Almanzor's death, reconstruction was swift. Alfonso V (999–1028) rebuilt the fortifications. Fernando I persuaded the caliph to release the bones of the great Visigothic saint Isidoro from Sevilla, and a major monastery, begun in 1056, was finished in time for the relics' arrival 7 years later. When the Muslim chronicler Idrisi visited in 1150, he found León to be "one of the most major and prosperous cities of Castilla, whose inhabitants, by nature warlike, noble, and prudent, dedicate themselves to commerce and industry, especially the raising of cattle" (144).

Actually, it was mainly sheep. In the newly reconquered pasturelands of the southern frontier, the herds multiplied. Soon the market centers of León and Castilla were hosting international wool fairs. Shopkeepers, artisans, money changers, manufactures, and traders of all sorts were drawn to León. A Moorish district established itself around today's Plaza de Santa Ana. Many of its residents worked in the construction trades. After the destruction of the Puente Castro Jewish community in the wars of 1196, a new Jewish *aljama* developed southeast of the Plaza Mayor, along what are now the streets of Santa Cruz, Malacín, Las Cercas, and Misericordia (#10 was the site of the principal synagogue). At its apex it extended beyond the city wall to what is now the Plaza de Santa Ana. Many of its inhabitants were farmers, at least until 1293, when Sancho IV decreed that Jews could not own land. Twenty years later they were forced to wear a yellow badge on their clothing. In the late 13ᵗʰ c. the *aljama*'s most famous citizen, Moses ben Sem Tov de León, wrote (or compiled) in León the *Zohar*, the principal text of Jewish mysticism (*kabbala*).

During these years so much money rolled into León from exports, from commerce, and from the fees (*parias*) that border Muslims now had to pay Christians to maintain peace, that in 1205 a larger cathedral was ordered in the revolutionary new French style. Astonishingly, it was completed in fewer than 100 years.

By the mid-14ᵗʰ c. almost all of Andalucía was in Christian hands, and the center of economic and political activity had largely shifted away from the Castilian Meseta. That, and the devastating effects of bubonic plague that decimated León, brought an end to the boom times.

PILGRIMAGE

León had numerous hospices, the principal one being the Convento de San Marcos (see below). In the Middle Ages it seems to have been a large, low building with interior patios, its own chapel, a corral, stable, hay barn, and some grazing meadows. The beds were separated by curtains, and rules limited to 2 the number of pilgrims per bed. The dormitory of women pilgrims was separate, because "it is a dishonest thing to have women and men in a single dormitory," and the "quality of people who come to the hospice are not of high caliber."

MONUMENTS: 1. **Catedral**. 2. Museo Diocesano. 3. **Roman wall**. 4. **Basílica de San Isidoro**. 5. **Panteón de Los Reyes** and **Museo de San Isidoro**. 6. **San Marcos**. 7. **Casa de Botines**. 8. Casa de los Guzmanes. 9. Palacio de los Condes de Luna. 10. Ayuntamiento Viejo. 11. **Iglesia de San Marcelo**. 12. Iglesia de Santa María del Mercado. 13. Iglesia de Santa Ana. 14. Colegio de Santa Teresa.

This seems like a lot and, compared to any place on the Road except Burgos and Compostela, it is. Moreover, most of what you will see here is of the highest quality. The cathedral, San Marcos, and San Isidoro are musts, and are likely to absorb you for 2 or more hours each. So, if you can manage it, don't rush. The Apostle's bones will wait for you an extra day or two.

1. **Catedral**. The building you see today is the fourth church on the site. The first, most likely a small, square, Visigothic-style church, was erected ca. 924 over ruins of a Roman bath on land donated by Ordoño II. The second, ca. 1084, was a medium-size Romanesque structure erected by Bishop Pelayo, complete with a palace, a library, and a hospice for the poor, the sick, and pilgrims. Alfonso VII of Castilla and León had himself crowned emperor in this church in 1135 with the king of Navarra, the count of Barcelona, the counts of Toulouse, Gascony, and France, and the Muslim ruler of Córdoba in attendance. (His dreams of empire came to nil: not only did he not unite Aragón and Navarra to his kingdoms of Castilla and León, he definitively lost Portugal.) The third cathedral, begun ca. 1175, was a showpiece, a magnificent large Romanesque structure meant to compete with the other monumental churches of the pilgrimage Road and to demonstrate León's wealth and political clout. Archaeological work under the current

cathedral has helped determine its dimensions. Many sculptures from this work are preserved in León's Museo Diocesano (see below).

The Gothic cathedral, begun ca. 1205, for the most part copies the Rheims Cathedral at ⅔ scale. Planned by Bishop Manrique de Lara (1181–1205) and begun in earnest by Bishop Martín Rodríguez el Zamorano (his tomb is described below), the cathedral was completed in record time, largely because it had the solid financial backing of both the monarchy and the papacy. Alfonso X contributed handsomely, in part to compensate morally for never having repaid a loan the Pope had given his father Fernando III for his war to conquer Sevilla. The papacy, in turn, granted indulgences (see ch. 88) to contributors, called off Italian creditors, signed over the papacy's third of the tithes from rural León, and forgave part of Fernando III's unrepaid loan. The whole kingdom joined the push. In 1258 a church council in Madrid offered 40-day indulgences to large contributors. Money was raised both for the whole of the structure and the parts. The chapels of Santiago and San Clemente were offered at bid. King Alfonso X himself endowed 2 chaplaincies. The chapels of the *cabecera*, begun in 1255, were completed in only 3 years. Contracts for carpenters, masons, and painters are still extant from the 1260s. To help recruit talented artisans, Alfonso X exempted a blacksmith, a glazier, and 20 sculptors from paying taxes. When work flagged, Sancho IV (1284–92) gave even more money.

By 1302 the cathedral was all but complete.

In the late 15th c., with the change to Renaissance tastes, several reforms and additions were undertaken. In 1495–1505 Juan de Badajoz the Elder built the library. The sacristy is from this period, as are several portals. In 1524 a new arch connected the cathedral with the cloister.

But unlike in Burgos, where the additions implant a 15th-c. Flemish-Gothic ambience to the whole structure, León's cathedral remains true to the spirit of 13th-c. Gothic architecture. It speaks strongly to the senses and is best savored slowly, first the whole and then the parts. You will probably hike into León in the early afternoon. After you have settled in, go rest for an hour on the benches in front of

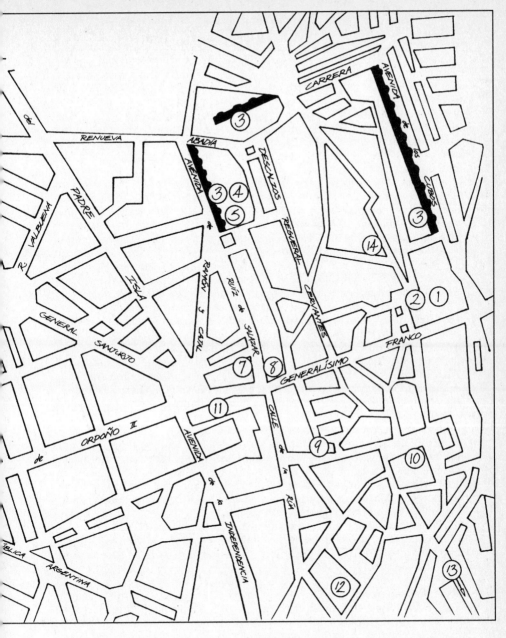

LEÓN

the cathedral's west façade and watch the afternoon sun play on the sculpted portals and on the spires of the towers. When the sunlight strikes full on the rose window, go inside and stand for a few moments in the middle of the nave breathing in
the colors of the light. Watch them change intensity as they glide across the floor
while the sun drops. Think of how these soaring towers of stone, this vast open
internal space, and these dancing colors must have blown the mind of your average
medieval pilgrim. Then come back tomorrow and look at the details.

Exterior:

• **West façade.** From across the street, take in the overall dimensions, shape, and harmony of the façade. You have much better perspective than medieval pilgrims had, for the spacious Plaza de la Regla in front of the cathedral was not opened up until the early 16th c. With the exception of the towers, most of the façade is pure 13th-c. Gothic, with an extraordinary sense of proportion and balance. The 3 portals matching the 3 naves is adopted from the French Gothic style and is uncommon in Spain. Their pointed arches lead the eye to the 4 windows of the triforium, which in turn rise to the rose window, which is also set into a pointed arch. The flying buttresses on either side of the nave seem to meld effortlessly into the arch of the rose window. The eye soars to the triangular frontpiece, flanked by pinnacles.

—Spires. The bell tower on the left, begun in the 13th c., was given an upper story in the 14th and capped with a spire by the architect Churriguera in the 18th. The clock tower on the right (1458–62) is in a style transitional between Gothic and Renaissance. It is crowned with a Burgos-style lacework spire. Despite their late dates, they harmonize with the 13th-c. Gothic façade.

—Theme. The west façade's overall message reflects the new enthusiasm for Mary in the 13th c. It links the exaltation of the Mother with the saving power of her Son. The left and right portals depict scenes from the life and death of the Virgin, each with a tympanum in 3 horizontal bands.

—Central portal. The 13th-c. tympanum of the **central portal** depicts the **Last Judgment**. Jesus, with angels bearing symbols of the Passion, is flanked by the kneeling Virgin and St. John. Angels weigh human souls. To the right of St. Michael on the lintel are the elect, including several happy souls seemingly engaged in conversation (such animation is almost never found in the Romanesque). To the left stand the damned, who continue on the archivolts in the fashion of Amiens, Paris, and the north portal at Chartres. Below the tympanum, on the mullion, the smiling **Virgen Blanca** welcomes worshipers to her house.

Two sculptural schools seem to be represented here. The Maestro de la Virgen Blanca is responsible for the Virgin and San Juan on the tympanum, the angel on the column, and the portal of San Juan in the south nave, which narrates the infancy of Jesus. The Maestro del Cristo del Último Juicio (ca. 1250) carved the Christ, the angel with the cross, and the lintel, as well as the sepulcher of Martín Fernández in the cloister, and the tympanum depicting the relics of San Froilán on the south façade.

—The line of large figures extending almost like a frieze across the jambs of the 3 portals appears to be by the sculptor who executed the south portal. Flanking the central portal are Saints Pedro, Pablo, **Santiago**, Tomás, Juan, and Judas Tadeo.

—Left portal (aka San Juan). The tympanum tells the story of the Virgin as mother of Jesus. The archivolts present the Tree of Jesse, with the genealogy of the Virgin, and finish with the life of St. John the Baptist. Here the frieze of large figures also relates the Old Testament precursors of Christianity: Kings David and Solomon, Saints John the Baptist and Paul. The 16th-c. Renaissance walnut doors, which narrate the Passion, seem to round out the story.

—Right portal. The tympanum focuses on the end of Mary's life: her Dormition, surrounded by angels and several of the Apostles; God receiving her soul; Jesus crowning her with glory. Again the jambs link figures from both Bibles: the Queen of Sheba, Saints Simeón and John the Baptist, the Eritrian Sibyl, Isaiah, and Jesus.

—The column between the central and left portals, bearing the arms of Castilla and León and the inscription *Locvs appellationis* ("The place for speaking out"), is where the public gathered to have their disputes resolved.

Behind the column, 2 15th-c. figures display a law book and a sword. Above them the smiling monarch seated on a lion throne appears to dispense justice tempered with mercy.
- North façade. The portal that used to open onto the cloister is blocked up by later construction. The window treatments and the rose window are typical of 13th-c. Gothic.
- **South façade.** Stand 10 m. in front of the central portal and look up. See how every element, from the arches to the sculpture to the flying buttresses, draws your eyes to heaven. This view is a textbook example of the Gothic emphasis on verticality.

This façade's 3 13th-c. tympana mirror those of the west façade. The central portal (aka the Portal of Revelation) also makes explicit reference to the Puerta del Sarmental in Burgos. Its tympanum portrays Christ in Majesty with Bible in hand as he reveals texts to the Evangelists. He is surrounded by angels and the old men of the Apocalypse. The Apostles stand on a frieze over the lintel. **San Froilán,** bishop of León (900–5), occupies the mullion. The right tympanum narrates the return of San Froilan's relics to León from the remote mountain monastery where they had been hidden during Almanzor's 988 raid.
- The **flying buttresses** (*arbotantes*), part of the original 13th-c. construction, were reinforced in the 15th c. They transmit the force generated by the weight of the roof to the ground, permitting the interior of the cathedral to be mostly open space. The 2 towers also serve as buttresses.

Interior:
As usual, we will visit the central altar and choir, the *trascoro*, and then the chapels.
- The **interior plan** measures 91 × 40 m. The *cabecera* with its ambulatory and radiating chapels facilitates movement around the altar, as in the pioneer pilgrimage churches. The central nave is 30 m. high. The walls and windows are Chartres-like: 3 stories high, with a triforium and clerestory. But unlike either of its French models, León's triforium is open, admitting even more light. This style later was popularized in France (Amiens, Paris, Strasbourg, and Cologne). The pillars, with small riblike columns arrayed around a central core, were common in France from the 1230s. The ribs permit arches at different heights to be supported by a single column. And the delicacy of the ribs communicates a sense of lightness belied by the enormous weight that the columns sustain.
- The **stained-glass windows** are why León is called the "Cathedral without Walls." León has more glass, and less stone, than any other cathedral in Spain.

> 📖 Francisco López de Úbeda, in his 1605 novel *La pícara Justina* (see ch. 58), was struck by the quality of light in the cathedral: "I went inside, but I was sure that I hadn't, and that I was still in the plaza, as the cathedral is so glassed and transparent. . . . You can drink from this church as from a glass cup" (Book II, part II, ch. 2).

The windows were executed at various times. Curiously, for until the 15th c. most artisans worked in anonymity, many of the glass painters in León signed their names, including 6 in the 13th c. Although some of the chronology is disputed, most agree that in the central nave the rose window, the first 5 panels on the north, and the first on the south are 13th-c. The fifth on the north shows a **hunting scene,** with lots of vignettes of medieval life: the trivium and quadrivium of the medieval university, falconers, ladies, etc. Tradition says that the glass came from a secular palace destroyed in the 15th c. In the ambulatory, the high central panels are 13th-c., the rest are 15th-c. In the aisles, the floral windows are 19ᵗʰ-c., though the **small rose windows** that cap them, depicting the capital sins, are 14ᵗʰ-c. In the transept, the north rose window is 13ᵗʰ-c.; the south, 19ᵗʰ; the remaining panels, 15ᵗʰ. By themselves these windows justify your having lugged your binoculars all these weeks.

📖 Although glassmaking techniques have been known since antiquity, stained-glass windows are relatively modern. The first examples of colored panes set into carved stone or wooden lattices are from 4ᵗʰ-c. Byzantium. A few simple figural panels appear in 9ᵗʰ-c. Carolingian art. But the expansive mosaics of light we know as stained-glass windows required the innovations of Gothic art—in which the weight of the vaults was sustained by massive buttressed pillars, allowing the thick stone supporting walls of Romanesque churches to be replaced by transparent Gothic walls of glass.

The medium required several techniques. Basic colors were obtained by mixing metals, or metal oxides, with the molten glass in the pot. To form flat panes, glassmakers blew long cylinders, cut them along one side, and let them slump onto a stone. Imperfections produced texture. To lighten the heavy opaque colors like red, a blown cylinder of clear glass could be dipped into molten colored glass to form a thin coating in a process called flashing. Artisans could also brush glass with enamel-like substances that they could fire to achieve various patinas, and these coatings could be etched away to produce 2-tone effects. Details could be added by painting the finished glass.

Artisans cut the colored panes with white-hot iron rods and then filed the pieces to achieve the required subtleties of form. They set the pieces into H-shaped strips of lead. When the entire panel had been laid out, it was soldered together and then fitted into grooves in the wood or stone window frames. The entire process was complex, lengthy, and enormously costly, which is why at first it was almost exclusively reserved for glorifying the houses of God. Fundraisers targeted stained-glass windows as an ideal medium for eliciting donations. Many were given by noble families and characteristically depict kneeling donors flanking the religious principal subjects; others were given by artisans' guilds, which explains why so many windows depict people at work. By the 15ᵗʰ c., when the new Renaissance merchant princes rivaled the princes of the Church, stained glass was used to glorify secular palaces.

• You will have noticed there is no retablo on the main altar. Gothic architects strove for a sense of openness, realizing that glory in glass palaces like León and Chartres lay in the unobstructed view of color.

📖 During the 15ᵗʰ–17ᵗʰ c., church planners strove to create theatrical backdrops for the altars where the miracle of the Eucharist was performed. Hence retablos were clogged into spaces never originally designed for them. You have seen them along the Road in 100 Spanish churches prior to León, and you have seen a few churches restored to their intended openness. Recall Santo Domingo de la Calzada's cathedral, where the Forment retablo was recently moved to a lateral altar. León's main retablo was taken apart in 1741. You will see several panels in the Diocesan Museum.

• The **choir stalls** (1467–81) are the work of several local sculptors. The details—clothing, interior views, etc.—reflect 15th-c. styles. The procession of large-scale patriarchs, Apostles, prophets, and saints on the seat backs is meant to stress the role of the Old Testament (in the lower register) in prefiguring the New (in the upper). Look, for example, on the left, where the wood that Isaac carries for his own sacrifice has 2 transverse beams, prefiguring the Crucifixion. The bread and wine given by Melchizedek to Abraham represents the Eucharist. The biblical figures are accompanied by Apostles and saints, the founders of the major religious orders, canons and friars. The themes of the continuity of human religious history and the unity of the Church set the pattern for choir stalls for the next 75 years, including several on the Road (Santo Domingo de la Calzada, Nájera, San Marcos in León, Logroño, Pamplona, and Santiago de Compostela). Also typical of these choirs are allusions to 15th-c. political events: the decapitation shown on one of the side reliefs here would undoubtedly have brought to mind the execution in 1453 of Álvaro de Luna, King Juan II's Condestable, once the most powerful man in Castilla.

The hundreds of secondary scenes carved on the backs, sides, armrests, and bottoms of the choir stalls are as engaging as the main figures. Like most Gothic choirs, León's castigates vices and says little about virtues, which are far less interesting. If you search, you will find a gambling nobleman being dragged off to hell by a demon. A glutton needs a wheelbarrow to carry his belly. A sadistic sodomite monk slaps the buttocks of a naked student. Another monk bathes with a woman, presumably a prostitute. A thief cuts a priest's purse during confession. Especially noteworthy are the carvings underneath each seat. They allowed monks, standing interminably in choir, to rest their nether quarters: hence their ironic name—**misericords**. Several of León's misericords are the work of a fine sculptor with an exquisite eye for detail. Take a close look at the Jewish doctor examining the urine vial, the physician administering an enema, the expert noble horsewoman, the male dancer, and the bagpiper and drummer.

• The *trascoro* that encloses the choir was started in 1529 by Juan de Badajoz the Younger, continued by Juan de Juní, and completed 50 years later by several other sculptors. Conceptually it is a triumphal arch, decorated with biblical scenes, statues of the virtues, and mythological figures, all framed with superb Plateresque decoration. The arch itself contains a schematic genealogy of the House of David and a Tree of Jesse giving the lineage of the Virgin. The framing elements are crowded with tiny figures of humans, children (the Italian Renaissance *putti*), monsters, and plants of every description.

• The **alabaster plaques** were executed in the 1570s by Esteban Jordán. With extraordinary detail they denote the life of the Virgin, the Apostles Peter and Paul, and Saints Isidro and Marcelo. Each plaque contains an upper and lower scene, joined both thematically and by various converging lines of construction, especially the triangular arrangement of the central elements of each scene. Each plaque seems to balance elements of symmetry and asymmetry. Note the subtlety in the use of architectural elements to frame the scenes.

• The chapels and walls of the aisles and ambulatory. The chapels are numbered counterclockwise beginning at the west end of the south aisle. Though each chapel and many of the walls contain significant works of art, the most interesting are the following:

—1. Capilla de la Virgen del Carmen. The 13th-c. **tomb of Bishop Rodrigo** depicts scenes repeated on a dozen other funeral monuments in this cathedral. Christ on the Cross promises redemption. The dead Bishop is accompanied by monks, dignitaries, and professional mourners (*plañideras*). He is shown distributing charity to the poor. Strategically placed angels assure the viewer that the Bishop's soul was saved. The chapel also has a small Rococo retablo of San José.

—2. Capilla del Calvario. The small 16th-c. **retablo by Juan de Bal-**

maseda. The 4 Evangelists are shown writing the gospels. San Lucas wears glasses, which were fairly common for the wealthy by the 16th c.

—3. The sacristy. The late-15th-c. sacristy displays the escutcheons of the Catholic Monarchs and of Bishop Alfonso de Valdivieso (1486–1500). The **Puerta del Cardo** (Juan de Badajoz the Elder, 1515) is a late Gothic jewel with complex arches and superbly detailed decoration.

—5. Capilla de la Virgen Blanca. The original 13th-c. statue of the Virgin, whose replica is on the central door of the west façade.

—6. The *trasaltar*. Across from the Virgen Blanca is the early Gothic **tomb of Orduño II**, which narrates Christ's Crucifixion with complexly structured realism. The arrangement of the Deposition is masterful: the 2 women embracing the body of Christ form a strong diagonal counterpoint to the dead Jesus. The woman holding his right hand and the woman kneeling at his feet bring the composition back into balance. The surrounding arches, with the castles and lions of Castilla and León and delicate foliated vines, were carved later.

—7. Capilla del Nacimiento. The modern-looking crèche was carved in the 15th c. in Flanders. The upper mountain scene, replete with shepherds, sheep, and a variety of plants, is a study in miniaturized realism.

—8. Capilla de la Virgen del Camino. Built by Juan de Badajoz the Younger, this chapel was intended to be a library. The brilliant **decoration around the door**, the ornate corbels (*ménsulas*), and the keystones on the ceiling arches are key elements of his style. Every surface is hyperdecorated with Italianate motifs that are typical of the early Spanish Renaissance and may derive in part from the taste for the textured patterning and abhorrence of vacuum that were characteristic of Mudéjar art.

• Next to the tomb of Ordoño II is a transition-to-**Renaissance tomb** by Juan de Badajoz the Younger. This was the very first break with Gothic in the main body of the cathedral. Its allegory of the triumph over death and the disposition of the figures is Flemish-Gothic, but the framing triumphal arch, the pillars with interesting grotesques, and massive Roman funerary urn reflect Renaissance humanism.

• In the wall of the north transept is the **tomb of Bishop Martín Rodríguez el Zamorano** (1232–42). The organization of the elements is late Romanesque, but the themes—the funeral procession and the emphasis on charity—are more Gothic. The detailing and delicacy of composition indicate the hand of a master, probably a foreign sculptor come to work in León.

• Entrance to the cloister and museum. A large Hispano-Flemish retablo has been reassembled in the passageway. Its painted panels depict the lives of several saints: Elena (lower and middle right), Gregorio (lower left and right), and Roque (upper right), among others. The overall ensemble is stunning, but the remounting lets you view the paintings right up close, allowing you to see that the details are largely mediocre.

• Around the corner is the <u>Puerta del Dado</u>, which once connected with the cloister. This is the oldest interior portal, ca. 1300. It still conserves its 1506 painting. The monumental figures, typical of the early Gothic, tend to be self-absorbed, revealing an inner spirituality rather than communicating directly with the viewer. This is especially true of the severe-faced Virgin, the monumental **Christ in his mandorla**, **Santiago Peregrino** with his conical hat, and the **Annunciation** on the jambs. Curiously, the 4 Evangelists, shown working at their desks, have the wings of angels.

Cloister:

• The late-13th-c. Gothic cloister was built over a Romanesque cloister of similar dimensions. In the 14th–15th c. it was a prestigious burial site; hence the large number of tombs.

• The **cloister vaults** were executed ca. 1540 by Juan de Badajoz the Younger and a corps of 20 sculptors who covered each of the Gothic arches with different Renaissance decoration. The ornate **capitals** and high-relief central **keystones**, surrounded by secondary keystones, are typical of his style (see San Zoilo in Carrión and San Marcos and San Isidoro here in León). Although the themes are varied, the life of Christ and the exaltation of Mary predominate.

• Many of the arches contain deteriorated mural **paintings** by Nicolás Francés. These compositions tend to be monumental and unified, but are often rigidly symmetrical. In the dramatically powerful **Crucifixion**, notice the naturalism of the soldiers casting lots, the powerful executioners tugging on the ropes, and the contrast between the serenity of Christ's body and the brutality of the tormentors.

2. **Museo Diocesano.** The museum is entered from the cathedral cloister. It is too rich to gallop through, but if you have time for only a brief visit, take a close look at these treasures:

• The first set of rooms:

— Ecclesiastical vestments, well displayed and well explained.

— **Hispano-Islamic textiles** that medieval Christian nobility prized to line their reliquaries and coffins.

— Two 10th-c. Bibles.

— An engaging 16th-c. statue of **Santiago Matamoros** presents the Saint as a late-medieval courtier.

— A "life"-size statue of Death will chill your bones.

— A Mudéjar storage chest. This massive 3 × 4 m. chest from the 13th or 14th c. is our favorite display. Each panel presents a different geometric design. Pieces like this make vivid the medieval Christian fondness for Islamic style.

• The second part of the museum is entered up a monumental **stairway** by Juan de Badajoz the Younger, rife with Italianate Renaissance decorative motifs. It is the first stairway in Spain with an oblique first course and double balustrade, a style that later became very popular.

— One room contains most of the surviving sculpture from León's late-12th-c. Romanesque third cathedral. Some of the pieces show the exquisite hand of the sculptor who carved Bishop Rodríguez's tomb in the transept.

— The statue of the **Knight and Lady** is labeled as depicting Santa Elena and her son Constantine, though the absence of references to the cross makes this doubtful. Instead, it may depict the return of a victorious nobleman from the Reconquest wars. The lady's crown, on the other hand, may identify her with the Church, in which case the scene may represent the triumph of Christianity over paganism. Your guess?

— Figures of a young woman and a standing Christ both look very French, although both are posed in Mudéjar-style horseshoe arches.

— Don't miss the stone on which the cathedral architect in the 13th c. sketched out the design for the rose window.

• Other upper rooms contain a miscellany of medieval art collected from the cathedral and from crumbling village churches around the diocese.

— One whole wall is filled with Romanesque and Gothic Virgins, giving you a good opportunity to contrast their different concepts of Mary and their evolving technical sophistication.

— There are 2 Jewish funeral stones, engraved in Hebrew, from Puente Castro.

— Retablo panels. The cathedral's main retablo was constructed by Nicolás Francés. It was dismantled and dispersed in 1741. The museum has collected 18 narrow panels in which you can see realistically faced saints in varied poses set against gold and brocaded backgrounds.

—There are several Gothic paintings, including a Last Judgment from Valderas with a frighteningly graphic—or perhaps amusing—mouth of hell.

—A grisly painting of San Erasmo shows executioners tearing out his intestines.

—Several pieces depict the pilgrim saints **Santiago** and Roque. The most unusual, despite its primitive workmanship, is a 14th-c. altar frontal from Adrados de Ordás showing the scenes from the Santiago legend: Santiago preaches to a disappointingly small throng; 2 disciples load the Saint's coffin in a boat; an oxcart carries his body up from the Galician shore. Since the village of Adrados has 2 patron saints, Santiago and San Cristóbal, the fourth panel depicts them together.

—The enormous **Plateresque silver chest** made for San Froilán's relics by the Renaissance metalsmith Enrique de Arfe. The chest is a thicket of intricate foliage that hides dozens of real and fantastic animals. The 10 saints framed in the arches include **Santiago**.

—An original **Christ on the Cross** by Juan de Juní (1576). The muscles of the stretched body and the cramped legs are extraordinarily realistic and contrast with the serene, almost sleeping, face of the dead Jesus.

3. **Roman wall.** The wall completed in the late 3rd or early 4th c. extended some 570 × 350 m. It was destroyed many times. Alfonso V (1010) undertook major rebuilding; most of what we see today behind the episcopal palace dates from this period.

4. **Basílica de San Isidoro**. This church, with its pantheon and museum (treated separately below), is likely to require at least 2 hours to visit. Its history makes it the cradle of the kingdom of León. Its exterior and interior Romanesque architecture established the artistic models for the whole of northwest Spain. Its treasury and museum are chock-full of high-quality art. And the paintings which cover its crypt are the best *in situ* Romanesque murals in Spain, and maybe in all of Europe.

The site once held a Roman temple to Mercury and then much later a medieval monastery dedicated to San Juan Bautista that was destroyed by Almanzor at the end of the 10th c. The current 11th-c. Romanesque complex is due largely to the efforts of Fernando I of Castilla and León, a great warrior and a deeply religious man who liked to dress as a monk and sing in the choir. He ravaged Extremadura until the Muslims sought peace. Unable to pay him in gold, of which by then they had little, they offered to the King instead the relics of some of the early Christian martyrs found in Andalusian cities, for which they themselves had little use. Elated, the King commissioned a church, constructed in its entirety from 1056 to 1067. The bishops of León and Astorga went on an expedition seeking the bones of Santa Justa, but were given the bones of San Isidoro. These were brought into León with great ceremony on Dec. 21, 1063.

> 📖 Isidoro of Seville (ca. 560–636) was indisputably the most important scholar-cleric of Visigothic Iberia. As archbishop for 36 years, he squelched the Arian heresy, built schools, and composed missals and breviaries. The most famous of his many writings, the *Etymologies*, is the world's first encyclopedia, ranging over topics from grammar and rhetoric to theology, history, mathematics, medicine, botany, and general science. It still makes good reading today. Isidoro was named a Doctor of the Church in 1722.

Fernando also founded a workshop for ivory in León to produce precious objects for the basilica (a crucifix carved here is now in Madrid's Archaeological Museum; another piece is in the Louvre). Goldsmiths and silversmiths also worked here.

After King Sancho II of Castilla was murdered in 1072, his sister, Princess Urraca, was the most powerful person in northwest Spain, even though her brother Alfonso VI was the king of Castilla and León. Urraca enlarged San Isidoro (ca. 1072–1101), largely with funds sent by Alfonso in the euphoria following his capture of Toledo from the Muslims in 1085. The refurbished church preserved the sculpted entrance portico and the crypt, which by then was already used as a pantheon for León's royalty. For the next century or so, San Isidoro was the most important religious institution in León.

Mid-12th-c. additions are commemorated by an immodest inscription in front of the baptismal font:

Here lies the servant of God, Pedro Deustamben, who rebuilt this church. He built the bridge called Deustamben's bridge and, because he was a man of admirable abstinence and many miraculous things came about through him, everyone spoke his praise. He was buried here by the Emperor Alfonso [VII of Castilla and León] and Queen Sancha.

The Church of San Isidoro fixed the 12th-c. Romanesque style for León the way that Jaca did for Aragón and eastern Castilla. Its principal elements include:

   —three-nave basilica with lateral apses;
   —naves covered with barrel vaults, sustained inside by buttressing arches supported by columns where they join the walls (a technique developed in Lombardy) and outside by massive buttresses perpendicular to the walls;
   —cylindrical arches over windows and doors;
   —sculpted corbels sustaining every roofline;
   —inside, segments separated by columns topped with floral Corinthian capitals;
   —horizontal lines of checkerboard decoration of the Jaca sort, with similar designs surrounding the windows.

San Isidoro suffered relatively few modifications in the post-Romanesque period. The church's central apse collapsed in 1513 and was replaced by a Gothic chapel. About the same time, the choir and cloister were added, and the south façade acquired some Renaissance decoration. The French invasion in the early 19th c., followed in 1811 by a lightning strike and fire, caused the loss of the Baroque retablos and the choir stalls.

Exterior:
The basilica has 2 portals on the south side.
   • **South transept portal**, also called the **Puerta del Perdón**, the rightmost of the 2 portals. This doorway created a school in León, characterized by a tympanum supported by a broken lintel, held up by figured *ménsulas*, and covered by an unadorned cylindrical archivolt capped by a checkerboard arch.

   The **tympanum** depicts the Descent from the cross, the 3 Marys' visit to the empty tomb, and Christ's Ascension (in which 2 beefy angels seem to have to give him a boost). Typical of this artist (probably Gelduinus, schooled in Toulouse) are faces with round jawlines and full cheeks, a strong vertical shin line, concentric curving drapery with folds fully modeled, and ribbonlike wing feathers on the angels.
   • **South nave portal** (on the left).

   The 2-level **Tympanum of the Lamb** depicts the Old Testament sacrifice of Isaac and the Christian Lamb of God. God's hand emerges to keep Abraham from completing the sacrifice. A mounted Ishmael—modeled on Roman centaurs—shoots an arrow into the air, while on the right, Sarah emerges from her tent. The carving is similar to the colonnettes of the Platerías portal in Compostela.

   The 2 large figures on the spandrels are Saints Isidoro (left) and Pelayo (right). Many of the figures on the spandrels seem to be by the sculptor who worked on the north transept portal in Compostela. His work tends to rigidly composed figures, softly rounded contours, and an emphatically plastic conception.

Interior:
- The heavy columns (alternating cruciform and complex pillars), the barrel vaulting, the elongated (*peraltados*) semicircular arches, and the **polylobed arches** of the transept and west door indicate a syncretism of Mudéjar, Asturian pre-Romanesque, and international Romanesque styles.
- *Altar mayor*: The retablo was constructed by Juan de Badajoz the Younger in 1513 in the Flamboyant Gothic style. The 24 painted panels of the life of the Virgin are by the Maestro de Pozuelo, ca. 1522. In the gloom of the poorly lit interior both are almost impossible to see. This is the altar with the urn of the relics of San Isidoro.
- San Isidoro is exceptionally rich in **capitals** and **corbels**. You will need your flashlight. The vegetable motifs are clearly antinaturalist and arbitrary, with bulbous plants and schematic or abstract foliage. They are carved in high relief, permitting the dramatic interplay of light and shadow. Numerous symmetrically positioned pairs of heads, cats, and monsters seem very oriental: they most likely derive from the Islamic ivory carving much prized by the Christian nobility. Note, too, the extraordinary profusion of human figures: jugglers, fighters, biblical figures, anatomically correct nudes. At least 3 artists' hands can be discerned: Pedro Deustamben, Maestro Esteban (of Compostela's Pórtico de la Gloria), and the so-called Master of the Tympanum of the Lamb.

5. **Panteón de los Reyes** and **Museo de San Isidoro**. These are visited on a single ticket, purchased in the bookstore. Tours are guided. The Panteón lies downstairs from the bookstore, the museum upstairs.
- **Panteón de los Reyes**. This was the original west narthex of Fernando I's church and served as a royal pantheon even before 1063. Its square shape and division by massive pillars into 3 naves of 2 bays each, covered by intersecting barrel vaults, is a Lombard technique.
- The 46 **capitals** are decorated with plants (palm-shaped ornaments, acanthus), animals, and humans. The two supporting the arch of the original doorway, showing the healing of a leper and the resurrection of Lazarus, were Spain's first to carry scenes from the Gospels and may also be the earliest portal with human sculpture, a full 100 years before Compostela's Pórtico de la Gloria. Other motifs include the sacrifice of Isaac, crossing the Red Sea, Moses and the tablets of the law, Balaam on his ass, some hunting scenes, and evocations of the monstrous world beyond the grave.

> 📖 By the late 11th c. the fusion of form and motif on decorative capitals was total. Historiated capitals were arranged like friezes, narrating various episodes on the 4 faces of the capital (remember San Pedro de la Rúa in Estella). The earliest ones were often done by master goldsmiths or ivory carvers. As the style spread, and demand increased, the less-skilled found work. Thus on Romanesque capitals, sophistication often indicates an early date, while cruder work tends to be later.

- The <u>fresco paintings</u> date from the first third of the 12th c. They are executed in tempera on a ground of white stucco, with ochre, red, yellow, gray, and black pigments. The general theme is the childhood, Passion, and glorification of Christ, together with saints, the zodiac, and the medieval annual agricultural cycle. The white background that separates the scenes from each other facilitates great variety in the composition. For example, the Annunciation is a straightforward narration. The message to the shepherds has a circular arrangement, and the Slaughter of the Innocents has a radial composition. The sense of spatial relationships largely disappears in the arrest and the Last Supper. The human figures are somewhat geometric, with the drapery clearly indicating social status: the holy figures are ductile and flexible, the peasants and executioners, rigid. Note the extraordinary realism of the **sheep and goats grazing** on the bushes, the mastiff drinking from the shepherd's hand. Some objects are labeled with their names (e.g. *gallus*), as if the painter, lacking confidence, thought they would be elsewise unrecognizable.

The episodes from Christ's life and Passion are arranged in accordance with a Mozarabic mass in which the priest breaks the consecrated host into 7 pieces and arranges them on the paten to form a cross, laying them in place as he invokes the mysteries: the 5 which form the body of the cross, from head to foot, are the Incarnation, Birth, Circumcision (much deteriorated), Epiphany, and Passion of Christ. His Death and Resurrection form the arms of the cross. Here the artist has added 2 additional scenes—Christ in Glory and Christ as King—to the right of the cross, and has broadened the scope of others: the Incarnation includes the Visitation, for example. The **Christ in Glory** is a masterpiece. He sits in His mandorla, bearing a book declaring *Ego sum lux mundi* ("I am the light of the world"), His right hand raised in blessing, His head flanked by alpha and omega (Christ is the beginning and the end of all things), surrounded by the 4 Evangelists. Follow how the rhythms are created by the drapery, the curves of the right elbow, the right knee, and the cloth draped over the left hand; the way in which Christ is made to seem to protrude from the surrounding framework by having His feet rest on the clouds of the nimbus and His right hand break the red frame.

Over the altar are scenes from the **life of Saint Catherine** (late 12th c.), arranged as in a retablo or an altar frontal: her dispute with the philosophers, her being visited in prison by an angel (the second woman in the scene may be the empress she converted), her torture on the wheel, her decapitation, and the transportation of her remains to Mount Sinai. The style hints at the transition to French-style Gothic.

On the arches are the **12 months**: GENVARIUS, a youth with 2 faces, old and new; FEBRVARIVS, a man warming hands and feet, covered with a cape; MARCIVS, a young peasant with a short tunic pruning vines; APRILIS, for whom the branch in each hand indicates the renovation of spring; MAGIUS, man ready to fight, since medieval wars tended to be summertime things; IVNIVS, a peasant harvesting barley; IVLII, harvesting wheat; AGVSTVS, thrashing stalks with a flail; SETENBER, harvesting grapes; OCTOBER, a peasant knocking down acorns, which fall in a pot (acorns were eaten raw or cooked, dried and ground to make flour, or converted to sausage by feeding them to pigs); NOVENBER, killing a pig (note the realistic grappling with the animal); DECENBER, rest and celebration, with a man at a table.

• The **tombs** contain 23 kings, 12 princes, and 9 counts, each with his epitaph. The best may be the **tomb of Count García**, with his body represented in outline.

• The cloister contains the **San Isidoro stone font** (ca. 1060) by a sculptor either unschooled or unskilled. It is one of the earliest manifestations in Spain of monumental plastically carved stone sculpture and appears to be derived from early-11th-c. Spanish ivory carving.

• The **treasury and museums**. Among the enameled reliquaries from Limoges, the chalices and church vestments, the Mudéjar chests, the fragments of the True Cross, and the cloth from Damascus, are these not-to-be-missed treasures:

    —An **ivory casket** (1059) depicting the Apostles. It is the first representation on ivory of the Romanesque checkerboard motif found on architectural arches, as in Jaca.

—**San Isidoro's reliquary.** Made of wood panels covered with silver plate. Inside, the box is lined with Muslim fabrics. The panels show the creation of man, original sin, the expulsion from Eden, and vivid details from 11th-c. daily life.

—**Doña Urraca's 11th-c. chalice** of agate, gold, and onyx, of Byzantine design. It incorporates 2 Roman onyx cups, covered with precious stones from earlier cultures, including a fine Roman cameo.

> 📖 This Urraca, who died in 1101, was Fernando I's daughter, the one who got Zamora when he split the kingdom. She was known for her charitable acts and donations. By contrast, Queen Urraca, Bishop Diego Gelmírez's staunch ally and the wife, for a time, of Alfonso I el Batallador, was known as the "despoiler," since in 1122 she confiscated much church gold and silver in order to wage war against her future ex-husband.

—A collection of late Gothic to early Renaissance silver crosses and chalices, many by Enrique de Arfe and his school, and an intricately worked 16th-c. Portuguese tray with repoussé figures of Judith and Holophernes.
• The **library**, one of Spain's richest, contains manuscripts from the 10th c. on, with many of them displayed. Especially prized is the illuminated *Codex Legionensis* Bible, finished in 960, with marginal notes in Arabic script.

6. **San Marcos.** Among León's many pilgrim hospices was one founded in 1152 by Bishop Juan Albertino next to the then brand-new bridge over the Río Bernesga. It was ceded to the knight Suero Rodríguez, one of the 12 founders of the military Order of Santiago, modeled after the Hospitallers of St. John and the Knights Templar.

> 📖 About 1160, Fernando II of León organized a brotherhood of knights and charged them with the defense of the city of Cáceres against the besieging Almohad troops. In 1171, these "Brothers of Cáceres" (*freiles de C.*) were renamed the Order of Santiago by agreement with Bishop Pedro Gudesteiz of Compostela, who promised them moral and material support in their war against the Muslims; he conceded them use of the red cross of Santiago. Dedicated to eliminating Islam, the Santiago knights' motto—*Rubet ensis sanguine Arabum* ("My sword is red with Arab blood")—suggests their temperament. They secured a charter in 1175 from Pope Alexander III and henceforth waged vigorous war against the Muslims in Extremadura. Some have asserted that the Order's corollary mission was to protect pilgrims, but there is no evidence to support the thesis. While from 1174 the Castilian branch of the Order was headquartered in Uclés, in the Mancha region of Castilla la Nueva, San Marcos remained the seat of the Order in León all through the Middle Ages. The Order of Santiago was the most prestigious association of nobles in Spain, with members in the forefront of both war and politics.

No trace of the earliest buildings remains. For a while the Order provided hospice services alongside the bridge, but by the time an inspection team examined the 1-story brick building with its internal patios in 1442, it was largely in ruins and had long ceased hosting pilgrims. The dormitory was a stable, its floor deep in manure. The team recommended reforms, but little was done.

In 1476, as part of his campaign to wrest power from the traditional nobility, King Fernando personally assumed the mastership of the Order of Santiago. In time he decided to impress the nobles by building the mother of all motherhouses. In 1514 he personally put up 300,000 maravedís for construction. Unhappy with the project's first architect, in 1515 he fired him and hired another, Juan de Horozco. Fernando's urgency had little effect: construction took 200 years. In another sense, however, Fernando succeeded. After he personally took over the mastership, the Order ceased being a military or political threat to the monarchy and instead became largely honorary. Both the painter Velázquez and the poet Quevedo proudly wore the red cross of Santiago on their breasts.

📖 Francisco de Quevedo was imprisoned in the basement dungeons (no longer extant) of this building from 1639 for allegedly writing a satire against Felipe IV, but really because he was a political enemy of the prime minister, the Count Duke of Olivares. As a member of the Order of Santiago, Quevedo was entitled to be kept here rather than in a civil prison. While in San Marcos he wrote three of his most profound philosophical works: the *Life of Saint Paul*, the *Providence of God,* and the *Constancy and Patience of Saint Job*. In the commentary on Job he wrote: "At the age of 71 . . . with eleven cancers, two of them still open, the court bailiffs came for me . . . and without a shirt, or cape, or servant, without having eaten supper, at 10:30 at night, the 7th of Dec., . . . they brought me here . . . in the rigor of winter, without telling me where or what was happening, some 55 leagues to the Royal Convent of San Marcos, in León, belonging to the Order of Santiago. . . . For 6 months I was locked alone in a cell. . . . I have now been here 2 years, without talking to anyone." After 5 years Quevedo was released and banished to his ancestral village of La Torre de Juan Abad, near Ciudad Real, where shortly after, he died.

San Marcos functioned as a monastery until the excloistration of the military Orders in 1837. It subsequently served as a high school, a Jesuit residence, a veterinary college, a hospital, a cavalry barracks, and a military warehouse. In 1961 the government transformed it into a superluxurious hotel and museum.

Exterior:
• The **façade of the main building**. The façade is a masterpiece of exuberant Renaissance Plateresque urban architecture, with an emphasis on sheer size. Built in 2 stages, due to a long cessation of funding, the right wing (from the church to the main door) is from 1533 to 1541; the rest, ca. 1615. Despite the difference, the exterior projects a sense of harmony. It is capped by a 1715 Baroque **Santiago Matamoros**.

The most striking decorations are the 48 **medallions**, executed by several important sculptors, including Juan de Badajoz and Juan de Juní. The medallions' unifying theme is human virtue, exemplified in an array of men (and a few women). The mix of classical myth with ancient, modern, and religious history is typically Renaissance. Each medallion is accompanied by a Latin inscription. The subjects include Hercules, Paris, and Hector; Judith, David, and Joshua; Julius Caesar and Octavian; Alfonso II el Casto, Fernando I, Isabel la Católica, the Cid, the legendary Bernardo el Carpio, Carlos V (between the warrior Trajan and law-giver Augustus), and Felipe II (flanked by patriotic Judith and virtuous Lucretia; the irony of contrasting him with his father by flanking him by women is probably unintentional). A 1716 addition, from the door to the tower by the river, displays medallions of the 15th-c. statesman Álvaro de Luna (who was beheaded), the Portuguese noble Beltrán de la Cueva (lover of the wife of

Enrique IV, called Henry the Impotent), and Felipe V (the last king of the Hapsburg dynasty, which by 1716 had been replaced by the Bourbons). No irony
intended?

The second most striking feature of the façade is the grotesques, an incredible array of sirens, sphinxes, winged horses, angels, plants and humans, dragons and fauns, dolphins and cornucopias, skulls and masks, garlands and vases.
Though several sculptors' hands are evident, the overall unity of design suggests
that they were working from a common pattern book.

Everything to the left of the church and museum is now the elegant Hostal de
San Marcos, one of Spain's premier hotels. If you can't afford to go in for a
drink, brush off your boots and go into the lobby and the room immediately to
its right, which has one of Spain's best-preserved **Mudéjar-style coffered ceilings**
(*artesonados*).

The **church**. Built in the exuberant style of the Spanish Renaissance, it was consecrated in 1514.

Exterior:
  • The **church façade** combines a Renaissance semicircular arch with a mix of
Gothic and Plateresque decoration. Note the **scallop shells** of Santiago, the impe-
rial coat of arms, and the plaque with the Descent from the Cross by Juan de Juní.

Interior:
  • The **church choir**. A signature under the prior's chair ascribes the work to
Guillermo Doncel in 1542, but most of the **carvings** (1537–43) are probably
early work of Juan de Juní, inspired by his study of Donatello and Michelangelo
while in Italy. They are notable for their technical mastery, the exalted mysticism of many of the faces (the prophet Esdras, for example), and their often violent dynamism. Some viewers find them more pagan than religious. The
Renaissance love of innovation is marked in the inscription *Omnia Nova Placet*
("Everything new gives pleasure").

Cloister:
The cloister, now part of the museum, is chock-full of mostly mediocre Roman
sculpture found in the environs of León. The cloister was begun by Juan de Badajoz the Younger (1549) and not finished until 150 years later. Badajoz's work is
characterized by a profusion of Renaissance motifs. The birth of Jesus in one angle
of the cloister is probably by Juan de Juní.

The **Museum**. The church, cloister, and several adjacent rooms are a treasure
house of Leonese art and historical objects, collected after their dispersal from area
monasteries after the 1835 *desamortización*. There are several significant pieces in
the church portion of the museum.
  • Reliefs of the Crucifixion and Descent from the Cross.
  • A **statue of Mary Magdalene** signed *Horozco me fecit.*
  • A superb Renaissance *reja*.
  • The stained glass of the *cabecera*, depicting Saints Joaquín, Ana, Pedro, Pablo,
Catarina, and Cristóbal.
  • The museum proper has 2 rooms.
  • Room 1.
      —Jewish gravestones from the Castro Judaeorum excavations.
      —The **Christ of Carrizo**, an 11th-c. ivory of Byzantine influence, dispro-
portionate but expressive.
      —The **cross of Ramiro II**, originally donated in the late 10th c. to the
monastery of Santiago de Peñalba, in León's Bierzo region, to celebrate the
defeat of 'Abd ar-Rahman III. Byzantine style.

—The **Calvario de Corullón**. These images of the Virgin and San Juan, from a late-11th-c. or early-12th-c. Crucifixion tableau, were found earlier this century in a trash heap.

—Four **capitals from San Facundo in Sahagún** that blend Corinthian and Mozarabic style. The historiated capital depicts 8 Apostles, individualizing only Peter with his keys.

—The **Retablo de San Marcelo**. This 14th-c. painted wood retablo depicts San Marcelo, his wife Nonia, their daughter, and 12 more children, each with the sword of martyrdom.

—Two statues of **Santiago Peregrino**. The 15th-c. image is from San Miguel del Camino.

—A **Pieta** by Juan de Juní. Note the violent contrast between Jesus's destroyed body and Mary's emotive concentration.

—A carved wood panel by Juan de Juní showing a **debate between Monks and Jews**, ending with the burning of books.

• Room 2. This **richly decorated Renaissance room** is by Juan de Badajoz the Elder (1549). The arrangement of the figures focuses attention on the retablo of Jeremiah and Isaiah contemplating God the Father on Mount Tabor.

—Below them is the apparition of **Santiago at the battle of Clavijo**.

—The cloth, from Damascus or perhaps Almería, was found in a 12th-c. tomb discovered in 1882 when fixing a wall.

7. **Casa de Botines**. The Catalán architect Antonio Gaudí (see ch. 64) began this palatial Art Nouveau commercial building in 1892 for the textile kings Simón Fernández and Mariano Andrés. A department store was to occupy the main floor, apartments the upper three. Its name recalls the store's first proprietor, Juan Homs y Botinás. Note the **neo-Gothic windows**, single, double, and triple, with their elegant decorative motifs, and how the horizontal emphasis of the friezes is counterbalanced by the verticality of the towers.

8. Casa de los Guzmanes. It was built in 1560 by the Renaissance architect Rodrigo Gil de Hontañón for the bishop of Calahorra. Felipe II stayed here in 1602. Inside are a splendid Plateresque patio and Renaissance staircase. The portal, with its 2 gigantic soldiers, displays Cicero's emblem: *Ornanda est dignitas domo: non ex domo dignitas tota quaerenda* ("Dignity of the house must be honored; should not all dignity be sought from a house?"). The iron grille-work prompted a pun from King Felipe II: "Es mucho yerro para un obispo" ("That's a lot of *yerro* for a bishop" [*hierro* means iron; *yerro* means sin]). Just right of the entrance is a Neoclassic plaque from the former Convento de las Augustinas Recoletas showing San Agustín washing the feet of Christ (except that Christ looks remarkably like **Santiago Peregrino**).

9. Palacio de los Condes de Luna. This 14th-c. mansion, which appears to be in a state of accelerated dilapidation, was erected by the Quiñones family. The knight Suero de Quiñones came to this house after the tournament of the *Paso Honroso* (see ch. 62).

The tympanum displays the family arms. The columned Romanesque windows were undoubtedly brought from elsewhere. The palace's magnificent *artesonado* ceilings and Mudéjar plasterwork were removed to archaeological museums in Madrid and León. The tower is late-16th-c.

10. Old Ayuntamiento. This old city hall in the picturesque Plaza Mayor has Herrera-style towers from 1677. Markets are held here on Wednesdays.

11. **Iglesia de San Marcelo**. This 17th-c. church, built over an early Romanesque church and since then much reformed, is dedicated to a centurion of the Seventh

Legion who was martyred for his Christianity in the 3rd c. The statue of San Marcelo carrying the cross is by Renaissance sculptor Gregorio Hernández, as is the marvelous **Pieta** in the church's Capilla de los Valderas. Fernández's contract specified that the image was to have ivory teeth and real fingernails.

12. Santa María del Mercado. The apse, with its fine corbels and square *metopes* and *modillones* is Romanesque, but the church has undergone many changes in the bell tower (14th c.), the vaults (15th c.), and the tower crown (1758). This site marks the center of the medieval Frankish neighborhood, just outside León's earliest wall. The Plaza del Grano behind the church is one of León's quietest and most picturesque.

13. Iglesia de Santa Ana. The retablo is Neoclassic, with a nice image of **Santiago** and some remnants of Mudéjar-style mural painting. The church is in the center of the old Jewish quarter. The Lepers' Hospital de San Lázaro was located nearby.

14. Colegio de Santa Teresa. In the courtyard still stands most of a 13th-c. palace with both Romanesque and Gothic elements. In the 16th c. the palace served as the seat of the Inquisition in León. The palace can be seen from Calle Pablo Flórez.

Wandering through the older sections of León affords you opportunities to find dozens of late medieval and Renaissance buildings, interesting plazas, and many additional worthwhile monuments. We recommend that you follow our dictum of never passing a church door without testing to see if it is open. With luck and perseverance you will get to see some of the following:

- Churches:
    —San Juan y San Pedro de Nueva. Splendid Baroque portal brought from the ex-monastery of Eslonza, and a nice 16th-c. crucifix.
    —San Martín. Gothic apse; Baroque crossing and cupola; fine Baroque Pieta.
    —Santa Nonia. Now a storage place of the processional images of several local brotherhoods, or *cofradías*.
    —San Pedro de los Huertos. Behind the cathedral, yet almost rural in character.
    —Santa Marina. Finely carved 17th-c. plasterwork; Virgin of the Rosary of Juan de Juní; several fine retablos.
    —San Salvador de Palaz del Rey. In origin the oldest church in León. Mozárabe in plan, the current church is largely 15th and 16th c. Its fine retablo is probably by Juan de Badajoz the Younger.
- Monasteries and convents:
    —La Concepción. 16th-c., with an interesting Gothic door; an ornate 18th-c. Baroque retablo. The convent's Mudéjar fireplace has been moved to the museum in San Marcos.
    —San Francisco. The current 19th-c. church houses a monumental Baroque retablo originally constructed for the cathedral.
    —Santa María de Carbajal. 17th-c., with some interesting paintings.
- Civil monuments: A large number of wealthy mansions and public buildings remain from the 15th to the 18th c. Some of the most notable, listed by streets or plazas, are:
    —Calle Ancha: Casa de los Marqueses de Villasinda. 16th-c. façade; now the Hotel Paris.
    —Calle del Cid: Fábrica de Hilados. Now part of Audiencia Provincial, in the 18th c. it was a thread factory. The royal escutcheon is flanked by allegories of Commerce and Fine Arts.
    —Calle Escurial: 16th-c. mansion with simple façade.

—Calle Fernández Cadórniga: 17th-c. palace with twin towers.

—Calle Juan de Arfe: 17th-c. palace with interesting balconies.

—Calle de San Pelayo: 14th-c. palace with simple Gothic decoration.

—Calle Serranos: Baroque façade with escutcheons of 4 noble families.

—Plaza de San Marcelo: Casa de los Manriques, with a classic façade. Also the Casa del Marqués de Torreblanca, with a 17th-c. tower and escutcheons.

—Plaza de San Martin: Casa de las Carnecerías. Constructed in the 17th c. as León's principal meat market.

—Plaza de Torres de Omaña: Casa del Cardenal Lorenzana. León's most opulent 18th-c. palace, with fine balconies.

61. León → Hospital de Órbigo

Route 1: León → Trobajo del Camino → **La Virgen del Camino** → Valverde del Camino → San Miguel del Camino → Villadangos del Páramo → San Martín del Camino → Hospital de Órbigo

Route 2: León → Trobajo del Camino → **La Virgen del Camino** → Aldea de la Valdoncina → Chozas de Arriba → Fojedo → La Milla del Páramo → Villarente → Hospital de Órbigo

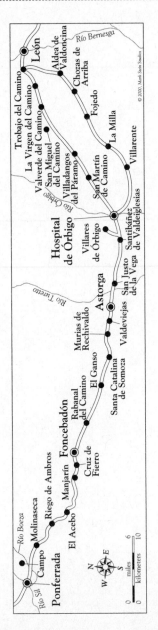

While Route 1 is the more common, and is marked, we prefer Route 2, which splits off to the south from La Virgen del Camino to traverse several small towns to the south of the modern highway via paths and farm roads. This route offers no significant monuments, and is not described below, but the scenery is pleasant and the road is quiet, sometimes shady, and is easy to find. It adds about 2 km.

Route 1:

✴ Trobajo del Camino A small Roman town was located on this hill. The church is dedicated to San Juan Bautista. It contains an image of **Santiago** taken from the nearby 18th-c. Ermita de Santiago.

✴ **La Virgen del Camino** This is the most modern church of artistic significance on the Road. Legend says that in 1505 the Virgin appeared to the shepherd Alvar Simón on this site and told him to have the bishop of León erect a hermitage there. The bishop was skeptical. To convince him that a miracle had happened, with his sling Simón hurled a stone that grew into a boulder. The bishop acceded, and ordered that a church be built. In 1522 Alonso de Rivera, held captive by Moors in Africa, asked the Virgin to allow him to visit his home for the pilgrimage to the Virgen del Camino. To scorn his belief, on the eve of the *romería* his jailers locked him in a chest, which the Virgin then miraculously transported to this site, along with some captured church bells which pealed from joy when they reached this site. The chains of Rivera's captivity are on display in the church.

In 1961 architect Fray Francisco Coello and sculptor José Subirachs were commissioned to build a new church on the site.

📖 Subirach's **standing Apostles**, who flank Mary on the façade, are shown with their traditional attributes. From left to right:

Matthias: with the stone of martyrdom; a bronze mark on his neck shows where he was decapitated after he was dead.

Philip: with his cross of martyrdom; he gave the fishes to Jesus to be multiplied.

Matthew: offers his Gospel.

Thomas: looks up incredulously, with a lance signifying unbreakable faith.

Santiago: shells; his right hand points to the Road.

John: the youngest; guards the Virgin; bears a chalice.

Mary: rises in Ascension; crowned as queen of Heaven.

Peter: blessing like a pope; the keys to heaven; the inverted cross of his martyrdom; on his left knee, Malco's ear that he sliced off in anger.

Andrew: his arms for the X-cross of his martyrdom.

Bartholomew: with the knife that flayed him.

James the Lesser: bishop of Jerusalem, with baculus and miter.

Judas Tadeo: with a canonical letter and the ax that decapitated him.

Simon: with his saw of martyrdom.

The door on the right narrates the miracle of the foundation of this church. At the base of the bell tower is represented the tomb of Christ: the carved wounds, feet, hands, and face serve as an outside altar.

Inside, the Baroque retablo holds an early-16th-c. wood statue of the Virgen del Camino on a 1715 silver base. Among the church treasures is a late-15th-c., roughly wrought silver Gothic processional cross with symbolic representations of the Evangelists and the self-sacrificing pelican.

✱ Valverde del Camino (aka Valverde de la Virgen) This town's church, like many along this stretch of the Road, is brand-new. This one bears a dedicatory plaque dated 1986. Also like many others, it incorporates an earlier *espadaña*. In 1998 this one was capped with 3 enormous storks' nests.

✱ San Miguel del Camino The town is documented as having had a hospice in the 12th c., located to the north on a small hill known as the Cuesta de Santiago. Nothing remains. The church of San Miguel is brand-new. The 15th-c. Santiago Matamoros from its precursor is in the San Marcos museum in León.

📖 The day the Italian pilgrim Albani walked through San Miguel in 1743 there was a disastrous fire. Of the town's 16 small adobe and straw houses, 9 were destroyed.

✱ Villadangos del Páramo On this fortified *castro* in 1111, the forces of Compostela's Bishop Gelmírez and doña Urraca and the infant king of León were defeated by Alfonso I el Batallador of Aragón. The 12th-c. *Historia compostelana* describes the events this way in Book I, chapter 68:

[The bishop's men] pitched their tents and awnings in a circle and, unaware that the treacherous Aragonese had set hidden spies and ambushes along the road, they slept that night without any fear. There were 266, no more. The perfidious Aragonese learned this from their spies and gathered their army of 600 mounted soldiers clothed in iron and 2,000 on foot with bows, swords, spears, and other arms. Emerging from their ambush, they attacked. [The brave but tragically outnumbered Gallegos (the Historia is shamelessly partisan) arrayed themselves in a line.] Brandishing their lances in their strong arms and spurring their swift steeds, with a terrible crash they engaged the vanguard, wounding almost all of them and knocking them to the ground, where in an instant a large number of Aragonese were killed. But even with their courageous fighting and unhorsing the enemy, surrounded on all sides by dust and enemy troops, attacked in the rear and on the flanks, they could not resist the impending disaster. Some were killed in the bloody combat, and others taken prisoner.

Bishop Gelmírez slipped away and took refuge 40 km. west, behind the walls of Astorga.

Villadangos's new church of Santiago conserves its 18th-c. bell wall. Inside, the chancel depicts the **battle of Clavijo**, where, allegedly with Santiago's help, Ramiro I defeated 'Abd ar-Rahman II. On the altar is an 18th-c. **Pilgrim Santiago**, with a 3-cornered hat bearing crosses and shells.

✻ San Martín del Camino The village dates from at least the early 13th c. A hospice is documented on the Calle Real from the 17th through the 19th c. San Martín's 1963 church has a 17th-c. tower capped by what appears to be a late-19th-c. *espadaña*.

The small inn (ca. km. 25) is said to have had an altar with the traditional protectors of pilgrims: Saints Roque, Martín, Antonio Abad, and Miguel.

This used to be dry wheat-farming country. Earlier this century, wells were dug to tap underground aquifers. These wells, called *norias*, were pumped by animals walking around in a circle. The water permitted some diversification of crops. In recent years a network of canals has brought abundant water to the flatlands bordering the Río Órbigo, and potatoes, corn, and sugar beets have flourished.

62. Hospital de Órbigo

History
   This ford over the Órbigo River was a strategic transportation control point, leading the Romans to establish a town here. The Suevi and Visigoths fought here in 452. Alfonso III (866–910) defeated the Moors here in 878. According to legend he was helped by Bernardo el Carpio, the renowned but probably fictitious hero of the early Reconquest wars.
   The town has 3 names. Its famous pilgrim hospice gave it the name Hospital de Órbigo. In the 13th c. the town belonged to the Knights Templar, leading to its alternate name: Encomienda de Órbigo. Its famous bridge contributed the third name: Puente de Órbigo.

The Paso Honroso
   Stand on the bridge and look south through the grove of poplars along the river. If you look closely, you can see colored pennants waving, and you can hear on the evening breeze the whinny of horses and the laughter of knights and their ladies.
   In 1434 the Leonese knight Suero de Quiñones held forth on this bridge against all comers in what may have been Europe's last true medieval tournament. Suero, scorned by his lady, wore an iron collar around his neck as a sign that he considered himself bound to her. When that failed to impress her, he resolved to challenge the best lances of Europe to meet him on the Órbigo Bridge. Suero went to King Juan II at Medina del Campo, where he secured the King's permission. In fact, the King had his herald ride through the kingdom reading out Suero's 22 conditions of challenge. The word spread like wildfire through a European nobility sated with the messy intricacies of court politics and gruesome dynastic wars and yearning for the simpler world they read about in *Amadís de Gaula* and their other books of chivalry. That fictitious world was a place in which a single knight, by the force of his personality and sword, could prove the virtue of his cause though the whole world be arrayed against him.
   The wooden lists were constructed in what is now the grove alongside the bridge: 146 paces long, with a palisade and spectator galleries. 1434 was a Jacobean Holy Year, so in addition to the contestants, their retinues, royalty, and the merely curious, the Órbigo road also thronged with pilgrims. Suero had the sculptor Nicolás Francés make him a life-size mannequin, sumptuously dressed like a herald, to set beside the pilgrimage Road with a sign pointing the way to the lists. The jousting began 2 weeks before St. James's Day, the moment of maximum traffic along the Road. Colorful battle tents were pitched everywhere; pennants fluttered in the breeze. The air rang with the shouts of squires and the clang of steel as the knights rehearsed for the upcoming contests.
   At dawn on July 11, 1434, the longed-for tournament began. Musicians blared out the fanfare, church bells rang, and the assembled knights and their retinues marched to the village church for mass. The jousting went on for several weeks, and after each day's contests the knights banqueted on the riverbank. Musicians played, and the knights and ladies danced in the flickering torchlight. On July 15 Suero was pitted against a Catalán challenger who, respecting Suero's reputation, dressed in a double thickness of steel. To mock him, Suero appeared in only light armor covered with a woman's blouse. The enraged, heavily encumbered Catalán was no match for the prancing Suero until a lucky blow to Suero's head knocked him from his horse. The crowd gasped. But a moment later Suero danced up, cry-

ing, "It is nothing." On July 20 Suero and his close companions stood off 9 knights of Gutierre de Quijada, who had stopped at the tournament on their way to Compostela. Gutierre, his knights beaten, rode off swearing vengeance.

On the last day of the tourney, August 9, a final great procession was held. Suero appeared and proclaimed that since he had proved his fealty to his secret lady by wearing the iron band and by breaking 300 lances at the jousts, he was now free. With that he removed the iron band and presented it to the judges. The crowd roared its approval. From the bridge Suero led a procession all the way back to León, where he vowed—now that he was free—to journey to Compostela as a pilgrim. This he did, and when he reached the cathedral, he deposited a jewel-encrusted golden bracelet as token of his release from the prison of love. You will see the bracelet in Compostela around the neck of the image of Santiago Alfeo in the cathedral museum.

> 📖 A footnote: 24 years later, after taking part in many battles in the 15th-c. civil wars, Suero de Quiñones was riding in open countryside when he chanced upon the still-rancorous Gutierre de Quijada. The 2 men dropped their visors and charged at each other. A moment later, the quixotic Suero de Quiñones lay dead.

PILGRIMAGE

The hospice for which the town is named belonged to the Knights of Saint John of Jerusalem, and nothing remains of it today. When the Italian pilgrim Domenico Laffi trekked through ca. 1670, he observed that the town's "inhabitants are so poor that they need alms, so you pay them for a shelter they provide in their huts" [Laffi; trans. Hall (1997), 149].

MONUMENTS: 1. Ermita de Nuestra Señora de la Purificación. 2. The **bridge**. 3. Iglesia de San Juan Bautista.

1. Ermita de Nuestra Señora de la Purificación. We have never found this church open. During our past several visits this whitewashed church at the east end of the bridge has been capped by 4 enormous storks' nests. We understand that the marshy riverbanks offer such succulent fare that these storks no longer migrate and can be seen here year-round.

2. This is one of Spain's best remaining **Gothic bridges**. Floods have swept away one or more of the arches at least 5 times since the 13th c. In 1809, as Napoleon's army chased Spain's English allies, headed by General John Moore, west toward Galicia, Moore blew up 2 arches to guard his retreat. Napoleon took another route. As it currently stands, counting from east to west: arches 3–6 are 13th-c., arches 7–16 are 17th-c., and arches 1–2 and 17–19 are 19th-c. The reconstructions have maintained the bridge's medieval aspect, and in the early morning, with the mist rising off the river to shroud the stone arches, you would swear you have journeyed back in time.

3. Iglesia de San Juan Bautista. New in 1184 , it was given to the Knights Templar to aid their mission of assisting pilgrims and protecting the road. Since 1874 the diocese of Astorga has administered it. The inside is unremarkable. San Juan is the central figure of its retablo.

63. Hospital de Órbigo → Astorga

Route: Hospital de Órbigo → Villares de Órbigo → Santibáñez de Valdeiglesias → San Justo de la Vega → Astorga

None of the monuments along this stretch of road is particularly significant, but the scenery is spectacular. Keep an eye on the horizon. Soon the banks of the clouds will reveal themselves to be chains of mountains, the Montes de León to the west and the Cordillera Cantábrica to the north. You are approaching the extreme northwest corner of the Castilian Meseta. The differential weather patterns spawned by the swirling winds and moisture streaming across the mountains have created a number of microclimates. In some of the gullies you will see groves of enormous chestnut trees. On the high, flat mesas (*páramos*) you will find mostly wheat and sheep. Where the land is too dry, or the soil too poor to support agriculture, the ground is covered with scrubby oak trees, or heather and broom. The red, sandy soil contains minute traces of gold, which in greater concentrations higher up in the Montes de León were mined by the Romans. It is laced with deposits of clay that in some of the villages supports a small brick-making industry.

By tradition (probably recent), pilgrims in these flatlands pick up the largest stone they feel they can carry and add it to their packs to be deposited at the summit of the Foncebadón pass 3 days west of here. Some pilgrims think of the rocks as sins, or as whatever other encumbrances of life that they hope the pilgrimage will help them leave behind.

✳ **Villares de Órbigo** The church has a **Santiago Matamoros** on the altar. This village raises lots of garlic. We have seen thousands of heads, their long stems braided together, laid out on the streets to dry. Once, when the wind was right, the perfume followed us halfway to Astorga. Above Villares is an early Iron Age *castro* called—anachronistically or ironically—El Santo.

✳ **Santibáñez de Valdeiglesias** La Iglesia de la Trinidad has images of **Santiago Matamoros** and the pilgrim San Roque.

One km. past Santibáñez are the ruins of a brick-making kiln. About 1 km. further is the clay quarry that supplied the kiln. The large-trunked, long-leafed trees seen here are the first of the chestnuts that dot the road all the way into Galicia.

✳ **San Justo de la Vega** The 16th-c. church of San Justo has a 17th-c. retablo. Records indicate that in the Middle Ages the town had a pilgrim hospice, now gone.

One km. from Astorga the hiking road, which parallels the highway on the right, crosses the remains of a small Roman bridge.

64. ASTORGA

HISTORY

Astorga is located at the intersection of the east-west Via Traiana and the north-south Vía de la Plata from Andalucía. In Roman times it guarded the mountain roads to the mines. Because it had been a capital of the ancient Astur tribe, the Romans named it Asturica Augusta. Pliny lauded it as an *urbs magnifica*. As an important Roman city it naturally became an early Christian center. Legend has it that both Santiago and St. Paul preached here. It is fact that it had a bishopric from at least the 3rd c. During invasions of the Germanic tribes, the Suevi settled the area. They were eventually conquered by the Visigoth Teodorico II (456), who largely destroyed the old Roman city in the process. In later Visigothic times the city prospered again, and in the surrounding mountains' hermitages flourished under Saints Toribio, Fructuoso, and Valerio. The Visigothic city was destroyed by Muslim invaders in 714. After its reconquest it was re-fortified as a Christian stronghold by Ordoño I (ca. 850). During Almanzor's raids on León (984–8), Astorga was untouched, and it became the *de facto* capital of the kingdom.

In the 11th c., as the pilgrimage blossomed and Leonese cities along the Road became commercial centers, Astorga prospered. Merchants from León, Castilla, and France set up their shops, and Jewish immigrants were numerous enough to have 2 separate neighborhoods. There was a synagogue as early as 1073, and a Jewish cemetery (site unknown) from 1092. One Jewish neighborhood, near the Puerta del Obispo, belonged to the church; today the site is still called the Paseo de la Sinagoga. Another area at the southeast corner of the city, near the Puerta del Sol, was called the *Castro de los judíos*. Unlike almost anywhere else in Spain, Jews here were welcomed in all aspects of city life. The *aljama* owned and maintained the guard towers near the gate, and Jews served in the armed night patrols. The Jewish quarters persisted in relative peace until the 1492 expulsion.

In the 15th c. the Marqués de Astorga built a large castle here (torn down in 1872). During the 19th-c. Napoleonic Wars the city was occupied by the French, who destroyed much of the remaining Roman wall.

PILGRIMAGE

Because the mountains that guard the entrance to El Bierzo and Galicia are formidable obstacles, and because the pilgrimage Road from the south, the Vía de la Plata, links up here, Astorga was a good place to gather strength for the climb to the west, and to recuperate on the way back east. At the pilgrimage's height, Astorga had 21 hospices, second only to Burgos. The hospice of San Roque hosted young Francis of Assisi on his 1214 pilgrimage. French pilgrims took comfort at Santa María de Rocamador, and the English (from 1195 to 1585) at Santo Tomás de Canterbury.

Astorga's many brotherhoods (*cofradías*) competed in sponsoring hospices, as did the workers' guilds. The carpenters financed Santa María; the carders, San Adrián; the leather workers, Santiago; and the shoemakers, San Martín. *Cofradía* members also hosted pilgrims in their homes. The *Ordenanzas* of the carpenters' guild legislated that if a male or female pilgrim died in any member's house, the guild had to pay for the burial. Other rules specified that the deceased's possessions should be sold at auction, with anything left after burial expenses going to the *cofradía*.

When the pilgrimage declined in the 16th c., 6 cofradías banded together and agreed to admit the indigent into their hospices. Statutes and ledgers from the time underscore problems that resemble those of today's urban homeless. Since poor people were sleeping in the streets, some of the indigent made a career of visiting the many hospices in turn, spending an entire year in the city. At least a portion of the pilgrims had paid for their lodging. With the shift to an indigent clientele, money needed to be found. In the 18th c. the hospices sold off land to meet operating costs. Many closed, and others were destroyed in the 19th-c. War of Independence.

The Hospital de San Juan Bautista, mentioned as early as 1187, was destroyed by fire in 1756. Rebuilt, it survives today as the Hospital de las Hermanas de la Caridad (Hijas de San Vicente Paul), the medical facility in front of the cathedral.

MONUMENTS: 1. **Catedral** and Museum. 2. **Iglesias de Santa Marta and San Esteban; Celda de las Emparedadas.** 3. **Bishops' Palace and Museum.** 4. **Walls.** 5. Chocolate Museum. 6. **Ayuntamiento.** 7. Iglesia de San Bartolomé. 8. Roman ruins: Ergástula; plaza; baths; "Synagogue" garden and Roman sewers. 9. Iglesia de San Andrés. 10. **Santuario de Fátima.** 11. Convento del Sancti Spiritus. 12. *Aljibe.* 13. Monasterio de San Francisco. 14. Convento de Santa Clara.

Astorga is not a big city, but there is a lot to see. We generally spend 2 nights here.

1. **Catedral** and Museum. The current building was erected over an earlier Romanesque church that stood from 1069 to the 13th c. The west transept retains some buttressing from that period and a cornice of carved leaves. The museum preserves a couple of the Romanesque capitals. The current building was begun in 1471. Most of the work was done in the 16th c. by Rodrigo Gil de Hontañón. The south façade is 18th-c. Damage resulting from the 1755 Lisbon earthquake led to late-18th-c. reforms, particularly in the cloister, which suffered again during the Napoleonic occupation. The cathedral's west façade and main retablo are among the Road's monuments not to be missed.

Exterior:
• The **west façade**. Finished in 1704, it resembles a grandiloquent Baroque retablo. The tympanum, divided into 3 wedge-shaped panels, narrates the Passion (on the left, in a curious anachronism, the pilgrim San Roque kneels before Christ). As in much Baroque monumental art, scenes are enclosed within scenes enclosed within scenes, and the pleasure for the viewer is often in the details. Architectural elements help frame the episodes. The heavily decorated columns, which are an anthology of Baroque column motifs, help give the whole composition its sense of theatricality. The façade is designed to overpower, and it does.
• The Renaissance-style south façade features the Assumption of the Virgin, crowned by a triangular tympanum depicting God the Father.

Interior:
• For a small cathedral the naves are unusually high, and the Flamboyant Gothic vaulting, with Renaissance-style painted keystones, is particularly elegant.
• The **retablo mayor** by Gaspar Becerra (1558–62), a disciple of Michelangelo and Raphael, is one of the best Renaissance ensembles on the Road. The design is monumental. The sculptures are solid, confident, and stunning. The retablo's theme is the life of Jesus and the Virgin Mary. As with the best Renaissance retablos, while each of the main narrative plaques is a work of art in and of itself, they are linked by theme, by color (here reds and blues), and by a variety of structural devices. Each of these panels has a roughly circular construction. In several the grieving Mary is highlighted by her position, her white face, and her dramatic gestures. Several of the attendant figures, such as the 4 women in the panels of the predella, are of classical inspiration.

• The **choir stalls** were begun in the Flemish style, with an upper Renaissance tier added ca. 1520. Unfortunately they are generally closed to the public. You will need your binoculars to savor the details. These seats are notable for their representation of the human form and the elegance of the clothed figures (if you visit Zamora's cathedral you will see their model). As on many choirs, the carvings on the misericords censure presumed moral abuses, often by the clergy themselves, as in the explicit depiction of homosexual acts. Astorga is unusual, however, in shifting the immoral acts to anthropomorphic animals, a cross between demons and monkeys. Try to find the misericord with the card-playing monkeys; one of them smokes a pipe, a mere 20 years after Columbus had brought the first samples of tobacco back to Europe.

• The **Chapel of San Miguel** (second from the west end of the south nave) is the cathedral's most interesting. The **retablo** (ca. 1530) is by the Maestro de Astorga, a close disciple of Juan de Borgoña. This Italianate master is noted for retaining the crumpled, sharp-edged draperies of Flemish Gothic, for his idealized lovely young women with elaborate headdresses, and for the realism in his depiction of suffering. The half figures are: on the left, St. Lawrence and **Santiago**; on the right, Saints Andrew and Martin, dividing his cloak with a beggar. It also has an exquisite **Plateresque frame**.

• **Nuestra Señora de la Majestad** (in the left apse; early 12th c.) is one of the most striking Romanesque images in Spain, with her rigid form and hieratic expression. Note the richness of the throne, covered with silver in the 13th c. The Child's hands and face were redone in the 16th c. The hole in the back is meant to hold relics.

• The Diocesan **Museum**. The museum is installed in the cloister and adjoining dependencies. Among the prizes here are a good collection of Romanesque Virgins and several tooled-leather altar frontals, the first we have seen along the Road. There is also a **pulpit** carved by Gaspar Becerra and the 10th-c. Mozarabic **chest of San Genadio** that was donated by Alfonso III el Magno to the bishop of Astorga ca. 900. Several of the pieces come from rural churches along the pilgrimage Road. In the first room is an ivory **Christ from Rabanal** (note the Baroque hyperrealism and the painted blood); and in the fourth room, a 12th-13th-c. stylized Crucifixion scene from Compludo. The museum contains many local images of **Santiago Peregrino** and **Matamoros**. The remnants of Romanesque sculpture on display suggest the existence of a high-quality workshop in Astorga in the 12th c.

2. **Iglesias de Santa Marta and San Esteban. Celda de las Emparedadas.** The fine retablos of the 18th-c. church of Santa Marta feature a 17th-c. image of San Pedro de Alcántara. San Esteban was built in the 16th c., next to the cathedral and over what was a chapel of the Hermandad de San Esteban in the 11th c. Between the 2 churches is a small 14th-c. cell where local prostitutes were imprisoned. Legend has it that pilgrims fed them through a slit in the door as an act of charity. There is a cautionary inscription over the window: "Consider how I have been judged, for

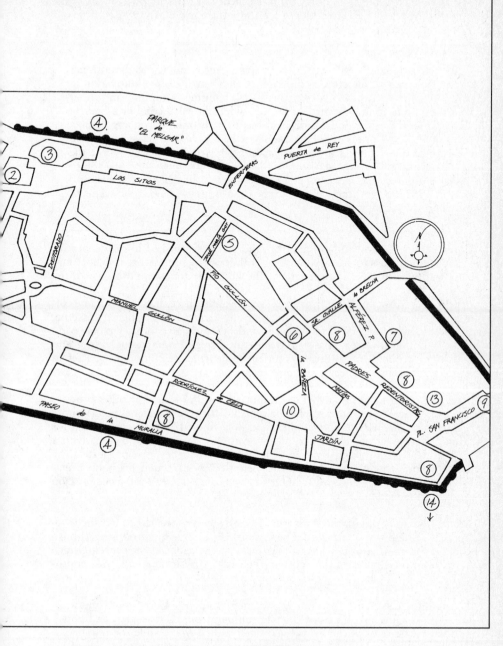

ASTORGA

your judgment will be the same: me yesterday, you today" (*Acuérdate de mi juicio, porque así será también el tuyo. A mí ayer, a ti hoy*).

3. **Bishops' Palace and Museum**. Antonio Gaudí designed this neo-Gothic palace for Archbishop Juan Bautista Grau Vallespinós. After various modifications man-

dated by the architects' Academia de San Fernando, construction began in 1889. The Archbishop's death, and other problems, led to a 20-year hiatus. The work was finished by Luis de Guereta in 1913. During the Civil War (1936–9) it served as the regional Falange headquarters.

> 📖 Antonio Gaudí (1852–1926) was Spain's most audacious practitioner of Art Nouveau architecture and design. Gaudí's art exhibits innovation in form, exciting mixtures of stone, tile, glass, painting, sculpture and other media, and harmoniously strident use of color. His work combines French, Victorian neo-Gothic, and Mudéjar elements with often surprising results. Most of his best work is in Barcelona, where he played a fundamental role in the turn-of-the-century Catalán *Renaixensa*. His most famous work, the new cathedral of La Sagrada Familia that he was commissioned in 1883 to design for Barcelona, has not yet been completed. In the Astorga Bishop's Palace (1887–93) and the contemporary Casa Botines in León, he seems to have had Gothic on the mind.

Construction mixes white granite from the Bierzo, varnished brick, decorative tiles, and stained glass to create a sense of both jewel-like miniature opulence and airiness and light. Even if it were empty, the building alone would be worth the visit.

In 1963 the Museum of the Pilgrimage was installed here. It contains a fine collection of Santiago imagery, shoes, hats, shells and other bits of pilgrim costume, and many documents related to hospices and other organizations having to do with the pilgrimage. Other parts of the museum display Romanesque virgins and capitals (one striking capital portrays an entire Benedictine community), Roman artifacts, and regional modern paintings.

In one of those miracles of coincidence that seem almost common on the pilgrimage Road, during our first visit to this museum in 1974 the only other browser turned out to be Walter Starkie, the 80-year-old Irish adventurer-scholar whose 1957 memoir, *The Way of Saint James,* had first kindled David's enthusiasm for the Road. Starkie had come by car, and was using a cane, but he told us with a twinkling eye that although that was his umteenth journey to Compostela, he hoped it wouldn't be his last. He seemed bemused to learn that his book's relationship to our pilgrim sally was similar to *Amadis de Gaula's* influence on Don Quijote. Starkie died in 1976.

4. **Walls.** Roman in origin, the walls were extensively reconstructed after the 9th-c. Reconquest. These walls witnessed a fierce battle in 1111 as the troops of Alfonso I el Batallador of Aragón besieged the forces of his estranged wife Queen Urraca and Archbishop Gelmírez of Compostela. The 12th-c. *Historia compostelana* provides a colorful—if partisan—description:

> The faithful Castilians, Asturians, and men from the Tierra de Campos, heeding the Queen's call, came quickly running from their castles, and put up their battle tents in the fields [below the walls]. Meanwhile the impious Aragonese had secretly gathered a large army with people from Nájera, Burgos, Palencia, Carrión, Zamora, León, and those who had come from Sahagún. . . . Among them were murderers, evildoers, fornicators, adulterers, hateful thieves, and execrable apostates. . . . And as they were marching against Astorga, look, and see a great crowd of soldiers appearing suddenly from among the bushes on the hills which you can see between Astorga and the Órbigo, and approaching the city they camped there, because they knew that the Gallegos were brave warriors.

The Aragonese sent for reinforcements, 300 armored knights on horseback, but the Gallegos (the "good guys" of the *Historia compostelana*) attacked them before they could arrive.

> [The Gallegos] armed themselves and, mounted on their chargers, they galloped out along the highway on which [the reinforcements] were coming. As soon as they saw them in the distance, their fierce eyes shone with the ardent desire to fight, and they galloped towards them at full speed, spurring their charges, their lances held in their powerful arms, and crashed into them, wounding them with fierce blows, making their entrails fall out below their breastplates and shields. The dead littered the field, and were stripped and despoiled. ... The survivors fled into the bush. ... The Aragonese, frustrated in their vain hope like another Herod thwarted by the three Wise Men, trembling with fear, worried and sleepless, at night lifted the siege and slunk back to Carrión. [Book I, ch. 73.3]

The walls were rebuilt yet again in the 15th c., so strongly that Alvar Pérez Osorio, the Marqués de Astorga, boasted: "Where my arms are placed they shall never be moved!" "*Never*" in this case equaled 4 centuries, for the walls were largely destroyed by Napoleon's troops during the War of Independence. Remaining today, in various states of reconstruction or disrepair, are more than 2 km. of wall, with 27 towers and 5 gates.

5. Chocolate Museum. This small museum celebrates the local industry that boomed in the 18th and 19th c. and has exhibits that show how chocolate is made. For obvious reasons this museum is a favorite of all but the most abstemious pilgrims. Now, if they only had a *café con leche* museum!

6. **Ayuntamiento**. The façade of the Baroque city hall (1683–1704), like those of León and Ponferrada, emphasizes its horizontal lines. The central *espadaña*, a 1748 addition, displays the national escutcheon surrounded by the Golden Fleece *Toisón* of the Hapsburgs. The Ayuntamiento preserves a banner reputedly carried by Astorgan troops in the 9th-c. battle of Clavijo. In the clock tower, typically dressed **figures of Maragatos** have come out to mark the hour since 1748. The male figure is the locally legendary Pero Mato, who allegedly fought alongside Santiago in the battle of Clavijo.

> 📖 The mountain people west of Astorga, known as Maragatos, are of uncertain origin. George Barrow (*The Bible in Spain*, 1834) speculated that they descend from Goths who sided with the Muslims during the 8th-c. invasion, adopting their religion, customs, and costume of tight bloomer pants, a large belt, and big hat. Some say they descend from (legendary) King Mauregato. Another etymology for their name is that because so many of them survived as carters and muleteers, unable to make a living from the rocky soil of these mountains, the Romans called them *mercator*, or merchants. Some believe they are an isolated group of Mozarabs who have preserved their customs. Others think them to be a remnant of Astures, Berbers, Visigoths, or even Carthaginians. Until the beginning of this century, the men's costume was wide breeches, white shirts, red garters, and slouch hats, while the women wore crescent hats, lacy mantles, heavy black skirts, and intricate filigree earrings that were noted by Arnold von Harff in the late 15th c. Whatever they may have been, their traditional culture has withered in the last few decades, surviving today mainly in museums and in tourist wares.

7. Iglesia de San Bartolomé. The oldest parts of the building are 11th-c. Note the Romanesque **tower** with its horseshoe arches. The main portal is Gothic. Notable in the interior are a 17th-c. **Ecce Homo** and a **Virgen de las Angustias** by José de Rozas.

8. Roman ruins. These are in 4 sets that may be visited in any order.
- Ergástula. This Roman tunnel or cave (between the Calle del Sr. Ovalle and the Plaza San Bartolomé) may originally have been an entrance to the city's forum, although popular legend holds it to have been a prison (Lat., *ergastula*) for slaves. The property was donated in 1120 to the church of Santa María by Queen Urraca. Until 1892 it was Astorga's jail. Only about a 50-m. stretch remains today.
- **Roman plaza and house.** These extensive ruins near the Plaza de San Francisco are well labeled and easy to visit.
- Roman baths. Remnants of 2 sets of baths exist. Little remains of the larger set, next to the Plaza de Modesto Lafuente. The smaller baths, near the west city wall, are well preserved.
- "Synagogue" Garden and Roman sewers. Site of one of Astorga's 2 Jewish quarters. In the southwest corner of the gardens are remains of the Roman sewer system. From the gardens one can see Mount Teleno, guarding the entrance to the Bierzo to the west.

9. Iglesia de San Andrés. This is a 20th-c. recreation of a Mudéjar-style church.

10. **Santuario de Fátima** (formerly San Julián) preserves the late Romanesque **capitals** on its main portal. Note the dragons, devils, and Saints Peter (keys and book) and Paul (beard and scroll). The interior of the church is known for its sculpted plasterwork, not particularly common in Road churches. On a capital just inside of the door is a scene rarely portrayed in Romanesque sculpture: an angel announces the coming Messiah to an Old Testament prophet, perhaps Zacariah (Luke 1:5).

11. Convento de Sancti Spiritus. This 16th-c. cloistered convent contains some nice ornamental vaulting and 18th-c. Baroque retablos.

12. The *aljibe* is a vaulted storehouse, of possible Roman origin, that served as a water reservoir for the medieval city.

13. Monasterio de San Francisco. The extramural monastery of San Francisco, by legend constructed to commemorate the Saint's passage through Astorga, preserves scraps of its medieval windows and capitals.

14. Convento de Santa Clara. You can get a good view of this extramural church from the "Synagogue" Garden (see #8, above). This church was part of a 14th-c. Franciscan convent that was pretty much destroyed in the War for Independence. Of the early church, the entrance portal and late Gothic cloister remain.

Route: ASTORGA → Valdeviejas → Murias de Rechivaldo → [Castrillo de los Polvazares] → Santa Catalina de Somoza → El Ganso → Rabanal del Camino → FONCEBADÓN

✱ Valdeviejas The church is dedicated to San Verésimo. The village's Hospital de Sancha Pérez was documented in 1481. The medieval Ermita del Ecce Homo was rebuilt in the 18th–19th c. Just past the town, you cross the modern *Autovía*.

✱ Murias de Rechivaldo This Maragato (see ch. 64) town supplied carters and pack-mule trains to the region. The 18th-c. Church of San Esteban has a tiny image of the Virgen del Pilar in a niche over the lintel of the door. It also contains an image of San Roque.

The landscape and townscapes change with each successive km. These are the first stone walls you have seen since before Burgos. The villages, too, are now made of stone. The low stone houses (*teitadas*) have roofs of locally mined slate or, in the more modest dwellings, of thatch.

In 1974 we found most of the thatched roofs (called *soberas*) in these towns intact. With each successive pilgrimage fewer remain. When the city-bred grandchildren reconstruct their family homesteads as weekend retreats, they tend to reroof them in slate, both because it is more durable and because there are few artisans today who remember how to weave thatch.

Windows in these houses are small in order to preserve heat. Overhanging balconies protect the doorways from the summer sun and winter rains and snows. Often a large stone set by the front door serves as a bench. The earth on these ridges is not very good for agriculture, and until recently the principal "crops" were sheep and cows, as attested by the dozens of stone corrals you will see to the left and right of the Road.

👟 Castrillo de los Polvazares This Maragato town, on the paved highway, just off the hiking Road to the north, was the setting for Concha Espina's 1913 novel *La esfinge maragata*, which chronicles life in the villages of the Maragatería in the early 1900s. Espina, like ourselves and everyone else caught up in the historical traditions of the Road, lamented change and romanticized the remaining sentinels of ancient ways.

The "vía de la plata" and the "pilgrim road" have been erased by a wide Spanish 18th-c. highway, on which the traditional carters are being extinguished, powerless before the swift railroad; centuries and generations have passed and fallen, along with sceptres and crowns, and through all those fleeting lives and all those ephimeral things, this fountain has pumped its fecund and eternal caress for every thirsty soul on the road. [Ch. 4]

Just southwest of the Castrillo, before km. 6, on a flat hill known as La Mesa, was a pre-Roman *castro*.

✳ Santa Catalina de Somoza Arnold von Harff in the late 15th c. merely called this village "Hospitale." The relatively modern church of Santa María contains a relic of San Blas.

✳ El Ganso In 1142, El Ganso had a small church and the Hospital de San Justo, run by Cluniac Benedictines. A small monastery dependent to Aguilar de Campóo (150 km. to the northeast) was founded in 1243. Nothing remains of either. The current modern church is dedicated to and has a 16th-c. statue of **San-tiago**. Built into an exterior wall is a medieval cross-shaped funeral stone, possibly from a pilgrim cemetery near the village.

El Ganso, whose main street was not paved until the mid-1990s, is one of the best places to view traditional Maragato architecture. In 1998 a few of the low stone houses here still had their thatched roofs.

As you climb higher on these long ridges the vegetation changes to scrub oak, heather, broom, and wild thyme. A little higher, the harsh climate eliminates the trees altogether, leaving only scratchy, near impenetrable brush. The rocky soil is now laced with hunks of white quartz.

✳ Rabanal del Camino The Knights Templar maintained a garrison in the town in the 12th c. to protect pilgrims crossing the pass over Monte Irago to Ponferrada.

Rabanal has 2 hermitages: the Ermita del Santo Cristo de la Vera Cruz and the 1733 Churrigueresque **Ermita de San José**, whose retablo contains images of **Santiago** and Santa Bárbara.

The late-12th-c. church of **Santa María de la Asunción** retains Romanesque elements, despite having been extensively remodeled in the 18th c. (north door and sacristy) and 19th c. (roof). The roughly decorated south door to the sacristy, recently discovered under its thick coat of plaster, probably once connected to the residence of the Templars. The church contains a 12th-c. image of San Blas and 18th-c. Baroque retablos.

The ancient **Hospital de San Gregorio**, also called Gaucelmo for the hermit who developed monasticism in these mountains, in which Aymery Picaud stayed in the 12th c., was recently rehabilitated and is now administered by the British Confraternity of Saint James.

> 📖 The Hospital de San Gregorio was visited several times in the 1720s by church authorities. In their reports they ordered that there always be a hospitaller on duty, that the Hospital continue to open its doors to "pilgrims who take refuge from the inclement weather," that in the interests of hygiene the straw on the floor be changed once a year [!], that the supporting brotherhood (*cofradía*) buy 4 cartloads of firewood, that the hospitaller "use it exclusively to warm the poor visitors and heat their meals," that men and women be lodged in separate rooms, and that any pilgrim dying in the hospice should be buried with a mass, and that yellow wax candles be burned during the service. The hospice also kept track of the number of pilgrims who were personally escorted up to Foncebadón (and sometimes down to El Ganso, depending on the weather), ranging from a low of 32 during 1804, to a high of 119 in 1832.

The large house known as the Casa de las Cuatro Esquinas housed the future Felipe II during his 1554 visit to Galicia.

👢 Just before km. 23 the hiking Road and asphalt road cross the remains of an old Roman Canal associated with the gold mines at Fucarona, a km. or so to the north. If you make the detour, you will see remnants of a strip mine, of 4 rectangular ponds that held water to sluice the ore, and of 2 heaps of tailings from which the ore has been washed out.

🚗 The modern entrance to western León's Bierzo region, and for some late-medieval pilgrims like Künig von Vach the preferred entrance, is the now-paved N-VI highway that crosses the mountains north of here over the Manzanal pass (1,230 m.). The 5th-c. hermitage of San Toribio was located there, and there in the 11th c. the hermit Gaucelmo built a church. A Roman road also traversed that route. The Cistercian Convent of San Miguel de las Dueñas is worth visiting along the way.

66. FONCEBADÓN

The Roman road through the Irago Mountains over the Foncebadón pass connected distant Italy, as well as the wheat lands of the Castilian Meseta, with the gold mines of the Bierzo region. Before Carlos III opened the Manzanal pass in the mid-18th c., this was by far the preferred entrance from León into the Bierzo and Galicia. The village of Foncebadón was of sufficient importance that in the 10th c. Ramiro II convoked a church council here. The village is nestled on a sheltered ridge below the pass, which makes it a good staging point for travelers. In 1103 the Church of San Salvador was built, and Foncebadón's Alberguería hospice petitioned King Alfonso VI for property rights in the region. Twenty years later the hermit Gaucelmo put up another hospice in the village. In the late 12th c. Fernando II gave sufficient importance to the hermitages and hospices along the Road through these mountains that he exempted them from paying taxes. A document dated 1790 justifies minor expenditures to improve pilgrim services at Foncebadón:

> The nature of the landscape is extremely rough and fearsome, and from nearly the first of September until the end of May the pass is closed, and the neighboring villages put up cairns to mark the route, and if this is insufficient, they dedicate themselves to guide, accompany, house and thaw out the poor pilgrims who come and go from Galicia. [Cited in Huidobro y Serna 2:700]

Today the village of Foncebadón is largely in ruins, although enough is left to convey a good sense of the characteristics of the popular architecture of the region. Everything is built of local slate. The houses have quoined corners, with uncut stones laid in horizontal layers filling in between the quoins. The roofs, steeply gabled against the heavy snows, are also covered with slate, or for the less affluent, with thatch. Slate is also used to enclose the chimneys: in several of the ruined buildings you can still see them leading down to stone or adobe hearths and ovens. In everything but the most recent constructions, nails are scarce and the rough beams are secured with pegs. Look at the way the walls are capped with flat horizontal stones. They keep the rain, snow, and heavy mountain dew from penetrating the walls, where it would freeze and crack the masonry.

When we first visited Foncebadón in 1974, the 2,000-year-old village was in its death throes. Only 4 human inhabitants remained to tend a couple of cows and a handful of sheep. Our pilgrims were permitted to lay sleeping bags on straw in one of the two houses in the village still having a semblance of a roof. The village's single team of oxen, yoked for plowing the stony slopes west of town, had their heads covered with fox skins, the legs and tails still in place to brush the flies from the oxen's faces. One black-clad old woman informed us that she had fought to retain the bells in the crumbling church, because in the winter she and her son were all alone in the town, and if there was trouble they could ring the bells, which—if the wind was right—could be heard in Rabanal, 6 km. down the mountain. By our visit in the mid-1980s only 2 residents were left in Foncebadón, and our pilgrim group took shelter from a raging sleet storm in an unfinished modern brick structure, itself half in ruins, near the spring. In 1993 that structure, too, had crumbled away. On our last visit, in 1996, a handful of former inhabitants had reconditioned some of the ruins as summer homes, but anyone wishing to spend the night needed a tent. In the church *espadaña* the bells were still in place. The rest of the church lay in rubble. The old woman was gone.

Route: FONCEBADÓN → **Cruz de Fierro** → Manjarín → El Acebo → Riego de Ambros → Molinaseca → Campo → PONFERRADA

Weather along this stretch can be treacherous in all seasons. In the winter, the Foncebadón pass is often buried in snow. The paved road is lined with snow poles all the way to El Acebo. Domenico Laffi reported that "here we were hit by a very violent storm, with wind and rain, which left us almost dead. But it was followed by a very hot sun, which dried our clothes" [Laffi; trans. Hall (1997), 151]. In 1987 gale-force winds tore open the zipped backpack of one of our group's pilgrims and scattered the contents all over the side of the mountain. The pilgrim, with her load lightened of *de facto* nonessentials, made it to the Cruz de Fierro with the stone from the flatlands still in her pocket.

The ruins 300 m. beyond Foncebadón before beginning the climb to the pass are the remains of the Hospital de San Juan established by the hermit Gaucelmo and granted privileges by King Alfonso VI in 1103.

✳ **Cruz de Fierro** The pass of Foncebadón over Monte Irago is 1,504 m. The enormous pile of stones at the summit may result from a variety of ancient customs. The pre-Roman Celts were in the habit of marking their high mountain passes with piles of rock (for which we still use the Gaelic word *cairns*). Roman travelers also customarily marked high passes by leaving stones, called *murias*, in honor of the god Mercury, the patron of travelers. The hermit Gaucelmo, who topped the pile here with a cross, essentially Christianized a pagan monument.

Many modern pilgrims who have picked up a large stone early in their journey as a symbol of the sins they hope to expunge by pilgrimage deposit them on the height of Foncebadón as an act of contrition. Or a photo-op. Be sure to climb to the top of the rock pile: from these heights you get your first glimpse of the wild mountains of Galicia to the west.

The small chapel of Santiago, ancient in appearance, was built in 1982 by the Casa de Galicia in Ponferrada.

✳ **Manjarín** This small town, first cited in 1180, maintained a hospice in medieval times. The tradition has been revived in the 1990s. When we first visited in 1974, Manjarín appeared to have been recently abandoned, and about half of the houses still had roofs. Now both roofs and walls have all but disappeared.

> 📖 A nearby cliff town to the southwest is called Labor del Rey. Legend holds that there a pilgrim fell from his horse and would have been killed had a miracle not kept him from tumbling to the valley below. An old woman saw him and exclaimed, "This is a work of the King!" (*¡Que labor de rey!*).

✳ **El Acebo** Despite its tiny size, this is a typical Road town: a single street coinciding with the pilgrimage route, with a church in the center. In former times the village was probably larger, for an important church council was held here in 946 at the now-vanished church of San Juan. In medieval times this town was freed from taxes so long as it maintained the winter snow poles marking the road over the Foncebadón pass. In the 15th c. the village council funded a small pilgrim hospice.

The current small 15th-c. church, dedicated to San Miguel, contains a Romanesque image most likely of San Juan Bautista (though possibly it is **Santiago**). At the exit to town by the *ermita* is a modern monument to the 70-year-old pilgrim cyclist Heinrich Krause, who died of a heart attack here in 1987.

From El Acebo, the road into the Bierzo descends through groves of magnificent chestnut trees. If the road were not well marked, it would be easy to get lost in these precipitous gulleys. In 1743 the Italian pilgrim Albani found the descent so confusing "that not even wild animals could have walked through them" (216). Eventually an old man who was collecting chestnuts led him to Ponferrada.

The smokestacks and cooling towers you see far across the valley—so far out of scale with the rest of the landscape that they look like implants from another world—are part of a nuclear power station that provides electricity to the Bierzo.

From El Acebo an alternate route to Ponferrada descends by a steep path to the left to the village of **Compludo**, in which San Fructuoso built a small monastery dedicated to Saints Justo and Pastor in the 7th c. The present church's ceiling, with both a nerved vault and wooden beams in the Mudéjar style, suggests a hybrid between late medieval and incipient Renaissance styles. The retablo, richly carved with heads and grotesques, angels and skulls, signed 1533, is the earliest datable Renaissance retablo in the Bierzo. In the center are paintings of Jesus's Transfiguration on Mt. Tabor and of Saints Justo and Pastor, both commemorated on August 6. Compludo also has a nondescript Ermita de la Asunción.

Compludo's **medieval iron forge** was rebuilt in the late 19th c. The technology was introduced into Spain in the 14th c: the oven is fired by an air blast regulated by a stream of water. Iron ore and carbon are heated together, releasing molten iron that flows out into ingot molds. It is then shaped in the forge with a water-powered trip-hammer.

✱ Riego de Ambros The town is cited in a late-12th-c. document. The 16th-c. church, dedicated to María Magdalena, has a nice Baroque retablo. There is also a small Ermita de San Fabián y San Sebastián. Note the popular architecture of the houses, with their lower courses in stone, topped with ornamental wood-planked balconies that overhang the street to provide shelter from rain and snow. Most of the houses have massive stone chimneys and slate roofs.

✱ Molinaseca The gorge cut by the Río Meruelo enters the broad central valley of the Bierzo at Molinaseca. As the valley terminus of the Bierzo side of the Foncebadón pass, the village prospered as a control point on the Roman gold road, called *Interamnio Flavio*. Two ancient bridges remain over the River Meruelo. In the 12th c. the village belonged to the Monasterio de Sandoval and was traded to the Monastery of Carracedo in the 13th c. The new owner granted it a charter favorable to Frankish businessmen, and the town burgeoned as a market and pilgrim-supply town. Molinaseca's wealth can be seen in the number of late medieval solid homes still lining its streets. The town maintained 4 hospices.

The Capilla de la Virgen de las Angustias, at the town entrance, has an 18th-c. Baroque retablo. The Iglesia de San Nicolás de Bari replaces a church funded by

Elvira Osoriz in 1173. It is Neoclassic and contains a Churrigueresque retablo from 1674 and a nice image of San Roque.

✶ Campo The village's ancient fountain is to the north of the Road. The mansions of the Villaboa and Luna families still sport their coats of arms. The Herrera-style parish church contains a small 18th-c. Churrigueresque retablo.

Next to the church is one of the largest live oaks (*encinas*) we have seen along the Road. This part of the valley is full of cherry trees, whose fruit always seems to be getting ripe as we walk through. With luck someone will offer you a branch.

68. PONFERRADA

Transportation and minerals have created Ponferrada. This site at the intersection of the Sil and Boeza Rivers, high on a crag that dominates the fertile central valley of the Bierzo, was already an ancient settlement when the Romans appropriated it. The village grew into a large city at the center of one of the Roman Empire's richest mining districts. The town was destroyed during the Visigoth invasions (ca. 456) and again by the Muslims in the 9th c. After its reconquest, it was rebuilt by Alfonso III el Magno. Bishop Osmundo of Astorga had a bridge constructed here for pilgrims in 1082. This bridge—reinforced with iron bars or perhaps with an iron railing—gave its name to the city: *Pons Ferrata*, Iron Bridge. In 1178, at the height of the pilgrimage, Ponferrada was entrusted to the Knights Templar to use as a base from which to protect the pilgrim roads. This they did until their expulsion from Spain a little over a hundred years later. The castle that commands the heights still retains a few elements of the Templars' construction.

In the Middle Ages Ponferrada was an important market town that early on outgrew its walls and sprawled across the river. It had a Frankish quarter and a Jewish quarter, which was located south of the castle along the river. Documents also cite a Jewish cemetery, at a place still called Campo judío, north of the bridge, about where the modern post office stands. The Jewish community was relatively well integrated with the rest of the town. In fact, Ponferrada resisted the 15th-c. laws requiring the forcible segregation of the Jewish neighborhoods, a resistance which lasted until 1484, when Queen Isabel sent an agent to ensure that the royal instructions were carried out.

In the late 15th c. warring noble families fiercely contested Ponferrada. In 1486 the Catholic Monarchs, in an attempt to end the strife, declared the city the property of the Crown. Ponferrada seems to have languished through the 16th c., and then it experienced a new economic boom in the 17th and 18th c., to judge from the fine public and private buildings constructed during that period. In 1882 the railroad to Ponferrada was completed. Yet in 1908, when it was officially made a city, it still had only some 3,000 inhabitants. The city's modern boom came with the exploitation of local coal deposits in the 1940s.

PILGRIMAGE
Ponferrada's iron bridge channeled pilgrim traffic. Before it was built, the Roman bridge, about a km. to the north, served pilgrims until it collapsed in the 18th c. and was replaced by a ferry. Clustered at the bridge's ends were the Iglesia de Santa María, a hospice, and the Ermita de San Blas. Nothing remains of any of them except 2 toponyms: San Blas, and Paso de la Barca. Today a modern bridge crosses the river there.

Ponferrada supported several hospices. The Hospital de la Reina at the entrance to the city was founded by Queen Isabel. In addition, the hospices of la Ponte Buesca, San Blas, San Juan, San Martín, San Nicolás, del Carmen, 2 hospices named San Lázaro, and the private hospice of Alvaro Pérez de Osorio lodged pilgrims in various parts of the city. They have all long since vanished.

📖 Domenico Laffi's ca. 1670 description of his visit to Ponferrada neatly combines the tourist and religious aspects of pilgrimage: "Ponferrada . . . [is] an excellent place that has . . . a large, attractive square, and many monasteries and fine houses. We stayed the night there, and next morning walked around the town. A funeral service was being performed, so we went into the church to observe the local customs. The close relatives of the deceased sit on a special bench while the Office is sung. After the service they go to the door of the church and give alms to the people leaving the church; and after this they go home, accompanied by all the mourners. They are dressed in black in a long garment like a monk's habit, with a tail and two sleeves that they trail along the ground. They wear a very large hat pulled down over their eyes, with a broad brim that falls down all round, so that you can hardly see who they are." [Laffi; trans. Hall (1997), 152–3]

MONUMENTS: 1. <u>Castle</u>. 2. Iglesia de San Andrés. 3. **Iglesia de Santa María de la Encina**. 4. Clock tower. 5. Ayuntamiento. 6. **Museo del Bierzo**.

1. <u>Castle</u>. The great medieval castle was erected over the pre-Roman *castro*, the Roman fort, and the Visigoth fort that was destroyed during Almanzor's raids in the 990s. Fernando II of León donated these ruins to the Templars in 1178. They built their enormous castle rapidly, between 1218 and 1282, but they got to enjoy the completed work for only 20 years.

📖 After the crusader Godfrey of Bouillon abandoned Jerusalem in 1118, 9 knights remained behind to protect pilgrims journeying to the holy cites. Because their house was near the Temple Mount, they termed themselves the Knights of the Temple, or Knights Templar. They adopted the rule of Saint Benedict and took vows of chastity, poverty, and obedience. During the 12th c. the growing Order waged war against the Saracens. Christian princes and wealthy private citizens donated lavishly to support the Templars' holy wars against the Muslims and to invest in their protection of highways. By the mid-13th c. some 20,000 Knights Templar were active in almost every part of Western Europe.

In Spain the Templars assisted in various campaigns against the Moors and played decisive roles in the reconquests of Valencia and the Balearic Islands. They were thanked with grants of lands, castles, towns, and urban districts, including one quarter of the Catalán cities of Tarragona and Lérida. Because the Order was both wealthy and international, it took on banking functions: you could deposit money in one place and withdraw it from another, carrying with you a letter of credit rather than heavy and tempting gold coins.

But before long the immense wealth, political power, and seemingly secretive ways of the Knights Templar aroused both fear and envy. When the Holy Land port city of Acre was lost in 1291 because—it was widely believed—the Templars had refused to fight, they began to lose prestige. Before long the Templars began to be regarded with similar opprobrium as the Jews. It was claimed that they were irreligious, that in their secret ceremonies they denied Christ and the Virgin, that they profaned the cross, that they adored demons, that they were all sodomites, and that they had sworn to enrich the Order through dishonesty. Many were arrested; some under torture confessed. In France a general edict of arrest was issued in 1307;

Spain followed a year later. The growing scandal about Templar excesses led the Vatican to dissolve the Order in 1312, and the Templars' vast holdings were dispersed.

After the dissolution of the Order in 1312, Alfonso XI entrusted the castle to the count of Lemos, Pedro Fernández de Castro, who added to it. Don Fadrique de Castilla inherited the castle in 1400. In 1467, during the *irmandiño* uprising (see ch. 76), Galician nobles took refuge in the castle, which was attacked, but not taken, by the mobs. In the dynastic wars of the late 15th c. Rodrigo Osorio, who opposed Fernando and Isabel, took the castle in 1483 by force. A settlement was negotiated. He vacated the site, then changed his mind and took it again in 1485. Unbelievably, the whole sordid process was repeated, and Osorio captured the castle a third time in 1507. This time the King's patience was at an end, and Fernando confiscated the castle for the Crown. He entrusted its care and defense to the Marqués de Villafranca, who ended up buying it from the Crown in 1558. The castle was garrisoned and attacked again during the early-19th-c. War of Independence, and subsequently was used as a quarry for buildings and sidewalks in the city.

On the west and north the castle is defended by cliffs that drop precipitously to the river, on the south by the heavily defended gate, and on the city side by enormous walls. Like many great castles, it served many functions simultaneously. It was a fort, a palace, a monastery, and a city in miniature, with its central plaza, reception hall, chapel, chapter house, and cemetery, as well as its stables, sleeping quarters, kitchens, and a dining room, its hospitality rooms for invited visitors, and its dungeons for visitors held under duress. The castle stuns with its size: 96 × 164 m. overall, nearly 16,000 square m.

The castle has been undergoing reconstruction ever since we have been visiting it, and clearly progress is being made. You may want to take a look at the castle exhibit in the Museo del Bierzo (see below) before you visit the castle itself. Though you still may have to stretch to picture these vast open spaces as a bustling castle-city, full of the clanking of blacksmiths, the shouts of young knights practicing at arms, the smells of the stables, the laundry flapping in the breeze, the giggles of the serving girls, and all of the colorful chaos and stench of a medieval castle in prime condition, it is worth an hour of your time to poke into whatever bits are currently open and to stroll the high ramparts, which offer broad views of the city and surrounding mountains.

• The **entrance gate** faces south. Like the entrances to many castles, it is a double gate. Attackers had to bridge the moat, fight through the barbican (the iron grille lowered to block the door), dodge the arrows from the bowmen in the 2 flanking towers, turn to the right (which put them at a disadvantage, most swordsmen being right-handed), and then breech a second defensive gate before—if they were lucky enough to still be alive and in fighting condition—confronting the massed troops waiting for them on the open ground.

The coats of arms over the entrance are a miniature history of the castle. You can see a cross, perhaps put there by the Templars; the yoke, arrows, and coat of arms of Fernando and Isabel's newly combined kingdom (prior to the 1492 addition of the pomegranate which symbolized the taking of Granada); the tau from the coat of arms of the Castro family; and Fadrique de Castilla's lion, castle, and zigzag staves.

• The **central tower** (*torre de homenaje*). You can still make out the Templar Latin motto, which translates: "If the Lord does not protect the city, those who guard it guard in vain."

2. Iglesia de San Andrés. The mostly 17th-c. church has a Baroque retablo and the Romanesque Cristo de las Maravillas, also called Cristo de los Templarios.

3. **Iglesia de Santa María de la Encina.** The 12th-c. church of Nuestra Señora de la Plaza was replaced with the current church between 1573 and 1660. Its elegant 17th-c. tower is sometimes called "La Giralda del Bierzo," likening it to the famous Moorish tower of the cathedral of Sevilla, which it does not resemble in any obvious way. The famous image of the **Virgen de la Encina** reputedly appeared miraculously in a tree trunk during the epoch of the Templars. It was made patroness of the Bierzo by papal order in 1958. It now stands in the center of the 1630 Baroque main retablo. On the north aisle wall is an almost naïve depiction of the **Last Judgment**, with souls in hell, purgatory, and waiting admittance into heaven. On the same wall is a fine 13th-c. Gothic crucified Christ.

However, it is the 3 **Baroque statues of Christ**, at the rear of the church, that rivet our attention. A patiently suffering, self-absorbed, almost otherworldly Christ on the cross is surrounded by 3 grieving figures. In a superbly emotive Pieta, Mary holds the dead body of her son in her lap. And in a coffin an emaciated dead Christ, stiff with rigor mortis, reminds worshipers of his human nature.

4. **Clock tower.** The tower was constructed over one of the gates of the medieval city walls. The coat of arms of Carlos I stands over the arch. Through the arch and along the street toward the church of Santa María are the old jail (now a museum, see below) and the Convent of the Madres Concepcionistas.

5. **Ayuntamiento.** This Baroque city hall was built from 1692 to 1705. Its most notable feature is the immense **imperial coat of arms** on the entrance.

6. **Museo del Bierzo.** A small museum has been installed in this former jail, which was constructed in the mid-16th c. Its collections are well displayed and well explained. Three rooms deal with the prehistory of the Bierzo, concentrating on the *castro* cultures. Another explains Roman mining operations. Another explains how archaeologists have determined how the castle was constructed over 400 years and displays artifacts from the excavations. Particularly interesting is the demythification of the Templars' contributions to the castle. One room contains linen-making implements and plays a video that explains the entire complex process. The basement contains temporary exhibits: at our last visit a photographic essay documented retablos in remote village churches all over the diocese.

The Bierzo region around Ponferrada is so rich in ancient and medieval monuments that pilgrims may want to spend an extra couple of days (for automobile visitors) or even more (for hikers). The high mountains that surround the Bierzo Valley, and the rivers that cut across it, mean that few of the access routes to these monuments are easy, and that all are beautiful and interesting. Here are 10 important sites. In our opinion, the first 3 all by themselves justify a trip to El Bierzo.

🚗 1. **Santiago de Peñalba** (19 km. south of Ponferrada). This village on a white rocky spur (*peña alba*) of the Montes Aquilianos was the center of a large community of *mozárabes*. Some of them joined the local hermits in building small monasteries and *ermitas* in the mountains surrounding the Bierzo Valley. Santiago's church was founded by San Genadio in the early 10th c. León's kings contributed to its building. The foundation walls of its monastery, which flourished until the 13th c., were discovered by archaeologists in 1985. Today the town derives its income from cherries, chestnuts, bees, and tourists.

The small **church** has the form of a Latin cross, with counterset apses. See how the **horseshoe arches of the entrance** are capped with other low-relief arches and are set into a square frame, an ensemble the Muslims called an *alfiz*. The **Corinthian capitals and marble columns** may well be reutilized from some other, perhaps Roman, structure. The church also retains bits of mural paintings. Its 10th-c. votive cross of Ramiro II is now displayed in León's San Marcos museum. The chalice of its Abbot Pelagio is in the Louvre in Paris.

On the mountain above the village is the cave of San Genadio. Below the cave a Roman canal directs water to distant mines.

🚗 2. **Las Médulas** (20 km. west). These **remains of Roman gold mines** are stunning for their size, color, weird shapes, and testimony to an ancient technology. In the 1st c. Romans noticed flecks of gold in the sandy soil, in a ratio of less than 1:1,000,000. The gold could be washed out if sufficient water could be brought to the site. More than 300 km. of canals channel water from the surrounding mountains to the Médula basin. Miners—archaeologists estimate some 60,000 slaves—dug out the sparkling soil by excavating long tunnels, and then washed the ore in huge sluices. The tailings and tunnels remain, reddish gold against the blue sky, set off by hundreds of enormous, dark green chestnut trees. The best overview is from the village of Orellán. For exploring the tunnels, a flashlight is useful, as well as sturdy shoes and clothes that you won't mind getting permanently stained.

🚗 3. **Cornatel** (10 km. west; Carretera N536, km. 13). This spectacular castle, perched on a crag halfway between Las Médulas and Ponferrada, is said to have been the site of the Templars' last resistance to their expulsion from Spain. It is one of the settings of Enrique Gil y Carrasco's 1835 Romantic novel *El señor de Bembibre* (see ch. 70).

👟 4. **Santo Tomás de las Ollas** (3 km. north, on the highway to Manzanal). The 10th-c. church is basically Mozarabic in style. There is a late-12th-c. **Romanesque doorway**. Note the curious way the slate is set on the corners of the building. Inside, the nave is Romanesque. The unique **Mozarabic** *cabecera* has a double horseshoe arch and a presbytery with a frieze of blind horseshoe arches. The **11-sided dome** is unique in Spain. In medieval times there was a ceramics factory nearby.

👟 5. **Iglesia de Nuestra Señora de Vizbayo** (2 km. south, in the village of Otero). This small Romanesque church, documented in 1028, is probably the oldest extant in the Bierzo. It mixes Mozarabic elements like horseshoe arches with others that are Romanesque.

🚗 6. **Ermita de la Santa Cruz** (14 km. south, just before San Pedro de Montes). The doorway conserves some Visigothic elements.

🚗 7. **San Pedro de Montes** (14 km. south). This important monastery was founded by San Fructuoso in the 7th c. and reconstructed by San Genadio toward the end of the 9th c. There are some early capitals in the tower and a Mozarabic inscription. The structure was rebuilt in the 12th c., and then again after it all collapsed in 1243. The sacristy was added in the 17th c. and the façade in 1756, when the cloister was also remodeled. Although much was destroyed in an 1842 fire, it has been tastefully reconstructed. Former monks are collectively remembered by the artful display of their bones.

Nearby is the pre-Roman *castro* of Rupiano.

8. Monasterio de Carracedo and **9. Monasterio de Corullón** (see ch. 69), and **10. Compludo** (see ch. 67).

69. PONFERRADA → VILLAFRANCA DEL BIERZO

Route 1: PONFERRADA → Compostilla → Columbrianos → Fuentes Nuevas → Camponaraya → [**Carracedo**] → Magaz → Cacabelos → Pieros → **Cerro de la Ventosa** → VILLAFRANCA DEL BIERZO

Route 2: PONFERRADA → Compostilla → Columbrianos → Fuentes Nuevas → Camponaraya → [**Carracedo**] → Magaz → Cacabelos → Pieros → **Corullón** → VILLAFRANCA DEL BIERZO

Route 2 is an alternate, unmarked route to Villafranca through Corullón. It adds about an hour and a half, but visits 3 high-quality Romanesque churches. We feel that both of these routes are equally rewarding.

During Visigothic times the Bierzo region was a center of religious fervor. The 7th-c. San Fructuoso and his disciple San Valerio founded several monasteries and inspired generations of hermit monks. Eventually there were 20 communities of hermits living in the Bierzo Mountains. Many of the small monasteries were destroyed during the Moorish invasions and then rebuilt by San Genadio in the late 9th c.

✳ Compostilla This ancient town, strategically perched over the river, has become an industrial suburb of Ponferrada. Today it belongs to the ENDESA Company, a large coal-processing concern. The 1960s company town is laid out in squares, with shady streets and lovely gardens. In the center of the complex, on the site of a medieval hermitage, stands the brand-new Nuestra Señora del Refugio, painted with pilgrimage iconography.

✳ Columbrianos Despite its modern appearance, Columbrianos is one of the oldest towns in the Bierzo. The parish church sits on a hillside just north of the town. The 2 large rounded hills further to the north each are capped with pre-Roman fortified *castros*. A necropolis was recently discovered near the water towers on the lower of the 2 hills.

✳ Camponaraya As you have probably noticed, you have been surrounded by vineyards for the last few km. In recent years the Bierzo has developed into an important wine-producing region, and this town is the site of a major wine cooperative.

Camponaraya has a church of San Ildefonso. During the Middle Ages the town maintained 2 hospices.

The main pilgrim Road proceeds from here to Cacabelos, but a worthwhile detour of 2 km. lets you visit the important monastery of Carracedo.

🐚 **Carracedo.** This early monastery, founded by Vermudo II in 990, incorporated an even earlier royal palace of Ordoño III. The monastery was intended to serve as a royal pantheon, much as San Juan de la Peña for Aragón or Santa María de Nájera for Navarra. It was extensively rebuilt ca. 1138 by Castilla's Alfonso VII. Ca. 1203 it affiliated with the Cistercians. Carracedo controlled 31 farms in the district, raising wheat, olives, grapes, flax, and fruit. In fact, at its height Carracedo owned estates from the Río Órbigo all the way to Galicia. From 1505 until the 19th c. it housed a community of Bernardian monks and prospered enough to be able to construct several new buildings. These were for the most part destroyed during its 1812 occupation by French troops.

What exists today is an anthology of construction techniques and styles. The delicately columned **chapter house** is 12th-c. Romanesque. The **royal palace** dates from the 13th c. It has a nice small rose window and interesting vaulting; one of the keystones depicts a *crismón*. The entrance to the kitchen has a 13th-c. **tympanum** depicting the death of the Virgin, surrounded by the Apostles. There are 3 cloisters (16th-, 17th-, and 18th-c.). Among the "modern" sections are the kitchen, tower, and Neoclassic church (with late Romanesque statues of Alfonso VII and the abbot Florencio). Largely in ruins following the 1836 *desamortización*, the buildings were consolidated in 1991 and now house a fascinating museum.

✳ Magaz The town has a small church of San Esteban and *ermitas* of San Juan and San Blas. In medieval times there was a hospice here.

✳ Cacabelos In existence since the 10th c., this village on the Río Cúa was destroyed by an early 12th-c. earthquake. It was rebuilt in 1108 by Bishop Diego Gelmírez and belonged to him personally. In fact, it pertained to the Compostela diocese until the 19th c. From 15th-c. tax records we learn that the town had a modest Jewish community as well.

Cacabelos is a typical long, thin Road town. In medieval times it was an important commercial center and supported 6 hospices: Santiago; de la Villa, now San Juan Bautista; Santa Catalina, documented in 1511; and the private hospices of Inés Domínguez and of Alfonso Cabrito. The Plaza San Lázaro, with its fountain, was formerly outside the walls and was the site of a hospice-leprosarium. In addition there were 8 other religious institutions.

Cacabelos has a number of other sites of interest:
Prada de Tope. At the entrance to Cacabelos is a private regional anthropological museum of sorts grafted onto a *mesón*, gift shop, and small factory where Bierzo products are prepared for shipping to customers around the globe. On our last

visit a dozen white-clad women were boiling and shelling freshly gathered chest-nuts.

Nuestra Señora de la Plaza (aka Santa María in Viam Francorum). The 16th-c. church preserves some minor Romanesque elements in its apse (which, strangely, is now a lateral chapel). On the modern concrete tympanum is a tiny 13th-c. Virgin, probably brought from another location.

Just before the bridge at the exit from town, on the right, are an old mill and an ancient wood olive press.

Santuario de las Angustias. This substantial *ermita* contains a retablo that for some reason depicts the child Jesus playing cards with San Antonio de Padua.

✷ **Pieros** According to an inscription, Pieros's Church of San Martín de Tours was consecrated in 1086 by Osmundo, the bishop of Astorga who built the iron bridge in Ponferrada. Pieros had a hospice administered by the Templars and also a lepers' hospice of San Lázaro (sometimes called the *Malatería*), documented in the 15th c.

Just beyond Pieros is the cutoff to Route 2, the detour to see the Romanesque churches of Corullón.

✷ **Cerro de la Ventosa** The large circular hill to the south of the paved road was the Castrum Bergidum of the Romans that gave the name Bierzo to this region. The western side of the old Celtiberian defensive wall has been recently excavated and is easily discernible if you look back from about 1 km. beyond the Cerro. On the other hand, we recommend that you climb the hill, both for the walls and for the view. A path just beyond Pieros leads to the top, and another on the west side snakes down through the vineyards to join the pilgrimage Road about 1 km. further along.

📖 The *castro* culture flourished from the 8th c. B.C.E. until the 2nd c. C.E. The semi-nomadic hunters and gatherers who had settled the northwestern third of the Peninsula were mostly Celtic. Around the 8th c. the tribes began to construct permanent villages. These were located near rivers. They chose flat hilltops or terraced hillsides that offered natural defenses, and they enhanced the defenses by constructing moats and walls. Their houses, usually semicircular, clustered against the inside of the defensive wall, leaving the center of the village for workshops, kilns, forges, and the like. The small size of these villages, generally no more than a couple of dozen houses, suggests that they were inhabited by extended clans. When the area was conquered by Rome—with great difficulty—the conquerors tended to appropriate the best *castros* for themselves. The Romans' main interest in the Bierzo was its mineral wealth, so that the smaller *castros* frequently became mining camps for the then-enslaved local population. More than 120 *castros* have been located in northwest Spain.

Route 2:

✷ **Corullón** This little town, the highlight of the second route to Villafranca, is strung out along the Río Burbia. It is the site of 3 extraordinary Romanesque churches.

✷ **San Esteban**. After its consecration in 1086, the church almost immediately collapsed. A new church was built from 1093 to 1100, financed by a local lord with better knowledge of the newest architecture of his time. The 17th-c. reforms replaced the apse and barrel vault. The Romanesque tower with its twinned window (recalling Frómista and Jaca) is topped with a modern bell. The **entrance** shows similarities with Compostela's Puerta de la Azabachería (before 1100) and the Puerta de las Platerías, which was being built about the same time. Its decorated archivolts, its capital moldings (*cimacios*) with palm leaves, its foliated capitals with nude men playing trumpets and symmetrically opposed birds, and its tympanum resting on lions' heads—all recall the Compostela model. The eaves are supported by a vivid series of **corbels**, on bestial, moral, human, and explicitly sexual themes.

✳ **San Miguel**. This mid-12th-c. church has a single nave and a semicircular apse. The buttressing tower was added later and the bells later still. It is noted for its **entrance capitals** (1 foliated capital is pre-Romanesque, reutilized from some other monument). Its **arcade** of columns and capitals depicting beasts and humans recalls San Isidoro de León.

On the hill above Corullón are remnants of a 14th-c. castle.

San Fiz. This simple, unadorned church, halfway between Corullón and Villafranca, is documented in the 13th c. In the 18th, when the *espadaña* was constructed, the church belonged to the Knights of San Juan de Jerusalén.

70. Villafranca del Bierzo

HISTORY

Judging from the number of pre-Roman *castros* in the immediate vicinity, this Road town has been an important communications center since antiquity. As is often the case, geography tells why: Villafranca lies at the confluence of the Burbia and Valcarce Rivers at the west end of the rich Bierzo basin, at the foot of the narrow valley leading up to the Cebreiro pass. The key location attracted merchants early on, for a document in 943 already calls the village Villafranca ("Foreigners' town"). Its major growth came with the pilgrimage in the early 12th c. By mid-12th c., half the inhabitants were foreign: French, Italian, English, German, Catalán, Jewish, Flemish, Portuguese, and even Scandinavian. In 1192 Alfonso IX of León granted a new charter to encourage further growth.

> 📖 With growth came the usual urban problems. According to a 15th-c. document, Villafranca's "streets were narrow and because of their size and their darkness, at night all sorts of crimes were committed. There were lots of poor people who had nothing at all. Its citizens were peasants who sold from the doorways of their houses their wine, bread, fish, fruit, olive oil, straw, barley, lambs and kids. Even the nobles did this."

From the late 12th to the late 15th c. the Osorio family ruled Villafranca. In 1486 the Catholic Monarchs established the Marquesado de Villafranca. The second Marqués, Pedro Álvarez de Toledo (1494–1553) built the castle.

> 📖 Pedro Álvarez de Toledo served Spain for many years as viceroy in Naples, and one of his illegitimate daughters married into the Medici family. His powerful friends included both the founder of the Jesuits, Ignacio de Loyola, and the Pope, who at Pedro's urging raised the priory of Villafranca to the status of abbey. Many of Villafranca's nobles who served with him in Italy returned with Italian tastes for art and luxury. Their mansions with their coats of arms line Villafranca's Calle de Agua. The third and fourth *marqueses* also served in Italy.

Unfortunately, Villafranca's development suffered several setbacks. Plague decimated the town in 1589. Floods destroyed much along the river in 1715. The French despoiled the city in 1808, to be driven out by English troops in January 1809. The English went on a rampage, wrecking the castle, robbing the churches, and burning the municipal archives, until General John Moore stopped them by having the leaders shot. In 1810 the city again changed hands, occasioning even more damage.

The Cortes of 1822 declared the Bierzo a province separate from León. During its 2-year independence Villafranca served as its capital.

Today Villafranca's center occupies the narrow terraces above the river plain. Steep flights of stairs lead both up and down from the picturesque Plaza Mayor. Unlike in Ponferrada, the modern Industrial Revolution has passed Villafranca by, allowing it to retain much of its late medieval and Renaissance atmosphere, particularly along the Calle de Agua and the narrow streets that parallel the river. Ironically, the increased tourist and pilgrimage traffic may change that. In the last few years modern hotels have replaced several of the medieval structures along the river, and many others have been allowed to go to ruin. Despite these changes, and the addition of several large, characterless apartment blocks, for the moment Villafranca remains one of the pilgrimage Road's most atmospheric "old towns."

PILGRIMAGE

Villafranca was the end of the tenth stage of the pilgrimage as laid out in the 12th-c. *Guide.* The town supported several hospices. In the early 11th c. the San Lázaro hospice tended to lepers: the site now holds the Iglesia de San Francisco. Santiago, now the Colegio de la Divina Pastora, near the Alameda, catered to general pilgrims. The hospice of San Juan, founded in the late 12th c., was at the end of the Calle de Agua. The Cluniacs added a hospice principally for French pilgrims. The medieval hospice of San Roque has become the Convento de la Anunciada. We know of 2 others: the 13th-c. private hospice of Pedro Veiga and the Sancti Spiritus. Künig warned late-15th-c. pilgrims off the wine in Villafranca: "Drink with care, because it makes some people dizzy and they let it flow like melted candle wax."

> 📖 Much in the same guise as the medieval private hospices, since the early 1980s Jesús Jato and his family have maintained an idiosyncratic plastic-tent hospice in front of the Iglesia de Santiago. Because the hospice was destroyed by fire and rebuilt a couple of times, Jato named it "El Fénix." The entire Santiago Road is sketched on the front half of its rustic bar. In 1998 Jato had begun constructing a new stone hospice on the site. In many ways, Jesús Jato seems to embody the medieval tradition of selfless hospitality to pilgrims. Like Padre José Alonso Marroquín's garlic soups in San Juan de Ortega, Jato's *queimadas* have become famous. He reports hosting 17,420 pilgrims from Jan. 1 through Nov. 1, 1999.

MONUMENTS: 1. **Iglesia de Santiago.** 2. **Iglesia de San Francisco.** 3. **Iglesia de San Nicolás.** 4. Iglesia de Santa María de Cluniaco. 5. Convento de las Franciscanas reformadas (aka La Anunciada). 6. Calle de Agua. 7. Castillo.

1. **Iglesia de Santiago.** The north portal of this Romanesque church, founded by the bishop of Astorga in 1186, is called the **Puerta del Perdón.** According to tradition, pilgrims too sick to go on could enter the church through this door, take communion, and receive pardon for their sins, a privilege reconfirmed by the 15th-c. Popes Urban II and Calixto III.

> 📖 Locals relate that in 1965 a French pilgrim who took sick here and knew the tradition begged authorities to open the door for him. He prayed, recovered, and went home content.

The **capitals** on the early-13th-c. north portal focus on the 3 Wise Men. We observe them riding to Herod's palace, animals coming to see them, and their siesta outside the gates of Bethlehem. Other capitals depict the Crucifixion, various animals—both real and fantastic—and vegetable motifs. The outermost archivolt has a small Christ in Majesty surrounded by pairs of Apostles. The church's interior, restored and given a new ceiling in 1958, is now used for exhibitions.

2. **Iglesia de San Francisco** (aka Nuestra Señora de los Angeles). Tradition holds that San Francisco himself founded this church in 1214 on his pilgrimage to Compostela. The entrance to the current 15th-c. Gothic church retains a few 13th-c. Romanesque elements, including a zigzag archivolt and some small stone heads probably meant to represent Franciscan monks. The door was probably moved from an early Franciscan monastery, built at the site of an even earlier municipal pilgrim hospice.

Inside are a late-17th-c. Baroque retablo and several nice Gothic sepulchers of the Marqués de Villafranca's family. They paid for the renovations, so the tau from their coat of arms is woven into the church's decorations. In a chapel on the left is the ca. 1555 **retablo de la Inmaculada**, replete with Renaissance decorative motifs, probably the best Renaissance retablo in the Bierzo.

The church's most stunning artistic monument is its **Mudéjar-style ceiling**, one of the largest in northern Spain, with beams painted in the 15th c. The intricate geometric patterns and the remnants of the formerly bright painting combining floral motifs with the arms of the Counts of Lemos that highlighted its designs must have made it difficult to keep one's eyes on the altar and one's mind on the mass.

During the mid-19th c., after the *desamortización*, this church served for a time as a military barracks. It has been restored recently.

3. **Iglesia de San Nicolás** (aka the Colegio de los Jesuitas). Founded in 1638, the costs for this church were underwritten by Gabriel Robles, a local boy who got rich mining silver in Peru. Domenico Laffi celebrated mass here on his 1673 pilgrimage. Since 1913 the church has pertained to the Paulist Fathers.

📖 The famous Jesuit essayist Juan Eusebio Nieremberg (1595–68) lived and wrote at the Colegio de San Nicolás. He composed several important books on mysticism and ascetic philosophy, as well as biographies of Jesuit saints. His works are known for their wide range of sources and their complex Baroque structure.

The building's most important feature is its **façade**. The original construction was severe and symmetrical, with 2 massive cubes bisected by an Herrera-style clock tower. The monumental stairway and Baroque decoration on the left were added later. They create an interesting interplay of geometric forms and contrasts between bare stone and intricate deep-relief escutcheons. Whether they unbalance and destroy the harmony of the original or whether they enhance an otherwise cold and dull façade is an open question.

Inside is a modest Baroque cloister. In the center of the church's main retablo is the Cristo de la Esperanza, patron of Villafranca. Because of its exotic appearance, people speculate that it may have been brought from America.

4. Iglesia de Santa María de Cluniaco (Cruñego). In 1120 Urraca, Alfonso VI's sister, gave this church to Cluny. The medieval church maintained a hospice for French pilgrims. In 1529 the Marqués de Villafranca funded the rebuilding of this church with monies raised through bulls authorized by the Marqués's friend, Pope Clement VII. The Pope made the former Benedictine monastery a *colegiata*, which within a few years controlled 60 parishes in the region. After a disastrous fire in 1754, the building was renovated in the 1790s. Work was not finished until the 18th c.

The church's overall design is by Rodrigo Gil de Hontañón. Don't miss the 16th-c. Plateresque retablo de la Trinidad in the Berruguete style. The central image of the **Trinity** is stunning, with a solid, smiling, seated God the Father lovingly sustaining his crucified Son. The background of fleecy clouds and *putti* and the overall sense of grandeur and serenity are typical of the best Italianate Renaissance sculpture. The cupola exudes confident Renaissance simplicity.

5. The Franciscanas reformadas (aka Convento de la Anunciada). This late-17th-c. convent occupies the site of the former Hospital de San Roque.

📖 María de Toledo y Osorio, daughter of the Marqués de Villafranca, refused the marriage arranged by her father, declaring she wished to be a nun. He locked her in the castle of Corullón, from which she escaped down a rope of twisted sheets. When she took her vows, he built this church for her, announcing, "If you must be a nun, you will be the founder." She was prioress from 1606 until her death in 1631. She also won modest fame as a poetess.

The façade is Italianate. Inside is the tomb of San Lorenzo de Brindisi.

📖 Lorenzo de Brindisi (1559–1619) was a Capuchin preacher endorsed by Pope Clement VIII, who gave him the mission to convert Rome's Jews. After a successful preaching campaign, he held various administrative and diplomatic posts for the Curia. As vicar general of the Christian Forces, he helped Emperor Rudolph push the Turks back from the gates of Venice. While on a diplomatic mission to Portugal, he died of gout and was buried in Villafranca.

In 1599 the Marqués brought the painter Jusepe Serena from Italy to paint a series of portraits of male hermits for the nuns' convent. Among the best are Bernardo, with his white habit and the apparition of the Virgin; Blas, shown with savages; Gil, with a wounded stag; Jerónimo at his writing table, wearing his cardinal's cape; and Antonio Abad, with a rosary and tau staff. These greenish blue landscapes with the hermits in the foreground are in a variety of Italian Renaissance styles. You can find the influence of Leonardo da Vinci in the glowing cities emerging from the backgrounds and in the dark, foreground vegetation. You will find touches of Patinir in the conventional blue-green craggy mountains that are pierced by bays and rivers. Flemish Mannerist influence is seen in the more realistic landscapes with exuberant vegetation.

6. Calle de Agua (aka Ribadeo). The street is lined with the mansions and coats of arms of the Torquemada, Álvarez de Toledo, and Omaña families. The romantic novelist Gil y Carrasco was born on this street.

📖 Enrique Gil y Carrasco (1815–46) was a diplomat, poet, essayist, and Romantic novelist whose 1844 *El señor de Bembibre* takes a tragic view of the expulsion of the Knights Templar from Spain. Almost all of the action of this novel takes place in the Bierzo, and its descriptions of local sites make fine evening reading for this part of the Road.

---

7. Castillo. The ancestral home of the Pimentel family, named the Marqueses de Villafranca by the Catholic Monarchs in 1486. Today the castle belongs to the Álvarez de Toledo family, the counts of Peña-Ramiro. The current castle was built

in the 1490s, burned by the French in 1812, and recently restored. Over the entry arch are the arms of the Pimentel family.

Villafranca has several other ecclesiastical monuments you might find interesting:
- The church of the Franciscanas Descalzas, built by Pedro Osorio in 1606.
- The Convento de la Concepción, which has a 19th-c. neo-Gothic retablo and an early Gothic crucifix.
- The Colegiata, which has a Neoclassic retablo from the 19th c.
- The Convento de San José (Calle del Agua) is 17th-c., with a splendid Baroque retablo.

Route: VILLAFRANCA DEL BIERZO → Pereje → Trabadelo → Portela de Valcárcel → Ambasmestas → Ambascasas → Vega de Valcarce → Ruitelán → Herrerías de Valcarce → Hospital Inglés → La Faba → Laguna de Castilla → O CEBREIRO

Although the legal limit of León extends almost to O Cebreiro, once you leave Villafranca the village architecture and culture are Galician. The valley villages are classic Road towns, strung out along the pilgrimage trail. The lateral villages, glimpsed on both sides of the valley, are smaller, more like hamlets than towns, with 4 or 5 large stone houses clustered around a tiny stone church with an *espadaña* or small square stone tower devoid of exterior decoration. The number of cows increases. Stone fences or bramble rows divide the fields into smaller and smaller plots. It is clear that most of these villages until recently practiced subsistence agriculture. You may still see oxcarts drawn up beside village houses (we saw several in every village in the 1970s). The older women wear dark clothing and wrap themselves in shawls and head kerchiefs as they go out into their garden plots. Mud and cow pies are a way of life here, and almost all the older farmers wear rubber boots or wooden shoes (*abarcas*) that are easy to hose down. The language changes, too: the vowels diphthongize and the rhythms of speech become more musical with each meter you climb.

Because of the rugged geography of the Valcarce Valley, in medieval times bandits made the 10-km. stretch of the Road just beyond Villafranca extremely dangerous. Two castles were erected to guard the route and to control the bandit problem: Castro de Veiga and Sarracín, both today in ruins. The Road is still dangerous, but now because of the trucks whizzing by on their way to and from Galicia. The new 4-lane *autopista*, under construction as we write, is bound to change that for the better, and—as far as pilgrims are concerned—almost everything else for the worse.

✱ Pereje Doña Urraca donated the hospice of Pereje to the monastery of Cebreiro in 1118. She charged it with helping pilgrims, which it did until the *desamortización* of 1835. The village of Pereje seems to have changed little in the last 2 centuries: the newest building is the pilgrim *albergue*. The great curved balcony that you will see on the house on the right as you exit town may be the longest balcony on the whole pilgrimage Road.

> 📖 Pereje is most famous for a lengthy lawsuit between O Cebreiro, which owned the hospice, and the Cluniac monks of Villafranca, who owned the town. Because King Alfonso IX of León did not have full jurisdiction over a matter of ecclesiastical property, the bishops of Astorga, Compostela, and Lugo handled the case. Their decision was appealed to the abbot of Samos. When he threw up his hands, the case went to Pope Urban II, who settled in favor of O Cebreiro.

✱ Trabadelo In 895 Alfonso III gave this town to Compostela. There is little left of the old town except a few stone houses and the Church of San Nicolás that reputedly contains a Romanesque Virgin. Two monuments were located between km. 419 and 420. As late as 1766 there stood the chapel and hospice of San Lázaro and just beyond it the Capilla de Nuestra Señora de la Asunción. Both have vanished without a trace.

The entrance to Trabadelo is lined with century-old chestnut trees that bloom in June and are harvested in late October. A lumber mill is the town's principal industry, and you may see logs piled along the side the highway. Several people in the village raise bees for honey. Look for hives on the hillside to your right.

At the exit of town, on the right just before the road to Parada, stood the castle of Auctares. Its lords supported themselves by taxing (i.e., extorting from) pilgrims, until Alfonso VI put a stop to the practice in 1072.

✱ Portela de Valcárcel In the 19th c. this hamlet's 16 houses were home to 70 inhabitants.

✱ Ambasmestas At the center of the village is a small 18th-c. stone church with a Churrigueresque retablo of little note. To the north, on the road to Balboa, on a bluff above the Río Balboa, there are remains of another castle.

✱ Vega de Valcarce The wide spot (*vega*) in the valley is better suited for agriculture than most locations along the Río Valcarce. Hence the village's existence and name. You will see vegetable gardens along the river, and tall stalks of chard (*berzas*) for making the famous *caldo gallego*. The village was large enough in the 15th c. to support a small Jewish quarter. The village's major claim to fame? Carlos V spent the night of March 20, 1520, here on his way to Compostela.

The tower of the small, heavy church of Santa Magdalena was added in 1587.

🥾 On a high hill to the southwest, across the Río Valcarce from Vega, was the castle of **Sarracín**, founded in the 9th c. Little is known about the early history of the castle, except that at one point the lords of Sarracín owned 35 small towns in the area. Current ruins are from the 14th or 15th c., when the castle was one of eight belonging to the Marqués de Villafranca. You can still make out the double wall on the castle's west side, 2 stone towers, and the remains of several interior buildings. On three and a half of the castle's 4 sides, sheer precipices protect it from unfriendly neighbors. The round-trip climb, about 45 minutes, will take you through a grove of age-old chestnut trees. We recognize that this day's walk is a long one, and almost all uphill. But if you think you can muster the energy, we believe you will be pleased with this short detour.

✱ Ruitelán In a leftover medieval historical anomaly, the 15th-c. church of San Juan Bautista belongs to the diocese of León rather than to Astorga. The chapel on the north as one exits Ruitilán is dedicated to San Froilán (833–905), who had a hermitage in these mountains before becoming bishop of León.

✱ Herrerías de Valcarce The large building across the river to the northeast was the town's principal forge, processing iron ore from the nearby mines of Caurel. In the late 17th c. it was described by the pilgrim Domenico Laffi:

[The place] is situated on the riverbank. Here they excavate iron from the hills and bring it to the village, where there is a furnace for smelting it. They have a large iron hammer which is driven by waterpower, as well as forging tongs and bellows. All these tools are of immense size. The village is small and nearly all its huts are roofed with straw. [Laffi; trans. Hall (1997), 155–6]

Excavations near the village's threshing floor (*era*) have discovered medieval pilgrim remains.

✳ **Hospital Inglés** Judging from its name, a hospice here was run by or belonged to the English. Even so, it is cited as early as 1178 as belonging to the Compostela Cathedral. Either way, it seems to have left no physical remains. In 1495 the German pilgrim Künig von Vach, who was not fond of mountains, described the split in the road here:

> [After leaving Villafranca] you will cross a bridge. At the second bridge, if you listen to me you won't go up to Allefaber [La Faba]. Leave it on the left and follow along the road to the right of the bridge.

Ignore his advice unless you want to add a couple of days to your route.

✳ **La Faba** Its small church of San Andrés, rebuilt in the 18th c., is the last parish in the diocese of Astorga, and its trees are the last before the windswept mountain heights of Traviesa that lead to O Cebreiro.

✳ **Laguna de Castilla** Although this is the last town in Castilla—the border is marked with a stele a few hundred m. to the west—this town is Galician to its core. Here you will see your first *pallozas* (see ch. 72). There is also an enormous corncrib (*hórreo*), again the first of the thousands you will see in Galicia. Take time to study it, because besides being your first, this *hórreo* is probably the largest and best preserved of the traditional *hórreos* you will see between here and Compostela. It is of a style peculiar to these mountains: large and square, resting on crisscrossed wooden beams, and with a thatched roof similar to the Celtic-style houses.

From here to O Cebreiro the Road climbs through brushy, open country, dominated by white broom, laburnum, and gorse, and punctuated by occasional groves of scrub oak. You might spot a small burrow with a cone of excavated earth at its entrance, home to the northern water rat, a relatively rare rodent who inhabits these heights.

72. O Cebreiro

History

This saddle of land, at the top of the 1,293-m. Cebreiro pass, has been occupied since ancient times. To the southeast lie the iron-rich Caurel Mountains. To the east rises the formidable Sierra de Ancares. A Roman way station here protected the road through the mountains west into Galicia. A battle here in 968 kept Norman pirates from entering Castilla. But the town did not come alive until the epoch of the pilgrimage. Medieval documents frequently refer to "Zebuaril" and "Zeberrium." The 12th-c. CC *Guide*, with what may be an ironic reference to the normally beastly weather on this high pass, calls it "Mons Februari."

In our first visit to O Cebreiro in 1974, the principal occupation of the handful of inhabitants was dairy farming. Since then the village has more than doubled in size. In 1998 we found a half dozen taverns, restaurants, and bed-and-breakfasts. It is clear that with the commercialization of the Road and of Spain's regional cultures, during this particular phase of its long history O Cebreiro is milking the seven fat cows of tourism.

Pilgrimage

The hospice here may go back to the 9th c. What is certain is that in 1072 Alfonso VI confirmed the privileges of the Benedictine monks of San Giraldo d'Aurillac who ran the hospice. From that time on, donations poured in. Doña Urraca gave the village of Pereje (see ch. 71) to the hospice in 1118. During 1186–87 Fernando II granted the hospice several houses in Villafranca and Santa María de Bercianos, free grazing rights in the mountains, and a cash endowment. For the next hundred years the successor kings made additional donations. Even so, when the Catholic Monarchs visited O Cebreiro in 1486 on their way to Compostela, they noted the poor state of the hospice. They donated 2 large gold nuggets and asked Pope Innocent VIII to transfer authority from the French Benedictines to the church of San Benito el Real in Valladolid. This he did, and he asked the bishops of León and Avila to take charge of its rebuilding. Young Carlos V confirmed the restored monastery's privileges on the occasion of his visit on March 21, 1520. The church sustained a small community of monks until the 1835 *desamortización*.

By tradition, the Holy Grail from which Christ drank wine at the Last Supper was hidden in O Cebreiro. In the 14th c. the Grail, an incredulous priest, and a wicked snowstorm combined to produce a famous miracle. A peasant from the hamlet of Barjamayor trudged up to Cebreiro in a snowstorm to hear mass. At the very moment he came in, the priest was raising the sacred host for the consecration. The skeptical priest berated the peasant for coming all that way in a storm just for a bit of bread and wine. At that instant the bread and wine literally turned into flesh and blood. Pope Innocent VIII certified the truth of the miracle in 1487. The miracle has been widely celebrated in painting, sculpture, and verse, such as this early-15th-c. poem by a Licenciado Molina:

Un caso ynefable - tambien dezir quiero	I want to tell you - a miraculous story
que en una ostia - que fue consagrada	about a host - which was being consecrated.
en carne perfecta - uereys trasformada	You will see changed - into perfect flesh

lo que cubierto - estaua primero	what at first - was [its] hidden [nature].
que un clerigo idiota - que	An idiot of a priest - who was
ensi lo profiero	offering it
dudando ser cierta - la consa-	doubted the truth - of the
gración	consecration.
le fue demostrada - tan santa	The holy vision - was demonstrated
uisión	to him,
según oy en día - se esta en	as it is today - in O Cebreiro.
el zebrero.	

The particles remaining from the miracle were eventually placed in a silver reliquary donated by Queen Isabel herself. The church's statue of the Virgin is said to have inclined her head so as to better view the miracle. Today she is known as la Virgen del Milagro, attracting pilgrims to her feast days of September 8 and 9.

MONUMENTS: 1. **Iglesia de Santa María**. 2. *Palloza* museum. 3. Valiña monument.

1. **Iglesia de Santa María la Real** (aka San Benito). In 1962 excavators found the meager foundations of a pre-Romanesque church under the streets of the village. Between 1965 and 1971 they rebuilt it from the ground up. Inside, all that remains of the medieval church are the Romanesque baptismal font and the chalice and paten. The statue of Christ on the altar is a reproduction of the original, which has been removed to the Archeological Museum in Madrid.

2. *Palloza* **Museum.** The *pallozas*, low, oval, stone houses, with ridge-hugging thatched roofs, are remnants of an ancient architectural style that goes back to Celtic times. They are found by archaeologists wherever there have been Celtic communities, from northern Scotland and Ireland to Brittany, Galicia, and the mountains of northwestern Morocco. Their rounded walls and aerodynamic straw roofs (*celme*), lashed firmly with twisted sprigs of broom (*veos*) to wooden ridge-poles against the fierce mountain winds, are perfectly adapted to their environment. *Pallozas* tend to have 2 rooms: one for animals and the other for humans. Generally both sets of inhabitants enter through a single door. *Pallozas* have no chimneys: smoke escapes through the straw roof, under which are hung joints of meat and sausages to be cured for eating during the long winters. Within the stone oval, the family side of the house is often divided into 2 levels by a wooden platform loft, with sleeping quarters upstairs, and the family kitchen, living quarters, and work spaces below.

You can visit one *palloza* that has been turned into a kind of local anthropology **museum**. Walking through the village, you will see others in various stages of reconstruction.

In 1974 we and our company of student-pilgrims, sleeping by the grace of don Elías Valiña in the loft of one of the *pallozas*, were awakened in the pitch-black wee hours of the morning by the noisy and redolent birth of a calf downstairs.

3. **Valiña monument.** The modern recuperation of O Cebreiro is largely the work of Father Elías Valiña Sampedro, the parish priest, who in addition to spending most of his time in these remote mountains, was a superb scholar.

> 📖 Valiña's 2 fundamental books on the pilgrimage Road (*Caminos a Compostela*, winner of the 1961 Premio Nebrija, and *El Camino de Santiago: Estudio Histórico Jurídico*, the 1978 Nebrija Prize winner) helped launch the field of modern pilgrimage studies. He also founded the journal *Peregrino*. Valiña's most widely read book, *El Camino de Santiago* (1985), was the first of the modern guides to the Road for walking pilgrims. His book introduced the format of map and text on facing pages.

In addition to his historical studies, Valiña was a dedicated anthropologist who scoured the mountains for artifacts of rural Galician culture and who oversaw the restoration of O Cebreiro's *pallozas* and the creation of the town's small museum. We can attest personally that he could also cook up a tasty stew and deliver a bone-jarring cup of coffee. Moreover, the concrete steles that mark the Road in Galicia are his doing, motivated—as was most everything he did—by his belief in the importance of recovering the Santiago pilgrimage for our times. In the 12th and 13th c. people were canonized for less.

Don Elías Valiña died in 1990. His bust in front of the church, erected almost immediately, is now covered with dedicatory plaques. On the church wall in 1996 we saw a painting recounting the Grail miracle, with faces of Jesus, Santiago, and Elías Valiña worked into the narration. By 1998 it had been removed as inappropriate.

Our first climb up the long mountain to O Cebreiro was on a day of record-breaking heat. One of our pilgrims, Beckie Sue Smith, was having a particularly hard time with the climb, and since the path from La Faba to O Cebreiro was clearly visible she told us to go ahead and that she would be along shortly. An hour went by, and we got nervous when she didn't appear. Finally, just as we were about to send out searchers, she staggered in, with an ecstatic expression on her face. "When I couldn't walk any more, I lay down by a bush to take a short nap, and when I awoke my ears were filled with the sound of angels singing. I was sure I had died and gone to heaven." "Close," we told her, "It was don Elías Valiña, entertaining the cows with a Bach *Magnificat* from the powerful loudspeaker system he has installed on the tower of the church."

73. O Cebreiro → Triacastela

Route: O CEBREIRO → Liñares → San Roque → Hospital da Condesa → Padornelo → Alto do Poio → Fonfría del Camino → Biduedo → Filloval → [As Pasantes → Ramil] → TRIACASTELA

To the north there is a splendid view of the Sierra de O Courel and the watershed of the Lor River, dotted by small villages. The path west from O Cebreiro flanks the ridge top, through fields scrubby with Scotch broom (*piornos*). The spiky green plants bordering the path are wild absinthe (*ajenjo*).

✳ Liñares This town, mentioned in an 8th-c. document and then in the 12th-c. CC, derived its name from the flax fields here that supplied linen for the looms in the Hospital do Cebreiro. The church of San Esteban, built from a chalky white stone prior to 1120, was restored in 1963. At that time the village had 4 inhabitants.

✳ San Roque To the right of this 1,264–m. pass was the Ermita de San Roque. Today J. Acuña's recent bronze statue of Santiago fighting the wind marks the pass. The rocks on this ridge are limestone (which is uncommon along the Road in Galicia), and the flowers that bloom here in the spring in profusion are therefore uncommon in most of the rest of the region: pimpernel (*pimpinela*), wild garlic (*ajo*), and blue lilies (*lirio azul*). The path borders a large grove of ash trees interspersed with occasional birch (*abedules*), holly (*acebos*), and hazelnuts (*avellanos*). This is a good place to search the sky for harriers (*aguiluchos*; hawks with long tails and broad wings) and short-toed eagles (*águilas culebreras*; small eagles streaked white underneath).

✳ Hospital da Condesa The only remnant of any hospice here is the town's name. Legend says that Egilo, wife of Conde Gatón, the repopulator of the Bierzo, founded one here in the 9th c. There was a church here in 1130. But the church you see today, with its scallop shells on the door and its tower with the cross of Santiago, is almost entirely a product of construction in 1963.

✳ Padornelo This hamlet, belonging to the bishop of Santiago, contained a priory of the Hospitallers of San Juan de Jerusalén. Its church of San Juan dates from the late 19th c. The modern cemetery is the site of an old pilgrim hospice and the former church of Santa María Magdalena. In 1985 Padornelo had 3 inhabitants.

The paths along here are lined with broom, blackberries, wild roses, and hawthorn (*majuelos*). To the north unfolds the panorama of the Río Navia basin and the Ancares Mountains. To the south, and much closer, is the Río Lóuzara basin, backed by the Caldeirón Mountains. During the day you won't see wolves along here, but you may spot their droppings along the trail. In the 18th c., pilgrims feared bandits in these wild and foggy forests. The Italian pilgrim Albani noted seeing small crosses stuck in the ground where travelers had been robbed or murdered.

✳ Alto do Poio In medieval times there was a hermitage at this 1,337-m. pass, one of the highest on the Road. The church of Santa María del Poyo belonged to the Hospitallers of San Juan.

✳ Fonfría del Camino 1,280 m. Its church of San Juan was restored in 1962. There used to be a hospice of Santa Catalina here, built ca. 1535. For a time it was hotly disputed between the bishop of Lugo and the Sancti Spiritus Church in Melide. A report to the bishop in 1789 describes its sorry state:

> The hospice for poor pilgrims is made of mud, covered with straw and slate, with a central patio or corral that contains an oven. The kitchen· is dark, with 2 areas divided by a wall. Two rooms are 2 Galician yards long by 2 and a half wide; the other 5 yards long by 4 wide. With the roof unsealed and the walls unchinked, it is ready to fall down, had not the hospitaller put up new ones at his own expense. The third area, which is the smallest, contains room for 3 cots and 2 beds on old planks, with straw and an old blanket, 2 linen sheets—ancient—for each bed. They spend 40–50 *reales* on pilgrims. The hospitaller's obligation is to keep the fire lit and to assist the pilgrims.

The hospice disappeared in the 19th c. Near the village are meadows of ferns, interspersed with patches of brush and occasional fields of rye and potatoes (potatoes, which came to Europe from Peru, would not have been part of the medieval landscape).

Beyond Fonfría the Road begins to drop precipitously until it reaches Triacastela (670 m.). The 600-m. drop takes you through several ecological zones with extraordinarily diverse flora. As you descend you will pass in turn groves of ash (in shaded gullies, often in limey soil), oak (from the heights to the valleys), pines (planted on the upper slopes as timber farms), and alders (along the rivers in the valleys). You will also pass thickets of broom, gorse, and other thick resilient shrubs, particularly in former pastures now gone to brush. These thickets are home to wild boar (*jabalí*), marten (*garduña*), weasel (*comadreja*), and ermine (*armiño*), none of which you are likely to see during the day. You may, however, catch sight of a sparrow hawk (*gavilán*; small—about 30 cm.—broad wings, long straight tail) or a goshawk (*azor*; twice the size, streaked white wings and tail). The large (64 cm.) black birds you see soaring, or flying with measured wingbeats, or perched in pathside trees will be common ravens (*cuervos*). If they are half the size, have red beaks, and make a lot of noise when you approach, they are probably choughs (*chovas piquirrojas*), a rare bird you are likely to see only on this stretch of the road.

✳ Biduedo This hamlet had a small hospice of the Hospitallers of San Juan and an Ermita de San Pedro belonging to Portomarín, but nothing remains of either. Its church is reputedly the smallest on the whole pilgrimage Road.

✳ Filloval The medieval hamlet belonged to the Order of San Juan de Jerusalén.

👟 As Pasantes This highway town, to the north of the walking path, contains the small chapel of Nuestra Señora de los Dolores. Not far to the north of the town is the pre-Roman Castro de Vilabella.

👟 Ramil Some houses in this ancient suburb of Triacastela preserve their coats of arms. To the north, near the highway, is the Castro de Triacastela.

74. TRIACASTELA

HISTORY

Count Gatón, the rebuilder of the Bierzo region, founded Triacastela in the 9th c. after the region's reconquest from the Muslims. The count donated money for a monastery dedicated to Saints Pedro and Pablo here, with the nearby village of Ramil to support it. The 3 castles that gave the town its name all dated from the early 10th c. All 3 seem to have been destroyed in the wars against Norman raiders, ca. 968, and nothing is left of them today. In the early 13th c. Triacastela was favored by the Leonese monarch Alfonso IX, who often spent time in the town and played a strong local role, personally naming the mayor and town council. Fernando III el Santo in 1248 gathered representatives of Galicia's town councils in Triacastela to raise money for his ultimately successful campaign to reconquer Sevilla. Prince Felipe II spent the night of May 16, 1554 here on his journey to England to contract marriage with his aunt, Mary Tudor.

The fields around Triacastela have fences made of vertical slabs of stone, a Galician style that you will see from here all the way to Compostela.

The language you are hearing is probably Galician (*gallego*). It is the westernmost of the Romance languages, splitting off from Latin in the early Middle Ages. During the reconquest wars of the 11th and 12th c., Galicia pushed south toward Coimbra, Lisbon, and the Algarve. Today the southern dialect of Galician is called Portuguese. You have probably noticed some spelling changes in the town names: the Castilian articles *el* and *la* have become *o* and *a* respectively, as in *O Cebreiro*. The letter *n* has become *ñ*, as in *camiño*. Your ear will have picked up how the sharp vowels of Spanish have become diphthongs (*-ero* has become *-eiro*) and how the final vowels in words tend to be pronounced *u*.

Gallego was considered the elegant court language in León as late as the 13th c. Troubadours sang Galician songs in the great halls, and King Alfonso X used the language for his *Cantigas* to the Virgin.

PILGRIMAGE

Though it is still about 670 m. high, Triacastela marks the end of the most mountainous section of the pilgrimage Road, what the 12th-c. CC *Guide* calls the "alpes Galliciae." In the 12th c. it was traditional for pilgrims to carry the calcium-rich stones found in this area to ovens near Castañeda, some 6 km. east of Arzúa, where they were made into cement for construction of the Compostela Cathedral.

The Casa Pedreira, in the center of town, is the site of the former Hospital de la Condesa. Skeletons found during the building's reconstruction suggest that it served as a pilgrim cemetery as well. Near the church, the Casa de Aira is also known locally as the Mesón del Peregrino.

MONUMENT: The Church of Santiago.

The apse is probably Romanesque, but the rest of the church is late 18th c. Its tower displays the 3 castles of the village's coat of arms. There is an image of **Santiago** inside.

This church's 15th-c. *sagrario*, the ark in which the consecrated hosts are kept, is now in Compostela's Museo das Perigrinacións. It is a 1-m. square chest of wood covered with several dozen carved scallop shells.

Also in Triacastela is the 1528 Casa do Concello, which was once the jail. The last old building as you leave the town, on the right-hand side, is called the Mesón da Ponte, a reference to its having served as an inn. It was also at one time a forge. In Triacastela, as in Puente la Reina and several other towns, there is a striking contrast between the ancient houses lining the town's medieval main street that carried pilgrim traffic west toward Compostela and the apartment houses along the modern highway that parallels the old pilgrimage Road.

> At the town's west exit a road to the left crosses a small river and becomes a path. If you follow the path about a km. downstream you will find ruins of a substantial old water mill.

Route 1: TRIACASTELA → A Balsa → San Xil → Alto de Riocabo → Montán → Fontearcuda → **Furela** → Pintín → Calvor → Aguiada → San Mamede do Camiño → San Pedro do Camiño → Carballal → Vigo de Sarria → SARRIA

Route 2: TRIACASTELA → San Cristobo do Real → Renche → **Samos** → Foxos → Teiguín → Frollais → SARRIA

From Triacastela to Sarria you will descend another 230 m. Two routes of roughly the same length lead to Sarria. Both are popular with pilgrims, both are marked, and we like them equally well. Route 1 has less vehicle traffic and passes through a number of picturesque hamlets (many too tiny to merit specific comment in this chapter) and a couple of minor monuments. Route 2, which has occasional truck traffic, follows a river gorge to the important monastery of Samos, where many pilgrims choose to spend the night.

The rugged hills here are mainly metamorphic rocks, schist, and slate. The humid gullies and streambeds abound with several species of lizards, salamanders, and frogs. Common small birds in these humid, low-altitude Galician copses include the redstart (*colirrojo real*; red belly, gray back, black cheeks and throat), the great gray shrike (*alcaudón real*; gray back, white belly, black mask, tail, and wings, hooked beak), and the wheatear (*collalba gris*; like the shrike, but without the hooked beak and with a prominent white patch at the base of its tail). Spiraling headfirst down the oak trees searching for insects you may see a nuthatch (*trepador azul*). In the chestnut groves you may see spotted thrushes (*zorzales*) looking for eatables among the fallen leaves. Along the edges of the cultivated fields you may roust up a partridge (*perdiz*) or a quail *(codorniz)*. The white-breasted black bird you may be lucky enough to see walking underwater on the bottom of the streams is a dipper (*mirlo acuático*).

Route 1:

✳ A Balsa Just north of this diminutive village is San Pedro do Ermo, site of an important 10th–12th-c. monastery. Only the ruins of a tiny chapel remain.

Just past A Balsa, on the left, is the modern Fuente Vieira, remodelled for the 1993 Holy Year.

✳ San Xil The church contains a 15th-c. chalice.

✳ Montán In 1985 the village housed 13 families. The nave of the church of Santa María is Romanesque.

✳ Fontearcuda The village has 3 houses. A detour of 1 km. to the left brings you to the rural Romanesque church of **San Román**. It has some peculiarly graphic corbels.

✳ **Furela** The chapel of San Roque has a beautifully expressive **naïve retablo**.

✳ Calvor Calvor occupies the site of the pre-Roman Castro Astorica. The town's original medieval name was Villa del Calvario. Its Egreija de San Esteban was founded by Adilano in 785, and its earliest parts are Visigothic, although what remains today is mostly 19th c. Inside, an alabaster Visigothic capital serves now as a baptismal font.

✳ Aguiada The town once had several hospices. The westernmost house in the hamlet is still known locally as "Hospital."

✳ San Mamede do Camiño Here the Road passes forests of imposing, moss-covered oak trees that seem to suggest why Galicians are reputed to believe in sprites and witches.

✳ Vigo de Sarria From this suburb, one road led straight to Sarria, one followed the river to the Ponte Ribeira (documented in 1280), and one cut off to the right to the Campo do Rollo, on whose gibbet medieval malefactors were executed.

Route 2:

✳ San Cristobo do Real Little has changed in this town of massive stone houses, hugging tightly together. By the Río Oribio are a small mill and a public washing house.

✳ Renche In medieval times there was an iron foundry here. The church has a statue of **Santiago Peregrino** on the altar.
   In this area, rich farming families were able to build large, almost palatial stone houses (*pazos*) in the center of their fields. One such stands halfway up the hill to the right of Renche.

✳ **Samos** The focal point of this village is its monastery, founded in the 6th c. by San Martín Dumiense. It preserves some Visigothic stones from that era. This monastery has played a central part in the history of Galicia and of León as well. Alfonso II el Casto was living and studying here when his father, Fruela I, was assassinated ca. 769. The area attracted Mozarabic refugees from the south, and their tiny chapel still stands nearby. Samos's wealth was so well known in the early middle ages that the monastery was sacked several times by pirates. In 922 Ordoño II brought monks from San Juan de la Peña, in Aragón (see ch. 7), to introduce the Benedictine rule in Samos. It is not surprising that from the early 11th c. the monastery maintained a pilgrim hospice. In the 12th c. it became part of the Cluny network of abbeys. Samos was so favored by monarchs and royalty that at its height it controlled 200 towns, 105 churches, and some 300 monasteries!
   From the latter Middle Ages until nearly modern times Samos was famous for its forge, pharmacy, farms, and schools. Its most famous monk was undoubtedly the 18th-c. encyclopedist and polymath Father Feijóo.

📖 Benito Jerónimo Feijóo y Montenegro (1676–1764) joined the Samos Benedictines at the age of 14. A brilliant student, and later a professor at various universities, he lectured and wrote on topics as diverse as mathematics, astronomy, physics, medicine, the social sciences, literature, religion, and theology. His 2 most influential books were the 1725 *Critical Universal Treatise* (*Tratado crítico universal o discursos varios en todo género de materias, para desengaño de errores comunes*) and his equally broad and diverse *Curious and Erudite Letters* (*Cartas eruditas y curiosas*, 1742–60).

Most of the abbey was destroyed in a huge fire in 1536. Rebuilding went on until the 18th c. Another fire in 1951 caused extensive damage and destroyed the library.

Exterior:
- Mozarabic chapel. You will find the diminutive chapel of El Salvador in a small park about 200 m. from the main monastery. It was built in the 9th or 10th c. with rough slate walls and 1 horseshoe arch.
- The monastery façade. At first glance the monastery is a massive stone cube that exudes strength. But the 18th-c. Baroque façade of the church is in fact an exercise in subtle contrasts. Massive rectangular pillars and paired Doric columns flank the large, rectangular, main door. Completing the frame are the zigzag lines of the double staircase, and the ornately framed statue of the Benedictine founder, San Benito. A horizontal frieze marks off the upper third of the building; its balustrade echoes the decorative touches on the staircase. The rounded forms of circular and oval windows, curved pediments, sculptural niches, and open arches with bells play counterpoint to the straight edges. At third glance, the upper corners of the façade's square frame prove to be the church's bell towers, incorporated into the overall design.

Interior:
One of the abbey's 13 monks (this was the number when we visited in 1998) will guide you through the monastery proper.
- **Claustro de las Nereidas.**
    —A modest Romanesque door remains in the northeast corner, with a **tympanum** showing a processional cross in low relief inside of a circle, perhaps symbolizing God without beginning or end.
    —On the vaults of this late-16th-c. Renaissance-Gothic cloister are 5 historiated keystones depicting themes related to the Benedictines: San Benito; his sister Santa Escolástica; his father, San Julián; and the child-martyr Santa Basilia. Another keystone contains an amusing hieroglyphic, which when deciphered, says "What are you looking at, stupid?" (¿Qué miras, bobo?).
    —In the center of the cloister garden is the Fountain of the Nereiads, constructed in 1713–7.
    —Annexed to the cloister are the refectory and library that suffered the 1951 fire. The Latin motto on the library door reads: Claustrum sine librario sicut castrum sine armentario ("A cloister without a library is like a fort without an armory").
- The Claustro de Feijóo (1676–1774) is reputedly the largest monastic cloister in Spain. Sober in style, it was added to accommodate a growing monastic community.
- Upstairs a seemingly endless modern mural, executed in 3 styles, depicts various episodes from the life of San Benito.
- The **sacristy** and **church** are stunning examples of the Baroque-classicist style, in which large-dimensioned, classical structures are arrayed, decorated, and lighted so as to dazzle the spectator. The 2 domes are particularly striking. The squinches of the church's dome depict 4 Doctors of the Church known for their writings about Mary. Our favorite is San Anselmo, wearing yellow glasses like some Baroque Elton John.

✳ Foxos Foxos (the name means "fire") once contained the forges that supplied iron to Samos. Today there is less than nothing to see.

76. SARRIA

HISTORY

Archaeological remains in the area point to considerable pre-Roman settlement, but the first documentary evidence for Sarria comes from the 6th c. After the Muslim invasion, the area was repopulated ca. 750 by Bishop Odoario of Lugo. Alfonso IX of León favored the city and funded several building projects. He died there in 1230. The oldest part of the city was located on the slopes of the hill around a castle that belonged to the counts of Lemos. Although this important Galician noble family had castles in many parts of the region, they considered Sarria their seat. During the later Middle Ages the Calle Mayor—it was also the pilgrimage Road—evolved as the major commercial street and the location of the principal noble palaces. Several conserve their coats of arms. The largest house belonged to the Saavedra Fajardo family. Other coats of arms indicate the Valle, Trancoso, Valcarce, Quiroga, and Losada families.

> 📖 In the Renaissance 2 native sons of Sarria made extraordinary contributions. One is the sculptor Gregorio Hernández (aka Fernández), whose works we have seen in various churches all along the Road. The other is Fray Luis de Granada (1504–88), a famous Dominican preacher who authored 2 16th-c. best-sellers: the *Guide for Sinners* (*Guía de pecadores*) and the *Introduction to the Symbols of Faith* (*Introducción al símbolo de la fe*). He is noted for writing about nature in terms both lyrical in their emotion and scientific in their accuracy of observation.

Several pairs of storks traditionally have nested in Sarria and its environs. Since storks are relatively rare in Galicia, they may be the last ones you will see on the Road.

PILGRIMAGE

In the 1670s the pilgrim Domenico Laffi praised Sarria and its Hospital de la Magdalena, founded by Italian monks in the 13th c.: "This is a very fine, prosperous town, with attractive houses and a monastery of the white friars who give pilgrims a *passada*" [Laffi; trans. Hall (1997), 159]. All that remains is a narrow door in the convent façade that used to lead to the hospice kitchen. The door is capped by an Augustinian emblem with the inscription *Charitas aedificat.*

In front of La Magdalena was the Hospital de San Antonio, founded by the Condes de Lemos. From the 16th c. it housed returning pilgrims free of charge so long as they presented their Certificate of Indulgences (see ch. 88). Much later the building became the Juzgado de Instrucción. Records indicate the existence of 2 other medieval hospices: San Lázaro and San Cosme.

Around the corner from the church of Santiago is Sarria's jail. In 1979, when we suggested in Spanish to one of our pilgrims that he try to lodge us in a local convent that reputedly had comfortable cells, the only word he caught was "cells." We ended up in the jail, which at that particular moment was devoid of prisoners. Sleeping on the planks that served as beds and washing in the cold-water fountain in the patio gave us a sense of the minimal facilities that often greeted medieval pilgrims in the locally run hospices. Sharing wine and conversation with the jailer and his wife brought home the traditional warmth of hospitality to pilgrims, even in meager circumstances.

MONUMENTS: 1. Iglesia de Santa Marina. 2. **Iglesia de San Salvador**. 3. Convento de la Magdalena. 4. Castle. 5. Ermita de San Lázaro.

1. Iglesia de Santa Marina. This undistinguished modern church is built over a 12th-c. predecessor. On the wall toward the street is a modern mural depicting pilgrims, painted in grays and beiges and black, melancholy and moving.

2. **Iglesia de San Salvador.** The apse is Romanesque, though the naves and portals date from the 14th c. The primitive-looking tympanum depicts Christ the Savior. The doors display some fine medieval ironwork.

3. Convento de la Magdalena. In the 12th c. some Italian pilgrims founded a hospice near the castle. In the 13th c. it became an Augustinian monastery. It now houses a community of Mercedarians. The façade is Plateresque; some Flamboyant Gothic elements remain in the cloister. In recent years it has run a hospice.

4. Castle. About all that is left of this 14th–15th-c. castle of the counts of Lemos is 1 reconstructed tower. The castle was destroyed in the 1467 civil wars between the *irmandiñas* and the Galician nobility.

> 📖 Several times in the 15th c. the oppressed underclasses of Galicia organized armed revolts against their feudal lords. In 1431 the vassals of Nuño Freire de Andrade organized a militia and sacked castles and palaces and killed many nobles until King Juan II sent an army against them and hanged the ringleaders. In 1464, as the result of political squabbling, the archbishop Alfonso Fonseca II was taken prisoner and held for 2 years by the lord of Altamira, Bernal Yáñez de Moscoso. The Archbishop's family raised a ransom. Yáñez attacked them in the Compostela Cathedral. In the resulting tumult the shops in the Plaza de Platerías were burned. In the aftermath the brotherhoods, the *irmandiñas*, demanded locally controlled government, reaffirmation of their traditional liberties, and law and order. Instead they provoked chaos. When the principal nobles fled Galicia, the mobs burned their castles. Among the dozens of castles destroyed were three along the Road: Melide, Arcos, and Sarria. They attacked the Conde de Lemos in the castle of Ponferrada, but failed to breach its impregnable walls. Meanwhile Archbishop Fonseca and several other nobles raised an army in Portugal and marched on Galicia, determined to destroy the rebels. By 1469 they had succeeded.

The castle was reconstructed by the Conde de Lemos to an extent that Laffi in the 1670s called it "a splendid, strong castle surrounded by very high walls, where the lord of the town lives" [Laffi; trans. Hall (1997), 159]. But eventually the reconstruction also fell apart. The ruins were dismantled in 1860 and the stones were used to make sidewalks.

Nearby, there used to be a Capilla de Santiago, also destroyed in the late 19th c. The cemetery west of the castle holds remains of Sarrians who died in a late-19th-c. cholera epidemic.

5. Ermita de San Lázaro. During the Middle Ages this small *ermita* outside the city's western wall was a hospice and leprosarium. The building on the site today is almost completely modern. The sidewalks in front of the *ermita* were decorated in the 1990s with mosaics with pilgrimage themes.

Route: Sarria → Vilei → **Santiago de Barbadelo** → Rente → Mercado da Serra → Mouzós → Xisto → Domiz → Pena Leimán → Peruscallo → [Belante] → Cortiñas → Lavandeira → Brea → Morgade → **Ferreiros** → [Paradela] → Mirallos → Pena → Rozas → Moimentos → [Santa María de Ribalogio → Cortes] → Mercadoiro → Moutras → Parrocha → Vilacha→ Portomarín

After descending from Sarria, the Road crosses the small medieval Ponte Aspera bridge over the Río Celerio. From here to Portomarín, gently rolling hills rise gradually higher until they drop steeply to the Miño River Valley. You will see jewel-like green fields, narrow lanes running between stone fences or rows of brambles, and everywhere redolent reminders of the dairy industry. The Gallego farmers hereabouts live in small hamlets of 3 or 4 houses (*caseríos*), most of which are named as if they were towns. Several of them have tiny chapels, rarely large enough to hold more than the *caserío*'s inhabitants. A circuit-riding priest comes periodically to say mass and to marry, christen, or bury villagers, as the circumstances warrant.

The houses are made from the stones you can pick up in every field, with windows and doors set into massive squared blocks that the builders would have purchased from a local mason. The houses ramble, generally incorporating a tractor shed, a henhouse or bit of barn, and several dark storage rooms. The family often lives in the upper stories. Next to every house is a garden of greens, mostly the tall-stalked *berzas*, ready to be picked for the evening's thick soup (*caldo*). Many homes have a raised corncrib (*hórreo*) alongside. If you look closely as you hike through these *caseríos*, you will see wooden rakes and scythes and other implements of farms past hung on the walls next to today's chain saws and spare tractor parts. In the 1970s we were rarely out of sight of a yoked team of oxen, hauling a groaning wagon up the narrow lanes or dragging an iron-tipped wood plow through the stony soil.

Most village churches along the Road in El Bierzo and Galicia were constructed either in the Romanesque style during the 12th through the 14th c., or in the Neoclassic style in the 18th or 19th c. From Villafranca del Bierzo to Sarria, the village churches have been almost entirely devoid of external decoration. From Sarria to Santiago many of the Romanesque churches have bits of interesting carving on their tympana, corbels, archivolts, or capitals. Barbadelo is the first of many fascinating examples.

✳ **Santiago de Barbadelo** In the *Veneranda dies* sermon in the 12th-c. CC, the author chooses Barbadelo as the place to rail against the commercialism of the hostelry business in Compostela:

> Another [innkeeper] goes to . . . Barbadelo, or Triacastela, and when he has found and greeted them and deceitfully talked to them about other matters, he then says to them: "My brothers who seek St. James, I am a fortunate citizen of his city, and I have not come here for the sake of hospitality, but so that I might speak with a certain brother of mine, who is staying in this village, and if you wish to have good lodging in St. James' city, stay as a guest

in my house, and tell my wife and my family that they should provide well for you out of love for me, and I will give you a token, which you can show to them." ... And when the pilgrims have traveled to his house and are lodged in it, and when they have been given the first course at the table of that inn, the lady sells them a taper worth four farthings for eight or ten. Thus are the pilgrims of St. James deceived by the innkeepers. [CC: Book I; trans. Coffey et al., 37]

None of this commercialism affects the comfortable new *albergue* in Barbadelo, in front of which we pitched our tents in 1996.

The original monastery in Barbadelo in 874 was duplex, housing communities of both monks and nuns. In 1009 it affiliated with the Monastery of Samos. By 1120 the monastery, by then for men only, was supporting a hospice. The current late-12th-c. church is noted for its **sculpture** and its fortlike tower, whose arches show a tendency to close toward a horseshoe shape. Several times we have seen a barn owl (*lechuza*) nesting in the bell tower of this church.

On the **archivolts of the north portal**, fantastic animals drink from a chalice. On the left are some Santiago scallop shells; on the right, some roses. The walls have 2 Jaca-style windows. The **west portal tympanum** is unusual in that it is carved on both sides. On the exterior the primitive male figure may be Christ. Below him is a Celtic-style laced knot. On the interior is another. The pinecones on which the tympanum rests symbolize both fertility and immortality. The church exterior also has several figural capitals.

The cemetery surrounding the Barbadelo church is typical of Galicia. Five or 6 stories of rectangular burial niches, constructed similarly to *hórreos* (and probably by the same masons), circle the church like a defensive wall. Many bear photographs of the deceased.

✱ Rente Along this stretch of the Road are many birch, oak, and chestnut trees. The gullies tend to be impenetrable tangles of roses, blackberries, and ferns.

✱ Mercado da Serra This crossroads was the site of a major medieval market that drew traveling merchants and artisans, as well as Jewish merchants from Portomarín, and shills for the hospices in Compostela.

> 👟About 100 m. south of Peruscallo is the hamlet of Belante, whose small Romanesque church has 2 entrances with figural capitals and corbels with well-carved tiny heads. The tympanum on its north door holds a crude cross.

A little before Ferreiros the gentle schist and slate hills we have been following become more abrupt and turn to granite. They are less suited to extensive agriculture and tend more to gorse and scrubby forests. Nearby are small deposits of iron.

✱ Ferreiros The village's name means "blacksmiths." The church of **Santa María de Ferreiros** retains bits of Romanesque decoration and a double-arched tympanum, similar to San Pedro in Portomarín. This church maintained a pilgrim hospice, San Mamed de Ferreiros, under the auspices of the Monasterio de la Magdalena in Arzúa. It has since vanished. In the village is the small *pazo* of the Barreiro family.

🚗 The automobile road from Sarria to Portomarín passes through Paradela (km. 145). The vilage is 7 km. south of Ferreiros. Paradela's 12th-c. Church of San Miguel has a plain exterior. Inside, a beautiful Romanesque arch with figural capitals separates the nave from the altar area. Local legend has it that any pregnant woman who rings this church's tiny bell will have an easy labor.

In front of the church is a roadside cross depicting a Crucifixion and the Virgen Dolorosa. A stone snake curls around the foot of the cross.

📖 Roadside crosses are documented in Galicia from the 12th c. They were erected by churches, towns, or individuals to mark road junctions or places where some misfortune or miracle was to be commemorated. Most—like this one—contain the image of the crucified Christ on one side, with Mary, or the symbols of the Passion, or a local patron saint on the other. Marking the intersections with stone reflects a pre-Roman Celtic tradition, for these crosses are common in other Celtic areas of Europe like Ireland and Brittany.

✳ **Mirallos** In the late 15th c. the German pilgrim Künig von Vach noted that the town manufactured nails for use by cobblers.

👟 Just south of Mercadoiro is the monastery of Santa María de Ribalogio. The name signifies the structure's location on the Río del Loyo. This monastery is one of Galicia's earlist: a 9th-c. document refers not to its founding but to its reconstruction. A sex scandal ca. 927 led the abbot to replace the entire community with presumably more pious monks. A legend surrounding the monastery attributes to it a close relationship with a mid-9th-c. group of 13 knights (symbolic of Jesus and the 12 Apostles) called the Caballeros de la Espada. The group was formed in 845 by Ramiro I to combat brigands in the area along the Road to Santiago. In the late 12th c. this monastery served as the first motherhouse of the military Orden de Santiago (see ch. 60).

A 1584 document notes that this church was already in ruins.

👟 **Cortes** About 200 m. from the parish church is the ancient Castro de Cortes, which preserves some vestiges of its ancient fortifications. Several artifacts found here are now in the Provincial Museum in Lugo.

From Moutras the path descends steeply to the Río Miño. As you cross the bridge leading to Portomarín look for the iridescent green flash of a kingfisher (*martín pescador*), or the snakelike neck of a cormorant (*alcatraz; cormorán*) fishing in the Embalse de Belesar, the dammed-up waters of the Río Miño. In the shallows you may see a large gray great egret (*garza*) or a small white egret (*garceta*) poised to spear a fish, and on the banks a smaller and more compact black-crowned night heron (*martinete*) waiting to ambush a frog. When the water level is low, long triangular eel traps will be set out in the river shallows.

78. PORTOMARÍN

HISTORY

Portomarín is located in the deep Miño Valley among rolling slate hills rich with iron deposits and marble quarries. A bridge over the Miño River gave life to this city perhaps as early as Roman times. What is certain is that a 993 document calls the town Villa Portumarini, so that a bridge must have existed by then. The bridge—a key control point on the major east-west highway across northern Spain—has been built and destroyed many times. Almanzor ravaged the area in the summer of 997 and presumably destroyed the span. Rebuilt, it was destroyed again ca. 1112 in the wars between Queen Urraca and her husband Alfonso I el Batallador. In 1126 Urraca commissioned an engineer named Pedro Peregrino to erect a new bridge, as well as a hospice named Dominus Dei and a residence for the Knights of the Order of San Juan. When Aymeric Picaud passed by ca. 1140 he knew the town as Pons Minei.

Because of the bridge, the town was of such strategic importance that it was always garrisoned. When the Order of Santiago was chartered, Portomarín was given to these knights. In May 1188, Alfonso IX and his mother Urraca transferred ownership to the Order of San Juan de Jerusalén, which for centuries continued to maintain a facility—and pilgrim hospice—in Portomarín.

The town grew along both banks of the Miño and became an important commercial as well as military center. It is mentioned in every medieval and Renaissance itinerary through the region. The Catholic Monarchs slept here in October of 1486, as did their grandson Carlos V (1520), his son Felipe II (1554), and many other notables. However, in the 19th c. the rapid growth of Lugo, some 30 km. to the north, and of the highway system that centered there, cut Portomarín off from the commercial flow, and the town withered. In fact, as late as 1919 it was still not reached by a single road that could accommodate wheeled traffic.

In 1956 construction began on the Embalse de Belesar Dam to provide hydroelectricity for the region. As the reservoir grew, it flooded the old town, whose major monuments were removed, block by numbered block, and reassembled in the new town of Portomarín created *ex nihilo* on the west side of the Miño gorge. By 1962 the move was complete. Francisco Franco's Ministerio de Educación y Turismo, in an attempt to breathe life into the region, constructed a tourist Parador here. It did not work, and by the mid-1980s the hotel had closed. In 1998 we noticed that it had reopened.

When we passed through Portomarín in early November 1998, the reservoir had been partially drained, and the ruins of old Portomarín, with its houses, streets, mills, eel traps, and old Roman bridge, could be seen sticking up through the mud.

PILGRIMAGE

Portomarín sustained several pilgrim hospices in the Middle Ages. In the 1670s Laffi was impressed with the region's wealth: "This is a fine town. Through the middle flows a large river with plenty of fish, particularly eels and excellent trout, which provided us with a magnificent supper. Along the river are large vineyards and many orchards. One half of the town lies on the near side of the river, the other half on the far side, the two parts being connected by a large, splendid bridge. . . ." [Laffi; trans. Hall (1997), 160–1]

The difficult terrain in this region posed problems for pilgrims and was a concern to many. In 1461 King Enrique IV donated a portion of the royal road tax paid by "all the animals and merchandise and other things which pass through the town" so that town authorities could make repairs to the church and hospice, and so that the Road to Santiago would be "well packed down and repaired so that travelers may come and go on it from one place to another."

Most of the bars in Portomarín—and other towns in the region—sell *torta de Santiago*, a compact almond cake adorned on top with a sugar-dusted cross of Santiago. We like a big slice for breakfast . . . on days when we are not walking.

MONUMENTS: 1. **Iglesia de San Juan**. 2. Casa del Conde. 3. Iglesia de San Pedro. 4. Pazo de la Marquesa de Bóveda. 5. Iglesia de Santa María.

1. **Iglesia de San Juan** (aka San Nicolás). This late-12th- or early-13th-c. church/fortress housed the Knights of Saint John. Its height and width make it the largest single-nave Romanesque church in Galicia, while its large regular stones speak to the wealth of its builders. The 4 corner towers lead to walkways protected by battlements that indicate the dual purpose of this church. Today it is the parish of San Nicolás.

Exterior:
Although it is an imposing fortress, monumental in size, the church is also wonderful for its innovative sculpture and decoration. In fact, there is so much decoration that on all 3 portals the cylindrical arch of the archivolt appears to be half swallowed up by encroaching decoration.
   • **West façade**. The **large arch** that frames the rose window emphasizes the building's height and width. The varied floral motifs on the **capitals** sustaining the 3 archivolts exhibit fine detail work. The **tympanum** shows Christ the Savior in his mandorla, surrounded by the 24 old men of the Apocalypse, who are grouped in pairs on the archivolts as on the Pórtico de la Gloria in Compostela.
   • The **north door**. The **tympanum** portrays the Annunciation with simple, fully rounded figures. An aggressive angel notifies a reticent Virgin Mary of her divinely designated role. The tympanum appears unbalanced, with the angel rendered large by his outstretched wings, which hug the tympanum's edge and offset Mary's undecorated background. The finely carved capitals of this portal are clearly by a separate hand.
   • The **south door**. On the tympanum 2 figures, carrying a book and a crozier, flank a bishop (San Nicolás) whose feet extend over a lintel that is held up by 2 engaging monsters with diverse body parts of unrepentant sinners dangling from their mouths. The capitals here, as on the north door, have some finely sculpted harpies (birds with human features).
   • The **apse**. It is solidly Romanesque in concept and execution, of a style pioneered in Jaca (see ch. 5). One difference here is the hatching inside the arches over the windows.

Interior:
The vast dimensions and clean structures create an impression of harmony and grandeur, reinforced by the simple geometric designs and architectural elements of the apse. It is easy to see where the Romanesque columns and sculptures give way to the slightly pointed Gothic arches of the vault. Though the rose window and the lateral windows are Romanesque in concept, their large size, making the church unusually bright, announces the new achievements of Gothic.
   • On each side of the altar are painted Gothic baldachins (see ch. 78 and 17) that must have sheltered Gothic images now long since disappeared. A flashlight will help you make out the remaining delicate touches of the half-deteriorated paintings.

2. Casa del Conde. The façade of this 16th-c. palace, reconstructed on the square in front of San Juan, now serves as the Ayuntamiento.

3. Iglesia de San Pedro. The Romanesque façade—all that was rescued of this church from the submerged town—dates from 1182. An inscription indicates that it was consecrated by the bishop of Lugo, Rodrigo II. In a style common in Galicia, derived from San Isidoro in León, 2 animal heads sustain the double-arched tympanum. You will find a similar arrangement in nearby Santa María de Ferreiros. The capitals are of 2 types: vegetable motifs with particularly broad leaves and simplified geometric forms, and symmetrically opposed birds and griffins.

4. Pazo de la Marquesa de Bóveda (aka Bebetoros). Raised from the riverbank, this 17th-c. palace has been reconstructed next to the church of San Pedro. The west wall bears 2 coats of arms. One refers to the Berbetoro/Pimentel family, the other to the Montenegros.

5. Iglesia de Santa María (aka la Virgen de las Nieves). The small chapel of Santa María, thought by local folk to protect them from drowning, once stood in the middle of the ancient bridge. It has been rebuilt at the end of the modern bridge.

79. PORTOMARÍN → PALAS DO REI

Route: PORTOMARÍN → Toxibo → Gonzar → Castromaior → Hospital → Ventas de Narón → Prebisa → **Lameiros** → **Ligonde** → Eirexe → Portos → **[Vilar das Donas]** → Lestedo → Valos → Alto do Rosario → PALAS DO REI

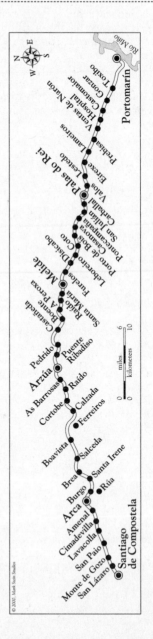

This section of the Road traverses reddish soil formed of Tertiary and Quaternary sediments with patches of impermeable flinty deposits. Near Palas the dominant rocks are gneiss and granite.

PILGRIMAGE

According to the *Veneranda dies* sermon in the CC, this stretch of the Road was famous as an open-air brothel, for which the author had little sympathy. "The whores[,] who ... are accustomed to come between the Minean Bridge and Palas del Rey in the wooded areas to meet the pilgrims, are not only to be excommunicated but also are to be held in shame by all and to have their noses cut off. Usually a single one appears to a solitary traveler." He similarly condemned "the innkeepers' servants on the route of Saint James who, for the sake of ravishing and of stealing money, are accustomed to go to the bed of any pilgrim at night at the instigation of the devil, are damned generally." [CC: Book I; trans. Coffey et al., 36]

✳ Toxibo The town is smaller than its name, but has a nice *hórreo* just north of the Road.

✳ Gonzar At the entrance to town are some enormous oaks. Gonzar is even smaller than Toxibo. Its nondescript Iglesia de Santa María is appropriately diminutive.

✳ Castromaior Ruins of a Roman camp have been discovered on the edge of the village. Just beyond the town to the northeast, over the river, is a small pre-Roman *castro* where some ceramics have been found.

> 📖 Local tradition holds the "Moors" inhabited the site. Legend recounts that once a pigherder girl left snouts of several pigs there for a traditional annual sacrifice. The next day she found a basket filled with lumps of coal rather than snouts. She threw all but one lump to the ground and took the basket home. The next morning she found a nugget of gold in the basket where the coal had been. When she went back to search for the rest of the coal, it was gone.

Castromaior's rustic 12th-c. Romanesque Iglesia de Santa María has simple capitals and a simple Baroque retablo. The church contains a seated 12th-c. moth-eaten wood Virgin.

The Road through San Bartolomé de Bagude passes several Celtic *castros*.

✳ Ventas de Narón Christian armies defeated the Muslims here in 820. This town is likely the *Sala Regina* referred to in the CC *Guide*. A small chapel dedicated to María Magdalena on the town's outskirts had a hospice.

For the next several km. the ground is poorly suited to farming. The Road traverses a high ridge (alt. 756 m.) composed of gneiss with large quartz and feldspar granules that in several places is commercially quarried. This is the watershed between the Río Miño (which flows into the Atlantic at Guarda, Portugal) and the Ulla (which joins the sea at Padrón). You will see few villages. Among the thickets of gorse and heather you are likely to see stonechats (*tarabilla común*; a small black-headed bird with a red patch on its chest and tail and a white belly), Dartford warblers (*curruca rabilarga*; a perky thin-billed, red-eyed bird with a dull red chest and belly and a long thin tail); and dunnocks (*acentor común*; a sparrow-sized bird with a greenish gray head). Where broom predominates, you may spot whitethroats (*curruca zarcera*, a white-bellied flycatcher with a gray back and reddish stains on its wings).

✳ Lameiros The hamlet's single house displays coats of arms of the Varela family (castle, fleur de lis, bars, and St. Catherine's wheel) and another family related to the Ulloas, Piñeiros, Riveras, and Gayosos. The adjoining tiny Capilla de San Marcos, with its graceful *espadaña*, also sports an enormous coat of arms. The chapel reputedly contains a retablo with statues of Saints Antonio, Gregorio, and Marcos. It is believed locally that San Marcos protects harvests against storms.

Just beyond is the roadside **Cross of Lameiros,** at the site of a former Capilla de San Lázaro. It depicts the Passion and the Virgin and Child. On the pedestal are Christ, with the symbols of the Passion at His feet, and the Virgen de los Dolores. The curving lines and tender pose of the Virgin, executed in an almost abstract style, make it, in our view, the most moving cross on the pilgrimage Road. A faint inscription with the date 1672 suggests it may have been donated by the Ulloa family.

Attesting to the antiquity of human settlement in this region, to the north and south of the Road over the next few km. are several significant pre-Roman settlements.
- The Castro de Ligonde, just northwest of the Road, is a large semicircle (120 × 80 m.) divided by a great wall, in places 7 m. thick and 10 m. tall.
- The Castro de Lardeiros, to the south of the road from Monterroso to Marco, has a 7-m.-wide ditch, and a 7-m.-wide wall leading to the built-up town area.

• The Castro de Gimonde lies 500 m. south of the Road at the beginning of the district of Palas do Rei.
• The conical hill to the north, now with the communications tower on it, is Castro de San Simón.

✳ **Ligonde** Ligonde is really 2 hamlets. The first, at the top of the hill, is known as Ligonde Ligonde. A large house at the entrance to town displays the coats of arms of the Ulloas, Travas, and Montenegros, and on the other side the Varelas. Carlos V stopped here in 1520 and in thanks for hospitality granted the house the right to offer sanctuary. Felipe II stayed here in 1554.

Several hundred meters further on is **Eirexe de Ligonde** (*eirexe* means "church"). Its **Church of Santiago** (1225–30?) has some unusual decorative elements. On its capitals are birds—incised lines indicate their feathers—picking at plants. Embedded in the church's south side is a large stone, perhaps formerly a lintel, depicting Daniel between 2 lions.

Opposite the church, at #7, is an unprepossessing building locally called Nabal del Hospital, or Casa do Rego. It was built by the Ulloa family as a pilgrim hospice and was still operating in the 18th c. Archaeologists have also located a pilgrim cemetery in the village.

Just up the hill from the church are the Road's first eucalyptus trees (see ch. 85).

👟 From Portos we always take the 45-minute detour to the north to visit the spectacular **Monasterio de San Salvador at Vilar das Donas**. It may originally have been a family monastery, which were common in Galicia, belonging to Juan Arias de Monterroso. The family gave it to the Order of Santiago in 1184, with the stipulation that Gallego members of the Order were to be buried here. It was much favored by Castilian royalty. Alfonso IX (1216), Fernando III (1232), and Juan I (1382) made donations. After the *desamortización* of the 1830s the monastery became a parish church. The current structure dates from the early 13th c.

Exterior:
• **Doorway**. The statues over the rain eaves depict Mary with Jesus, and Saints Miguel and Bartolomé. Note the ancient forged **hinges** on the door.

Interior:
The architecture has been called early post-Romanesque, with high, unbuttressed walls—made possible because of the reduced weight of the wood ceiling—and a simple crossing of the transept and nave.
• **Altar**. Made of granite, the retablo depicts an emotional Descent from the Cross and the miracle of the Eucharist, which may refer either to the legend of San Gregorio or to the miracle at O Cebreiro (see ch. 72).
• The **baldachin**. This 15th-c. canopy, constructed to resemble a castle, may mirror the nearby Castle of Pambra.

📖 Stone canopies are common in Galicia, perhaps because the 12th-c. cathedral in Compostela had one (it and its 15th-c. replacement have both vanished). The Compostela baldachins were imitated in rural churches all over the region, and some 60 still exist. The most notable ones are in Portomarín, Serantes, Xurenzás, Baiona, Noia, Ventosa, and this church of Vilar das Donas.

• The escutcheons on the tombs indicate the Amarante, Ulloa, Varela, Seixas, Gayoso, and Piñeiro families, many of whom have *pazos* along the pilgrimage Road in this region.

• The <u>frescoes</u> in the apse are this church's treasure. They probably date from the early 15th c. The female portraits have provoked fanciful speculation. Most probably they refer to the parable of the 10 virgins, in which Christ cautions watchfulness since no one knows the hour of His return. Therefore they are a kind of *memento mori*, a reminder of human mortality. One of the women in the frame, in fact, bears the words *Vos bela he mi* ("You watch, and I do, too"). Curiously, this inscription has led some people to believe that the portrait is of a doña Bela.

✳ Lestedo The Church of Santiago stands in the middle of the typical Galician atrium-like cemetery. The interior has traces of 12th-c. wall paintings in lamentable condition.

✳ Alto do Rosario From this height, to the west you can see the cone of the Pico Sacro (see ch. 87), and to the south the 1,000-m.-high Monte Faro, with its Ermita de Nuestra Señora. There are enormous oak trees along this section of the Road.

80. Palas do Rei

HISTORY

Legend holds that Visigothic king Witiza (701–9), the last of the militant Arian heretics (who held that Jesus was not human or divine, but supernatural), constructed the palace here that gave the town its name. The town appears frequently in documents from the 12th c., such as the CC *Guide*. In the Middle Ages the area around Palas was filled with small agricultural hamlets, and it has not changed much. Of the 43 parish churches in the district of Palas, 20 are Romanesque.

MONUMENT: Iglesia de San Tirso.

Documents from the 9th c. refer to a church on this site. The current church of San Tirso retains a modest 12th-c. Romanesque portal with a plain tympanum and foliated capitals, but most of the church is much newer and unremarkable.

Route: PALAS DO REI → Carballal → San Julián del Camino → Pontecampaña → Casanova → Porto de Bois → Coto → **Leboreiro** → Disicabo → **Furelos** → MELIDE

The fields just west of Palas, called the Campo dos Romeiros, marks the beginning of the last segment of the 12th-c. CC *Guide*. From here to Melide, the road traverses several forests of eucalyptus (see ch. 85), planted for paper and for lumber. These forests, and the interspersed cornfields, are relatively sterile with regard to bird and animal life. The occasional cork oaks and thickets of bamboo are signs of the more temperate climate as you descend westward toward the Galician coast.

✳ San Julián del Camino This church has several 12th-c. Romanesque elements. The simplicity of the foliated capitals and the undecorated corbels suggest Cistercian models. The slightly horseshoed arches recall Asturian or Cordoban styles. The small retablo is Neoclassic.

> 👟 A little more than a kilometer south of San Julián is the fortified *pazo* of the Ulloa family, one of the most powerful of the medieval Galician nobles. In the 12th c. Queen Urraca, ally of Compostela's Diego Gelmírez, was a frequent guest here. What remains is a massive rectangular structure with a solid 15th-c. arched door capped by the family arms. This was the setting for Pardo Bazán's novel, *Los pazos de Ulloa*.
>
> > 📖 Emilia Pardo Bazán (1852–1921) was Galicia's most prominent novelist. Born into a moneyed, noble family, she traveled extensively in Europe and soaked up the techniques of the French naturalist Zola. Her 1886 *Los pazos de Ulloa* was the first in a series of novels thick with Galician ambiance. Pardo Bazán was prolific: her short stories, essays, poems, and historical works (biographies of St. Francis of Assisi and Hernán Cortés) fill 43 volumes.

> 🚗 Ten km. further south, perched on rocky crags above the river, is the 14th-c. **Castle of Pambre**, built by Gonzalo Ozores de Ulloa. Although it is private property, and you cannot go inside, it is one of the most complete and spectacular castles anywhere near the pilgrimage Road.

The Road crosses the Río Pambre. Birches, willows, and narrow-leafed ash trees, shading a large variety of wild flowers and ferns, border the banks.

✳ Pontecampaña Here the remains of an ancient granite bridge cross the Pambre River.

✳ Casanova Just before this village is a stand of centuries-old oak trees.

✳ **Porto de Bois** At this small bridge a decisive battle was fought between Enrique II de Trastámara and the Conde de Lemos, Fernán Ruiz de Castro, who fought on behalf of King Pedro I el Cruel. Pedro's death at age 35 in 1369 led to the establishment of the Trastámara dynasty in Castilla. Lemos fled to Portugal and then to England, where he died in exile. People say the stream ran red with blood all the way to the Ulla River.

To the left of the Road, as you descend to the bridge, is yet another small noble house with the escutcheon of the Varela family. Another noble property bearing the arms of the Ulloa family is in the house-cluster of Vilacendoy some 1.5 km. further west.

> 🚗 North of the Road is the castle of the Felpós family, who early in the 14th c. made their living as brigands on the pilgrimage Road. Compostela's Archbishop Berenguel besieged the castle. It fell on July 29, 1321.

The soil in this region is laced with good deposits of clay that for centuries have supported a cottage brick-making industry. You will see occasional small kilns to the side of the Road.

✳ **Leboreiro** The village boomed from the 11th to the 13th c., offering important support services for pilgrims. The CC *Guide* calls it "Campus Levurarius" (Rabbit Field). The fact that the village is not mentioned in later itineraries probably speaks to its decline.

The 13th-c. Church of Santa María was rebuilt in the 18th c. and given a wood roof. The tympanum depicts the Virgin and Child with flanking angels swinging censers. Supporting the roof are a variety of interesting Romanesque corbels, including one very obvious phallus. Inside are 15th-c. wall paintings (San Sebastián, the Visitation, the Descent from the Cross). In the apse is a cross bearing the Lamb of God.

> 📖 A legend describes the founding of the Church of Santa Maria. A heavenly odor and, at night, a shining light emanated from a nearby fountain. Villagers dug up an image of the Virgin there and placed it on the altar of their church, but the next day they could not find the image, for it had returned to the fountain. This happened for several days, until the villagers carved this tympanum and dedicated the church to her, at which point the image remained calmly on the altar. This **Virgin**, with the lovely smile of someone who has gotten what she wants, is still in the church. Reports indicate that in the 1960s some villagers believed that she returned to the fountain every night to comb her hair.

Across the street is the Casa de la Enfermería, an old pilgrim hospice. A document dated 1172 says that it belonged to the Monastery of Sobrado (see ch. 84). By the 15th c. it was another of the many properties of the Ulloa family, whose escutcheon is still on the building. In recent times it has served as a hay barn.

Beyond Leboreiro the landscape changes to fields of heather.

✳ **Disicabo** The medieval bridge over the Furelos River is named for María Magdalena.

✱ **Furelos** The village once belonged to the Hospitallers of San Juan. You enter the town over an elegant medieval **bridge** with 4 arches. The old house just past the bridge on the left was a pilgrim hospice. A 12th-c. document says that it was maintained by a Brother Martinus. Another large house in the village was originally part of the Hospitaller holdings. Its coat of arms designates the Varela family.

Furelos's church of San Juan, reconstructed during the last century, preserves 1 wall and some mediocre corbels from the 13th c.

The parish of Furelos, like much of this area, was inhabited long before the Roman conquest. To the south of the Road are several *mamoas*, 2,000-year-old funeral barrows about 1.5 m. high and 8 m. around. One proved to have been constructed of old Roman roof tiles (Lat.: *tegulae*), and thus must have been contemporary with the Roman settlement. Just north of the hamlet of Piñor is the Castro de Piñor, a fortified hill town that preserves most of its parapet, 3 to 9 m. high.

82. MELIDE

HISTORY

Many nearby Neolithic dolmens (Maruxosa, Peña de Doraposo, La Capela) and *castros* (Reboredo, Lavacolla, Graña) attest to the dense settlement of this region in prehistoric times. The town was an important transportation hub where the Roman Via Traiana and the Cantabrian roads crossed. Curiously for a market town and transportation center, the town was largely defenseless. Only in 1316 were citizens granted permission to erect a wall, but the project was never finished.

If you are in Melide on Sunday noon—or for that matter anyplace else in Galicia on Sunday noon—you are likely to see a large black kettle steaming on one of the street corners and find a woman dispensing slices of octopus onto wooden plates, which you and the locals will wash down with cups of white *ribeiro* wine.

PILGRIMAGE

In medieval times the pilgrimage Road was Melide's most important feature, and the town strung its businesses, hospices, and residences in a long, thin line along the highway, called locally merely "la Calle." A 1575 document indicates that of the town's 100 families, the greatest number were innkeepers. During much of the Middle Ages the town sustained 4 large hospices.

In 1375 Fernán López, a notary in Melide, and his wife Aldara González donated money to a hospice just outside Melide run by the Franciscans of the Sancti Spiritus monastery:

> [The hospice] currently has 12 beds with mattresses and blankets to house and sleep poor people and pilgrims who seek lodging in the name of God, which beds can hold 24 people, 2 to a bed. . . . [We] donated a property so that its products would provide a hearth and beds and lodging and food and charity . . . ; the poor people and pilgrims should receive in charity 12 pieces of bread each day, and every day a mass should be said in the Monastery of Sancti Spiritus.

Castilian monarchs seem to have favored this hospice as well, for ca. 1400 Juan I exempted all of its staff from paying the head tax (*tributo y pecho*), and Juan II also exempted them from having to serve in the army in times of war. This hospice existed up to relatively modern times. In 1732 the bishop visited it and reported:

> There were 2 rooms, an upstairs, and a downstairs which served mainly as a bakery and dormitory for the monastery bakers. In the upstairs hospice against one wall were 4 beds each with its straw, sheet and cover, and a straw pillow, and the other wall was piled with firewood. Above this room is a high room where the families who visit the monastery can stay.

But by 1852 the former pilgrim hospice had been converted to military barracks.

MONUMENTS: 1. Iglesia de San Pedro. 2. **Iglesia de Sancti Spiritus**. 3. Oratorio de San Antonio. 4. Casas Consistoriales. 5. Iglesia del Carmen.

1. Iglesia de San Pedro. When the former church of San Roque, located on Melide's principal street, fell to ruin, its Romanesque door was moved to San Pedro. The interior is a mélange. Several 14th-c. tombs sport coats of arms of the

Ulloa and Galo families. There are some fragments of late-15ᵗʰ-c. mural painting. The retablo is from 1717.

In front of the church is a **14ᵗʰ-c. cross**, one of the finest in Galicia, depicting God the Father and the Crucifixion with María and San Juan Bautista.

2. **Iglesia de Sancti Spiritus**. This church was part of a monastery built in the 14ᵗʰ c. At the time it was the richest Franciscan monastery in Galicia, housing 30 monks. Parts were rebuilt in 1498 (using stones from Melide's ruined castle) and the 18ᵗʰ c. The interior plan is a simple Latin cross, covered by a Neoclassic barrel vault. There are various 15ᵗʰ-c. tombs of the Ulloa family. The **Baroque retablo** contains 2 parts, which are not very well joined. The lower section has some fine Baroque statues of Franciscan saints, whose haunting eyes gaze from beneath their hoods. The upper part depicts the Assumption of the Virgin contemplated by the 12 Apostles in a composition that gives a distinct sense of upward movement.

3. Oratorio de San Antonio. This prayer chapel was begun in 1671 as a small church. The façade is Baroque. Beside the altar are 2 kneeling statues. The man on the left with the long curly hair and fine clothes that show him to be a Knight of Santiago is Antonio Varela de Segade, who endowed the oratorio and who founded the Obra Pía confraternity. The man dressed as an ecclesiastic is Mateo de Segade Bugueiro, who became a bishop in Mexico.

Unlike most monuments in Melide, the Oratorio is almost always open, which makes it a convenient quiet place to meet or to take refuge from Galicia's nearly omnipresent rain.

4. The Casas Consistoriales. The town hall was once part of the palace of the Marqués de Corvera. By the late 17ᵗʰ c. it belonged to the archbishopric of Santiago.

5. Iglesia del Carmen. The church is located at the west end of the city, at the foot of the hill that was an ancient *castro* and later the site of a castle. The 1755 church has a nice *espadaña*, but not much else worthy of attention.

🚗 **San Antolín de Toques**. Six km. from Melide on the Toques road and then 2 km. uphill on the left (the sign says simply "Capella"), you will find the remains of an important, wealthy monastery. The site is entrancing: in a deep crevice halfway up a mountain, with a gushing stream pouring through the remnants of an ancient mill. The half-overgrown monastery dependencies, scattered along the gully, are delightful to explore.

The monastery is documented as early as 1067. But the small church is probably even earlier. It is typical of rural Galician Romanesque: a single nave and square apse, both covered with barrel vaults. The church appears to have been influenced by several 10ᵗʰ- and 11ᵗʰ-c. styles. The little rose decorations and the swastikas seem Visigothic, the sawtooth decorations in the apse seem Mozarabic, and the use of brick resembles Toledan Islamic architecture. The arch of the door is slightly elongated (*peraltado*), suggesting an Asturian influence. The series of blind arches on the walls of the apse seem related to international Lombard Romanesque. Inside, there are fine mural paintings and a 13ᵗʰ-c. Crucifixion. On one wall is a relief of an armed man confronting some sort of quadruped.

One km. before San Antolín, the tiny church of Santa Eufemia has an engaging series of Romanesque corbels.

Two km. beyond San Antolín is the 4ᵗʰ–1ˢᵗ-c. B.C.E. *castro* of A Graña.

83. MELIDE → ARZÚA

Route: MELIDE → **Santa María de Melide** → San Lázaro → Raído → A Peroxa → Santiago de Boente → Santa María de Castañeda → Pomariño → Pedrido → Puente Ribadiso → ARZÚA

There is very little net loss of altitude on the Road from Melide to Arzúa, but you will find yourself continually walking uphill or downhill, as the numerous small rivers in the region have cut deep valleys. Many of the smaller hamlets preserve their ancient—or at least premodern—rural Galician atmosphere. You will see *palleiros* (haylofts for cattle); the straw-covered huts called *pallotes*; and outside ovens for cooking cornbread (*brona*). You may see oxen pulling a cart with wood wheels and axles. Traditionally, people could recognize their family cart from a distance just by its sound. In the 1970s we saw many dozen carts on the Road, but in 1996 only one actually in use. Instead, we saw the carts parked in sheds, behind houses, and in barnyards, generally falling into ruin. By 1998 some of these had been reconditioned as planters for flowers. Others will surely end up in the hands of antiquaries, as the age-old material culture of rural Galicia passes from functional to decorative.

✳ **Santa María de Melide** This 12th-c. rural **Romanesque church** 1 km. from Melide has 2 decorated entrances, one of which has a simple tympanum. The west door has a triple archivolt with unusual inset geometric designs and some decorated capitals. One portrays Daniel flanked by 2 lions. Two windows on the south side are columned, arched, and capitaled in the Jaca style.

Inside, the single nave is covered with a barrel vault. Check out the **frescoes**. Although the iconography is archaic, almost Romanesque, they date from the 15th c. The central deity is the Trinity rather than the Romanesque Pantocrator or Virgin, but it is still surrounded by the Tetramorphos and the Apostles (**Santiago** is on the left). On the vault, angels play musical instruments. The bands of painted geometric decoration are also archaic.

✳ **San Lázaro** Just beyond Santa María a bridge crosses the small Río Lázaro. The small house with an anthropomorphic tomb in front, reutilized as a planter, is what is left of the medieval Capilla de San Lázaro. Santa María de Melide maintained a leprosarium here; a 1375 document records an annual donation of 6 pairs of shoes for the lepers. Just beyond, the 14th-c. roadside cross of San Roque portrays Christ in Majesty and, on the back, under the fleur de lis, Christ's divine judgment.

> 🥾 About 400 m. north of A Peroxa is the late-13th- or early-14th-c. chapel of **San Vicente de Vitiriz** (also called Rocamador). The portal contains a tympanum with a naïve Crucifixion scene. Some simple but expressive corbels support the roof.

Just before Santiago de Boente is an enormous Mediterranean pine tree, common in Andalucía and on the eastern coast of Spain, but relatively rare in Galicia.

✻ Santiago de Boente This church is documented from the 8th c., although the building you see dates from the 20th. Two capitals from the 12th-c. Romanesque church are incorporated into the external wall of the apse. The church contains a 19th-c. seated **Santiago** of no particular artistic merit. The escutcheons display the wolves of the Altamira family.

To the south of the modern highway are some stretches of medieval and Roman paving and a small, recently reconstructed Roman bridge over the Río Boente.

✻ Santa María de Castañeda The church of Santa María has a Baroque retablo.
    In the 12th-c. CC *Guide* the author says that the ovens that produced lime for the Santiago Cathedral construction were in Santa María de Castañeda, and that pilgrims were asked to bring stones with them from Triacastela to be processed here. Nothing remains of this operation. Nearby are 2 pre-Roman *castros*: Castromil and Boente.

👟 Beyond Santa María, on a low hill, is the 17th-c. square stone Pazo de Sedor, a manor house bearing the coat of arms of the important Galician Osorio family. In 1515 its tenth owner, Alonso Pita de Veiga, was reputedly the man who took French king François I prisoner at the battle of Pavía, a victory that for a time gave Spain supremacy in southwestern Europe. Carlos V held François for nearly a year before releasing him to return to France.

✻ Puente Ribadiso A bridge has spanned the Iso River here from at least 572. Records indicate another was built in 1188, and another in the 13th c. Pilgrims, punning on the name, called it Puente Paradiso (Paradise Bridge).
    The hospice of San Antón was at the site of the first house on the right past the bridge. It was administered first by a small convent of Franciscan nuns from Compostela and later (1523) by the Compostelan silversmiths' guild. It has recently been restored and again functions as a pilgrim *albergue*.

84. ARZÚA

HISTORY

Numerous *castros* nearby indicate that this region was intensively settled prior to Romanization. Several Roman roads also cross the region. To judge from its name, after the Christian reconquest Arzúa's new inhabitants came from the Basque region. The resettlement must have been fairly late, for the town is called Vilanova in the 12th-c. CC *Guide*. During most of the Middle Ages Arzúa was a small, walled village. It is still small, but the wall is gone.

Arzúa sits in the middle of fine dairy country. It is known for its cheeses and, since 1975, for its cheese festival in March of every year. In the plaza is a modern statue of a cheese maker.

PILGRIMAGE

In times past, Arzúa supported 2 hospices for pilgrims.

MONUMENTS: 1. **Iglesia de Santiago**. 2. Iglesia de La Magdalena.

1. **Iglesia de Santiago**. Several earlier churches dedicated to Santiago on this site have disappeared. The current structure was built from 1955 to 1957. The most interesting feature of its 19th-c. main retablo is its crowning **medallion,** held up by angels, depicting **Santiago's** intervention in the battle of Clavijo. The Rococo Retablo del Carmen is late-18th c. The Retablo del Rosario (1779–92) is undoubtedly the best artistically, harmoniously proportioned and with fine detail work. The Retablo de la Inmaculada was completed in 1907 in neo-Gothic style.

2. Iglesia de La Magdalena. The church is a former Augustinian monastery, founded in the mid-14th c. as a dependency of Sarria. In the 16th and 17th c. the Sarria monks maintained a small pilgrim hospice here. A 1607 document refers to 5 guest beds and to 3 monks in residence.

The church is rectangular, with a single nave. Its tower was destroyed in 1836 during the Carlist Wars (see ch. 25). The main entrance could not be more nondescript. Inside are some *ojival* arches and several 16th-c. tombs with coats of arms. There is also a modern statue of **Santiago Matamoros**.

At the north edge of Arzúa on the Sobrado road are 2 churches, San Salvador and Santa María, of no particular interest.

Nearby are 2 monasteries worth visiting:

—Sobrado de los Monjes. This early hermitage and small independent monastery became in 1142 the first Cistercian abbey in Galicia. Eventually the Cistercians had 16 abbeys in the region. Sobrado itself grew enormously in power and wealth: at its height it owned 130 villages, 13 monasteries, 20 churches, and 5 islands. From the first it offered services to pilgrims using the northern routes to Compostela. A logbook for 1773 indicates that Sobrado's 80 monks hosted more than 8,000 pilgrims that year alone.

The end came swiftly. One of the monks had a brother who was a prominent Carlist, and the monastery raised funds for the Carlist cause. In 1834

Queen Isabel II kicked out the monks and turned the buildings into military barracks. The *desamortización* scattered the extensive library and the monumental retablos and paintings all over the world. Some of the statues, in fact, were shipped to Australia. The cloister was demolished to use for gravel. In the early 1900s some attempts were made to preserve the ruins, and in 1954 a Cistercian monk, Antonio Fernández Cid, began restoration work.

Although almost nothing of the early medieval buildings remains, there are things to see. The Baroque façade is profusely decorated. The tunnel leading to the Renaissance sacristy, designed by Juan de Herrera, is decorated with carvings of plates of food. The church houses Baroque choir stalls on permanent loan from the cathedral of Compostela.

Medieval monks dammed the nearby Río Tambre to make a lagoon, which is today a preserve for aquatic birds.

—San Pedro de Mezonzo, a ruined monastery whose church is a 13th-c. Romanesque structure, is 21 km north. Among the remains are several pre-Romanesque and Romanesque capitals.

Route: ARZÚA → As Barrosas → Capilla de San Lázaro → Laberco → Raído → Fondevila → Cortobe → Pereiriña → Tabernavella → Calzada → Ferreiros → Boavista → Salceda → Brea → San Miguel → Santa Irene → Rúa → Burgo → ARCA

The route list looks long, but most of the hamlets are minuscule in size and notable merely for their Gallego popular architecture and beautiful scenery. We have signaled a couple of monuments to look for, but none will detain you long.

When we hiked here in 1974 it seemed as though every open field contained a few cows and a cowherd, often an older woman, umbrella in hand, patiently watching her charges manufacture milk for the region's well-known cheeses. Each time we have returned we have noted fewer pastures and fewer cows, now enclosed by fences, no cowherds in sight. Increasingly the hillsides are planted with eucalyptus trees, used for furniture and for the manufacture of paper.

📖 Several of the 134 species of Australian eucalyptus were brought to Spain in 1865 for use in construction, for which the wood proved to be unsuitable. These fast-growing imports have no natural controls, drive out the local species, mess up the ground with their leaves, nuts, and bark, and are enormously consumptive of water, which fortunately is not in short supply in Galicia. Their biggest "advantage" is that their owners do not have to stand all day, umbrella in hand, watching them grow, but instead can work in the factories in Lugo or Compostela.

✳ Capilla de San Lázaro Just outside Arzúa, just past the small stream called Regato das Barrosas, is the nondescript Capilla de San Lázaro.

✳ Calzada The name refers to its location on the Roman and pilgrimage Roads.

✳ Ferreiros Just past km. 72 is this hamlet, named for its ironworkers. The small church of San Verísimo was rebuilt in 1933, although an earlier structure on the site may date back to the 9th c.
    Some 300 m. to the south is the small church of San Mamede, with 2 small unremarkable Baroque retablos.

At the top of the hill just before Santa Irene is the pre-Roman Roda do Castro. Its circular defensive wall, in some places 3 m. thick, is hidden among trees and blackberry bushes. There are also some massive oak trees along this stretch of the Road.

✳ Santa Irene Near km. 80, between the old and new highways, is the small 18th-c. chapel of Santa Irene, with a small Baroque retablo. A nearby covered fountain contains an image of Santa Irene dating from 1692.

Just past the village the view opens to the south over the Ulla River basin and the distant Pico Sacro.

CC Book III narrates how the martyred St. James's body was brought to Galicia for burial. The lady Lupa, the region's ruler, set Santiago's disciples many trials in order to secure her permission to bury the Saint. The last was to take the body to Mt. Ilicino and to harness to the burial cart the wild oxen they would find there. She neglected to mention the fierce dragons that were terrorizing the mountain's inhabitants. With faith, and some judicious exorcisms, the disciples banished the dragons, and the ferocious oxen, cowed by the miraculous example, came placidly to the cart. The mountain was renamed the Pico Sacro. Centuries later, Christians built a small chapel to Santiago on the mountain. Today the small Romanesque *ermita* of San Sebastián is all that remains.

✱ Rúa Just before the hamlet are some of the largest eucalyptus trees you will see along the Road. Along this section you may catch a glimpse of a fox, attracted by the unfortunate local custom of depositing garbage in open dumps and of disposing of animal carcasses by throwing them into the woods.

86. ARCA

Near the former chapel of San Antón de Arca, of which nothing remains, recent excavations have discovered a pilgrim cemetery. Presumably this was the site of the Hospital de Santa Eulalia de Arca, whose 2 beds and kitchen were supported by the donation of several properties in the village.

The Church of Santa Eulalia de Arca is modern.

Just across from the town hall on the road to the church are 3 enormous cork oaks. The thick, gnarled bark is harvested once a decade.

Route: ARCA → San Antón → Amenal → Cimadevila → San Paio → **Lavacolla** → **Monte de Gozo** → San Lázaro → SANTIAGO DE COMPOSTELA

✳ **San Paio** After flanking the runway of the Lavacolla Airport, and just before descending into the village of Lavacolla, you will find the small rectangular church of San Paio (Payo, Pelayo) de Sabugueira, whose dedicatory plaque is dated 1840. A 12th-c. monastery that used to be on the site belonged to the Compostela Cathedral.

✳ **Lavacolla** Lavacolla, called Lavamentula in chapter 6 of the CC *Guide*, was an obligatory ceremonial stop for pilgrims. In the Middle Ages Christians washed seldom (and ridiculed Muslim and Jewish enthusiasm for personal hygiene); travelers tended to wash not at all. And yet some sort of ritual purification seems to have been required before entering the holy city of Compostela. Thus in the small river here pilgrims used to wash themselves (well, at least their genitalia: the Latin word *mentula* means phallus; in medieval Romance *colla* signifies scrotum). The CC *Guide*'s author carefully explained that pilgrims were attentive to more than the etymological minimum: "there the French . . . wash not merely their virile member, but, having taken off their clothes, wash off the dirt from their entire body" (CC: Book V, trans. Melczer, 88-90). Laffi's group "refreshed themselves" in the river and changed their clothes. Some historians believe that the tradition, and the toponym, may reflect a pre-Christian purification rite associated with the nearby Pico Sacro (see ch. 85).

In medieval times the Compostela tourist industry pitched its wares in Lavacolla. Documents tell us that just like today's merchants, 12th-c. Compostelans posted advertisements, in a variety of languages, touting the virtues and prices of their inns, restaurants, and taverns. Advance men from the hospices accosted weary, excited pilgrims with tales of how the scarcity of lodgings in the city required them to make decisions about, and payment for, lodging on the spot. Shills from the tavern industry, with wineskins from which the pilgrims could have a taste, booked people into tavern lodgings where the wine was seldom up to the quality of the sample.

MONUMENTS: 1. Iglesia y Cruz de Benaval. 2. Ermita de San Roque. 3. Stream.

1. Iglesia y Cruz de Benaval. The modern Neoclassic-style parish church is on a small hill in the center of the village. In front of the church is the Cruz de Benaval.

> 📖 Legend holds that Juan Pourón, the leader of a revolt in 1319, was to be hung. He asked the Virgen de Belén to demonstrate his innocence, crying out, "Ven e valme" ("Come and save me"). At that moment he died instantaneously, saving him from the pain and humiliation of a public hanging.

The cross that marks the miracle is named for his cry. On one side is the crucified Christ; on the other the image of the Dolorosa with a dagger in her breast.

2. Ermita de San Roque. At the exit of Lavacolla, this small rectangular chapel is now a barn, although it reputedly still preserves a small retablo with an image of the Saint.

3. The stream. Lavacolla's famous stream is barely a trickle of water. Near the center of the village it runs south of and parallel to the highway to Compostela. The marked hiking road crosses it on a small bridge, which is the best place to scramble down to wash your *colla*, or whatever you deem appropriate.

🚗 North of the highway, opposite the Monte de Gozo, is the pre-Roman Castro de Lavacolla, with a well-preserved defensive wall.

✳ **Monte de Gozo** The last hill that must be traversed before Compostela is the Monte de Gozo (Mount Joy, Monxoi), so named because of the euphoria experienced by pilgrims reaching its height and catching their first glimpse of Compostela's towers.

Pilgrims traditionally race up the 5-km. slope from Lavacolla. The first member of the group to reach the summit earns the right to call him- or herself "king." Many believe that this is the origin of the popular French name *Leroy* (the king = *le roi*). Another tradition holds that even pilgrims who came on horseback had to walk from the Monte de Gozo.

📖 Several miracles are associated with the Monte de Gozo. CC Book II's miracle 4 recounts the most famous of them. In 1080 a group of 30 pilgrims embarked from Alsace-Lorraine. Twenty-nine swore that they would assist each other along the Road; only 1 refused to take the oath. In Gascony one of the band fell sick and was carried on horseback for 15 days by his companions until, at the foot of the Pyrenean Puerto de Ciza, he could go no further. All of his companions abandoned him, except the one who had refused to swear the oath. After praying all night, he tried to help his sick friend across the pass, but in the evening the friend died on the freezing heights. As the faithful pilgrim waited for dawn to bury his friend, a passing knight offered to help. He took the corpse in his arms and lifted the pilgrim to the flank of his horse. The 3 rode all night, and when dawn broke, they found themselves atop the Monte de Gozo. The dead pilgrim was buried in Compostela, and his friend completed his pilgrimage with the help of their benefactor, Santiago.

Many of the pilgrims who have written about their journeys describe the rapture of this first sighting. Bartolomé de Villalba wrote in the late 16th c.: "[The pilgrims] looked like those tortured souls at sea when they first spy the safety of port" (1:381). Laffi described the experience in some detail:

We climbed for about half a league to the top of a hill called the Monte del Gozo. From here we could discern Santiago, the city we had so much longed to reach, some half a league away. On seeing the city we fell to our knees and, with tears of great joy falling from our eyes, we began to sing the *Te Deum*. But we had sung no more than two or three verses when we found ourselves unable to utter the words because of the copious tears which streamed from our eyes, so intense were our feelings. Our hearts were full and our unceasing tears made us give up singing, until finally, having unburdened ourselves and spent our tears, we resumed singing the *Te Deum*. Singing as we walked, we carried on down to the outer suburbs of Compostela. . . . [Laffi; trans. Hall (1997), 161]

Albani's group of Italian pilgrims in 1743 saw the bell towers, knelt down and kissed the ground a thousand times, took off their shoes, and began to sing hymns. The group of students with whom we trekked to Compostela in 1974, although largely secular in outlook, reacted in almost exactly the same fashion. The summit then was mainly small vegetable gardens. As we looked across the cabbages and spied the distant cathedral towers, most of us fell to our knees as tears welled up in our eyes. For a few moments none of us could speak. Then we pulled ourselves to our feet, hugged each other, and descended to Santiago singing not Laffi's *Te Deum*, but the CC's most famous pilgrim hymn, "*Dum pater familias.*"

The summit used to be marked by the small chapel of Santa Cruz. In 1105 Archbishop Diego Gelmírez led a procession of all the city's clerics, dressed in their finest church vestments, preceded by altar boys swinging censers of fragrant incense and accompanied by silver processional crosses and embroidered banners, from the Compostela cathedral all the way to the new chapel for its consecration. Today a modest new chapel of San Marcos sits just to the north of the summit.

Alas, Monte de Gozo today is much different than what it was in the Middle Ages—much different, in fact, from what we experienced in 1974. The cabbage field through which we glimpsed the cathedral spires has been replaced by hectares of neatly mowed lawn, in the center of which rises an impressive monument to the Road, built for the 1993 Holy Year. To the south are communication towers and a sprawling hospitality complex with beds for several thousand pilgrims. Compostela itself has grown, so that the Monte de Gozo is encompassed by the city's eastern suburbs, and a gigantic apartment and commercial complex has been allowed to block the view of the old city, the city which for medieval pilgrims, exhausted and exhilarated after months on the Road, used to rise above the rolling pastoral landscape of Galicia like a longed-for Jerusalem.

From the Monte de Gozo to the Compostela cathedral you have an hour or more of city walking. Once you have crossed the bridge over Compostela's new multi-lane circumferential highway, you will climb a gentle but very long hill toward the city center. At the top, you will find on the left the small Capilla de San Lázaro. In 1149 the monks of Santa María del Sar founded a leprosarium on this site, but nothing remains from that early period.

88. Santiago de Compostela

Compostela is the end of the pilgrimage.

Your pilgrimage and this book have led you through more than 350 towns and villages on your way to Compostela. Now you are here! Your first desire—and depending on your motive, your first duty—is to hurry to the cathedral to see the Apostle's tomb, and to fulfill the age-old rites of pilgrimage. Therefore, we begin this last chapter of the book with a new section, the Rites of Pilgrimage. We recommend that you read this section first, then visit the cathedral and do your thing. Later, when you have shaken off the dust of the Road and have begun to step down from the euphoria of arrival, you can take time to enjoy the artistic splendors of this unique city of pilgrims and bishops, of merchants, students, and kings.

RITES OF PILGRIMAGE

Medieval sources prescribe and describe numerous activities for pilgrims arriving in Compostela. Traditionally, once they had been hosteled, pilgrims spent their first night in the city in vigil in front of the cathedral, or—if the church doors were open—in front of the high altar. They would group by country and language, singing hymns and playing whatever instruments they had brought with them. Pilgrims often fought with each other to get a good spot at the altar. In fact, the competition was so bloody in 1207 that the church had to be cleansed and reconsecrated.

A 13th-c. source suggests this order of activities for the next morning. Pilgrims offer their personal prayers and deliver the prayers and offerings that they had been entrusted to bring to Compostela. Midmorning, a bell would ring for mass, and from the high altar a priest would announce—in the languages of whatever pilgrims were present—the indulgences being granted that particular day. He would then invite the pilgrims to deposit their offerings. The first invariably went to Santiago, and then to whatever favorite saint the pilgrims could find in one of the lesser chapels. After the offerings, pilgrims would confess to a priest who spoke their language, and then in the Capilla del Rey de Francia obtain the certificate—called the *compostelana*—that they had completed the pilgrimage and received their indulgences. The oldest extant *compostelana* was granted to André le Breton in 1321.

In 1974 we obtained our *compostelanas* in the cathedral sacristy, after having been interviewed at length to certify our legitimacy as walking pilgrims. Nowadays there are so many pilgrims that the certificates—of religious or of secular pilgrimage—are given in the Oficina de Acogida de Peregrinos opposite the Puerta de Platerías.

Next, pilgrims climbed the stairs behind the altar to touch the statue of Santiago. The German pilgrim Arnold von Harff reported in 1497: "On the high altar is a great wooden shrine made in honour of St. James. On it is a silver crown, and the pilgrims ascend behind the altar and place the crown on their heads, wherefore the inhabitants make fun of us Germans" (Harff; trans. Letts, 275). In the 16th c. we have reports of a golden crown that pilgrims put on Santiago's head, but by the end of the century it had disappeared. By the late 17th c., pilgrims were hugging the statue and some of them put their own hats on the image, a custom that Cosimo de Medici found ridiculous.

📖 Unlike pilgrims at many religious shrines and pilgrimage sites, Compostela pilgrims seem always to have had the right to touch the altar, embrace the Saint, and to put on the crown. Pilgrimage, after all, is based on the belief that certain places have a special link to the divine, and that physical contact—being there, touching the relics, in some shrines drinking from the sacred spring—somehow brings the spiritual power directly to bear on the individual pilgrim.

Domenico Laffi, whose commentaries have accompanied you on your journey, recorded that he and his companions celebrated their arrival in this order: They knelt before the altar and gave thanks for their safe arrival. Next they climbed the stairs to embrace the statue, noting that "if you kiss it reverently you will be granted plenary indulgence, though you are not allowed to touch the sacred body itself. Pilgrims put their cape on the statue and their hat on its head while they embrace it, and then stay a few moments." Laffi's group prayed before the altar a second time. Then, their goal having been reached, their prayers recited, and their vows fulfilled, Laffi notes how they—like every pilgrim before and since—underwent a fundamental transformation from pilgrim to tourist: "we walked round the church, marveling greatly at everything" [Laffi; trans. Hall (1997), 163].

Modern pilgrims usually enter the cathedral from the Obradoiro Plaza, climbing up the monumental Baroque steps. They pause in the Puerta de la Gloria to view the serene image of Santiago that welcomes pilgrims from the *parteluz* in the center of the door. This is a place to pause in prayer, and to initiate your physical contact with the mystery of Compostela by touching your hand to the column that holds the Saint. In fact, over the centuries so many pilgrim hands have caressed the central column that 5 finger holes are worn deep into the marble. From the portal, pilgrims march up the central aisle to the altar rail, where again they pause in prayer. Next, they climb the stairs behind the altar to embrace the Baroque statue of the Saint. And from there they descend to the crypt to view the casket with the relics. So many pilgrims seem to leave a bit of their journey in the crypt—their walking staff (*bordón*), the cross or scallop shell that they have carried with them—that each night the cathedral staff has to truck away the day's offerings. It is not a new problem: regulations written in 1250 destine for the altar all donated candles, wax, cloth, and incense, and for the cathedral workshops the staffs, crosses, swords, bells, candelabra, and anything else old, unserviceable, or able to be melted down.

During Holy Year (when the Saint's day falls on a Sunday: 1993, 1999, 2004, 2010, 2021) pilgrims enter the cathedral through the Puerta del Perdón on the east side. The door is solemnly opened on the eve of the Holy Year and closed with equal ceremony at midnight on December 31. In the summer months, and particularly around July 25, the lines to embrace the statue or to descend to the crypt may circle the entire church.

Since many pilgrims undertook the journey to earn forgiveness for their sins, the indulgences they received were of prime importance. Each indulgence annulled a certain number of sins, or lessened by some number of days the time a sinner would have to spend in purgatory. Medieval pilgrims collected these treasures avidly, keeping tabs for themselves and their loved ones, and seeking out places and activities that would grant the most substantial pardons. Compostela was a prime source.

A 13th-c. catalog, echoed in 1456 by the British pilgrim William Wey, records these indulgences:
    —for making the trip to Compostela: remission of one third of one's sins; if you die on the Road, total remission
    —for taking part in each religious procession in the city of Compostela: 40 days' indulgence; if the procession is led by a mitered bishop, 200 days more
    —if the procession is that of July 24: 600 days
    —hearing mass at which an archbishop, dean, or cardinal officiates: 200 days
    —hearing mass at the Monte de Gozo: 100 days

In 1576 a Church synod confirmed that pilgrims who visit the cathedral on July 25 and confess their sins will receive plenary indulgence. Pilgrims in Holy Years also receive plenary indulgence.

HISTORY

Archaeological evidence—such as an ancient tomb discovered near the Iglesia de María de Salomé on the Rúa Nova—indicates that the gentle hill between the Sar and Sarela Rivers was already occupied in pre-Roman times. Excavations under the cathedral floor have turned up a variety of Roman remains, including an altar dedicated to Jupiter. Suevi remains from the Visigothic period have also been found. After that there is a gap in the archaeological record until the 9th c.

Legends surround the discovery of Santiago's tomb ca. 813 (see Introduction). What is certain is that the site began drawing pilgrims, and that a succession of ever-larger churches were built to venerate the relics. The city's importance as a commercial, religious, and political center grew apace. As Compostela grew wealthy it became a tempting target. Normans assaulted the city and burned many buildings in 968, killing Bishop Sisnando Menéndez. Some 30 years later, when word reached Compostela of Almanzor's imminent arrival, Bishop Pedro de Mezonzo hid Santiago's bones. When the Cordoban warlord strode into the church, he found Mezonzo praying at the altar and, recognizing him as a holy man, spared his life. On the other hand, Almanzor destroyed the cathedral, made off with the bells, and all but razed the city.

Actually, Santiago's bones were hidden several times in successive centuries to keep them out of the hands of various threatening parties, such as Drake, who wanted them for England, and various Spanish monarchs, who coveted them for the Escorial. Eventually their exact location was forgotten altogether, although pilgrims continued to venerate an urn on the altar that they believed held the bones. Excavations in 1878–9 unearthed some bones that—when the discoverer went temporarily blind—were held to be

SANTIAGO DE COMPOSTELA

those of the Apostle. Six years later Pope Leo XIII issued a bull verifying the validity of the relics, thus—at least officially—ending all controversy.

After Almanzor's raid, rebuilding of the city's walls and towers began immediately. Bishop Mezonzo undertook a grandiose new church on the basis of money contributed from the far corners of Christendom. As Christians gradually gained the upper hand in the Reconquest wars, Muslim border princes increasingly bought peace by paying protection money (*parias*), a percentage of which purchased stone in Compostela. The funding, and building, continued well into the 13th c. In 1236 Fernando III finally captured the city of Córdoba and forced Muslim captives to carry back to Compostela the bells that Almanzor had stolen 239 years before.

Perhaps the most important—as well as colorful—figure in medieval Compostela, and the force behind the extraordinary popularity of the 12th-c. pilgrimage, was Diego Gelmírez, who was bishop from 1100 to 1140. His achievements as a builder are legion. He constructed Galician coastal defenses and helped create a navy. His hydraulic engineers brought fresh water to the burgeoning city and created public fountains. His vision of an architecturally grandiose Compostela gave impulse to the construction boom of the early 12th c.: the cathedral, the archbishop's palace, and the churches of Santa Susana, San Fructuoso, and San Benito. He was a master of both religious and secular politics. He got Compostela named an archbishopric, and he nearly persuaded the Pope to transfer the primacy of Spain to there from Toledo. In politics, his support for the succession of King Alfonso VI, his alliance with the King's sister Urraca in her war against her son Alfonso VII, and his successes in staving off conquest by Aragón's Alfonso I el Batallador were all key events in Castilian history. In 1108 he even persuaded King Alfonso VI to permit him to coin money in Compostela.

In Gelmírez's Compostela, national politics played themselves out at the local level. His autocratic ways led the burghers of Compostela to side with Alfonso VII against him and Urraca and, in perhaps his most difficult moment, to rise up against him in revolt. As you stand in the Plaza del Obradoiro, looking at the façade of Gelmírez's palace, imagine the tumultuous events of 1116, so vividly described in the present tense in the pro-Gelmírez *Historia compostelana*:

> The Church of the Apostle is assaulted. Across the altar fly stones, arrows, darts. The battling traitors commit sacrilege.... The perverse aggressors burned the church of Santiago, setting fire to one side and the other, burning the furnishings and hangings.... Men and women cry out in grief and curse the authors of so much evil. Oh! And how they cry, the pilgrims who had come from diverse regions to visit the body of the Apostle!

Gelmírez and the Queen take refuge in one of the towers of his palace, but the mob follows:

> They run, steal, throw down vestments and goblets of gold and silver and all the possessions of the Bishop and Queen. Everything is destroyed, and divided among the evil enemies.

Gelmírez's men bravely defend the tower, and the mob below is momentarily halted:

> They protect their heads under their shields which they had joined together, and manage to introduce fire through a window in the lower part of the tower, tossing on anything which would fuel the flames.

Gelmírez, stoically mouthing comparisons with Shadrach, Meshach, and Abednego, leads his men to the highest part of the tower. The mob offers Urraca safe conduct, and with Gelmírez's encouragement she goes down:

> They throw themselves on her, seize her, hurl her to the ground in the mud; they fall on her like wolves, tear her dress, and leave her face down on the ground with her body shamefully naked to everyone's eyes.

Gelmírez prepares himself for martyrdom, and holding before his face a cross given to him by the abbot of San Martín Pinario, descends to meet his fate. The *Historia compostelana* treats what follows like a miracle:

What a marvel! He walks among the fighting troops, through the ranks of his fiercest enemies (more than three thousand in number), without being recognized by a single one. He reached the place where the queen lay in the mud, trod on by the multitude of aggressors; and seeing her so cruelly naked and debased, transfixed by grief he walked on by, and went into the church of Santa María de la Corticela [ch. 114].

Many of the Bishop's followers were killed trying to escape from the tower. Eventually Urraca dragged herself up and made her way to the Church of Santa María to join Gelmírez, and from there—after a number of picturesque adventures and narrow escapes—to link forces with King Alfonso VI and fight their way back to power.

Eventually the tumult subsided, at least for a while. For the next several centuries tensions persisted between the Compostelan see and the papacy, the peasants and their lords, Portugal and Castilla, and the nobles and the burghers. Still, there were occasional islands of calm. Bishop Juan Arias's tenure (1237–66) was one of these periods of peaceful prosperity. Yet trouble always lay just below the surface. In 1366 King Pedro el Cruel had the new archbishop Suero Gómez and the dean of the cathedral Pedro Álvarez murdered because he thought they supported the upstart Trastámara rebels. The dynastic wars of the late 14th c. enveloped Galicia and Compostela. The city was even occupied for a time by the duke of Lancaster, who claimed the throne of Castilla by virtue of his marriage to a Castilian princess. Even while all this was going on, pilgrims continued to come, new churches were built, and the towers were added to the cathedral.

The Fonseca family, three of whose members were archbishops, dominated 15th- and early-16th-c. Compostela history. Alfonso de Fonseca I worked hard to pacify the archdiocese after more than a century of violent conflicts with the city's burghers. His successor, Alfonso de Fonseca II, continued the process. He was embroiled in the *irmandiñas* wars of the 1460s (see ch. 76). Once the rebellious burghers were quashed, he supported Isabel de Castilla in the dynastic war against her half brother Enrique IV. He hosted Isabel and Fernando de Aragón in 1486. Alfonso de Fonseca III (who subsequently served as archbishop of Toledo) supported the succession of Carlos V in 1520 and hosted a session of the royal *Cortes* in Compostela that year. As enthusiastic promoters of the new Renaissance Plateresque style, the Fonseca family left a visual stamp on the city, as can be seen in the Hostal de los Reyes Católicos and the Colegio Mayor de Fonseca.

Throughout the 16th and 17th c. pilgrims continued to come. The cathedral accountants logged donation after donation. The expulsion of the Jews, the bubonic plague of 1560, raids on the Galician coast by Turkish pirates and by Sir Francis Drake, and the war with Portugal in 1640 all dealt blows to the local economy. Municipal and hospice records document that along with true pilgrims were increasing numbers of beggars and false pilgrims, *coquillards* who sported the scallop shell as their ticket to free board and lodging. Also affecting the pilgrim flow was the northern European Protestant Reformation, which derided pilgrimage as one of the external, Romanist manifestations of probably false piety. On the other hand, cathedral records of those years note many visits by Irish and English Catholic pilgrims presumably fleeing religious persecution in their own lands, or atoning for their reactions to that persecution.

Attention focused on Compostela in the early 17th c. when Santa Teresa de Ávila was nominated to replace Santiago as the official patron of Spain. Militant religious conservatives like Francisco de Quevedo argued that Santiago was Spain's traditional protector, and that the nation risked much if it opted to switch divine horses in the middle of the historical stream. Eventually the Santiago forces triumphed, James remained as patron, and King Felipe IV's conscience was assuaged by increased donations to the cathedral.

With all the attention, both the national and Church leadership felt that the old cathedral was a bit shabby for the home of the patron of Spain. Its sober straight Romanesque lines seemed dowdy when compared to the effervescence of the new Baroque styles. The canon in charge of the church's physical spaces, the architect José de Vega y Verdugo, was delighted with the direction of the debate. When King Felipe IV came through in 1643 with a promise of several thousand ducats in annual donations, matched by the Order of Santiago, Vega had his license to build. The first project was the main altar, its design drafted that same year. Next came revisions to the Pórtico de la Quintana. Then the bell tower. Master architects and masons flocked to Compostela, launching a hundred-year boom in Baroque architecture that included grandiose projects like the Obradoiro façade, retablos and chapels and church façades all over town, and new urban palaces for all of Compostela's merchant elite. The building campaigns transformed the appearance of both the cathedral and the city, and spurred the development of a Baroque style that was uniquely Compostela's. The new watchword was *grandeur*.

The early 19th c., on the other hand, dealt harshly with Compostela. Napoleon's troops destroyed most of what was not made of stone. The *desamortizaciones* of the 1830s stripped the religious Orders of their bases of economic support and emptied the monasteries. In 1835 the annual national *ofrenda* of the *Voto de Santiago* was annulled. Late in the century, when industrialization led to the modernization of port cities like La Coruña and Vigo, Compostela remained a backwater capital crammed with musty monuments, the home of a second-class university and a pilgrimage center whose glory days had passed.

Recovery probably began in 1878, when the new "scientific" interest in Spain's historical roots led excavators to find Santiago's bones. Scholarly erudition was followed by a minor popular revival of the pilgrimage. In the ideological battles of the late 19th and early 20th c., when traditional Catholic Spain felt itself threatened by the twin forces of modernization and secularization, the pilgrimage became a kind of symbol of the link between Catholicism and Spain's destiny. In the Civil War Galicia backed Francisco Franco—who hailed from the city El Ferrol, near La Coruña—as the champion of their traditional values. Falange party faithful made mass pilgrimages to Compostela. The Nationalist armies rallied to the ancient cry of "¡Santiago y cierra España!" After the war Franco gave substantial attention to the annual *ofrenda* and pumped funds into making Compostela a showpiece of Catholic Spain. The university, too, prospered from national attention. Today's Compostela reflects this half century of investment, as well as the renaissance of international interest in the pilgrimage over the last 20 years.

MONUMENTS: 1. Casa Gótica y **Museo das Peregrinacións**. 2. Catedral. 3. Palacio Arzobispal de Gelmírez. 4. **Hostal de los Reyes Católicos**. 5. Ayuntamiento y Palacio de Rajoy. 6. Colegio Mayor de Fonseca. 7. Monasterio de San Francisco de Valdediós. 8. **Monasterio de San Martín Pinario**. 9. Iglesia de Las Ánimas. 10. Iglesia y Hospital de San Roque. 11. **Monasterio de San Paio**. 12. **Monasterio de Santo Domingo de Bonaval**. 13. Monasterio de San Agustín. 14. Iglesia de San Fiz. 15. Universidad. 16. Iglesia de la Compañía. 17. Iglesia de Santa María Salomé. 18. Casa del Deán. 19. **Casa del Cabildo**. 20. **Convento de Santa Clara**. 21. Casa de la Troya. 22. **Monasterio de Santa María del Sar**.

You have met your pilgrim obligations, and now it is time to tour. Leave yourself 2 days minimum (we usually take four). Compostela's art includes almost all periods and genres from the early Middle Ages until sometime last week, so that as you tour you can test yourself on all that you have learned on your journey. However, 2 styles predominate: Romanesque, from the time of Gelmírez and the apex of the pilgrimage; and Compostela Baroque, from the period of the city's major economic boom in the 17ᵗʰ and 18ᵗʰ c.

You will see so much Compostela Baroque in the city that it is useful to set out here its principal characteristics.

—The dominant medium is stone.

—Large buildings with large, well-cut stones and large decorative elements combine to create a sense of wealth and grandeur. Lots of marble (or when the budget would not permit, faux marble).

—The clean lines of classicism are interrupted by ornamental swirls, broken arches, and ornate encrustations.

—Interplay of sharply angled and round geometric shapes.

—Decorations predominantly in high relief, so that the interplay of sun and shadow changes continuously during the day.

—Contrasting textures of plane surfaces and low-relief columns with protruding high-relief decorations and ornately decorated eaves and cornice railings.

—Complex *estípites*, columns incorporating inverted pyramidal shapes.

—As with almost all Baroque architecture both in Compostela and elsewhere, frames within frames, and altars within altars; contrasting lines of movement; and perfection in both the whole and its parts (see ch. 28).

1. Casa Gótica y **Museo das Peregrinacións**. We recommend you begin your tour here rather than at the cathedral. The Casa Gótica itself is not so interesting, but the museum has superb cutaway **models of the Compostela Cathedral** in each of its various stages of construction that should help you understand that building's intricacies. There are additional displays detailing the discovery of Santiago's tomb and the development of the pilgrimage. The museum also contains dozens of Medieval, Renaissance, and Baroque sculptures, and the famous Renaissance **painting of Santiago** by Juan de Juanes.

2. **Catedral**. This cathedral has many parts worthy of a detailed visit. For the exterior we will describe the **Obradoiro Façade**, the **Pórtico de la Gloria**, the **Puerta de Platerías**, the **Puerta de Perdón**, and the Puerta de la Azabachería. On the inside we will detail the overall layout of the naves and transept, and then the **Altar Mayor**, the Crypt of the Relics, the principal **chapels**, the **Tesoro** (treasury), the **Museo de la Catedral**, the **crypt**, and the cloister. As with Burgos, we recommend you make repeated visits rather than try to absorb this all at once.

The site of the cathedral has been holy for eons: excavations under the crypt beneath the Pórtico de la Gloria have found remnants of a pre-Roman necropolis. Remains of a Roman cemetery were found under the naves. Shortly after the relics were discovered in the early 9ᵗʰ c. a chapel was built, soon to be replaced by a larger chapel. About 896 Alfonso III of León had bishop Sisnando Menéndez erect a new church to accommodate the increasing streams of pilgrims (its foundations were revealed in the 1945–55 excavations in the nave). After Almanzor destroyed it in 997, Bishop Pedro de Mezonzo erected another in 1003.

In the late 11ᵗʰ c. Diego Peláez, dreaming of a grandeur to surpass anything in France, knocked it all down and began anew. The building's footprint was so large that it incorporated several nearby structures, such as the Corticela church, which became a chapel in the new cathedral. Though Peláez was replaced in office in 1088 with a French Cluniac bishop, the work went forward. The ambulatory was begun in 1075 and finished a remarkable 2 years later. Work was begun simultaneously on the transept, the nave, and the western portal. The Puerta de Platerías was begun in 1103, and enough of the church was completed so that the building could be consecrated in 1105. The next bishop, Diego Gelmírez, added a chapter house and cloister. Maestro Mateo completed the Pórtico de la Gloria in 1188. Judging from masons' marks on the stone (see ch. 15), more than 50 different sculptors worked on the cathedral. During the 13th to the 15th c. a number of chapels were added to the nave and *cabecera*. The cloister was rebuilt in the 16th c., and the Obradoiro façade added in the 18th.

📖 The Muslim chronicler Idrisi was impressed during his 1150 visit to the cathedral: "This famous church, to which come travelers and pilgrims from every corner of Christendom, yields in size only to that of Jerusalem, and rivals the Temple of the Resurrection for the beauty of its construction, its size, and the wealth of gifts it receives in donations. These are both large and small, and include over 300 crosses worked in gold and silver, encrusted with zircons, emeralds, and other stones of various colors, and around 200 images of these same precious metals. 100 priests attend to the religious needs, without counting the acolytes and other clerics. The temple is of stones, cemented with lime, and it is surrounded by the houses of the priests, monks, deacons, clerics, and readers" (140).

Exterior:
• **Obradoiro Façade.** If you are reading this at the foot of the monumental staircase, you are too close to appreciate the overall effect of this façade. Go out into the middle of the plaza or, better yet, stand just in front of the Ayuntamiento. The best time is late in the day when the façade catches the full light of the setting sun.

The bell tower was built in the 17th c., as was the innovative double stairway leading up to the west doorway. The monumental stairs served as a focal point for what became one of the largest projects during Compostela's 18th-c. boom: the complete renovation of the Obradoiro Square and the construction of a glorious new façade for the cathedral. Fernando de Casas y Novoa built the platform and 70-m.-high façade (1738–50). His design emphasizes vertical symmetry, cut irregularly by horizontal lines to give the whole a sense of shimmering balance. As with any great Baroque work, each of the details is a semiautonomous composition, centered in decorative elements. In turn, each forms part of the frame for other points of interest. Look first at the simple rectangular door/window capped by a simple semicircular arch. Then take in Casas y Novoa's masterful repetitions of those basic geometric shapes with variations in size, ornamentation, texture, location, and complexity. The massive amounts of glass, of course, are designed to let maximum light reach the Pórtico de la Gloria.

The façade's central portion is topped with a figure of **Santiago Peregrino**. Over the central windows is a representation of the urn containing his remains, flanked by his disciples Teodoro and Atanasio. The towers contain images of Santiago's parents, Zebedee and Salomé.

As you zigzag up the stairway, notice how the complex Baroque patterns change in shape and emphasis. They will vanish altogether as you pass through the unornamented door and find yourself suddenly in the late 12th c.
• **Pórtico de la Gloria**. This ambitious entrance to the cathedral was undertaken by Maestro Mateo from 1168 to 1188. Though conceived and executed in the Romanesque idiom, it shows an awareness of the *ojival* advances of Cluny, introduced by Abbot Suger in St.-Denis in 1144. To even up the irregular ground—picture the building set on its hill without the Plaza de Obradoiro or the Baroque staircase—Mateo built a basement, or understory, and then constructed the narthexlike porch above it. The portal was almost undoubtedly polychromed in the 12th c. Today it still shows traces of its 17th-c. repainting.

As with many Romanesque portals, here the theme is the Last Judgment and the saving power of Christ and of the Church. But the complexity and narrative coherence of this portal far exceed anything else sculpted in the 12th c. Old Testament pre-Christian history is represented on the left, the triumph of Christ in the center, and the redemption and condemnation of human souls on the right. The right and left doors have decorated archivolts but no tympana.

For the art historian Kingsley Porter in 1923, this door was simply "the most overwhelming monument of medieval sculpture." Given the international clientele of Compostela, it is not surprising that the Pórtico de la Gloria in turn influenced compositions not only in Galicia but also in France (Chartres and Rheims), Switzerland (Lausanne), and England (York). (Note: the portal lauded by the author of the CC *Guide* was an earlier west entrance to the cathedral, for he wrote several decades before this portal was built).

—The **left (north) door.** Here the theme is Judaism and Old Testament history as the precursors of Christianity. In the center of the inner archivolt is a tiny, smiling Christ the Savior, one hand raised in blessing, the other holding the book of truth. To his right are tiny figures of Eve, Moses, Aaron, David, and Solomon; and to his left, Adam, Abraham, Isaac, Jacob, and Judah. The exterior archivolt contains 10 figures that are wrapped around the cylindrical arch as if they were sitting at a table. They are thought to be pre-Christian Jews in the Limbo of the Just, awaiting the coming of the Messiah to effect their salvation.

—The central door. The **tympanum** depicts the resurrected **Christ,** crowned with majesty rather than thorns. He is surrounded by the 4 Evangelists, 8 angels with symbols of the Passion and 2 bearing *incensaria,* and 40 figures representing saved souls. His serene expression shows that here He does not judge, but rather shows the elect what He has suffered for their redemption as per Apocalypse, chapters 4 and 5. The 24 old **musicians** are drawn from the same text. One is tuning; another tinkers with the bridge of a viola da gamba; one adjusts the tension of a string on a psaltery, while another gives the pitch. Their **musical instruments** are so realistically sculpted that they are a fundamental source for understanding the nature of medieval music. Several reproduced instruments are displayed in the cathedral crypt and in the Museo das Pregrinaciós. The angels that sustain the nerves of the vault have an Aquitanian air, and the whole arrangement—similar to Vézélay, Saint Gilles, Toulouse, and Moissac—proclaims the French roots of this art.

—The **jambs** of the central door contain both **Old and New Testament figures** and represent God's kingdom on earth, surmounted by Christ in heaven. Among the Old Testament figures, the young, smiling Daniel is one of the most expressive images of its century. Daniel, Isaiah, Moses, and Jeremiah (with his curly beard) are balanced by Peter, Paul, and **Santiago** and his brother John, who seem to be engaged in conversation. **Santiago,** whose face is the same as the Santiago on the *parteluz,* bears a scroll proclaiming how God has sent him to Spain: *Me misit dominus.* As at the proto-Gothic churches of St.-Denis and Chartres, architectural function and figure are merged, with only the head and hands protruding from the single sculpted block. These figures are one of Maestro Mateo's most significant achievements, innovative for their size and placement as well as for their idealized naturalism with vivid expressions and graceful movement. They were much imitated and helped create the new sculptural style known as Gothic.

📖The Gallega poet Rosalía de Castro described them this way:

¿Estarán vivos? ¿Serán de pedra	Can they be alive? Are they of stone,

aqués sembrantes tan verdadeiros,   these faces that are so true,
aquelas túnicas maravillosas,   these marvelous tunics,
aqueles ollos de vida cheos.   these eyes blinded by life?
                                                 ["N'a catedral"]

—The *parteluz* depicts the Tree of Jesse, the often-represented genealogy of Christ, but here with several iconographic innovations. The figure
of Mary, at the top, is not touched by the twining branches, indicating
that she alone is free of original sin. The capital above the column presents
the temptations of Christ, temptations that He, unlike Adam, is able to
resist. And of course the welcoming figure is not Jesus but **Santiago**, with
his pilgrim staff, smiling to greet pilgrims after their arduous journey. His
halo is studded with jewels. This Tree of Jesse sustains not only Jesus, but
the entire Trinity, represented on the capital over the column: the holy
assemblage keeps monstrous sin—in this case the toads at the foot of the
parteluz—in its place.

Maestro Mateo's self-awareness as an artist is unusual for the
Romanesque period. After securing the King's and the Cathedral Council's
explicit permission, with pride he sculpted himself on the base of the *parteluz*
in the guise of a kneeling worshiper looking toward the distant high altar.
Today, stressed-out students clunk their heads against this kneeling figure,
the *Santo dos Croques*, to ensure success on their examinations.

—The **right (south) door**. These archivolts proclaim the promise of the
future. God the Father and God the Son are in the center. To their left are the
condemned, to their right the resurrected elect, whose childlike souls are carried heavenward by angels. The sinner at the top, his neck still ringed with
the noose with which he has hanged himself, is Judas. While the picturesque
torment of sinners in hell is a common Romanesque theme, this arch intro-
duces several local variants. A glutton is compelled to eat an *empanada*
(meat pie), while a demon keeps him from swallowing. A drunkard hangs
upside down, trying unsuccessfully to drink from a wineskin. Octopus tenta-
cles ensnare another sinner.

—The **vaults, west face, and other elements of the porch**. This porchlike
narthex was part of the original design for the portal. **Angels** at the 4 corners
of the porch, the curve of their wings perfectly fitting the arch, blow trumpets to signal that Judgment is at hand. On the Old Testament side of the
door stand **Job, Judith,** and **Queen Esther**, who seems to be flirting with
Daniel across the way. On the New Testament side are 2 unidentified figures
and **John the Baptist**, who carries a plate on which sits a proud, confident
Lamb of God—symbol of the Eucharist. Even the foliated **capitals** in this
assemblage are complex and show close attention to detail. Our favorite is
over the head of Santiago chatting with his brother: intricately interwoven
heads, legs, and foliage create an abstract design that only reveals its identity
as 2 birds upon close study. The leftmost of the **figural columns**—which
seems to be by a different sculptor than the others—contains detailed scenes
of warfare and hunting: knights in chain mail, archers, centaurs, birds taking
refuge in trees, etc.

• **Puerta de las Platerías**. The plaza and portal are named for the artisans who
fashioned trinkets in silver (*plata*) for pilgrims to take home with them. After
800 years the shops here still offer silver souvenirs to pilgrims.

Begun in 1103, this south portal was the most splendid Spanish construction
of its time. When the urban riots of 1117 severely damaged this part of the
church, the remnants of several portals were reassembled here, with their elements unfortunately scrambled. Although what we see today is a haphazard

and largely incoherent mishmash of sculptures of different types, materials, artists, and dates, it is nonetheless majestic.

—The overall composition presents 2 stories separated by a horizontal eave sustained by carved corbels and metopes. The polylobed arches of the upper story recall the Mozarabic-influenced transept you saw on San Isidoro in León.

—The **left tympanum**. The main scene is the temptation of Christ by fantastic demons. There are 2 sets: the monsters nearest Christ are rather crude, ugly demons, with little attention to detail. The **demons** to their right are rhythmically carved creatures with sinuous legs and long claws. Above them, a figure bent nearly horizontal rides a clawed beast. The figure appears so contorted in its current position that it may originally have been set vertically. Christ seems to be guarded by angels with *incensaria*; one of them is enmeshed in a thicket in which you can also see a snake.

The **Adulterous Woman** (or perhaps Eve, or perhaps María Magdalena) is much more expressive than the surrounding figures. Her rounded features, the sensually draped cloth, the flowing disarray of her hair, and the extraordinary attention to anatomical detail of her left leg indicate an accomplished sculptor familiar with classical models.

Our pilgrim-students always find this tympanum exciting, and they have good precedent, for when the author of the CC *Guide* visited Compostela in the 12th c., he was so dazzled that in his ninth chapter he described the tympanum in detail:

> ... above the doors, the Temptation of the Lord is sculpted. Before the Lord, in fact, there stand some repellent angels looking like monsters who set Him on the pinnacle of the Temple; others offer Him stones and urge Him to transmute them into bread; and still others display before Him the kingdoms of the world feigning to hand them over to Him if, on His knees, He adored them—may that never happen! There are, however, other angels—white, that is to say, good ones—some behind him and some above, who are ministering to Him with censers.... Eleven columns flank the portal.... Some of these columns are of marble, others of stone, all of them admirably sculpted with figures, flowers, men, birds, and beasts. The marble of these columns is white. And one should not forget to mention that there is a woman next to the Temptation of the Lord, who holds in her hands the filthy head of her lover beheaded by her own husband; and this one forces her to kiss it twice a day. Oh, what a great and admirable punishment meted out to the adulterous woman, to be recounted to everybody! [CC: Book V; trans Melczer, 124-5]

—The **right tympanum**. The central theme is the condemnation and flagellation of Jesus. Its sculpture is inferior to the left tympanum, though its narrative structure is more coherent. The best group may be Christ curing the paralytic man on the far left: compare the sense of movement in Christ and in the head of the sick man to the static quality of Judas on the left. Herod's throne has interesting details.

—The 2 tympana rest on monstrous *ménsulas*. The one on the far left has his head twisted back to bite the next person who enters.

—The door jambs. The 4 static, vertical figures, with elongated bodies and elegant clothing, probably came from another composition. On the far right, the woman with a lion cub in her arms is thought to make reference to legendary prodigious births in Toulouse where 2 women were said to have given birth to a lion and a lamb, symbols of the nature of the coming Messiah.

—The **figured columns**. As these are carved in the round, they were probably originally freestanding columns supporting a stone baldachin. This type of column is common in France but relatively rare in Spain. These three are particularly well done, with variation in the poses and expressions of the figures and in the columned arches in which each individual stands.

—The **capitals**. The capital on the far left is remarkable for its workmanship and for the young face of **God expelling Adam and Eve from Eden**.

—The buttress figures. On the left are **God creating Adam** and **David playing a rebec**. You have seen this cross-legged pose in Santo Domingo de la Calzada and in Carrión de los Condes. The rounded, expressive features and rhythmic—but not realistic—interplay of the looping drapery are characteristic of the sculptor called Maestro Esteban, who probably carved the Adulterous Woman on the left tympanum. You have seen his work in San Isidoro in León and perhaps in the Pamplona museum.

—The spandrels over the tympana. As in Sangüesa, these spandrels are an anthology of figures drawn from other locations and are incoherent in theme and structure. Sculptors of varying degrees of skill are discernible. For example, of the 4 angels blowing trumpets, only the angel at the left corner of the right tympanum is at all sophisticated. Several of the individual figures on this assemblage are masterpieces.

Figures toward the left:

    —**God chastising Adam**.

    —The centaur, probably Sagittarius, may be from a series representing the months of the year, as in León's San Isidoro.

    —San Pedro, identified by the keys to heaven that he carries.

Figures toward the center:

    —The hieratic **Christ** in the center and the 6 small Apostles to the right with expressionless faces and stylized anatomies and draperies are the work of the so-called Maestro del Cordero.

    —**Santiago** between the 2 ornate cypress trees, stepping on a monster. The style of the image is French, closely resembling another one in Toulouse. Many of the details—the schematized undulations of the hemline, the gathered folds, the articulation of sleeve hem and folds, the articulation of the eyeballs and the arched brow, and the ornamental border—resemble the great San Pablo in Moissac, on one of the pilgrimage routes in France.

    —Below Santiago in the center: the white stone plaque depicting the **transfiguration of Abraham**.

Figures toward the right:

    —**San Andrés**.

• Puerta de Perdón. Flanking the door are 24 saints and prophets that formed part of Maestro Mateo's original **Romanesque stone choir stalls**. They are displayed in pairs, exhibiting variations in pose and expression. Some pairs seem to be engaged in vigorous conversation. As on the Obradoiro façade, above them are **Santiago Peregrino** and his 2 disciples Atanasio and Teodoro.

• Puerta de la Azabachería. In this plaza artisans fashioned trinkets in black jet (*azabache*) for pilgrims to take home. The shops here still sell jet.

📖 Jet is a dense, coal-black variety of lignite, formed by the petrification of wood submerged in the ocean floor's mud. It is found in small quantities throughout the world and has long been prized as a gemstone. Greek artisans carved jet in the second c. BCE. It was popular among native Americans and later among British Victorians, for whom it denoted mourning. Its English name—jet—derives from the name of a Greek town where it was mined.

The Arabic name by which it is known in Spain—*azabache*—signifies "black stone." In the Middle Ages people believed that jet would protect the wearer against both snakes and the evil eye.

From at least the 13th c. high quality Asturian jet was carved in Compostela into trinkets which were sold to pilgrims as *mementi*. The art reached its height in the 15th and 16th c. when the jet-carvers' guilds dominated this area northeast of the Cathedral. The Italian pilgrim Cosmi de Medicio commented on the trade in the late 17th c. Excavations in Germany and Switzerland have turned up carved jet scallop shells, *higas*, and images of the Saint.

There is a splendid collection of Compostelan jet in Madrid's Museo de Valencia de Don Juan and another in New York's Hispanic Society of America.

Through the early 12th c. this was the principal entrance to the cathedral, sometimes called the French entrance. Its portal—described in loving detail in the CC *Guide*—had 2 doors, 13 columns (some are in the cathedral museum), and probably a tympanum with a Christ in Majesty. In the plaza stood a fountain so large, says the CC *Guide*, that 15 people could bathe in the water that spewed from the mouths of its 4 stone lions. An inscription indicated that it was paid for by Bernard the Treasurer "for the salvation of my soul and that of my parents" (CC: Book V; trans. Melczer, 122). The fountain was dismantled in the 15th c.

Nothing remains of the Romanesque portal except what has been incorporated into the reconstructed Puerta de las Platerías. The current structure dates from the mid-18th c., with a Baroque lower story finished off in the Neoclassic style. It lacks the pizzazz of Compostela's best façades.

Taken together, the 3 main Romanesque portals would have exhibited a certain unity of theological concept, progressing from the Incarnation (Azabachería), through Christ's appearance to the world (Platerías), to his Resurrection and the triumph of Salvation and Judgment (Gloria). It has been termed "the first effort anywhere to coordinate the decoration of multiple ensembles with parallel compositions" (Hearn). The ensemble probably had a political element as well. In 1116 Alfonso VII had just defeated the Almorávides near Toledo, and the inscription of the King's name on the Platerías Santiago relief suggests the joint mission of the Church and the monarchy to reconquer Spain from the Muslims for the glory of Christ.

Interior:
• Overview of the naves and transept. This is a pilgrimage church, a model developed in the 11th c. to handle the throngs of people who began streaming in to view relics. The earliest church with this plan is Saint-Martin in Tours, followed swiftly by Sainte Foy de Conques, Saint Martial in Limoges, Saint-Sernin in Toulouse, and then Santiago. These churches are **basilicas, with 3 naves, a transept to create a floor plan like a Latin cross, and a *cabecera* with radiating chapels.** Their major innovation is the **ambulatory**, a circular walkway projecting from the lateral naves around behind the high altar, where the principal relics were housed, allowing traffic to flow smoothly. The pilgrimage churches are gigantic, larger than almost anything built in western Europe from the fall of the Roman Empire until then. Compostela's cathedral is 87 m. long and 65 m. wide in the transept, with an audacious central nave 8.5 m. wide and 21 m. high, an unheard-of width and height for something that had to support a barrel vault. The 32-m.-high cupola that caps the crossing of the transept and nave was completed in 1445.

In a development that anticipated Gothic advances, in these churches the **weight of the vault is sustained by pillars**, since the walls are largely replaced by soaring arches that line the aisles. In Compostela the arches are elongated (*peraltados*), as in pre-Romanesque Asturian art, emphasizing their height. In both the central nave and the transept of the pilgrimage churches, the airy second-story **triforium** reduces the weight of the wall and provides indirect lighting. This Compostela triforium is unique in the Romanesque period because it runs completely around the church. In the pilgrimage churches the **pillars are complex and cruciform**, allowing columns of different heights to be joined in a single harmonious construction. The building stones are large and evenly cut, reflecting the wealth of resources poured into these churches. Massive round and squared blocks of masonry define the enormous, geometrically simple volumes of interior space. Here, as in the other classic pilgrimage churches, the decorative details are exquisite, even when—as is the case with many of the capitals sustaining the heavy arches of the vault—they are too high and too dimly lit to be clearly seen without binoculars and a strong light.

—The **Botafumeiro**. The *botafumeiro* ("smoke-belcher") must be Catholicism's largest *incensario*. On special occasions it is suspended from the cupola. The 1851 silver-plated brass censer in use today—the third of Compostela's majestic thuribles—replaces one donated in the 15th c. by French king Louis XI that was stolen by Napoleon's troops. Laffi's description of its use ca. 1670 could have been written yesterday:

> Before the high altar is a great thurible in the shape of a large lamp, attached by a rope to the ceiling at the very top of the dome. It is lowered when they put in the incense and light it. Then they draw it to one side, to such a height that only a few can still reach it, and then they give it a push. It swings from one door to the other, that is, from south to north, along the arms of the cross. Because of its size and speed it makes a great wind. The burning incense and other odours produce a thick, fragrant smoke, which permeates the whole church. [Laffi; trans. Hall (1997), 171–2.]

• **Altar Mayor**. Several artists intervened in this dazzling **Baroque assemblage**, in which every available surface is covered with ornate decoration, often in silver and gold: busts, crowns, chubby cherubs, curlicue frames, twisted columns and delicate balustrades, statues and candlesticks; each complex segment both a center of focus and a part of the frame of adjoining sections. The altar dates mainly from 1658–67, with reconstructions ca. 1890. The tabernacle (*sagrario*) is early-18th-c.

—One unusual feature of this altar is Domingo de Andrade's early-18th-c. baldachin, which is sustained by iron rods masked by 8 oversize angels. The 4 corners depict the cardinal virtues. Below the baldachin is a standing **Santiago Peregrino**.

—The **Santiago Matamoros** that crowns the ensemble was carved by Mateo de Prado in 1677.

—The **Romanesque seated image of Santiago** in the central niche, of painted stone, has been much reworked. It sits on a silver throne. Stairs lead pilgrims into a small chamber (*camarín*) behind the altar, where they can embrace this image.

• Crypt of the Relics. Under the altar is a crypt that recalls the Roman mausoleum in which the Apostle's bones were buried. The silver chest that holds the remains of Santiago and his disciples San Atanasio and San Teodoro was constructed in 1886.

• The **chapels** and other art on the cathedral's perimeter. The visit is ordered counterclockwise from the Puerta de la Gloria. While all of the chapels contain interesting works of art, in our view the most significant are the following:

—2. The **Capilla de las Reliquias** (1527). Note the starry effects of the dome. The 140 relics on the altar, of recent arrangement, were donated by pilgrims and notables over the centuries. Though pilgrims came to Compostela to see Santiago's relics, they found comfort knowing that their other favorite saints were represented here, too (José, Juan Bautista, Bárbara, and so forth). This chapel's small painted alabaster 15th-c. English retablo, with a delightful scene of Jesus calling his disciples from their fishing, was donated in 1456 by John Goodyear, an English pilgrim from the Isle of Wight.

The entrance to this chapel has served as a royal pantheon. The funerary statues mark the **tombs** of such notables as Ramón de Borgoña, father of Alfonso VII; Alfonso IX of León; Juana de Castro, wife of Pedro I el Cruel; and **Fernando II of León**, whose tomb was probably carved by Maestro Mateo in 1188. Another tomb is of Berenguela, the wife of Alfonso VII.

> 📖 The figure of Alfonso VII's wife is so pretty and serene that local girls still say that when someone is all dressed up she is trying to "be a Berenguela."

—4. The south transept. On both sides are interesting Plateresque doors leading to the sacristy and to the cloister. Another entrance, no longer functional, contains an 11th-c. **tympanum** representing **Santiago Matamoros at the battle of Clavijo,** one of the earliest to display this scene.

—5. Capilla del Pilar (aka Caballeros de Santiago). 18th-c. Galician Baroque by Andrade and Casas y Novoa. The octagonal cupola seems alive with decoration. The clean lines of the retablo's basic structure are complicated by profuse Baroque ornamentation.

—6. The Capilla de Mondragón (1521–6). Note the delicate nerves of the vault and the Gothic balcony. The terra-cotta altar with a Descent from the Cross by Miguel Ramón combines a Renaissance sense of balance with Mannerist details such as the hyperrealism of the dead Christ and Mary's gesture of grief, which is both tenderly introspective and theatrical.

—8. The painted Puerta Santa, flanked by painted Romanesque statues carrying scrolls. The *crismón* over the door incorporates a sun and moon along with the traditional alpha and omega.

—9. Capilla del Salvador. Built ca. 1075, it is probably the first chapel constructed in the cathedral. The current granite retablo is Plateresque.

—12. Capilla de San Bartolomé. The Romanesque architecture contrasts with the Plateresque retablo and showy Plateresque mausoleum.

—14. The Capilla del Espíritu Santo. Founded in the 13th c. and rebuilt in the 17th c. by Andrade and Casas y Novoa. The tombs date from the 14th to the 16th c. The 17th-c. retablo of Nuestra Señora de la Soledad used to be in the cathedral's *trascoro.*

—15. **Capilla de la Corticela.** In the 9th c. this was a church, one of Compostela's oldest. It was administered by the Benedictines of San Martín Pinario, who continued to have jurisdiction even after the church was incorporated into the expanded cathedral in the 12th c.—and in the process almost entirely rebuilt.

The portal to this chapel has a superb **tympanum,** either by Maestro Mateo or his workshop, depicting the adoration of the Wise Men. An unusual feature are the 2 riderless horses on the left archivolt. At the right rear is the 15th-c. sepulcher of an anonymous pilgrim woman from Bourgogne whose richly decorated attire, together with the location of her tomb in the cathedral, suggests that she was someone of wealth and status. On the left wall of the chapel's interior is a rough-featured 15th-c. Christ in the Garden of Gethsemane in polychromed granite.

📖 Students believe this image of Christ will bring them luck, so they often pass their written themes through the image's hands.

—18. **Santiago Matamoros.** This small chapel in the north transept is dominated by an animated, and often reproduced, 18th-c. statue of Santiago, his sword raised high, his horse trampling Muslim soldiers under his feet.

—20. Capilla del Cristo de Burgos. The beard and hair on this emotive 1754 crucified Christ remind us of the much-revered statue in the Burgos Cathedral. On the sides of the chapel are statues of the kneeling donors and small high-quality Renaissance retablos depicting San Jerónimo and Christ's entry into Jerusalem.

• **Crypt, treasury, and museum.** One ticket admits you to all 3 complexes. Together they contain a rich collection of church vestments, crosses, chalices, jewels, lamps, tapestries, and numerous images of **Santiago.**

—The **crypt.** Maestro Mateo designed this ingenious basement complex in 1168 to support the Pórtico de la Gloria. Its key is the massive **central column,** which holds up more weight than you would care to calculate as you stand next to it. Mateo carved the capitals and the arch's **keystones** that represent angels holding images of the sun and moon. Several chambers of the crypt are used to display impressive fragments of medieval sculpture, among them figures that were once on the crypt's own monumental entrance. Several cases hold reproductions of the musical instruments depicted on the Pórtico de la Gloria.

—The **treasury.** Among the masterworks on display are a 1544 **monstrance** by the goldsmith Antonio de Arfe depicting various episodes from the life and death of Santiago. (You saw a similar monstrance by his brother Enrique in Sahagún.) The 14th-c., jewel-encrusted bust of **Santiago Alfeo,** which contains some relics of this Apostle brought to Spain in 1108, still wears the necklace brought by Suero de Quiñones after the 1434 *Paso Honroso* episode at the Órbigo bridge (see ch. 62). At the entrance to the treasury is the **tomb cover of Bishop Teodomiro,** the man who authenticated Santiago's relics in Compostela and launched 1,200 years of pilgrimages.

—The **museum.** The museum's chambers honeycomb the walls facing the Plaza del Obradoiro. Excavations in the floor of the lowest level turned up a stretch of Roman street. Among the museum's treasures are many fragments of Romanesque sculpture, including a re-creation of Maestro Mateo's stone choir (being installed as we write). Wood panels from the 16th-c. cathedral choir depict several episodes from Santiago's life. Also pictured is the triumphant return of Compostela's bells from their exile in Córdoba after Almanzor's raids. And if you like 17th- and 19th-c. **tapestries,** this museum has the best collection in Spain outside of Madrid, including several designed by Goya.

• **Cloister.** A sober 16th-c. masterwork by Juan de Alava and Rodrigo Gil de Hontañón, mixing late Gothic and Renaissance elements.

3. **Palacio Arzobispal de Gelmírez.** Gelmírez's original palace was destroyed in the 1117 urban revolt. This new palace was begun 3 years later, and even though it was not finished for another 150 years, it still bears Gelmírez's name. This is the only large Romanesque palace extant in Spain. You can still see its 12th- and 13th-c. great hall, refectory, and festival hall. The large upstairs hall is covered by one of the

widest (8.4 m.) Spanish Romanesque vaults. Lighting comes from the rose window and from the other large-paned windows, separated by delicate columns and capped by polylobed arches. The room undoubtedly hosted the Church synods of the period. The graceful nerved arches, hinting at Gothic but still in the Romanesque idiom, rest on 13 **decorated corbels** that are the palace's most famous feature. Their theme of secular feasting seems to allude to royal wedding festivities. One corbel depicts a royal couple holding hands over bread, a priest reading from a book, and a juggler making a bear dance. Another shows the monarchs cutting with knives, a server with a soup pot, and a violist. On yet another the royal couple help play an *organistrum*, a musical instrument like the modern Galician *zanfoña*.

4. Hostal de los Reyes Católicos. When Fernando and Isabel visited Compostela in 1486, officials bemoaned the decrepit state of the old pilgrim hospice. Despite the fact that they needed every maravedí for the Granada War, the Catholic Monarchs promised the funds to build a new one, and dedicated one-third of the special Granada tax to its construction.

> 📖 Added to these funds were taxes on the wine, meat, cloth, and fish sold in Compostela markets, and the import duties collected in the Galician ports of Padrón, Villagarcía, Noya, and Pontevedra. Many wealthy pilgrims also made donations. But a large portion of the funds was eaten up by the administrators' high salaries and lawyers' fees in the lawsuits arising from land confiscation.

In all, it took 10 years to acquire the property and formulate the plans, so that the first stone was not laid until 1501. The architect was Enrique Egas, famous for his work in Toledo and Sevilla. Documents show that the Monarchs nearly drove him crazy with their micromanagement, intervening on the choice of stone, the placement of the chimneys, the kinds of fountains in each patio, etc. By 1509, although work still continued, the Hostal opened to pilgrims, with a dedicatory plaque on the second floor: *Magnus Fernandus: et grandis Helizabeth: peregrinis: divi: iacobi: construi: Iussere: anno salutis MDI* ("The great Fernando and the powerful Isabel ordered this to be constructed for pilgrims. The year of their health 1501"). In 1526 Carlos V expropriated property in front of the Hostal, closing an ugly, open sewer and demolishing buildings to leave an open view from the plaza. In 1542 the Hostal and the town collaborated in paving the plaza, creating the space we see today.

From the start, the Hostal combined 2 traditional functions: pilgrim hospice and infirmary. The 1524 *Constituciones* stated that the Hostal should open its doors to all sick people, except of course people with contagious diseases such as plague and leprosy. They legislated the staff: 1 attending doctor, 3 lawyers, a druggist, nurses, and a cleaning woman. They decreed how water was to be boiled for the sick, how the rooms were to be perfumed and ventilated, and how each sick bed was to have a bell for summoning the nurses.

> 📖 In 1550 Bartolomé Sagrario de Molina had only the best to say about the Hostal: "I believe that this hospital is so well known in every part of the world that all I can say about it will be readily credited. In the three large wards there are few days when there are fewer than 200 sick people, and the number is much larger in jubilee year. Yet every patient is treated with as much care as if the hospital had been erected for his particular benefit." [attributed to B. de Medina by Huidobro y Serna 3:210]

Similar care was taken with regard to pilgrims, even though the administrators believed them often to be a scurvy lot. The *Constituciones* prohibited the use of arms, or cards, or dice, or even playing ball. They permitted pilgrims to reside for 3 days in summer, 5 in winter. The 8 chaplains on staff were required to know a variety of languages, and 1 or 2 men were to scour the city every afternoon for French pilgrims who might not be aware of the hospice's services.

From time to time the Hostal added a third function: orphanage. A *torno*, a kind of lazy Susan in the outside wall, was provided to facilitate the receipt of infant bastard children. A 1541 register lists 131 orphan children housed in the facility. The administration paid nursemaids who cared for the children, but the orphans also were expected to render service as maids and cleaners.

The Franco government made the Hostal de los Reyes Católicos the jewel of their network of Paradores, tourist hotels in historic buildings.

By tradition and by Fernando and Isabel's charter, pilgrims walking to Compostela were entitled to 3 days' free food and lodging at the hospice. When we arrived in Compostela in 1974 with our group at the end of our first pilgrimage, the doorman's eyes popped with surprise, but we were duly housed and fed for free. Our lodgings were opulent, but in a dormitory-like room with bunk beds (and free toothbrushes). We were served delicious meals, but with the staff in the kitchen, 3 hours before normal Spanish mealtimes. We were welcomed with respect, but we were encouraged not to lounge in the salons with the paying guests. Alas, with the rebirth of the mass pilgrimage, these traditions are no longer possible to uphold.

• **Façade.** The central composition opens like a retablo around a **Plateresque door.** Each segment of the minutely detailed decoration is symmetrical around a vertical axis. On the pilasters are sculptures of Adam and Eve and of Spanish monarchs. The frieze depicts the Apostles and various saints, including a pilgrim **Santiago** and a **San Roque.**

—The gargoyles were an afterthought. Since there was no money left in the contract, 2 stonecutters were commissioned to make 32 at 6 *reales* each. The artisans obviously had a sense of humor (check out the sixth from the right, for example).

📖 Gargoyles are so named because their hollow throats serve as waterspouts. The same Latin root gives us *gargle, gurgle, gorge,* etc. Carved grotesques that do not channel water are not technically gargoyles.

—The balconies with their exotic corbels were added in the late 17th c.
• **The patios.** Each of the 4 interior patios with its columns and arches and canopial doorways was designed by a different architect. There was 1 patio each for healthy and sick men, and for healthy and sick women.
• **The chapel.** The intricate nerves of the vaulting and the soaring cupola recall those of the Burgos Cathedral. The entrance to the chapel is closed by an elegant *reja* with its escutcheons of Fernando and Isabel, together with their yoke-and-arrows device (see ch. 24). The carvings on the side walls of the chapel are so finely detailed that they look as if they were done in plaster, not stone.

5. Palacio de Rajoy (Ayuntamiento). The late-18th-c. Neoclassic façade, arranged around several vertical axes, nicely counterbalances the massive Baroque mountain of the cathedral's west face. The Palacio's central segment depicts **Santiago's apparition at the battle of Clavijo** on its triangular pediment.

6. **Colegio Mayor de Fonseca** (aka **Santiago Alfeo**). Founded by Archbishop Alfonso de Fonseca III in 1525, this was the humanities center of the Compostela University until the 19th c. It now houses the university library.

📖 For students all over Spain, this building, called simply "Fonseca," was emblematic of university life. Perhaps the most popular song played by the student street bands, the *tunas* or *estudiantinas*, begins by saying how sad the city is when the students have gone home for the summer: "Triste y sola, sola se queda Fonseca, triste y sola, se queda la universidad."

The building blends Renaissance and Plateresque styles. The monumental doorway, with its doubled Ionic columns and coat of arms with the 5 five-pointed stars of the Fonseca family, opens to a harmonious Plateresque cloister (resembling that of the Colegio de Irlandeses in Salamanca—another Fonseca project). To the left is the great hall, formerly the refectory. On one side is the pulpit from which edifying texts were read to the presumably silent diners. This room has a spectacular **Mudéjar coffered ceiling**.

Immediately next door is the Instituto de Estudios Gallegos. The corner building facing the Plaza del Obradoiro is the Colegio de San Jerónimo, now serving as the university rectorate. It dates from the early 16th c. Its striking **portal**, originally gracing a pilgrim hospice in the Plaza de la Azabachería, was carved in the 15th c. in the retro–Romanesque style.

7. Monasterio de San Francisco de Valdediós. San Francisco de Asís reputedly founded a community on this site during his pilgrimage to Compostela ca. 1214. The Franciscans paid their landlords, the Benedictines of San Martín Pinario, an annual rent of one basket of fish right up into the 18th c. The monastery's late Gothic chapter house makes a good meeting hall: 20-year-old Carlos V held *Cortes* here in 1520. The building is still a Franciscan monastery, surviving now on revenues from the attached luxury hotel.

- The **chapter house**. Of the original Gothic structure only a few arches remain at the entrance from the cloister into the chapter house, but these are worth a moment's look. The capitals and arches are covered with elegant harpies and elongated Franciscan monks.
- Cloister. The monastery's other notable feature is its second cloister, Neoclassic in style and perfectly proportioned to create a sense of harmony and calm. The second story of the cloister has been outfitted for a **Museo de Tierra Santa**, a repository of Holy Land artifacts ranging from the spearheads of the Neolithic through the grenades of the 1948 Israeli War of Independence. Most striking, and informational, are the models of the Second Temple, of the city of Jerusalem in Christ's time, of the Church of the Holy Sepulcher, and so forth.
- The Church. The monastery church next door is a massive 18th-c. Baroque structure, inspired by Italian classicist models. The central nave is so high it easily accommodates a spacious upstairs gallery overlooking the congregation far below. The classic-style dome over the crossing is higher still. The central retablo, with tall, elegant faux-marble columns, speaks more of power than of wealth. This church is designed to overwhelm, and it does.

In front of the monastery, the large statue dedicated to the Franciscan Order was completed in 1930 by the Compostelan sculptor Francisco Asorey (1889–1961).

8. The **Monasterio de San Martín Pinario**. Here in the 10th c. stood the small oratory of Bishop Sisnando, which grew into one of the most powerful monasteries in

Galicia. At one point it had over 30 dependencies. The gargantuan current building (20,000 square m.) dates mainly from the 17th c. The San Martín complex has 2 basic parts: monastery and church.

• The monastery. The imposing **monastery façade**, completed in 1697, combines the massive, sober elegance of the late Renaissance with the theatricality of the high Baroque. It is capped by Herrera-style pinnacles and a San Martín dividing his cloak.

The monastery has 3 cloisters. The largest encloses a graceful fountain by Casas y Novoa. Monumental staircases lead to the upper stories. The monastery today serves as a diocesan seminary and a student dormitory.

• The church.

Exterior:

• The **façade's** most interesting feature is the late-18th-c. Baroque staircase that winds down to the front door. The façade itself is one of the few in Compostela organized like a Baroque retablo.

Interior:

• The interior of the 17th-c. church, much of it the work of Mateo López, continues the sense of monumental Mannerism.

• The **retablo mayor**, by Casas y Novoa and Miguel de Romay, is one of the most ostentatious and engaging constructions of the Spanish Baroque. Its intricate design, based on ascending and intersecting triangles, its exuberant angels, and its daring blend of architectural and sculptural elements is unique. It features paired lateral sculptures of the warriors **Santiago and San Millán** (in Benedictine robe, with the wavy sword). In the center the Trinity crowns the Virgin Mary.

• The fine Baroque lateral retablos—which would be the center of attention in almost any other church—narrate episodes from the life of San Benito and that of the Virgin.

• The **low choir**. The 149 **plaques by Mateo de Prado** (1639–47) are in 3 tiers: scenes from Mary's life (lower tier), militant Counter-Reformation saints (middle), and the life of San Benito (upper). The contorted figures, with their emphasis on musculature (see, for example, San Juan Bautista), recall those of Burgos's Hospital del Rey, and are among Spain's best from the mid-17th c.

• The high choir demands attention for the wizardry of its nearly flat arch.

9. Iglesia de Las Ánimas. The sculpted polychromed relief of Souls in Purgatory gives the church its name. The famous 18th-c. architect Ventura Rodríguez is thought to have intervened in the design of this church. The **façade**, like so many of this period in Compostela, projects a sense of monumentality with massive volumes and solid forms. The interior houses notable works such as the Crucifixion of the main retablo and the high reliefs in the aisle chapels.

10. Iglesia y Hospital de San Roque. The 18th-c. church is attached to the 16th-c. hospital. The church's façade is severely classicist. Inside is an ornate 1742 Churrigueresque **retablo** by Simón Rodríguez. The hospital façade—under reconstruction in 1998—features statues of Saints Cosme and Damián. Inside is a small elegant cloister.

11. **Monasterio de San Paio** (aka San Pelayo de Antealtares). Galician King Alfonso II el Casto founded this monastery in the 9th c. for the Benedictines who took care of the Apostle's tomb. The current building dates from the early 18th c. The sober **façade** is transitional: it still echoes the Baroque in its interplay of massive structures with contrasting lines and in the weight of the cornice over the columns, while at the same time it projects a Neoclassic monumental simplicity.

Inside are 5 rich **Baroque retablos**. Legend holds that the marble ark is a Roman construction that was consecrated by Santiago's disciples. On the retablo of the north transept, angels draw aside a theatrical curtain to reveal the **Virgen de la O**. For a treat, visit when the cloistered nuns are singing vespers.

12. **Monasterio de Santo Domingo de Bonaval**. When Santo Domingo de Guzmán visited Compostela ca. 1220, he founded this monastery of his new Dominican Order. In keeping with the aggressive, high-visibility program of the Preaching Friars, the monastery occupies a dominant height northeast of the city. The church is 12th–16th-c.; the Baroque convent, 16th-c.; and the cloister, 17th-c. The complex now houses an art museum and archive.
   • The church. The *cabecera* is transitional from Romanesque to Gothic. Some stained-glass windows remain from the Gothic period, as well as some fine 15th-c. sepulchers. The right nave is the pantheon of illustrious Galicians and includes the grave of the sculptor Francisco Asorey and the poetess Rosalía de Castro (1837–85).

> 📖 Galicia's most famous poetess, Rosalía de Castro, during her long years in Castilla with her husband, wrote with yearning of her native hills and rivers in an intense interior biography, composed in both the Castilian and Galician languages.

Artisans from several guilds were also buried under the church floor, and you can make out some of the symbols of their trades on their stones.
• **Circular staircase**. The triple concentric staircase by Domingo de Andrade (1696) is a marvel of Baroque ingenuity, at once simple and puzzling. He also designed the monastery's façade and cloister.
• The museum houses a variety of fine images, including the 16th-c. stone Virgen de Bonaval and a Baroque retablo dedicated to San Vicente Ferrer, scourge of Spain's Jewish communities, who preached from this pulpit. Each section of the ethnological museum displays some sector of traditional Galician society, from fishermen on the seacoast to farmers in the high valleys. Several rooms are given over to professions: potters, silversmiths, jet carvers, etc. Another section re-creates elements of Galician popular architecture.

13. Monasterio de San Agustín. This former Augustinian monastery of the early 17th c. now houses a community of Jesuits. The massive classic façade and severe Neoclassic interior, with its unadorned arches and simple dome, are in striking contrast to the Church of San Francisco. The Solomonic columns on the main altar may be Compostela's largest. In the right transept is a good Baroque **Christ tied to the column**, with the twisted body, haunted expression, and exaltation of suffering typical of Counter-Reformation sculpture on this theme.

14. Iglesia de San Fiz de Solovio (aka San Félix). Tradition holds that the hermit Pelayo was praying here when he saw the lights gleaming over the tomb of Santiago. Be that as it may, this is most likely the site of Compostela's earliest church: archaeologists have located a 6th-c. necropolis on the site.
   The current, mostly modern, building preserves its Romanesque entrance, built by Diego Gelmírez after Almanzor had destroyed the structure a century earlier. The polychrome 14th-c. **Adoration of the 3 Kings** in the tympanum was carved by an enthusiastic, if not very talented, sculptor, for both the composition and the details are awkward.

> 📖 The Adoration of the 3 Wise Men, or Kings, is one of Compostela's most popular themes, since they are held to be the earliest Christian pilgrims, and they traditionally represent the diversity of peoples who go on pilgrimage.

The Baroque bell tower is early 18th-c. Inside the church reputedly there is a nice 15th-c. retablo.

Next door is the Mercado de Abastos (produce market). It was created toward the end of the 19th c. to congregate in one place all of the produce sellers, who were making passage through the city's arcaded streets impossible.

15. The university. Founded in 1501 by Archbishop Alfonso de Fonseca III, and augmented by King Felipe II, its period of greatest importance was the late 18th c. The current building—housing History and Geography—was part of the former Jesuit monastery whose church is next door. The university has an elegant cloister and a good 18th-c. **Baroque library,** which houses various medieval manuscripts and incunabula (books printed before 1500). There is generally an interesting selection on display.

16. Iglesia de la Compañía. This building was formerly a Jesuit church. It has been part of the university since 1769, when the Jesuits were expelled from Spain. It is a typical Jesuit basilica: a Latin cross with 3 naves, a triforium, and a light, soaring cupola. When the university took it over, the Jesuits' anagram in the center of the façade was reworked to transform it into the royal coat of arms. Inside, the 1727 **Baroque retablo** is dazzling.

17. Iglesia de Santa María Salomé. Today's largely 15th-c. church preserves a 12th-c. simple, rural Romanesque façade. A 14th-c. Virgen de la Leche and a 15th-c. Annunciation were at some point added to the entrance portal. Its Baroque tower dates from 1743. The inside is unremarkable, except for 2 angels wearing glasses on a retablo in the left nave.

18. Casa del Deán. 1747–53. Typical of Compostela Baroque is the interplay of the solid masses of wall with the decorative shell formed by the balcony and doorway. Curiously, and by the architect's design, the main door is not in the building's center. Instead, the door is the center of the view of the house from the Plaza de Platerías. In 1993 the building was reconditioned to house the Oficina de la Acogida del Peregrino.

19. **Casa del Cabildo.** This mid-18th-c. palace facing the Platerías Portal is one of the best examples of **Compostela Baroque,** noted especially for its interplay of sharply angled and round geometric shapes. In the middle of the square is Compostela's finest fountain, the Fuente de los Caballos, which is contemporary with the palace.

20. **Convento de Santa Clara.** This convent of Franciscan nuns was founded ca. 1260 by Violante, wife of Castilian king Alfonso X, only 45 years after San Francisco's pilgrimage to Compostela. The current building dates largely from the 18th c.

On the south corner is another of Compostela's superb **Baroque façades,** work of Simón Rodríguez, ca. 1719. The architect created tension by 2 devices: contrasting cylinders and cubes (the church is often called Los Cubetes), and the top-heaviness that seems somehow threatening. Curiously, this façade leads not to the church but to a charming garden, beyond which is the church proper. Inside the church are a Gothic stone pulpit and a Churrigueresque retablo by Domingo de Andrade (ca. 1700).

> 📖 Many Compostelans believe that a gift of eggs brought to the Convento de Santa Clara will insure good weather for an upcoming event.

21. Casa de la Troya. Compostela's "other" pilgrimage is to this late-19th-c. boarding house. Members of student street bands, called *tunas*, revere this house as the setting of Alejandro Pérez Lugín's novel about student musicians and university life in Galicia in the 1880s. Pérez Lugín lived in the house during his own student days, which he immortalized in his novel *La casa de la Troya*. The house has been outfitted as a period museum. It contains lots of Pérez Lugín memorabilia, as well as dedicatory plaques, gifts from *tunas* around the world, and samples of the more than 100 different editions of the novel.

22. **Monasterio de Santa María del Sar.** On the east side of the city, on the banks of the Río Sar, a half-hour walk from the Plaza del Obradoiro, this **12th-c. complex** is important both artistically and historically. Diego Gelmírez consecrated the original church in 1136; the current building dates from some thirty years later. At some time in the 12th c. it belonged to the Knights Templar. Due to engineering errors, or sinking soil along the river, the entire building has gone cockeyed (some even believe it was built askew—you know how weird those Templars were!).
- Its walls are propped up on the outside by what must be the most massive **flying buttresses** in all of Spain, added in the 18th c. to forestall impending ruin.
- Inside you will find narrow, peculiarly **leaning naves,** and the classic Romanesque semicircular apses. The height of the original construction can be seen in the arch over the central apse. The aisles were raised much higher, permitting the rose window, and were vaulted using transitional *ojival* arches. Note also the several tombs from the 13th to the 16th c.
- In what remains of the **cloister** are some **capitals** by the school of **Maestro Mateo.**

If you still have time and energy, several other civil and religious monuments in Compostela are worth your attention.

- Civil monuments:
    —All of the old city of Compostela. The city's ancient ambience is vigilantly preserved by the city government (if only they had included the Monte de Gozo within their mission!).
    —Especially all of the Rúa Nova. A well-preserved 18th-c. colonnaded merchant street.
    —Casa das Pomas. A late-17th-c. palace on the Rúa Nova, designed by Domingo de Andrade, whose windows are adorned with carved strings of fruit.
    —Casa de los Canónigos. An 18th-c. palace by Domingo de Andrade south of the Plaza de Quintana.
    —Arco de Mazarelos. Mentioned in the CC, this early medieval gate next to the university is the only surviving remnant of the city walls.
    —Pazo de Bendaña. This 18th-c. palace, topped with a statue of Atlas, is another splendid example of Compostela civil Baroque architecture.
    —Casa de Monroy. An elegant palace of Italian inspiration.
    —Casa de la Parra. This 18th-c. Baroque palace on the Plaza de la Azabachería is named for the bunches of grapes that adorn its windows.

- Religious monuments:
    —Convento del Carmen. Mid-18th c. The sober, well-proportioned façade contrasts nicely with Santa Clara across the street.

—Colegio de las Huérfanas (aka Orfas). Built in the early 18th c., mostly by Casas y Novoa, to educate orphan girls for domestic service. The church proper predates the façade by a half century. Its most striking feature is the elegant Neoclassic dome.

—Convento de la Merced. The massive convent and church was built in the 1680s. The façade, flanked by 2 street-to-roof fluted columns and adorned with large coats of arms, is elegant and somewhat Italianate. In the entrance is a polychromed Romanesque Virgin. The interior of the church is unremarkable.

—Convento de Santa María la Real del Conxo. Archibishop Gelmírez founded the Benedictine convent in 1129, although legend ascribes its beginning to a woman named Roswinda, who built it to entomb her lover Alberico Canojio, who was assasinated on his pilgrimage to Compostela. The current structure is mostly from the 18th c., with a few Romanesque bits in the cloister. Inside are several showy Baroque retablos and a sculpture of Christ by Gregorio Hernández that is much venerated locally. It is now a psychiatric hospital.

—San Benito del Campo. Neoclassic, dating mostly from the 18th c., and heavily reconstructed. Inside you will find a Gothic Visitation and a 14th-c. Romanesque tympanum **showing the Adoration of the Kings**.

—San Fructuoso. This small mid-18th-c. church sports a showy Baroque façade, topped with an oversized coat of arms. The entablement at the top contains statues of the cardinal virtues: Temperance, Strength, Justice, and Prudence. The views of the façade from the Obradoiro terrace and from the street are strikingly different: which perspective do you think the architect had in mind? Inside the church is a high, austere dome.

—Santa María del Camino. 18th–19th-c. Baroque façade distinguished by 4 large Ionic pillars. Inside is a high-quality Baroque retablo.

—San Miguel dos Agros. Sober, Neoclassic façade. Inside is the image of the Virgen de los Dolores. Condemned prisoners were brought here to pray, and after their executions their bodies were placed here before their burial.

Well, now you have seen just about everything.
Except Padrón, which will take you another couple of days. And Finisterre.

If you can manage it, walk home. Remember that everything looks different when viewed from west to east.

And don't forget to take a picture of your calluses, so that your grandchildren will believe your incredible tales of the time you went walking on pilgrimage to Compostela. As for us . . .

> We've been to see the Apostle
> and we've walked 500 miles,
> and we won't forget the laughter
> and we won't forget the smiles,
> and we won't forget Cirauqui,
> and we won't forget León:
> for we'd rather walk on pilgrimage
> than spend our life at home.

PART II

The Reference Points

Abbreviations

aka	also known as
alt.	altitude
b.	born
B.C.E.	before the common era
c.	century
ca.	circa
CC	*Codex Calixtinus*
C.E.	common era
ch.	chapter
d.	died
km.	kilometer(s) [1 kilometer = approximately $5/8$ of 1 mile]
LSJ	*Liber Sancti Jacobi*
m.	meter(s) [1 meter = approximately 39 inches]
ms., mss.	manuscript(s)

SPANISH-ENGLISH GLOSSARY

We have maintained the Spanish names of towns and provinces (e.g., Castilla, not Castile) and most saints and rulers (e.g., Juan, not John). In this handbook we have also preserved other Spanish terms that are readily understandable and that you will encounter almost daily. Here is a list of recurring terms for which a translation or explanation may be useful:

abadía, abad	abbey, abbot; an abbey is a large monastery often with dependencies; in the monastic world, abbots are equivalent to bishops
acequia	irrigation ditch
aljama	Jewish neighborhood or community (Arabic term)
amapola	poppy
ampolla	blister
arzobispo	archbishop; a bishop who coordinates a group of dioceses
autopista	highway
ayuntamiento	city hall
barrio	neighborhood
bodega	wine cellar
calle	street
capilla, capellán	chapel, chaplain; chapels are secondary or private worship areas annexed to a church or other building; chaplains are responsible for saying mass in the chapel
caserío	small village (from the Spanish *casa*, meaning "house")
castro	a circular or oval fortified hilltop town dating from the Bronze Age to Roman times
catedral	cathedral; the administrative center of a diocese (also called a see), presided over by a bishop
cofradía	brotherhood; organized group of people who care for pilgrims
colegiata	a secular (i.e., not affiliated with a religious Order) church large enough to be staffed by a community of priests
convento	convent or monastery; term used for both men's and women's institutions
converso	convert from Judaism to Catholicism
cortes	a council of eligible citizenry assembled to advise a king; at times almost a parliament
desamortización	disentailment; early 19th-c. expropriation that removed monasteries from religious control, causing many to fall into ruin
ermita	hermitage; originally the small church maintained by a hermit; now, any small nonparish church, often away from centers of population
Franco(s)	foreigner(s); medieval term used often to refer to those from France or elsewhere, especially those who settled in Spanish towns
frontón	court on which jai alai (or *pelota*) is played
fuero	a royal charter granted to a municipality or other corporate body offering certain privileges, demanding certain services, and confirming certain rights. *Fueros* were crucial

	instruments of royal policy in developing cities along the Road.
Guerra Civil	Civil War (1936–1939)
hospital	lodging supplied, in the Middle Ages, by towns, religious groups, or *cofradías*; global term used in the Middle Ages for hospital, hospice, and hotel, which today we consider separate institutions
iglesia	church
judería	[see *aljama*]
llanura	plains
loma	a rounded hill
mesa	table land, flat-topped hill
meseta	Castilian plain
mesta	medieval corporate body governing the sheep and wool business
monje, monja	monk, nun
monte	mountain; also wasteland of forest or scrubby vegetation; often but not necessarily mountainous
morería	Muslim neighborhood
morisco	a Muslim converted to Christianity
moros	generic term referring to Spanish Muslims, no matter what their ethic background
mozárabe	a Christian living in Muslim territory
mudéjar	a Muslim living in Christian territory
obispo	bishop, the head of a diocese
orden	generic term for monastic or military associations adhering to a rule
páramo	[*see mesa*]
parias	sums of money paid by Muslim caliphs to keep Christian kings and warlords from raiding their territories. The Cid collected *parias* for Alfonso VI of Castilla
peña	cliff
priorato, prior	priory, prior; a small monastery, sometimes dependent to an abbey
rollo	gibbet; a large column to which malefactors were tied and punished
romería	generic term for a short, generally one-day, pilgrimage to a local shrine
regla	rule; body of regulations governing a religious congregation or order
san/santo/santa	saint

[Spanish art terms are found in the section devoted to artistic styles.]

ART STYLES OF THE ROAD

abacus (*ábaco*)   the upper part of a capital, often an undecorated slab [*see drawing #6*]

ajedrezado   checkerboard decoration

ajímez   a window divided in two by a column

alero   [*see* eave]

alfiz   a low-relief frame around a window or arch, common in Islamic architecture [*see drawing #2*]

ambulatory (*girola*)   a processional passageway surrounding the choir or chancel

apse   a vaulted, semicircular extension at the head of a church [*see drawings #5, #8*]

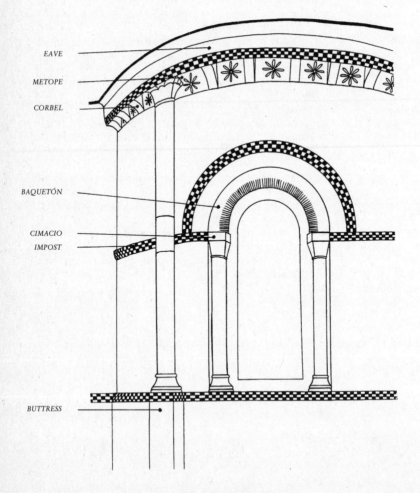

EAVE

METOPE

CORBEL

BAQUETÓN

CIMACIO

IMPOST

BUTTRESS

1. ROMANESQUE APSE

arbotante	[*see* buttress, flying]
arch	a curved structure, usually of wedge-shaped stones, that spans an opening
arch, blind (*ciego*)	a decorative arch with no opening
arch, canopial	[*see drawing #2*]
arch, horseshoe (*herradura*)	a circular arch that closes more than 180° [*see drawing #2*]
arch, lobed (*lobulado*)	[*see drawing #2*]
arch, Lombard	decorative blind arcade composed of small arches separated by columns or pilasters

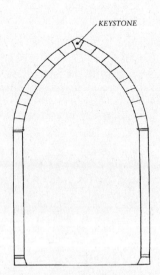

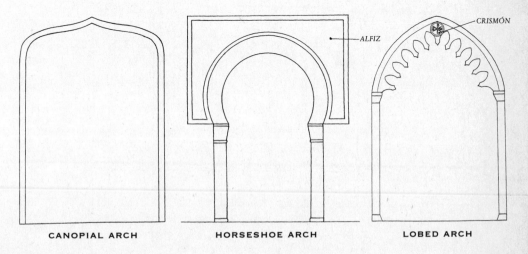

2. ARCHES

archivolt
the continuous molding on the face of an arch [*see drawing #7*]

arco ciego
[*see* arch, blind]

arco de herradura
[*see* arch, horseshoe]

arco lobulado
[*see* arch, lobed]

arco peraltado
semicircular arch whose sides project below the circle's diameter

arcos formeros
heavy semicircular arches supporting a barrel vault

arista
[*see* vault, groin]

artesonado
[*see* coffering]

ashlar
large rectangular blocks of stone laid in regular courses

astragal
(*astrágalo*)
the small molding placed around the top or bottom of a column; sometimes resembles a twisted rope [*see drawing #6*]

atrium
the forecourt of a church

baldachin
ornamental canopy over a throne or altar

baquetón
a tubular arch [*see drawing #1*]

Baroque
pan-European stylistic movement from the late 16th to the early 18th c., characterized by spectacular visual effects, violent contrasts, emphasis on complexity and movement, mixed media, and combinations of genre, often fusing architecture and sculpture

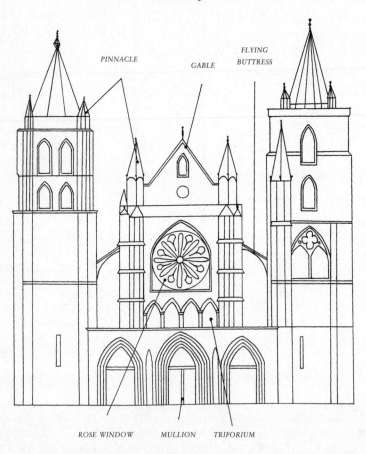

PINNACLE   GABLE   FLYING BUTTRESS

ROSE WINDOW   MULLION   TRIFORIUM

3. GOTHIC FAÇADE

basilica	rectangular church plan, with a high central nave and 2 lower flanking naves, ending in an apse
buttress	a projecting support built against a wall to counteract the lateral thrust of an arch or vault [see drawings #1, 11]
buttress, flying (arbotante)	an arch or half arch serving as buttress, transferring the thrust of the vault to a lower support [see drawing #3]
cabecera	[see chevet]
canecillo	[see corbel]
capital	the decorated form transitioning between a column and whatever it supports [see drawing #6]
chancel	east end of a church containing the altar and sometimes the choir
chancel screen	separates the chancel from the rest of the church
chapter house	the room where a religious community convenes for business; it generally opens to the east side of the cloister [see drawing #5]
chevet (cabecera)	French term for east end of a church
choir (coro)	part of a church where the divine service is sung; generally between the altar and the crossing [see drawing #5]

4. CRISMÓN

Churrigueresque	a phase of Spanish Baroque launched by José Churriguera ca. 1700; extravagant, theatrical design featuring high-relief sculpture, twisted columns, and elaborate leaf work
ciborium	a canopy on columns over the altar of a church; also a vessel holding the consecrated host
cimacio	decorated molding crowning a capital [see drawings #1, 6, 7]
clave	decorated pendant attached to the intersection of ribs of a vault
clerestory	the upper stage of a nave, rising above the aisle roofs, pierced with windows
cloister	a monastery or church open courtyard with its surrounding covered passage [see drawing #5]
coffering (artesonado)	ceiling decoration consisting of sunken square or polygonal panels
column	a freestanding upright member intended as a support [see drawing #6]
column, estípite	composite column including elongated inverted pyramids; popular in the late Baroque [see drawing #6]
column, Solomonic	a twisted column, presumably echoing prototypes in Solomon's temple [see drawing #6]
corbel (canecillo, ménsula)	small block of stone supporting a beam or cornice, often decorated [see drawing #1]
Corinthian	[see order]
cornice	a projecting, ornamental molding along the top of a wall
coro	[see choir]

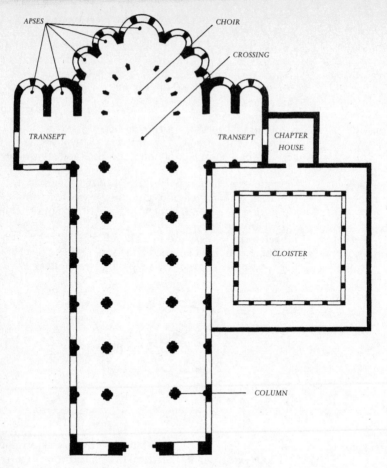

APSES

CHOIR

CROSSING

TRANSEPT

TRANSEPT

CHAPTER HOUSE

CLOISTER

COLUMN

5. GOTHIC FLOOR PLAN

crismón	a rosette symbolizing the Trinity, whose symbolic design contains the cross, the chi-rho that begins the name *Christus* in Greek, and the alpha and omega indicating that Christ is the beginning and end of all things. [*see drawing #4*]
crossing	the space where the nave and the transept of a church intersect [*see drawing #5*]
crypt	an underground chapel or chamber, often beneath an altar
cupola	a small dome
custodia	[*see* monstrance]
dintel	[*see* lintel]
diptych	a painting or relief of 2 panels
Doric	[*see* order]
dosel	canopy
eave (*alero*)	a roof's projecting edge that overhangs the side [*see drawing #1*]
enamel	colored powdered glass fused to a metal surface by extreme heat
enjuta	[*see* spandrel]
espadaña	bell gable

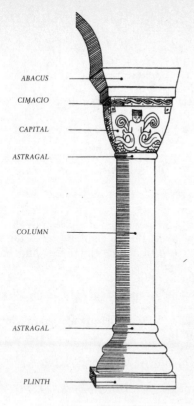

ABACUS

CIMACIO

CAPITAL

ASTRAGAL

COLUMN

ASTRAGAL

PLINTH

ROMANESQUE COLUMN

FLUTED COLUMN

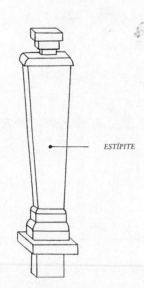

ESTÍPITE

COMPOSITE COLUMN

SOLOMONIC COLUMN

6. COLUMNS

estípite	[*see* column]
estrellada	[*see* vault, starred]
extrados (*trasdós*)	the exterior curve of an arch
fresco	mural painting on fresh, moist lime plaster
frieze	a sculptured or decorated horizontal band [*see drawing #7*]
frontal	the decorated panel covering the front of an altar; may be painted, carved, enameled, embroidered or otherwise decorated
gable	a triangular portion of a wall at the end of a pitched roof [*see drawing #3*]
girola	[*see* ambulatory]
Gothic, Flamboyant	15th- and 16th-c. phase of Gothic featuring elaborate tracery work
grille (*reja*)	—chapel screen; ornamental iron gate closing off a chapel
Hispano-Flemish	late-15th- and early-16th-c. style popularized in Spain by the royalty's taste for Flemish art. Blends Flamboyant Gothic decoration with a hyperrealism in the depiction of humans and the realia that surround them
hórreo	corncrib, common in Galicia
impost	the top of a pier or pillar supporting the curve of an arch [*see drawings #1, 7*]
intaglio	a gem with incised carving; by extension, any incised carving
intrados	the internal curve of an arch
Ionic	[*see* order]
jamb	the vertical face of an arch, doorway, or window [*see drawing #7*]
keystone	the central stone of an arch or vault [*see drawings #2, 11*]

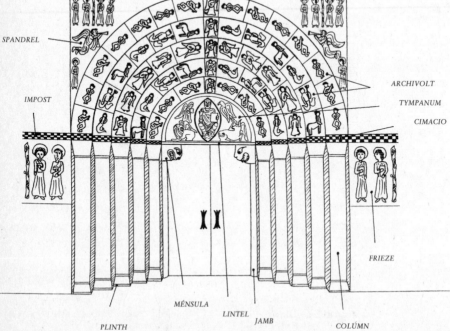

SPANDREL
IMPOST
ARCHIVOLT
TYMPANUM
CIMACIO
FRIEZE
MÉNSULA
LINTEL
JAMB
PLINTH
COLUMN

7. ROMANESQUE FAÇADE

lantern	a small, circular, or polygonal turret with windows all around
lintel (*dintel*)	a horizontal beam bridging an opening [*see drawing #7*]
Lombard	[*see arch, Lombard*]
mamoa	Celtic tomb mound common in parts of Galicia
mandorla	[*see nimbus*]
Mannerism	16th-c. reaction against the simple classic lines of Renaissance aesthetics; characterized by elongated and twisted figures, dramatic lighting, aggressiving coloring, and contrasts of scale
medio cañón	[*see vault, barrel*]
ménsula	[*see corbel*]
metope	one of a series of decorated square spaces between corbels [*see drawing #1*]
misericord	a projection on the underside of a hinged seat in a church choir against which a standing cleric could rest
modillion	one of a series of small, square decorative brackets supporting a cornice
monstrance (*custodia*)	an open or transparent artifact, usually of precious metal, to display the consecrated host
Mozárabe	a Christian living in Muslim territory; the Islamicized art of those Christians
Mudéjar	a Muslim living in Christian territory, often working as an artisan; the Islamicized architecture they built for Christians
mullion (*parteluz*)	a vertical post dividing a door or window [*see drawing #3*]
narthex	the enclosed porch at the entrance of a church
nave	the congregational area of a church, usually the western end, flanked by aisles
nerve (*nervio*)	[*see vault, rib*]
nimbus (*mandorla*)	the cloud framing a sacred figure, generally Christ; often almond shaped [*see drawing #10*]
oculus	a circular window in a wall or dome
ogival (*ojival*)	early Gothic; so called because of its pointed arches (ogives) [*see drawing #11*]
order	a column with its base, shaft, and capital; the most common are Doric (no base, simple round capital devoid of decoration), Ionic (scrolled capital), and Corinthian (complex capital made of leaf forms)
parteluz	[*see mullion*]
pazo	the Galician term for manor house
pediment	a low-pitched gable over a portico, door, or window
peraltado	[*see arco peraltado*]
pier	a solid freestanding masonry support, generally noncylindrical [*see drawing #8*]
pilaster	a shallow rectangular column projecting from a wall
pillar	a freestanding upright member which, unlike a column, need not be cylindrical [*see drawing #8*]
pinnacle	a small, ornamented termination to a spire or buttress [*see drawing #3*]
Plateresque	a Renaissance ornamental style incorporating classical motifs (scrolls, twisted columns, grotesques, urns, flowers, and *putti*). Framed Plateresque low-relief panels, arranged symmetrically around a vertical axis, were used to decorate façades, retablos, furniture, and tombs. Cristóbal de Villalón coined the term *Plateresque* in 1539 while

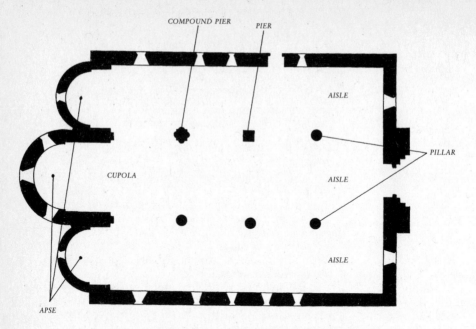

COMPOUND PIER   PIER

AISLE

PILLAR

CUPOLA

AISLE

AISLE

APSE

8. ROMANESQUE CHURCH FLOOR PLAN

	comparing one of León's cathedral façades to the art of silversmiths
plinth	the unadorned projecting base supporting a column [*see drawing* #6]
polyptych	a painting or relief of more than 3 panels
portico	a roofed space, open or partly enclosed, forming an entrance or façade
predella	platform on which an altar is set; a set of paintings, or panels, sustaining an altar [see *drawing* #9]
pulpit	an elevated stand for a preacher or reader
quoin	the stones or bricks used to form the external angle of a wall or building, often through contrast of color, shape, or pattern of placement
reja	[*see* grille]
reliquary	receptacle for a sacred relic
reredos	[*see* retablo]
retablo	the multisectioned structure behind an altar, frequently divided into rows (streets) or columns, each framing carved figures with architectural elements [see ch. 23] [*see drawing* #9]
rib	a projecting band separating the cells of a groined vault
Rococo	the last phase of Baroque style, substituting for grandiloquence and overstatement a presumed refinement of sensibility featuring decorations with arabesques, scrolls, shells, flowers, and oriental motifs
Romanesque	style of architecture, sculpture, and painting predominant in western Europe in the 11th and 12th c. The imitation of certain building techniques from extant Roman ruins gave the style its name. Characteristics: small basilica churches with rounded naves, radiating chapels, barrel vaults, narrow doors and windows

Romanist	16th-c. sculpture imitating Italian models. Poses tend to be sober and static, almost Mannerist; figures suggest solidity; hair in large curls; painted with bright colors; fondness for nudes [see ch. 25]
rose window (*rosetón*)	large circular window at the end of the nave or transept of a Gothic church [*see drawing #3*]
sacristy	room near the altar in which sacred vessels and the priests' vestments are stored
sagrario	[*see* tabernacle]
spandrel (*enjuta*)	a triangular area between the outer curve of an arch and the rectangle of the moldings which enclose it [*see drawing #7*]
squinch (*trompa*)	an arch placed diagonally to support a polygonal or round superstructure on a square base

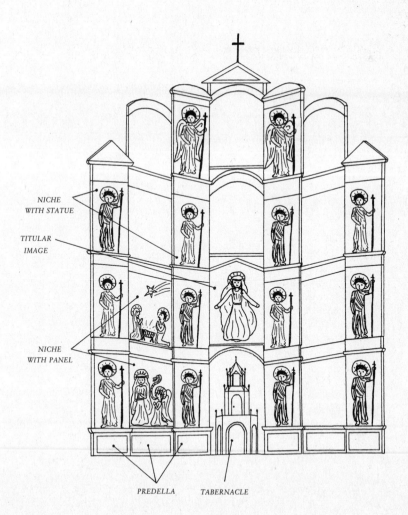

NICHE
WITH STATUE

TITULAR
IMAGE

NICHE
WITH PANEL

PREDELLA   TABERNACLE

9. RETABLO

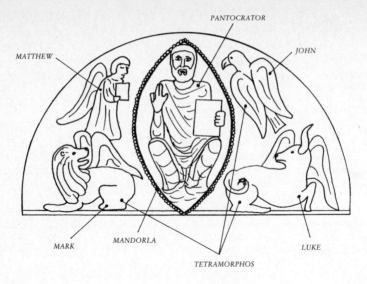

PANTOCRATOR

MATTHEW

JOHN

MARK

MANDORLA

LUKE

TETRAMORPHOS

10. ROMANESQUE TYMPANUM

tabernacle (*templete, sagrario*)	ark in which the consecrated hosts are kept on the altar [*see drawing #9*]
templete	[*see tabernacle*]
tracery	ornamental intersecting stonework in a window, screen, or panel

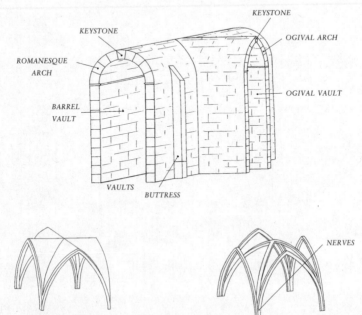

KEYSTONE

KEYSTONE

ROMANESQUE ARCH

OGIVAL ARCH

OGIVAL VAULT

BARREL VAULT

VAULTS

BUTTRESS

NERVES

GROIN VAULT

11. VAULTS

transept	the transverse arms of a cross-shaped church [*see drawing #5*]
triptych	a painting or relief of 3 panels
trascoro	the external part of the wall enclosing a choir
trasdós	[*see* extrados]
triforium	an arcaded wall passage facing the nave (above the arcade, and below the clerestory) [*see drawing #3*]
trompa	[*see* squinch]
tympanum	semicircular area between the lintel of a doorway and the arch above it [*see drawings #7, 10*]
vault	a masonry roof or ceiling supported by arches
vault, barrel (tunnel, cannon)	a continuous, semicylindrical section unbroken by crossvaults [*see drawing #11*]
vault, groin (*arista*)	the intersection of 2 barrel vaults [*see drawing #11*]
vault, rib (nerve, *nervio*)	a vault sustained by a framework of arched, diagonal ribs, in-filled with lighter stone [*see drawing #11*]
vault, starred (*estrellada*)	a vault whose decorative ribs form a star, flower, or other tracery figure
verja	[*see* grille]
window, paired (*ventana geminada*)	window of 2 arches separated by a column

ARTISTS CITED

Alava, Juan de (1505?–1537). Architect and mason. Known for incorporating classical Renaissance elements into late Gothic architecture. His masterwork is San Esteban in Salamanca. Also worked in Plasencia and in Compostela on the Cathedral cloister.

Anchieta, Juan de (ca. 1530–1588). Sculptor. Studied in Italy, where he absorbed Renaissance influences, particularly of Michelangelo. His work is not passionate, but stolidly classical. His stocky figures and somewhat monotonous heads suggest imitation of other artists' work rather than a study of the human form. Works in Jaca, Obanos, Pamplona, Burgos.

Andrade, Domingo de (1639–1712). Best-known Baroque architect in Galicia. Very influential. Famous for Compostela Cathedral's clock tower and main altar baldachin and Santo Domingo de Bonaval's triple circular staircase.

Aponte, Pedro de (1490–1529). Painter active in Aragón in the early 16th c. Known for his portraits and his religious paintings inspired by Flemish prints. One of the first Spanish painters to work in oils.

Arfe, Antonio de (el Mayor) (ca. 1510–1574). Silversmith son of Enrique de Arfe. Antonio introduced the Greco-Roman Plateresque style to Spain. His midcentury monstrances are found in Compostela and in Santa María de Rioseco.

Arfe, Enrique de (ca. 1475–1545). The Arfe (or Harf) family were German artisans from Cologne active in Spain in the early 16th c. Enrique is documented working in León in 1501. His Sahagún monstrance is from 1515. Others are in Córdoba (1513) and Toledo (1515–24, with gold and silver from America). He executed a large processional cross for the Burgos Cathedral, and the Arca de San Froilán in the cathedral of León. He is known for his finely wrought Gothic miniature figures and for the exquisite architectural details of their setttings.

Badajoz, Juan de (el Mayor) (?–1522). Architect and sculptor; employed as Master of the Cathedral Works in León. One of the architects of Salamanca's new cathedral, the vaults in Sevilla, and the cathedral tower in Oviedo.

Badajoz, Juan de (el Menor) (ca. 1495–1552). Part of his father's workshop, he designed Plateresque cloisters for San Marcos in León, the Leonese Cathedral, San Zoilo de Carrión, and several other churches.

Balmaseda, Juan (ca. 1488–1548). Sculptor and stained-glass artist.

Becerra, Gaspar (ca. 1520–1568). Architect, sculptor, and painter in the Romanist style. Studied with Michelangelo, but sweetened his anguished figures. Liked fleshy, contorted figures, anatomically correct classicism. Hired by Felipe II in 1562. His followers, such as the Haya brothers, imitated the showiness of his ensembles and the idealized, stereotyped features of his human subjects. Best work at Astorga. Several paintings in the Prado.

Berruguete, Alonso (ca. 1489–1561). Sculptor, painter, and architect, son of Pedro Berruguete. He studied in Florence and Rome and was active in Spain from 1517. One of Spain's most important Renaissance sculptors, known for his Mannerist figures, expressing strong religious emotions from anguish to ecstasy.

Berruguete, Pedro (ca. 1440–1504). Vizcayan. Probably studied in Flanders and surely studied in Italy at the court of Urbino. Court painter to Queen Isabel and to her daughter's husband, Philip the Fair, who came to Spain in 1502. His most famous picture today is of victims about to be burned in an *auto-da-fé*. His style blends several elements: international Renaissance (architectural elements, particularly framing arches; sumptuous costumes), Flemish (modeling in chiaroscuro; delight in multiplication of small details; contorted drapery), and Spanish (gold brocade, sumptuous background cloth; fabric canopies; Mudéjar ceilings).

Bigarny, Felipe [*see* Vigarny]

Borgoña, Juan de (ca. 1470–1536). From Langres, Burgundy. Educated in Italy. Active in Toledo (he gilded the main retablo), Salamanca (retablo of Vigarny chapel), and Ávila. By 1494 working with Pedro Berruguete. Active in Burgos, 1522–40. Figures tend to be grave and idealized, in somewhat rigid poses. Works also in Astorga, in the Cathedrals of Ávila and Toledo, and in the Meadows Museum in Dallas. His son, also named Juan de Borgoña (1500–65), was a painter active in Castilla.

Bruselas, Arnao de (?–1565). Sculptor; probably Flemish or Dutch. Active in La Rioja from 1545.

Casas y Novoa, Fernando de (1680–1749). Showy Baroque architect whose works are seen all over Galicia. His most famous achievements are the Compostela Cathedral's Fachada del Obradoiro and San Martín Pinario's retablo.

Cerezo, Mateo (1626–1666). Painter of the Madrid school, with several works in Burgos. His Crucifixions show an influence of Rubens, with sketchy, jagged composition and brush strokes.

Churriguera, José Benito de (1665–1725). Sculptor and architect who launched the style called Churrigueresque, noted for deep-relief Solomonic columns, heavy moldings, and foliated decoration. Masterworks in Salamanca and Madrid, but influences seen all along the Road. Head of a large family, all of whom seem to have designed façades and retablos, plazas and fountains.

Colonia, Francisco de (ca. 1470–1542). Sculptor, son of Simón de C., grandson of Juan de C. Was Master of Stonecarving in Burgos in 1511, and built the Burgos Cathedral's Puerta de la Pellejería.

Colonia, Juan de (ca. 1410–1481). Born Meister Hans von Köln (Cologne), he was brought to Burgos by the *converso* bishop Alonso de Cartagena after the Council of Basel in 1440. Several of his 6 children became artists. He was made Master of the Burgos Cathedral Works in 1454. His contributions include the Burgos Cathedral towers, the Capilla de la Visitación (1454–6), Cartagena's monumental tomb (1447), and the Burgos Cathedral's dome (it collapsed in 1539). He designed the Cartuja de Miraflores, which was largely built by his son Simón.

Colonia, Simón de (1445?–1511). Architect and sculptor, son of Juan de C. He worked in Burgos, finishing up his father's projects. His masterwork: the Burgos Cathedral's Capilla del Condestable.

Cristóbal, Juan (aka Juan Cristóbal González Quesada; 1898–1961). Popular Andalusian sculptor much influenced by Italian Renaissance sculptors. Famous for sculpted portraits, such as that of Ganivet in the Alhambra, and grandiose heroic figures.

David, Gerard (?–1523). Dutch painter, the last great master of the Bruges school. Noted for his intensity of expression, the realism of his portrayal of human forms, and the ordered architecture of his compositions.

Egas, Enrique (?–1534). Architect famous in his day for incorporating simple classical geometric forms on Italian models. Best work on the Road: the Compostela Hospital de los Reyes Católicos.

Fernández, Gregorio [*see* Hernández]

Forment, Damián (1470?–1540). Valencian sculptor trained in Italy. He designed retablos in Zaragoza's Seo, the Cathedral of Huesca, and the Monastery of Poblet, generally with frames and with compositions still Gothic in character, while introducing colors, designs, and classical simplicity, balance, and decorum related to the Renaissance aesthetic. Best late work, in an almost mannered style, with twisted figures and looming entablatures, is the monumental retablo in Santo Domingo de la Calzada.

Gallego, Fernando (1440?–1507). Painter of biblical subjects in the Flemish style. Centered in Salamanca. Founded a school of painters who worked extensively in Castilla.

Gaudí, Antonio (1852–1926). Architect in the Art Nouveau style. Though his most important buildings are in Barcelona, there are 2 on the pilgrimage Road: in León and in Astorga.

Gil de Hontañón, Juan (1480?–1526). Architect and sculptor who apprenticed with Simón de Colonia in the Burgos Cathedral and then designed the Salamanca Cathedral. Patriarch of a large family of artists.

Gil de Hontañón, Rodrigo (1500?–1577). Architect and theorist, son of Juan. Published an influential treatise on architecture.

Goya y Lucientes, Francisco (1746–1828). Spain's most innovative and significant romantic painter. He designed cartoons for tapestries, painted royal portraits, chronicled the horrors of the French invasion in *Disasters of War*, and explored the deepest reaches of the human psyche.

Goyaz, Juan de (?–1556). Guipuzcoan architect and sculptor of the Vigarny school who worked in the Rioja in the mid-16th c. and also in Carlos V's constructions in Granada.

Gumiel, Pedro de (1460?–1518). Painter and architect patronized by Cardinal Cisneros. Known for Mudéjar-style decoration and adoption of Italian motifs.

Haya, Martín and **Rodrigo** (active 1561–86). Brothers active in Burgos as architects, sculptors, and painters. Designed the Burgos Cathedral's Capilla Mayor.

Hererra, Juan de (ca. 1530–1597). Architect who finished the Escorial, designing steep dormered gables and spires sheathed in slate, which were imitated first in the Spanish court and then all over Spain.

Hernández, Gregorio (1576–1636). Baroque sculptor, painter, and architect, known for his intense, emotional figures and hyperrealism. He carved retablos, processional figures for Holy Week, and a number of rivetingly pathetic reclining Christs.

Jordán, Esteban (ca. 1534–1598). Student and son-in-law of Alonso Berruguete. Collaborated with Juan de Juní. His work has somewhat less movement and exquisite detail than theirs.

Juanes, Juan de (1523–79). Son of the painter Vicente Juan Macip; lived in Valencia. Painter, known for his religious fervor and mystic idealism. Often combining late Gothic detail work with Renaissance idealized forms, he adapted the new Roman style to the Spanish sensibility. The bulk of his work is found in Valencia; good examples in Burgos and Compostela.

Juní, Juan de (1507–1577). Italian sculptor, painter, and architect active principally in Spain. His sculpture studies human form, draped and undraped, and incorporates the classicism of Michelangelo and his school. But unlike his masters, he tended to twist and deform his subjects in poses often verging on the grotesque. Besides Burgos, major works are found in Segovia, Valladolid, and Osma.

Leodegarius (active from 1155 to early 13th c.). Burgundian sculptor who worked in Sangüesa and carved doña Blanca de Navarra's sepulcher in Nájera.

López, Mateo (late 16th c.). Master of Gallego Mannerism. Worked on the church of San Martín Pinario beginning in 1593.

Mateo, Maestro (active 1168–88). At Fernando II's behest, in 1168 Mateo took over construction of the Compostela Cathedral. Nothing is known about his life, except that his work shows Burgundian, Italian, and northern European influences, and that his masterful large-scale sculpted figures are often considered to have initiated the new Gothic style.

Memling, Hans (ca. 1430–1494). Flemish painter avidly collected by the Trastámara and Hapsburg monarchs. Though he worked almost exclusively in Bruges, his diptychs and triptychs graced churches all over Europe. Known for eye-catching details, particularly of interiors: brocades, mirrors, tile floors, furniture.

Mengs, Antonio Rafael (1728–79). Mengs was a Bohemian who moved to Rome and worked for various royal patrons. Carlos III brought him to Spain in 1761 with a nice stipend (house, coach, painting expenses, etc.). Despite tuberculosis, Mengs was prolific during his years in Spain, leaving more than 2,000 works, many portraits of the Spanish royalty. Working in the Neoclassic style, Mengs favored bright colors like blue, red, and yellow, and avoided black and other dark tones. One of the apprentices who sketched out tapestries for him was Francisco Goya.

Moretto, Giovanni (aka Juan de Moreto; active 1530–40). Florentine sculptor and architect who worked mostly in Spain. Worked with Damián Forment in Aragón. Combined the hyperrealism of late Gothic with the new modes of Plateresque.

Nájera, Andrés de (active 1504–33). Sculptor specializing in wood choir stalls. Carved stalls in Santo Domingo de la Calzada and San Benito in Valladolid; collaborated with Vigarny on the Burgos stalls.

Nicolás Francés (?–1468). Painter. Workshop in León in 1430s. Designed stained glass. Influenced by Italian artists working in Salamanca. Mixes international style (figures in contemporary dress, minute episodical details, engraved gold patterning in lieu of sky) with Spanish touches (rich costumes, ceremonial scenes). Good at delineating character, almost caricature. Designed Suero de Quiñones's clothing for the *Passo Honroso*.

Obray, Esteban de (active 1517–56). A French sculptor whose best-known works are the Flamboyant Gothic choir of the Cathedral of Tudela and the Plateresque choir of the Cathedral of Pamplona.

Paret y Alcázar, Luis (1746–99). Neoclassic painter, printmaker, architect, transla- tor (from Greek and Latin), and designer of fountains (one in Pamplona). Known for interesting, informative, elegant works, with luxurious fabrics, flowers, porce- lains, and jewels. Major works in Viana and in the Museo del Prado. Banished to Puerto Rico because of some outrageous love affairs.

Pereyra, Manuel (1614–67). Noted Portuguese sculptor of saints who worked largely in Madrid from the 1640s. He did several St. Brunos for the various Iberian Carthusian monasteries.

Picardo, León (?–1547). French painter and gilder, active in Spain from 1513. Took the *comuneros*' side in the 1520 war. Strong sculptural sense in his paintings. Works in Santo Domingo, Burgos, Briviesca, Oviedo, and in the Prado in Madrid.

Prado, Mateo de (?–1677). Baroque sculptor whose choir stalls in San Martín Pinario are among Spain's best from the 17th c.

Ribera, José de (1591–1662). Painter and printmaker. Created and popularized dozens of types: philosopher beggars, penitents, ascetics, happy drunks, Virgins, realistic saints. Psychological painter, revealing the inner dramas of his subjects. Good at skin tones and at rich draperies. Decreased the number of secondary char- acters in order to focus on the principals of the story. Enormously popular throughout Europe. Byron mocked: "Il Spagnoletto tainted / his brush with all the blood of all the Sainted."

Ricci, Giovanni [Juan] Pietro (1600–1670?). Son of the Bolognan artist Antonio Ricci. Was brought by Felipe II to work on the Escorial. A professed Benedictine, expelled from the monastery of Montserrat in 1627 for his wild character, Ricci subsequently earned his living with his brush, decorating Benedictine monasteries in Silos, Madrid, Burgos, Cardeña, Sopetrán, Rome, and Monte Casino, and espe- cially San Millán de la Cogolla. His only non-Benedictine saints are in the Burgos Cathedral.

Rodríguez, Simón (1679–1752). Baroque architect and sculptor whose works are seen all over Compostela. His masterworks are the façade of Santa Clara and the *retablo mayor* in the Compañía.

Siloé, Diego de (1490–1563). Son of Gil. Diego studied in Florence in his teens. He formed part of a group of young artists (Pedro de Berruguete, Simón de Colonia, Felipe de Vigarny) working in the late Flemish-Gothic and early Renaissance styles. By 1519 he was working in Burgos, where Bishop Acuña contracted him for his sepulcher in his chapel of Santa Ana. Other masterworks in the Burgos Cathe- dral include the Escalera Dorada (1519) and the Santa Ana retablo (1522). Diego later worked in Granada, and he designed the chapter houses for the cathedrals of Toledo and Sevilla.

Siloé, Gil de (?–pre 1505). Came from Flanders in the mid-15th c. to work in Spain. His prestige was such that Isabel summoned him to sculpt the tombs in the Cartuja de Miraflores (1489–93). His style is noted for the expressive realism of his figures, his minute attention to detail, particularly the texture of the sculpted textiles, and his appropriation of Mudéjar elements of design. He left a half dozen major works in Burgos: the Virgin and Child over the cloister entrance in the cathedral, the sepulcher of Prince Alfonso, the retablo of the Capilla del Condestable, and others.

Vallejo, Juan de (1505–1569). Architect and sculptor. Designed the openwork vault and other works in the Cathedral of Burgos. Also designed nobles' palaces in Burgos.

Valmaseda, Juan de (1488–post 1548). Sculptor, known for combining the emotional pathos of late Gothic with the exaggerated postures of Renaissance Mannerism.

van der Weyden, Roger (1399–1464). Painter from Brussels who launched the Golden Age of Flemish painting. His stark settings and shallow backgrounds emphasized the importance of the foreground figures. A genius at expressing emotion, such as the diversely expressed sorrow of the witnesses to the Crucifixion and the Descent from the Cross.

Vigarny, Felipe (ca. 1470–ca. 1542). He had emigrated to Burgos by 1498. With his wife Mary Sáenz Pardo he had 5 children, including the artist Gregorio Vigarny; he had 5 more with his second wife. His sculpture is transitional between late Gothic, noted for its superb attention to detail and heightened narrative sense, and Renaissance, with its interest in perspective, its classicist Plateresque decorative motifs, and its sense of calm theatricality. Other works in Santo Domingo de la Calzada, and in Granada and Zaragoza.

Ysenbrant, Adriaen (1510–51). Dutch painter, known for his nudes and his portraits. Was popular in Spain and painted many works for Spanish export.

Saints and Religious Iconography

Agnes [*see* Ines]

Agnus Dei. Lamb of God. Symbol of Christ's sacrifice and of the Eucharist. Lamb often depicted with cross and flag. Sometimes held by John the Baptist.

Águeda/Agatha (Sicily; 3rd c.). Maiden who preferred Christian virginity to marriage. Her rejected suitor, Quintianus, had her tortured, cutting off her breasts and threatening her with fire. St. Peter healed her breasts, and an earthquake saved her from the fire. She prayed to die, and did. A silken veil taken from her tomb saved villagers from a Mount Etna eruption. Emblems: palm of martyrdom, breasts on a tray, veil. Patron of bell makers and cheese makers, from the shape of the breasts. Feb. 5.

Agustín/Augustine (354–430). Converted to Christianity while a rhetoric professor in Milán. Became bishop of Hippo. Wrote *Confessions*, the chronicle of his spiritual life. Emblems: bishop's miter, book and pen; sometimes flaming heart pierced by arrow, the symbol of his flaming piety. Aug. 28.

Alodia [*see* Nunila]

Amador (France; ?). Hermit. Legend: founded shrine of Roc-Amadour in central France. Tomb discovered on cliff there in 1162. Legend quickly developed saying that it belonged to San Amador, servant of the Virgin Mary, husband of Santa Verónica, and missionary to Gaul. Aug. 20.

Ambrosio/Ambrose (Italy; 339–97). Governor of Lombardy; upon his conversion elected bishop of Milán. Preached so well that bees stopped to listen. Converted San Agustín. Patron of beekeepers. Dec. 7.

Ana/Anne. Mother of Mary; wife of Joachim. Emblems: green mantle (immortality) and red dress (God's love). Often shown teaching Mary to read or to sew; or at the presentation of the Virgin in the Temple. Invoked against sterility. July 26.

Andrés/Andrew. Apostle, brother of Peter. By tradition a missionary to southern Russia. Fearing his power, the governor of Patras had him crucified on an X-shaped cross. Emblems: X-shaped cross; occasionally a fishing net. Patron of Russia and Scotland. Nov. 30.

Annunciation [*see* María]

Anselmo/Anselm (England; 1033–1109). Benedictine monk, later archbishop of Canterbury. Theologian noted for his ontological proof of God's existence. His refusal to recognize a schismatic Pope led to his banishment from England. Later political troubles led to a second banishment. At several church councils he insisted on greater clerical celibacy. Apr. 21.

Antonio Abad/Antón/Anthony the Abbot (Egypt; 4th c.). After parents' death, gave away their possessions; lived 20 years as hermit by the Nile, struggling with temptations or demons. As an old man, sought out the hermit Paul, and they created a community. Considered a founder of monasticism. A Frenchman prayed to Anthony to cure his son of a burning form of leprosy and founded the Order of St. Anthony to care for lepers; the disease became known as St. Anthony's fire. Emblems: monk's robe, on left shoulder a blue tau (for the Greek *Theos*, meaning God); crutch (for old man); bell (exorcist); pig (exorcised demons); fire in his hand; landscape with phantasmagorical temptations. Patron of Castrogeriz. Jan. 17.

Antonio de Padua/Anthony (Italy; 13th c.). Francis of Assisi recognized his preaching ability. Taught divinity at many universities. Legend: a heretic of Padua said he'd not believe in the Eucharist unless Anthony made an ass leave its stable and kneel before it; the ass did. Emblems: Franciscan robes, kneeling ass, lily, flowered cross, basket of bread. June 13.

Apolonia (Egypt; ?–249). Deaconess of Alexandria. Martyred by having her teeth broken out with pincers. Threatened with being burned alive if she did not renounce her Christianity, she forthrightly stepped into the fire. Protects against toothaches. Emblems: teeth and pincers. Feb. 9.

Assumption [*see* María, Dormition]

Aurea [*see* Oria]

Babil (early 8th c). He ran a school at Leyre for Mozarabic children.

Bárbara (?). Legendary virgin martyr, allegedly killed ca. 303. According to the *Golden Legend*, her father, Dioscurus, imprisoned her in a tower to keep her from men's eyes. When she became a Christian against her father's wishes, he nearly killed her, then handed her over to a judge who condemned her to death. A lightning bolt killed her father. Barbara protects against sudden death and is the patroness of things that go boom: lightning, artillery, mines, and explosives. Emblem: tower. Dec. 4 (cult suppressed in 1969).

Bartolomé/Bartholomew. Apostle. Legend: traveled to India where he cured King Polemón's daughter and converted his court. Returning, he was captured by Armenian heathens, mistreated by King Astiages, flayed, and crucified. Patron of tanners. Emblems: flaying knife; sometimes a flayed skin over arm. Aug. 24.

Basilia (?–304). Nine-year-old martyr in the Diocletian persecutions. Withstood scourging, fire, and beasts before finally succumbing. Sept. 3.

Baudillo/Baudelius/Boal (France; ?–ca. 380). Native of Orleans, missionary in Gaul. Beheaded at Nîmes when he insisted on preaching during a festival to Jupiter. Over 400 churches dedicated to him in southern France and northern Spain. May 20.

Benito/Benedict (Italy; ca. 480–550). Hermit who attracted many followers. Established 12 Benedictine monasteries, with the mother house in Monte Cassino. Wrote a comprehensive monastic rule, which shaped all subsequent monasticism. Emblems: Benedictine robes, flowing beard; dove (his sister Escolástica's soul, which he saw ascend to heaven); raven (which fed him when he was a hermit); broken cup (enemies tried to poison him); sometimes index finger at lips (vow of silence). July 11.

Bernardino de Siena (Italy; 1380–1444). Franciscan preacher who reputedly could make the deaf hear. Known for sermons on the Holy Name of Jesus. The monogram IHS contained in the sun appeared to him in a vision. May 20.

Bernardo/Bernard (France; ca. 1090–1153). Nobleman who became a monk at the poverty-stricken abbey of Clairvaux, which flourished under his leadership and made him abbot. Active reformer and innovator, strongly influenced development of the Cistercians. Lobbied for the creation of the Knights Templar (see ch. 68) to fight the infidels and protect pilgrims. Preached the Second Crusade. Supported the election of Innocent II as Pope, and the white-robed Cistercians prospered under their alliance. Prolific writer: his treatise on God's Love is a classic of Catholic spirituality. By his death, there were over 400 Cistercian houses, many in Spain. Aug. 20.

Blas/Blaise (Armenia; 4th c.?). Bishop. During the persecutions he hid in a cave where, among his miraculous cures, he aided a boy choking on a fish bone. The boy's mother brought him food and 2 candles in thanks. Martyred by being torn with carding combs and then beheaded. Protects against diseases of the throat (after prayer and the application of 2 candles to the neck). Emblem: carding combs. Feb. 3.

Braulio (?–646). Studied with San Isidoro in Sevilla. Became bishop of Zaragoza. Biographer of San Millán. Mar. 26.

Bruno (France; ca. 1030–1101). Deposed as diocesan chancellor at Rheims for denouncing the new archbishop. Retired with 6 companions to Chartreuse (near Grenoble) to found the Carthusian Order in 1084. The Order's rule limited each monastery's membership to 12 monks (later 24) and a prior, and stipulated that the bulk of their time be spent in solitary, silent prayer. They were permitted to speak only during 1 hour each week. Oct. 6.

Caprasio (France; ?–303). Bishop of Agen. Implausible Spanish legend: he retired from the active world to a cave in Belorado (Burgos). Beheaded during the Diocletian persecutions. June 1.

Carmen [*see* María, Virgen del Carmen]

Casilda (?– ca. 1050). Toledan Christian of Moorish parents. Won fame as a hermit near Briviesca (Burgos). Apr. 9.

Catarina/Catalina/Catherine of Alexandria (Egypt; 4th c.?). Cult began in 9th c. Legend: noble woman who rejected marriage to the emperor Magencio as she considered herself a virgin bride of Christ. She defeated in debate 50 philosophers called to dissuade her from Christianity. The emperor tortured her on a wheel of knives, which broke before it did her serious damage. He then beheaded her. Her neck bled milk rather than blood. Patron of young girls, philosophers, nurses, and artisans who work with wheels: spinners, potters, millers, etc. Emblem: broken wheel of knives. Nov. 25 (cult suppressed in 1969).

Cecilia (Italy; 3rd c.). Roman martyr of whom nearly nothing is known. Fifth-century legend makes her a Christian from a wealthy family who refused to wed the pagan Valerian because she had pledged her virginity to God. Compelled to marry, she sang along with the organ at her wedding that God would help keep her pure. Refused to consummate the union. Her husband became Christian and was martyred. She was sentenced to be suffocated. This failed. Eventually beheaded. Patroness of music. Emblem: an organ. Nov. 22.

Celedonio [*see* Emeterio and Celedonio]

Céntola (?– ca. 304). Martyred with her colleague Elena near Burgos during the Diocletian persecutions. Aug. 13.

Cernín/Saturnino (France; 3rd c.). Missionary from Rome to the Pyrenees. Became the first bishop of Toulouse. Dragged to death by a bull when he refused to sacrifice to pagan gods. Legend: one of Santiago's disciples. Nov. 29.

Crismón. A rosette symbolizing the Trinity, devised to distinguish Catholic monuments from those of Arian heretics. Its symbolic design contains the cross, the chi-rho that begins the name *Christus* in Greek, and the alpha and omega indicating that Christ is the beginning and end of all things.

Cipriano (France; 6th c.). Bishop of Toulon. Oct. 3.

Clara/Clare (Italy; 1194–1253). Born at Assisi; influenced by and then colleague of Francis. Founded Franciscan nuns. Their strict rule and aggressive adoption of poverty led to their being called the Poor Clares. Her Order was particularly popular in Spain, with over 45 convents founded in the 13th c. Emblem: the brown robes of her Order. Aug. 11.

Colomba (?–853). When her father died, she refused marriage, preferring to become a nun. During the persecutions of Mohammed I in Córdoba, ca. 853, she was pressured to convert to Islam, but instead she tried to convert her judge to Christianity. Beheaded, her body was tossed into the Guadalquivir River; after 6 days it surfaced incorrupt. Her bones lay for 2 centuries in the church of Santa Eulalia in Córdoba before being taken to Nájera. Sept. 17.

Cosme/Cosmas and **Damián** (?). Legend: Arab twin brother doctors who cured for no fee. Reputedly they grafted a white leg onto an injured Black man. Patrons of doctors and veterinarians. Emblem: bicolored patient. Sept. 26.

Crispín and **Crispiniano** (?–ca. 285). Shoemaker brothers, beheaded in France during the Diocletian persecutions. Patrons of cobblers. Emblem: making shoes. Oct. 25.

Cristóbal/Christopher (3rd c.?). Legendary martyr. The *Golden Legend* says he was a Canaanite giant who served Satan until he found that the Devil feared Christ, and then he switched allegiance. A hermit educated him and set him to carrying travelers across a river. Once he carried a child who was so heavy Christopher could barely manage. The child said that he was Christ, that Christopher had carried the weight of the world, and that if he planted his staff he would receive a sign. He did: it bore flowers and dates. Patron of travelers; invoked against death by water or plague. Legend holds that whoever sees St. Christopher will not die before having time to confess. Emblem: giant carrying child Christ; in Spain often painted large on the wall near the church entrance. Classic Spanish kids' joke: "How did that giant get in through that little door?" "In a paint can." July 25 (cult suppressed in 1969).

Damián [*see* Cosme and Damián]

Deposition (aka Descent from the Cross) [*see* Jesus]

Doctors of the Church. Writers whose works are deemed to be of supreme value to the Church. In the early Middle Ages the 4 doctors were Gregory the Great,

Ambrose, Augustine, and Jerome. Later additions include Spanish saints Isidoro (in 1722) and Teresa de Ávila (in 1970). Today there are 33 Doctors.

Dolorosa [see María]

Domingo de Guzmán/Dominic (1170–1221). Founded the Dominican Order of Preaching Friars. Augustinian canon in Osma (Soria) until 1203, when he accompanied the bishop on a diplomatic mission. Pope Innocent III had him preach to the Albigensian heretics in the Languedoc (France), which he did both before and during Simon de Montfort's cruel military crusade that all but wiped them out. Dominic's Inquisition against the Albigensians was a precursor of the 15th-c. Spanish Inquisition, which was run by Dominicans at its inception and during most of its history. Dominic's Order believed monks should leave their cloisters to preach in the world. The idea caught on, and within 5 years of his death there were 60 Dominican friaries. Emblem: the black and white robes of the Dominican Order. Pejorative folkloristic name #1 for Dominicans: *urracas* (magpies), for their black-and-white robes and loud voices. Pejorative name #2: dogs of the Lord (Lat: *domini canni*). Emblems: star; dog with torch in mouth. Aug. 4.

Domingo de la Calzada (?–1109). Shepherd from Viloria who, after washing out as a monk in San Millán and Valvanera, became a hermit in the Sierra de la Demanda. Disciple of Cardinal Gregorio Ostiense, accompanying him to Compostela. When the cardinal died in 1043, Domingo devoted the rest of his life to helping pilgrims by building roads, bridges, churches, and hospices (see ch. 36). May 12.

Domingo de Silos (ca. 1000–73). Born to a peasant family in Cañas (La Rioja). Entered San Millán de la Cogolla and rose to be prior. A dispute over property rights led to his banishment by the king of Navarra and his founding of the monastery of Silos under Castilian protection. He built it into a powerful center of learning. Believed to cure the sick and to free captives. His abbot's crozier, said to assure safe childbirth, was kept at the bedside of pregnant Spanish queens. In the 1990s Silos's monks released a best-selling CD: *Chant*. Dec. 20.

Dormition and Assumption [see María]

Dorotea/Dorothy (Cappadocia, Turkey; ?–ca. 313). Legend: virgin martyred by Diocletian. On the way to execution, a skeptical lawyer asked her to send him fruits from paradise. She agreed. After her death, an angel delivered a basket with 3 apples and 3 roses. Emblem: basket of fruits and flowers. Feb. 6.

Ecce Homo. Latin for Pilate's words "Behold the man" (John 19:6). In art, the term designates Christ crowned with thorns, beaten and suffering, exhibited to the mob.

Elena/Helena (Turkey; ca. 250–330). Mother of Emperor Constantine. He persuaded her at age 60 to become Christian. Pilgrim to the Holy Land, where she identified the site and remains of the True Cross, which she validated by having it resuscitate a dead woman. She established the sites of many other New Testament events. Emblem: displaying the Cross; resuscitating the woman. May 21.

Elizabeth [see Isabel]

Eloy/Éloi/Eligius (France; ca. 588–660). Bishop of Noyon and Tournai (France). Before entering the priesthood he won fame as a gold- and silversmith. Patron of smiths. Emblem: horseshoe. Dec. 1.

Emeterio and **Celedonio** (4th c.?). Soldiers in Calahorra martyred for their faith. Mar. 3.

Epiphany [*see* Jesus]

Erasmo [*see* Telmo]

Escolástica/Scholastica (Italy; ?–ca. 543). Sister of St. Benedict. Founded first nunnery of the Benedictine Order and is its patroness. Benedict had a vision of her soul ascending to heaven as a dove. Emblem: black habit, often with crozier; white dove flying from mouth. Feb. 10.

Esteban/Stephen (Palestine; ?–ca. 35). First Christian martyr. His life is sketched in Acts, chapters 6–7. Probably a Hellenistic Jew, one of 7 early Christian deacons. When he preached that Jesus was the Messiah, the crowd stoned him. Patron of deacons. Invoked against headaches. Emblem: large stone(s). Dec. 26.

Eulalia (?–ca. 304). Cordoban virgin and martyr. During the Diocletian persecutions she criticized her judge for causing souls to be lost. She resisted flattery, bribes, and tortures before being burned alive. (There may be a second contemporary Saint Eulalia, from Barcelona.) Dec. 10.

Evangelists [*see* Tetramorphos]

Fabián (Italy; ?–250). Pope. First martyr of Decius's persecution of the Church. Jan. 20.

Facundo (?–ca. 300). He and his friend Primitivo were Diocletian martyrs who were twice burned and then had their eyes torn out. Their bodies were thrown in the River Cea near Sahagún. Nov. 27.

Felices (5th c.) Tutor of San Millán.

Felipe/Philip. Apostle. Emblem: cross of martyrdom.

Félix [*see* Voto]

Fermín (1st c.). Santiago's disciple Cernín converted Fermín, who later, as bishop, evangelized Navarra. Preaching in France, he converted 3,000 in 3 days, for which he was imprisoned and tortured before his miraculous—though temporary—release. He was martyred in Amiens by losing his head (and is thus a model for the young people who throng to his annual festival in Pamplona). July 7.

Francisco de Asís/Francis of Assisi (Italy; 1181–1226). Founded the Preaching Order of Franciscans. Son of a cloth merchant. Rejected a business career to help poor people and lepers. A vision that told him "repair my house, which is falling down," led him to use family money for church repairs. Eventually gave away all his possessions and embraced poverty. His followers increased. Went on pilgrimage to Compostela in 1214, founding many Franciscan congregations along the way. Journeyed to the Holy Land, grew disillusioned with the dissolute Crusaders, and returned to Italy. In 1224, during a mystic vision, he was favored with stigmata, wounds like the crucified Christ's, which scarred his hands, feet, and side. Emblem: kneeling receiving stigmata; Franciscan robes. Oct. 4 (stigmata, Sept. 17).

Francisco Javier/Francis Xavier (1506–52). Son of a Basque noble family. While studying in Paris, he joined Ignacio de Loyola as one of the first 7 members of his new Jesuit Order. His first missionary assignment in 1541 was to Goa. Spent several years doing mission work in southern India. In 1549 he sailed to Japan, the first European to do missionary work there. His body is preserved in Goa. Dec. 3.

Froilán (?–1006). Native of Lugo. Hermit in the Bierzo. Reorganized Galician Benedictine monasticism. Later became bishop of León. Oct. 3.

Fructuoso (?–ca. 665). Born in Toledo to a Visigothic royal family. Left the court to become a hermit in the Bierzo. He sought solitude, but his disciple Valerio (who became his biographer), Toribio, and many others flocked to him. Retired to the mountain again, and again they came, building the monasteries of San Pedro de Montes, Compludo, and Santiago de Peñalba. Eventually accepted post as bishop of Braga. In 1102 Diego Gelmírez (see ch. 88) secured his relics for Compostela. Apr. 16.

Gabriel. Archangel who helped Daniel understand his visions (Dan. 8, 9), prophesied the birth of John the Baptist, and brought Mary the news of her conception of Jesus (Luke 1). Mar. 24 (recently moved to Sept. 29).

Gadea [*see* Águeda]

Genadio (?–936). Monk from Ponferrada who rebuilt several Bierzo monasteries destroyed by the Muslims (e.g., San Pedro de Montes). Alfonso III of Asturias appointed him bishop of Astorga. After 10 years he renounced to return to monastic life. May 25.

George [*see* Jorge]

Gertrudis/Gertrude (1256?–1302). Benedictine mystic known for her visions during the Divine Liturgy. Her writings popularized devotion to the Sacred Heart of Jesus. Nov. 15 (sometimes 16, or 17).

Gil/Giles (France; early 8th c.). Founded a monastery in Provence (Saint-Gilles) that became a major pilgrimage site. Tenth-century legend: he was a royal Athenium who became a hermit near Nîmes. One day King Wamba, hunting a deer, shot an arrow that wounded Giles as the deer took refuge with him. Another legend: an emperor (Charlemagne?) craved forgiveness for a sin he did not dare confess. At mass Giles saw an angel bearing a written record of those sins; as Giles prayed, the letters faded and disappeared. Penitents believed he could broker divine forgiveness even without their making full oral confession. Patron of lepers, cripples, and nursing mothers (related to his giving refuge). His churches are often at crossroads. Emblems: abbot with staff, or monk protecting a deer. Sept 1.

Gregorio/Gregory the Great (Italy; 540?–604). Founder of monasteries, Roman ambassador to Byzantium, and eventually Pope, in which role he negotiated important treaties and sent Augustine as missionary to the Britons. His attention to detail and to serving as an effective instrument of temporal and divine power helped create the modern papacy. Noted for his love of music, especially the style of chant that still bears his name. Copious and learned writer. Legend: while Gregory was saying mass the wounds on the image of the crucified Jesus bled real blood to convince skeptics of the literal truth of the eucharistic miracle. Emblems: in the act of writing (with inspiration from the the dove of the Holy Spirit); or as one of the Doctors of the Church; or in the miracle of the mass. Sept. 3.

Gregorio Ostiense (?–1044?). Benedictine cardinal and bishop sent by the Pope to the Rioja to quell a plague of locusts. There he met and mentored Domingo de la Calzada from 1037 until Gregorio's death in Logroño in 1041. May 9.

Helena [*see* Elena]

Ignacio de Loyola/Ignatius (1491–1556). Youngest son of a Basque noble family. Spent his early years soldiering; badly wounded in the siege of Pamplona. He wanted to convalesce with favorite books of chivalry, but was given the lives of the saints and of Christ. He converted, wrote the first draft of his *Spiritual Exercises*, went as a beggar on pilgrimage to Jerusalem. Studied in Paris; with 6 colleagues (including Francisco Javier) decided to dedicate his life to Christ and to serving the interests of the Church. Founded the Society of Jesus, the Jesuits, as a spiritual army to counteract the Protestant Reformation. July 31.

IHS. First letters of Greek word for Jesus. Often misinterpreted as abbreviation of Constantine's statement of devotion to the cross (*in hoc signo*) or to the saving power of Christ (*Iesus hominum salvator*). The monogram, contained in the sun, appeared in a vision to St. Bernardino of Siena.

Ildefonso/Ildephonsus (ca. 607–77). Archbishop of Toledo. Wrote a treatise on baptism and another on the virginity of Mary. In gratitude she personally gave him a chasuble. Emblem: Mary placing the chasuble over him. Jan. 23.

Indalecio (1st c.). By tradition one of Santiago's 7 disciples. Served as the first bishop of Urci (Almería) and of Auca (Villafranca de Montes de Oca). May 15.

Inés/Agnes (Italy; ca. 304). Teenager who preferred Christian virginity to marriage; martyred in Rome by being stabbed in the throat. Emblem: a lamb. Jan. 21.

Irene (Greece; ?–304). With Agape and Chione, martyr during Diocletian persecution. Even after her companions were burned, Irene steadfastly refused to eat Roman sacrificial food. She was cast naked into the soldiers' brothel, but no one dared touch her. Eventually she, too, was burned. Apr. 3.

Isabel/Elizabeth. Mother of San Juan Bautista; wife of Zachary. Nov. 5.

Isidoro (ca. 560–636). Succeeded his brother as bishop of Sevilla ca. 600. Became the outstanding churchman of his time. Converted the Arian Visigoths; sponsored several significant church councils; founded schools in each town of his diocese. His most famous work, the *Etymologies*, is the first medieval encyclopedia, treating at length topics of theology, astronomy, geography, history, biography, etc. Canonized in 1598; made a Doctor of the Church in 1722. Emblem: bishop with a quill pen. Apr. 4.

Isidro (1070–1130). A farmer who worked near Madrid for Juan de Vargas. When he tarried in church, angels did his farmwork for him. Patron of Madrid. Emblem: yoked oxen and plow, often with angel plowing. May 15.

James the Lesser [*see* Santiago el Menor]

Jerónimo/Jerome (ca. 341–420). Well-educated in Latin rhetoric as a young man, he converted, became a monk, and eventually a hermit. Mastered Hebrew and Greek. Responsible for the standardized Latin translation of the entire Bible known today as the *Vulgate*. Known for his energy and wisdom, but also for his temper and scathing wit. Eventually settled in Bethlehem to write, teach, and live a simple monk's life. Emblems: as a hermit in the desert, he beats his naked chest with a rock as a sign of penance; as aide to Pope Damasus, he wears a cardinal's hat; as a Doctor of the Church, often dressed—anachronistically—as a Pope. Often with a lion (who befriended him in the desert; see ch. 40) at his feet. Sept. 30.

Jerónimo Hermosilla (?–1861). Native of Santo Domingo de la Calzada. Dominican missionary in the Philippines and Vietnam. Tortured and beheaded. Canonized 1988. Nov. 1.

Jesus. You will see many episodes from the life of Jesus. Here is a list of the most frequently depicted. The Nativity. The Annunciation of His birth to the shepherds. The shepherds adore Him. Twelve nights later, at the feast now called Epiphany, so do the 3 Wise Men (Magi or Kings). Mary presents Him at the temple. He is circumcised at the temple. The Holy Family flees to Egypt to escape Herod's order that all male children be killed: Mary, carrying the infant, rides an ass, Joseph walks ahead and leads the animal. Returned from Egypt, Jesus disputes the law in the temple with several rabbis. John baptizes Jesus. He prays in the desert and is tempted by demons. He calls His Apostles from their boats. He cleanses the temple. He presides at the marriage at Cana, turning water to wine. He raises Lazarus from the dead. Jesus, praying with John, James, and Peter, undergoes a Transfiguration, shines with light, and is visited by Old Testament figures. Mary Magdalene washes His feet.

The Passion: Entry to Jerusalem. Jesus washes the disciples' feet. The Last Supper. Praying in the Garden of Gethsemane. The Betrayal and Judas's kiss. Christ appears before Caiaphas. And before Pilate. The Flagellation, where Christ is tied to a pillar. The crowd mocks Him. The Ecce Homo. The Road to Calvary with its 14 episodes, often called the Stations of the Cross: Jesus is condemned; receives the cross; falls the first time; meets His mother, Mary; Simon of Cyrene helps Him carry the cross; Veronica wipes His face; Jesus falls a second time; speaks to the women of Jerusalem; falls a third time; is stripped of His clothes; is nailed to the cross; dies; is taken down from the cross (Deposition); is laid in the tomb.

Joaquín/Joachim. Husband of Ana, father of Mary, according to apocryphal Gospel of James. Childless, Joaquín and Ana offered a sacrificial lamb at the temple. It was refused. Joaquín retired to the wilderness to pray, Ana to her garden. Each was visited by an angel to announce Ana's pregnancy. Often shown rejected at the temple door, lamb in arms; or advised by an angel of Mary's conception. July 26.

Jorge/George (?–ca. 303). Probably a soldier, martyred during Diocletian persecutions in Roman Palestine, near Lydda. Venerated as patron of the Byzantine army. The *Golden Legend* tells the story of a dragon that terrorized the country with its poisonous breath and demanded human victims, even the king's daughter. George wounded it and led it back to the city with the Princess's mantle, promising that if the people adopted Christianity he would kill the monster. They did, and he did, accepting no reward but that the king protect the Church and succor the poor. George was adopted by the Crusaders—particularly the English—as their patron. Since he personified the ideals of Christian chivalry, he was later adopted as patron by Portugal, Cataluña, Venice, and Genoa. Apr. 23.

José/Joseph. Husband of Mary. Often depicted as an old man, frequently dozing to one side of scenes relating to Jesus's birth. Mar. 19.

Juan Bautista/John the Baptist. Recognized by Christ as the greatest prophet. He was sanctified in the womb of his mother Isabel and thus freed from original sin. Baptized Jesus in the Jordan River. Was martyred under Herod, at the instigation of Salome, who called for his head on a platter. Emblem: young man, dressed in the rough skins of a shepherd; or a head on a platter. June 24.

Juan de Ortega (?–1163). Juan Vélazquez, from Quintana, assisted Domingo de la Calzada in his engineering work on behalf of pilgrims (see ch. 40). Patron of civil engineers. June 2.

Juan de Sahagún (1419–79). Juan González de Castrillo studied at Sahagún and Salamanca. Joined Augustinians; became one of his age's most famous preachers, known for his visions and ability to read men's souls. Later years spent in Burgos. He was a scathing moralist who probably died poisoned by the mistress of a man whom he had led back to a more virtuous life. June 12.

Juan Evangelista/John the Evangelist. Fisherman of Galilee, son of Zebedee, brother of Santiago. Often identified as the Beloved Disciple. Exiled to Patmos; later resident in Ephesus. Traditionally the author of the Fourth Gospel, 3 epistles, and the book of Revelation. Emblem: eagle. Dec. 27.

Judas Tadeo/Jude. Apostle and martyr. Patron of people in desperate straits. Emblem: the ax that decapitated him in Persia. Oct. 28.

Julián. Probably mythical. The *Golden Legend* relates that a stag told him he would kill his parents. To avoid his destiny, Julian left home, made his fortune in a distant kingdom, and married a widow named Adela. His parents came to visit, were welcomed by his wife, and went to bed. Julian returned, saw the couple asleep, thought his wife was adulterous, and killed them both. In remorse Julian and his wife left home and near a river established a hospice for travelers. He helped a leper, who later granted him a vision of his forgiveness. Patron of innkeepers, boatmen, travelers. Jan. 29.

Justo and Pastor (?–ca. 304). Christian martyrs in Complutum (Alcalá de Henares) under the Diocletian persecutions. The 2 friends were 13 and 9 when they suffered scourging and beheading. Aug. 6.

Lesmés/Adelelmus. (France; ?–1097). Adelelmo Lesmés, of noble family, gave his inheritance to the poor and as a young Benedictine wandered for years as a pilgrim. Became abbot at Chaise-Dieu (France). Alfonso VI's wife Costanza de Borgoña brought him to Spain to oversee the imposition of the Roman liturgy over the Mozarabic (see ch. 7). Lesmés helped Alfonso VI reconquer Toledo and then retired to Burgos to establish a hospice and help pilgrims. Jan. 30.

Lorenzo/Lawrence (Italy; ?–258). A Roman deacon of the early Church, martyred in the Valerian persecution by being burned alive. Legend: when asked if he'd had enough, he requested to be turned over so he could roast evenly on all sides. Emblem: the gridiron of his martyrdom. Aug. 10.

Lucas/Luke (1st c.) Evangelist. A Greek gentile, probably from Antioch. Physician. Accompanied Paul on his journeys. Said to have been a painter. Emblem: ox. Oct. 18.

Lucía/Lucy (Italy; ?–304). Virgin martyred at Syracuse in the Diocletian persecution. Legend: Sicilian noblewoman who gave away her fortune and refused a noble suitor, who had her prosecuted. The judge ordered her sent to a brothel, but by miracle she could not be moved. He also failed in an attempt to have her burned. Her torn-out eyes were miraculously returned to her face. Eventually she was killed by sword. Emblem: eyes, often presented on a plate. Dec. 13.

Magdalena [*see* María Magdalena]

Marcelo (?–298?). Roman Centurion. Spaniards believed he lived in León. At the Roman Emperor's birthday celebration Marcelo threw off his uniform, crying "I serve only the eternal King." His martyrdom may have been in León, or perhaps Tangier. He may have been the husband of Santa Nonia [Nona], who was also martyred. Oct. 30.

Marcos/Mark. Evangelist. Preached in Cyprus and probably Alexandria. Associated with Venice, which acquired his relics in the 9th c. Emblem: lion. Apr. 25.

María/Mary. Mother of Jesus. Aug. 15. The most commonly depicted episodes and manifestations are:

Annunciation. The archangel Gabriel tells Mary, still a virgin, that she has conceived a child by the Holy Spirit. Often she is depicted kneeling in prayer or interrupted reading a prayer book. The Holy Spirit is represented by a dove.

Visitation. Mary, pregnant with Jesus, visits her older cousin Elizabeth, pregnant with John the Baptist. Elizabeth was the first to recognize Jesus's true nature. Often depicted embracing.

Nativity. Jesus is born in a stable, attended by various farm animals, often an ox and an ass (Isaiah 1:3).

Presentation. Fulfilling a vow made when she prayed to be granted a child, Ana took 3-year-old Mary to the temple to dedicate her to the service of God.

Pieta. Mary, sometimes with Mary Magdalene, weeping over the body of Jesus after the Crucifixion.

Dormition and Assumption. After many years Mary yearns to be reunited with Jesus. Six episodes are related. An angel promises that within 3 days they will be joined, and gives her a palm branch to be carried at her funeral. Mary bids farewell to the Apostles. The Apostles gather at her deathbed, as do many angels, who carry her soul heavenward. Her body is taken to its tomb. She is entombed. Mary's body and soul, reunited, are physically transported to heaven.

Mary is commonly portrayed in a variety of manifestations. Here are five frequently seen along the Road:

La Dolorosa. Depictions of the weeping Mary. Sometimes shown with a dagger piercing her heart. The 13th-c. Servite Order popularized Mary's 7 sorrows: hearing Simeon prophesize the Crucifixion; the flight into Egypt; the loss of the child Jesus in the temple; meeting Jesus on the road to Calvary; standing at the foot of the cross; seeing Jesus's removal from the cross; the burial. Fri. before Palm Sun., and third Sun. in Sept.

Virgen del Carmen. Elijah, praying on Mount Carmel for rain to assuage a drought, saw a cloud approaching (I Kings 18:4). Christians later interpreted the cloud as Mary, and the arrival of rain as the birth of Christ. The Carmelite Order, founded during Crusader times, popularized the Virgen del Carmen. Patroness of the Spanish armed forces and of businessmen. July 16.

Virgen de la Nieve (V. of the Snows). Two legends evolved about the 4th-c. church of Santa Maria Maggiore in Rome. 1. Mary appeared to Pope Liberius and told him to build her a church where snow would fall on Aug. 5. 2. A barren couple vowed to do whatever the Virgin asked if she granted them a child. When it snowed on Aug. 5, and the wife conceived, they built a church. Cult popular in mountain regions. Aug. 5.

Virgen de la O. Representation of the pregnant Mary.

Virgen del Pilar. Mary bringing the pillar of Jesus's flagellation. Emblem: standing with, or on, a pillar (see Introduction).

María Egipciaca/Mary of Egypt (5th c.?). Egyptian prostitute who was converted in Jerusalem and then lived as a solitary penitent in the wilderness. She is often shown near-naked, modesty provided by her long hair, contemplating a crucifix. Sometimes kneeling before a skull. Apr. 2.

María Magdalena. Repentant sinner; her demons were cast out by Jesus. She stood by the cross, went to anoint Jesus's body, and was granted a vision of the risen Christ (Luke 7). Legends add many biographical details. Patron of repentant sinners. Emblems: the pot of ointment; long hair, often covering her near-naked body. July 22.

Marina (?). Legend: when her father became a monk, she did, too, disguised as a boy. An innkeeper's daughter accused the "boy" of getting her pregnant. Expelled from the monastery, Marina begged faithfully at its gates without revealing her gender. Readmitted 5 years later, together with her putative son; until her death she was assigned the monastery's most menial tasks. When the monks dressed her corpse her secret was revealed. Feb. 12.

Martín de Tours (France; ca. 316–97). A Roman soldier who renounced the army when he became Christian. At Amiens he divided his cloak in half to clothe a naked beggar, after which Christ appeared to him wearing the half cloak. He became a monk, gathered followers, and established monasticism in Gaul. Eventually made bishop of Tours, but continued to live humbly in a poor cell, and devote his efforts to Christianizing the pagans. Since weather turns cold around his feast day, it is the traditional date to slaughter pigs and make sausages (*A cada puerco le llega su San Martín*—"Every pig has a St. Martin's Day"). Emblem: man on horseback dividing his cloak. Nov. 11.

Mateo/Matthew. Apostle and evangelist. Tax collector for the Romans before following Christ. Usually depicted as a man, since his gospel emphasizes Christ's family and humanity. Emblem: a man, often with wings. Sept. 21.

Matías/Matthias. Apostle and martyr. Chosen by lot to take Judas's place among the 12. Almost nothing known of his life or death. Emblem: stone of martyrdom. Feb. 24.

Mauro/Maurus (Italy; 6th c.). Monk, associate of San Benito, possibly sent to organize monasticism near Tours and Nantes (France). Often depicted as monk saving Plácido from drowning. Jan. 25.

Miguel/Michael. Archangel. Name means "who is like unto God?" General of the heavenly armies fighting against the Devil (Rev. 12:7–9). His power can rescue souls from hell. His cult was near universal in Christendom, and he is patron of dozens of cities, regions, and nations. Churches on rocks or other militarily apt sites are often dedicated to him. Emblems: sword; scales of judgment; vanquished devil at his feet. Sept. 29.

Millán (473–574). Hermit in the Rioja (see ch. 33).

Nativity [*see* María]

Nicolás/Nicholas of Bari (Turkey; 4th c.). Bishop of Myra, of whose life little is known. When Muslims took Turkey, his bones were brought to Bari (Italy). Legends: gave 3 bags of gold to poor unmarried girls to save them from becoming prostitutes (whence Santa Claus and Christmas gifts, as well as the pawnbrokers' 3 golden balls). Resuscitated 3 young boys who had drowned in a vat of brine; rescued 3 innocent men from execution; saved 3 sailors from death by storm. In death a fragrant perfume emitted from his tomb. Patron of children, unmarried girls, perfumiers, saliors, pawnbrokers, apothecaries, etc. Emblems: the 3 balls/sacks of gold; the 3 boys in the tub. May 9.

Nunila and **Alodia** (?–840) Legend: natives of Huesca; 2 sisters with a Muslim father and Christian mother. Raised Christian and then orphaned, they refused to convert to the faith of their Muslim guardian. They were sentenced to decapitation, which they accepted with Christian resignation. The Mudéjar ivory casket of their relics is now in the Museo de Navarra in Pamplona. Oct. 22.

Nonia [*see* Marcelo]

Oria/Aurea (1042–69). Hermit who walled herself up in a cave next to the monastery of San Millán de Suso (see ch. 33). Mar. 11.

Orosia (8th c.). Christian noblewoman who took refuge in caves of the Basa Valley near Sabiñánigo. Muslims captured and tried to convert her. She resisted torture, losing her arms, legs, and eventually her head. An angel is said to have revealed her relics to a local shepherd. Patroness of the Serrablo region of Aragón.

Pablo/Paul (1st c.). Roman, known as Saul before his conversion on the road to Damascus. With Barnabas, took the message of Christianity to gentiles all over the eastern Mediterranean. Tireless missionary and writer. Beheaded in Rome. Emblems: sword and book. June 29.

Pastor [*see* Justo]

Payo/Paio/Pelayo/Pelagius (911–25). Sent to Córdoba at age 10 in a hostage swap for his uncle the bishop of Tuy. The Caliph, taken with his beauty, offered inducements for him to convert, but he loudly proclaimed, "I am a Christian." inducements became threats, then tortures. Eventually he was slain and his body thrown into the Guadalquivir River. His relics were sent to León in 967 and later to Oviedo. June 26.

Pedro/Peter (1st c.). Fisherman called by Jesus to become the leader of the Apostles, the rock (*petrus*) on which the Church was to be built. Jesus entrusted him with the keys to heaven. The first Pope. By tradition, crucified head-down during Nero's reign. In Romanesque art he was the first of the Apostles to be distinguished by an attribute. Emblem: keys. June 29.

Pedro de Alcántara (1499–1562). From Extremadura. Franciscan reformer. Served as provincial of his monastery, then retired as a hermit to the Mountains of Arábida (Portugal). A mystic and an extreme ascetic: slept 1 hour per night, on the floor; ate only bread and ashes, etc. Writings extremely popular in the 16th c. Patron of Brazil and Extremadura. Oct. 19.

Pedro Mezonzo (?–ca. 1000). Pedro Martínez was a Galician Benedictine in the monastery of Mezonzo. Became abbot of San Martín de Antealtares in Compostela, and in 986 was made archbishop. Legend: author of the hymn *Salve regina*. Sept. 10

Pelayo [*see* Payo]

Pelican. Legend: draws blood from its own breast to feed its young. Therefore it became a symbol of Christ's sacrifice. Often shown nesting on the cross.

Pentecost. As Mary met with the Apostles, after Jesus's crucifixion, suddenly they were struck by a great wind, and tongues of fire danced on their heads. Filled with the Holy Spirit, they began to speak with other tongues (Acts 2:2–4).

Philip [*see* Felipe]

Pieta [*see* María]

Plácido (6th c.). Monk associated with San Benito in Subiaco. Nearly drowned but rescued by San Mauro. By tradition (now proven false) martyred in Sicily. Jan. 25.

Presentation [*see* María]

Primitivo (?–304). One of 18 Zaragozan martyrs (Facundus is the other popular one) under the Diocletian persecution. Apr. 16.

Quiteria (5th c.). Legend: daughter of a Galician prince; fled to avoid marriage and preserve her Christian identity. Her family tracked her to Aire (Gascony) and had her beheaded. A popular ditty goes: *Santa Quiteria parió por un dedo; podrá ser verdad, pero no lo creo* ("Saint Quiteria gave birth through her finger: it could be true, but I don't believe it"). May 22.

Rafael. Archangel, known as a healer, mentioned in the Book of Tobit. Often depicted with Tobit, and carrying a fish. Oct. 24 (now with Gabriel, Sept. 29).

Rocamadour [*see* Amador]

Roque/Roche/Rocco/Rock (France; ca. 1350–ca. 1380). Left his wealthy French family to become a hermit and then a pilgrim. Near Rome he caught the plague and was fed and tended by a dog. He probably died in prison, suspected of spying. Patron of people afflicted with plague. Emblems: pilgrim garb (staff, bottle gourd, pilgrim insignia), knee with lesion on it, dog carrying bread. Aug. 16.

Ruperto (Germany; ?–ca. 710). Bishop of Worms and Salzburg; missionary along the Danube. Credited with developing salt mines near Salzburg. Emblem: barrel of salt. Mar. 27.

Santiago el Menor/James the Lesser/Santiago Alfeo. Apostle. Son of Alphaeus. Head of Jerusalem Christians, martyred by stoning. Emblems: baculus and miter. May 1.

Saturnino [*see* Cernín]

Sebastián (ca. 300). Roman martyr of the Diocletian persecution. Legends hold him a Roman soldier and member of the Praetorian Guard who helped other secret Christians. He was reproved by the emperor and ordered executed by being shot full of arrows. He miraculously recovered, reproved the emperor in turn, and was beaten to death. Patron of archers. Emblem: half-nude body with lots of arrows (popular pretext for studying the nude male figure). Jan. 20.

Simeón (1st c.). Reached out to hold the infant Jesus at his presentation in the temple and prophesied regarding the resurrection and Mary's pain at Jesus's death (Luke). Called Holy Simeon, but not considered a saint.

Simón (1st c.). Apostle and martyr. Nothing known about him. Legend: martyred in Persia. Emblem: his saw of martyrdom. Oct. 28.

Sixto/Sixtus (?–258). Pope, martyred by Valerian. Aug. 6.

Stations of the Cross [*see* Jesus]

Stephen [*see* Esteban]

Tecla (1st c.). Legend: impressed by Paul's teaching, she chose perpetual virginity over marriage. She was ordered burned, but a storm extinguished the flame. In Antioch, with Paul, she was condemned to be thrown to wild beasts, but they would not harm her. She escaped to Myra disguised as a man, and there spent 72 years as a hermit. Even by the 4th c. she was considered apocryphal. Patroness of Tarragona. Sept. 23 (cult suppressed in 1969).

Telmo/Elmo/Erasmos (?–ca 300). There are few facts about his life. Legend 1: Syrian bishop who fled Diocletian's persecution to become a hermit. When discovered, he was rolled in pitch and burned. Legend 2: he preached during a fierce thunderstorm, and is thus invoked against storms, which makes him a particular favorite of sailors. The atmospheric discharges of electricity from the top of masts of ships during storms was known as St. Elmo's Fire. Spanish legend 3: he was from Frómista (Palencia). His most common emblem, a windlass, was misinterpreted to be an instrument of torture used to winch out his intestines. By logical extension, patron of people with digestive problems and of children suffering from colic. June 2.

Teresa de Ávila (1515–82). Founder of the Order of Discalced Carmelites. Mystic, author, and the first woman declared a Doctor of the Church. In early 17th c. nominated, unsuccessfully, to replace Santiago as patron of Spain. Emblem: fiery arrow or dove above her head. Oct. 15.

Tetramorphos. Symbols of the 4 Evangelists: Matthew (ox), Mark (lion), Luke (man), and John (eagle).

Tirso (3th c.?). One of 3 martyrs whose relics were brought from Constantinople to Spain and France. Much revered by Mozarabs. Jan 28.

Tomás/Thomas. Apostle. Doubted the resurrection until Christ appeared to him and he touched the wound. Legend: missionary to Indian state of Kerala. Emblem: lance signifying unbreakable faith. Dec. 21.

Tomás de Canterbury (England; 1118–70). The monk Thomas Becket was made royal chancellor by King Henry II. Served as statesman, courtier, diplomat, and even soldier. Made archbishop, he did an about-face, became an ascetic, and quarreled with the King. Murdered in his Cathedral. His shrine at Canterbury became England's greatest pilgrimage site. Dec. 29.

Toribio [*see* Fructuoso]

Transfiguration [*see* Jesus]

Tree of Jesse. Representation of the genealogy of the Virgin Mary. A tree springs from the breast of King David's father, Jesse (Isa. 11:1–2), and winds heavenward, where it culminates in Mary.

Valerio [*see* Fructuoso]

Veremundo (?–1092). Abbot who built Irache to great prominence. Champion of the Mozarabic rite (see ch. 26). Miracle: produced food for 3,000 worshipers during a famine. Mar. 8.

Verónica. Wiped Jesus's face as he walked to Calvary. His true image (*vero iconos*) remained on her handkerchief. Emblem: the hanky. Bullfighting term: a particular pass with the large cape is called a *verónica*. July 12.

Vicente Ferrer (1350–1419). Dominican preacher from Valencia who converted many Jews. Supported schismatic Pope Benedict XIII (Pedro de Luna) until 1416, when he withdrew his support and helped heal the breach. Patron of Valencia. Died and buried in Vannes in Brittany. Apr. 5.

La Virgen. Name given to Mary and, with modifiers, to her infinite manifestations. For Carmen, Dolorosa, de la O, Pilar, de la Nieve, *see* María.

Victoriano (Italy; ?–558). Italian priest who became abbot at Asan near Barbastro (Aragón). Jan. 12.

Virila (?–1000?). Abbot of the Monastery of Leyre (see ch. 10).

Visitation [*see* María]

Vitores (?–ca. 950). Late medieval legend: Spanish priest martyred by the Muslims near Burgos. Emblem: severed head held in hand. Aug. 26.

Voto and **Félix** (?–ca. 750). These 2 brothers joined the hermit Juan in founding the Monastery of San Juan de la Peña. May 29.

Zacarías/Zachary. Father of John the Baptist. Nov. 5.

Zoilus/Zoilo (?–ca. 304). Young Cordoban martyr who was tortured by having his kidneys torn out and then killed along with 20 companions under the Diocletian persecution. In the 7th c. he revealed the location of his tomb to the Cordoban bishop San Agapio in a dream. The relics were given to the son of the counts of Carrión by the Muslim caliph in return for certain services and were brought to Carrión ca. 1050. June 27.

Time Line of Rulers
and Events

Date	Navarra	Aragón	Castilla	León
895				Alfonso III el Magno King of Asturias 866–910
900				
905	Sancho I Garcés 905–25 King of Pamplona			
910				Garcia I 910–14 Ordoño II 914–24
915				
920				Fruela II 924–925 Alfonso IV 925–30
925	García I Sánchez 925–70 King of Pamplona		Fernán González 929–70	
930				Ramiro II 931–51
935				
940				
945				
950				Ordoño III 951–55
955				Sancho I el Gordo 955–58
960				Ordoño IV 958–59 Sancho I el Gordo 959–967
965				Ramiro III 967–84
970	Sancho Garcés II Abarca 970–94 King of Navarra & Count of Aragón		García Fernández 970–95	
975				
980				Vermudo II el Gotoso 984–99
985				
990	Garcia II Sánchez el Temblón 994–1000			

Muslims	People	Events	Arts
		899: 1st basilica of Santiago	
'Abdar-Rahman III 912–61 Apex of Cordoban caliphate		910: Cluny founded	
939: Battle of Simancas			
			ca. 950: *Glosas emelianses* 950: Mozarabic churches of Serrablo begun
		961: Hospital of St. Bernard founded in Swiss Alps	
968: University founded in Córdoba			
978: Almanzor named chief minister of Córdoba			
	Capetian dynasty in France		

Date	Navarra	Aragón	Castilla	León
995			Sancho García 995–1017	Alfonso V el Noble 999–1027
1000	Sancho III Garcés el Mayor 1000–1035			
1005				
1010				
1015				
1020			García Sanchez 1017–29	
1025			[Protectorate of Navarra 1029–35]	Vermudo III 1027–37
1030				
1035	García III Sánchez el de Nájera 1035–54	Ramiro I 1035–63	Fernando I el Magno de Castilla (1035–) y León (1037)–1065	
1040				
1045				
1050	Sancho Garcés IV el de Peñalén 1054–76			
1055				
1060		Sancho Ramírez I 1063–94		
1065			Sancho II 1065–72	Alfonso VI 1065–72
1970			Alfonso VI of Castilla (1065–) y León 1072–1109	
1075	Sancho Ramírez I of Aragón y V of Navarra 1076–94			
1080				
1085				
1090	Pedro I of Aragón y Navarra 1094–1104			

Muslims	People	Events	Arts
Almanzor ravages northern Christian kingdoms			
1002: Almanzor dies			
	1019: Domingo de la Calzada born		
Caliphate dissolves into Taifa states			
	1045: Rodrigo Díaz de Vivar, El Cid, born		
	Urraca inherits Zamora from Fernando I, her father		
		Benedictines of Cluny invited to San Juan de la Peña	
			1076: Rebuilding of Compostela Cathedral begins
	ca. 1080: Juan de Ortega born		
1085: Toledo captured by Christian forces			
Almorávides invade Córdoba Caliphate from Morocco			

Date	Navarra	Aragón	Castilla	León
1095				
1100	Alfonso I el Batallador of Aragón y Navarra 1104–1134			
1105			Urraca 1109–1126	
1110				
1115				
1120				
1125			Alfonso VII of Castilla y León 1126–57	
1130	García Ramírez IV el Restaurador 1134–50	Ramiro II el Monje 1134–37		
1135		Petronilla 1137–62		
1140				
1145				
1150	Sancho VI el Sabio 1150–94			
1155			Sancho III el Deseado 1157–1158 Alfonso VIII 1158–1214	Fernando II 1157–88
1160		Regency of Count of Barcelona 1162–1164 Alfonso II el Casto 1164–96		
1165				
1170				
1175				

Muslims	People	Events	Arts
	1099: El Cid dies	1098: Monastery of Cîteaux: Cistercian reform begins 1099: Jerusalem conquered by 1st Crusade Christian forces	
	1100–40: Diego Gelmírez: Compostela archbishop		ca. 1100: *Chanson de Roland*
	ca. 1109: Domingo de la Calzada dies		1107: *Historia compostelana* begun
	Pope Calixtus II 1119–24		
		1128: Templar Order officially recognized	
			ca. 1140: *Liber Sancti Jacobi* ca. 1140: *Poema de mío Cid*
		1147–9: 2nd Crusade	
1147: Almohads invade Córdoba Caliphate			1154: Idrisi's *Geography* published
			1056: León's San Isidoro begun
	1163: Juan de Ortega dies		
			1066: Frómista's San Martín begun 1067: Ivory Arca de San Millán
	1173: Thomas of Canterbury canonized		
		1175: Order of Santiago chartered 1179: Portugal independent	1076: Jaca Cathedral begun

Date	Navarra	Aragón	Castilla	León
1180				
1185				Alfonso IX 1188–1230
1190	Sancho VII el Fuerte 1194–1234			
1195		Pedro II 1196–1213		
1200				
1205				
1210		Jaime I el Conquistador 1213–76	Enrique I 1214–17	
1215			Fernando III el Santo 1217–52	
1220				
1225				
1230	Teobaldo I (Champaña) 1234–53		Fernando III el Santo of Castilla y León 1230–52	
1235				
1240				
1245				
1250	Teobaldo II 1253–70		Alfonso X el Sabio of Castilla y León 1252–84	
1255				
1260				
1265				

Muslims	People	Events	Arts
	1180: Gonzalo de Berceo born		
		1187: Jerusalem reconquered by Muslims 1189–92: 3rd Crusade	
1195: Almohads defeat Castilla's Alfonso VIII at Alarcos			
		1202–4: 4th Crusade 1204: Crusaders take Constantinople	
			1209: 1st Gothic church in Spain built at Roncesvalles
1212: Christians defeat Almohads at Las Navas de Tolosa. Andalucia is opened to Christians	1214: Francis of Assisi on pilgrimage to Compostela	1207: Franciscan Order founded	
		1215: Dominican Order founded; Magna Carta signed	
			1221: Burgos Cathedral begun
1229: Aragonese conquer Mallorca	1228: Francis of Assisi canonized		
		1230: Leprosy arrives in Europe via Crusaders	ca. 1230: Berceo's poems
1236: Córdoba falls to Castilla; bells taken back to Compostela 1238: Valencia falls to Aragón			
1248: Sevilla falls to Castilla	1248: Gonzalo de Berceo dies		
			ca. 1250: *Poema de Fernán González* 1251: *Siete Partidas*
			ca. 1261: Alfonso X's *Cantigas*
			ca. 1265: Jacobus de Voragine's *Golden Legend*

Date	Navarra	Aragón	Castilla	León
1270	Enrique I el Gordo 1270–4			
1275	Juana I 1274–1305	Pedro III 1276–85		
1280			Sancho IV el Bravo de Castilla y León 1284–95	
1285		Alfonso III 1285–91 el Liberal		
1290		Jaime II 1291–1327		
1295			Fernando IV de Castilla y León 1295–1312	
1300				
1305	Luis I 1305–16			
1310			Alfonso XI el Justiciero de Castilla y León 1312–50	
1315	Felipe I 1316–22			
1320	Carlos I el Calvo 1322–28			
1325	Juana II 1328–49	Alfonso IV el Benigno 1327–36		
1330				
1335		Pedro IV el Ceremonioso 1336–87		
1340				
1345	Carlos II el Malo 1349–87			
1350			Pedro I el Cruel de Castilla y León 1350–69	
1355				
1360				
1365			Enrique II de Castilla y León 1369–79 Trastámara dynasty begins	
1370				
1375			Juan I 1379–90	

Muslims	People	Events	Arts
		Pope Boniface VIII proclaims Jubilee Year for Rome	1302: León Cathedral completed
		1305: Popes in Avignon 1308: Templars disbanded	
		1337: Hundred Years' War between France and England begins	
s			ca. 1355: Sem Tob's poems
		1378: Start of schism in papacy	

Date	Navarra	Aragón	Castilla	León
1380				
1385	Carlos III el Noble 1387–1425	Juan I 1387–95		
1390		Martin I 1395–1410	Enrique III el Doliente de Castilla 1390–1406	
1395				
1400				
1405			Juan II 1406–54	
1410		Fernando I el Justo 1412–16		
1415		Alfonso V 1416–58		
1420				
1425	Blanca 1425–41 (m. prince Juan II of Aragon)			
1430				
1435				
1440	[Carlos, Principe de Viana 1441–58, claims throne]	Prince Juan II claims throne of Navarra		1441–58: crown
1445				
1450			Enrique IV el Impotente de Castilla y León 1454–74	
1455		Juan II 1458–79		
1460	Blanca II 1461–64 Leonor I 1464–79 (m. Gastón de Foix)			
1465				
1470				
1475		Fernando II 1479–1516	Isabel I la Católica 1474–1504	
1480	Francisco de Foix 1479–83			

Muslims	People	Events	Arts
			ca. 1387: Chaucer's *Canterbury Tales*
		1391: Riots and mass conversions of the Jews	
		1417: End of papal schism	
		1431: 1st *Irmandiñas* War 1434: Passo Honroso	
disputed in Navarra			
		1453: Constantinople conquered by Muslim Turkish forces 1453: Gutenberg printing press	
	1456: Wm. Wey's pilgrimage	1458: Carlos, Príncipe de Viana, poisoned	
		1462–4: 2nd *Irmandiñas* War	
		1469: last *Irmandiñas* War	
		1478: Inquisition founded in Spain	
			Flemish artists migrate to Burgos

Date	Navarra	Aragón	Castilla	León
1485	Catalina de Foix 1483–1512 (m. Juan de Albret)			
1490				
1495				
1500				
1505		Fernando as regent for Juana la Loca 1504–16		
1510	Fernando incorporates Navarra			
1515		Carlos V 1516–56		

Muslims	People	Events	Arts
1492: Granada surrenders to Christian forces		1492: Jews expelled from Spain; 1st C. Columbus voyage	
	1495: Künig von Vach's pilgrimage 1496: Arnold von Harff's pilgrimage	1499: Fernando and Isabel mandate pilgrims' hospice in Compostela 1499: Forced mass conversion of Muslims in Spain	
		1504: Pope Julius II establishes university in Compostela	
	1515: Teresa of Ávila born 1519: Carlos V named Holy Roman Emperor	1514: In Cuba, town of Santiago named capital 1517: Martin Luther posts his theses at Wittenburg: Beginning of Reformation	

BIBLIOGRAPHY OF WORKS CITED

Albani, Nicola. *Viaje de Nápoles a Santiago de Galicia*. Ed., trans. Isabel González. Biblioteca facsimilar compostelana, 1. Madrid: Consorcio de Santiago, 1993.

Alfonso X el Sabio. *Cantigas de Santa Maria*. Ed. Walter Mettmann. 3 vols. Madrid: Clásicos Castalia, 1986–1989.

Alonso, Pilar, and Alberto Gil. *Santiago de Compostela*. Guías para viajeros tranquilos. Madrid: Celeste, 1992.

Alvarez-Coca González, María Jesús. *Escultura románica en piedra en La Rioja Alta*. Biblioteca de temas riojanos, 18. Logroño: Gonzalo de Berceo Instituto de Estudios Riojanos, 1978.

Andrés Ordax, Salvador. "Arte románico. Arte gótico." *Historia de Burgos*. Vol. 2. Burgos: Caja de Ahorros Municipal de Burgos, 1987.

———. *Villalcázar de Sirga: La iglesia de Santa Maria*. Palencia: Diputación, 1993.

Arraiza, Jesús. "De Pamplona a Puenta la Reina." *Peregrino* 2nd. epoch. 46 (Dec. 1995): 11–17.

———. "Reportaje: Pamplona, la primera del camino." *Peregrino* 2nd. epoch. 30 (May 1993): 11–17.

Azanza López, José Javier. *Arquitectura religiosa del barroco en Navarra*. Pamplona: Gobierno de Navarra, Departamento of Educación y Cultura. Institución Príncipe de Viana, 1998.

Bango Torviso, Isidro. *Edificios e imágenes medievales: Historia y significado de las formas*. Madrid: Historia 16: Información e Historia, 1995.

Barrow, George. *The Bible in Spain*. 1834. New York: G. P. Putnam's Sons; London: John Murray, 1901.

Berceo, Gonzalo de. *Obras completas II. Los Milagros de Santa María*. Ed. Brian Dutton. London: Tamesis, 1971.

———. *La "Vida de San Millán de la Cogolla" de Gonzalo de Berceo*. Ed. Brian Dutton. London: Tamesis, 1967.

———. *Vida de Santo Domingo de Silos*. Ed. Teresa Labarta de Chaves. Madrid: Clásicos Castalia, 1972.

Bernard of Clairvaux, St. *Apologia ad Willelmum*.

Bernès, Georges, Georges Vernon, and L. Laborde Balen. *The Pilgrim Route to Compostela. In Search of St. James*. Trans. Robertson McCarta. 2nd rev. ed. London: Randonnées Pyrénéennes, 1990.

Bertaux, E. "La sculpture chrétienne en Espagne des origines au XIV siècle." *Histoire general de l'art*. Ed. A. Michel. Vol. 2.1. Paris: n.p., 1906.

Biggs, Anselm Gordon. *Diego Gelmírez: First Archbishop of Compostela*. Washington: Catholic University Press, 1949.

Biurrún [y] Sútil, Tomás. *El arte románico en Navarra*. Pamplona: Aramburu, 1936.

Borde, Andrew. *The Fyrst Boke of the Introduction of Knowledge*. 1544. Ed. Frederick J. Furnivall. EETS, es 10. London: Kegan, Paul, Trench, Trübner, 1870.

Bravo Lozano, Millán. *Guía práctica del peregrino. El camino de Santiago*. León: Everest, 1993.

Butler's Lives of the Saints. Eds. Herbert Thurston and Donald Attwater. 4 vols. New York: P. J. Kenedy, 1963.

Camón Aznar, José. "Arquitectura española del siglo X; Mozárabe y de la repoblación." *Goya* 52 (1963): 206–19.

Cantera Burgos, Francisco. "Las juderías españolas y el camino de Santiago." *XII semana de estudios medievales, 1974*. Ed. Vicente Galbete Guerendiáin. Pamplona: Diputación Foral de Navarra; Institución Príncipe de Viana. Amigos del Camino de Santiago, 1976. 73–119.

Castro, Rosalía de. "N'a Catedral." *Follas novas II*. 1880. In *Obras Completas*. Ed. V. García Martí. Madrid: Aguilar, 1960.

Castro Vázquez, Josefina. *El camino de Santiago (entre Portomarín y Compostela)*. Lugo: Diputación Provincial de Lugo, 1991.

The Chronicle of San Juan de la Peña. A Fourteenth-Century Official History of the Crown of Aragon. Trans. Lynn H. Nelson. Philadelphia: University of Pennsylvania Press, 1991.

Codex Calixtinus. See *Liber Sancti Jacobi*.

Conde Roa, Juan. *Santiago de Compostela*. El viajero independiente. Madrid: Júcar, 1995.

Contín, Sebastián. *La baronia de Sigües y el Camino de Santiago*. Zaragoza: Cuadernos NS, 1964.

Cosmen Alonso, María Concepción. *El arte románico en León: Diócesis de Astorga*. León: Universidad de León, 1989.

Coverdale, John F. *The Basque Phase of Spain's First Carlist War*. Princeton: Princeton University Press, 1984.

Deben, Carmen. *El Hostal de los Reyes Católicos en la historia de Santiago*. León: Everest, 1968.

———. *El Hostal de San Marcos*. León: Everest, 1972.

Días Fuentes, Antionio. *O Cebreiro—Sarria: un recorrido por el Camino de Santiago*. N.p.: Consellería de Cultura, 1994.

Díez y Díaz, Alejandro. *Puerte la Reina y Sarria en la historia*. Sarria: Verbo Divino, 1989.

Dodds, Jerilynn D. *Architecture and Ideology in Early Medieval Spain*. University Park, Pa.: Pennsylvania State University Press, 1989.

Enciclopedia vniversal ilvstrada evropeo-americana. 70 vols. Madrid: Espasa-Calpe, 1907–1930.

Encyclopaedia Britannica Online. Web site. Address http://www.eb.com.

Espina, Concha. *La esfinge maragata*. Ed. Carmen Díaz Castañón. Madrid: Castalia, 1989.

"Estella." *Encyclopaedia Judaica*. Jerusalem: Keter, 1902. 6:905.

Estella Marcos, Margarita. *La imaginería de los retablos de la Capilla del Condestable*. Valladolid: Junta de Castilla/Cabildo Metropolitano, 1995.

Estepa Díez, Carlos, T. Ruiz, J.A. Bonachia, and H. Casado. *Burgos en la edad media*. Valladolid: n.p., 1975.

Federación aragonesa de montañismo. Comité nacional de senderos de gran recorrido. *Senderos de gran recorrido. Camino de Santiago. Somport-Undués de Lerda (tramo aragonés)*. GR 65.3. Zaragoza: Prames, 1991.

Fernández de Arratia, Fernando. *Itinerario jacobeo*. Pamplona: Gobierno de Navarra, 1990.

Fuente Gallardo, Concha de la. "Mirar un retablo: su historia, sus artifices, su estilo, sus mensajes. . . ." *Peregrino* 2nd. epoch. 61 (Oct. 1998): 13–24.

"Fuero de Estella." Peregrino 2nd. epoch. 8 (May 1989): Servicio de documentación 1–6.

García de Cortázar, José Angel. *El dominio del Monasterio de San Millán de la Cogolla*. Salamanca: Universidad de Salamanca, 1969.

García Gaínza, María Concepción, dir. *Catálogo monumental de Navarra*. Vol. 2. *Merindad de Estella: Abáigar-Eulate*. Pamplona: Dpto. Educación y Cultura. Institución de Príncipe de Viana, 1982.

Giménez de Azcárate Cornide, Joaquín, Ignacio Munilla Rumbao, and Rafael Romero Suances. *Guía de la naturaleza del Camino de Santiago en Galicia*. [Compostela?]: Hércules/Consellería de Cultura, 1995.

Goicoechea Arrondo, Eusebio. *Rutas jacobeas: Historia de la Peregrinación-Arte en la Peregrinación-Caminos para la Peregrinación*. Estella: Los Amigos del Camino de Santiago, 1971.

Gómez Moreno, Manual. *Catálogo monumental de España. Provincia de León*. 1925–6. 2 vols. Madrid: Ministerio de Instrucción Pública y Bellas Artes, 1979.

Gudiol Ricart, José, and Juan Antonio Gaya Nuño. *Ars hispaniae. Historia universal del arte hispánico. 5. Arquitectura y escultura románicas*. Madrid: Plus-Ultra, 1948.

Guerra Campos, José, and Jesús Precedo Lafuento. *Guía de la Catedral de Santiago de Compostela*. Vitoria: Aldeasa. División Palacios y Muesos, 1993.

Gutiérrez Eraso, Pedro María. "Francisco Santiago Liscler peregrino jacobit alemán nacido en Estella en 1759." *Ruta jacobea* 3.22 (Apr. 1965): 2.

———. "San Antón de Castrogeriz y el 'mal de los ardientes'." *Ruta Jacobea* 1.3 (1963): 4–5.

Harff, Arnold von. *The Pilgrimage of Arnold von Harff, Knight, from Cologne, through Italy, Syria, Egypt, Arabia, Ethiopia, Nubia, Palestine, Turkey, France and Spain, which he accomplished in the years 1946 to 1499*. Trans. Malcolm Letts. London: Haklyut Society, 1946.

Hearn, M.F. (Millard Fillmore). *Romanesque Sculpture: The Revival of Monumental Stone Sculpture in the Eleventh and Twelfth Centuries*. Ithaca: Cornell University Press, 1981.

Helguera Quijada, Juan, Nicolás García Tapia, and Fernando Molinero Hernando. *El canal de Castilla*. 2nd ed. Valladolid: Junta de Castilla y León, 1990.

Hernández Perera, Jesús. "Alabastros ingleses en España." *Goya* 22 (Jan.–Feb. 1958): 216–22.

Historia compostelana. Trans., ed. Emma Falque Rey. Clásicos latinos medievales. Madrid: Akal, 1994.

Hita, Joaquín, Belén Itxaso, and Jesús Maeztu. *Estella, posta y mercado en la Ruta Jacobea*. Estella: Caja de Ahorros de Navarra, n.d.

Huidobro y Serna, Luciano. *Las peregrinaciones jacobeas*. 3 vols. Madrid: Publicaciones del Instituto de España, 1949–1951.

Idrisi. *Geografía de España*. Ed. Antonio Ubieto Arteta. Textos medievales, 37. Valencia: Anubar, 1974.

Itúrbide Díaz, Javier. *Estella*. Colección Panorama, 21. 2nd. ed. Pamplona: Panorama, 1995.

Jacobus de Voragine. *Legenda aurea. The Golden Legend*. Trans. Granger Ryan and Helmut Ripperger. 2 vols. London: Longmans, Green, 1941.

Jimeno Jurío, José María. "Sangüesa y el camino." *Peregrino* 2nd. epoch. 23 (Dec. 1991): 14–15.

Kraus, Dorothy, and Henry Kraus. *The Gothic Choirstalls of Spain*. London and New York: Routledge & Kegan Paul, 1986.

Künig von Vach, Hermann. "*Die Wallfahrt und Strass zu Sant Jakob*. 1495. La Peregrinación y camino á Santiago." Trans. Antonio G. Vázquez Queipo. In Antonio López Ferreiro. *Historia de la Santa A.M. Iglesia de Santiago de Compostela*. Santiago: Seminario Conciliar Central, 1907. 9: 178–194.

Labeaga Mendiola, Juan Cruz. *Sangüesa en el camino de Santiago*. Sangüesa: Ayuntamiento de Sangüesa, 1993.

Lacarra, José María. "Roncesvalles." "Monjardín entre la historia y la leyenda." *Melanges offerts à Rita Lejeune. 1: Estudios de historia navarra*. Liège or Pamplona: [J. Duculot], 1971. 459–69.

Laffi, Domenico. *A Journey to the West: The Diary of a Seventeenth-Century Pilgrim from Bologna to Santiago de Compostela*. Trans. James Hall. Leiden: Primavera Pers, 1997.

———. *Viaje a Poniente*. Trans., ed. Clemente Crespo Caamaño. Biblioteca mágica del peregrino, 2. Santiago de Compostela: Editorial Sildavia, 1991.

Lampérez y Romea, Vicente. "Iglesia parroquial de Villalcázar de Sirga." *Boletín de la Real Academia de la Historia* 75.5 (Nov. 1919): 387–98.

Liber Sancti Jacobi. Codex Calixtinus de la Catedral de Santiago de Compostela. Madrid: Kaydeda, 1993. See also *Miracles of Saint James*, and *Pilgrim's Guide to Santiago*.

Lomax, Derek. "La Orden de Santiago y la peregrinación." *Peregrino* 2nd. epoch. 12 (Feb. 1990): Servicio de documentación. 1–3.

López, Carlos María. *Leyre: Historia, arqueología, leyenda*. Pamplona: Gómez, 1962.

López de Mendoza, Íñigo (Marqués de Santillana). *Poesías completas*. Ed. Miguel Ángel Pérez Priego. 2 vols. Madrid: Alhambra, 1983–1991.

López de Úbeda, Francisco. *La pícara Justina*. In *La novela picaresca*. Ed. Angel Valbuena y Prat. Madrid: Aguilar, 1962. 700–880.

López Ferrerio, Antonio. *Historia de la Santa A[postólica] M[etropolitana] Iglesia de Santiago [de Compostela]*. 11 vols. Santiago: Seminario, 1898–1909.

———. *El Pórtico de la Gloria, Platerías. El primitivo altar mayor de la Catedral de Santiago*. 1893. Rpt. Santiago: Pico Sacro, 1975.

Losada Díaz, A., and E. Seijas Vázquez. *Guía del Camino Francés en la Provincia de Lugo*. Madrid: Gráficas Cóndor, 1966.

Luengo y Martínez, José María. "Notas sobre el hospital de peregrinos de San Gregorio, de Rabanal del Camino." *León* 225 (1973): 3–5.

Madrazo, Pedro de. *Navarra y Logroño. España. Sus monumentos y artes, su naturaleza e historia*. Barcelona: Daniel Cortezo, 1886.

Manier, Guillaume. *Pèlerinage d'un paysan Picard à St. Jacques de Compostelle au commencement du XVIIIᵉ siècle*. Ed. Baron Bonnault d'Houët. Montdidier: Abel Radenez, 1890.

Marías, Fernando. *El largo siglo XVI. Los usos artísticos del renacimiento español*. Madrid: Altea, Taurus, Alfaguara, 1989.

Martínez Díez, Gonzalo, and Santiago Francia Lorenzo. *De Itero de la Vega a San Nicolás del Real Camino: Piedra y Vida*. Palencia: Diputación, 1994.

Martínez Liébana, Evelio. "La aljama de Sahagún en la transición del siglo XIV al XV." *Hispania* 53.2 (1993): 397–429.

Medicis, Cosme de. *Viaje de Cosme de Medicis por España y Portugal (1668–9)*. Eds. Angel Sánchez Rivero and Angela Mariutti de Sánchez Rivero. Junta para ampliacion de estudios e investigaciones científicas. Central de estudios históricos. Madrid: Sucesores de Rivadeneyra, [1927].

Mendoza, Fernando de. "Con los judíos de Estella." *Príncipe de Viana* 44–5 (1951): 235–71.

The Miracles of Saint James. Translations from the Liber Sancti Jacobi. Trans., eds. Thomas F. Coffey, Linda Kay Davidson, and Maryjane Dunn. New York: Italica, 1996.

Molina, Licenciado. 15th-c. poem. See Valiña Sampedro, *Camino de Santiago*.

Mulertt, Werner. "Libro del famoso passo que el onorable caballero generoso S. de Quiñones tuvo en el Puente de Órbigo." *Homenaje a M. Artigas*. Madrid: Boletín de la Biblioteca Menéndez y Pelayo, 1932.

O'Callaghan, Joseph F. *A History of Medieval Spain*. Ithaca: Cornell University Press, 1975.

Olarte, Juan B. *Monasterio de San Millán de la Cogolla*. León: Edilesa, 1995.

Oses, José. "Navarrete: alfar de historia y arte." *Peregrino* 2nd. epoch. 41 (Feb. 1995): 14–15.

Passini, Jean. *Aragón. El Camino de Santiago. Patrimonio edificado*. Collection de la Casa de Velázquez, 45. Estudios y monografías, 21. Madrid: École des hautes études hispaniques. Casa de Velázquez. Departamento de Cultura y Educación. Diputación General de Aragón, 1993.

———. *Aragón: Los núcleos urbanos del Camino de Santiago*. Zaragoza: Diputación General de Aragón, 1988.

———. *El Camino de Santiago: Itinerario y núcleos de población*. Madrid: Ministerio de Obras Públicas y Transportes, 1993.

Paz López, G. *Portomarín (Puertomarín)*. Zaragoza: Departamento de Geografía Aplicada del Instituto Elcano, 1961.

Pérez Lugín, Alejandro. *La casa de la Troya*. 8th ed. Madrid: Pueyo, 1918.

The Pilgrim's Guide to Santiago de Compostela. Ed., trans. William Melczer. New York: Italica, 1993.

Peter the Venerable. *De miraculis*.

Poema de Fernán González. Ed. John Lihani. Medieval Texts and Studies, 4. East Lansing, Mich.: Colleagues Press, 1991.

Poema de mío Cid. Ed. Colin Smith. 1972. 4th ed. Madrid: Catedra, 1978.

Porter, Arthur Kingsley. *Romanesque Sculpture of the Pilgrimage Roads*. 10 vols. in 3. 1923. Rpt. New York: Hacker Art Books, 1966.

Post, Chandler Rathfon. *A History of Spanish Painting*. 14 vols. in 18. Cambridge, Mass.: Harvard University Press, 1930–1966.

Postal, Bernard, and Samuel Abramson. *Traveler's Guide to Jewish Landmarks in Europe*. New York: Fleet Press, 1971.

"La Pretiosa." In Fidel Fita y Colomé. "Roncesvalles." *Boletín de la Real Academia de la Historia* 4.3 (Mar. 1884): 172–84.

Ptolemy, Caludius. *The Geography*.

Rabanal Alonso, Manuel Abilo, dir. *El camino de Santiago en León: Precedentes romanos y época medieval*. León: Universidad, Secretariado de Publicaciones, 1992.

Rahlves, Friedrich. *Cathedrals and Monasteries of Spain*. Trans. James C. Palmes. New York: A. S. Barnes, 1966.

Reguera, Iñaki. "Las cárceles de la Inquisición en Logroño." *Perfiles jurídicos de la Inquisición española*. Ed. José Antonio Escudero. Madrid: Instituto de la Historía de la Inquisición/Universidad Complutense de Madrid, 1989. 415–38.

Revuelta, Manuel. "Frómista: Ráfagas de historia." *Peregrino* 2nd. epoch. 22 (Nov. 1991): 14–15.

Rivera, Javier. *La Catedral de León y su museo*. León: Nebrija, 1979.

Rodríguez Alba, J. *El Monasterio de Santa María de las Huelgas y el Hospital del Rey*. Burgos: n.p., 1950.

Rodríguez de Lena, Pero. *El Passo Honroso de Suero de Quiñones*. Ed. Amancio Labandeira Fernández. Madrid: Fundación Universitaria Española, 1977.

Ruiz, Teófilo. *The City and the Realm*. Aldershot, Hampshire, Great Britain: Ashgate Publishing; Brookfield, Vt.: Variorium, 1992.

Santiago de Compostela. Guía del viajero. Madrid: Susaeta, 1991.

Sem Tob. "Proverbios morales." *Poetas castellanos anteriores al siglo XV*. Ed. Tomás Antonio Sánchez. Madrid: Atlas, 1952.

Soria y Puig, Arturo. *El Camino a Santiago. II: Estaciones y señales*. Madrid: Ministerio de Obras Públicas y Transportes, 1992.

Starkie, Walter. *The Road to Santiago. Pilgrims of St. James*. London: John Murray, 1957.

Stokstad, Marilyn. *Santiago de Compostela in the Age of the Great Pilgrimages*. Centers of Civilization. Norman, Okla. University of Oklahoma Press, 1978.

Strabo. *Geography*.

Ubieto Arteta, Antonio. *Los caminos de Santiago en Aragón*. Eds. M. D. Cabanes Pecourt and M. I. Falcon Pérez. Zaragoza: Gobierno de Aragón. Dpto. de Cultura y Educación, [1993].

Urbina Marino, Angel. "El *Fuero de Logroño*." *Peregrino* 2nd. epoch. 43–44 (July 1995): 23–26.

Valdivielso Ausín, Braulio. *Burgos en el Camino de Santiago*. Burgos: Aldecoa, 1992.

———. "Hospital y hospitalidad en San Juan de Ortega." *Peregrino* 2nd. epoch. 42 (Apr. 1995): 14–15.

Valiña Sampedro, Elías. *El Camino de Santiago: Estudio histórico-jurídico*. Monografías de historia eclesiástica, 5. 1967. Madrid: CSIC, 1971. 2nd ed. Lugo: Diputación de Lugo, 1990.

———. *El camino de Santiago. Guía del peregrino a Compostela*. Vigo: Galaxia, 1992.

Varela Jácome, and A. Rodríguez González. *Santiago de Compostela*. León: Everest, 1971.

Vázquez de Parga, Luis, José María Lacarra, and Juan Uría Riu. *Las peregrinaciones a Santiago de Compostela*. 3 vols. Madrid: CSIC, 1949. Rpt. Asturias: Excma. Diputación Provincial, 1981. Rpt. Pamplona: Iberdrola, 1992.

Villalba y Estaña, Bartholomé. *El pelegrino curioso y grandezas de España*. 1580. Ed. Pascual Gayangos. 2 vols. Madrid: Sociedad de bibliófilos españoles, 1886.

Viñayo González, Antonio. *San Isidoro de León: pintura románica del Panteón de los Reyes*. León: Edilesa, 1993.

Voces Jolías, José María. *Arte religioso de El Bierzo en el siglo XVI*. Ponferrada: Gráficas Mar-Car, 1987.

Von Hagen, Victor W. *The Roads that Led to Rome*. Cleveland: World Publishing, 1967.

Weber, Cynthia Milton. *La portada de Santa María la Real de Sangüesa*. Pamplona: Príncipe de Viana, 1984.

Wethey, Harold E. *Gil de Siloé and His School: A Study of Late Gothic Sculpture in Burgos*. Cambridge, Mass.: Harvard University Press, 1936.

Wey, William. "An English Pilgrim to Compostela." Trans. James Hogarth. *Medieval World* 5 (Mar.–Apr. 1992): 15–9.

Suggestions for Additional Reading

The pilgrimage to Santiago has generated a tremendous amount of bibliography, as have the history and culture of Spain along the Road. The following resources will help you get started:

American Friends of the Road to Santiago. [For your pilgrim's passport. For information. For networking with others in the USA who are going or who have already trekked to Compostela. A semiannual newsletter with queries, information, and updates on recent publications about the pilgrimage. E-mail: dgitlitz@aol.com.]

British Confraternity of St. James. [A vigorous society of nearly 2,000 members in 1999. Bulletins, activities, good publications, including some useful guides. Write: Confraternity of St. James, First Floor. Talbot Yard. 87 Borough High St. London SE1 1YP England.]

Dunn, Maryjane, and Linda Kay Davidson. *The Pilgrimage to Santiago de Compostela: A Comprehensive, Annotated Bibliography*. New York: Garland Publishing, 1994. [Annotation of 2,970 titles.]

Frey, Nancy Louise. *Pilgrim Stories: On and Off the Road to Santiago*. Berkeley: University of California Press, 1998. [Study of today's pilgrim phenomenon in the pilgrims' own words.]

Hitt, Jack. *Off the Road. A Modern-Day Walk Down the Pilgrim's Route into Spain*. New York: Simon & Schuster, 1994.

Hoinacki, Lee. *El Camino: Walking to Santiago de Compostela*. University Park: Pennsylvania State University Press, 1996.

Peregrino. [The quarterly journal, in Spanish, produced by the Association in Logroño and Frómista. Articles are interesting, usually well focused; photography is excellent. News on the happenings around most of the European confraternities. Write: *Peregrino*. Aptdo de Correos 315. 26001 Logroño, La Rioja, Spain.]

Stanton, Edward F. *Road of Stars to Santiago*. Lexington: University of Kentucky Press, 1994.

INDEX

"Pilgrimage" is not indexed since it is the prime material of this Handbook. Likewise, since Saint James (Santiago el Mayor) appears on nearly every page, we index only the most important references to his legend. We index artists and art styles of the Road only if they receive special treatment in the text. For biographies of the artists and descriptions of art styles, see pages 386–91 and 374–85 respectively. Boldface page numbers indicate detailed treatment.